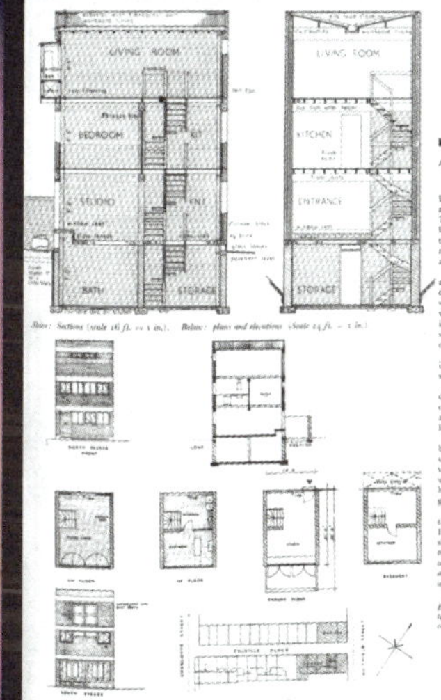

HOUSE IN SOHO, LONDON

Alison and Peter Smithson

"The attempt was made to build in Central London, and failed because of difficulty with adjoining owners. It seemed that a series of Trusts held the surrounding land (all bombed) but it turned out to be one man who intended to build kitchens to the left, W.C.'s to the right and restaurants to the rear—this contract was about to be signed after nine months' work.

On the normal city site costing between 15s. and 25s. per sq. ft. one can apparently do little different from the Georgian, but it was considered that a different internal order must be visualised. The air and sunlight of the attics in the daytime suggests that living quarters should be up top, with the bathroom in the cool of the dim basement.

It was decided to have no finishes at all internally—the building being a combination of shelter and environment.

Bare concrete, brickwork and wood. The difficulty of unceiled rooms was satisfactorily overcome by the disposition of rooms which were also placed high up or low down according to light-sunlight desired.

Brickwork may suggest a blue or double burnt or coloured pointing; but the arbitrary use of colour and texture was not conformed with, and common bricks with struck joints were intended. The bars and colour variation have some sort of natural tension when laid by a good bricklayer.

In fact, had this been built it would have been the first exponent of the "new brutalism" in England, as the preamble to the specification shows: "*It is our intention in this building to have the structure exposed entirely, without internal finishes wherever practicable. The Contractor should aim at a high standard of basic construction as in a small warehouse.*" P.D.S.

Erratum: The four houses shown above were inadvertently incorrectly listed in the contents on the front cover of last month's issue of "A.D."

342

That's Brutal, What's Modern?

The Smithsons, Banham, and the Mies-Image

Mark Linder

PARK BOOKS

Contents

Introduction

In the name of New Brutalism, and in pursuit of what this book calls the Mies-image, Alison and Peter Smithson initiated a manner and mode of late modernism that remains provocative, puzzling, and pertinent. Their pursuit began with their design of the Hunstanton School (1950–54) in Norfolk, UK, as an effort to see something new in Mies van der Rohe's Chicago work. It continued when they began to see something new in Hunstanton as it was being built, and then for several decades afterward in their incessant reimaging of their own work and that of Mies. New Brutalism first coalesced as a "scene" in the last months of 1953, when Hunstanton reached what the Smithsons would later call the "layering of reflection at the glazed stage,"[1] when the phrase "New Brutalism" first appeared in print,[2] and when *Parallel of Life and Art*, the exhibition they devised with their friends and fellow Independent Group members Nigel Henderson and Eduardo Paolozzi, was staged in London at the Institute of Conteporary Art and then restaged at the Architectural Association (fig. 1). It gathered renewed momentum in the late 1950s when Peter traveled twice to America, and it intensified after 1967 when they presented a seminar on Mies in Berlin. It culminated in the imaging practices of the Smithsons' subsequent books, lectures, exhibitions, and design work, which in varied ways reconfigure the latent potential of the scene that launched their careers.

FRONT ENDPAPER

Fig. 1

The confluence of events and experiences that launched New Brutalism in 1953 exemplify what Jacques Rancière terms a "scene" in his book *Aisthesis* (2011). In that "counter-history of 'aesthetic modernity'", the writing of each chapter articulates the "sensible fabric and intelligible form" of a scene—a historically and discursively entangled moment —from Johann Winckelmann's musings on the Belvedere Torso (1764) to James Agee's account of the lives of Alabama sharecroppers in *Let Us Now Praise Famous Men* (1941): "The scene is not the illustration of an idea. It is a little optical machine that shows us thought busy weaving together perceptions, affects, names and ideas, constituting the sensible community that makes such weaving thinkable." Scenes are "microcosms in which we see the logic of [the aesthetic] regime being formed, transformed, incorporating unexplored territories and forming new patterns in order to do so." In an interview with Oliver Davis, Rancière describes his "method of the scene" as "choosing a singularity whose conditions of possibility one tries to reconstitute by exploring all the networks of signification that weave around it." Rancière characterizes this approach as "the method of the 'ignorant', in a sense, as opposed to a method that first takes a set of general determinations that function as causes and illustrate their effects in a certain number of concrete cases. In the scene, the conditions are immanent to their effectuation. This also means that the scene [...] is fundamentally anti-hierarchical. It is the 'object' that teaches us how we can talk about it, how we can treat it. The scene abolishes the difference between the language of the object and the language of its explanation. It defines a poetics of translations and paraphrases that maintain the equality of the discursive fabric. But the scene is also important for the reflections on art which maintain that art is defined only through a specific regime [...] of perceiving, of phrasing that perception, of constructing its intelligibility."

Two words complicate and confuse the scene: "imaging" and "new." The first complicates our theoretical and historical understanding of modernist visuality. Launched with the onset of the "age of mechanical reproduction" and then exacerbated by digital media—from printing and fabricating to screening and scanning to modeling and animating; from the ubiquitous and banal to the esoteric and rarefied—imaging has superseded (but by no means replaced) prior paradigms of representation and abstraction. Imaging practices, as post-photographic modes of production, exchange, and experience, have radicalized the proliferation and efficacy of visual materials. As modes and matters of extralinguistic iteration and affiliation, imaging taps our evolved cognitive capacities for pattern recognition, serial processing, and spatial imagination in old and new ways. *That's Brutal, What's Modern?* reconsiders the entirety of the Smithsons' work as an ongoing effort to invent and use transdisciplinary imaging practices that were inspired not only by Mies but also by the Independent Group (1952–55) and its sources in art and popular culture. But this book does not attempt to reconstruct a stable meaning or significance for the legacy of New Brutalism. Instead, it offers a capacious and robust understanding of New Brutalist motives, methods, and influence by considering the Smithsons' work as a wide-ranging series of provisional and productive experiments in the early history of imaging practices that redefine the particular techniques and approaches that constitute the work of the architect and the production of architecture. It aims to recover a specific and integral, yet overlooked, aspect of its peculiar newness by showing how, from the beginning, and increasingly over time, the figure at the heart of the Smithsons' production was a variation of the modernist imaginary that I am calling the Mies-image, which exemplifies and anticipates the kinds of cognition and intelligence that dominate our architectural imaginations today.

The second word, "new," creates confusion because it is essential as often as it is superfluous in both contemporary and historical discussions of New Brutalism, which was never intended to be simply new, or simply modern. The missing word "new" in this book's title repeats a symptom that is, in effect, a subterfuge of architecture's history and, in fact, an object lesson in the ordinary and typical degradation and intrigue of theoretical discourse. After the Smithsons' first published mention of New Brutalism in December 1953, they and others around them—architects, editors, critics, artists—were inconsistent in their use of the word "new." That was in part a colloquial shorthand, but it contributed to the later confusion of "New Brutalism" with "Brutalism" in the popular knowledge and discussion of postwar architecture. The implications and effects of the lapse are enormous. It is a peculiar fact that New Brutalism preceded Brutalism and that the latter's success overshadows the former's distinctiveness. Hear the word "Brutalism" and we conjure images of massive concrete forms and the settings of dystopian films, not the Smithsons' audacious, optimistic, and ambitious project to relaunch European modernism in Britain after World War Two. That is only one, but perhaps the greatest, of the confusions of New Brutalism: the initial inspiration the Smithsons found in Mies van der Rohe's Chicago idiom of steel, glass, and brick was soon displaced by a fascination with the *béton brut* of Le Corbusier's Unité d'Habitation (1947–52). The peculiar question of how New Brutalism came to be mistakenly associated with the monumental, concrete Brutalist architecture of the British welfare state is a curious slippage of language, sequence, and memory.[3]

As many of the quotations in this book demonstrate, New Brutalism began to be called simply Brutalism in most discussions even before Brutalism coalesced as a style in the late 1950s. That elision of the "new" has continued ever since in the writing of both astute scholars and casual reporters. Even the most influential contemporary commentator on New Brutalism was in on the game. Reyner Banham's inconsistent use of "new" in his 1966 book *The New Brutalism: Ethic or Aesthetic?* as well as in his famous 1955 essay "The New Brutalism" might be scrutinized as an ambivalent stance, an unconscious symptom, or even a devious tactic. But it was hardly an oversight. Rather, it effectively compounds multiple ambiguities in both the history of New Brutalism and in the 1953 scene. Crucially, both Banham's book and his essay discounted the importance of Mies. In 1966 he implicitly ratified the transposition of the Marseille Corbusier and the Chicago Mies as New Brutalism's progenitor: his discussion of the influence of Corbusier precedes that of Mies, and seven pages of images of the Unité appear before four pages of images of Mies's Alumni Memorial Hall (1945–47), one of his early projects at the Illinois Institute of Technology. Banham wrote:

> Behind all aspects of the New Brutalism, in Britain and elsewhere, lies one undisputed architectural fact: the concrete-work of Le Corbusier's "Unité d'Habitation" at Marseilles. And if there is one single verbal formula that has made the concept of Brutalism admissible in most of the world's western languages, it is that Le Corbusier himself described that concrete-work as "béton brut." Word and building stand together in the psychological history of post-war architecture.[4]

In just those few sentences, and in the sequencing of the book's plates, Banham managed to jumble the distinctions between, and precedence of, Mies and Corbusier as well as New Brutalism and Brutalism. While his explanation of the influence of Mies gets the chronology right, it is derisive, characterizing the Smithsons' "imitation" of his "assembly of highly finished synthetic materials" as not much more than a first step toward the subsequent discovery and embrace of "Le Corbusier's honesty in demythologizing concrete." The effect is a reductive conflation of New Brutalism and Brutalism as variations of modernist moralism:

> The first completed building to carry the title of "New Brutalist" was not Corbusian; rather, it was the most precise imitation of the building style of Mies van der Rohe to have appeared outside the USA by that time [. . .]. Yet the morality that approved the raw concrete of the "Unité" could equally well approve the use that Mies van der Rohe had made of steel, glass and brick in the campus buildings for the Illinois Institute of Technology at Chicago.[5]

In the end, Banham argued, New Brutalism's dual sources in two modernist "masters" generated a popular "fusion of the Mies-image with the Corb-image [that] was an understandable, if philosophically reprehensible, step toward the creation of the kind of single vision of a real and convincing architecture that this generation sought."[6] That conceptual fusion, Banham concluded, led to practical confusion. For Banham, the meaning, intent, and implications of New Brutalism were already lost in its very beginnings. By the time the Hunstanton School was completed in 1954, "the situation was becoming confused by the many things that happened to the Smithsons, to architecture in Britain and the world, and the word Brutalist itself, which was being heavily overworked already."[7]

Thus, Banham deviously demonstrated that the newness of New Brutalism was always ambivalent, not radical. The Smithsons would certainly agree, but for different and more basic reasons. The kind of modernism to which New Brutalism aspired was neither "neo" nor "novel." The word "new" was crucial to New Brutalism's distinctly polemical and sarcastic dissemblance of the presumed novelty of older modernist movements, from Art Nouveau to Neue Sachlichkeit to New Empiricism.[8] It was also an acknowledgment of the lateness of the Smithsons' generation relative to what they saw as a more legitimate claim to newness in what they called the "heroic period of modern architecture," the time "just before and just after the first world war [when] a new idea of architecture came into being."[9] Thus, as Robin Boyd noted in a review of Banham's 1966 book, "Brutalism"—without the word "new"—becomes more serious, harsh, and agonistic: "It was the adjective that gave the name its special force. The noun was bold and powerful yet the 'new' relieved it with a slightly ironic twist. One understood that the brute force was to be applied in this movement at the intellectual level."[10] For an orthodox modernist like Boyd, the Smithsons' ideas were not new enough and their buildings were not brutal enough. New Brutalism was simply "the most articulate of all the attempts to re-establish the original integrity and strength of modern architecture [. . .]. Yet it cannot be inflated more than that."[11] Ten years earlier, John Summerson had leveled a similar critique in his introduction to the catalogue of the Arts Council exhibition *Ten Years of British Architecture: '45–55*, writing that "the New Brutalism is a sub-jocular expression of the moment" and "a nickname for an attitude. 'The Old Rigour' might have done as well—perhaps better, seeing that the attitude involves a recapitulation, a reassessment of ground which the modern movement has covered more than once in its history [. . .] a lively background of experience to be revisited often and with profit."[12] More important, however, Boyd's and Summerson's specifically architectural—and reductive—understandings of New Brutalism disparaged the ways in which the Smithsons' intellectual inflection of modernist principles was derived from a complex of sources in and around architecture, especially those circulating among the artists, critics, and architects in the Independent Group. But it was precisely this "intellectual level," and transdisciplinary scene, that introduced the kind of imagination and the range of imaging practices that gave New Brutalism its peculiar newness.

Banham understood this well in his decidedly intellectual first take on New Brutalism. But he focused on the suffix, insisting that any claims of newness must be understood in the context of a contemporary historical sophistication about "the 'isms' which are the thumb-print of Modernity. [. . .] One cannot begin to study the

New Brutalism without realizing how deeply the New Art-History has bitten into progressive English architectural thought. [. . .] The New Brutalism has to be seen against the background of the recent history of history, and, in particular, the growing sense of the inner history of the Modern Movement itself."[13]

As the irresolution of the many subsequent attempts to explain the origins of the name suggests, and given that the Smithsons' tendency, like Banham, was to be belligerent, combative, and contentious, New Brutalism began as a playful, performative, and even funny name that seemed aimed to provoke nervous laughter and to clarify who was in on the joke. That was true at its beginning but especially so for decades afterward in the Smithsons' efforts to rethink what New Brutalism was, what it was becoming, and what it might yet be. In doing so, they continually refreshed both the "ethic" and the "aesthetic" of New Brutalism by persistently reimagining it. They came to understand its viability, versatility, and potential again and again in the years that followed. For them, New Brutalism appeared through the Mies-image, and the means of its appearance was an ongoing, opportunistic, idiosyncratic, and contrarian imaging practice. The Smithsons insisted on reasserting the newness of New Brutalism by repeatedly demonstrating that a newer New Brutalism is not only always possible but, for them, always necessary and never entirely new. New Brutalism was not so much retrospectively redefined as insistently rediscovered. The Smithsons' emphasis was always on constant research into and reassessment of their earliest insights, imaged in fresh ways and as new work. Their development as architects, and the development of their sensibility and ways of looking, was complicated by the persistent revision of their own work. Each project succeeded the others without superseding or dismantling earlier achievements or aspirations.

New Brutalism always operated as a kind of situated and timely renewal. That recursive method is most clearly, complexly, and creatively pursued in the texts, images, and graphic organization of the Smithsons' later books, *Ordinariness and Light* (1970), *Without Rhetoric* (1973), *The Shift* (1982), and *Changing the Art of Inhabitation* (1994). As much as any of their design projects, those books are sophisticated imagings that renew New Brutalism. That is the explicit aim of *The Shift*, which creatively curates three decades of work to imagine latent connections and affiliations that only "looking back" can reveal. All four books were predominantly republications of prior work. Each offered an imaging of a different version of the New Brutalist story and sensibility. In the two earlier books, the Smithsons rewrote essays from the 1950s and 1960s, revised the selection of images, and combined them into new wholes. Two decades later, the strategy of *Changing the Art of Inhabitation* was different: their prior writings (published and unpublished, in full or in part) were simply repeated and reorganized. It includes many of the same writings and favorite images that appear in *Ordinariness and Light* and *Without Rhetoric* but curates them as an annotated and illustrated anthology or atlas. In *Changing the Art of Inhabitation* they also had an explicit historical aim to situate their work and ideas as the last voices in a discourse of "Three Generations" of modern architects who are named in the book's subtitle: *Mies' Pieces, Eames'*

Dreams, The Smithsons. The curated content and graphic organization of the 1994 book present the Mies-image as the implicit subject of the Three Generations discourse.

Banham's insistence on the crucial importance of the term "image" in his 1955 essay is itself crucially important to the history of New Brutalism, even though he did not persist with his early ideas and would explicitly reject them as "my own pet notions" in the final chapter of his 1966 book.[14] His conceptualization of image was provocative, but hardly precise or cogent; he always was a better proselytizer, critic, polemicist, and historian than a theorist. But he was on the right track in 1955, when he was an enthusiastic participant in and exponent of the ideas and insights circulating in, around, and through the Independent Group. He still was on the right track one year later, when he made an astonishing conceptual leap. In his review of the group exhibition *This Is Tomorrow* (1956) at the Whitechapel Art Gallery in London, Banham identified a surprising affinity between two very different projects in the show: *Patio and Pavilion* by the Smithsons, Henderson, and Paolozzi, and the playful multimedia installation by Richard Hamilton, John Voelcker, and John McHale: "The clue to this kinship would appear to lie in the fact that neither relied on abstract concepts, but on concrete images—images that can carry the mass of tradition and association, or the energy of novelty and technology, but resist classification by the geometrical disciplines."[15] Banham's concept of concrete images not only offered a canny insight into the ethic and aesthetic of New Brutalism; it also codified what would turn out to be a droll distinction between New Brutalism (concrete images) and Brutalism (concrete buildings) even before Brutalist architecture existed as a style. The tension between the power of his insight and the significance of his distinction contributes to the enduring intrigue of New Brutalism. As Beatriz Colomina wrote in 2017: "This encounter with what Banham called 'concrete images' is stronger than the encounter with concrete itself. [. . .] For Banham, the opposition is not the escapism of mass media imagery vs. the confrontation of brutal materiality. Mass media images themselves have a brutal materiality and in reverse, Brutalism is first and foremost a play of images."[16] *That's Brutal, What's Modern?* strives to recover the historical importance and theoretical coherence of imaging in New Brutalism. Banham initiated that insight but did not pursue it. The Smithsons pursued it, but only allusively acknowledged it. It coheres in the Mies-image.

Banham's discarded fascination with imaging resurfaced near the end of his life in *A Concrete Atlantis* (1986). He described that book as "an inquiry into the connections between North American industrial building and the classic modernist architecture of the International style in Europe," and in his introduction he focused on the powerful and enduring influence of fourteen photographs of American concrete warehouses and grain elevators that were famously published in Europe in 1913.[17] Although he does not mention it, New Brutalism could be seen as a recurrence of that formative instance of transatlantic photographic influence, when the Smithsons first saw photographs and drawings of Mies's American buildings and based their design of the Hunstanton School on those published images.[18] In both cases, Banham's writings reveal his skepticism about the willful

misapprehensions engendered by that kind of influence. In *A Concrete Atlantis* he argued that, despite the aggrandizing rhetoric of early European modernists, the photographs of American industrial structures merely evoked a reductive reaffirmation of reverence for "the eternal and fundamental verities underlying all great architecture, old as well as new."[19] In seeing those images and their influence in that limited way, Banham was returning to the muddled conflation of image and concept that was the most conventional and confusing aspect of his 1955 essay, where he claimed: "All great architecture has been conceptual, has been image-making."[20] Banham's account of photographic influence in *A Concrete Atlantis* revived that traditional philosophical equivalence and effectively demonstrated that he had forgotten or abandoned the more adventuresome concept of concrete images that he had proposed three decades earlier in his review of
ARRAY 0.1 *This Is Tomorrow*.

But *A Concrete Atlantis* begins in a spirit closer to his 1956 insight, with Banham's account of a personal experience that seems something like the apprehension of a concrete image and which he memorialized in a seemingly ordinary snapshot of the remains of an industrial building in California that, he remarked, was demolished soon after he took the photograph. He described the building as "three tall, fat, crusty-black vertical cylinders that had probably once been oil tanks. Next to them, however—and this is what made the site so intriguing to me—was an apparently unfinished concrete structure, a flat, square ground-slab carrying one story-height of vertical square columns whose heads were joined by equally simple concrete square beams."[21] Banham recollects and explains that encounter as the moment when the "main currents" of his book's thesis "seemed to spark together most enlighteningly within my eyes."[22] It happened "not in the presence of some monumental structure or provocative text, but among the abandoned installations of the defunct sardine fisheries on Monterey Bay."[23] Unlike his account of the pure forms the European modernists perceived in the photographs of concrete American factories and grain elevators, or his 1955 conflation of concept and image, Banham's encounter provoked a "spark" of imagination or instance of recollective imaging, which he augmented with a literary image of that same site as it may have appeared over fifty years earlier. The second paragraph of *A Concrete Atlantis* is a passage from John Steinbeck's novel *Cannery Row* (1945) that, Banham explained, "gives a very plausible account
ARRAY 0.2 of the disposal of some obsolete industrial equipment" in the same area in 1932. Banham's factual and fictional flash of recognition—and the documentary snapshot—was not (at least not at that moment) a mere reaffirmation of known formal concepts. Rather, the scene that evoked his condensation of Steinbeck's fictional description, of iconic photographs of industrial buildings, and of a recurrence of his own "pet ideas" of 1955 exemplifies the operations of imaging. It enacts something like Walter Benjamin's theorization of dialectical images, in which one's experience of the present is imagined as prefigured in reproduced images from the past. As Benjamin wrote in his *Arcades Project* in the 1930s: "It's not that what is past casts its light on what is present, or what is present its light on what is past; rather, image is that wherein what has been comes together in a flash with the now to

0.1

METALS AND MINERALS RESEARCH BUILDING

ILLINOIS INSTITUTE OF TECHNOLOGY

DESIGNED BY MIES VAN DER ROHE

This is the first of Mies van der Rohe's buildings to be erected in the USA, and has been designed to form part of a large educational group for the Illinois Institute of Technology.

It has that purity and integrity of expression, that simplicity of design, and that extreme care in structural detail which distinguish his earlier work in Europe.

The building was erected for the Armour Research Foundation to house several industrial research activities involving the use of delicate precision apparatus and fairly heavy industrial equipment including several types of furnaces, presses and metal rolling mills. This equipment, however, is not fixed or permanent and a major requirement was that flexibility possessed by a modern factory. As a war expedient the building has been used to house equipment other than was originally intended, but the building is first and foremost a foundry.

The materials used are structural steel framework, which is exposed and painted, brick, concrete and glass. The roof is a combination of steel and concrete.

pollock

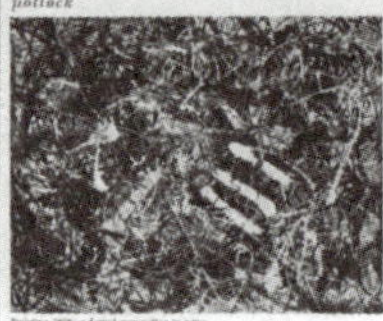

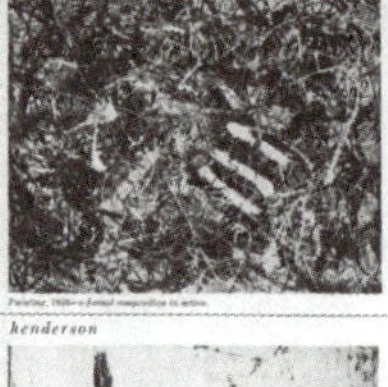

burri

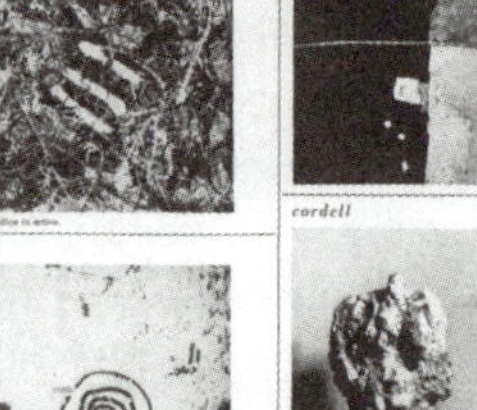

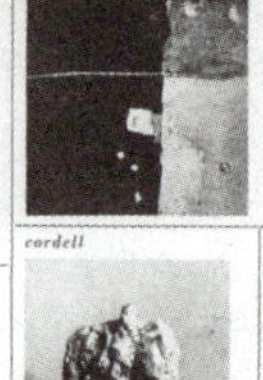

NEW BRUTALISM

henderson

cordell

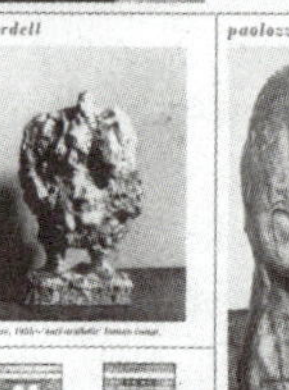

paolozzi

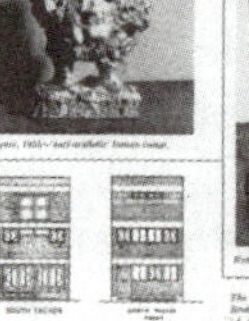

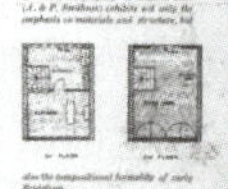

to reduce the means employed to a set of recognizable elements, classifiable under the heads of Structure, Plasticity, Symbol and Sign, even if pictures were merely hung on a wall these four elements were all employed, if only accidentally.

Some concept of structure—geometry clothed in substance—proved to be the basic, or unifying postulate of most groups' offerings, and in one case, the partnership of John Weeks and Adrian Heath, structure was the totality of the exhibit, a wall of standard bricks

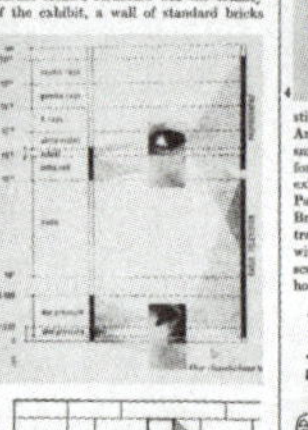

which were displaced or omitted, 3, to give it the plasticity and symbolic significance of an abstract sculpture.

More complex structure-sculptures were seen in the Catleugh-Thornton-Hull screen, 4, but a note of ambiguity, more consciously exploited in other sections, appears in the composition of curved planes on which Peter Carter, Colin St. J. Wilson and Robert Adams collaborated. Normal scale-effects are reversed, and that part which is large enough to admit a standing man, 5, is clearly sculptural in feeling, while the manifestly structural element beyond is sited and displayed like a free-standing statue.

This ambiguity was part of a general feeling of broken barriers and questioned categories that constituted the most

stimulating aspect of the whole exhibition. And yet the technique of category-smashing could not be used as a basis for forming value-judgments about the exhibits. Thus, the Smithson-Henderson-Paolozzi contribution showed the New Brutalists at their most submissive to traditional values. They erected a pavilion within a patio, 6, and stocked it with sculptures signifying the most time-honoured of man's activities and needs.

Concrete frame and abandoned tanks, Cannery Row, Monterey, California. (Photo, author)

Washburn-Crosby Elevator, Buffalo, as photographed by Erich Mendelsohn, 1924

Fiat-Lingotto, aerial view of test track, ca. 1970. (Photo, Fiat)

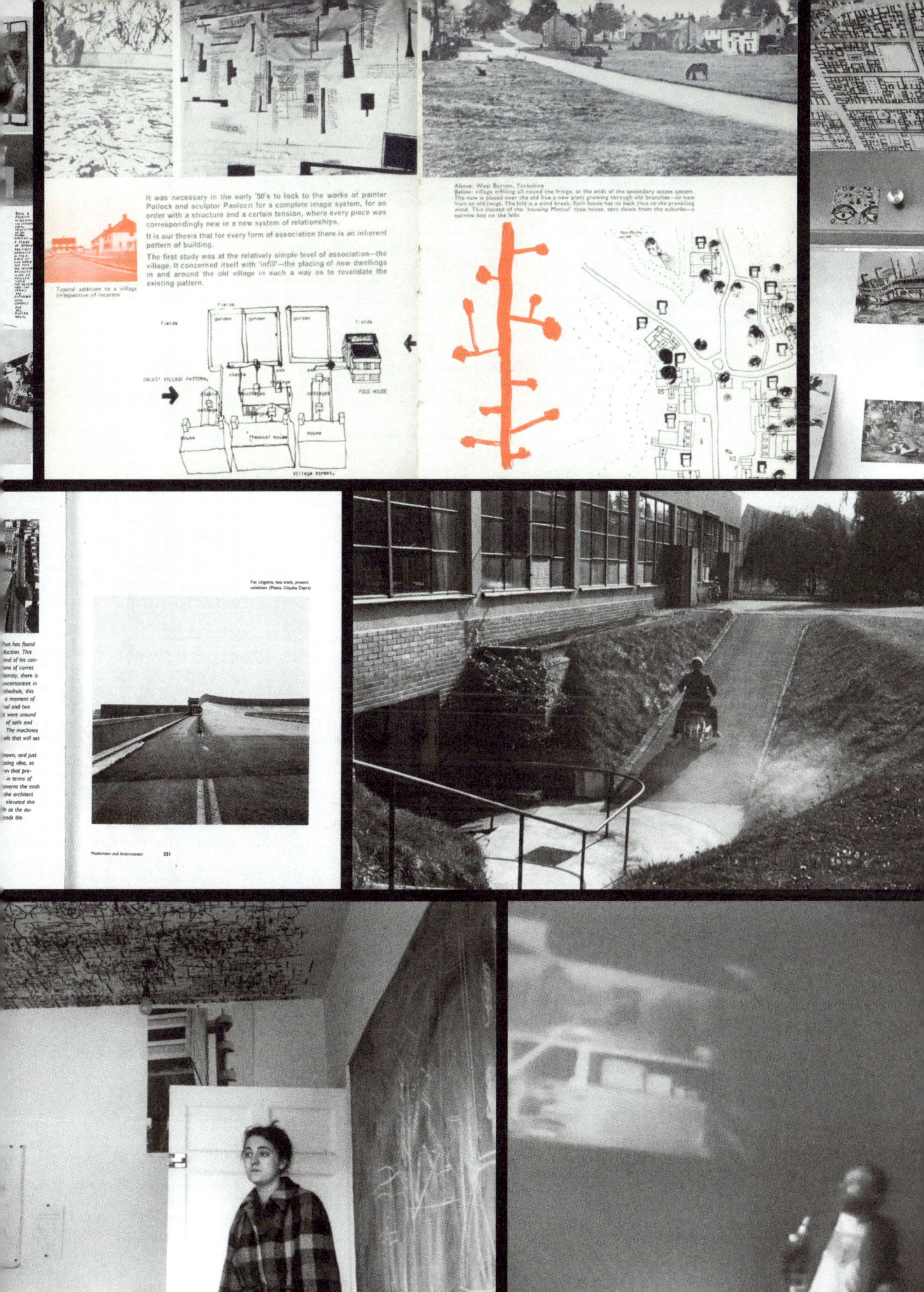

It was necessary in the early '50's to look to the works of painter Pollock and sculptor Paolozzi for a complete image system, for an order with a structure and a certain tension, where every piece was correspondingly new in a new system of relationships.

It is our thesis that for every form of association there is an inherent pattern of building.

The first study was at the relatively simple level of association—the village. It concerned itself with 'infill'—the placing of new dwellings in and around the old village in such a way as to revalidate the existing pattern.

Typical addition to a village irrespective of location

Above: West Burton, Yorkshire
Below: village infilling all round the fringe, at the ends of the secondary access system. The new is placed over the old like a new plant growing through old branches—or new fruit on old twigs. The fold is a wind break. Each house has its back thus to the prevailing wind. This instead of the 'housing Manual' type house, sent down from the suburbs—a barrow boy on the fells

Fiat Lingotto, test track, present condition. (Photo. Claudio Dapra)

Modernism and Americanism 251

0.2

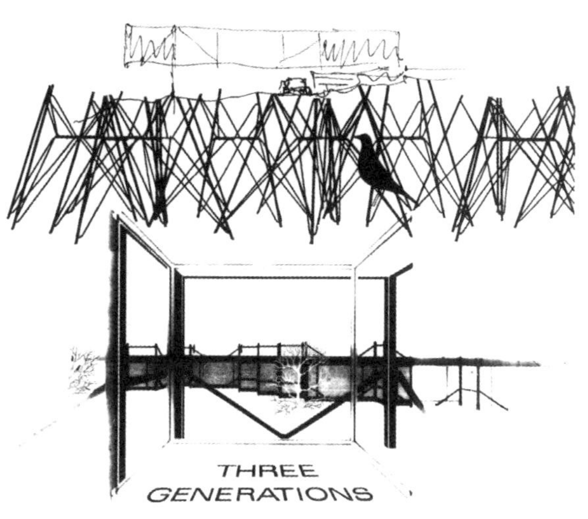
THREE
GENERATIONS

form a constellation. In other words, image is dialectics at a standstill." Such an image, according to Benjamin, does not convey essences, facts, or ideas: it operates as a vital and virtual "historical index."[24]

Yet Banham's subsequent discussion of the meaning of the creative "spark" that he experienced in Monterey is far from Benjaminian. Instead, his second description of the abandoned industrial site converts his surprising recollection, and seeming return of a repressed New Brutalist imaginary, into his own version of a familiar recognition of "fundamental principles" of "great architecture." His account becomes a reassertion of the classicizing abstraction of "European views of American industry": "Indeed it was barely architecture at all; it was like the merest diagram of an idealized reinforced concrete-frame structure, the sort of thing that used to appear in worthy books claiming to instruct lay people in the fundamental principles of modern architecture, an image as familiar as any of the other older furniture of my mind."[25] Banham's language—"barely architecture," "merest diagram," "idealized," "fundamental principles," "older furniture of my mind"—reduces that moment of imaging into "familiar" *concepts*. For Banham, in the end, both his snapshot and the early photos of industrial architecture were not concrete images. They were pictures of concrete buildings that offer "an available iconography, a language of forms."[26] His reading of photography in 1986 adopted the then pervasive methods of visual studies and formal analysis, which converted "dialectical" or "concrete" images into linguistic codes or geometric concepts as a means to control, extract, and stabilize their historical, political, and aesthetic significance. Later in his introduction he confirms that attitude, and it becomes clear that he has adopted a fully *anti-visual* position to replace the "anti-art," "anti-Academic," and "anti-beauty"[27] position he had articulated in 1955 as the basis of New Brutalism: "Architecture remains a predominantly visual art; this may be regrettable but it is a historical and cultural fact, and it means that architects are educated and influenced primarily by the force of visual example."[28]

In his explanation of the powerful influence of the photographs of factories and grain elevators on early modernist architects, Banham did more than emulate the methods of visual studies and formal analysis: he reinforced ideas about photography as mechanical, automatic representations that epitomize—or signify—scientific, technological, and even journalistic objectivity:

> The power of the photographs comes from the fact that, like the works of engineering they represented, they were understood to be the product of the scientific application of natural laws. Having come into the hands of their European admirers in the guise of news photographs, rather than that of "art" photography, they were supposedly free from those elements of personal selection and interpretation that must inevitably infect any artistic rendering, or even the traditional production by architectural draftsmen of finished drawings from measured field notes. The photographs represented a truth as apparently objective and modern as that of the functional structures they portrayed.[29]

The contrast between Banham's understanding of photography in *A Concrete Atlantis* and the New Brutalists' understanding of photographic images is too clear to ignore. In fact, it was precisely an impulse against seeing documentary and scientific photography in terms of objectivity that inspired the New Brutalists' first tests of an imaging aesthetic in projects such as *Parallel of Life and Art* and *Patio and Pavilion*, or in the Smithsons' photo-collages for the Golden Lane Housing competition (1952) and their uses of Henderson's photographs in their CIAM Grille (1953), and which they continued to explore in their later essays and books. Most peculiar and symptomatic of all, at the end of the introduction to *A Concrete Atlantis*, Banham invited a comparison of classic modern architecture with New Brutalism by repeating a crucial phrase he had used in 1955. In "The New Brutalism," he declared that *Parallel of Life and Art* constituted the "*locus classicus* of the movement," and in *A Concrete Atlantis* he called the much earlier Fiat factory in Turin (1916–23) "the *locus classicus* of modernism."[30] But in *A Concrete Atlantis* his argument was quite literally classicizing:

> Any search for an understanding of why those factories and grain elevators look so good to us now must also involve some attempt to understand the ambitions, expectations, and frame of mind that drove the founding fathers of the modern movement to adopt these monuments as the models for their new architecture—which was also, somehow, expected to rediscover and then embody the eternal and fundamental verities underlying all great architecture, old as well as new.[31]

As Banham's argument develops in the introduction, it becomes entirely clear that he, like the early modernists, saw the fourteen photographs as well as his own snapshot as imaginatively powerful not because they are concrete images, but because they are technical, optical images of things that "had concrete—literally concrete—presence here on earth."[32] The photographs depicting the "idealized but concrete industrial architecture of North America" manifested the idea of science and technology that, Banham argued, fueled the "simultaneous quest for pure modernity and also ancient certainty"[33] that was shared by Adolf Loos, Walter Gropius, Le Corbusier, Nikolaus Pevsner, and Sigfried Giedion, and that was evident above all in Edoardo Persico's 1927 essay praising the "ancient order" of the Fiat Factory, which Banham quotes nearly in its entirety to make "the last argument of the book."[34] Thus, *A Concrete Atlantis* ratifies and finalizes his rejection two decades earlier of his own pet ideas about the importance of concrete images for New Brutalism in the 1950s.

That's Brutal, What's Modern? attempts to recuperate both Banham's rejected theorization of, and the Smithsons' recursive practice of, New Brutalism as ways of making and scrutinizing concrete images. It builds on Banham's original but not quite coherent theorization of New Brutalism in 1955 as an imaging practice that "requires that the building should be an immediately apprehensible visual entity, and that the form grasped by the eye should be confirmed by the experience in use," or, as he elaborated in reference to the Smithsons' entry in the Golden Lane Housing competition, results from the "determination to create a visual image by non-formal means [. . .] and fully validating the presence of human beings as part of the total image."[35] The following year, Banham offered his crucial "concrete images" reformulation, yet only one year after that, in a letter to the editor of *Architectural Design* defending his ideas about New Brutalism, he would neglect his imaging theories, leaving it to John Voelcker, in a letter in the same issue of the journal, to offer what remains perhaps the most eloquent expression of those ideas: "Brutalism aims to invent those unique images from bits and pieces (stone, door handle, standard metal window, polythene pipe, etc.) which communicate and are inevitable in the historical/ecological/technological situation 'as found'."[36] Fast-forward yet another ten years, and another evocative version of those ideas would appear in Robin Middleton's review of Banham's book. Seemingly responding to Banham's misleading discussion of a "fusion of the Mies-image and the Corb-image," Middleton suggested a different pairing of sources for the Smithsons' "Brutalist" imaging practices:

ARRAY 0.3

> Mies van der Rohe's beautifully articulated buildings for the Illinois Institute of Technology suggested a point of departure—the buildings were reticent, clean and easily apprehended. They provided a ready-made aesthetic. But the Smithsons' real discovery [. . .] was more personal in inspiration. They realized that they would have to build up their architecture from whatever fragments were available. [. . .] But the problem remained how to relate one to another and then to the building as a whole so that the result might be architecture. Charles and Ray Eames [. . .] provided the Smithsons with a clue. Objects could be arranged, apparently casually, against a neutral background to forceful resultant effect. The combination of the Mies aesthetic with the Eames concept of arrangement proved electrifying when interpreted by the Smithsons. The wash-handbasins and kitchen stoves at Hunstanton seen against the walls of glass convey still the strongest impression of the Brutalist image. But clearly architecture could not be composed like a pin-up board; at worst the method might be equated with flower arrangement.[37]

Thus Middleton, like Banham, advanced imaging as crucial to New Brutalism but then retracted it as not adequately or fully architectural. Banham and Middleton distrusted image-thinking, whether "pet notions" or "flower arrangement," just as images and imaging have been denigrated as ephemeral or deceitful for centuries in Western culture. It should be no surprise that the vast majority of post-Enlightenment models of visuality attempt to counter that presumed weakness by emulating language or science. But imaging theories and practices offer a counter-move: they propose that alternative modes of thoughtful looking and seeing can be as intelligent, intellectual, and constructive as geometry, language, or modernist models of visuality, especially in today's age of ubiquitous digital media when the incessant distribution, replication, and recording of digital images threatens—or promises—to launch what Vilém Flusser has called, in a book published just one year before *A Concrete Atlantis*, "a universe of technical images" that will "take over the task formerly served by linear texts, that is, the task of transmitting information crucial to society and to individuals."[38] Flusser argues that these "calculated and computed mosaics" are not only superseding texts, they operate very differently than previously established modes of representation.[39] They perform "a concretizing gesture" that "neither abstracts, nor steps backwards; just the opposite, it concretizes, it projects."[40]

A different theorization of the procedures of imaging is elaborated in Jacques Rancière's explanation of *graphisme* in his 2002 essay "The Surface of Design."[41] He characterizes the graphic layouts of Stéphane Mallarmé's poetry and the product designs of Peter Behrens in the early twentieth century as "practices that configure the shared material world" by imagining a simultaneously literal and abstract (or material and ideal) "surface of conversion where words, forms and things exchange roles."[42] This "surface of equivalence" (or ambivalence between "reality and illusion") enacts the "reconfiguration of a shared material world by working on its basic elements, on the forms of the objects of everyday life."[43]

Maryanne Wolf offers another basis upon which to understand the contemporary status and uses of imaging in relation to language. She argues that global culture is now undergoing a profound stage in "the evolution of human intelligence" as we "transition from a reading brain into an increasingly digital one."[44] She summarizes over a decade of her own research in cognitive neuroscience and developmental psycholinguistics by saying: "*human beings were never born to read*. The acquisition of literacy is one of the most epigenetic achievements of *Homo sapiens*."[45] Over thousands of years, humans have traveled through a "long developmental process of learning to read deeply and well [. . .] which rewired the brain, which transformed the nature of human thought."[46] By enabling crucial "cognitive processes such as critical thinking, personal reflection, imagination, empathy," deep reading became the "best-known path to developing whole new pathways in the cerebral evolution of our species."[47] Most important for Wolf, and for the argument of this book, reading is a cognitive ability that must be learned by every individual and is challenged today by the very different "cognitive capacities emphasized by digital media."[48] Wolf offers an extended argument for new research and projects that can preserve and enhance the deep reading brain in the face of an unexpected and paradoxical historical outcome that has accelerated radically over the last few decades: "In our almost complete transition to a digital culture we are changing in ways we never realized would be the unintended collateral consequences of the greatest explosion of creativity, invention, and discovery in our history."[49] Wolf focuses singularly on reading and does not develop arguments about the tensions between reading and imaging. Yet her ambition aligns with the aims of this book. She does not oppose a culture of deep reading to a digital culture but believes we must begin to understand and develop the potential of a deeper digital culture as we undergo a "historical transition to new ways of acquiring, processing, and comprehending information."[50] Such an ambition is supported by new knowledge of the neural basis of reading: "Underlying the brain's ability to learn reading lies its protean capacity to make new connections among structures and circuits originally devoted to other more basic brain processes that

0.3

One final thought concerning an aspect of our inheritance the existence of which has only risen into consciousness during the months of the preparation of this reflective genealogy: that much of our inheritance reaches us through the female line...
Lily Reich
Charlotte Perriand
Ray Eames
For the invention of a new spacial container needs the separate invention

of Cards: Charles and
ames, 1952.

airs: Charles and Ray
1952.

45

10] THE ARCHITECTS' JOURNAL for January 3, 1946

Above, the central part of the building open to the full height of two storeys to give flexibility for various, and changing, equipment. Below, one of the laboratories. Partitions have been omitted as far as possible. Right, the second of the two main laboratories used as a lecture hall.

Charlotte Perriand
"Our generation are used to Le Corbusier being able to give form to a changed situation. As one would expect, the Unite kitchen, by Charlotte Perriand, is as much part of the architectural whole as are the pilotis, and certainly had as great an impact on young architects as did the pilotis."
A fragment from an essay by A.M.S. on "the Future of Furniture".
First published in Architectural Design, April 1958.
Edited, October 1990

together.
So too, the Gropiuses at breakfast together in their house in Lincoln, Massachussets; designed in the late nineteen thirties, the style of the container and the style of the contents are inseparable.
And the Eames, from the next generation.
And to the end, in conscious homage to the founding mothers – Sunday breakfast at our house in the country.

By the third generation nothing built is without pre-existing meanings. For us in that generation the commonest elements of building carry with them a [illegible] architecture itself.

95

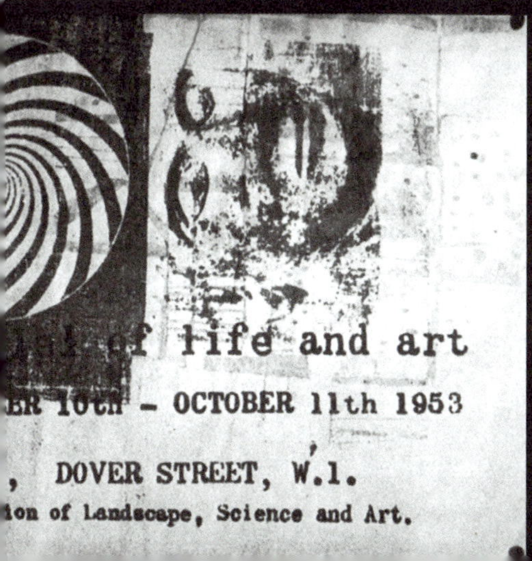

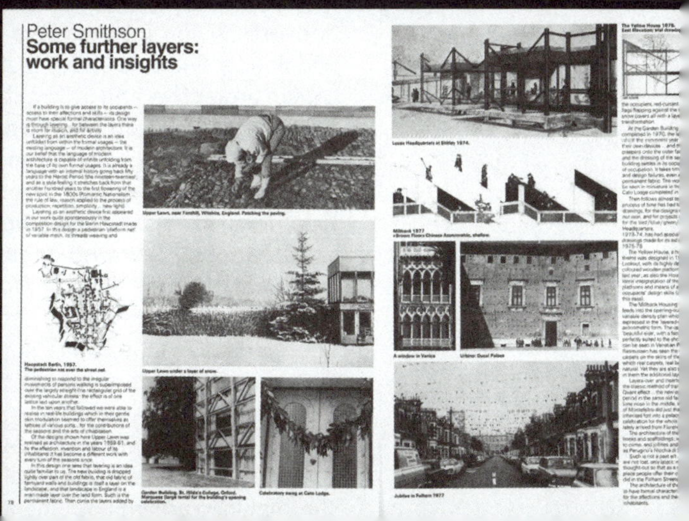

Peter Smithson
Some further layers: work and insights

Upper Lawn, near Fonthill, Wiltshire, England. Patching the paving.

Hauptstadt Berlin, 1957.
The pedestrian net over the street net.

Upper Lawn under a layer of snow.

Garden Building, St. Hilda's College, Oxford. Marquees (large tents) for the building's opening celebration.

Celebratory swag at Cato Lodge.

Lucas Headquarters at Shirley 1974.

Milbank 1977

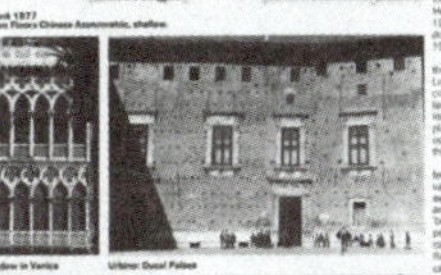

A window in Venice

Urbino: Ducal Palace

Jubilee in Fulham 1977

The Yellow House 1976.

have enjoyed a longer existence in human evolution, such as vision and spoken language."[51] Quite simply, "recycling existing visual circuits made the development of reading possible."[52]

Thus imaging, like reading, involves cognitive capabilities that preceded language by tens of thousands of years and which have been developing, or in some ways atrophying, in coincidence with it.[53] Imaging theory that draws on the writings of Wolf, Rancière, Flusser, and others in combination with a historical understanding of the emergence of post-photographic imaging practices can demonstrate new modalities of their long-standing and still latent potential. Is it possible to develop imaging practices that rival deep reading and "the more time-demanding cognitive processes nurtured by print-based mediums"?[54] How might "deep imaging" produce and operate as knowledge or as architecture at this critical moment in the history of "deep reading"?

Art historian Barbara Stafford offers some initial answers to those questions. She suggests that scrutinizing the history of art is a way to better understand the history of our ever-evolving, plastic brains, including in today's digital culture, where "new media's electronic mash of images refocuses experience through an increasingly aberrant lens. Blocking, filtering, and layering digital technologies are generating shifting and drifting ways of seeing, as well as producing seamless repetition."[55] For her, every innovation in the history of art is a kind of intuitive or critical discovery of a latent neurological capacity of human cognition. She proposes a transdisciplinary alliance between neuroscience and the humanities as a "new meta-field" to explore the coevolution of cognition and culture. Media theorist Mark Hansen exemplifies that approach. He argues for a definition of "image as a temporal process rather than a spatial/visual figure."[56] For Hansen, media literally involves mind and matter in a "microtemporal pattern of cognitive activity."[57] Drawing on recent neuroscientific research and philosophers such as Henri Bergson, Gilles Deleuze, and Gilbert Simondon, Hansen's concept of the "fluid image" explains media as "a continuum connecting mental and material images" that activates a "convergence between microtemporal media and microtemporal cognition."[58] Stafford and Hansen clarify how imaging technologies as seemingly different as fMRI, video, and digital modeling each employ digital media as a kind of artificial imagination that converts vision into matters of processing and calculation.[59] Those imaging technologies have fostered a kind of human–machine cognition that is projective and affirmational but often in ways that refuse or are opaque to dominant or conventional thinking, especially the predominance of language. The concern with imaging in this book centers on how humans (as well as other life forms and artificially intelligent machines) produce, exchange, value, and react to images as a specific way of tapping evolved cognitive capacities and understanding the potential of those capacities. New Brutalism is nothing less than an early episode in the history of imaging practices that offers basic but useful lessons in how imaging finds potential or virtuality in material, including the material of our brains.

The imaging arrays in this book operate as equal partners with the text to demonstrate, as vividly, precisely, and concretely as possible, the imagined affiliations among objects, sites, and events that circulated in the New Brutalist sensibility. Each array coalesces and organizes multiple visual references as they appear and are discussed in the text. They provide historical and actual evidence of New Brutalist design aspirations. Many individual images are repeated in multiple arrays, just as the book's six chapters return to, and reconsider, some of the same events, artifacts, and texts. Each chapter or array can be read or engaged with separately or in any order, but the argument develops more fully and reiteratively if they are read as a series. The chapters and arrays offer different approaches to develop a basic thesis: that New Brutalism is best understood as the Smithsons' pursuit of the Mies-image. Chapters One and Two establish the general historical context of New Brutalism and British modernism. Chapter Three presents theoretical arguments for imaging both in the early 1950s and today, drawing especially on the recent aesthetic theory of Rancière. Chapter Four, the core of the book, presents a close reading of the complex interrelationships and repetitions of texts and images in the Smithsons' later books as the best evidence and explanation of their imaging practices. Together, those books recollect, reformulate, resituate, and reactivate variations of New Brutalism as the pursuit of the Mies-image. Chapter Five tracks the development of Banham's shifting explanations and evaluations of both New Brutalism and Mies. It presents his antagonistic and polemical positions as a counter-project to the Smithsons' that helps to clarify their thinking. It offers a reassessment of Banham's first formulation of New Brutalism as a topological imaging practice and, building on his ideas about concrete images, argues that *Patio and Pavilion* has surprising affinities with the work of Mies that would be pursued in the Smithsons' later work. The final chapter offers a general theoretical discussion of imaging and its implications for architecture. It introduces versions of theories that appeared in the broader context of an emerging image culture in postwar Britain, looking at philosophical debates (especially the ideas of H. H. Price, Gilbert Ryle, and Ludwig Wittgenstein) and their appearance in the world of art (the activities of the Independent Group and the writings of Anton Ehrenzweig and Ernst Gombrich). It ends with the contemporary ideas and questions that fuel the historical investigation of the Smithsons' New Brutalism and draws on recent approaches to image theory, including those of Rancière, Flusser, Stafford, Hansen, and others, to elaborate the ways New Brutalism engaged versions of the multimedia practices that would intensify in the latter half of the twentieth century and which are now the basis of architectural production, imagination, and experience.

While the Smithsons did not embrace the technological potentials of contemporary media such as television, video, or computers and were even disinterested in them, they were attuned to their import and impact. Their approaches can be understood as cautious yet curious responses to the full range of new media and new audiences. Cautious because they never risked losing or diluting the modernist architectural discipline and its history that they learned in their youth. Curious because they never seemed to tire of finding new ways to investigate, revise, and communicate the potential of those sources and influences. The Smithsons' imaging practices fundamentally yet cunningly reconfigured architecture's disciplinary knowledge and operations. They explored architecture as a recollective effect of their deep, rich, malleable, and imperfect post-photographic memories and imaging practices. Recasting New Brutalism in terms of imaging and examining the Smithsons' work as a historical case study situates both in an intellectual and visual culture that had been emergent long before them, and which continues today without apparent paradox or reduction in our computational, automated, and mediated realities of production and exchange. Just as Mies began to be understood in the 1980s—when, not coincidentally, the Barcelona Pavilion was being reconstructed—in terms of media, effect, and technologies of reproduction, New Brutalism's complex beginnings allow a similarly complex understanding of its motives and aspirations.

That's Brutal, What's Modern? attempts to correlate and couple New Brutalism and the Smithsons by detailing and assembling the scene out of which their New Brutalist Mies-image emerged in the early 1950s and, more importantly, how that scene was recollected and rethought in their later work. Most attempts by scholars, contemporaries, and followers to untangle the complexities of New Brutalism's history and its influence tend to make sense of particular episodes or just a few strands of this complicated and tightly bound knot. This book arrays the evidence and makes the case that the identity and influence of the Smithsons' New Brutalism was constructed retrospectively as they persistently reimagined the "Miesian" qualities and efficacy of concepts such as "a random aesthetic," "the as found," "patterns of association," and "conglomerate ordering" and developed later ones such as "the lattice idea" and "treillage'd space."

Finally, while this book focuses on the Smithsons, it is motivated by a more general question and a broader research project. The question is intended to be timely and contemporary, but is posed with both historical and polemical purpose: What would architectural practice become if its acknowledged means and ends were imaging? A series of other questions follows: What distinguishes the imaging practices of New Brutalism? What is the alliance between New Brutalism and imaging? How did today's world of imaging practices, imagery, and imaging technologies emerge in history? How is New Brutalism still *new* and increasingly pertinent for architecture's production, reception, and dissemination? And what is the potential for a *newer* New Brutalism that draws and builds on a coherent and comprehensive understanding of recent imaging theory? New Brutalism in the early 1950s and the pursuits it inspired afterward for Alison and Peter Smithson exemplify the kinds of discovery provoked by those questions. Their own answer is most evocatively posed in their 1967 Berlin seminar, where they claim that Mies's architecture conveys a disciplined "quietness, that up to now our sensibilities have not recognized as architecture at all, let alone seen clearly enough to isolate its characteristics."[60] As I understand them, what the Smithsons seem to have been saying, at that moment of a crucial shift in their sensibilities, is that they came to understand how Mies's architecture is almost nothing like a building, and almost something like an image.

Notes

1 The phrase first appears in Peter Smithson, "Reflections on Hunstanton," *ARQ*, 2, no. 3 (Summer 1997), p. 38, but also in the introductory text (which may have been written as early as 1974, probably by Alison Smithson) to the 28-page section on the Hunstanton School in *The Charged Void: Architecture*, New York: Monacelli Press, 2001, p. 40: "We saw layering of structure at the naked stage, layering of reflection at the glazed stage." In a gallery talk in 1975, Alison discussed their design for the Lucas Headquarters (Shirley, West Midlands, 1973–74, unbuilt) as a study of the "reflections and the build-up of transparency" that they first observed at Hunstanton. "Alison Smithson – A Line of Tree … A Steel Structure," Art Net, London, October 31, 1975, www.youtube.com/watch?v=QHnaEwRWJ-0, accessed June 22, 2018. The earliest published discussion of Hunstanton in similar terms appeared in Alison and Peter Smithson, *The Shift*, London: Academy Editions, 1982, and is also discussed in *Changing the Art of Inhabitation: Mies' Pieces, Eames' Dreams, the Smithsons*, London: Artemis, 1994, pp. 64 and 153, which quotes a passage from an unpublished essay by Alison, dated 1991–92: "'Afterthoughts on Reflections', the Outcome of the Questions of the 1950s."

2 Alison and Peter Smithson, "House in Soho, London," *Architectural Design*, 23, no. 12 (December 1953), p. 342.

3 The chronology is further complicated by prewar projects that could be characterized as both proto-New Brutalist and proto-Brutalist: Mies's Concrete Office Building (Berlin, 1923, unbuilt) and the elegant and functional reinforced concrete buildings by the English engineer Owen Williams, such as the Boots pharmaceutical factories (Beeston, Nottinghamshire, 1930–32 and 1935–38) and especially the Pioneer Health Centre (London, 1933–35), which has intriguing programmatic and formal affinities with Hunstanton.

4 Reyner Banham, *The New Brutalism: Ethic or Aesthetic?*, New York: Reinhold, 1966, p. 16.

5 Ibid., p. 17.

6 Ibid., p. 18. Banham was especially critical of those who mistakenly treated Mies as a master of proportional systems.

7 Ibid., p. 20.

8 In 1955 Banham identified the most specific target for New Brutalism as "'The New Humanism', which was in itself a reworking of a title invented (by the 'Architectural Review') for the Swedish retreat from Modern Architecture: The New Empiricism," which was influential among the Archtects' Department of the London County Council after the war. Banham, *The New Brutalism*, p. 12.

9 Alison and Peter Smithson, "The Heroic Period of Modern Architecture, 1817–1947," *Architectural Design*, 35, no. 12 (December 1965), p. 590.

10 Robin Boyd, "The Sad End of New Brutalism," *Architectural Review*, 142, no. 845 (July 1967), p. 10.

11 Ibid., p. 9.

12 John Summerson, "Introduction," in *Ten Years of British Architecture: '45–55*, exh. cat., London: Arts Council of Britain, 1956, p. 11.

13 Reyner Banham, "The New Brutalism," *Architectural Review*, 118, no. 708 (December 1955), pp. 355–56.

14 Banham, *The New Brutalism*, p. 134.

15 Reyner Banham, "This Is Tomorrow," *Architectural Review*, 120, no. 716 (September 1956), p. 188.

16 Beatriz Colomina, "Brutalism and War," in *Brutalism: Contributions to the International Symposium in Berlin, 2012*, Zurich: Park Books, 2017, p. 24. More than anyone else, Colomina has recognized the importance of the Smithson–Mies connection in numerous essays. See especially "Couplings," *OASE*, 51, special issue: *Rearrangements, A Smithsons Celebration* (June 1999), pp. 22–33.

17 The photographs appeared in the *Jahrbuch des Deutschen Werkbundes*, Jena: Eugen Diederichs, 1913.

18 An even more famous, and much more robust and consequential, instance of transatlantic influence occurred over a half-century earlier in Gottfried Semper's encounter with a reconstruction—an imaging—of a Caribbean hut at the Great Exposition in London in 1851.

19 Reyner Banham, *A Concrete Atlantis: US Industrial Building and European Modern Architecture, 1900–1925*, Cambridge, MA: MIT Press, 1986, p. 21.

20 Banham, "The New Brutalism," p. 358.

21 Banham, *A Concrete Atlantis*, p. 2.

22 Ibid., p. 1.

23 Ibid.

24 Walter Benjamin, *The Arcades Project*, trans. Howard Eiland and Kevin McLaughlin, Cambridge, MA: Harvard University Press, p. 462.

25 Banham, *A Concrete Atlantis*, p. 2.

26 Ibid., p. 7.

27 Banham, "The New Brutalism," p. 358.

28 Banham, *A Concrete Atlantis*, p. 9.

29 Ibid., p. 18.

30 Banham, "The New Brutalism," p. 356; Banham, *A Concrete Atlantis*, p. 21.

31 Banham, *A Concrete Atlantis*, p. 21.

32 Ibid., p. 8.

33 Ibid., pp. 8, 9.

34 Ibid., pp. 248–53.

35 Banham, "The New Brutalism," pp. 358, 361.

36 John Voelcker, "Letter," *Architectural Design*, 27, no. 6 (June 1957), p. 184.

37 Robin Middleton, "The New Brutalism; or, A Clean, Well-Lighted Place," *Architectural Design*, 37 (January 1967), pp. 7–8.

38 Vilém Flusser, *Into the Universe of Technical Images* [1985], trans. Nancy Ann Roth, Minneapolis: University of Minnesota Press, 2011, p. 5.

39 Ibid., p. 170.

40 Vilém Flusser, "A New Imagination," in *Writings* [1990], ed. Andreas Ströhl, trans. Erik Eisel, Minneapolis: University of Minnesota Press, 2004, p. 114.

41 Jacques Rancière, "The Surface of Design," in *The Future of the Image*, trans. Gregory Elliott, London and New York:

Verso, 2007, pp. 91–107. First published as "Les Ambivilences du graphisme" in *Design ... Graphique?*, ed. Annick Lantenois, Valence: École Regionale des Beaux-Arts de Valence, 2002.

42 Rancière, "The Surface of Design," pp. 91, 106.

43 Ibid., p. 101.

44 Maryanne Wolf, *Proust and the Squid: The Story and Science of the Reading Brain*, Harper Collins, 2007, p. 4.

45 Maryanne Wolf, *Reader, Come Home: The Reading Brain in a Digital World*, New York: Harper Collins, 2018, p. 1 (italics original).

46 Ibid., p. 2.

47 Ibid., pp. 8, 2.

48 Ibid., p. 8.

49 Ibid., p. 3.

50 Wolf, *Proust and the Squid*, p. 17.

51 Ibid., p. 5.

52 Ibid., p. 12.

53 For a fascinating and comprehensive acount of the evolutionary basis of the neural systems underlying reading, see Todd Feinberg and Jon Mallatt, *The Ancient Origins of Consciousness: How the Brain Created Experience*, Cambridge, MA: MIT Press, 2017, especially the chapter "Consciousness Gets a Head Start: Vertebrate Brains, Vision and the Cambrian Birth of the Mental Image," pp. 69–100.

54 Wolf, *Reader, Come Home*, p. 8.

55 Barbara Stafford, "Crystal and Smoke: Putting Image Back in Mind," in *A Field Guide to a New Meta-Field: Bridging the Humanities–Neurosciences Divide*, Chicago: University of Chicago Press, 2011, pp. 33–34.

56 Mark Hansen, "From Fixed to Fluid: Material-Mental Images between Neural Synchronization and Computational Mediation," in *Releasing the Image: From Literature to New Media*, ed. Jacques Khalip and Robert Mitchell, Stanford: Stanford University Press, 2011, p. 104.

57 Hansen, "From Fixed to Fluid," p. 87.

58 Ibid., pp. 104, 111.

59 Artificial imagination encompasses the use of any mechanical or digital imaging technology to activate a synthetic (human–machine) collaboration and generate new varieties of visual perception and cognition by exacerbating and expanding the established, latent, and potential capacities of our brains to process visual information and assemble images. Media such as fMRI, video, and digital modeling are thus recent predecessors of today's understanding of artificial imagination—ranging from machine vision to novel image generation using neural networks—as a subfield of artificial intelligence.

60 Alison and Peter Smithson, "Mies van der Rohe," Architectural Design, 39, no. 7 (July 1969), p. 363.

Fig 1. Jacques Rancière. *Aisthesis: Scenes from the Aesthetic Regime of Art* [2011], trans. Zakir Paul, London and New York: Verso, 2013, pp. xiii, ix, xi, xii; Jacques Rancière and Oliver Davis, "On Aisthesis: An Interview," trans. Steven Corcoran, in O. Davis, ed., *Rancière Now: Current Perspectives on Jacques Rancière*, Cambridge: Polity, 2013, pp. 202–3.

Chapter 1

That’s Brutal

Alison and Peter Smithson's initial, brash, and tenacious declaration of their ambition to redirect modern architecture in the wake of World War Two first appeared in Britain via Chicago in the image of a New Brutalist Mies. Acquainted with Ludwig Mies van der Rohe's new Chicago work only through photographs and drawings published in a 1946 article in the *Architects' Journal* and in Philip Johnson's 1947 catalogue for the *Mies van der Rohe* exhibition at the Museum of Modern Art, New York,[1] the Smithsons' competition-winning design for the Hunstanton Secondary Modern School (1950–54) adopted and ARRAY 1.1 revised the startling clarity, directness, and raw materiality of the steel, glass, and brick buildings Mies had begun to design in the early 1940s for the Illinois Institute of Technology (IIT). The Smithsons believed they had found the means to assert a rigorous, frank, and open architecture during a time of austerity and conflicted cultural values and in anticipation of an uncertain but hopeful future. Miesian restraint, practicality, and logic seemed to offer an assured exit from British ambivalence toward modernism as well as the potential to resume, relocate, and redirect the prewar continental legacy that the Smithsons would later call the "heroic period of modern architecture."[2]

But during the long four years when the Smithsons' first building was under construction, an altered version of what this book theorizes as their Mies-image began to emerge. By 1953 they had begun to see everything differently, and to see more in Hunstanton than they anticipated. The new imaginary evoked and provoked by the appearance of the constructed building was enabled by new sensibilities, interests, and awareness they had developed through their participation in the Independent Group meetings at the Institute of Contemporary Arts (ICA) in London beginning in 1952.[3] During the interval between winning the Hunstanton competition in the spring of 1950 and the building's completion in 1954, the Smithsons had moved from a commitment to Mies motivated primarily by modernist ideas about program, form, space, structure, detailing, and materials, to seeing their building as a complex architectural apparatus that was as tangible and direct in its material means as it was elusive and mutable ARRAY 1.2 in its virtual effects. By the summer of 1953, when the building reached the "layering of reflection at the glazed stage,"[4] the Smithsons began to see the ways that architecture was implicated in—and susceptible to—the same kinds of observation and imagination required in a much broader and more enticing visual and intellectual contemporary culture. In the years that followed, the Smithsons' interests and working methods expanded rapidly. Their initial understanding of Mies had been altered profoundly by a scene that was dense with timely and fresh sources both outside and inside architecture:

> 1954 has been a key year. It has seen American advertising equal Dada in its impact of overlaid imagery; that automotive masterpiece, the Cadillac convertible—parallel-with-the-ground (four elevations) classic box on wheels; the start of a new way of thinking with CIAM; the revaluation of the work of Gropius; the repainting of the Villa at Garches?[5]

The Smithsons' new sensibility was most directly influenced and advanced by their close friendships and collaborations with the sculptor

1.1

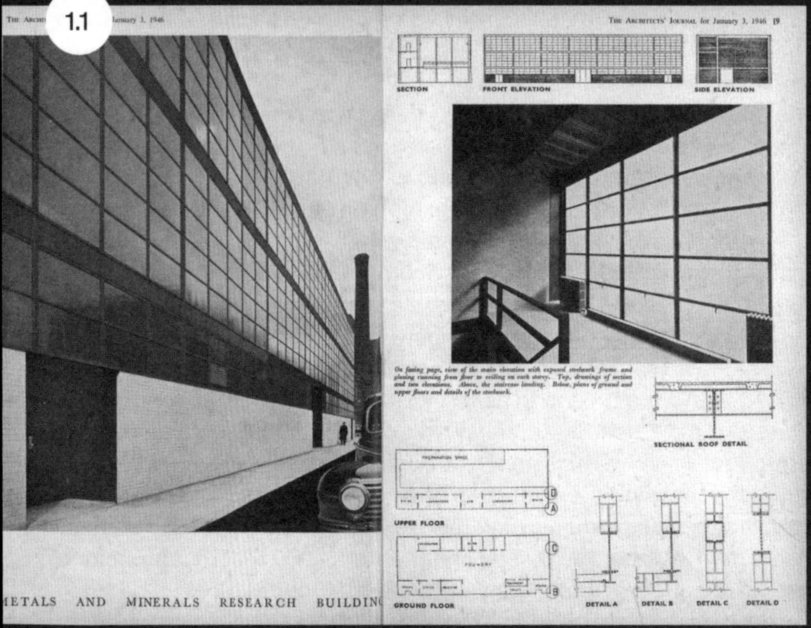

THE ARCHITECTS' JOURNAL for January 3, 1946

METALS AND MINERALS RESEARCH BUILDING

THE ARCHITECTS' JOURNAL for January 3, 1946 9

SECTION FRONT ELEVATION SIDE ELEVATION

On facing page, view of the main elevation with exposed steelwork frame and glazing running from floor to ceiling on each storey. Top, drawings of section and two elevations. Above, the staircase landing. Below, plans of ground and upper floors and details of the steelwork.

SECTIONAL ROOF DETAIL

UPPER FLOOR

GROUND FLOOR

DETAIL A DETAIL B DETAIL C DETAIL D

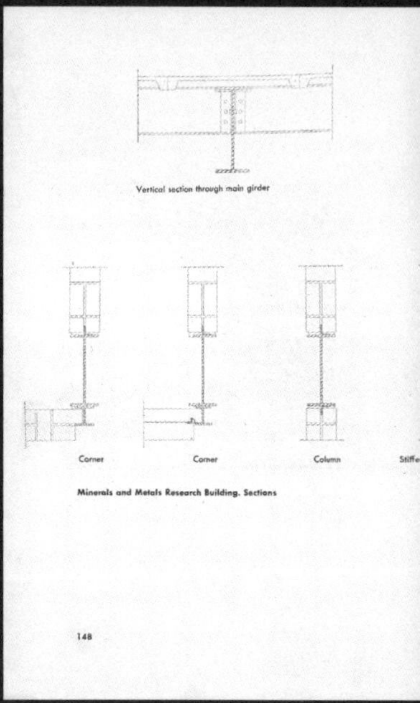

Vertical section through main girder

Corner Corner Column Stiffe

Minerals and Metals Research Building. Sections

148

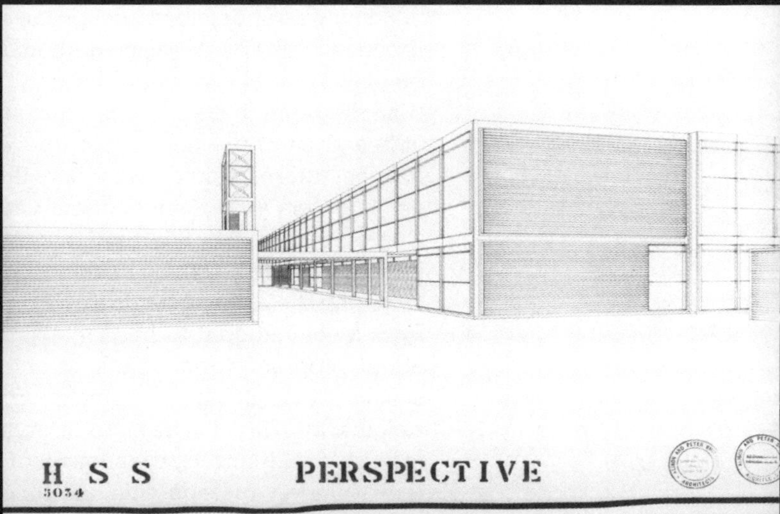

H S S PERSPECTIVE

3034

10 THE ARCHITECTS' JOURNAL for January 3, 1946

Above, the central part of the building open to the full height of two storeys to give flexibility for various, and changing, equipment. Below, one of the laboratories. Partitions have been omitted as far as possible. Right, the second of the two main laboratories used as a lecture hall.

METALS AND MINERALS RESEARCH BUILDING *BY MIES VAN DER ROHE*

DRAWINGS FOR TH
ADMINIST
BUILDING, ILLINO
DESIGNED BY MIES

The original drawings of a project for the Library and Administration Building, part of a construction programme of fourteen buildings for the Illinois Institute of Technology, which Mies van der Rohe has been commissioned to design, are illustrated here. The construc-

tion is similar to the Building shown on the pages, and will form p same group.
This building, like the Building, has that se line and that precisi and sincerity of design

Minerals and Metals Research Building. Laboratory
149
14
SECTION THROUGH THE LIBRARY BLOCK
1:24
15

1.2

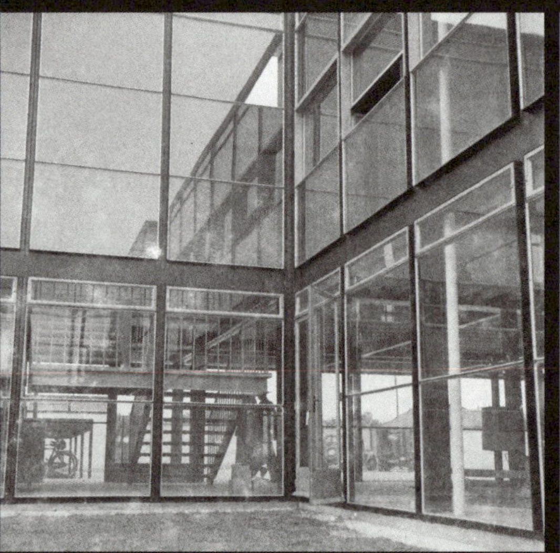

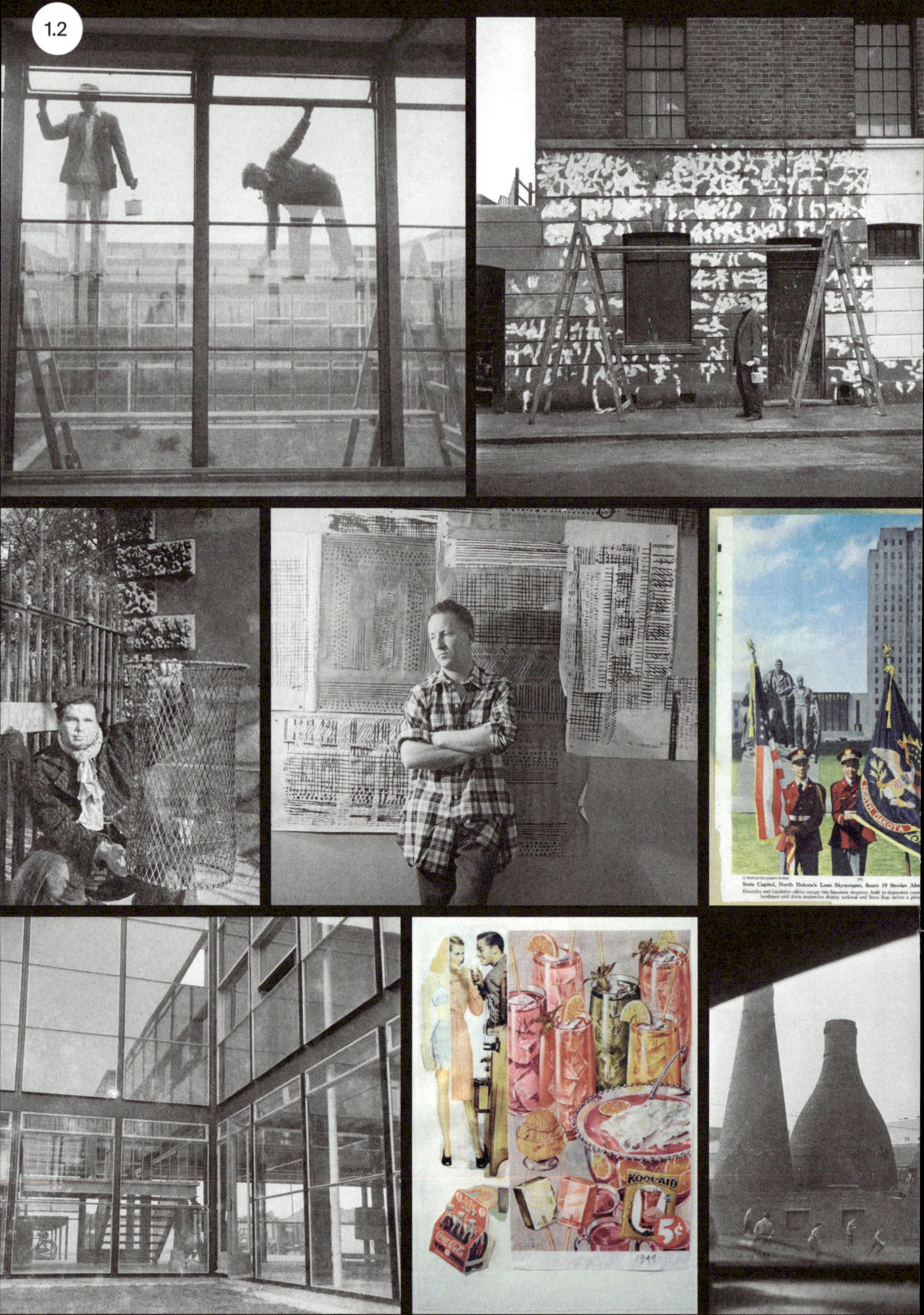
State Capitol, North Dakota's Lone Skyscraper, Soars 19 Stories Abo
KOOL-AID
5¢
Coca-Cola
1949

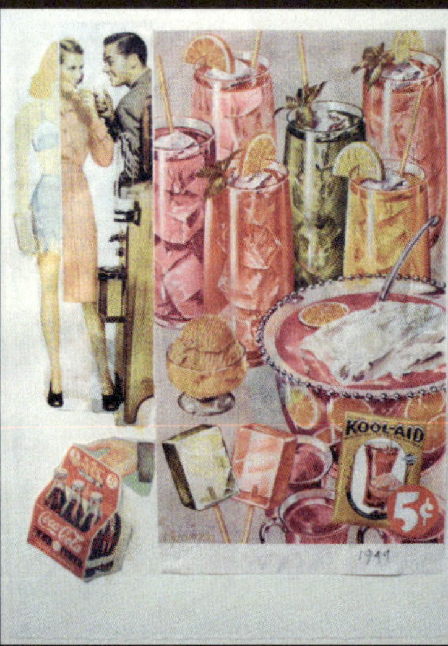

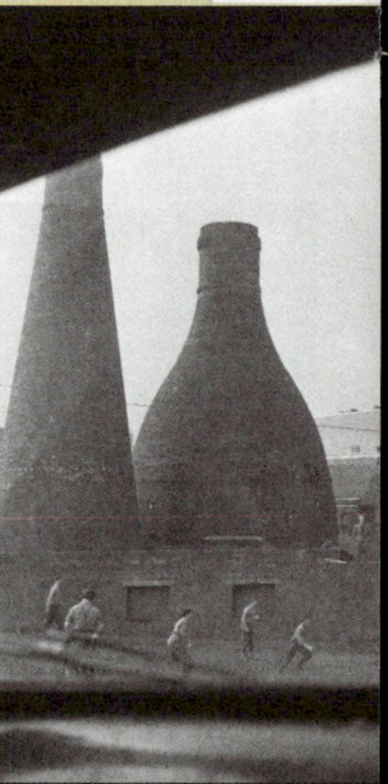

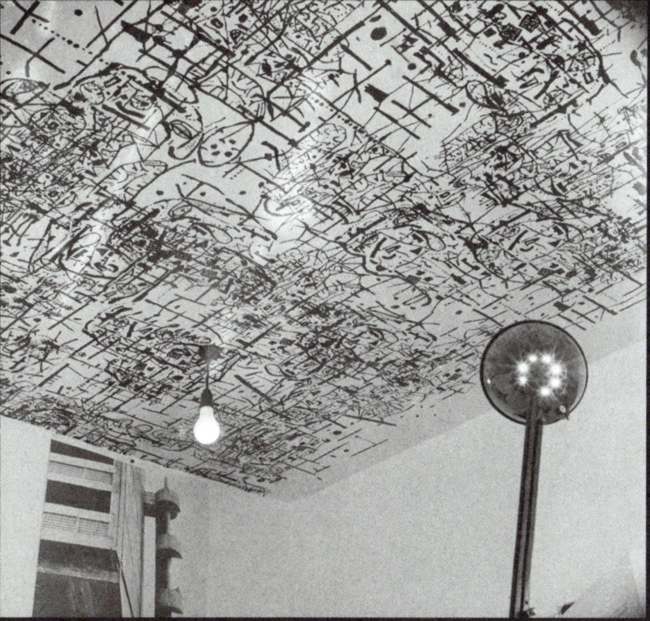

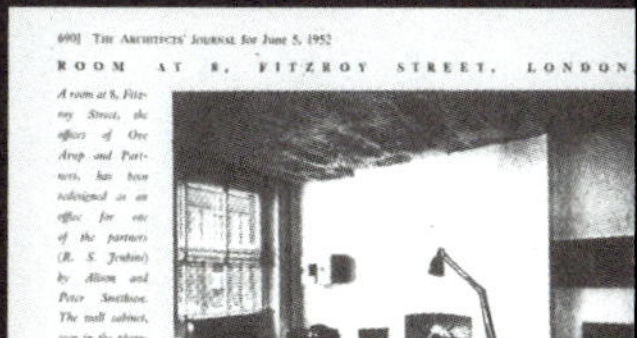

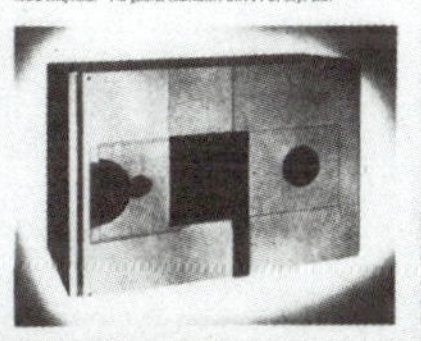

690] The Architects' Journal for June 5, 1952

ROOM AT 8, FITZROY STREET, LONDON

A room at 8, Fitzroy Street, the offices of Ove Arup and Partners, has been redesigned as an office for one of the partners (R. S. Jenkins) by Alison and Peter Smithson. The wall cabinet, seen in the photograph, bottom left, was designed by Victor Pasmore. The case is mahogany with a double front, side hung on piano hinges, so that when the doors are open flush with the sides a different pattern is obtained. The front is faced with panels of "Perspex" and other plastics. The table, which appears in the top photograph, was designed by the architects, and is made of ebonised blackboard, with legs of ½-in square section solid steel rods. The ceiling, part of which is seen bottom right, was designed by Eduardo Paolozzi and is printed on white lining paper by the silk screen process. The screens can be turned in different directions to vary the basic pattern. The colour scheme of the room is entirely black and off-white except for the radiators, which are painted battleship grey. One wall, which appears in the photograph, centre right, has a large blackboard fixed to it. This is of hardboard, treated with three coats of blackboard compound. The general contractors were F. C. Cape Ltd.

tions and projects by the foursome, whom the artist Richard Hamilton called "Paosmithend,"[6] operated as a collective, almost familial intensification of the aesthetic of imaging that suffused the Independent Group meetings, epitomized by Paolozzi's famous epidiascope presentation to the group in April 1952 in which he projected images of magazine pages and his collages made from them. The group's explorations continued in the seminars convened that fall by Reyner Banham, and their development can be tracked in a series of adventurous ICA exhibitions such as Hamilton's *Growth and Form* (1951), *Memorable Photographs from Life Magazine* (1952), *Opposing Forces* (1953), and *Wonder and Horror of the Human Head* (1953). More intimately, the Smithsons were learning from Henderson's street photography of London's East End—which Peter emulated—and from Paolozzi's prints, wallpapers, and collages, which inspired Alison to produce similar scrapbooks of images.[7] Most directly, they were learning from Henderson's photography of Hunstanton at various phases of construction (Fig. 2).

Fig. 2

SECONDARY SCHOOL AT HUNSTANTON

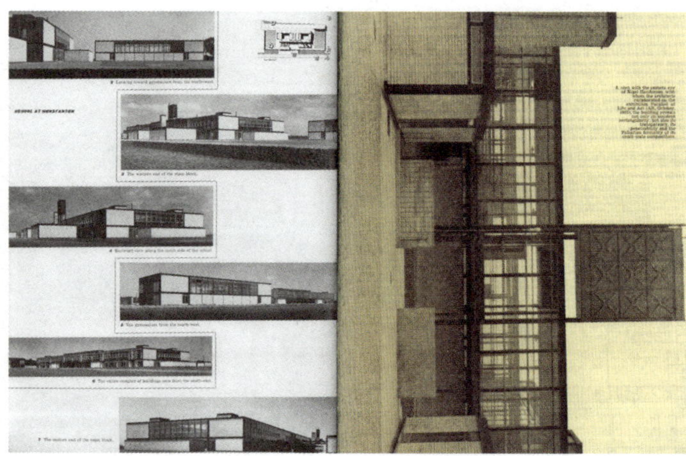

Numerous photographs taken of Hunstanton as the glazing was being installed capture its subtle and powerful effects. The first to be published, a large, artful photograph on the first page of an article in the *Architects' Journal* in September 1953 shows the interior corner of one of the two courtyards. Taken at an oblique angle to the glazing, it emphasizes the opposite effects of mirroring (the oblique surface) and transparency (the frontal surface across the courtyard) as well as the intricacy of the detailing and the large painted dots on the glass, which seem to mirror patches of sand on the ground. In many ways it is similar to the numerous photographs taken by Henderson during construction. It also resembles a photograph published that same month in *Architectural Design* (dated to June 1953), and one of the finished building with cleaned glazing in *Architectural Review* in September 1954. Another photograph in the 1954 article offers another take on the glazing. It shows a section of the north elevation, including the water tower, and is rotated 90 degrees as a full-bleed image with the caption (certainly written by Reyner Banham, whose own essay is referenced), "seen with the camera eye of Nigel Henderson, with whom the architects collaborated on the exhibition *Parallel of Life and Art* (AR, October 1953), the building reveals not only its insistent rectangularity, but also its transparency, its penetrability and the Palladian formality of its small-scale compositions." That image, with its Independent Group sensibility, appears opposite (and sets up a debate with) the page with the famous cinematic series of images (mistakenly characterized in many histories as Picturesque) as if moving around the school.

In late 1953, multiple aspects of the Smithsons' expanding world converged, and for the remainder of their careers they strived to understand what they had been seeking from the beginning by reiterating, revising, and augmenting their explanations of New Brutalism and their speculative scrutiny of the Mies-image. While the profound expansion of the Smithsons' sensibility in the early 1950s may seem like an alteration beyond recognition, it was not a radical break. Rather, it was an uneasy but enduring intensification of their aesthetic sophistication and of their understanding of modern architecture, as well as the beginning of a productive and ongoing effort to position and promote architecture as central to and effective within an emerging image culture of advertising, film, magazines, photography, and other mass media. Hunstanton's design, New Brutalism's ethos, and the Independent Group's radicality are bound up together as the sources of insights and an acumen that the Smithsons never stopped unpacking, scrutinizing, and developing. Increasingly, in many ways and over many years, beginning in the late 1950s, their aesthetic circulated and evolved around and through their ongoing, yet fitful, and acknowledged fascination and coming-to-terms with the potential they saw and found in Mies. To the extent that the Smithsons insisted that their aesthetic discoveries first appeared in Hunstanton, and as they were continuously reconsidered for the next fifty years in later projects and publications, New Brutalism can be defined as the Smithsons' enduring pursuit of the Mies-image.

This book focuses on images and imaging practices as the crucial aesthetic context for New Brutalism and the kinds of aesthetic procedures integral to the Smithsons' subsequent efforts as designers, writers, and observers to understand and engage their rapidly changing postwar world. Their creative approaches gradually assimilated and utilized the kinds of serial processing, restless scanning, and pattern recognition that were becoming ubiquitous aspects of daily life. The persistence and appeal of New Brutalism and the continuing interest in the work of the Smithsons can be elucidated at least in part, and in critical ways, by understanding how they and their architecture serve as imperfect but instructive and powerful exemplars of the emergence of the varieties of imaging practices that have been changing and challenging architecture's production and mediating its effects for at least the last century, from mass media to digital design. Rather than the usual (partially accurate and partially misleading) association of New Brutalism with Le Corbusier's *béton brut* projects, most notably the Unité d'Habitation in Marseille (1947–52), or the emphases on popular culture and consumerism, on ordinariness and the "as found," on everyday urbanism and the Smithsons' matter-of-fact attitude, this book brackets and re-brackets the exploration of imaging practices by the Smithsons within a brief period of time, from their design of the Hunstanton School in 1949 to *Patio and Pavilion* in 1956, their collaborative installation with Paolozzi and Henderson for the *This Is Tomorrow* exhibition.

ARRAY 1.3

In the first half of the 1950s, the Smithsons began to develop new ways of seeing. The story of the Smithsons' imaging practices and their pursuit of the Mies-image begins with the design of Hunstanton, but it soon swerved, intensified, and advanced with several projects just before and contemporaneous with the beginnings of the Independent Group and Hunstanton's "glazed stage": most notably, the little-known but crucially important interior for Hunstanton's structural engineer which they called Jenkins Room (1952, London), the Golden Lane competition entry (1952), *Parallel of Life and Art* (1953), their Sheffield University competition entry (1953), and the Urban Re-Identification Grid (or CIAM Grille, as it is better known) (1953). The after-effects of those projects and their sensibilities appear most

1.3
HOUSE
STREET
RELATIONSHIP
CIAM 9
HOUSE
ASSUMPTIONS
PHYSICAL COMPONENTS

DISTRICT
CITY
UR
office
ceremonial
craft
factories
WEST ELEVATION OVERLOOKING PARK WITH LAKE IN FOREGROUND
LIBRARY & ARCHITECTURE

vividly in their later publications, lectures, and projects, in which they re-examined, furtively or overtly, the imaging potential they found in Mies and often saw, too, through the surrogate lens of the work of Charles and Ray Eames. By situating the Smithsons' work in the pervasive cultural and intellectual condition of imaging, an entirely different explanation of New Brutalism as "part of the mythology of Modernism in Britain" emerges.[8]

All accounts of New Brutalism agree that the effects and influences of the first half of the 1950s, especially the Smithsons' participation in the Independent Group and their collaborations with Henderson and Paolozzi, were formative for their understanding of modern architecture and urbanism. The Smithsons, who had "come from the North to conquer London with a driving, rather fierce ambition," contentiously and audaciously inserted themselves into ongoing debates between generations and among various camps, even though their strident confidence masked ways in which they were still somewhat naively groping for a way forward.[9] The first published use of the term "New Brutalism" was in November 1953, in a brief text accompanying drawings of their unbuilt House in Soho. They had adopted the term as a catchy, somewhat cheeky, and evocatively vague name for their attitude and approach, which they and their peers attempted to explain and define only afterwards.[10] But the timing was apt for the Smithsons and architectural discourse in Britain. It is impossible to understand the enduring appeal and influence of either New Brutalism or the Smithsons without considering the confluence and aftereffects of the issues, ideas, events, personalities, and sources that were circulating in the early 1950s, both within architectural discourses and in the broader intellectual and popular culture. New Brutalism, however vague and contested the meaning and origin of the term may be, is inseparable from the distinct postwar British scene of aesthetic experimentation and the theorization of imaging in art criticism, architecture, and philosophy of which the Independent Group was a crucial part and to which it made a crucial contribution.

There is little agreement about how New Brutalism, the Independent Group, and the Smithsons align and intersect with one another and with that scene, or how the ideas that developed in and around the Independent Group affected the Smithsons' later thought and work. Many see irresolvable conflicts among their initial intense and dogged attempt in Hunstanton to find, and found, a renewed, robust modern architecture, their subsequent fascination with popular culture and mass media, and their leadership roles in founding the urban design collective Team 10 beginning in 1953. But their collaborative and transdisciplinary development of imaging practices suffuses all their thinking in the 1950s and afterwards. The confusion and debate about the significance of New Brutalism among the Smithsons' varied endeavors derives largely from the fact that New Brutalism was so short-lived and ill-defined, that the Independent Group is so strongly associated with the emergence of Pop art, that the work and history of Team 10 are so well documented, and that Banham's ideas and influence were so great then and still are for so many of the historical and pervasive accounts of New Brutalism. Yet perhaps the greatest source of confusion is the Smithsons' incessant reconsideration of their past and insistent repositioning of themselves in the present. Discerning the Smithsons' ideas and positions is complicated by the ways their thinking is bound up in a tangled chronology of histories and hagiography, recollections and reproductions, collaborations and contestations, claims and criticisms, many of them produced or encouraged by the Smithsons themselves. Yet that constant revisioning of their thinking and their modes of documenting its results are also the evidence of New Brutalism's significance, even if the Smithsons' work appears to be an idiosyncratic, inconsistent, and inscrutable resituating of themselves and of their contribution in response to contemporary trends and their own changing imaginations and reputations. Certainly the Smithsons' disposition was contrarian, and their polemics and declarations were simultaneously subversive and reactionary. Their persistent reimagings varied as the times changed and as they changed with time. They would never arrive at decided positions, and that productive indecision plays into the general and pervasive critique that their thinking and approaches were inconsistent and incoherent, or at least inchoate. The Smithsons were public figures and published profusely, yet they purposely evaded clear and contemporaneous articulations or explanations of their thinking in lectures, essays, or project briefs. Their thoughts and insights, even in essays, notebooks, and lectures, are more like musings, asides, and provocations that were constantly revised, republished, and restated. The cogency of their sensibility and approaches emerged only gradually over several decades of relentless production and reconsideration.

The variability of the Smithsons' fascination with Mies is especially confounding. Yet its importance and coherence are hiding in plain sight. Their initial interest in his Chicago work in the late 1940s is often dismissed as a temporary adulatory phase that is unrelated to their later, much more inscrutable, extended, and generally overlooked preoccupation with Mies beginning in the late 1950s.[11] But that enduring commitment demonstrates that the Smithsons' embrace of the Chicago Mies was not just a first attempt but also a truly formative event in an ongoing effort to redefine the ethos and modes of modernism. Like many younger British architects, the Smithsons' aim was to creatively continue the experimentation and vision of prewar work on the Continent. Their choice of Mies and their adaption of his Chicago approach to conditions and possibilities in Britain might also be understood as their first instance of engaging what they called the "as found"—in this case, their reimagings of his Minerals and Metals Research Building (1942–43) and Library and Administration Building (1944–45, unbuilt) at IIT as found in and through photographic media—as well as an early demonstration of their canny ability to work with concepts or idioms that interested others, but to do so while declaring a fundamentally different purpose or meaning. The untimely afterimage of their initial ardent and contrarian engagement with Mies turns out to be the enduring aide-mémoire of their lifelong reimagining of New Brutalism in books, buildings, exhibitions, essays, and lectures. The Smithsons' divergent ideas, projects, approaches, interests, and affiliations cohere as a persistent effort to apply New Brutalist sensibilities to architecture through their ongoing reconsideration and reimaging of Mies. Looking back repeatedly and relentlessly at what they were doing in the early 1950s, they realized over and over again, in different ways, that when they designed Hunstanton they were barely beginning to understand what they thought they saw in Mies. That pursuit was both specifically architectural and broadly transdisciplinary. Their constant return to the Mies-image and revisioning of New Brutalism was motivated by questions about the legacy and potential of not only modern architecture but also modernist visuality and post-photographic imaging practices.[12]

Those pursuits gathered new momentum in a phase starting in the late 1950s when the Smithsons relaunched their engagement with Mies. Peter's first trips to the United States in 1957 and 1958, which were announced as a consequential event in his 1958 "Letter to America,"[13] took him to New York and then to Chicago and Los Angeles, where he met Mies and the Eameses and encountered their work. In 1959 Mies visited London to receive the RIBA Gold Medal and during that visit was celebrated at the Architectural Association with a presentation and discussion of slides of his work, many of them Peter's recent photographs—of the Farnsworth House (1945–51), the dormitories at IIT (1954), and the Seagram Building (1958)—many of which were taken from unusual angles and emphasized the surface qualities and effects of the glazing. Thirty-five years later, the Smithsons affirmed how those photographic impressions of Mies in the late 1950s were as formative as their fascination with published photographs of his work a decade earlier. First in the 1980s—when the Barcelona Pavilion and *Patio and Pavilion* were both reconstructed—and then most definitively in their 1994 book *Changing the Art of Inhabitation*, the Smithsons would characterize themselves as third-generation Miesians. The opening pages of that book's first section, "Mies' Pieces," feature more of Peter's late 1950s photographs of Mies's Chicago buildings—860–880 Lake Shore Drive (1949–51), Alumni Memorial Hall (1945–46), and other buildings at IIT—along with writing excerpts from those years: an essay on the Seagram Building, a letter to Alison remarking on Mies's Chicago buildings, and a 1959 lecture on the same subject.

ARRAY 1.4

Scrutinizing the later work of the Smithsons, especially their books and other publications, offers a way to understand the continuities and interdependence between the two young architects' precociously sophisticated and tough-minded design of a glass, steel, and brick school and their subsequent fascinations with advertising and "the popular arts," which they would most famously articulate in their 1956 essay "But Today We Collect Ads":

> The advertisements which appear in the *New Yorker* or *Gentry* [. . .] are good "images" and their technical virtuosity is almost magical. Many have involved as much effort for one page as goes into the building of a coffee bar. And this transient thing is making a bigger contribution to our visual climate than any of the traditionally fine arts. [. . .] As far as architecture is concerned, the influence on mass standards and mass aspirations of advertising is now infinitely stronger than the pace setting of avant-garde architects, and it is taking over the functions of social reformers and politicians. [. . .] Mass-production advertising is establishing our whole pattern of life—principles, morals, aims, aspirations, and

standard of living. We must somehow get the measure of this intervention if we are to match its powerful and exciting impulses with our own.[14]

Those competing desires and raw tensions in their thinking—between the viability of "heroic" modern architecture and the appeal of mass culture—converged slyly a decade later in a wholly original and deeply personal reassessment of Mies that both reflects and affirms their ambivalence throughout the 1950s and 1960s about architecture's immersion in popular culture.[15] In a 1967 seminar that they led at the Berlin Technical University, a version of which they published two years later—a month before Mies's death, as a kind of homage to his influence—the Smithsons imagined a wily Mies who connects and integrates disciplinary rigor and popular entertainment: "Those who think 'Mies is all the same' or who confuse a Braun toast-maker with a record player" are unable to see that he "is surprisingly tuned in to our culture. His [...] big-box in Berlin accepts *and* clarifies what is going on—that art now [. . .] has become show-business."[16] They admired Mies for working across the spectrum of aesthetic experience and between the competing experiences of slow architecture and fast entertainment, discreet immersion and distinct stimulation.[17] What the Smithsons saw in Mies in the late 1960s, and characterized so eloquently in their writing, was an extension of what they saw in "ads" in the 1950s: the potential for architecture to "somehow get the measure" of both "mass production" and "mass standards"[18] while also conjuring an image of disciplined "quietness, that up to now our sensibilities have not recognized as architecture at all, let alone seen clearly enough to isolate its characteristics."[19] Their unique reading of Mies's work, beginning with projects as early as 1920 and continuing into the 1960s, identified "a kind of mode-shift in the discipline of architecture, which makes itself more and more obvious in his work in America." They believed that Mies had established "two separate but reciprocal themes" as the basis of modernism: an "almost autonomous repetitive neutralizing skin" and an "open-space-structured [...] recessive, calm, green, urban pattern." Out of their regard for that legacy, the Smithsons conjured their Mies-image as an enticing and subtle version of "the new, softly smiling face of our discipline."[20]

There is a complex coherence and significance for New Brutalism to be found in the Smithsons' consistently creative reviewing and rethinking—in a word, *reimaging*—of Mies as a site or scene of aesthetic exploration. Their efforts, in their buildings, essays, lectures, exhibitions, and books, at seeing "clearly enough" how Mies is a replenishing source for variations of modern architecture is a case study in the development of post-photographic imaging practices in the second half of the twentieth century (Fig. 3). Those possibilities and potentials of architectural design as imaging were nurtured by their involvement in the Independent Group and advanced through their collaborations with Paolozzi and Henderson. But they first became actual and vivid as architectural qualities and effects in 1953 in "the layering of reflection at the glazed stage" of Hunstanton: that is, in the building's actual reflections as well as in their own reflections on the building's reflections, then and after, as a model for the New Brutalist architectural imaginary. As Peter auspiciously remarked in

1.4

1

12 September 1958.
Letter from PS to AS
Carman Hall, IIT Campus, 60 East 32nd Street, Apt 16, Chicago 16.
Postmarked 25 September 1958.

Some notes on what I've seen so far of Mies. Structural steel used as such has a quality that nothing else has, and even its having to be painted seems an advantage.

Aluminium is quite useless for cities; it corrodes away and filthies in about four to six years.

860 Lake Shore Drive[1] (the undoubted Parthenon of Mies) is being repainted, I assume for the first time. The aluminium window frames are being painted grey and the steel black. The result is that original idea is so re-established it can, just, ride-over the additions of fifty types of air-conditioner and blower which have been put into the lower window panel.

This painting business seems to give a solidness and historical existence to things. Boats repainted, no matter how bashed about, look OK. Smart yet not new. Old things cannot look new.

Mies' new black anodised-aluminium blocks next to 860 Lake Shore Drive have the imitation look and already the surface anodising is beginning to peel off in sheets like sunburnt skin.[2, 3] So it looks as if even Mies can make Miestakes.

2

3

4

5

Certainly at IIT[4–6] there are many er
early buildings in concrete and wood wind
sumably built during the war) and later
and steel windows, 1958, are very very
Especially as the Campus is dumped in th
of a slum/industrial area. Krefeld was
the starting point and he suppressed bo
those early buildings here. Of course th
much good – 75 per cent is successful, 10
terrific and the rest somewhat studied
tough enough for their use. I can't really bl

The concrete, brick and aluminium wir
the building] I am in are really excellent bu
by shabbiness which mars the external c
I have come to the conclusion that it's
try and make a building which can get c
We have to do away with smoke from tow
and dwelling areas. It's uncivilised and wa
labour and effort not to.

Mies uses concrete blocks in the I
Commons building (Union) and then spra
with a spotty cold glaze (he also cold-glaz
lifts) which is textured, rough and is tough
ily cleaned. He is an old fox.

6

Mr. Smithson's travels were confined to the East Coast. He was therefore unable to check his generalisations against the reality of F. U. Wright, Mies (except at Seagram), Neutra, Rudolph, Eames or Soriano

All photographs have been taken specially to show the ordinary way one sees the buildings in their environment, and this of course includes chance optical effects

Left: downtown New York where the streets are medieval

Letter to America

Peter Smithson

Before I went to America, I thought I would be asked to compare the state of architecture in America with that in Europe, and I prepared the short formal statement printed below:

The architectural situation in the U.S.A., as far as one can judge from photographs and written material, is that there is still basically a belief in square, 'rational' architecture—a continuing to live off the impulses of 1913.[1]

Even when new structural forms (e.g. doubly curved shells) are introduced, or new materials (e.g. plastics), they are styled in the old International Style Architecture way.

The exception to this, at the unconscious level, seems to be the curtain wall building (as in Lever House), which whilst consciously being 'square' architecture, actually transcends this discipline. (What is supposed to be academic Mies ends up as something else.) The conscious exception is in the, to me, half comprehended, ideological writing and project work of Louis Kahn, where something approaching the European new way of thinking seems to be present.

And, of course, there is Charles Eames.

In general, from our side of the Atlantic it looks as if the American architect accepts the social and building-type status quo. He takes the given object and styles it up 'Modern'.

The situation in Europe is that the 1913 impulses have become pretty weak, and they no longer seem spiritually valid, or their formal solutions applicable to architecture.

The rejection of the Modern Architecture canon means that we have had to examine the situation 'as found' and interpret this situation. This attitude is producing what we have called elsewhere an 'æsthetic of change'.

Of course the average architecture of either Europe or America does not reflect these ideas except terribly indirectly. But certainly the trend in Europe which I have described, can be observed in the 'old masters', Le Corbusier and Alvar Aalto, side by side with hang-over concepts from their first period.

In younger architects the trend is ideologically well established; in fact, I think that the ideological period of the New Modern Architecture is over and only awaits opportunity to get on to the ground and into our lives.

You may ask what are the characteristics of the New Modern Architecture in Europe: I think that it is pragmatic (its basis is a sort of active socio-plastics) rather than old styled rational (i.e. diagrammatic with right angles).

As to its imagery, the magic having flown from the rectangle it is much freer in its use of form, more rough and ready, and less complete and classical.

(continued on page 95)

[1]. The first 'constructions' were done by Tatlin in 1913, as a direct result of his encountering Picasso's reliefs. At this point Cubism became architecture.

128. Penn Cen
winning – build

becomes 'art
American arc
images and d
are used wi
folk-art.

This is n
magazines, w
and where th
when the bu
bi-axially sy
comes to reg
by purist sta

For in ne
so kicked a

[31] Of course there a
category in Americ

The Professor was asked whether he had found it difficult to train his structural engineer to let him do these things, or had it been necessary for him to do them all himself.

Mies van der Rohe *We tell him what we want to have, and he will tell us i[f] possible. Most of the structural engineers, with ver[y few] exceptions, do not know what they are doing. They can [figure] it out, but they do not know the meaning of it. You have [to tell] them exactly what you want. We had some trouble wi[th the] engineer on this building. He wanted to have sheer walls [in the] building. Normally we do not use them. Since he was in [favour] of it, I told him to go ahead and do it his way. That i[s why] you see that in the back of the building there are sheer wa[lls].*

[12]7. Who is

129. Two curtain-wall buildings facing one another – and bang!

[...]rations of 'fine' or 'folk' are relevant. Most [...]-art of the first category; old-style European [...]as trabeated space definition and symmetry, [...]ding and are therefore transformed into

[...]when the buildings are known only from [...]graphs isolate the building from its context [...]e at a time with long intervals between. But [...]gone specially to see mostly turn out to be [...]ever the circumstances or programme, one [...] buildings of metal working peasants which [...]chitecture at all.[31]

[...]ldings the accepted discipline (symmetry) is [...]ally ignored as to convince one that the

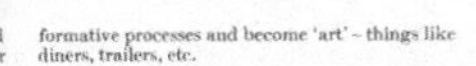

[...] formative processes and become 'art' – things like [...] diners, trailers, etc.

Above: American architecture has not yet had its Pollock
Below: Mondrian's 'Broadway Boogie-Woogie', coloured cars in gridded streets

Above: Penn Centre, Pittsburgh – or how boring can you get!

Philip Johnson's own house at New Canaa[n]
Above: the kitchen end, with reflections
Below: general view of the bedroom end

Above: 'Cape Cod' houses in Levittown

Symmetry and crypto-symmetry in New Canaan
Below: New Canaan. At left is Johansens miniature Villa Capra and (right) a more conventional 'American Modern' house in the New Canaan woods

Below left: view from the fireplace looking [...]
Below right: interior of the guest house, w[...] forms, which are used in the Synagogue at [...]

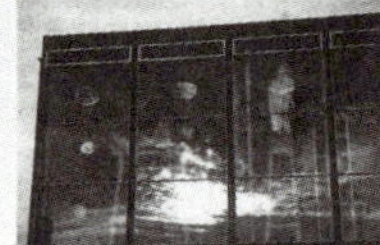
82

On discovering reflections in Hunstanton,[87] 1953–54, we could better read the photographs of MIT' and understand what the Barcelona Pavilion, the Glass Exhibit, 1934, and so on, must have been like or intended to be like.

In 1953 we were to see Krefeld.''

Mies must have been informed by van der Leck, for suddenly (after his Otterlo, the Dutch commission) the plans come apart, walls glide off as if on ice skates – the glass the ice?

Then there is the 'glass-stone'. Is this Mies' variation of the Glasen-kette of Taut and Scharoun? Of all architects perhaps since the Goths Mies knew about stone, in an artisan-like way it was part of him; more and more he went as a monumental mason, dressing with the discretion and air of an undertaker.

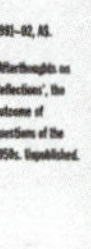
1981–82, AS.

'Afterthoughts on Reflections', the outcome of questions of the 1950s. Unpublished.

Which PS would not to see until 1952.

Directions given by Sam Stevens who had served with the Friends' Ambulance Service in Germany

The Hunstanton school, now nearing completion, will provide secondary school facilities in a large rural area. In addition, it will serve as an evening institute (it has the only decent hall in the district) and a gardening centre for the neighbouring primary schools. Designed by Alison and Peter Smithson, for the Norfolk Education Committee, it stands on a twenty-acre site on the top "edge" of Hunstanton—an early Victorian seaside resort. It is planned so that formal teaching areas have south aspect and Sandringham prospect; practical rooms have north aspect and little prospect; "contemplative" rooms face east and west on to the enclosed courts. The plan is universal and the structure—welded steel H-frames—is one of the first in this country to be designed according to the "plastic theory." Both plan and structure were dealt with at the discussion between the architects (left and centre in photo) and the engineer and Editors of the Journal, recorded below. The design of the school was the subject of a competition won by the architects in 1950. It will be described and illustrated in detail when completed.

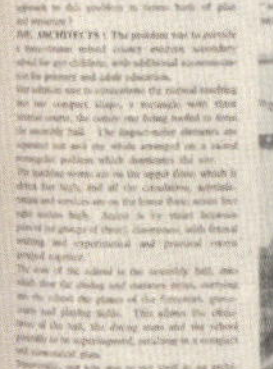

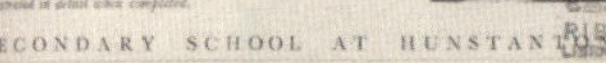

SECONDARY SCHOOL AT HUNSTANTON

A discussion between the architects (Alison and Peter Smithson), the engineer (R. S. Jenkins of Ove Arup and Partners) and Editors of the Journal, referred to below by their respective numbers (see page 305).

EWS
ORLD

the May 1966 issue of *Bauen + Wohen*, a celebration of Mies's eightieth birthday, "Mies' thought runs very deep and is not easily accessible—not even one suspects to himself [. . .] the re-direction of the mainstream of architecture itself, which my instinct tells me lies in his work, will take some years for us to comprehend and to grow upon."[21] That humble remark should be seen as the subtext of the Smithsons' brash assertion a few years later that "we believed New Brutalism to be the direct line of development of the Modern Movement."[22]

Fig. 3

On May 27, 1959, architect H. T. Cadbury-Brown hosted a presentation and discussion of slides of various buildings by Mies, including several photographs by Peter. The images and transcript were published as "Ludwig Mies van der Rohe: An Address of Appreciation by H. T. Cadbury Brown to the Guest of Honour, Professor Mies van der Rohe. Illustrated by Slides of his Work. On page 46 a note reads: "Photographs on pages 33, 34, 39, 42–6 were taken in September 1958 by Peter Smithson." In his introduction to the event, Brown remarks (and reveals what must have been a pervasive attitude) that Mies's buildings demonstrate that photography, like drawing, is no substitute for actual encounters: "The photograph is too often the end in view of many architects and the only end in view of most architectural magazines. The result is a special form of graphic design where the contrived viewpoint of the camera is the dominant factor. The real quality of Mies' work is apparent only when these buildings are seen. Only a shadow is caught by the camera. It is significant that there never seem to be 'arty' photographs of his work." It is striking that he did not recognize Peter's photographs as arty, and after his opening caveat he did not call attention to the failings of the photographs. Seeming to contradict himself, he makes this statement: "Images capture the imagination, and sometimes dominate our lives." He even credits Mies with having created "two of the most important images of the century. They are the German Pavilion at the Barcelona Exhibition in 1929 and the Tugendhat House in Brno, built in 1930". It is unclear whether he is referring to the iconic photographs or the buildings.

Yet the most vivid and succinct published instance of the Smithsons' many versions of the Mies-image appears in *Changing the Art of Inhabitation*, near the end of "Mies' Pieces." Page 64 includes just a single unattributed photograph (but likely taken by Peter) of Hunstanton, with the caption (slyly displaced, like all the others, in an index at the end of the book), "Reflections of the sky in the glass on the south side during construction." Adjacent to the photograph is a passage from an unpublished piece of Alison's writing, "Afterthoughts on Reflections, the Outcome of the Questions of the 1950s" (1991–92), which begins: "On discovering reflections in Hunstanton, 1953–54, we could better read the photographs of MIT [*sic*, IIT] and understand what the Barcelona Pavilion, the Glass Exhibit, 1934, and so on, must have been like or intended to be like."[23] That single, largely blank page crystalizes the strategy of *Changing the Art of Inhabitation* and demonstrates the Smithsons' recursive approach. Although New Brutalism was launched in the intensity and density of influences in the early 1950s, "the outcome of the questions of the 1950s" was achieved gradually, over several decades, through a persistently creative and even obsessive preoccupation with realizing and refining the Mies-image.

The Berlin seminar and *Changing the Art of Inhabitation* were crucial instances in their extended and compulsive engagement with Mies, but their definitive declaration of his importance for them occurred halfway in between, in 1980, when they formulated their idea of "Three Generations" of modern architects.[24] In Peter's contribution to the *ILA&UD Annual Report*, he charted parallel developments in the Renaissance and in the twentieth century in which "messages [...] passed in an instant across the generations in the artisan way that each generation speaks to the other—through the single image half understood, the thought half heard, the detail seen in passing on site or drawing-board, the detail studied and reflected on in silence."[25] The three sections of *Changing the Art of Inhabitation* fully elaborate the Three Generations concept. The Smithsons' careful collection and graphic presentation of mostly unattributed photographs by themselves and others, text excerpts of their own published or unpublished writings from 1956 to 1993, and drawings operates as a curated imaging atlas of hints, clues, claims, and gestures toward an understanding of the conjunction, or involution, of New Brutalism and the Mies-image.

The Smithsons' imaging approach in *Changing the Art of Inhabitation* is intentionally complex and refuses the presumption that New Brutalism ever was or could be a stable set of principles and convictions that might be discerned or traced in a lineage of their or others' buildings, theoretical explanations, or design principles. In that way, the Smithsons half-agreed with Banham's dismissive conclusion about the movement's formation and legacy in *The New Brutalism*. Banham's book includes an extensive discussion of New Brutalism's beginnings, aims, and impact in a broader context, but its conclusion and catalogue of buildings were intended as an announcement of New Brutalism's end and an attempt to have the last word. The book's alternating sections—an illustrated history of the beginnings and sources of New Brutalism (in sections printed on matte paper) and a catalogue of captioned photographs and drawings of buildings (in sections printed on glossy paper) that exemplify the international profusion of "Brutalist" architecture from the early 1950s to the early 1960s—aim to demonstrate the deficiencies and unfulfilled promise of what Banham identified as the original "ethic" of New Brutalism. The book concludes with a tragic narrative:

> It has been a salutary lesson to me as a critic historian to watch a movement being created—to gain a glimpse, thereby, of the manner in which movements as portentous as Gothic architecture could start from the interaction of a few lively minds around Bishop Suger, or the art of the Renaissance from a group of friends few enough to be listed in the dedication to Alberti's "Della Pittura." But the process of watching a movement in gestation and growth was also a disappointment in the end. For all its brave talk of "an ethic, not an aesthetic," Brutalism never quite broke out of the aesthetic frame of reference. For a short period, around 1953–55, it looked as if an "other architecture" might indeed emerge, entirely free of the professional preconceptions and prejudices that have encrusted architecture since it became an "art."[26]

For Banham, the Brutalist architecture that subsequently emerged across the world was hardly what he had imagined a decade earlier as "*Une Architecture Autre*."[27] New Brutalism had transmogrified into Brutalism: "an architecture of massive plasticity and coarse surfaces" and "a craftsmanly exercise within the great tradition."[28] Thus the evidence for the failure of New Brutalism was the success of an idiom of building design that was related in name only. Rather than contesting that conflation and misnomer, Banham reversed the charges. The pervasion of the international Brutalist aesthetic became Banham's evidence to support his claim that New Brutalism as launched by the Smithsons in Britain had failed: "The biggest and most important fact about the British contribution to Brutalism is that it is over."[29] New Brutalism became, simply, Brutalism. When New Brutalism was still new, it was still only British, still only the Smithsons, and still an ethical imperative. Thus Banham was indirectly, but not entirely subtly, claiming that the Smithsons were over too.[30]

Banham not only declared the New Brutalism case closed after a protracted diffusion and decline. He also wondered if the Smithsons had "abandoned their extreme anti-traditionalist position" as early as 1956 with their installation *Patio and Pavilion*, which he described as "an appeal to fundamentals in architecture" in the form of "a garden shed [. . .] [which] had been excavated after the atomic holocaust and discovered to be part of [the] European tradition of site planning that went back to archaic Greece and beyond."[31] But Banham was protesting too much. In a variety of both surreptitious and obvious ways—although Banham did not acknowledge it—*Patio and Pavilion* is better understood as an intensification and exemplification of the Smithsons' post-Hunstanton pursuit of the Mies-image. As photographed by Henderson and the Smithsons, its reflective surfaces and rough frame-structure operate much like the glass, steel, and brick of Hunstanton. Its reflections and textures generate a simultaneously direct and evasive image that envelops and organizes its varied and scruffy contents, which were installed as the final step in the project by Henderson and Paolozzi without the Smithsons' involvement.

ARRAY 1.6

Although Banham was a principal ally of the Smithsons and the primary advocate for New Brutalism in the 1950s, he had always dismissed Mies as a significant influence for them or as a source for the movement. By the early 1960s, Banham became openly critical of the Smithsons' increasing preoccupation with what he more than once, offhandedly and apparently derisively, called "the Mies-image."[32] In 1961, when he was still attempting to reinforce the revolutionary *bona fides* of their youth (and was perhaps hopeful that their recent renewed engagement with Mies would not last), he wrote, in praise, that when Hunstanton was under construction, "they suddenly kicked the Mies image—an almost unbelievable piece of boldness when they had a virtual corner in the style."[33] It is crucial to note that while Banham's primary derision was directed toward Mies, he was also ambivalent about imaging. As he was moving away from the Smithsons and New Brutalism in the early 1960s, and endorsing Pop in his writings, he offered this double-edged praise for their work: "In spite of their stylistic variability, or because of it, they care deeply about what their buildings look like, and their aim is always to create an image that will convince and compel."[34] For the Smithsons and Banham, the revision and reassessment continued for decades in their disagreements over the legacy of the New Brutalism, but especially in their divergent and irreconcilable assessments of the significance of Mies (see Chapter Five). The Smithsons' Mies was not Banham's. Their understanding and uses of imaging were not his, either. Those tensions and differences first surfaced publicly in 1965 with Banham's criticism of their Economist complex in London (1959–64) as a rearguard and genteel urban monument: an implicitly Miesian "*tabula rasa* on which to execute an historically well-informed exercise in civic design." The project's raised plaza, Banham declared, is in effect the "lid of the large dustbin underneath, into which have been swept the parked cars," as if the Smithsons were attempting to have "largely disposed of the 20th century."[35]

By 1966, Brutalism was most definitely no longer new, and New Brutalism had lost its currency. But New Brutalism was not over for the Smithsons. They never stopped reviewing its past significance or present vitality. They repeatedly insisted that the initiation and sources of the most salient aspects of their work could be traced back to the moment in late 1953 when New Brutalism became the name for a sensibility in which ethics and aesthetics were tightly bound in ways that required new kinds of transdisciplinary thinking and imagination. New Brutalism had emerged amid the rapid evolution of the Smithsons' earliest ideas, and those youthful imagings were reimagined, however unevenly and argumentatively, as they reverberated in their thinking over the next fifty years.

The late 1950s were the beginning of both the Smithsons' reengagement with Mies and their pattern of explaining and understanding New Brutalism and themselves though recollection. From that point on, virtually all their work would be treated as, and would contain, implicit and explicit reassessments of prior work and resonances of the Mies-image. This recursive approach became their mainstay in the mid-1960s, soon after the publication of "A Smithson File" in 1966, an issue of *Arena: The Architectural Association Journal* that was "intended to be a definitive description of the Smithsons' work in their first 40 years" presented as a chronological, annotated list of "all their published essays, projects, competition entries and completed buildings" as well as "significant unpublished works."[36] At the same time as the *Arena* issue was produced, the Smithsons began working on a series of books that revised and compiled their previous work in a concerted effort to understand its significance for and refresh its applicability to the present: *Ordinariness and Light* (1970 [using materials from 1952–60]), *Without Rhetoric* (1973 [1955–72]), *The Shift* (1982 [1950–78]), and *Changing the Art of Inhabitation* (1994 [1956–93]). The subtle and never "expressive" or "formal" graphics of text and image in the seemingly casual layouts of each of those books is in effect an attempt to gather, refine, update, revise, and reassemble the strands of New Brutalism. Increasingly, from *Ordinariness and Light* to *Changing the Art of Inhabitation*, Mies is the inescapable antagonist of their efforts.[37]

New Brutalism thus remained, as it began, an unstable but redolent label. The Smithsons introduced the term in December 1953 precisely at a time of transition, historically and personally. The first publications of a nearly complete Hunstanton had appeared three

1.6

HE TEMPORARY EXHIBITION GALLERY

months earlier in two major architecture journals[38] that coincided with the Smithsons' most intensive involvement in the Independent Group: the opening in September of *Parallel of Life and Art*, their collaborative exhibition with Henderson and Paolozzi at the ICA, and in October the beginning of the Independent Group's "Aesthetic Problems of Contemporary Art" seminars, convened by Banham. Those events were the culmination of an intense and productive year for the Smithsons during which they also began their involvement with CIAM, a swerve that ran parallel to New Brutalism and intersected with its preoccupations in important but tangential and intermittent ways.[39] The CIAM and early Team 10 years were in effect a partial hiatus from New Brutalism that made their gradual return to Mies, and turn away from Le Corbusier (who departed CIAM in 1955, in effect turning the group over to the younger members who would form Team 10), beginning in the late 1950s that much more powerful and productive. Most important, that diversion was initiated with one of the most notable and famous byproducts of their experiences with Paolozzi, Henderson, and the Independent Group. The sensibility of the Smithsons' CIAM Grille, which was produced for the July 1953 CIAM 9 meeting in Aix-en-Provence as a presentation of their Golden Lane Housing project (1952), builds on the Smithsons' earliest explicit explorations of imaging: the three famous photocollages that were produced for their entry to the Golden Lane competition. One is the horizontally attenuated perspective of the project's street deck (with photographs of Marilyn Monroe and Joe DiMaggio inserted), and the other two are aerial and street views (the latter with photographs of Jawaharlal Nehru, the French film star Gérard Philipe, and other recognizable public figures inserted) of the buildings emerging in a state of partial completion from a bombed-out urban site. Only the street view collage appears in the Grille, and then only as a small image. The left portion of the Grille's horizontally elongated panel included nine large photographs by Henderson of children playing in an East London street. They were inserted into its gridded format in a way that resonates with the glazed framework and program of Hunstanton as well as early studies produced by Henderson and Paolozzi for *Parallel of Life and Art* in the spring of 1953.[40] The right portion of the Grille inserts Paolozzi-inspired branching and layered urban-structuring diagrams that explain Golden Lane's strategy and patterns of siting and growth.

ARRAY 1.7

The Smithsons' turn toward imaging intensified beginning in 1953, the year after the Independent Group first convened and the Smithsons produced their entry for the Golden Lane competition. It was also the year when, as a further development and explanation of Golden Lane, the Smithsons completed their "Urban Re-identification" (*UR*) manuscript, which would be revised and refined, textually and graphically, and in ways that continued to advance their imaging practices, as the first half of *Ordinariness and Light*.[41] It is also the year of Hunstanton's "glazed stage," of *Parallel of Life and Art*, and of the Sheffield University competition. From then on, image-thinking was latent and generative in all the Smithsons' work. Their CIAM Grille was produced in the same months they were beginning to work with Paolozzi and Henderson on *Parallel of Life and Art*,[42] and was an attempt to convey their "random aesthetic" by subverting the codified orthogonal layout specified by CIAM for project submissions.

The Smithsons used the grid not as boxes or modules to contain or categorize information of various kinds, but as a framework to interrelate an array of images. Though not as visually sophisticated as work by Henderson or Paolozzi, the broad range of materials, including Henderson's photographs, the diagrams, plans, and photomontages of Golden Lane, and the Urban Re-identification logo, operates associatively and visually as aspects of an image-world. Like the multiple overlapping and interwoven patterns and figures in Paolozzi's drawings, or the posters, magazines, and products displayed in the rectilinear panes of shop windows photographed by Henderson, the gridded structure of the panel echoes within the panels at multiple scales, from the children's chalk drawings on the street surface in the photographs to the branching networks in the Smithsons' urban diagrams. In that way, the CIAM Grille demonstrates the Smithsons' rethinking of the rationalist concept of circulation as they began to explore it in the Golden Lane project. Rather than understanding urban circulation as the managed, calculated, and optimized movement of bodies, objects, and vehicles in physical space, the Smithsons conceived of circulation as a much more varied network of "communications and dispositions,"[43] such as the delivery of milk, newspapers, or mail, the exchange of pleasantries and gossip in social interactions, or views of corridors and landscapes. That shift emphasized the ways in which infrastructure enabled the mobilization of virtual content and actual effects: circulation for the Smithsons was the exchange of information and images in a world of "human associations," and it was "the job of the architect and planner [. . .] to make these groupings apparent as tangible reality."[44] The CIAM Grille and *Parallel of Life and Art* share a commitment to "a random aesthetic reaching-out to town-patterns not based on rectangular geometries, but founded on another visual world,"[45] which one "reads" in the panel from left to right as an imaging system. The CIAM Grille thus extends the generative and originary devices and sensibility of *Parallel of Life and Art* to architecture and urban design. It converts conventional and traditional uses of grids as conceptual and physical structures into matrices that distribute the associative and affiliative imaging of patterns. In 1953 the Smithsons were seeing the same aesthetic possibilities in the nearly complete structure and glazing of Hunstanton, again aided by Henderson's photography of the building under construction.

But an earlier and less known and much smaller project is as significant as the CIAM Grille for understanding the Smithsons' turn toward imaging. Jenkins Room (1952, London) was a collaboration with Paolozzi and the artist Victor Pasmore to design an office space for Ronald Jenkins, the engineer at Ove Arup who had used "plastic theory" to design the "all-welded" steel structure at Hunstanton and who would provide financial support for *Parallel of Life and Art*.[46] While not even as large as the coffee bar they referenced four years later in "But Today We Collect Ads," the project was a crucial departure for the Smithsons. Its design was, in effect, an explicitly architectural prototype for *Parallel of Life and Art*. As documented in several photographs by Henderson and J. R. Pantlin, the design activates multiple horizontal and vertical surfaces, including a patterned ceiling wallpaper by Paolozzi, an enlarged photograph of Le Corbusier's Marseille Unite d'Habitation mounted high on a wall

ARRAY 1.8

1.7
HENDERSON
PAOLOZZI

MERCURY
BOUGHT
BAG-WASH
COLOURS
AND
WHITES
Cleaned and
Pressed
BAG-WASH
PLEASE HELP
BAG
WASH
STREET
RELATIONSHIP
CIAM
9
HOUSE
STREET
DISTRICT
CITY
UR
ASSUMPTIONS
UR
PHYSICAL COMPONENTS

1.8

THE SHIFT

Images happening beyond images: the introduction of a plane, the tempo of whose images were contrapuntal to that of its setting. These spatial manoeuvres interested us (and lay behind our attempt to get Norfolk Education Authority to purchase Paolozzi fabric curtains for the Assembly Hall at Hunstanton, 1953). We achieved the upturning and re-tuning of existing space to make it indisputably of its present in the room for Ronald Jenkins, Charlotte Street, 1952, with its Paolozzi wallpapered ceiling stitched up in black poster paint into a single composition by Eduardo himself (sighing heavily the while, interspersed by our remarks about Michelangelo's socks). Contrapuntal fragments in collage decorated the box for the Arup projector, c.1952. And from that same period the tuning of space by the collage of Greek newspapers cut polygonally and stuck on the basement stairwell (after much repair of plaster) in Limerston Street, winter 1953?, a re-play of the temple podium wall, Delphi, as if first seen in the dark at the back of that grocer's shop but seen by us in summer sun, 1951.

Slide projector box for Ove Arup and Partners, 1952

Ronald Jenkins' room in Charlotte Street, 1952 (Photo: J.R. Pantlin)

Opposite
Hunstanton. Perspective of exterior view of kitchen court with water tower. Drawn P.S., 1950

Interior view of hall (Photo. de Burgh Galwey)

Perspective of interior, view through hall. Drawn P.S., 1950

12

abutting the ceiling, an immense wall-sized blackboard with the slate set flush into the wall surface, large slab-like desks topped in glass, and a slide projector box decorated with what the Smithsons later called "contrapuntal fragments in collage."[47] Likely influenced by exhibition designs for the ICA, many of which incorporated patterned panels suspended from the ceiling,[48] Paolozzi's wallpaper was printed with the help of the art theorist Anton Ehrenzweig, who taught printmaking at the Central School of Art, where Peter Smithson, Henderson, and Paolozzi also were instructors at that time.[49] In his 1967 book *The Hidden Order of Art*, Ehrenzweig explained: "I myself acted as a screen printer for the young Eduardo Paolozzi, who [. . .] made silk-screens that could be overprinted on top of each other in almost any position. They would always produce meaningful results. [. . .] Once [for Jenkins Room] Paolozzi printed rolls of ceiling paper in ever varying overprints."[50] Ehrenzweig added, in a caption to an image of the screen print, "Paolozzi printed the paper by superimposing semi-realistic images, a double profile, an aeroplane insect and an architectural grid. He allowed the workmen to put up the rolls of paper at random so that 'accidental' joints were produced. Paolozzi touched up only a few roughnesses."[51]

Jenkins Room was effectively an immersive environment like *Parallel of Life and Art*, with various images—photographs, posters, drawings, patterns, chalk drawings and writing, projected slides, reflections on desktops, views from the two large windows—deployed and oriented diversely throughout the space. But Jenkins Room was a more disciplined display, with images organized by type, use, medium, and content. The images were not as enveloping, as all-over, or as uncategorizable, interchangeable, and indeterminate as the mixture of scales, patterns, textures, and associations of the similarly enlarged, mounted, and printed images that made *Parallel of Life and Art* so intellectually challenging and visually seductive. The didactic distinctions between media and among patterns, pictures, collages, and degrees of resolution in Jenkins Room were adventurous but only a step toward the similarly reproduced photographs mounted on individual panels and arrayed as affiliated image-objects that would be installed the next year at the ICA. Yet the ceiling wallpaper, with its visible but "touched up" seams, variable alignments, and mutable figures, textures, and patterns, did operate similarly to the arrayed images of *Parallel of Life and Art*, which also suggest a kind of suspended ceiling or faceted tenting with its edges draping down onto the walls. The connection between Jenkins Room and *Parallel* is obvious and crucial, but other than a brief mention in the *Architects' Journal* in 1952 it was not published for thirty years, as the second project (following a two-page spread of *Parallel of Life and Art*), and as the second example of "Working Drawings" (after Hunstanton), in *The Shift*, the Smithsons' highly personal retrospective monograph that aimed to show "that a shift took place in the aesthetic of our architecture in the late 'sixties."[52]

In 1982, looking back at their evolution over three decades, *Parallel of Life and Art*, Jenkins Room, and Hunstanton were the first three projects in *The Shift*, suggesting that the Smithsons saw them as the key achievements in "the first group" of their early projects: "All three are arrangements of straight lines and flat planes overlaid with other sorts of images."[53] That simple description explains how the Smithsons saw Jenkins Room, along with other projects and events from 1952 and 1953, as interdependent with *Parallel of Life and Art*, which, according to Henderson, began as a shared effort to "ferret about for some common ground [. . .] and build up a sort of pool of imagery and maybe a spin-off of ideas."[54] After collaborating intermittently for most of a year, the four collaborators selected 122 photographic images for the exhibition from their books, journals, and collections of magazine and newspaper clippings. The reproduced and enlarged images (actually photographs taken by Henderson from the source material using a plate camera[55]) were mounted on variously sized panels and attached to the walls or hung from the ceiling of the ICA gallery to create an image environment that conveyed, in Henderson's words, their "common aesthetic, although we could none of us formulate a verbal basis for it."[56] Two years later, Banham famously stated that *Parallel of Life and Art* was the "*locus classicus*" of New Brutalism and that it exemplified its central aspiration "to create a coherent visual image by non-formal means [. . .] and fully validating the presence of human beings as part of the total image."[57] Banham's claim, along with mentions of affinities with numerous other examples of contemporary art in the text and illustrations, drove home the point that the Smithsons were developing a transdisciplinary practice and refining their version of the sensibility that circulated through and around the Independent Group as a shared imaginary. As much as or more than any of the others involved, the Smithsons continued to pursue and develop that aesthetic in multiple imaging practices: architecture, urbanism, exhibitions, publications, slide lectures, and other kinds of design.

Reviewers of *Parallel of Life and Art* were interested and perplexed as much by the exhibition's seemingly arbitrary organization as by its challenging aesthetic, both of which provoked either ridicule or amazement. Yet the skeptical reactions and negative assessments reveal something other than the usual smugness about the modernist or avant-garde ambitions of the ICA. The critics' target was less the pretentiousness of esoteric artworks than the pretentiousness of mystifying obvious similitudes and intellectualizing ordinary visual experience. In different ways, disinterested or hostile critics acknowledged, missed, or dismissed the show's effort to neither declare nor prove anything but, instead, to demonstrate and evoke the strange new potential and alternative aesthetic of documentary photographic imaging as commonly experienced, from microscopy and X-rays to newspaper photographs to reproductions of artworks. The *Glasgow Herald* mocked, as a departure from the ICA's usual "ineffable" intentions, the "promising unintelligibility" of the show's title and the "modesty" of the organizers' admission in their press release that "there is no watertight scientific or philosophical system demonstrated" and "no single aim."[58] The *Scotsman* was equally sarcastic and dismissive: "Anybody equipped with three hands or who could write intelligibly while waving the Union Jack could probably make some very penetrating sense" of the "highbrow" attempts"to prove the obvious with 122 photographs. [. . .] there is a potential picture in every article, in every kind of material, and in every way of looking at things."[59] Similarly, the London art critic

David Sylvester was not impressed, despite his strong interestin the relationship between architecture and painting and the seeming affinities between his concept of "afocalism" and the exhibition.[60] He argued in *The Listener* that the show simply proved that photography generates a reduction that allows us to compare anything to anything else. Sylvester might have been expected to be sympathetic to the show's content, if not its approach, because he collected images from magazines and newspapers to use in lectures or to give to his friend the painter Francis Bacon.[61] Yet he found that the Smithsons, Paolozzi, and Henderson had "displayed the exhibits with a consummate inconsequentiality" and been "equally unhelpful in the catalogue," the organization of which he considered "arbitrary, inconsistent and perverse" as well as "obscure and muddled."[62]

But there were also admirers. The *Times Educational Supplement* praised the show as "an ambitious attempt to counteract the purely rationalist approach to art. [. . .] The editors have assembled an encyclopaedic range of photographic material, past and present, to show how the findings of the sciences and arts are aspects of a cultural whole." The result was "bewilderingly complex" and "reveal[ed], even to the layman, the astonishing potential range of the camera."[63] In the *Art News and Review*, Bryan Robertson, the innovative curator of modern art and director of the Whitechapel Art Gallery at that time, offered a backhanded compliment: "This beautiful and rewarding exhibition" conveys "a freshness and air of discovery which entirely surmounts the possible dangers of pigeon-holing or providing specious arguments or comparisons. There are indeed no arguments at all."[64] In the *Architects' Journal*, the regular anonymous columnist called Astragal, whose job was generally to politely satirize or gently scandalize, was unusually positive:

> The exhibition makes some steep assumptions about [photography's] status and importance, which one can accept or not as one thinks fit, but it does include some of the most extraordinary photographs that Astragal has ever seen. They make one realize that though the camera cannot lie, it is apt to take a pretty queer view of truth on occasions, and that looking at two wildly different objects it is apt, unlike the human eye, to make them look the same. A further interest that this exhibition will have is that among its organisers are Peter and Alison Smithson, designers of the school at Hunstanton that was lately discussed in the Journal. If you are wondering about the visual education of architects who could be guilty of such unprofessional conduct as to use the word "ugly" in public, then here is some of it at least. And while we are speaking of visual education it is very much to be doubted that either yours or mine is so complete that we won't see *something* which is new to us in this show.[65]

Not surprisingly, the most insightful review was Banham's, in *Architectural Review*, which featured one image from the show on its cover (a grainy photograph of an Alaskan carved whalebone mask) and seven in the article.[66] He found the show both captivating and concerning, writing that "The organizers of this exhibition are obviously sensitive to many of the implications of the camera. It is creating a new visual environment" and has "established its manner of seeing as the common visual currency of our time, and we have come to think of the photographic experience as the equivalent of personal participation."[67] For Banham, the appeal and radicality of the show was not its demonstration of the problematic and compelling uses of photography, but its effort to understand that "camera eyed western man" was both producing and experiencing a new visual world that required the same degree, but an entirely different kind, of precise scrutiny and acquisitive knowledge that informed the academic approach of Neoclassical architects like John Soane, "who had measured every stone of the orders of the Colliseum [*sic*]."[68] For Banham even to suggest an analogy between Soane and the Smithsons, Henderson, and Paolozzi as studious and assiduous collectors was a provocation. His parallel between the collection of photographic reproductions at the ICA and the collection of unique artifacts in the Sir John Soane's Museum, London, focused attention on the differences between two very different visual regimes: representational depictions and photographic reproductions. While Soane's collections also included reproductions such as books, casts, prints, and models, they all operated representationally or textually. While many of the images in *Parallel of Life and Art* were also representational, the manner of enlarging and printing and the deployment as an immersive array effectively overcame that. Banham's critical insight was that the investigation at the core of *Parallel of Life and Art* was not simply a technical exploration of the aesthetic potential of new media or a facile interplay of visual similarities but a demonstration of a different kind of intellectual engagement, awareness, and experience that required new but as yet undeveloped kinds of erudition and theorization.[69] Distancing himself and his colleagues from the attitude that photography is either objective or reductive (or both), Banham was making an appeal to architects to thoughtfully consider the very issues, questions, and possibilities that he, Richard Hamilton, Toni del Renzio, and Lawrence Alloway would be addressing that fall and winter in the Independent Group seminars they led: "the impact of technology," "new sources of form," "non-formal painting," and "the human image."[70]

The significance and implications of the distinctions Banham was making in his review became all too apparent when *Parallel of Life and Art* was reinstalled for five days later that fall at the Architectural Association. The shift in context from an art gallery to an architecture school provoked different kinds of reactions. At a public discussion with students on December 2, in an attempt to stifle any talk of humanism, beauty, or classical knowledge and to emphasize the motivations of the exhibition, Peter Smithson prefaced his remarks with an oblique reference to Banham's criticism and a direct dismissal of contemporary architectural interest in classical or mathematical theories, announcing: "We are not here to talk about symmetry and proportion."[71] Most important, his comment was also a retort to an Independent Group seminar given just a few days earlier, on November 26, by the architect Colin St. John Wilson, titled "Proportion and Symmetry," which referenced very different intellectual sources than the Independent Group talks that had preceded it. Smithson was not only drawing lines of division among the members of the

Independent Group. His remark was a preemptive defense of the broader ambitions of the Independent Group against the kinds of preoccupations and critiques he expected to hear from a large subset of architects who embraced the certainties of mathematical and geometric systems exemplified in Le Corbusier's *Modulor* (1948), Colin Rowe's essay "Mathematics of the Ideal Villa" (1947), or Rudolf Wittkower's *Architectural Principles in the Age of Humanism* (1949).[72] New Brutalism proposed and practiced an entirely different imaginary that more deftly navigated the British ambivalence toward modernism and the sense of new possibilities in a rapidly changing cultural and intellectual scene.

Notes

1 The *Architects' Journal* of January 3, 1946, included four pages of photographs and drawings of the Minerals and Metals Research Building (1942–43) and five pages of drawings of the Library and Administration Building (1944–45, unbuilt) at IIT. In 1949, Alison, then in London, cut them from the *Architects' Journal* and sent them to Peter, when he was still at school in Newcastle. The couple had purchased the Philip Johnson monograph earlier that year. See Peter Smithson, "Reflections on Hunstanton," *ARQ*, 2, no. 3 (Summer 1997), p. 35. Johnson's book has similar images to the *Architects' Journal* article, plus photographs of the Alumni Memorial Hall, a photograph of the steel frame of the Chemistry building under construction, and drawings of several other proposed buildings at IIT. Near the end of their 1969 essay "Mies van der Rohe," and repeated in *Without Rhetoric* as a footnote with slight grammatical revisions and the addition of the word "precisely," the Smithsons say that the Minerals and Metals Building "captured our personal interest in Mies when it was first published in England in 1946: a wonderfully clear exposition—because the things it is assembled from are so humble—of how his handling makes us see their richness." Alison and Peter Smithson, "Mies van der Rohe," *Architectural Design*, 39, no. 7 (July 1969), p. 366; Alison and Peter Smithson, *Without Rhetoric: An Architectural Aesthetic, 1955–1972*, Cambridge, MA: MIT Press, 1974, p. 42 (first published London: Latimer New Dimensions, 1973).

2 *The Heroic Period of Modern Architecture* was begun and substantially completed in 1955 and 1956. It was originally published as the December 1965 issue of *Architectural Design*. The book was intended as a definitive annotated catalogue of familiar published images of the original and distinct works of high modernism. It reproduces well-known, iconic photographs and drawings and includes very little text other than captions. It is thus an image atlas displaying a collective and personal history of the period of "absolute conviction" about modern architecture, 1917–34. Their ambition in their own work was not to be radical or programmatic in that "heroic" sense but to continue the modernist project in ways that extended its tough-minded engagement with the facts and circumstances of modern living. The Smithsons saw their photographic catalogue as "probably the last collection of its kind. The next collection in forty years' time of the architecture of our own period will be quite different for it will not record 'buildings', but built-places, and the documents will be mostly air views, sequential photographs, and system explorations. Our documents are still very much like those in Bannister Fletcher on the Italian Renaissance." Alison and Peter Smithson, *The Shift*, London: Academy Editions, 1982, p. 5.

3 For the most extensive documentation and chronologies of the Independent Group, see David Robbins, ed., *The Independent Group: Postwar Britain and the Aesthetics of Plenty*, Cambridge, MA: MIT Press, 1990, and Anne Massey and Gregor Muir, ed., *Institute of Contemporary Arts, 1946–1968*, London: Institute of Contemporary Arts, 2014. The Independent Group began early in 1952 with the ICA's reluctant sponsorship of the activities of a "young independent group" to provide an outlet for views and projects of its younger members that diverged from the agenda of its founders, especially the Surrealist and Cubist inclinations of Herbert Read and Roland Penrose. Projects by these members had been ongoing for several years, nurtured by informal gatherings at the ICA's bar. Persistent attempts by advocates of the younger members, chief among them the managing director, Dorothy Morland, unsuccessfully promoted initiatives such as the Smithsons' interest in exhibiting their model for the Coventry Cathedral competition or suggestions for lectures by lesser-known artists and intellectuals. The first attempts were in late 1951, and the first mention of the group was various requests for speakers in the ICA lecture series discussed at a meeting of the "subcommittee on lecture policy and programme" on January 29, 1952, and raised again in the April 16 meeting. Those requests were building on the first successful event staged by members of the younger group, despite continuing resistance from programming committees: Richard Hamilton's *Growth and Form* exhibition (July–August 1951), which had begun as a collaboration with Paolozzi and Henderson, though only Henderson remained involved to assist Hamilton in the show's production *Growth and Form* was approved only after Hamilton's two-year effort to obtain funding from sources in industry. Support also increased after Le Corbusier's visit to the show, and his high praise for it, when he was in Britain for CIAM 8 at Hoddesdon. Richard Lannoy held the first organized meetings of the Independent Group, beginning with Paolozzi's epidiascope lecture in April 1952. Banham became the convener in fall 1952, and Lawrence Alloway succeeded him in 1954, shifting the focus to mass media, popular culture, and advertising. Notably, for three consecutive weeks in December 1954, the Independent Group seminar series discussed "Books and the Modern Movement," including Le Corbusier's *Vers une architecture* (1923), Pevsner's *Pioneers of the Modern Movement* (1936), and Roger Fry's *Vision and Design* (1920). The group's last meeting was in August 1955. In the 1966 *Arena* monograph on their work, the Smithsons include a list of original Independent Group members in 1952 that augments the rosters found in most histories: "Frank and Madge Cordell, Peter Reyner Banham, Sam Stevens, Alan Colquhoun, Richard Hamilton, Terry Hamilton, Eduardo Paolozzi, Alan Davie, Martin Richmond, Enid Euvlonger, Toni del Renzio, Nigel Henderson, William Turnbull, Sandy Wilson, and Alison and Peter Smithson." *Arena: The Architectural*

Association Journal, 81, no. 899, special issue: *A Smithson File*, compiled by Jeremy Baker (February 1966), p. 182.

4 See Introduction, note 1, on the origins of this phrase.

5 Theo Crosby, "The New Brutalism," *Architectural Design*, 25, no. 1 (January 1955), p. 1. This statement of principles by the Smithsons was requested for publication and "somewhat edited" by Crosby, who wrote an introductory paragraph.

6 See Richard Hamilton, "Retrospective Statement," in Robbins, ed., *The Independent Group*, p. 188.

7 See Peter's photographs of wheelbarrows (1952) and a tenement (1951) in Alison and Peter Smithson, *The Charged Void: Urbanism*, New York: Monacelli Press, 2005, p. 21, and illustrations of Alison's scrapbooks in Christine Boyer, *Not Quite Architecture: Writing around Alison and Peter Smithson*, Cambridge, MA: MIT Press, 2017, pp. 156, 162, 384. Henderson's family connections to Peggy Guggenheim and the Bloomsbury Group legacy were also important. See Victoria Walsh, *Nigel Henderson: Parallel of Life and Art*, London: Thames and Hudson, 2001, pp. 9–16.

8 Alan Powers, *Britain: Modern Architectures in History*, London: Reaktion Books, 2007, p. 98.

9 See "Conversations between Eduardo Paolozzi and Alvin Boyarski, May 1984," in *Eduardo Paolozzi: Writings and Interviews,* ed. Robin Spencer, Oxford: Oxford University Press, 2000, p. 316. Previously published in Eduardo Paolozzi, *Underground Design*, Folio X, London: Architectural Association, 1982.

10 Alison and Peter Smithson, "House in Soho, London," *Architectural Design*, 23, no. 12 (December 1953), p. 342. The Smithsons' House in Soho was one of four houses featured in a three-page spread: "In fact, if it had been built it would have been the first exponent of the 'new brutalism' in England as the preamble to the specification shows: 'It is our intention in this building to have the structure exposed entirely, without internal finishes whenever possible. The Contractor would aim at a high standard of basic construction as in a small warehouse'." The project is attributed in the byline to Alison and Peter Smithson and the text is initialed P.D.S., but the Smithsons insisted that Alison wrote it. See Alison and Peter Smithson, "Banham's Bumper Book on Brutalism, Discussed by Alison and Peter Smithson," *Architects' Journal* (December 28, 1966), pp. 1590–91.

11 For a few years in the early 1950s, Le Corbusier's Unité d'Habitation became the iconic project for New Brutalism. The Smithsons' return to Mies in the later 1950s is often dismissed either as a move away from the basic tenets of New Brutalism and the pervasive preoccupation with Le Corbusier, or as a minor concern compared with their intense involvement in Team 10. Peter's famous quote from the late 1950s, "Mies is great, but Corb communicates," further complicates the issue. The phrase first appeared in print, in all caps, in the transcript of a symposium on Le Corbusier held at the Architectural Association on March 4, 1959, two months before Mies would participate in a discussion there on May 27. See "Le Corbusier: A Symposium," *Architectural Association Journal*, 74 (May 1959), p. 254.

12 Theoretical and historical research into these aspects of Mies were launched in the late twentieth century in essays such as K. Michael Hays, "Critical Architecture: Between Culture and Form," *Perspecta*, 21 (1984), pp. 14–19; Stan Allen, "Mies's Theater of Effects: The New National Gallery, Berlin," in *Practice: Architecture, Technique and Representation*, Amsterdam G+B Arts, 2000; and the broad range of essays in Detlef Mertins, ed., *The Presence of Mies*, Princeton, NJ: Princeton Architectural Press, 1994.

13 Peter Smithson, "Letter to America," *Architectural Design*, 28, no. 3 (March 1958), pp. 93–102.

14 Alison and Peter Smithson, "But Today We Collect Ads," *Ark*, 18 (November 1956), n.p.

15 The Mies seminar marks a crucial turning point in the Smithsons' thinking about Mies. It was conducted a year after the publication of Banham's book and the *Arena* monograph, the first two attempts to assess and historicize their work, which seems to have provoked their own subsequent, persistent attempts at retrospective revision and recollection.

16 The text and slides of their December 1967 seminar at the Berlin Technical University were later published in the form of an essay, "Mies van der Rohe," *Architectural Design*, 39, no. 7 (July 1969), pp. 363–66 (here p. 366). The text was reworked and reappears as paragraphs distributed throughout *Without Rhetoric* in 1973.

17 The two 1956 projects by the Smithsons that are so often seen as incommensurable, *Patio and Pavilion* and House of the Future, exemplify the range of that aesthetic spectrum. A comparison in terms of immersion and stimulation can elucidate the ways in which each project engages different aspects of Mies and imaging.

18 A. and P. Smithson, "But Today We Collect Ads."

19 A. and P. Smithson, "Mies van der Rohe," p. 363.

20 Ibid.

21 Peter Smithson, "For Mies van der Rohe on his 80th Birthday," *Bauen + Wohnen* (May 1966), p. 206. The statement reappears in *Without Rhetoric.*

22 A. and P. Smithson, *Without Rhetoric*, p. 2.

23 Alison and Peter Smithson, *Changing the Art of Inhabitation: Mies' Pieces, Eames' Dreams, the Smithsons*, London: Artemis, 1994, pp. 64, 153. All the captions in the book are included in an index on its final six pages. A note regarding "MIT" appears near the bottom of the page: "Which PS would not see until 1957."

24 The idea stems from a lecture presented in 1980 at the International Laboratory of Architecture and Urban Design (ILA&UD) that draws an analogy between three generations of Renaissance architects—Filippo Brunelleschi, Leon Battista Alberti,

Francesco di Giorgio (or Donato Bramante)—and three generations of modern architects: Gropius, Mies and Le Corbusier, Prouvé and the Eameses, the Smithsons. See Peter Smithson, "Three Generations," *ILA&UD: Annual Report, Urbino 1980* (1980), pp. 88–98. The following year the Smithsons would publish two versions of a "poster"—one by Alison, one by Peter—with a compound image, or ideogram, of the three modern generations (now just Mies, the Eameses, the Smithsons) that focuses on the "late" appearance of "the diagonal brace as an architectonic device" in "the language of modern architecture." The three images are a 1934 Mies sketch of "a glass house on a hillside" (in Philip Johnson, *Mies van der Rohe*, New York: Museum of Modern Art, 1947, p. 109), the patterns of the legs of the Eameses' Wire Mesh Chair of the early 1950s, and a perspective drawing of the Smithsons' Lucas Headquarters (1973–75). This fascination with the diagonal brace evolves into "the lattice idea" in 2000 and builds on the patterns of the "random aesthetic." That ideogram reiterated the Smithsons' use of a similar image device in a poster for a lecture at Harvard about the Renaissance triad, with fragments of church plans by Brunelleschi, Alberti, and Bramante arrayed as an exquisite corpse to form a single plan-body. See Peter Smithson, "The Masque and the Exhibition: Stages toward the Real," *ILA&UD: Language of Architecture* (1981), p. 62.

25 P. Smithson, "Three Generations," p. 94.

26 Reyner Banham, *The New Brutalism: Ethic or Aesthetic?*, New York: Reinhold, 1966, p. 134.

27 Reyner Banham, "The New Brutalism," *Architectural Review*, 118, no. 708 (December 1955), p. 361.

28 Banham, *The New Brutalism*, pp. 47.

29 Ibid., p. 134.

30 Two reviews of Banham's book, by Robin Middleton and Robin Boyd, each contested Banham's conclusion and offered alternative, and opposing, narratives: Middleton affirmed New Brutalism's importance and influence and claimed that "the link," "the doorstep," and "the pattern of a route system" are the true legacy of New Brutalism. His review ended: "Brutalism marches on." Robin Middleton, "The New Brutalism; or, A Clean, Well-Lighted Place," *Architectural Design* (January 1967), pp. 7–8. Boyd's review, as its title suggests, "The Sad End of New Brutalism," *Architectural Review*, 142, no. 845 (July 1967), pp. 9–11, characterized New Brutalism as just another version of a postwar attitude of "aggressive candour" and a "revival of the rebellious spirit of early modern architecture" (p. 9). He wrote: "New Brutalism was certainly the most articulate of all the attempts to re-establish the original integrity and strength of modern architecture that occurred after the soft decade following the war. Yet it cannot be inflated more than that" (p. 9). Boyd saw New Brutalism as simply a commitment to "absolute basic architecture" and dismissed the idea that there is or was an aesthetic (there was just an "over-strained aesthetic argument"), even ridiculing the importance of advertising images and claiming that in their own review of Banham's book, the Smithsons "did not dispute the Banham thesis that a real New Brutalism, or an ethic of building technology, must exclude art, and they seemed to agree that the New Brutalism was dead" (p. 11). In fact, he suggested that New Brutalism was neither ethical nor "anti-artistic" enough: "The greatest hope of every architectural evangelical movement like New Brutalism is that it will lead the world away from seductive aesthetic pleasures to the pure intelligence of building" (p. 11).

31 Banham, *The New Brutalism*, p. 65.

32 In the early 1960s, Banham seemed to use the word "image" more in Richard Hamilton's "pop" sense of consumer marketing than Henderson's, or even that of his own philosophical concepts in his 1955 essay. See Richard Hamilton, "Persuading Image," *Design*, 134 February 1960), pp. 28–32.

33 Reyner Banham, "Apropos the Smithsons," *New Statesman* (September 8, 1961), p. 317. In 1962, Banham wrote a respectfully critical essay on Mies as the final installment of his six-part "On Trial" series in *Architectural Review*, interrogating various architects' uses of technology: "When we have got over trying to build him up as an aesthetic absolute we shall have the less comfortable prospect of having to live with him as a moral example" whose "peculiar authority" derives from his "almost unique attitude to technology—he accepts it." Reyner Banham, "Mies van der Rohe: Almost Nothing Is Too Much," *Architectural Review*, 132, no. 786 (August 1962), p. 128.

34 Banham, "Apropos the Smithsons," p. 317. Writing about the magazine *Archigram*, Banham criticized the consumption of images and their significance for architecture: "The essence, and the value [...] is in its running dialogue with current images immediately they appear. It is the instant assignment of values, however temporary, to each new image, however puerile and improbable, the moment it swims into the architectural viewscreen, that justifies the fuss we all make over Archigram." Banham, review of Peter Cook's *Architecture, Action and Plan*, in *Architectural Design*, 37, no. 7 (August 1967), p. 352. In his contribution to a later book, Banham reiterated that pejorative idea of images: 'Archigram is [...] in the image business and they have been blessed with the power to create some of the most compelling images of our time." Reyner Banham, "A Comment from Peter Reyner Banham," in Peter Cook, ed., *Archigram*, Basel: Birkhauser, 1972, p. 5.

35 Reyner Banham, "Crowther's Acropolis," *New Statesman* (January 15, 1965), pp. 83–84.

36 *Arena* special issue, p. 180.

37 Other key evidence of the timing of this shift are the revisions to a 1981 edition of "The Heroic Period of Modern Architecture", which was first published in 1965. In the 1981 edition, the most significant changes (other than the addition of a section of color images at the end) are three new images of and two short texts about

Mies's work, as well as the consolidation of the images of the Tugendhat House on two pages.

38 Two British journals published extensive documentation of a nearly complete Hunstanton in the same month that *Parallel of Life and Art* was staged: *Architects' Journal*, 118 (September 10, 1953), pp. 323–28, and *Architectural Design*, 23, no. 9 (September 1953), pp. 238–48. The earliest publication of the building under construction was "Welded Steel Fabrication Used at Hunstanton Secondary Modern School," *The National Builder* (April 1953), pp. 280–81. A more elaborate presentation, including a brief essay by Philip Johnson praising the design as "not only radical but good Mies van der Rohe," appeared the following year in *Architectural Review*, 116 (September 1954), pp. 149–62. The official opening of the building was not until March 17, 1955. The competitionwinning design was published three times in 1950 (in *Architect's Journal*, May 11, pp. 576–77; *The Builder*, May 12, pp. 642–44; and *The Architect and Building News*, May 12, pp. 486–88). In both "The New Brutalism" (1955) and *The New Brutalism: Ethic or Aesthetic?* (1966), Banham misstates a key aspect of the chronology of New Brutalism, claiming that Hunstanton was not published until 1954, after the term New Brutalism first appeared in print in December 1953. Yet he rightly points out how intertwined *Parallel of Life and Art* and Hunstanton were in discussions of New Brutalism. In 1955 Banham remarked that the publication of Hunstanton (one year after *Parallel of Life and Art*) redirected discussion of New Brutalism with "a sharper and less humorous tone, for here in three-dimensional and photographic reality, and in the classic Modern Movement materials of concrete, steel and glass, was the Smithsons' only completed building" (p. 357). All the 1953 publications of Hunstanton focused on the structure and building systems. Each of the September 1953 articles included several photographs of the building under construction, with the glass partially installed.

39 The CIAM 9 meeting, in July 1953, was the beginning of the Smithsons' involvement with CIAM. Team 10 took shape between then and CIAM 10, in July 1956, with the preparation of the Doorn Manifesto in January 1954. The CIAM 8 meeting, in 1951, was held in Hoddesdon, England, and Peter Smithson may have attended for part of a day.

40 "Memorandum. March 27th, 1953," Tate Archive, London, 9211.5.1.1. The first proposal for *Parallel of Life and Art*, then titled "Sources," was submitted in April 1952, the same month as the first meeting of the Independent Group.

41 The *UR* manuscript was begun in 1952 and "was finished" in "early 1953." See Alison and Peter Smithson, *Ordinariness and Light*, Cambridge, MA: MIT Press, 1970, pp. 9, 103.

42 "Memorandum. March 27th, 1953."

43 A. and P. Smithson, *Ordinariness and Light*, p. 62.

44 Ibid., p. 43.

45 Ibid., p. 11.

46 For a contemporary account of plastic theory see the full-page explanation accompanying the publication of the Hunstanton School: Dargan Bullivant, "The Plastic Theory of Bending and its Application to the Design of the Hunstanton Steel Frames," *Architectural Design*, 23, no. 11 (September 1953), p. 248.

47 A. and P. Smithson, *The Shift*, p. 12.

48 The design may also have been imagined as an alternative interior design approach to compete with and critique the ICA interiors designed by Jane Drew.

49 Henderson began teaching at the Central School in 1951, and Peter taught there from at least early 1951 until mid-1952. Ehrenzweig taught at the Central School from 1948 to 1964 as a dye technician in the Printed Textiles Department, and Paolozzi was at the school from 1950 to 1954 in the Printed Textiles Department, the only position available when he was looking to teach after returning from Paris. See Robbins, ed., *The Independent Group*, pp. 15, 19; Martin Harrison, *Transition: The London Art Scene in the Fifties*, exh. cat., Barbican, London: Merrell, 2002, p. 102; and Beth Williamson, "Paolozzi, Anton Ehrenzweig and Art Education in Post-War London," in *Eduardo Paolozzi*, ed. Daniel F. Herrmann, exh. cat., London: Whitechapel Gallery, 2017, pp. 42–48. Of the collaboration between Paolozzi and Ehrenzweig, Beth Williamson writes: "The exchanges that took place between them were largely pragmatic and focused on the practical matter of printing. [...] Ehrenzweig acted as his dye technician and screen printer and their exchanges continued after Paolozzi left the Central School in 1955."

50 Anton Ehrenzweig, *The Hidden Order of Art: A Study in the Psychology of Artistic Imagination*, Berkeley: University of California Press, 1967, p. 100. The Smithsons explain in *The Shift*, p. 12, that Paolozzi "stitched up [the connections between sheets] in black poster paint" to create "a single composition [...] (sighing heavily the while, interspersed by our remarks about Michelangelo's socks)."

51 Ehrenzweig, *The Hidden Order of Art*, caption to plate 4, a full-page bleed of the screen print.

52 A. and P. Smithson, *The Shift*, p. 9. Jenkins Room merits only a brief mention in the chronology in the 1966 *Arena* catalogue of their work: "JUN 05 52 AJ, JENKINS ROOM, Room at Ove Arup and Partners, 8 Fitzroy Street, W1, for R. S. Jenkins, designed by the Smithsons and having a ceiling by Eduardo Paolozzi and a wall cabinet by Victor Pasmore. Project Completed.") *Arena* special issue, p. 182.

53 A. and P. Smithson, *The Shift*, p. 73. As if inviting us to see Hunstanton as a malleable and recursive image, photographs of Hunstanton appear intermittently in *The Shift*, out of chronological order on spreads with other projects.

54 The quotation, from an unused interview with Reyner Banham for the film *Fathers of Pop* (1979), appears in Robbins, ed., *The Independent Group*, pp. 124–25.

55 See Walsh, *Nigel Henderson*, p. 95.
56 Henderson, handwritten notes for presentation at the Architectural Association, December 2, 1953, sheet 2, Tate Archive, 9211.5.1.5.
57 Banham, "The New Brutalism," pp. 356, 361.
58 The *Glasgow Herald* article is quoting from the August 31, 1953 press release, Tate Archive, 9211.5.1.2.
59 "Three Photographic Shows," *The Scotsman*, September 11, 1953, Tate Archive, 955.1.12.48.
60 See David Sylvester, in "Curriculum Vitae," the introduction to *About Modern Art: Critical Essays, 1948–1997*, New York: Henry Holt, 1997, p. 117, where he mentions his "invention of a new movement called 'Afocalism'" in the late 1940s inspired primarily by the paintings of Paul Klee, which, importantly, in a 1951 essay in *Architectural Review*, he recommends as "a source of inspiration for the contemporary architect" because they "are unified not by a balance of masses but by an equipoise of forces (movement directed in space), which demand that the spectator [...] project himself into it in imagination." David Sylvester, "Architecture in Modern Painting," *Architectural Review*, 109, no. 650 (February 1951), p. 88. Ben Highmore makes a compelling argument for the affinities between Sylvester's afocalism and New Brutalism in "Brutalist Wallpaper and the Independent Group," *Journal of Visual Culture*, 12 (2013), p. 217. He describes afocalism as "a sort of roaming, peripatetic seeing" that is exemplified by the paintings of Klee or Jackson Pollock, but "is also the condition of the image-field in a mass-media environment where multiple images are clamouring for attention simultaneously," which requires a kind of perception that "is practised in drifting and distracted looking."
61 See Harrison, *Transition*, p. 54. "Although Sylvester did not write about Bacon until 1952, he was close to him at this time [1949] and in 1950 shared living premises with the artist. [...] Sylvester, who had grasped the significance of photography for Bacon's work, began to collect clipings of images from newspapers and magazines, and to show them in his lectures."
62 David Sylvester, untitled review, *The Listener*, September 24, 1953, Tate Archive, 955.1.12.48.
63 Untitled review, *Times Educational Supplement*, September 19, 1953, Tate Archive, 955.1.12.48.
64 Bryan Robertson, untitled review, *Art News and Review*, September 19, 1953, Tate Archive, 955.1.12.48.
65 Astragal, *Architect's Journal* (September 1953), p. 224.
66 Reyner Banham, "Photography: Parallel of Life and Art," *Architectural Review*, 114, no. 682 (October 1953), pp. 259–61.
67 Ibid., p. 261.
68 Ibid., pp. 260, 261.
69 Banham never mentions Aby Warburg, who had been working on his *Mnemosyne* atlas in London from 1924 to 1929 and whose iconographic approach was extended by others in different ways after World War Two, such as Fritz Saxl and Rudolf Wittkower. Surprisingly, as late as June 1955 the use of cameras was still novel enough among architects that *Architectural Review*, in conjunction with a competition titled "Photographing Modern Architecture," ran a five-part monthly "tear-out" series (June–October) by Sam Lambert, "Notes on Architectural Photography," featuring technical advice and instruction on camera use. Examples of earlier tear-out series include "Office Practice," "Design Data," and "Building Science."
70 For the most complete list of the seminar titles, topics, and number of members in attendance, see Anne Massey, *The Independent Group: Modernism and Mass Culture in Britain, 1945*–59, Manchester: Manchester University Press, 1995, pp. 80, 139–41.
71 In *Arena* special issue, p. 184, the only text about *Parallel of Life and Art* is three brief excerpts from Banham's review in *Architectural Review* and, printed in all capital letters, Peter's statement. Banham mentions Peter's statement in "The New Brutalism," p. 361. The announcement card from the Architectural Association for "Evening Forum 3: A Discussion on the Implications of the Exhibition Parallel of Life and Art, with Eduardo Paolozzi, Peter Smithson, and Nigel Henderson, 2 December 1953," notes that the exhibition was reinstalled from November 30 to December 4. Tate Archives, 955.1.12.48. Strangely, John Voelcker (who became one of the most compelling advocates for New Brutalism and a key collaborator with the Smithsons in the early years of Team 10) would coauthor a definitive article on systems of proportion with Ruth Olitsky one year later, "Form and Mathematics," *Architectural Design*, 24 (October 1954), pp. 306–7. Also see a series of articles on the proportion system of Harry Roberts, by his son, A. Leonard Roberts, in *Architectural Design* from September 1949 through February 1950.
72 A letter to the editor, to which Banham alluded (without citation) in his 1955 essay "The New Brutalism," reported on the responses of many students: "As one of the initiators of the AA Forum on 'Parallels [*sic*] of Life and Art' at which both Peter Smithson and Basil Taylor were speakers, I was particularly interested to see the student feeling was running very strongly against the exhibition—the aesthetic source of the New Brutalism. It was variously condemned as shallow, eclectic, and an example of the New Picturesque and denying the spiritual in man. As a result of this discussion one of your editorial colleagues at a recent seminar at the Institute of Contemporary Arts labelled the AA students a reactional body!" Hugh Pope, "Letter to the Editor," *Architectural Review*, 115 (June 1954), p. 364.

Fig. 2 *Architects' Journal* (September 10, 1953), p. 323; *Architectural Design*, 23, no. 9 (September 1953), p. 245; *Architectural Review*, 116 (September 1954), pp. 149, 115.

Fig. 3 H. T. Cadbury-Brown, "Ludwig Mies van der Rohe: An address of Appreciation by H. T. Cadbury Brown to the Guest of Honour, Professor Mies van der Rohe. Illustrated by Slides of his Work," *Architectural Association Journal*, 75 (August 1959), pp. 26–46.

Chapter 2

What's Modern?

Prior to World War Two, as evident in British architecture journals, interest in modern architecture was both sporadic and tepid. With the exception of regular articles by Howard Robertson and others featuring examples of European modernism in the *Architect and Building News* beginning in the early 1920s, and the occasional publication of modernist projects in the then more traditionalist *Architectural Review* (most notably those of Le Corbusier on the occasion of the English translation of *Vers une architecture* in 1927), it was not until after the founding of the Modern Architecture Research Group (MARS) as the British representatives to CIAM in 1933, and as the editorial changes implemented by Hubert de Cronin Hastings started to take hold at *Architectural Review* and *Architects' Journal* around that time, that modern architecture began to have numerous British advocates in practice and in the press.[1] It was not until much later, in the late 1940s, that modernism truly began to flourish in the arts.[2] Francis Bacon's *Three Studies for Figures at the Base of a Crucifixion* was first exhibited in 1945, the Institute of Contemporary Arts was established in 1946 (although its first shows were not staged until 1948), and the sculptors Henry Moore and Barbara Hepworth would represent Britain with solo shows at the Venice Biennale in 1948 and 1950. A few years later, simultaneous with the beginnings of New Brutalism and the Independent Group, a new kind of controversy about modernism and the future of British art occurred: "Between 1951 and 1953 a 'ferocious squabble about abstract art,' otherwise known as the abstraction versus realism debate, enlivened the correspondence columns of *The Listener* and *The New Statesman and Nation*."[3] By early 1953, when the Smithsons, Henderson, and Paolozzi began working on *Parallel of Life and Art*, the quarrel had intensified as a personal argument between the artist-critic Patrick Heron and the Marxist critic John Berger, who were "battling out the contrary views of art-for-itself—and so for the elite—and art-for-the-people—and so for propaganda."[4] The immediate impetus for the debates was *Looking Forward*, an exhibition of contemporary realist painting curated by Berger at the Whitechapel Art Gallery in fall 1952. The show was intended as an inclusive catalogue of otherwise unrelated artists who exemplified the range of possible future directions for realism in British painting. Soon after, architecture was implicated in the controversy. Beginning in January 1953, the ICA staged an exhibition of entries in an international competition (secretly funded by the United States with anti-Soviet intent) for a monument to the *Unknown Political Prisoner*. Berger attacked several abstract entries, including the eventual winner, which would be announced in May: Reg Butler's brass wire model, which appeared something like a cross between a guard tower and a radio antenna. Joshua Sperling, in his biography of Berger, characterizes the moment as a cultural and political convergence in which "everything changed. All intermediate space dried up" and "there were two—and only two—choices left."[5]

Yet New Brutalism and the Independent Group avoided choosing sides. Both evaded divisiveness in favor of deviousness, although the arguments and positions on modernism affected art and architecture differently. In the interval between early 1950, when the Smithsons submitted their entry to the Hunstanton School competition, and 1954, when the completed building was published in three major journals, including a positive appraisal by Philip Johnson in *Architectural Review*, the status of modern architecture in Britain was not in question, especially in school design.[6] But the Smithsons were more adventurously modernist than their elders and most of their peers in the profession. As they wrote at the time they were designing Hunstanton, "Only a person familiar with the pathetic figure of English functionalism supported since the war on a crutch of pseudo-science can understand why it was necessary to make such an obvious statement and design such a didactic building."[7] Hunstanton and the rhetoric of New Brutalism provoked strong reactions, even though, by 1954, few influential architects or critics continued to oppose modernism to British traditions. As Alan Powers explains, "For the first time in the history of Modernism in Britain [. . .] the enemy outside, in the form of traditional styles, was nearly defeated."[8] The pervasive question in the journals, the schools, and at the Royal Institute of British Architects (RIBA) was how to devise a successor to European modernism that could evolve uniquely in the postwar British context. The shock of war and the urgency of rebuilding in its aftermath had unleashed debates about British identity and Britain's new role and engagement in international culture. When the Smithsons began designing the Hunstanton School in 1949, they looked at Mies's first Chicago buildings through the lens of postwar austerity and systematic efforts by the British government to revive the culture and restructure the economy of a victorious but depleted nation.[9] Hunstanton's "ruthless" and "abstemious"[10] logic resonated uneasily with the harsh realities of postwar scarcity and its politics of rationing,[11] as well as with the commitment to state-sponsored planning and social services initiated by the Beveridge Report (1942) and pursued in the policies and agenda of Clement Attlee's Labour government (1945–51).[12]

Yet the emphasis on disciplinary rigor and "exposed materials and untreated surfaces" that came to define New Brutalism is a huge oversimplification of what the Smithsons meant by their statement in 1957 that the "essence" of New Brutalism is its "attempt to be objective about 'reality'—the cultural objectives of society, its urges, and so on."[13] For the Smithsons, the plea for objectivity was not aligned with the technical and functional objectivity of *Sachlichkeit* as espoused by Hermann Muthesius in Germany. Instead, objectivity meant an insistence on unsentimental, nondogmatic, clear-eyed attention to actual problems and conditions of modern life.[14] Usually only the Smithsons' first phrase, "to be objective about 'reality'," is quoted, and even then the quotation marks around the word "reality" go unnoticed or unremarked upon. But more important, the Smithsons' "attempt to be objective" was not a desire for objectivity in any modernist or idealist sense, but a plain declaration of objectives—aims, goals, aspirations, hopes, imagined futures—and, perhaps most important, an honest acknowledgment of the urges that fuel them. Yet *Sachlichkeit* is precisely the attitude that many ascribed to New Brutalism. Among them was John Summerson, who described New Brutalism as merely "a recapitulation, a reassessment of ground which the modern movement has covered more than once in its history." But Summerson did accurately characterize an important aspect of the New Brutalist attitude as entirely of its time: "Already in 1951 there was a perceptible hostility to whatever was idiomatic and a tendency to go in search of principles. Not, it should be understood, theoretic principles, but principles embodied in actuality, principles announced as buildings."[15]

That characteristic British aversion to "theoretic principles" is also a central theme in Banham's "Biography" of Howard Robertson in the September 1953 issue of *Architectural Review*. Writing when Robertson was at the midpoint of his two-year presidency of the RIBA, Banham described him as "the first occupant of that august position who has been in any active manner associated with the Modern Movement," and he saw this as "a tribute to the manner in which Modern Architecture has taken command in England."[16] But he also characterized Robertson as a moderate figure who had long played the role of a "liaison between the extreme moderns and the established tradition"[17] and whose characteristic judiciousness had had both progressive and stifling effects on the reception of modernism in Britain. On the one hand, his education at the École de Beaux-Arts had instilled a "most un-English passion for the logic of plans" that was "uncontaminated by the picturesque"; on the other, he epitomized "the rather diffuse and muddled way in which the Modern Movement got under way in England" and personified the "undefinable qualities which make it unmistakably English."[18] Yet Banham's essay ends with qualified hope for the future role Robertson could play in achieving a complete "change of heart" toward modernism at the RIBA: "No-one is better equipped to perform this piece of surgery with the minimum of bloodshed, and so that the beneficial effects may be most immediately felt."[19]

Banham's backhanded praise captures the tensions of a transformational moment when modernism was pervasive and even dominant but hardly established or fully accepted. Though he was certainly and necessarily being diplomatic, it was deeply ironic that Banham endorsed Robertson, however ambivalently, for possessing the same attitude of gradualist "adaptability"[20] that New Brutalism resolutely rejected and which was given official sanction two years earlier in the "Contemporary Style" of the Festival of Britain, a government-funded exhibition marking the hundredth anniversary of the Great Exhibition of 1851 and celebrating the nation's cultural, technological, and scientific progress.[21] Social historian Harry Hopkins has explained the Contemporary Style and the festival itself as both the last flourish of British complacency about cultural and social modernity and the event that marked the start of a "new phase of life" in which "the nation groped towards a new balance between its past, its present and its future" by looking "to the modest, model social democracies of Scandinavia":

> The strength of the English had long lain in a quiet conviction of their own innate superiority [. . .]. Down the years the idea had modified: a capacity for adjustment without-apparent change was part of its strength. Then, somewhere in the interwar years, between the brittle Twenties and the sleep-walking, finally nightmarish, Thirties, the capacity for adjustment had been overrun. The impact of the war, like electric convulsion therapy for the mentally confused, had wiped the slate, provided a new start. Tentatively remodelled, the idea had begun to re-form.[22]

The New Brutalist generation saw any kind of modernist moderation as a missed opportunity to challenge British taste directly rather than assuage it.[23] Hostility toward the Contemporary Style and the Swedish sources it was modelled upon (generally known as the "New Empiricism," which many saw as one of New Brutalism's primary targets) had provoked architects, artists, and designers to take principled stands on modernism.[24] Those positions found some support at the recently founded ICA, which by 1951 was flourishing, influential, and fully established in its new Dover Street premises, exerting influence on the arts as well as architecture. As early as August 1948, the ICA sponsored two lectures by Sigfried Giedion on "Modern Architecture," and in 1951 it hosted another by Giedion and one by Philip Johnson. Regular "discussions" on architectural criticism began in late 1952, led by J. M. Richards and others, as public seminars to inculcate a new vocabulary and support particular projects and practices, such as Powell & Moya's Pimlico Flats and Churchill Gardens (on November 27, 1952) and Tecton's Hallfield Estate (on January 20, 1953).[25]

The Smithsons' ardent modernism was not only an explicit rejection of the tempered approach of their elders like Robertson, Casson, Charles Holden, or even the refined functionalism of Maxwell Fry and Jane Drew (who began their practice together in 1946), but also an overt departure from the stylistic formalism of the first generation of modern architects in Britain, such as Wells Coates, Ernő Goldfinger, Berthold Lubetkin, Edward Mills, and Ward Connell.[26] In different ways, either too compromising or too imitative, both groups exemplified the tepidness of early British modernism in art and in architecture that Nikolaus Pevsner characterized in his 1955 radio lectures, *The Englishness of English Art*, as a disposition for "conservatism" and a "national character of practical sense, of reason, and also of tolerance" that had the negative effect of lacking the kind of "intensity which alone can bring forth the greatest in art."[27] Like many British historians and critics, Pevsner repeated the Burkean truism that British revolutions are "unbloody,"[28] an attitude that can be traced to the late eighteenth-century aversion to the "despotic 'system' of French Revolutionary art." Instead, as David Solkin explains, "the British School embraced pluralism and originality as the very stuff of its identity, but only to the extent that this valorised the individualistic ideology and cultural pretensions of the commercial middle class."[29] David Corbett has suggested that British modernism was always a "struggle of competing definitions, the majority of which were marked by retreat, evasion, and concealment of modernism's impact,"[30] while Charles Harrison has characterized British modernism between the world wars as marked by "reproving timorousness, the invoking of unspecified 'essential realities,' the recall to order, the vaunting of a conservative concept of professionalism, the attaching of value to 'sincerity' in the absence of criteria for deciding truth."[31]

Elizabeth Darling offers an alternative view of modernism in Britain that turns gradualism and realism into its primary virtues and which helps clarify the contrarian appeal of New Brutalism's evasion of both overt emulation of European sources and acceptance of endemic British attitudes. She argues that it misses the point to label an aversion to strident modernism as conservatism. Her emphatically political and cultural understanding of both modernism and its history in Britain identifies a continuous concern with design as an institutionalized tool for social and political reform: "The emergence, development, and ultimate hegemony of modernism in Britain can only be understood if we see it as one of a range of attempts in the inter-war decades to engage with the problems of modernity through radical approaches to social and cultural reform."[32] Defined that way, "by 1939 modernism was well-established in Britain," much earlier than it was accepted as a style: [33]

> So rather than seeing the Le Corbusier-influenced work of Connell, Ward and Lucas, or the Miesian borrowings of Fry, as a wholesale and thoughtless copyism, and evidence of the lack of a true modernism in Britain, we might, instead, understand their deployment of such radically different forms as a rhetorical device to propagandize whichever cause the building served. Furthermore, a look beyond the rhetorical form to the rhetorical content might also allow a reassertion of the Britishness of this modernism. For while their surfaces may have been borrowed from elsewhere, they cloaked programmes which derived from peculiarly British approaches to social reform. It would be through this hybridization of progressive reform with progressive content that modernism was able to capture some of the most significant discourses of inter-war reform.[34]

As Banham suggested in 1955, positioning oneself as a modern architect in Britain after World War Two required a new sophistication toward the complexity of both the present and the past: "New Brutalism has to be seen against the background of the recent history of history, and, in particular, the growing sense of the inner history of the Modern Movement itself."[35] That same year, the Smithsons stated directly that New Brutalism was "the only possible development *for this moment* from the Modern Movement."[36] At the outset, New Brutalism, as exemplified in the Hunstanton School and the "warehouse aesthetic" of the Smithsons' unbuilt House in Soho, was a bold announcement that modern architecture in Britain could be an unapologetically advanced and challenging extension of Heroic Modernism. While the Soho house exemplifies the ethos of unadorned, sober design that Adolf Loos had admired in English building at the turn of the century or that Muthesius examined in *Stilarchitektur und Baukunst* (Style-Architecture and Building-Art, 1902), it would be more accurate to understand the ambition of New Brutalism as a desire to initiate the next stage in the historical progression from "William Morris to Walter Gropius" that Pevsner had detailed in *Pioneers of the Modern Movement* (1936), a narrative that he continued to promote and refine for decades in multiple editions of his book. Its second edition appeared in 1949 (with numerous revisions that reinforced and augmented his support for modernism), the same year that he presented a summary of its argument as a BBC radio talk in which he characterized Morris as the inventor of "a whole system of aesthetic socialism or socialist aesthetics" that directly informed and inspired Gropius's program for the Bauhaus, "*the most* remarkable effort towards combining creative freedom in art and craft with disciplined work for industrial standards."[37] Modernism, he argued in the second edition of *Pioneers*, recognized "the essential unity of architecture" as an integration of social conditions, systems of production, and aesthetics from its nineteenth-century British sources to its emergence in Germany as "the genuine and legitimate style of our century."[38] In the last lines of the 1949 book (unchanged from 1936), Pevsner's described Gropius's Fagus Factory in Alfeld (1914) in a way that could almost be mistaken as a description of both Hunstanton and life in postwar Britain: "The glass walls are now clear and without mystery, the steel frame is hard and its expression discourages all other-worldly speculation. It is the creative energy of this world in which we live and work and which we want to master, a world of science and technology, of speed and danger, of hard struggles and no personal security, that is glorified in Gropius's architecture."[39]

Although the Smithsons emphasized sources other than Pevsner's, both historical and contemporary, in architecture and in popular culture, the ethos and appeal of New Brutalism were infused with affects and ideas derived from British origins, from the moral imperatives of Augustus Pugin's *True Principles* (1841) and John Ruskin's *Seven Lamps* (1849) to the sheer technical ingenuity of the Crystal Palace (1851), the social project of Morris, and the practical comforts of the English house admired by Muthesius (1904).[40] That deep sense of a British architectural and cultural legacy is evident in the Smithsons' famous reference to Robert Smythson's Hardwick Hall (1590–97) as a precedent for the interior space of Hunstanton, an example that also reflects an understanding of modernism informed not only by Pevsner, who admired that building's "basic affinity" with modernism,[41] but also by J. M. Richards, who adopted, simplified, and popularized Pevsner's narrative in his widely read 1940 book *An Introduction to Modern Architecture*.[42] Richards foregrounded the practical and technological aspects of modernism and expressed skepticism toward Pevsner's characterization of modernism as a style. He ably condensed Pevsner's argument into the simple explanation, in sympathy but not allied with New Brutalist attitudes, that architecture is "a social art related to the life of the people it serves" and that modernism is "the revival of architecture as a live art" that strives "to solve problems for which history has no precedents."[43]

As much as the appeal of New Brutalism must be understood as aligned with the broad outlines of Pevsner's and Richards's books, it was also a distinct evasion of the specific positions that the two men would advocate during and after the war in their roles as editors of *Architectural Review*.[44] In different ways, they each advanced programs for specifically British and decidedly nondogmatic variations of modernism that adapted the principles of the English Picturesque, which, in the words of Pevsner, was "the first feeling-your-way theory of art in European history and far the greatest contribution England has made to aesthetic theory." Most important, "albeit unconsciously, the modern revolution of the early twentieth century and the Picturesque revolution of a hundred years before had all their fundamentals in common."[45] In many ways, the New Brutalist aesthetic, or sensibility, shares Pevsner's and Richards's recognition of the significance of the Picturesque, although the Smithsons took pains to distinguish their position. This was necessary because, beginning in January 1944,[46] and continuing for a decade, Pevsner worked with Hubert de Cronin Hastings at *Architectural Review* to advance an editorial policy that promoted the Picturesque as a sophisticated yet ingrained and familiar mode of visuality that was not only quintessentially modern but "that might be called perennially English" and could make "possible our own regional development of the International Style, as a result of our own self-knowledge—technics in marriage to psychology."[47]

A provocative example of that "marriage" appeared in September of that year as an intriguing pair of essays by the architect Hugh Casson and the artist Julian Trevelyan that outlined the aesthetics and the technique of camouflage and its applicability to urban design.[48] The editorial introduction to the essays, under the shared title "Art by Accident," makes explicit the relationship to the

ARRAY 2.1

Review's rationale for advocating Picturesque theory: "Camouflage is functional design *par excellence*," and its results "often have a distinct visual charm and a curious similarity to the conscious creations of modern art."[49] Illustrations included aerial reconnaissance photographs, abstract paintings, and color sketches of streetscapes that demonstrated how the combined visual effect of camouflaged infrastructure sited among vernacular buildings conveyed a Picturesque sense of variety, ruin, and decay through devices of "contrast, concealment, surprise and balance—the surface antagonisms of shape."[50] Casson's essay, "The Aesthetics of Camouflage," concluded with the claim that "the scientific use of texture, tone and colour, to complement instead of to disguise form" could, if "used with imagination, control and the knowledge gained from war-time experience [...] surely be of the greatest and most stimulating assistance to those who will be faced with the task of bringing coherence and vitality into the post-war street scene."[51] While the intent and implications of these essays were polemical, their arguments and the sensibility of the illustrations aligned with the more moderate and practical interpretations of the Picturesque that would later inform the Townscape movement promoted by *Architectural Review* beginning in 1949.[52] Early versions of those arguments and their manner of illustration appeared in John Piper's May 1945 essay "Colour in the Picturesque Village," which praised a naturalism in which "there are no violent colour contrasts with the surroundings; the village looks as if it has grown from the soil. Its beauty springs from the fact that here man's interference with nature is camouflaged from the start, and the camouflage becomes more complete with the passage of time."[53] Those ideas and a similar visual sensibility were taken in a less nostalgic direction in the artist Michael Rothenstein's 1946 essay "Colour and Modern Architecture; or, The Photographic Eye." He blamed the "austere," "untextured," "colourless idiom" of modern architecture on the "clearcut but colourless" character of "the Photographic Eye which sees in terms of black and white and which habitually dissociates form from colour. For here in England the architect must sometimes have relied on photographic representation when forming impressions of those great continental buildings which have influenced him so decisively."[54]

Seven years later, *Parallel of Life and Art* offered the New Brutalist counterargument to Rothenstein's characterization of the photographic modernist eye even as the exhibition's attitude toward photography had much in common with the aerial images in

2.1

…tep[s in] engineering

…e relation, if … the vernacular and functionalism has never been …ely studied. …ould say they are two words for the same thing—…ctional building. But there is at least one outstanding difference, and that … in the mentality which evolves them. Whether vernacular architecture …ecessarily functional, may be contested. What can be put down as certain, …ever, is that the vernacular is by definition the product of instinct and …it. The cult of what has come to be known as functionalism on the other …d is nothing if not self-conscious and deliberate. Between the two, equally …inct from the one as from the other, lies the corpus of humanist tradition. …manism is as deliberate as functionalism (all isms are), but, whereas the …ctionalist is out to express function in terms of æsthetic values, the …nanist's aim is to achieve the æsthetically valuable in terms of Art with a …ital A. He has a strong bias against a purely functional ideal. The three …ges Vernacular—Humanist—Functionalist are fairly familiar in archi…tural history. The object of this note is to show that over a much shorter …iod, not more than a hundred years, very much the same stages can be …erved in the field of engineering. While this raises the question if it might … be possible and in more than one way illuminating to try and classify …man activities of other kinds—of all kinds, perhaps—on a similar basis, the …mediate interest lies in the stylistic distinctions that can be made (morpho…cally, not historically) between stages of engineering. It is contended here …t there is a "primitive" state in modern engineering which exhibits all … characteristics of vernacular building; that at a given point the psy…logically developing engineer breaks out of this "innocence" into full…oded humanism as exhibited by a strong tendency towards curly bits; …d that this again is only a stage in a cultural evolution which brings about …lly and inevitably a deliberate and self-conscious pursuit of the functional.

…eps in architecture

…VERNACULAR FUNCTIONAL. *The first flow of … outhouse at Bibury, in the …wolds, is reached by the simplest …stairs, the type as children build … with their building blocks. …h step is one block higher than … preceding one. There are no …bellishments whatever, not even a …drail. All relations in space are …ctly rectangular.*

2 ART APPLIED TO FUNCTION. *The straightforward block of a provincial town hall (Poole) has been embellished by the addition of a double-flight staircase of Georgian stateliness and elegance. The vigour of the double curve is contrasted against the sturdy solidity of the pedimented landing.*

3 ART AND FUNCTION INTEGRATED. *At first nothing here (Lowestoft) seems to go beyond the functional. Closer observation, however, reveals subtleties which cannot be coincidental. The sweeping curve of the stair stands dramatically against the vast surface behind, and the handrail recessed in the wall throws a delicate double line across the rough texture of the stone.*

…eps in engineering

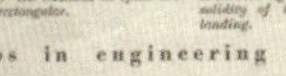

…VERNACULAR FUNCTIONAL. *Again no embellishments at all. …plain a statement in iron as was the …wold stair in stone, and as convinc… a statement too. Note the contrast …slender stem and energetic ascent of … ladder.*

2 ART APPLIED TO FUNCTION. *The water tower decorated in the buoyant mid-Victorian manner. The stair has the same buoyancy, but achieved by sheer engineering. A discrepancy results between functional jollity in the stair and applied-art jollity in the tower.*

3 ART AND FUNCTION INTEGRATED. *The dramatic way in which the stair clings to the huge surface of the gas container and sweeps into the picture and out of sight again, is the conscious and deliberate work of the twentieth century functionalist.*

had been lavished on its decoration, and yet within an hour it was entirely consumed. A quarter of an hour after we had used all the precautions possible against fire, it broke out behind us, in front of us, to right, to left, and we were unable to see who set it going. There it was in a dozen places at once, and flaring from every attic window.

"The general immediately called for the sappers to try to cut the fire off, but it was impossible. We had no pumps and not even any water. . . . The utmost we could do was to save some pictures and a few other valuables, amongst which were Imperial ornaments, velvet mantles lined with ermine, besides many other precious things which we afterwards had to leave behind. About half an hour after the fire broke out, a furious wind got up and in less than ten minutes we were hemmed in by the fire and could neither advance nor retreat. Several men were hurt by falling pieces of burning timber. It was two o'clock in the morning before we could get out of this hell, and we then found that the fire had spread for more than half a league all round—for the whole of this quarter was built of wood and was very beautiful."

Concepcion in 1835

(from *The Voyage of the Beagle*).

"*March 4* (1835).—The next day I landed at Talcahuano, and afterwards rode to Concepcion. Both towns presented the most awful yet interesting spectacle I ever beheld. To a person who had formerly known them, it possibly might have been still more impressive; for the ruins were so mingled together, and the whole scene possessed so little the air of a habitable place, that it was scarcely possible to imagine its former condition. The earthquake commenced at half-past eleven o'clock in the forenoon. If it had happened in the middle of the night, the greater number of the inhabitants (which in this one province amount to many thousands) must have perished, instead of less than a hundred; as it was, the invariable practice of running out of doors at the first trembling of the ground, alone saved them. In Concepcion each house, or row of houses, stood by itself, a heap or line of ruins; but in Talcahuano, owing to the great wave, little more than one layer of bricks, tiles and timber, with here and there part of a wall left standing, could be distinguished. From this circumstance Concepcion, although not so completely desolated, was a more terrible and, if I may so call it, picturesque sight.

"After viewing Concepcion, I cannot understand how the greater number of inhabitants escaped unhurt. The houses in many parts fell outwards; thus forming in the middle of the streets little hillocks of brickwork and rubbish. Mr. Rouse, the English Consul, told us that he was at breakfast when the first movement warned him to run out. He had scarcely reached the middle of the courtyard, when one side of his house came thundering down. He retained presence of mind to remember, that if he once got on the top of that part which had already fallen, he would be safe. Not being able from the motion of the ground to stand, he crawled up on his hands and knees; and no sooner had he ascended this little eminence, than the other side of the house fell in, the great beams sweeping close in front of his head. With his eyes blinded, and his mouth choked with the cloud of dust which darkened the sky, at last he gained the street. As shock succeeded shock, at the interval of a few minutes, no one dared approach the shattered ruins; and no one knew whether his dearest friends and relations were not perishing from the want of help. . . . The thatched roofs fell over the fires, and flames burst forth in all parts. Hundreds knew themselves ruined, and few had the means of providing food for the day.

". . . Pools of salt-water were still standing amidst the ruins of the houses and children, making boats with old tables and chairs, appeared as happy as their parents were miserable. It was, however, exceedingly interesting to observe, how much more active and cheerful all appeared than could have been expected. It was remarked with much truth, that from the destruction being universal, no one individual was humbled more than another, or could suspect his friends of coldness—that most grievous result of the loss of wealth. Mr. Rouse, and a large party whom he kindly took under his protection, lived for the first week in a garden beneath some apple trees. At first they were as merry as if it had been a picnic; but soon afterwards heavy rain caused much discomfort, for they were absolutely without shelter.

"The town of Concepcion was built in the usual Spanish fashion, with all the streets running at right angles to each other; one set ranging S.W. by W., and the other set N.W. by N. The walls in the former direction certainly stood better than those in the latter; the greater number of the masses of brickwork were thrown down towards the N.E. . . . The different resistance offered by the walls, according to their direction, was well exemplified in the case of the Cathedral. The side which fronted the N.E. presented a grand pile of ruins, in the midst of which door cases and masses of timber stood up, as if floating in a stream. Some of the angular blocks of brickwork were of great dimensions and they were rolled to a distance on the

THE BAROQUE—PHOTOGRAPHED WELL AND PHOTOGRAPHED BADLY

On the right a photo of the head of Thomas Thynn by Thomas Quellinus. The photographer has done what most photographers would do: placed his artificial lighting dead in front of the head, and his camera too. On the left is the same head photographed by Mr. Gernsheim under the supervision of Dr. R. Wittkower, an example of the outstanding recording and reviving technique used in the Westminster Abbey photographic campaign which the Warburg Institute carried out last year on behalf of the National Buildings Record and which is discussed in detail on pages 2—12. Thomas Thynn's is a reclining figure. He looks up heavenward, and his expression seems to ask for mercy—mercy at the hand of God, or at that of the highwayman who murdered him on February 12, 1682? The photographer, by putting his lighting apparatus into the position of the sun shining through the windows of the choir aisle, has intensified the effect aimed at by the sculptor instead of destroying it. The bad photograph reminds us of the plaster-casts that still haunt us in the art schools. The eyes are dead, the mouth flabby. In the good photograph the head at once achieves the sentients of the Baroque. The bold and sweeping shadows throw into prominence what is expressive. The photographer may lose a little too much of the detail in the hair, but then the Baroque never quibbled over detail. It is the large effects that matter, and they come out to a degree which would no doubt enrapture Quellinus, if he could come back to see them.

level plain, like fragments of rock at the base of some high mountain. The side walls (running S.W. and N.E.), though exceedingly fractured, yet remained standing; but the vast buttresses (at right angles to them, and therefore parallel to the walls that fell) were in many cases cut clean off, as if by a chisel, and hurled to the ground. Some square ornaments on the coping of these same walls, were moved by the earthquake into a diagonal position. . . . Generally speaking, arched doorways or windows stood much better than any other part of the buildings. Nevertheless, a poor lame old man, who had been in the habit, during trifling shocks, of crawling to a certain doorway, was this time crushed to pieces.

"I have not attempted to give any detailed description of the appearance of Concepcion, for I feel that it is quite impossible to convey the mingled feelings which I experienced. Several of the officers visited it before me, but their strongest language failed to give a just idea of the scene of desolation. It is a bitter and humiliating thing to see works, which have cost man so much time and labour, overthrown in one minute; yet compassion for the inhabitants was almost instantly banished, by the surprise in seeing a state of things produced in a moment of time, which one was accustomed to attribute to a succession of ages."

Rheims in 1919

(from *Those Were the Days*, by Osbert Sitwell, Macmillan, 1938).

"Of this lost world, Rheims was the capital, a metropolis of the dead as remote from current life as those drowned cities which men, on the coasts both of the Atlantic and Mediterranean, believe yet to stand down below, claiming sometimes of a quiet night, when there is only a gentle swell on the waters, to hear the bells of their minsters ringing in the tide's wash.

"As Irene and her party approached, they could see from a great distance the towers and vast façade of Rheims Cathedral, rising up from this immolated plain and clad at this hour in the golden armour of the setting sun. Plainly now, they would stand sculpiturally, burnt and pounded and battered and inexorably smashed though they were. The lapse of four years, so short a period out of a lifetime of nine hundred, seemed to have invested them with especial qualities, both of symbolism and perpetuity. Thus, upon their stone, it seemed for once to have made visible the same lacerating and disintegrant process that it had wrought in secret upon the hearts of human beings, whether by involving them personally in the killing, or by proxy, through the persons of those they loved. Further, the passage of this comparatively brief space of time had substituted the very fabric of the walls for another, changing them, as it were, from a work of man into a work of God. Often people have wondered at the sacked and gutted cities of the antique world, trying to imagine by what alchemy it was, for example, that the great buildings of Rome, such as the Colosseum or the Pantheon, differed so completely, in their apparent substance and texture, from those which were erected only a few centuries later, seemed so much more noble in their ruin than the others in their full splendour? Here fire and sword—or

An image of Christ of that violent, somewhat sensational realism which the Spaniards brought from home and the Aztecs and Mayas took up with glee.

must have been one of the quietest scenes in the world, and yet at the same time one of the most exciting. A forest of ventilators! Never had I seen so many ventilators. Nor of such varying sizes.

I hope you will not think my photograph is touched up, for it is an exact record of what I saw. They stood about, all facing in different directions, like people on a railway platform; and their round, void faces had a calm, silent look, which did much to assuage me.

A fortnight later, in a little town several hundred miles from the sea, I took a photograph of a crowd of men at a street corner. They seemed to have something in common, these two groups. The faces of the men have so much the void expression of the ventilators' faces that they almost look as if they *were* the ventilators, but had acquired eyes and noses.

Any day, in any place in that country, you may see groups of Mexicans looking precisely like that group. And whereas the ventilators had a visual effect of calm in the midst of an aural pandemonium, the group of men had a visual effect of pandemonium in the midst of an aural silence.

All over Mexico one sees examples of Spanish architecture, wildly baroque in its pastrycook extravagances. And like erections of actual sugarcake, it is all crumbling away. They don't repair anything in Mexico, and the Spanish rococo is going the way of all plaster.

But when the four centuries of Spanish occupation have become only a tiny vignette on a page of history, and all their convents, palaces and haciendas have crumbled back into the hard red soil; when nothing is left of that story save a few Spanish names among the people who have utterly absorbed the tyrants of yesterday; there on the plains and the high plateaux, vast and unchanging, will stand the pyramids and temples of the first Americans, those far-distant predecessors of the Aztec and the Maya, with their surprising carvings as fresh and clearcut as when they were new from the sculptors' chisels more than six thousand years ago.

The Mexicans are a very lazy, gentle and truly religious people. If they had not been lazy and gentle, they would have overthrown their oppressors long before they did. And if they were not a truly religious people they would not have closed all the convents and monasteries, confiscated the churches, and made it a crime to appear in public dressed as a priest. It would, however, be as big a mistake to conclude that the Mexicans are irreligious because they got tired of supporting a number of monks, nuns and priests out of all proportion to the population, as it would be to imagine that the Mexicans are prudes because they put frilly drawers on the figures of Christ hanging on wayside crosses. The drawers are gifts offered in deep respect by loving hearts.

No; the Mexicans share with the English the valuable gift of inconsistency, which is one of the jewels in the crown of free peoples. Pleasing anomalies exist to charm the traveller and benefit the inhabitants. (This is one of the many things in which free peoples differ from the Germans, who are strictly consistent, a characteristic of backward races.) Thus in the enormous church at Taxco, which, along with the rest, was appropriated by the Government, I several times attended services as one of a crowded congregation of all ages and sexes. The priests were obliged to come to the church dressed as civilians, and put on their uniforms in a vestry where they had no official right to be.

There is no doubt that the Mexicans are interested in religion. The realism of their life-size models of martyrdoms is horrifying: the twisted limbs; the awful, agonized expressions; the gaping wounds; the puddles of Ersatz blood. One finds them in rows in their dusty glass cases, in such churches as have not been cleared out for other uses. Village congregations in England are quite accustomed to saying, ". . . was crucified, dead, and buried." But their imaginations, bless their hearts, aren't particularly active, and idolatry is popery. Unless he is one of those people who have been to India, for example, the Englishman really has no conception what the sun can do to someone who is without a hat, is starving, is hanging up on a tree, nailed through the palms of the hands and the middle of the feet.

But the Mexicans are determined that the congregation shall realize to the last detail, *exactly* what it is like to have your eyes gouged out, and your stomach opened up with red-hot pieces of iron. (By the way, that was one of the few things I felt didn't *quite* come off. The red-hot-ness was too like mere bloodfulness. Possibly the effect was better years ago, when it was new.)

In 1939, there were a great many Germans in Mexico, running clubs, hotels and businesses of all kinds, and generally organizing Central America to be taken over by the Herrenvolk. I was able to do two of these deserving creatures a friendly service one day, to which he and the female German with him instantly reacted gratefully. We were strolling round an old church particularly rich in martyrs. At length we all paused before the most startling. It was of a female saint, and a newly born baby. Both were in the final stages of agony, their bodies ripped apart. I looked, raised my eyebrows and passed on. I wasn't being superior, you understand. I merely had seen all I required. The German and his woman remained, gazing.

A quarter of an hour or so later, when I had been all over the building, I found them still staring, fascinated. I joined them for another glance. A moment later, prompted by some intuition, I uttered a groan, followed by a short throaty sound as suggestive as I could make it, of unspeakable pain. My intuition had been unerring. The two German faces lit up with pleasure. It had all been perfect, that representation in the glass case—perfect but for one thing. One thing was missing—alas! The screeches, the uncontrolled groans of agony.

Suddenly I had supplied these. The Germans beamed with the simple joy of satisfied desire. They beamed at me with their mild Prussian eyes, taking me for a sympathetic soul. They linked their hands together and, with smiles and bows to me, walked away, laughing like two happy, podgy children.

On the road out of Cuernavaca to the east, there is a group of fourteen iron crosses. They commemorate a meeting that didn't quite take place not very long ago, between two generals. One sent word inviting the other to meet him so that they might discuss a plan together. The reply came back that he would be there at the appointed hour. So the inviting general and his staff ambushed the accepting general and *his* staff, and shot them all dead. They buried them where they fell, and, of course, put up a cross to each of them. I was unable to find out if the smaller crosses signified that the one lying beneath it was younger, or of a junior rank, or merely that he had been a smaller man. (Or possibly the first general had only been able to get a job lot of mixed crosses.) I was driving along the road in comparative silence when all of a sudden the general and his staff shouted wordlessly at me, deafening my eyes.

This is not a fantasy of Paul Nash at his most surrealist, but an untouched photograph by Lance Sieveking of ventilators on S.S. Mexico. There could be no better illustration of the chief theme in last month's issue: the pleasures of open-eyedness and of susceptibility to the visual as well as to the utilitarian connotations of objects. We may not be allowed in the twentieth century to indulge in such reckless ornamentation as the old Aztecs. But we can in our machine-minded age still bring about a good many picturesque thrills if we set our minds to do it.

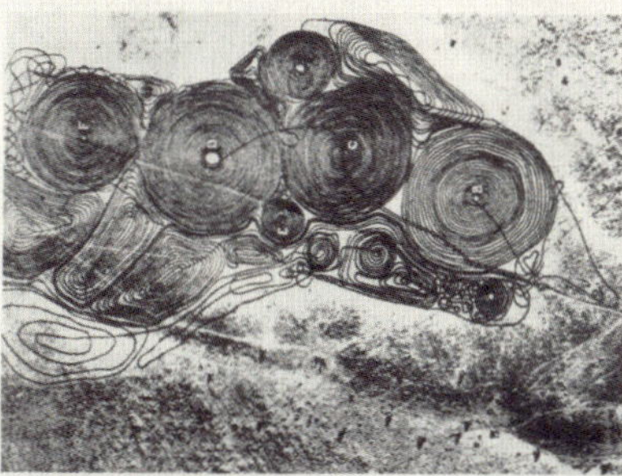

MOUFLAGE

thetics
and technique

THE NATURAL PATTERN

The contrast is impressive enough between the English fields, hedgerows, individual trees and spinneys, and the much more intense and matter-of-fact cultivation of France with its close rectangular pattern (first and second from the left). Again quite different is the arid surface near the sea in Malta. Note the characteristic long dividing walls. A surprise is the Chinese design on the right, close to one of the many tributaries of the Yangtze. The land looks curiously European in scale and in colour too. Such varied patterns the camouflage expert has to conceal.

THE PATTERN DISTURBED

However, the camoufleur's life would be easy if he had only to cope with natural patterns. In fact his worst bug-bear is the artificially disturbed pattern. Any airfield, camp, industrial build in the open country, even any road or track forms such a disturbance and gives away information to enemy reconnaissance. Here is one of the most spectacular examples of the aesthetic thrills which the observer in his plane might meet on reading the ground over which he flies. This is not a Paul Klee picture but a deserted German airfield in North Africa after it had been ploughed up by three tractors. All three started from A. Tractor one went to B and started ploughing from the centre outwards. He was a bit jerky on his driving. Tractors two and three proceeded to C, where tractor two started ploughing from the centre outwards. He ploughed very closely. Tractor three went on from C to D, where he started ploughing from the centre outwards. He made a specially neat job of it. Tractor two, after finishing C, made the little circle at E, and then went on and did circle F. Tractor three, after circle D, made circle G. At this point they either packed up for lunch or for the day. At any rate they subsequently came back, but now having exhausted shapes to fill in, they started at the outside and worked inwards. Hence the uncertainties of some of the other parts. To camouflage such a complicated and intensive pattern would be an impossible task. Fortunately it is beyond what the expert is usually called upon to do.

THE DISTURBANCE CONCEALED

This concealment of a headquarters post in the Tobruk area is a very simple netting affair, yet it is both effective and of rich intricacy of pattern.

ART BY ACCIDENT

Camouflage is functional design par excellence. Its only raison d'être is to conceal effectively. Whether this is done with aesthetically valuable or indifferent results, cannot matter in the least to those who commission it and pay for it. Yet—as it is mostly done by artists or at least experts of aesthetic sensibility—the results of camouflage often have a distinct visual charm and a curious similarity to the conscious creations of modern art. THE ARCHITECTURAL REVIEW is interested in both aspects of camouflage, the consciously functional and the accidentally aesthetic. However, any thorough treatment of camouflage and its spectacular progress as a craft between 1939 and 1944 is, of course, out of the question. As much of the technique and development of camouflage as can at this stage safely be disclosed is told in an article on pages 68 to 70 by Mr. Julian Trevelyan, who has had years of experience in army camouflage. Mr. Hugh Casson's work is connected with Air Force camouflage. He has chosen for his article, which begins below, a frankly aesthetic approach. Another difference between the two articles is that Mr. Casson is dealing exclusively with the camouflage of buildings against high-level or long-distance air attack, whereas Mr. Trevelyan rather stresses the concealment of smaller objects against level army attack. The illustrations are by the authors of the articles in which they occur.

Hugh Casson: the aesthetics of camouflage

ART criticism is not among the extractive industries mentioned in the Scott Report and, to the casual observer, the professions of miner and critic would seem to have little in common with each other. Yet the characteristics which they share—the skilled laborious search for the rare amongst the worthless, the tireless prospecting, the "lucky strikes" and ensuing "gold-rushes"—are perhaps similar enough to permit the analogy. The contemporary critic, like the miner, is faced with fast diminishing resources. For him the mines of discovery, as Sir Kenneth Clark has recently pointed out, are nearly exhausted. The richest seams, of the Antique and the eighteenth century, have long since yielded up their wealth. To-day they lie deserted and only rarely disturbed by the fitful spouting lamp of some obscure scholar scavenging his way along the abandoned workings. Raw material is not so easy to reach as it once was, and when found it is of uncertain quality. For this problem there are three possible solutions open to the critic. By elaborating his machinery of research—if the technical parallel may be pursued a little further—he can dig a little deeper and thus open up less accessible veins; or he can pick over the slag heaps discarded by his predecessors, select the likeliest-looking lumps, burnish them with his wit and learning, and then hold them up to the light so persuasively that they seem to sparkle like the Best Kitchen Brights; or he can adopt the fashionable wartime technique of "open-cast mining"—scratching for such material as lies on or immediately beneath the surface—the architecture of A.R.P. perhaps, or the iconography of military insignia. When such prodigies of effort are needed, it is difficult for him to avoid exaggerating—if only in self-justification—whatever results he may obtain. There is a danger of becoming over-serious about the trivial, of enveloping the commonplace with so thick a fog of teutonic documentation and technical jargon that the true outline is obscured or falsified.

Such a charge, perhaps, may be levelled at the subject or at least at the attitude of this article. Camouflage, it will be rightly said, has nothing to do with aesthetics. It is not, intentionally at least, a question of shapely patterns, sophisticated line or sensitive colour contrasts. It is merely a scientific solution of an exact technical problem. In purpose it is as practical and unpretentious as a stirrup pump. Any connection with beauty is, as the film credit titles say, purely coincidental.

Yet beauty most certainly exists: the sort of bold irrelevant beauty flaunted by a string of multi-coloured signal flags fluttering from a mast head. Beauty, as it were, "off the record." To see a camouflaged building looming through a grey November morning or aflame in the angry light of a June sunset, is to receive a tremendous visual thrill from the flow and flicker of its fantastic patterns and strange colours. The fact that this aesthetic experience is, so to speak, accidental does not blunt the sharpness of its impact, but its nature perhaps cannot be accurately assessed without some knowledge of the true aims and principles of camouflage of which this beauty is so exciting a by-product.

Camouflage is not magic. Despite popular belief to the contrary, parti-coloured patterns, violently contrasted, confer no mantle of invisibility upon the object to which they are haphazardly applied. They may, indeed, do the reverse. Nobody, for instance, with even the smallest flying experience could have perpetrated or placed trust in those dazzle-painted monuments to the

given visible antiquity to a church tower by means of something so much a part of commonsense nature as mantling ivy—as in Gray's *Elegy*:—

"Save that from yonder ivy-mantled tow'r
The moping owl does to the moon complain." (1750)

or Warton's *Pleasures of Melancholy*:—

"Save the lone screech-owl's note, who builds his bow'r
Amid the mould'ring caverns dark and damp,
Or the calm breeze, that rustles in the leaves
Of flaunting ivy, that with mantle green
Invests some wasted tow'r. . . ." (1747)

—which Gray obviously had in his mind.

Going back to Gilpin, his *Forest Scenery* would assuredly have been read by Samuel Palmer, and weighed with him rather more than the architecture and lichens in Sir Uvedale Price's *Essay on the Picturesque* (1794). Price objects strongly to daubing, plastering and white-washing "some antient castle-like mansion or the mossy weather-stained tower of an old church." He has a good note on lichens and brickwork: "When brick becomes weather stained and mossy, it harmonises with the colours that usually accompany it, and has often a richness, mellowness, and variety of tint, infinitely pleasing to a painter's eye; for the cool colour of the greenish moss lowers all the fiery quality, while the subdued fire beneath, gives a glow to what without it would be cold and insipid." Observe, he asks earlier on, "observe the process by which time (the great author of such changes) converts a beautiful object into a picturesque one. First, by means of weather stains, partial incrustations, mosses, etc., it at the same time takes off from the uniformity of its surface, and of its colour; that is, gives it a degree of roughness and variety of tint. Next . . ."—and he describes how the stones loosen and fall, sedums and wall-flowers find nourishment in the decayed cement, and birds bring in the seeds of yew and elder and ivy. A few pages on Sir Uvedale Price writes of the extreme picturesqueness of water-mills, with the "intricacy of the wheels and the wood work," with lights and shadows "mosses and weather stains from the constant moisture," and plants "springing from the rough joints of the stones." The water-mill would have been more in Palmer's taste, when he was a boy; but, if he read it, he might have taken still more from J. T. Smith's *Remarks on Rural Scenery with Twenty Etchings of Cottages, from Nature* (1797)—to which the subscribers included Constable—two copies—and William Blake. Cottages, Rainy Day Smith remarks, have been neglected by artists, rather less so by poets. He points out Gainsborough's contribution, refers to Payne Knight on cottages in *The Landscape*: "the retired antiquated cot" with a roof of reeds and mosses, talks of 'neat' and 'neglected' cottage-scenery; and then:—

"We (i.e. artists) turn from this neatness and regularity, to what we must esteem a far more profitable subject—the neglected fast-ruinating cottage—the patched plaster, of various tints and discolourations . . . the weather-beaten thatch, bunchy and varied with moss—the mutilated chimney top—the fissures and crevices of the inclining wall—the roof of various angles and inclinations—the tiles of different hues—the fence of bungling workmanship—the wild, unrestrained vine. . . ."

One of Smith's etchings, *At Cobham, in Surrey*—curling hops, thatch, walls of corn, children by the door—is Palmer, without Palmer. The difference between Palmer's "primitive cottage" and Rainy Day Smith's is that Palmer paints life and not decay; but still with the mosses, "weather stains" and the creeping plants. I do not know of a Palmer drawing which would correspond either to Sir Uvedale Price or Crabbe—with detailed lichen upon stone work; but he records and observes, not only the round mosses—actual mosses—upon thatch, and lichens upon tree trunks, but lichens upon the weather-boarding of farm buildings.

Plenty of lichen is poetically observed between Gilpin, Price and Coleridge in the seventeen-eighties and nineties, and Palmer in the late eighteen-twenties. Besides Crabbe in 1810, there was Wordsworth, who in the same year first published his *Guide to the Lakes*. Wordsworth wrote of the "bluish, or hoary grey" tint of the lichens mixed with the red tinge of the rocks as a main element in the colouring of the mountains; he observed how "the mosses and lichens are never so fresh and flourishing as in winter, if it be not a season of frost," and he noticed the lichens again on roadside walls, and on the walls and slate roofs of the cottages. Years later, Southey describes a walk to Walla Crag in Borrowdale:—

"After a steep ascent you reach one of those loose walls which are common in this country; it runs across the side of the hill, and is broken down in some places; the easier way, or rather the less difficult, is on the inner side, over loose and rugged stones, the wreckage of the crags above. They are finely coloured with a yellow or ochrey lichen, which predominates there to the exclusion of the *lichen geographicus*: its colour may best be compared to that of beaten or unburnished gold: it is richly blended with the

Leafy Lichen: "Specimens of this very fine and rare lichen were sent to Mr. . . . by Mr. Slater, who found them in the mountainous part of Denbighshire . . ."

Coralline Lichen: "Observed first by Mr. Dickson on rocks in Scotland . . . [illegible] in doubt respecting this species, and yet it can scarcely have been unseen by . . ."

[illegible] illustrating this article are by James Sowerby from Smith and Sowerby's *English Botany* [illegible] and the captions are quotations from the same work.

white or silvery kind, and interspersed with the stone-fern mountain-parsley; the most beautiful of our wild plants, resemb[ling] the richest point-lace in its fine filaments and exquisite inden[ta]tions." (*Sir Thomas More; or, Colloquies on the Progress* [and] *Prospects of Society*.)

Beyond Palmer, again, in the æsthetics of lichenology, come Rus[kin] and the Pre-Raphaelites, and Browning, and in the fifties the fi[rst] and about the last, *Popular History of British Lichens*, by the [?] lichenologist, Lauder Lindsay. Lindsay, in his introduction, str[ikes] me as a bit too glum. Lichens "have ever been the acknowled[ged] *opprobria* of Cryptogamic Botany. The delicate waving frond of [the] fern is anxiously tended by jewelled fingers in the drawing-rooms [of] the wealthy and noble; the rhodospermous seaweed finds a pl[ace] beside the choicest productions of art in the gilt and broidered albu[m;] the tiny moss has been the theme of many a gifted poet; and even [the] despised mushroom has called forth classic works in its praise. But Lichens, which stain every rock and clothe every tree . . . have b[een] almost universally neglected, nay despised." Which was not tr[ue,] as Lauder Lindsay would have discovered had he but read or loo[ked] round himself a little more. Without going back to Wordsworth a[nd] Southey (Crabbe he did quote), he could have seen lichenous tru[nks] and at least one lichenous brick wall in Pre-Raphaelite painting[;] for honour to lichens he could have drawn upon Ruskin, in *Mod[ern] Painters*, upon Ruskin declaring that "the harmonies of colour am[ong] the native lichens are better than Titian's," Ruskin calling lich[ens] "the most honoured of the earth-children," and saying that "to the[m,] slow-fingered, constant-hearted, is entrusted the weaving of the da[rk] eternal tapestries of the hills; to them, slow-pencilled, iris-dyed, [the] tender framing of their endless imagery. Sharing the stillness of [the] unimpassioned rock, they share also its endurance; and while [the] winds of departing spring scatter the white hawthorn blossom l[ike] drifted snow, and summer dims on the parched meadow the droop[ing] of its cowslip gold—far above, among the mountains, the silver lich[en] spots rest, star-like, on the stone; and the gathering orange sta[in] upon the edge of yonder western peak, reflects the sunsets of a thousa[nd] years."

Ruskin wrote that panegyric upon lichens, was able to write it o[nly] because, for the best part of a hundred years before him, liche[ns] (like much else in nature) had been crawling out of the obscure. A[nd] without the lichenologists, the collectors, the illustrators, Gilpin, S[ir] Uvedale Price, Crabbe, Wordsworth, Southey, and so forth, it wou[ld] not have been possible for Browning to notice lichens so minute[ly] upon a tombstone; as he did in *Earth's Immortalities* (it was publish[ed] in 1845):—

. . . Headstone and half-sunk footstone lean awry,
Wanting the brick-work promised by-and-by;
How the minute grey lichens, plate o'er plate,
Have softened down the crisp-cut name and date!

The Pre-Raphaelite use of nature, in literature and painting, was [what] that Coleridge would have condemned as picking nature's pock[et.] For Coleridge, landscape (for example) was not only itself, it was la[nd] imagery: "The land imagery of the north of Devon is most delightful[."] Seeds were seeds, and the seeds of life: "September 1 [1800]—T[he] beards of thistle and dandelions flying about the lonely mountai[ns] like life." "A poet ought not to pick nature's pocket; let him borro[w,] and so borrow as to repay by the very act of borrowing. Examin[e] nature accurately, but write from recollection; and trust more to you[r] imagination than to your memory"—which is perennially sound advic[e.] The Pre-Raphaelites and their kin wrote and painted from detaile[d] immediacy, not from memory. If one examines the lichens upo[n] Pre-Raphaelite trees—for instance in Holman Hunt's *Two Gentlemen* [of] *Verona*, or in *The Long Engagement* by Arthur Hughes (both are in th[e] Birmingham Art Gallery), one realises they are only one of ver[y] many accurately noted elements, in a picture which is an ordere[d] notebook. In *The Long Engagement* the emphasis is sharp on every[-]thing, on moss, lichen, ivy, dog rose, leaves, squirrels, eye-balls, velve[t] cloak, bracken, the sleekness of the dog. In a drawing by Palmer [a] tree rises and twists from the ground, as the principal of the vision, upo[n] the strength of which the coloured lichen is visible.

Pickpocketing of one kind and another, if it has not disappeared[,] has declined in the arts, and with it the visibility of such natura[l] minutiæ as lichens. We would be at one with Gilpin again when h[e] said that, in painting, lichens, or 'moss,' "touches not the great parts [of] *composition and effect*"; but that is no reason for not seeing lichen[s] at least as Wordsworth and Southey saw them. And there is reaso[n] for seeing them not only on mountain rocks and trees, but as part o[f] the texture of buildings, up the country and down. The most luxurian[t] of lichenous and ferny church towers I know are those of the Gowe[r] peninsula; made not with flint, like Crabbe's church tower, but o[f] limestone, which, of all rocks and building stones, is the one most favourable to lichens. Especially I recommend the tower, only a few feet from and above the sea, of Oxwich Church; there the lichens

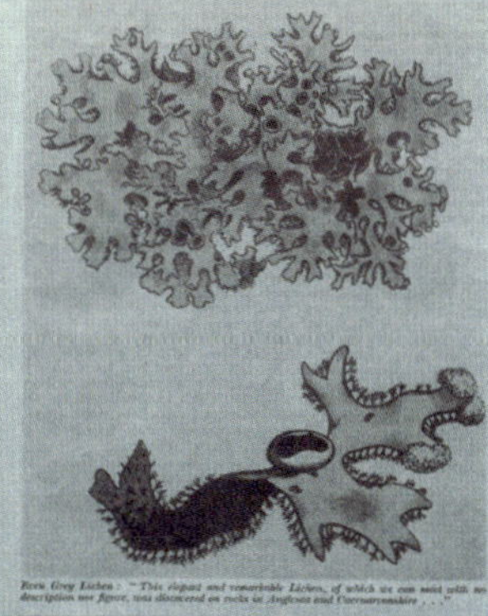

Rosy Grey Lichen: "This elegant and remarkable Lichen, of which we can meet with no description nor figure, was discovered on rocks in Anglesea and Caernarvonshire . . ."

Downy Shrubby Lichen: "First found in Britain by Mr. W. Borrer, on clay at [illegible] in Scilly Island in April, 1804."

Casson's "Aesthetics of Camouflage" or with another fascinating Picturesque-inspired essay in *Architectural Review*, the poet, curator, and naturalist Geoffrey Grigson's "The Aesthetic of Lichens,"[55] which appeared in the same issue, presumably in opposition to the attitudes informing Rowe's famous "Mathematics of the Ideal Villa." Grigson took the Picturesque in a simultaneously more literary and more scientific direction that came closer to anticipating the visual sensibility of the photographs in *Parallel of Life and Art*. His essay was an effort to convey how lichen on stonework was a "part of the texture of buildings," and included long quotations of eighteenth- and nineteenth-century poetry as well as numerous scientific illustrations of lichen by James Sowerby, taken from Sowerby and James Edward Smith's 36-volume encyclopedia *English Botany* (1791–1814). The aesthetic that concerned Grigson was less that of naturalism than a literary practice of what he called "lichenology": the way lichens are "poetically observed" in writing and drawings of the past: "The visibility of lichens followed their slow classification and recognition in science." Both artistic and scientific representations contributed to this altered imagination. "Towards the end of the eighteenth century they came out of the invisible; they stayed visible until after the climax of Pre-Raphaelite vision; and have since sunk back to being slightly in, but more out of, our public sight."[56] Grigson was interested in how imagining an "aesthetics of lichenology" enabled a critic like Ruskin to see "that 'the harmonies of colour among the native lichens are better than Titian's.'"[57]

Other reconsiderations of visual sensibilities in *Architectural Review* explored the playful use of photography. Perhaps the most striking and emblematic was an uncredited spread in January 1944, the same issue that initiated the advocacy of the Picturesque in the journal, which juxtaposed two photographs (a closely cropped eye-level view of the varied cargo ventilators on the deck of the SS *Mexico* and a close-up of ornamentation on an unidentified Aztec frieze) and included a caption describing the pairing as an "illustration" of "the pleasures of open-eyedness and of susceptibility of the visual to the utilitarian connotation of objects. We may not be allowed in the twentieth century to indulge in such reckless ornamentation as the old Aztecs. But we can in our machine-minded age still bring about a good many picturesque thrills if we set our minds to do it."[58]

Richards elaborated a much more earnest and wistful attitude toward the Picturesque in *The Castles on the Ground* (1946), a book written while he was stationed in Cairo during the war (and when Pevsner was temporarily filling his editorial position at the *Architectural Review*). Richards argued that the "elaborately synthetic picture" that constitutes "the charm of the suburb" and the "essence of the suburban environment" is "in many senses identical with the English Picturesque tradition."[59] The suburbs' "scenic effects" were an indigenous and "genuine vernacular" that challenged the "geometrical purism and the inspiration of new techniques [. . .] that justifies [. . .] modern architecture's claim to be something other than an alternative style."[60] Like Pevsner and Hastings, Richards saw political virtues in the British "suburban character" and believed that Picturesque theory could help advance the aims of modern architecture and planning: "If democracy means anything, it means deciding—

for a change—to pay some attention to the expressed preference of the majority," even if architects "may despise what they want. We [...] can only progress democratically at a speed which does not outpace the slow growth of the public's understanding, in particular its assimilation of social and technical change."[61] Thus Richards's divergence from Pevsner—his shift away from explaining modern architecture as an advanced style while still understanding how the emergence and viability of British modernism might build on an endemic and still viable culture and sensibility—suggests a more direct line of descent from the ideas and practices of Morris and the Picturesque.

The Smithsons both resisted and assumed aspects of those varied narratives of British modernism. New Brutalist polemics advanced a savvy, negotiated stance toward the range of issues affecting British modernism after World War Two: the adoption of Continental styles, interest in social and political reform, and the aspiration of advocates of the Picturesque to develop a more nuanced visual perception that was sensitive to popular taste. The Smithsons' aim was to devise a specifically British idiom, but one that was as uncompromising as the heroic European sources they admired, without being recognizably mimetic of their style. Their choice to claim and revise the Chicago Mies was an adventurous and shrewd acknowledgment and evasion of pervasive ideas about modern architecture. The Mies exhibition at the Museum of Modern Art (MoMA), New York, in 1947 had brought widespread attention to the architect's Chicago practice and reestablished him as a newly relevant figure. Embracing Mies allied New Brutalism with American culture and building technology but also with the new and very different work of an architect who seemingly had produced relatively little after emigrating from Germany in 1937. The Smithsons recognized Mies's new idiom as an inventive redirection of the interest in luxurious surfaces and abstraction in the two projects that had been most widely published in Britain before and after the war: the Barcelona Pavilion (1929) and the Villa Tugendhat (Brno, 1930).[62] They were joined in the early 1950s by others who also saw potential in Mies's new work.[63] As Stephen Kite has noted, Colin St. John Wilson and Peter Carter's entry to the Coventry Cathedral competition (1950–51) was inspired by the space-frame airplane hangars of Konrad Wachsmann that later would be the basis for Mies's Chicago Convention Hall project (1954), while Wilson and others at the London County Council Architect's Department designed the housing estate at Albert Drive in west London (1950–52) to simulate the steel structure of the buildings at IIT through a combination of painted concrete slab edges and black brick cladding.[64] Another more ingenious, perhaps ingenuous, and even original variation of the Chicago Mies is Walter Segal's facade at Ovington Square in Chelsea (1955), which superimposes a light wooden grid supporting and containing the window units, painted black and easily mistaken for steel, in front of the two-tone brick cladding, creating a subtle geometric pattern of frames, voids, and surfaces of glass and brick as well as a sense of lightness in an otherwise conventionally constructed infill apartment block.

More than most of their peers, however, the Smithsons were also aware of Mies's German work of the early 1920s: Johnson's MoMA catalogue included the glass skyscrapers and the concrete

ARRAY 2.2

2.2

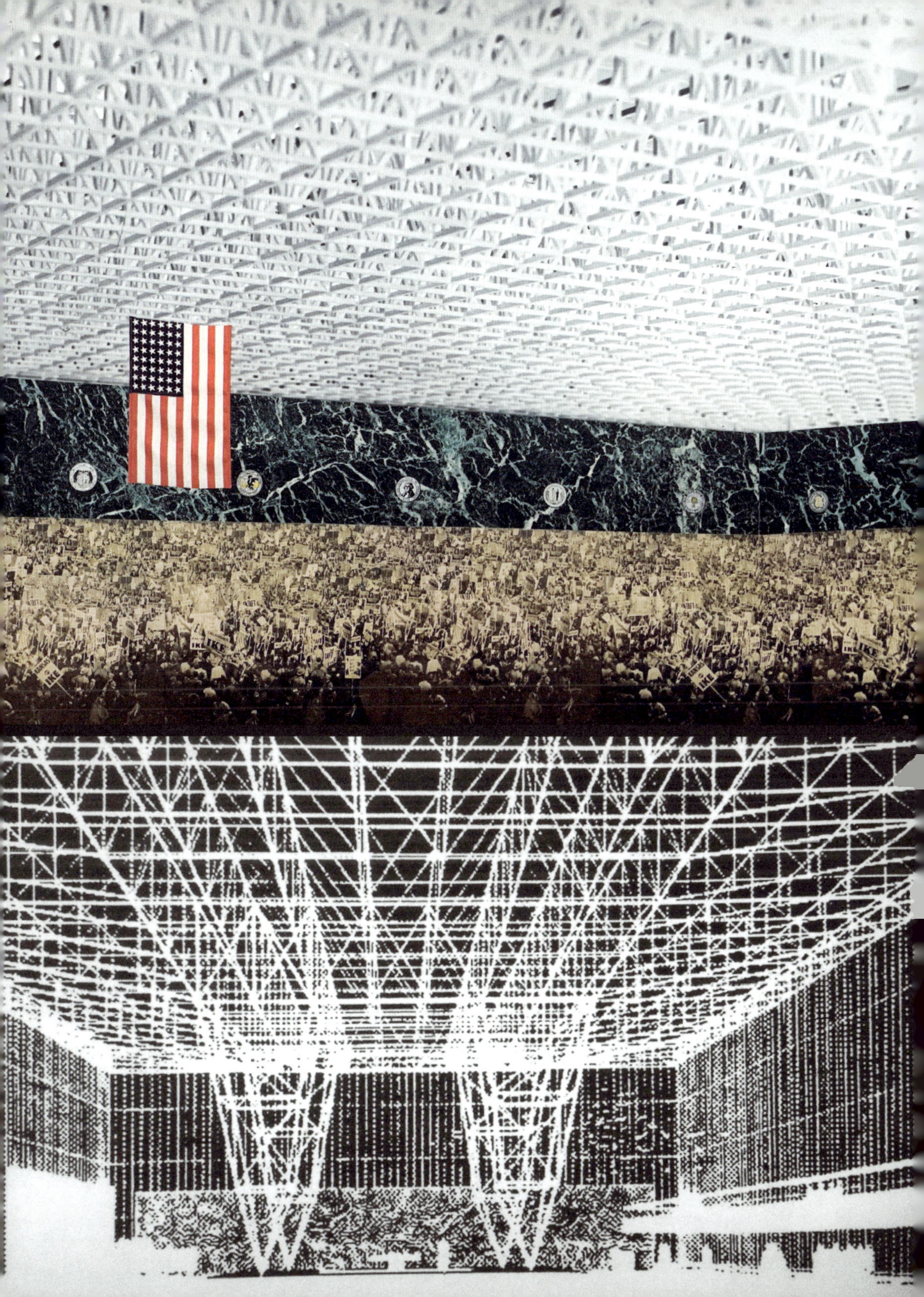
IKE
IKE
TAFT
IKE

2.3

15

HE FORMAL GARDEN FROM THE POOL

METALS AND MINERAL
RESEARCH BUILDIN
ILLINOIS INSTITUTE OF TECHNOLOG
DESIGNED BY MIES VAN DER ROH

This is the first of Mies van der Rohe's buildings to be erected in the USA, and has been designed to form part of a large educational group for the Illinois Institute of Technology.

It has that purity and integrity of expression, that simplicity of design, and that extreme care in structural detail which distinguish his earlier work in Europe.

The building was erected for the Armour Research Foundation to house several industrial research activities involving the use of delicate precision apparatus and fairly heavy industrial equipment including several types of furnaces, presses and metal rolling mills. This equipment, however, is not fixed or permanent and a major requirement was that flexibility

METALS AND MINERALS
RESEARCH BUILDING
BY MIES VAN DER ROHE

17
THE BACKS

office building that were published in *G*, as well as the Weissenhof exhibition and his brick houses. In 1953 the Smithsons would learn about and visit the Verseidag factory complex (1931–35) in Krefeld, which they saw as something of a clarifying precedent for the sensibility of Mies's Chicago work. Several Krefeld projects are in Johnson's book, but not the more prosaic-looking factory buildings, which, even more than the famous Lange and Esters houses (1928–30) there, became a touchstone for the Smithsons' extended identification with Mies and an enduring influence on their pursuit of the Mies-image. As they affirmed multiple times in their later books, it was thrilling for them to see the factory for the first time, just as Hunstanton was nearing completion, as a confirmation of their approach and their fascination with Mies's later work.

ARRAY 2.3

Mies first appears in the Smithsons' work in Peter's final student project, a design for a new Fitzwilliam Museum, Cambridge, that is a careful study of Miesian devices of assembly, space planning, and representation. In 2001 Peter described the project, completed in 1949 at the Royal Academy just before the Smithsons designed Hunstanton,as "an attempt, using English rolled-steel sections and the English scale, to extend the steel frame and glass language of Mies van der Rohe: an exercise that was to bear fruit in Hunstanton."[65] The Smithsons were excited by the potential of the Chicago work as an extension and revision of Mies's earlier approaches, but it must have appeared absolutely startling to them in comparison with his work from before 1930. Looking back in 1966, Peter explained: "In '49, I spent £4 on Johnson's book on Mies. It was worldshaking. Those IIT workshops really were worldshaking. But what we wanted to find out was how to use Mies methods without any mannerisms. At the time, there were economic reasons for all that dead-pan detailing. If we had the money, we wouldn't have made it more elaborate."[66] As they would discover in 1953 in Hunstanton's "layering of reflection at the glazed stage" and in their pursuit of the Mies-image for rest of their careers, they did not have to.

Notes

1 Robertson began writing books on modern design in 1922 and had been nominated to be the first British representative to CIAM in 1930. He attended the first two congresses but did not join, according to Elizabeth Darling in *Re-Forming Britain: Narratives of Modernity before Reconstruction*, Oxford: Routledge, 2007, p. 42. He later served as a member of the design team for the United Nations. Hastings became editor of both *Architectural Review* and the *Architects' Journal* in 1927. For a brief account of the appearance of modern architecture in British journals and Robertson's role, see Anthony Jackson, *The Politics of Architecture: A History of Modern Architecture in Britain*, Toronto: University of Toronto Press, 1970, pp. 16–21. Trevor Dannatt notes the changes at the *Architectural Review*, which "began to take on a bizarre aspect, to bleed edges, to illustrate off-centre things, to cultivate a wicked alliance of voguishness and erudition." Trevor Dannatt, *Modern Architecture in Britain*, London: Batsford, 1959, p. 14. For a different account of the appearance of modern architecture in the British architectural journals, see Darling, *Re-Forming Britain*, pp. 27–31. For a detailed account of British architectural publications, see Andrew Higgott, *Mediating Modernity: Architectural Culture in Britain*, Oxford: Routledge, 2007, and "Visual Sensibility and the Search for Form: *The Architectural Review* in Postwar Britain," in *Modernism and the Professional Architecture Journal: Reporting, Editing and Reconstructing Postwar Europe*, ed. Torsten Schmiedeknecht and Andrew Peckham, Oxford: Routledge, pp. 93–111. Nikolaus Pevsner, in his foreword to *Pioneers of Modern Design* (1936), described his book as "the first to be published" on the British sources in the "development of the Modern Movement" and mentions the essays by P. Morton Shand published in *Architectural Review* from 1933 to 1935 as "excellent" but unknown to him when he was writing his book.

2 As Harry Hopkins explains, by the late 1940s "'Modern Art' was no longer considered either uproarious or outrageous," as evidenced in 1947 when "the queues winding around the Tate Gallery, waiting to enter the Van Gogh Exhibition, were so long that police were needed to marshal them." Hopkins, *The New Look: A Social History of the Forties and Fifties in Britain*, London: Readers Union, 1964, p. 237.

3 Margaret Garlake, *New Art New World: British Art in Postwar Society*, New Haven: Yale University Press, 1998, p. 40.

4 Robert Hewison, *In Anger: British Culture in the Cold War, 1945–60*, Oxford: Oxford University Press, 1981, p. 112.

5 Joshua Sperling, *A Writer of Our Time: The Life and Work of John Berger*, London and New York: Verso, 2018, p. 30. Sperling writes: "In Britain, 1953 was the year when the Cold War became a full-fledged culture war. Battle lines were drawn and the ICA controversy marked the true start of combat. [...] And ideology was soon unavoidable" (p. 31). The context of these debates is important. A scandal involved the ICA in June 1951 when it was reported that two missing Soviet spies, Guy Burgess and Donald Maclean, had been members of the ICA beginning in 1950. At that time, Americans were involved financially and programmatically with the ICA: Antony Kloman, the brother-in-law of Philip Johnson, became the director of public relations at ICA beginning in April 1951 and helped organize the *Unknown Political Prisoner* competition, which was funded by the CIA and was boycotted by the Soviet Union. Thus, between 1951 and 1953 the ICA became a conduit for American art and culture into Britain.

6 On modernist architecture's emergence in Britain see, for example, Nicholas Bullock, *Building the Post-War World: Modern Architecture and Reconstruction in Britain*, Oxford: Routledge, 2002; Darling, *Re-Forming Britain*; and Alan Powers, *Britain: Modern Architectures in History*, London: Reaktion, 2007.

7 Peter Smithson, "Reflections on Hunstanton," *ARQ*, 2, no. 3 (Summer 1997), p. 36. Smithson is quoting here from an unnamed text written "at the time of design and construction."

8 Powers, *Britain*, pp. 89–90.

9 Mark Crinson describes the culture of postwar Britain as "veering back and forth between the experience of austerity and deindustrialization on the one hand and a selected sense of affluence and American-style consumerism on the other." Mark Crinson, "'A House which Grows': Stirling and Gowan, the Smithsons, and Consumer Society," in *Neo-avant-garde and Postmodern: Postwar Architecture in Britain and Beyond*, ed. Mark Crinson and Claire Zimmerman, New Haven: Yale Center for British Art, 2010, p. 177.

10 Reyner Banham, "The New Brutalism," *Architectural Review*, 118, no. 708 (December 1955), pp. 357, 358.

11 Possible affinities between New Brutalism and the British government's Utility Furniture Scheme (1941–January 1953) are unexplored. As part of the rationing policies during and after World War Two, furniture was a controlled commodity (and extensive austerity measures continued even until 1954 for many commodities, such as paper and sweets). Initially, the Board of Trade sanctioned a limited set of simple designs for manufacture, which were explained to the public not as efficient and functional modernism but as characteristically British solutions to practical needs. According to Harriett Dover, a 1944 article in *Art and Industry* promoted the program as "an opportunity to put into production a design of furniture that would re-educate the public, not through its bombastic modernism, but through its sane, wholesome simplicity." After the war, the designs were less restricted but still controlled. Yet Misha Black, in *Picture Post* in January 1945, praised the Utility scheme as part of the "enforced break with tradition that this war has brought." See Harriet Dover, *Home Front Furniture: British Utility*

Design, 1941–1951, Aldershot: Scolar Press, 1991, p. 20.

12 During Attlee's Labour government, a fundamental cultural tension developed between those who advocated the development of a progressive social welfare state and internationalism in culture and politics, and those who were committed to restoring British traditional cultural values and society. The division was not necessarily along political lines: even among the intellectual left (F. R. Leavis in literary criticism, Richard Hoggart in social history, John Berger in art criticism) there was a strong affection for working-class values and ways of life that was antagonistic toward both European high culture and American mass culture.

13 Reyner Banham, *The New Brutalism: Ethic or Aesthetic?*, New York: Reinhold, 1966, p. 47; Alison and Peter Smithson, "Thoughts in Progress: The New Brutalism" (statement at the end of the discussion), *Architectural Design*, 27, no. 4 (April 1957), p. 113.

14 The Smithsons' point was as much a concern with tough-minded engagement with problems of building and function, as a refusal to allow idealism to cloud their understanding of the actual problems and limitations of contemporary culture, politics, and communication.

15 John Summerson, "Introduction," in *Ten Years of British Architecture: '45–55*, exh. cat., London: Arts Council of Britain, 1956, pp. 10–11.

16 Reyner Banham, "Howard Robertson," *Architectural Review*, 114, no. 681 (September 1953), p. 161.

17 Ibid., p. 167.

18 Ibid., pp. 162, 163.

19 Ibid., p. 168.

20 Ibid., p. 163.

21 Banham writes of the festival: "The younger generation, viewing these works, had the depressing sense that the drive was going out of modern architecture, its pure Dogma being diluted by politicians and compromisers who had lost their intellectual nerve." Banham, *The New Brutalism*, p. 13. It was soon after the festival that the Attlee government was replaced by the Conservatives, in the miscalculated nap election of October 25, 1951. An overlooked but important component of the festival was the Telekinema, designed by Wells Coates and completed in 1950. It reopened after the festival ended as the National Film Theatre. The building doubled as a television studio and a cinema, the first in the world with the capacity to project both film and television images. The program during the festival included "a feature film, fourteen documentaries, four experimental films and four 'stereoscopic' [3D] films." See www.theinfolist.com/php/SummaryGet.php?FindGo=Telecinema. The major architecture journals did not publish articles on the Telekinema, though *The Builder* published plans and photos, calling it "a gem in its scale and kind," and the *Architects' Journal* had a brief feature in the May 24, 1951 issue. The BBC broadcast a radio show about the Telekinema on August 2, 1951. The building was promoted widely in the film industry press as a new prototype. See Sherban Cantacuzino, *Wells Coates: A Monograph*, London: Gordon Fraser, 1978, pp. 78–80, and Elizabeth Darling, *Wells Coates*, London: RIBA Publishing, 2012, pp. 119–25.

22 Hopkins, *The New Look*, p. 271.

23 See "Foreword" to the issue of *Architectural Review* on the Festival of Britain, 110, no. 656 (August 1951), pp. 72–79. Robertson had not been involved in the design and planning of the festival, but he was a member of the government's Council for Architecture, Town Planning and Building Research, which advised Hugh Casson, who led the architecture and site planning. A domestic version of the popular arts allied with the Contemporary Style was promoted by Barbara Jones in numerous publications and in *Black Eyes and Lemonade*, a 1951 exhibition at Whitechapel Art Gallery.

24 See anonymous article, perhaps written by J. M. Richards, "The New Empiricism," *Architectural Review*, 101, no. 606 (June 1947), pp. 199–204.

25 See Anne Massey and Gregor Muir, eds., *Institute of Contemporary Arts, 1946–1968*, London: Institute of Contemporary Arts, 2014.

26 Peter Smithson published a brief note on Connell, Ward & Lucas in the *Architectural Association Journal*, 72 (December 1956), p. 138, in response to the prior issue on that firm. Looking back on his prewar student years, he writes that Connell, Ward & Lucas "made me realise [...] what architecture was all about. [...] Of all the English modern architects, C., W., and Lucas seemed to be the most uncompromising, and the most exciting [...] the nearest we had in England to the first generation of modern architects. [...] But what C., W., and Lucas lacked was the absolute ruthlessness of Stam or Oud, who could drive the aesthetic right through the organization—into the window detailing, into the furniture, and into the lives of the occupants." Excerpt in *Arena: The Architectural Association Journal*, 81, no. 899, special issue: *A Smithson File*, compiled by Jeremy Baker (February 1966), p. 194.

27 Nikolaus Pevsner, *The Englishness of English Art*, London: Peregrine Books, 1956, p. 206.

28 Ibid., pp. 80, 82: "Revolutions in England are unbloody, like that of 1688 and that of the last twenty-five years. [...] There are two causes for this, both equally English. One is reasonableness, and [...] the other is conservatism."

29 David Solkin, "The British and the Modern," in *Towards a Modern Art World*, ed. Brian Allen, New Haven: Yale University Press, 1995, p. 4.

30 David Corbett, *The Modernity of English Art, 1914–1930*, Manchester: Manchester University Press, 1997, p. 1.

31 Charles Harrison, *English Art and Modernism, 1900–1939*, London: Allen Lane, and Bloomington: Indiana University Press, 1981, p. 165.

32 Darling, *Re-Forming Britain*, p. 3.

33 Ibid., p. 6.

34 Darling, *Re-Forming Britain*, p. 50. For

Darling, the overtly modernist style of famous 1930s buildings such as Wells Coates's Isokon flats (1934), Owen Williams's Pioneer Health Centre (1935), and Tecton's Finsbury Health Center (1939) is much less significant than the social programs the buildings contain and that their images publicize. But that characterization of the rhetorical image of modernism is quite distinct from the Smithsons' ethical and technical uses of imaging.

35 Banham, "The New Brutalism," p. 356.

36 Theo Crosby, "The New Brutalism," *Architectural Design*, 25, no. 1 (January 1955), p. 1. This statement of principles by the Smithsons was requested for publication and "somewhat edited" by Crosby, who wrote an introductory paragraph.

37 Pevsner gave the talk "From William Morris to Walter Gropius" on March 6, 1949, as the first part of a three-part lecture series on the Bauhaus, with subsequent parts presented by others. Stephen Games, *Pevsner: The Complete Broadcast Talks*, Farnham: Ashgate, 2014, pp. 84, 88.

38 Nikolaus Pevsner, *Pioneers of Modern Design: From William Morris to Walter Gropius*, 2nd edn, New York: Museum of Modern Art, 1949, pp. 20, 38. Pevsner made numerous changes in the 1949 edition that not only clarified his argument but altered his account of the influence of graphic design and painting on modern architecture. The phrase "essential unity of architecture" does not appear in the 1936 text. The 1949 edition inserts the word "legitimate" in the place of "adequate" in 1936.

39 Ibid., p. 135.

40 Crosby, "The New Brutalism," p. 1.

41 Pevsner, *The Englishness of English Art*, p. 120.

42 In one of only two footnotes in his book (the other references Gropius's *The New Architecture and the Bauhaus*), Richards refers his readers to Pevsner's book for a fuller elaboration of the "early history of modern architecture." J. M. Richards, *An Introduction to Modern Architecture*, Harmondsworth: Pelican, 1940, p. 61.

43 Ibid., pp. 1, 15.

44 Richards was an editor at *Architectural Review* from 1937 to 1971, with Pevsner serving during the war as acting editor from 1943 to 1945. Hastings wrote in "Exterior Furnishing, or Sharawaggi: The Art of Making Urban Landscape," *Architectural Review*, 95 (January 1944), p. 8: "So we propound a simple thesis. That England has a traditional way of seeing things which was brought into full consciousness and raided to an art, in Picturesque theory and practice, known to the eighteenth century as the Modern Manner. [...] Pick up the theory, rediscover the prophets, and apply the principles." Boyer characterizes the Picturesque as "a blend of popular modernism with English traditionalism, an aesthetic theory that [...] was an art of compromise, a specifically English form of synthesis." M. Christine Boyer, "An Encounter with History: The Postwar Debate between the English Journals of *Architectural Review* and *Architectural Design* (1945–1960)," p. 136, www.team10online.org/research/papers/delft2/boyer.pdf. Also see John Piper, "Colour in the Picturesque Village," *Architectural Review*, 97, no. 581 (May 1945), pp. 149–50; John Macarthur, "The Nomenclature of Style: Brutalism, Minimalism, Art History and Visual Style in Architecture Journals," *Architectural Theory Review*, 10, no. 2 (2005), pp. 100–108; John Macarthur, "'The Revenge of the Picturesque', Redux," *Journal of Architecture*, 17, no. 5 (2012), pp. 643–53; John Macarthur and Mathew Aitchison, "Oxford versus the Bath Road: Empiricism and Romanticism in the *Architectural Review*'s Picturesque Revival," *Journal of Architecture*, 17, no. 1 (2012), pp. 51–68.

45 Nikolaus Pevsner, "C20 Picturesque," *Architectural Review*, 115 (April 1954), p. 229. The article summary in the issue's table of contents explains that Picturesque principles "are demonstrably the same as those of functionalism, even if the words are different. The picturesque was the first, but not necessarily the ultimate, aesthetic discipline which was not based upon the grid, the axis, the module and other academic preconceptions, but rather upon the free grouping for parts, free juxtaposition of different materials, upon taking things on their own merits, upon an experimental and tentative approach which is the guiding principle of the modern movement and the planner's life-line in a world of visual chaos" (p. 221).

46 The Editors [Hubert de Cronin Hastings], "Exterior Furnishing, or Sharawaggi: The Art of Making Urban Landscape," *Architectural Review*, 95 (January 1944), pp. 2–8.

47 I. de Wolfe [Hubert de Cronin Hastings], "Townscape," *Architectural Review*, 106, no. 636 (December 1949), p. 355. Alan Powers, in *Britain: Modern Architectures in History*, pp. 10–11, embraces the Picturesque attitude, claiming that "it is not unlike systems theory that entered architectural discourse in the 1950s and remains the ideological model and a practical tool today. Perhaps my approach to this [book] has been a Picturesque one, evoking a changing parade of images and characters, not easily reduced to simple generalizations, but operating quickly and making up their own rules as they go along." Powers characterizes the Picturesque as an enduring approach in which "rules were to be tested by subjectivity, rather than established by logic. It meant that opposites could be brought together without cancelling each other out. It has often been claimed that the Picturesque was the only original English contribution to aesthetics, and its effects have been profound. During the twentieth century it provided plenty of grounds for controversy, and there was a current fashion among academics to condemn it. The picturesque [still] seems relevant however because of its concern with human sensations and responses, and its sensitivity to national processes."

48 Hugh Casson, "The Aesthetics of Camouflage," and Julian Trevelyan, "The

Technique of Camouflage," *Architectural Review*, 96 (September 1944), pp. 63–68 and 69–70, respectively.

49 "Art by Accident," *Architectural Review*, 96 (September 1944), p. 63.

50 Casson, "The Aesthetics of Camouflage," p. 67. This phrase appears in Casson's article as part of quotation taken from the article by Hastings that launched the journal's advocacy of the Picturesque. The Editors [Hastings], "Exterior Furnishing, or Sharawaggi," p. 8. For a list of "the key Pevsner articles" in *Architectural Review*, see Reyner Banham, "Revenge of the Picturesque," in *Concerning Architecture: Essays on Architectural Writers and Writing Presented to Nikolaus Pevsner*, ed. John Summerson, London: Penguin, 1967, p. 265.

51 Casson, "The Aesthetics of Camouflage," p. 68.

52 For detailed accounts of the *Review*'s policy and its implications, see John Macarthur, "Townscape, Anti-Scrape and Surrealism: Paul Nash and John Piper in *The Architectural Review*," *Journal of Architecture*, 14, no. 3 (2009), pp. 387–406; Mathew Aitchison, "Townscape: Scope, Scale and Extent," *Journal of Architecture*, 17, no. 5 (2012), pp. 621–42; Boyer, "An Encounter with History"; and M. Christine Boyer, "Compromising Modernism: Architectural Polemics in Postwar England," in *Not Quite Architecture: Writing around Alison and Peter Smithson*, Cambridge, MA: MIT Press, 2017, pp. 1–36.

53 Piper, "Colour in the Picturesque Village," pp. 149–50.

54 Michael Rothenstein, "Colour and Modern Architecture; or, The Photographic Eye," *Architectural Review*, 99, no. 594 (June 1946), p. 159.

55 Geoffrey Grigson, "The Aesthetic of Lichens," *Architectural Review*, 101, no. 603 (March 1947), p. 79.

56 Ibid., pp. 79–80.

57 Ibid., p. 81. Grigson was quoting Ruskin from *Modern Painters.*

58 *Architectural Review*, 95 (January 1944), p. 33. The page of photographs follows a travel essay on Mexican architecture.

59 J. M. Richards, *The Castles on the Ground: The Anatomy of Suburbia*, London: Architectural Press, 1946, all p. 24, except "essence of the suburban environment", p. 20.

60 Ibid., pp. 32, 30, 18–19.

61 Ibid., pp. 19, 20.

62 The Tugendhat house was featured in both F.R.S. Yorke, *The Modern House*, London: The Architectural Press, 1934, and J. M. Richards, *An Introduction to Modern Architecture*, London: Pelican, 1940, and the Barcelona Pavilion in the latter. It is interesting to note how Richards's characterization and presentation of Mies changes in the numerous editions of his book. The original 1940 edition includes illustrations and descriptions of Barcelona and Tugendhat and mentions the plans for a new campus at IIT. In the second, revised edition of 1962, the Minerals and Metals Reseach Building is on the cover and is the only Mies plate: the Barcelona and Tugendhat plates are absent. There are almost no articles on Mies in the British architectural journals in the 1940s or early 1950s. Rare examples are two articles in *Architectural Design* by Mark Hartland Thomas: "The Mies Influence?" (July 1952), and "Mies van der Rohe: Recapitulation and Two New Projects" (December 1953), pp. 331–39.

63 Another important interest in Mies was the theory of "endlessness" advanced by John Weeks and Richard Llewelyn-Davies in the early 1950s, which is discussed by Banham in his 1966 book (p. 18) and more extensively in "Revenge of the Picturesque," p. 272. See Richard Llewelyn-Davies, "Endless Architecture," *Architectural Association Journal*, 67 (November 1951), pp. 106–13.

64 See Stephen Kite, "Softs and Hards: Colin St. John Wilson and the Contested Visions of 1950s London," in *Neo-avant-garde and Postmodern*, ed. Crinson and Zimmerman, pp. 62 and 72.

65 Alison and Peter Smithson, *The Charged Void: Architecture*, New York: Monacelli Press, 2001, p. 28.

66 *Arena* special issue, p. 180. The comment is appended to the mention of Peter's Royal Academy thesis project (1948–49) for a new Fitzwilliam Museum.

Chapter 3

New Brutalist Imaging

Banham's conclusion in 1966 that "Brutalism never quite broke out of the aesthetic frame of reference" is surely accurate on its face.[1] But it should not be construed in the negative terms he intended. By the fall of 1953, when the Hunstanton School was nearly complete, *Parallel of Life and Art* was being staged, and Banham was convening the Independent Group's "Aesthetic Problems of Contemporary Art" seminars, he and the Smithsons were explicitly and intuitively tapping into what, two years later, Banham called "the general body of anti-Academic aesthetics currently in circulation."[2] Those interests, which they shared with fellow Independent Group members Henderson, Paolozzi, Hamilton, and Lawrence Alloway, among others, would inspire Banham's ingenious argument in 1955 in "The New Brutalism" that architecture should be conceptualized and actualized "as 'an image.'"

> *An Image*—with the utterance of these two words we bridge the gap [. . .] between the meaning of [New Brutalism] as applied to architecture and its meaning as applied to painting and sculpture. The word *image* in this sense is one of the most intractable and the most useful terms in contemporary aesthetics.[3]

Just over a decade later, in *The New Brutalism: Ethic or Aesthetic?*, Banham would disavow those earlier aesthetic speculations as an "attempt to father some of my own pet notions," ones that were not "truly representative of the state of the Brutalist movement at that important time in its evolution."[4] Yet those pet notions have proven to be the most important, accurate, apt, and enduring insights in his essay. Banham's theorization of imaging was nascent and schematic, but it brilliantly illuminated what the Smithsons had begun to see and pursue in the early 1950s and continued to explore for decades: the potential for architecture to be understood and operate as "something which is visually valuable, but not necessarily by the standards of classical aesthetics."[5] Most important, "image" was, and remained, a crucial word for the Smithsons: "Image was the favourite word of the period [. . .] 'a good image' was the highest possible praise, for a newspaper photograph, for an advertisement [. . .] in fact for anything."[6]

Neither Banham nor the Smithsons would fully develop explanations of those not necessarily classical aesthetic standards for "a coherent and apprehensible visual entity,"[7] and the Smithsons never explicitly embraced or rejected the theories and judgments in Banham's 1955 essay.[8] But they lambasted his 1966 book as "instant history" that contained numerous factual errors and offered only a "fully authenticated myth. For the period up to 1958 Banham is well up to *Time* standards. [. . .] From 1958 onwards he seems not to have been paying attention and the reality of what we were all up to has got away from him."[9] Banham's outlook and support did indeed shift in the late 1950s, but his argument in 1966 also diminished key aspects of what the Smithsons, Henderson, and Paolozzi "were all up to" in the early 1950s. That is clear at the end of his book when he offers a constrained and pithy definition of the New Brutalist ethic as "an idea that the relationships of the parts and the materials of a building are a working morality."[10] Banham did not identify the features of that ethic explicitly in "The New Brutalism"—the word never appeared in the essay—

but even he would have considered his 1966 characterization to be misleading and inadequate back in 1955. If an ethic was implicit at that time, it was not a positive assertion of architectural or aesthetic principles or values about design or building: rather, it was an intellectually complex, historically informed, and emotionally raw attitude that refused conventional or received wisdom about modernism, especially the kinds of casual composition and stylistic detailing that he called "the doldrum of routine-functionalist abdications,"[11] which operated on "the assumption that if structure and function are served then the result must be architecture."[12]

In 1955 Banham argued that New Brutalism emerged in a context of heightened sophistication about "the inner history of the Modern Movement," which had fueled a "suspicion of crypto-academicism," a rejection of "the most insidious myths" of modernism, and a desire to avoid "quasi-historical" explanations of its newness.[13] He characterized the New Brutalist alternative as "*je-m'en-foutisme*, its bloody-mindedness," which took the "basic moral imperatives" of "honesty in structure and material" entirely and extremely seriously as a means to call attention to "the thing itself, in its totality, and with all its overtones of human association. [. . .] Basically, it requires that the building should be an immediately apprehensible visual entity, and that the form grasped by the eye should be confirmed by the experience of the building in use."[14] For Banham, the kind of *thing* that a New Brutalist building is, is a kind of inhabitable image. His crucial but puzzling and only partly developed insight is that "grasping" or "apprehending" the "overtones" and "totality" of that kind of image—including its historical, technical, spatial, functional, and experiential aspects and qualities—is equally ethical and aesthetic. In 1955 Banham argued that a New Brutalist building asserts the latent ethos of contemporary society by advancing and implementing new kinds of aesthetic approaches and experiences, and in 1966 he remarked that that aim was evident in the Smithsons' concern with "social ethics" in the design of housing and their "attempt to visualize the total environment in which this ethic could be realized."[15] In 1966 Banham lamented the disintegration of that original New Brutalist synthesis of ethical rigor "inextricably entangled" with aesthetic experimentation. Yet he inflated his criteria of success beyond what they had been when New Brutalism was new. In 1955 he was constructingan aesthetic argument for New Brutalism as *une architecture autre* allied with developments in painting, sculpture, and music. By 1966, Banham had moved on from so-called "anti-Academic aesthetics" and concluded that New Brutalism had failed to fulfill much grander ambitions: it had not radically altered the established practices and purposes of the architectural discipline. New Brutalism's ethical impulse had lapsed and it had returned to "the notion of the art of architecture that has been current since the Renaissance," namely "the structure/space synthesis": "the idea that the prime function of the architect is to employ structure to make space."[16] His new hope lay in Buckminster Fuller's "quest for ever-higher environmental performance" and in the promise of "sophistication for all" in "Pop-Architecture."[17] He saw no point in revisiting or affirming the powerful yet undeveloped criteria and concepts in his 1955 essay. Instead, Banham's revised historical

ARRAY 3.1

assessment focused on the attitudes that were part of New Brutalism's original reception by its audience, all of which he found deficient. Apparently, he thought the New Brutalist ethic was both inadequate and had been lost on its followers from the beginning. "By 1954–55 one could see at least three different conceptions of the New Brutalism circulating in architectural gossip and criticism," he wrote: "a 'rappel à l'ordre', a search for the traditional fundamentals of architecture," "judging each case on its merits in the best traditions of British pragmatism," and an "aesthetically sophisticated body of opinion [...] in favour of direct physical and emotional response and involvement in the creative process."[18]

The books the Smithsons published after 1966 suggested that while their understanding of the New Brutalist ethos aligned most with Banham's third category, they did not accept his dismissive and revisionist description (in comparison to the much broader and more obscure range of influences in his 1955 essay) of the "aesthetically sophisticated" sensibilities of the 1950s. In 1966 Banham reductively aligned New Brutalism with action painting and kitchen-sink theater. The Smithsons' approach also had nothing to do with professionalism in the "art" of building, which converted it "from a violent revolutionary outburst to a fashionable vernacular."[19] This, Banham claimed, was the actual, ultimate legacy of New Brutalism. For the Smithsons, however, the aesthetic potential of New Brutalism remained vital and was moving closer to achieving what Banham had characterized in 1955 as an "anti-Academic" yet still aesthetic "determination to create a coherent visual image by non-formal means [...] and fully validating the presence of human beings as part of the total image."[20] Over and over in their later work, the Smithsons continued to operate with that basic framework of an aesthetics that, as Banham wrote in 1955, "fully matches up to the threat and promise of *Parallel of Life and Art*."[21]

Banham's most vivid and wry articulation of those ideas appeared in a remarkable footnote at the end of "The New Brutalism," where he suggested that a shift to "image and topology," as "more generalized concepts" than "beauty and geometry," could be the basis for an "other" architecture and an aesthetics "which, though essentially primitive, can be reached only through immense sophistication. Once this state of sophistication has been achieved, and the new concept digested, it suddenly appears so simple that it can be vulgarized without serious distortion."[22] Banham's footnote effectively and irreverently demonstrates key aspects of the ideas and attitudes that he would later call pet notions. It is at once the most "sophisticated" statement of aesthetic theory in the essay and a digressive reference to a "vulgar" source. The footnote ends with a condescending suggestion to his readers to "acquire a copy of *Astounding Science Fiction* for July 1954" as "a handy back-entrance to topology without using the highly complex mathematics involved." He did not explain that he was not referencing any of the articles or stories in the magazine but was referring instead to its cover illustration's visual lesson in the basics of topology (with a discreet label near the bottom warning of the issue's "INAPPROPRIATE" content). The image depicts a young man—from the rear, nude, seated cross-legged on a blanket—holding a human heart in one hand and facing a blueprint of a comic book robot design that fills the background like wallpaper.

3.1

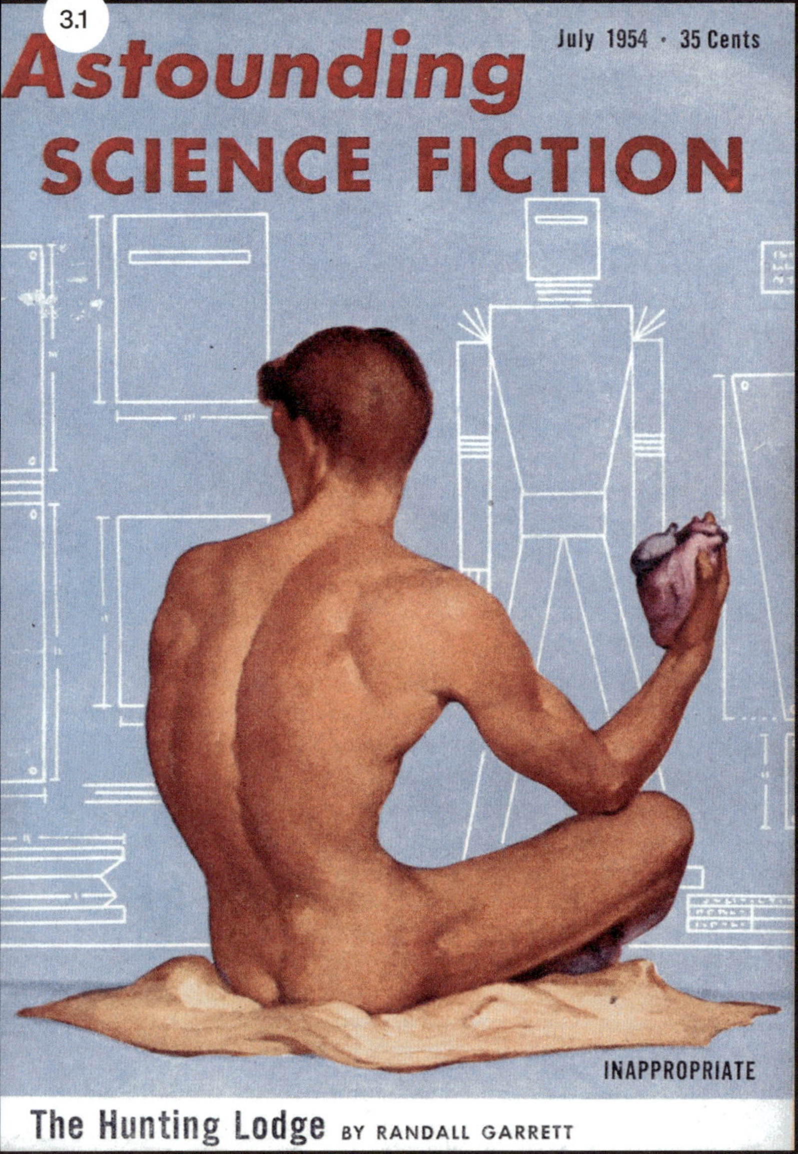

July 1954 · 35 Cents

Astounding SCIENCE FICTION

INAPPROPRIATE

The Hunting Lodge BY RANDALL GARRETT

pollock

Painting, 1953—a formal composition in action.

henderson

Sgraffiti on a Window (photograph)—image of human as well as formal value.

Parallel of Life and Art—exhibition of 100 Brutalist images.

[4] This analogy could probably be rendered epistemologica
beauty and geometry, hitherto regarded as ultimate properti
now appear as linguistically refined special cases of more gene
—image and topology—which, though essentially primit
reached only through immense sophistication. Once this sta
tion has been achieved, and the new concept digested, it sud
simple that it can be vulgarized without serious distortion,
back-entrance to topology without using the highly comp
involved, the reader could not do better than acquire a cop
Science Fiction for July, 1954.

NEW BRUTALISM

Painting on burlap—typically Brutalist in his attitude to materials, Burri accords the burlap the same visual value as the paint it carries.

Coventry Cathedral competition entry (A. & P. Smithson) dramatic visual image created by spectacular structure, raised on a plan of Neo-Palladian symmetry—their last formal plan, 1951.

paolozzi

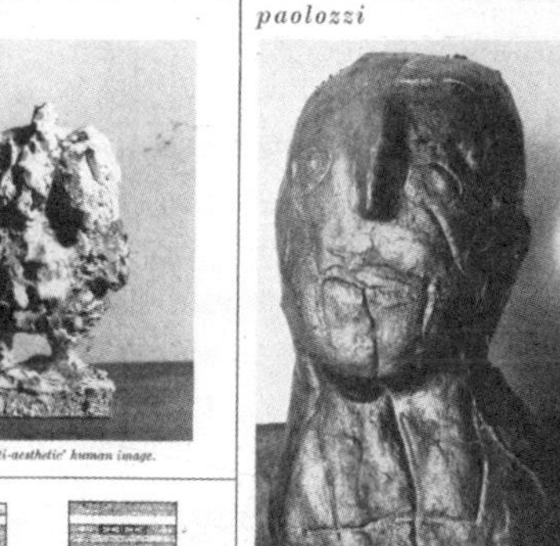

...nti-aesthetic' human image.

Head, 1953—'sophisticated primitivism.'

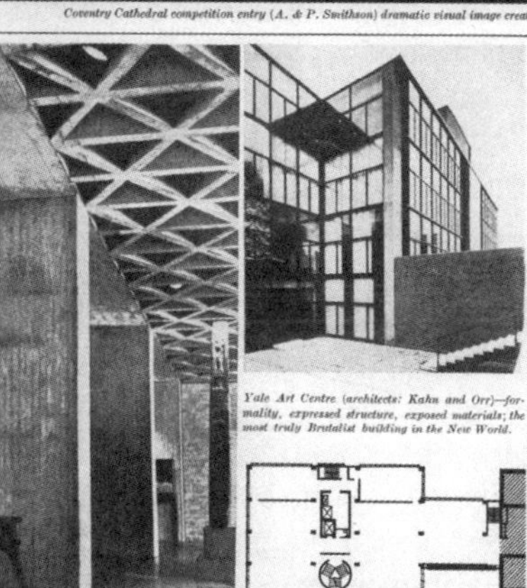

Yale Art Centre (architects: Kahn and Orr)—formality, expressed structure, exposed materials; the most truly Brutalist building in the New World.

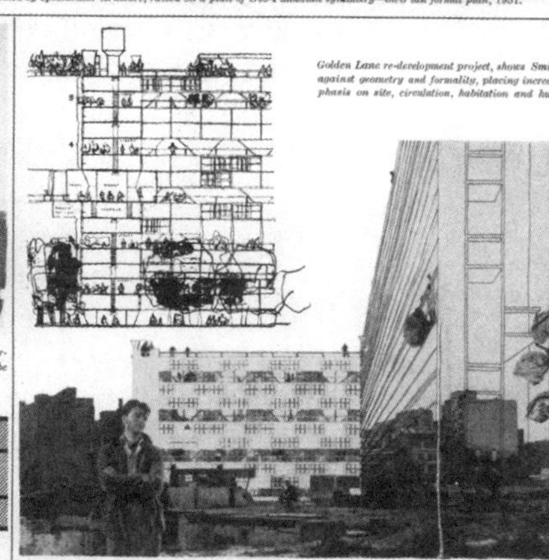

Golden Lane re-development project, shows Smithso... against geometry and formality, placing increased ... phasis on site, circulation, habitation and human...

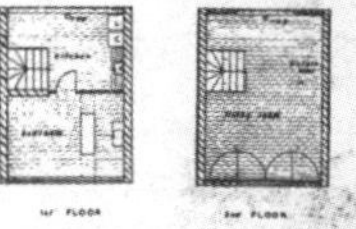

The first building to be categorized as Brutalist, this project for a house in Soho (A. & P. Smithson) exhibits not only the emphasis on materials and structure, but also the compositional formality of early Brutalism.

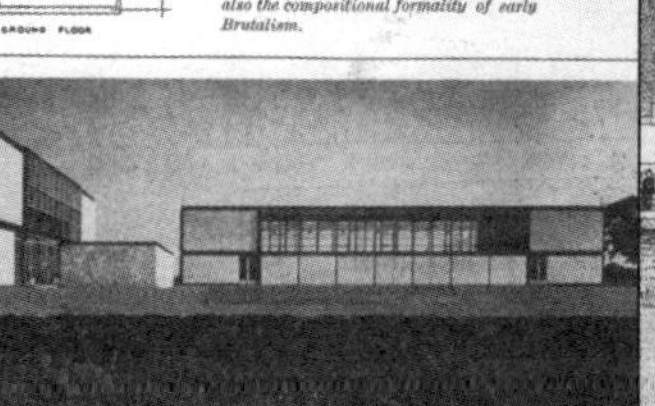

...on (A. & P. Smithson), first completed New Brutalist building, view toward gymnasium.

Sheffield University extensions (competition entry b... Smithson)—furthest development of New Brutalist a... toward the completely a-formal, anti-geometric, yet ... compositional methods exemplified in painting by P... Burri. Raised walk-ways, one suspended beneath a b... services, connect the main entrance, under 1, with ... dept., 3, Senate House, 2, and other buildings on sit...

rict—both
the *cosmos*,
d concepts
have been
sophistica-
appears so
r a handy
athematics
Astounding

Banham's footnote playfully exemplifies what could be termed "vulgar sophistication" in two distinct ways. On the one hand, his idea of an aesthetics based in "a-formal, anti-geometric"[23] imaging practices is an anti-academic vulgarization of philosophical and mathematical sophistication; on the other hand, he finds evidence of aesthetic sophistication in a vulgar source. "Vulgar sophistication" is also a fascinating and appropriate description of the implicit aspiration and operative subject of each of the Smithsons' books and many of their essays and projects, all of which pursue the subtleties, peculiarities, and inseparability of the connection between aesthetics and ethics. But while Banham seems to have understood vulgarization in ironic terms as the shrewd reduction and effective popularization of intellectually difficult ideas, the Smithsons' attitude or ethic aligned more closely with the word's Latin root, *vulgus*, meaning "the common people," and was manifest in the Smithsons' passion to understand the mass appeal and aesthetic subtleties of presumably crude or banal realities. Thus Banham's "sophistication" was also of a different kind than the Smithsons'. As Banham would imply in the early 1960s with his Pop concepts of "sophistication for all" and "design by choice," his idea of New Brutalist sophistication required an uneasy alliance of cultivated discernment and popular taste. It assumed the position of an educated consumer or trained critic awash in a commercial culture of products and brands, who needed to make wise choices that affirmed their status among new cultural hierarchies.[24] Banham, as both a self-declared intellectual expert (unafraid to deploy art historical technique and knowledge) and wise man-on-the-street (eager to display his hip contemporaneity), played each against the other as a subversive game in which he aimed to be declared the winner. The Smithsons, as they made clear in "But Today We Collect Ads," were at home in the same world but treated it as a "visual climate" that was "beating the fine arts at their old game." They believed advertisements and other "popular arts" were worthy objects of intellectual study and scrutiny but could not be understood on the same terms or with the same methods as fine art because they should be "seen as a pattern of social organization, not as a stylistic source." They saw them as "packed with information—data of a way of life and a standard of living which they are simultaneously inventing and documenting."[25] That sophisticated ethos suffused not only New Brutalism but also many practices in postwar British intellectual culture. It was evident in the new artistic and intellectual approaches that emerged in a range of fields, from ordinary language philosophy to Free Cinema to cultural studies.[26]

That enduring "brutalist" attitude and aesthetic approach pervades each of the Smithsons' books, beginning with the collection of iconic architectural images in *The Heroic Period of Modern Architecture* and continuing with the magazine advertisements for cars, playgrounds, cigarettes, furniture, or toilet paper that they included as illustrations in *Ordinariness and Light* and *Without Rhetoric* to show "ourselves as we now wish to be."[27] Perhaps the most succinct and overt plea for the value of vulgar sophistication—on the Smithsons' terms as a kind of aesthetic aspiration or achievement—is the last sentence of *Without Rhetoric*: "Things need to be ordinary and heroic at the same time."[28] Twenty years later, *Changing the Art*

ARRAY 3.2

of Inhabitation presented the most sustained, clear, and nuanced version of that approach and argument. The book's design operates as a display or atlas of accumulated evidence—anecdotal, historical, photographic, textual—of recurrent tendencies and a latent sensibility in their own work and in that of the Eameses and Mies. Each image and "verbal illustration" in the book was curated, juxtaposed, cropped, captioned, or annotated to generate an updated, inflected, and seemingly fleeting coherence across the three generations of architects.[29]

ARRAY 3.3

The subtitle of *Without Rhetoric: An Architectural Aesthetic, 1955–1972* also affirms the Smithsons' ongoing commitment to aesthetics, as does the first image and its caption in *Ordinariness and Light*. Their urban design slogan "reaching out to a random aesthetic" is printed below a nearly full-page image of the striking and memorable ideogram that they devised in the early 1950s as an emblem of the branching urban strategy of the Golden Lane project and which clearly emulates the patterns and shapes of the sculptures, paintings, and prints that Paolozzi was producing at that time.[30] The Smithsons' passionate pursuit of another aesthetic in their work and their attempts to discern it in others' work, combined with their insistence that those pursuits were inseparable from an ethic, was at the core of their disagreement with Banham.[31] Quite simply, for the Smithsons, to minimize aesthetic motives or insist on distinguishing them from ethical motives, as Banham did in 1966, is to impose a categorical mistake.

The Smithsons' first explicit, if still cursory, discussion of aesthetics was their 1957 essay "Aesthetics of Change," where they proposed "an architecture of involvement" that they distinguished from the "finite relationship" of "the part and the whole" in classical aesthetic theory. Instead of a "closed" system of discrete, timeless forms, they outlined a general theory of a "transient" aesthetic that "postulat[es] a relationship with something that does not yet exist and possibly cannot even be imagined."[32] That aesthetic is inherently political and engaged. "Transient" buildings actively and effectively participate in changing conditions rather than propose ideal or utopian solutions. "To sum up," they wrote, "the new modern architecture is objective about the human and built situation, and acts in it, making use of change. Its aesthetic is necessarily 'open', non-geometric, and if necessary, impermanent."[33] The essay offered several positive examples of this aesthetic: Alvar Aalto's "a-geometric" Säynätsalo Town Hall (1949–51), the "genuine impermanence" and "expendability" of the Eames House (1949), and the "continuous 'flow' complex" of their unbuilt competition entry for Sheffield University.[34] To illustrate the counterpoint, the Smithsons identified Mies's plan for IIT, which, they claimed, uses "traditional solutions" derived from "neo-classical aesthetic principles."[35] But they did not maintain that understanding of Mies for long. "Aesthetics of Change" was written not long before Peter's first trip to Chicago, and in the revised—and much abbreviated—version of the essay that appeared in *Ordinariness and Light*, the negative reference to IIT was removed, as were any discussion and images of Säynätsalo.[36] Most important, the Smithsons also excised the phrase "and possibly cannot even be imagined." In 1970 the sentence simply ended with the assertion that an aesthetic of change "postulat[es] a relationship with something that does not yet exist." Did

3.2

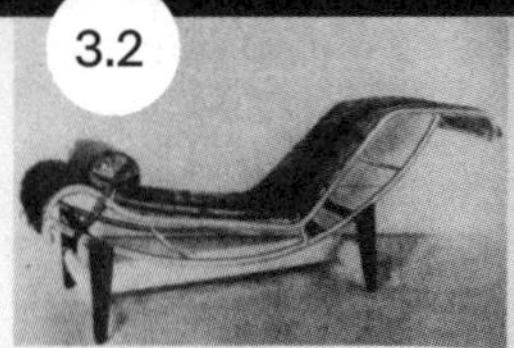

Le Corbusier, P. Jeanneret, with Charlotte Perriand, chair for Thonet, Paris, 1929
Casteels, L'Art Moderne Primitif

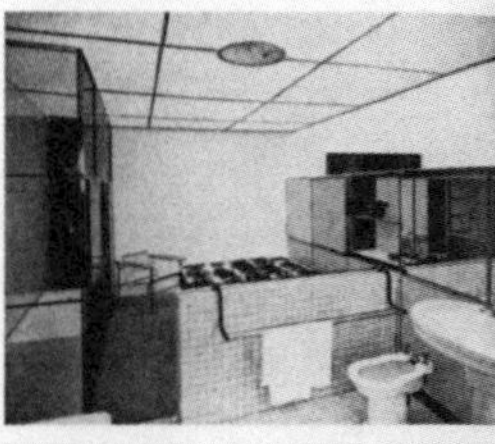

salon

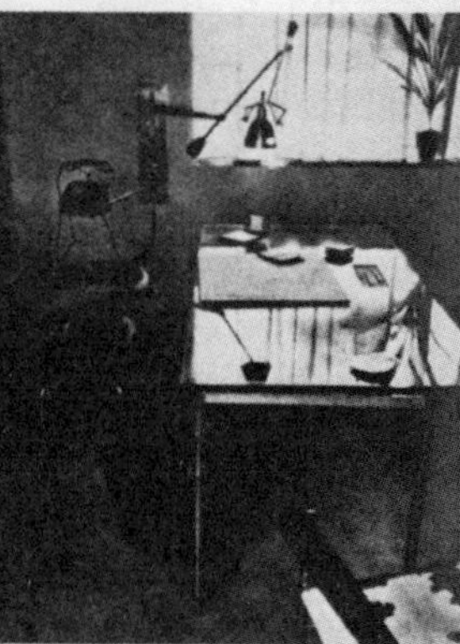

ON MIES VAN DER ROHE

No other men have succeeded as have Le Corbusier and Mies van der Rohe in building complete systems.
Their concentration is such that the nature of their systems is implicit even in the fragment. One has, for example, a perfectly clear notion of the sort of city and the sort of society envisaged by Mies van der Rohe, even though he has never said much about it. It is not an exaggeration to say that the Miesian city is implicit in the Mies chair.
Le Corbusier's system is of course more familiar because of his constant reiteration of the part even his smallest objects play in his general scheme of things. And what validates both their systems is that they are conceived in the terms of the technology of their time and that both men have a capacity for rejection and reconsideration in the face of changing circumstances.

P.S., from a *"Footnote on the Seagram Building"*, published in the *Architectural Review*, December, 1958.

Mies van der Rohe, Barcelona Pavilion, 1929
Johnson, Mies van der Rohe

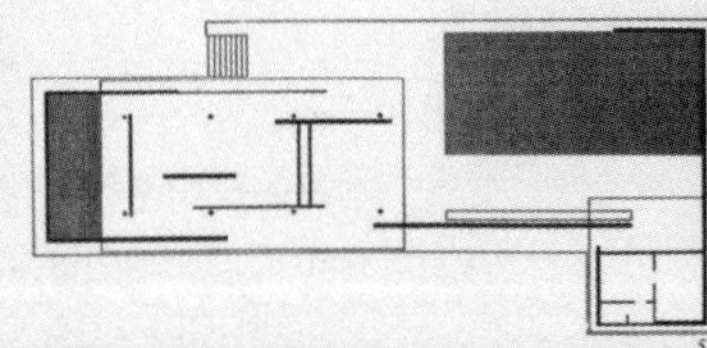

57

Above : light in the city : Buenos
Below : cars as a spectacle : Los A

(continued from previous pag

Housing in the mass presen face. There are few eye rest see what the man can eat, c wear, buy. The mind wants for action—or relaxation— if it has no wish or need to The clerk, the mechanic, se when going home. A few ga ing, but forty tiny plots are hurries past head down.

The approach to the house link with society as a whole stair or down into a basem an estate road past twenty houses; along an air-conditi corridor.

These are men's links with down which man looks at h

In the housing areas there a 'principles of mobility.'

A road must: feel as if it's g North or South; towards o you, even if it's pitch dark

Car movement is flow mov gular: stopping and starting turning around, of the walk

To flow means to move eve functions, from fast on natio house access roads.

The car is not good at turni space, and it is dangerous w ing under such conditions. ing estate cul-de-sac is there grouping of houses where t livery vehicles, doubly usele

Right: 'our cities—an extension to be'

1910

1911

Gropius, Fagus Works, Alfeld, 1911
Giedion, Work and Teamwork

Gropius, Fagus Works, Alfeld, 1911
Giedion, Walter Gropius

Gropius, Fagus Works, Alfeld, 1911
Gropius, Bauhaus Bücher I

TRIBUTE TO FRANK LLOYD WRIGHT

Frank Lloyd Wright remained until the end an architect of the art nouveau. His buildings were always with rare exceptions private worlds into which artifacts from the outside entered with difficulty. At the turn of the century there were two really important architects, F.L. Wright and C.R. Mackintosh. Both men included in their vocabulary highly developed rectangular systems of building derived presumably from a common oriental source.
Systems of square sectioned, overlapping, obviously jointed, natural finished constructions, which could be extended to light fittings, to furniture and to decoration.
Neither man used this system exclusively but it was this particular manner in the hands of F.L. Wright which was seen in Europe before 1914 and the sense of liberated space that went with it that fired the imagination of the generation of Rietveld, Mies and Le Corbusier. It was as if a door had opened on a new world. That world they constructed for themselves and it was in fact a world full of light and the spirit of ordinariness quite opposed to art nouveau. And one which the master found unacceptable to the end.
Frank Lloyd Wright was seminal to the architecture of the twentieth century.

Peter Smithson, Paris, April 1958.

1914

Le Corbusier, Pierre Jeanneret, Maison Dom-ino, 1914
Oeuvre Complète, 1910-1929

1915

A. and G. Perret, Docks, Casablanca, 1915
L'Arch. Vivante, 1926

2

Villa at Garches, under restoration Summer 1954, photographed during visit with Alfred Roth who had worked on the drawings in the office of Le Corbusier.
NB: the modern van only comes half way up the garage which was made for tall cars that ladies could get into in dust-coats and elaborate hats. P.S.

Scorning the sociologists of that time for collating past aspirations, we turned to this forever renewed source material so that we could be in a position to give form to people's aspirations at the same moment as they discovered they had them.
1954 was for us a key year . . . American advertising equal to Dada in its impact of overlaid imagery . . . that automotive masterpiece the Cadillac convertible – parallel with the ground, four elevations – classic box on wheels . . . the start of a new way of thinking by CIAM[1] . . . the revaluation of the work of Gropius . . . the repainting of the Villa at Garches; all these events we selected as meaningful and encouraging. We believed New Brutalism[2] to be the direct line development of the Modern Movement.

1 Developed by Team 10 after Otterlo 1957.
2 Coined on sight of a newspaper paragraph heading which called (by poor translation of Beton Brut?) the Marseilles Unité 'Brutalism in architecture' – that was for us: 'New', both because we came after le Corbusier, and in response to the going literary style of the Architectural Review which – at the start of the 'fifties – was running articles on the New Monumentality, the New Empiricism, the New Sentimentality, and so on.

entified as a 'road without issue', and where ogress through a housing area from points A to is a series of infuriating and dangerous false arts and turnarounds.*

new layouts the road/building relationship ould indicate the relative importance of the ute. In an existing road system this could be ne with coloured markers, and at night by loured light. (Louis Kahn has a wonderful draw- g showing the possibilities of light in *Perspecta* Yale architectural students' magazine.)

oads are also places.

onsider for example the social implications of e arrangement of houses around a small green, rking lot, or turn-around, which puts all move- ent under continuous social scrutiny.

one American 'Package Township' housing ourt' described in the *Organization Man*. To- therness was taken to the point that the doors the side away from the courts were done away th altogether. In such conditions even Americans, hose privacy threshold is renownedly low, und the consequences of mutual surveillance tolerable.

he opportunity for opting-out of a given social uation seems to be one of the reasons why ople have chosen to live in cities—even if their ighbourhood is in Surrey or New England. To free in one's associations and not forced by the ze or structure of the community into unchosen lationships from which it is impossible to escape a genuine twentieth-century necessity.

This was one of the many reasons why in 1952 we developed the pedestrian street-in-the-air idea for high buildings, so that people could 'choose to go a different way home', and generally have much greater possibilities for free movement than is possible in Point Blocks or Unités d'Habitation.

Where many routes are available even a recluse benefits, for it is easier for the others to go away.

In conclusion: to fly; ride a horse; sail a boat, are all distinct sensations. We must have this directness and sensation of freedom for the car.

The first step is to realize a system of urban motorways. Not just because we need more roads but because only they can make our cities an extension of ourselves as we now wish to be.

t is worth while remembering that cul-de-sac planning d the detailed æsthetic techniques of Parker and Unwin ere developed for a horse and cart society.

a

b

c

d

173. Advertisements exploiting the desire for relaxation: *a*, the mountain cabin; *b*, Seine type; *c*, the open air; *d*, the woods

st of four full page advertisments, Ladies Home Journal, early 'fifties.

141. Tokyo Expressway No. 4, near Kandabashi. Built movement

142. Garage; advertisement tear-sheet. Our cities – an extension of ourselves as we now wish to be?

3.3

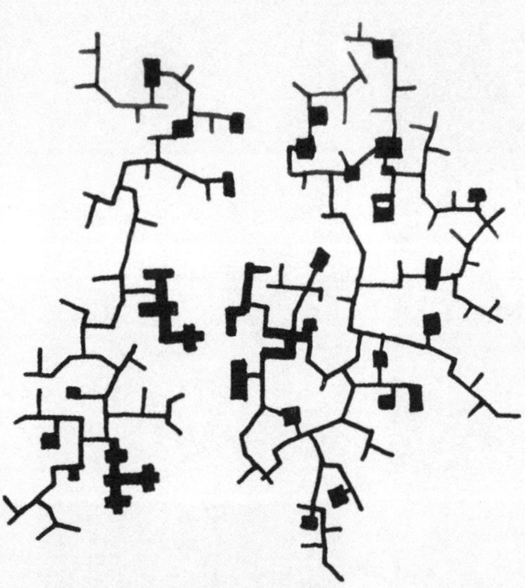

1. Reaching out to a random aesthetic

programme'; for the document – intended originally for publication as a popular general statement of an idea (its format based on Le Corbusier's classic work '*Urbanisme*') – was in fact never published as a whole, and has lain unread over the intervening years.

10

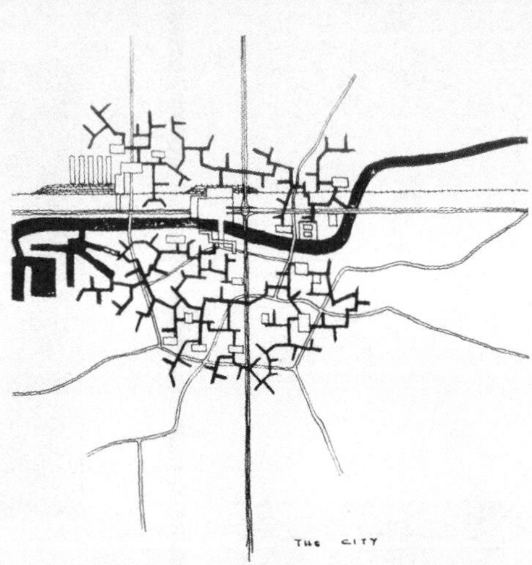

37. Golden Lane city

The difference between towns and cities is only one of size, for both are arrangements of districts.

The city is the ultimate community, 'the tangible expression of an economic region'.

It is extremely difficult to define the higher levels of association, but the street implies a physical contact community; the district an acquaintance community; and the city an intellectual contact community.

To maintain looseness of grouping and ease of communication, the density must increase as the population increases; and with high densities, if we are to retain the essential joys of sun, space and verdure, we must build high.

48

38. Ni
elemen

D

In 1949 at Peggy Guggenheim's palazzo in Venice we saw the first manifestation of the new ordering, in the painting of Jackson Pollock.

In a roomful of academic abstract painting Pollock seemed too good to be true: the ghost of the twenties had at last been laid and the way was clear.

At last we were free from the shadow of our international grandfathers, free to solve our problems in our own way.

The painting of Jackson Pollock is a different sort from any that we had ever seen before. It is more like a natural phenomenon, a manifestation rather than an artifact; complex, timeless, n-dimensional and multi-vocative.

Comparable developments have taken place in structural design, in which the actual behaviour and the properties of the materials are more accurately accounted for. This has led, as in art, to the consideration of the parts not as simply acting, but as things in themselves with their own internal disciplines complexly acting in a total system of forces.

In Le Corbusier's book on his Unité d'Habitation at Marseilles there is one very significant page which shows the plan of St Dié and a student sketch of the Carthusian monastery of Ema in Tuscany. Of this sketch Corbu says: 'L'organisation harmonieuse du phénomène collectif et du phénomène individuel, y est résolue dans la sérénité, la joie et l'efficience.'

69. Eduardo Paolozzi. Sculpture from 'This is Tomorrow' 1956

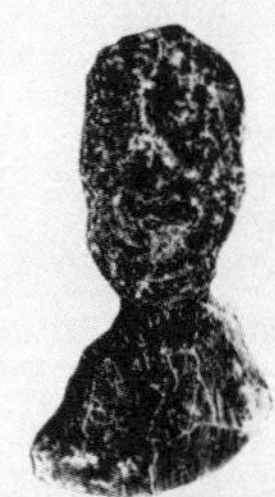

70. Eduardo Paolozzi, *Man's Head* 1954

86

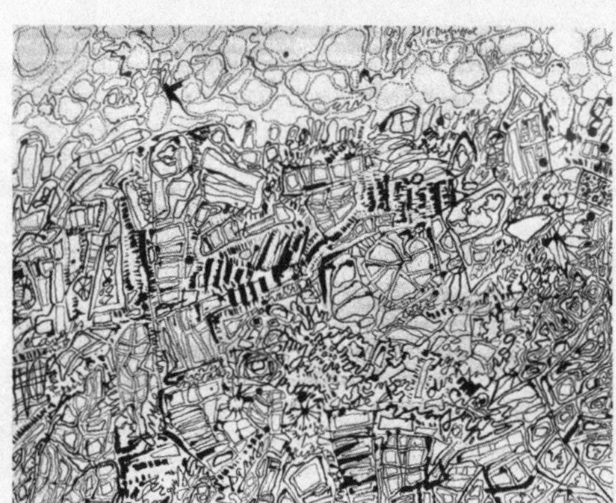

71. Jean Dubuffet, *Dématérialisation*; ink drawing 1952

No-one can doubt the validity (in the middle ages) of the monastic system, or fail to be moved by the serenity of the plastic resolution – for resolution of relationships *is* architecture. But the assurance and clarity of St Dié[18] rest on an invalid relationship between the individual and the collective.

Families do not now (nor did they in the fifteenth century) live an introspective scholastic life where the only relationship that matters is that of God and Man. That was the life at Ema, and Ema is the seed from which Unité and St Dié have grown.

In Unité seen negatively the out-turned cell faces impersonal sun and space. Man scurries along from Victorian lifts down gloomy corridors to the solitary confinement of his private drawer.

[18] 1966. Yet it is indisputable that the unbuilt plan for St Dié contained more of value than all the ghastly new town areas the French have built.

87

ing room, Bethnal Green, east London, 1952. Silk screen
zi, used as wallpaper

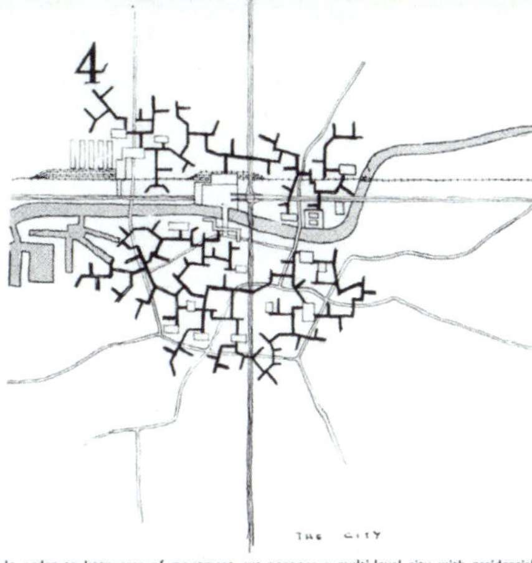

In order to keep ease of movement, we propose a multi-level city with residential streets-in-the-air. These are linked together in a multi-level continuous complex, connected where necessary to work and to these ground elements that are necessary at each level of association. Our hierarchy of association is woven into a modulated continuum representing the true complexity of human associations

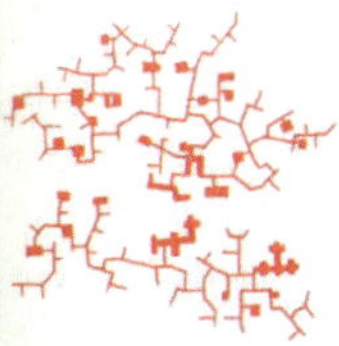

Streets-in-the-air are linked together in a multi-level continuous complex, connected where necessary to work and to those ground elements that are necessary at each level of association. Our 'hierarchy of association' is woven into a modulated continuum representing the true complexity of human associations.

Districts in association generate the need for a richer scale of activities which in their turn give identity to the ultimate community.

THE CITY

Any new combinations of dwellings with their immediate access that would make for a new way of living in the city must nearly always expect to have to lace-in between existing buildings and mesh over existing road and service networks. Their function is renewal; of the dying centres and derelict areas among railway

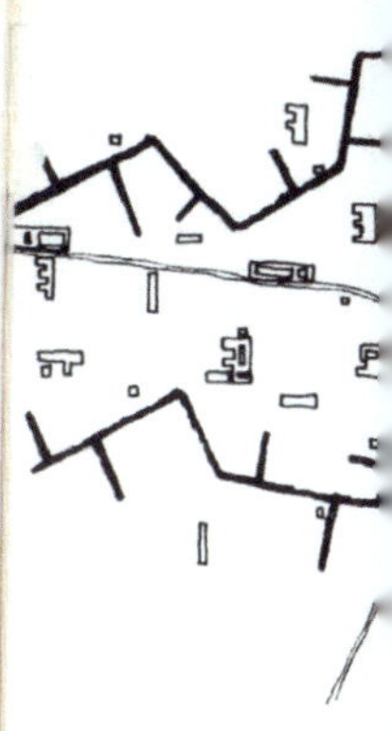

viaducts and old industrial
help from their surrounding
their unblemishable newnes
for renewal in themselves.

The horizontal street mesh
of other buildings in an a
multi-level buildings already

July 1950 Eduardo Paolozzi

Eduardo Paolozzi

the Smithsons think that the phrase they removed was unnecessary hyperbole, or did they come to think such transient, changing relationships actually could be imagined? The latter seems to be the case, and the change was, at least in part, an effect and affect of their return to Mies. The transient aesthetic is a kind of imaging design that operates with the same kinds of malleability, formats, patterns, and potential that operate in visual organizations, from ornamental wallpaper to video screens to urban plans.

The revised version of "Aesthetics of Change" ends with a simple yet sophisticated spread featuring two images of the Sheffield project and one of the Eames House.[37] Overall, eight of the images in the original article were removed from the new version, and two new images (one of Sheffield and one of the Eames House) replace others in the final spread. Its new layout operates as a textual and visual imaging array, not simply as three individual illustrations of two specific projects. It is a graphic exemplification of a broader aesthetic that replaces and supersedes the use of illustrations in the 1957 article. The intricate patterns and subtle abstraction of the spread's three very different kinds of image are enhanced by their juxtaposition, which generates reciprocal alterations and fluctuating affinities in and among them. A simple yet highly articulated and dynamic line drawing of the Sheffield site plan (which was produced by Alison around the time of the book)[38] floats in the white expanse of the upper left page. Below it, an elevation of Sheffield (produced for the 1953 competition) is framed by its pale gray background, which reinforces the layered depth and superimposition of the building elements that are emphasized in the drawing. On the right page is a single large photograph of the Eames House showing an oblique view of its gridded exterior, mottled by the shadows and overlapped by the speckled trunks of eucalyptus trees. The spread's positive demonstration of the fluctuating patterns of a "transient aesthetic"—an "aesthetic of expendability quite outside of the European tradition"—makes the negative critique of Mies or the distinction between "non-geometric"
ARRAY 3.4 and "a-geometric" in the first version of the essay unnecessary. The array of images on that spread, like many others in the 1970 book, is evidence that the Smithsons had moved fully into exploring "the threat and promise" of design as imaging.

That pursuit, and the crucial significance of the Eames House as a variation of the Mies-image, is clearly stated in a 1990 lecture by Peter on the occasion of the reconstruction of *Patio and Pavilion*:

> So, somehow through Mies, through a rejection of much of Mies, but still through Mies, or so it seems to me, we get the 1949 house [. . .]. The house was an Eames-defined territory, established by the pavilions set into it which reinforced the line of trees; with, on occupation, an Eames content. [. . .] The framing, the skin, of the pavilions are a notation against which was played a content. Both house and content are perceived in graphic terms—an American phenomenon—to set in contrast with the very concrete, very European, *Patio and Pavilion*. [. . .] The Eames House is a picture of the Eames.[39]

Two other essays in *Ordinariness and Light* affirm the impact of Peter's American encounters with Mies, or the Smithsons' reinterpretation of his influence. In "Fix: Permanence and Transience," which was first published in 1960, after Peter's trips, the notion of a transient aesthetic was elaborated further as a dialectic of "fixes" and "transients" similar to the urban strategy of the Golden Lane project, which had proposed a new branching network of linked housing slabs weaving through the remaining historic and civic monuments and the new and old infrastructures of the postwar cityscape: "'Fixes' should look fixed and 'transients' transient, even if their actual life as buildings (so-called permanent constructions) is the same. To give an example: Mies van der Rohe's Crown Hall at IIT is a fix, and looks it, while Charles Eames's own house is a transient, and looks it. Both are built of steel and glass, and have roughly the same standard of permanence."[40] Such an interplay of actual and implied temporalities, they explained, operates across the range of scales, from transportation systems to "small buildings, particularly shops and houses," to the "non-architectural environment" of "illuminated signs," "shop windows, clothing magazines," and "posters," which "arrive and disappear with great rapidity, in cycles related obscurely to each other."[41] The essay concludes with a crucial statement: "An 'aesthetic of change', paradoxically, generates a feeling of security and stability by supplementing our ability to *recognize the pattern* of related cycles."[42]

Recognition, as a temporal interplay of memory and imagination, and *pattern recognition*, as the specific modality of the Smithsons' transient aesthetic, applies as much to urban environments and architecture as to their own process of developing ideas and their constant revisioning of them over decades. The complexity of that temporal and cognitive process is evident in the way their prior work is reimagined in each of their books. It is also enacted in the complex temporal structure of Peter's "Letter to America," which comments upon his first trip to the United States. Published in 1958, it includes a text written before the first visit (outlining his expectations and preconceptions) and one written after (in effect, correcting his image of America), as well as numerous photographs taken during the trip, as an effort "to try to measure that preconception of America against the reality."[43] In *Ordinariness and Light* the text of "Letter to America" is only slightly abridged from the original, but, more important, the book chapter increases the temporal instability by also including a previously unpublished text on Chicago that was written after the second trip. The importance of the "Letter" for the Smithsons is explicit: a note on the title page to the chapter reads, "The following letter is printed more or less fully because in it are the seeds of virtually all subsequent essays right up to the present time."[44] It is significant that each part of the chapter—"Letter to America" and "Chicago"—ends with an evocative statement about Mies, each of which would be developed further a few years later as the key ideas in their Berlin seminar. The ending of the "Letter" is unchanged from its 1958 version: "And there are moreover magical distortions when two straight-up-and-down [glass- and metal-faced] buildings are opposite one another. A blue glass city, no matter how organizationally banal, is never optically boring. Seagram, of course, in dark brown glass and bronze, plays it so cool that everything else now looks like a

3.4

145. Sheffield University competition project. Site plan

146. Sheffield University. Library façade seen from the park, the route entering from the right

This building's aesthetic of expendability is quite outside the Euro[...] tradition, but if we need transient buildings we must face up to cre[...] transient aesthetic.

147. The Eames's house, Santa Monica, California. (cf illustration 171)

[...]ssical tradition, Mies van der [...] of Technology, layout

[...]stitute of Technology, Archi-[...]to Engdahl, Hedrich Blessing)

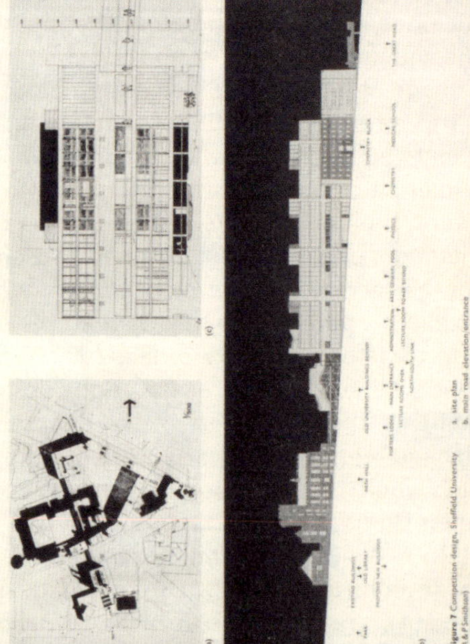

(a)

(b)

(c)

Figure 7 Competition design, Sheffield University (A & P Smithson)

a. site plan
b. main road elevation/entrance
c. library façade

7 The stuff and decorati[...] the urban scene

The Heroic Period of modern architecture finished in [...] subsequent to this can be regarded as exploratory for t[...] creative period beginning now. Both periods are [...] simultaneous parallel development in architecture, engin[...] and sculpture; the attitudes, theorems and images [...] unsought consonances in the others.

It was inevitable that the International Style whic[...] this Heroic Period, and which derived much of its inv[...] reduction of problems to their basic elements and relat[...] lose its dynamic when most of the problems had been th[...] after all, when the basic kitchen has been achieved what can[...]

Only Dada followed another road which we have tak[...] to rediscover.

The cult of simplicity does not necessarily produc[...] problems grew larger the simple surfaces and volumes [...] into which applied neo-plasticist ornament (Royal Festiva[...] and technique (U.N.O., New York) were sucked.

The position can be stated thus. In the twenties a [...] piece of architecture was a finite composition of simple ele[...] which have no separate identity but exist only in relati[...] the problem of the fifties is to retain the clarity of intent[...] but to give the parts their own internal disciplines and co[...] kind of ordering, as opposed to geometric ordering, mus[...] all creative endeavour from the city to the object.

The concept of society should be one of motion and c[...] and plastically this should be apparent.

People and objects in motion and change are both the stuff a[...] decoration of the urban scene.

68. Jackson Pollock at work

jumped-up supermart."[45] "Chicago" ends, after a critical comparison of "normal" and "poetic" aspects of the work of Frank Lloyd Wright, Le Corbusier, and Mackintosh, by celebrating Mies: "And in a curious way Mies van der Rohe's work in Chicago has both these characteristics, normality *and* light-filled poetic space."[46] The Smithsons had come to recognize the vulgar sophistication of the Mies-image: cool and never optically boring, normal and poetic, threat and promise, ethic and aesthetic.

Many disagreements about New Brutalism can be attributed as much to limited understandings of what the Smithsons were struggling to say or see as to reductive understandings of ethics and aesthetics and their interrelationship. The Smithsons' combination of strident tone and idiosyncratic turns of phrase certainly has contributed to those misunderstandings, but no more than the difficulty of what they were trying to convey.[47] A key source of confusion is their famous response to the fourth and final "Thoughts in Progress" panel discussion in the April 1957 issue of *Architectural Design*, which debated the significance of New Brutalism. The statement ends with the declaration: "Up to now Brutalism has been discussed stylistically, whereas its essence is ethical."[48] As much as any statement by the Smithsons, that assertion of the ethical essence of New Brutalism is both instructive and prone to misinterpretation. Responses to the "Thoughts in Progress" discussion (published two months later as Letters to the Editor) reveal several aspects of the confusion that the Smithsons' statement engendered regarding their ideas as well as about aesthetics and ethics generally. A reactionary letter from Edward Armitage repeated the typical modernist justification for the autonomy or purity of art: "'Ethics' in one way or another has been at the bottom of all the really nasty things in this poor world. The arts should be outside ethics."[49] Letters from Banham and the Smithsons' friend and collaborator John Voelcker each opposed that view and expanded on what New Brutalist aesthetics might mean. Banham was not among the many who misconstrued the Smithsons' point at the time. He understood that the Smithsons were not dismissing stylistic discussion of New Brutalism but were noting its limitations. More important, Banham also understood that "stylistic" is not a synonym of "aesthetic" and that neither term excludes ethics. His letter succinctly reiterated some of the ideas about aesthetics that he had formulated somewhat abstrusely in his 1955 essay, but, in an indication that he was already changing his mind about his "pet notions," he omitted any mention of "images" (a topic that was not raised in the "Thoughts in Progress" discussion, either). Banham defended his argument that a second, mature phase of New Brutalism began after Hunstanton, when the Smithsons realized that they could "define their relationship to the visual world in terms of something other than geometry."[50] He explained that "my gearshift from formality to memorability, from geometry to topology" was a "second version of the deducible principles (not dogmas) of Brutalism," and it "in no way excludes the Hunstanton School, but simply recognizes the fact [. . .] that the Brutalists were in search of a wider frame of reference for their design-activities. They rejected routine-Palladianism, not Hunstanton."[51] Nor did they reject Mies, which seems like a logical conclusion, but one that evadedBanham then and perturbed him later.

Voelcker's letter insisted empathically on the importance of images and offered a more eloquent, nuanced, and rich explanation of "the development of Brutalism," the potential of Banham's ideas, and the Smithsons' evolving approach:

> A profoundly significant extension of the movement occurred after Hunstanton had been designed. [...] This extension of architecture cannot be understood through stylistic analysis. [...] Brutalism aims to invent those unique images from bits and pieces (stone, door handle, standard metal window, polythene pipe, etc.) which communicate and are inevitable in the historical/ecological/technological situation "as found."[52]

Voelcker was building directly on Banham's suggestion in his 1955 essay that "many things have been called 'an image'—S[anta] M[aria] della Consolazione at Todi, a painting by Jackson Pollock, the Lever Building, the 1954 Cadillac convertible, the roofscape of the *Unité* at Marseilles, any of the hundred [*sic*] photographs in *Parallel of Life and Art*."[53] Voelcker easily could have expanded Banham's list to include artists represented in that essay's illustrations, such as Alberto Burri and Magda Cordell, or whom Banham had mentioned in his text, such as Jean Dubuffet and Karel Appel. Banham himself soon would expand the list in a 1958 essay that claimed New Brutalists admired "with equal fervor peasant houses on Santorin, and the chrome-work on Detroit cars; the *Cutty Sark*, Chiswick house, Camels cigarette packs, and Le Corbusier's chapel at Ronchamp; Pollock, Paolozzi and Volkswagens."[54] In his 1966 book, Banham developed a much fuller discussion of aesthetic sources for New Brutalism, but he avoided any discussion of images or any elaboration of the specific intellectual sources that in 1955 he had called "the general body of anti-Academic aesthetics currently in circulation." Crucially, in both 1955 and 1966 he dismissed Mies as an aesthetic exemplar or source. Yet New Brutalism and the Smithsons' imaging practices emerged in 1953 precisely from a confluence of imaging and Mies when Hunstanton was nearing completion and the Independent Group meetings were beginning to debate a rough constellation of ideas and sources informing "anti-Academic aesthetics." As Banham commented in 1966, even as he disavowed his own earlier ideas, his 1955 essay "retains some validity as a demonstration of the kind of intellectual climate in which discussions of the New Brutalism, and of architecture in general, were conducted in London, by a certain circle, at that time."[55] Many of those intellectual sources are well known—Marshall McLuhan's *The Mechanical Bride* (1951), Paul Klee's *Pedagogical Sketchbook* (1925, English translation 1953), André Malraux's *Le Musée imaginaire* (1947, English translation 1951),[56] László Moholy-Nagy's *Vision in Motion* (1947), and Sigfried Giedion's *Mechanization Takes Command* (1948)—but Banham and the Smithsons were alsoalmost certainly aware of, and likely influenced by, the diverse ideas about imaging advanced by others affiliated with the ICA: Peter Rose Pulham on photography as an art, Humphrey Jennings's documentary films and his notion of "imaginative history," Ernst Gombrich's theories of representation, and Anton Ehrenzweig's psychoanalytic theories of art.[57]

ARRAY 3.5

ARRAY 3.6

3.5

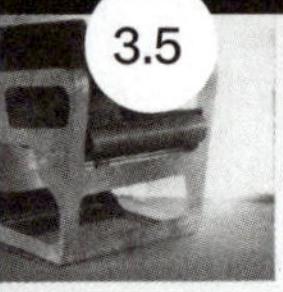

O Charles Niedringhaus, 1939
armchair
ir is one of the most ingenious
which Niedringhaus designed in
tute of Design. It weighs only
and the springiness of the seat
sult of the use of manifold ply-
nding (covered by U.S. patent)

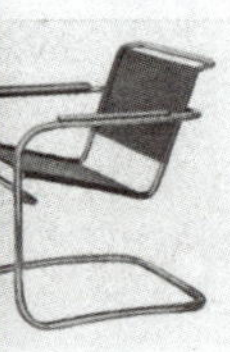

Marcel Breuer, 1926
armchair (constructed from
steel tubing)
material, steel, allowed this two-
olution of a chair, making it par-
advantageous at places where, es-
in a motor car, an extension is
for leg space for the sitter behind
seat. This chair—in contrast to
ions—avoids contact of the body
metal by pulling back the bars at
der and knee, as well as insulat-
rms of the chair with wood. By
the chair's back from cloth or
the spine has a good support
ressure caused by the usual back
hard material

O Jack Waldheim, 1944
armchair in laminated wood
cation of the tubular steel chair
The Institute of Design made
periments for furniture, especially
was found that no chair is satis-
which the position of the sitter
It is a human habit to change
ion of the body after sitting for
Chairs in which such movements
easy should be considered more
eous. Such a chair is illustrated
sing the principle of the wood
vented at the school, see Figs.

Fig. 23. O L. Moholy-Nagy, 1940
Compressed air holds up a chisel, dancing in the air
The shape of things is generally not the result of individual effort but a process of development in the fields of art, science and technology in a certain period for which the designer has an understanding. Thus functions can be solved in different periods with different means. Excellent wooden chairs have been made in previous periods with three and four legs. Today we can make chairs with two legs from tubular steel or plywood, and in the future we may be able to eliminate legs entirely and support the seat with compressed air

disposal. Today new chair forms can be produced, seats with two legs instead of the usual four, and with four joints or none at all in place of the customary forty or fifty. Tomorrow there may be just a seat on a compressed air jet.•

established paths of thought

It appears then that the best designer is the person who knows all contemporary resources and can understand their trend most completely. This goal does not seem to be very difficult to attain. One would think that the present scientific and technological information would speed the application of the potentialities at hand. This, however, turns out to be an illusion. It took a hundred years after plumbing was introduced in the kitchen to create the design of a water kettle that dared to exchange the small spout for a large one, which could be held directly under the faucet, filling the kettle without taking off the lid.

• *Difficulties may arise as far as public acceptance of such revolutionary designs is concerned. The plywood chairs made in the Institute of Design, Chicago, looked so incredibly light that people at first hesitated to use them. A similar reaction retarded the general recognition of the first steel tube chair by Marcel Breuer; and when it was accepted, it was often misused. Steel is a heat conductor. Breuer considered this, and designed his chairs so that the human body did not touch the metal structure. The imitators, copying only the appearance, did not consider this important feature. I recall another incident. In 1916, the police in Rotterdam, Holland, ordered an architect to place two columns under his cantilevered balcony of reinforced concrete, even if he would only make them from cardboard, because "the projection may frighten the public."*

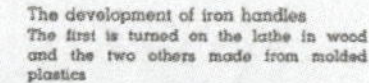

The development of iron handles
The first is turned on the lathe in wood and the two others made from molded plastics

Figs. 24 a, b,
handles, 1941
Since the handl
the designer
principle of ha
of imitating th
handle

The heat-insulated handle of a flatiron shows a similar lag in de
handle was covered with rags, then it was hand-carved from w
the lathe. This handle was then literally translated into plastic
been redesigned in accordance with the properties and mass-pr
of the new material independent of lathe turning.

Figs. 25 a, b. Water kettles
It took 130 years after the introduction of plumbing before a waterkettle-spout was devised, large enough to be filled directly —from faucet to spout—instead of having to take off the lid

LE MUSÉE IMAGINAIRE

Le rôle des musées dans notre relation avec les œuvres d'art est si grand, que nous avons peine à penser qu'il n'en existe pas, qu'il n'en exista jamais, là où la civilisation de l'Europe moderne est ou fut inconnue; et qu'il en existe chez nous depuis moins de deux siècles. Le XIXe siècle a vécu d'eux; nous en vivons encore, et oublions qu'ils ont imposé au spectateur une relation toute nouvelle avec l'œuvre d'art.

⑫ **Exercises**

(based on the Trichotomy):

First organ active (brain),
Second organ medial (muscle),
Third organ passive (bones).

a) **Waterwheel and Hammer** (Fig. 25):

Fig. 25

I The Waterfall (active). II The Wheels (medial). II The Hammer (passive).

Drums of the big wheel. Spokes of the small wheel.

Transmission belt.

b) **The Watermill** (Fi

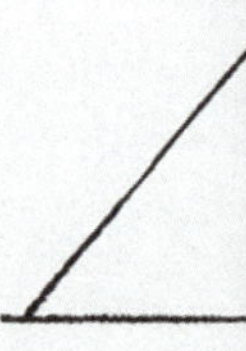

Fig. 26

I Two energies: a) gra
II Diagonal force to en
III The turning wheel (p

320. Rockefeller Center. *Photomontage. Expressions of the new urban scale like Rockefeller Center are forcefully conceived in space-time and cannot be embraced in a single view. To obtain a feeling for their interrelations the eye must function as in the high-speed photographs of Edgerton.*

mous slabs which makes it impossible to bind them rationally together. The Time and Life Building, completed in 1938, has through its free orientation the decisive force of planes separated by air but moved and combined unconsciously by the observing human eye. Out of these well-calculated masses one

becomes aware of a new fantastic element inherent in the space-time conception of our period. The interrelations which the eye achieves between the different planes give the clearly circumscribed volumes an extraordinary new effect, somewhat like that which a rotating sphere of mirrored facets gives to a ballroom when the facets reflect whirling spots of light in all directions and into every dimension.

Space-Time
Rockefeller

Such a great building complex presupposes not the single point of view of the Renaissance but the many-sided approach of our own age. The difference can be indicated by comparing it with such thirteenth-century structures as the leaning towers of the two noble families of Asinelli and Garisenda in Bologna (*fig.* **319**). Private patrician fortresses, they rise up magnificently into the sky, but they can be embraced at a single glance, in a single view. There is no uncertainty in the observer concerning their relation to each other. On the other hand,

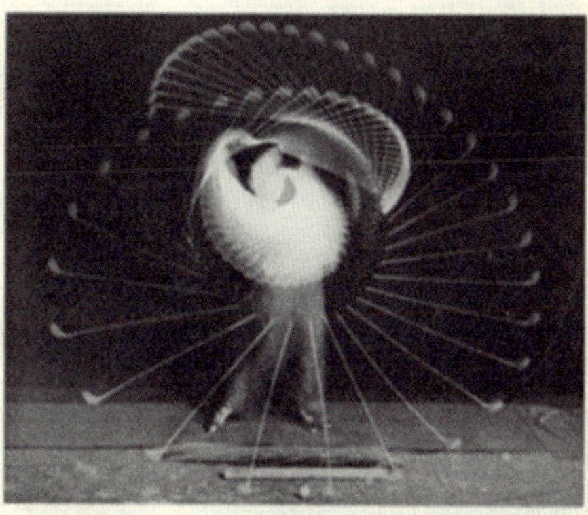

321. EDGERTON, Speed photograph of golf strike. *In Edgerton's stroboscopic studies, in which motions can be fixed and analyzed in arrested fractions of 1/100,000 of a second, a whole movement is separated into its successive components, making possible comprehension in both space and time.*

Iℓ

II

III

ng mountain (active).
Waterfall (medial).

say 'Goodbye, darling . . .' We got every one of the fifteen Japs, and then we hustled to move this kid, but it was too late . . . we pried open his hand, and it held this picture of you—the bullet had gone through it . . ."

Maybe that picture had been torn out of our magazine. We don't know.

But we do know that a *lot* of people see *Modern Screen* every month, overseas and at home.

This month, *millions* of people will look for the exclusive life story we run in each issue . . . and they'll read about the incident of the bullet-pierced picture in our new life story of Betty Grable.

They'll read intimate, private-life items about Betty—anecdotes never before released for publication. They'll see pictures of Betty in many of her great roles—as "Sweet Rosie O'Grady"—as "Pin-up Girl" —and as *herself* . . .

—the girl who is now Mrs. Harry James . . . the girl who works tirelessly, as do other great film stars, for "her boys" at Army camps and canteens and benefits . . . the girl with the "pearl-and-gold" freshness who can talk to anybody and make them love her—yes, and the girl who cried when she got the letter and the picture we've shown you on this page.

We're sure you'll like our October issue of *Modern Screen*. Please *share* your copy—lend it to your friends if their newsstands run short. Although we're printing 1,300,000 copies, these just have to be enough, in these times, to go around.

This blurb accompanying the ad is delivered with the slick aplomb and automatic tones of profound human interest and understanding so necessary to the moving of emotion and merchandise. The meaning of war and the glory of death, we are to suppose, are nobly expressed by this "episode." What is more moving than to think that this soldier fought and died for the fantasies he had woven around the image of Betty Grable? It would be hard to know where to begin to peel back the layers of insentience and calculated oblivion implied in such an ad. And what would be found as one stripped away these layers, each marked with the pattern of sex, technology, and death? Exactly nothing. One is left staring into a vacuum such as is created by the techniques for "developing your executive ability" and found in the philosophies of revolution described in a recent book, *Zero*, by Robert Payne.

The European nihilists were conscious, logical, ar-

ticulate. But the
type, unconscious,
even bigger effect
Mr. Payne, must
self-hatred within
meeting and wou
cultures converge.
ditions of rapid
systematic change

Out of this situa
that send ads like t
meet a somnambu
ically. Otherwise,
in the name of the
An alert and cons
this ad emphatical
publication. The
have been glad to
large sections of
grows.

While junior w
the Pacific, his mo
at home. A news
24, 1946, was capt

MATRONS ASK M

A group of San
the emphasis on
wood to provide
forty."

The organiz
. . . submitted
swer to Van Jo

"We demand
ford, who is v
with the cinema
filmic love to ac
and Greer Gars

The ad and the
the futility of any
solutions to such
"constructive" wh
nosis has been re
very people who
centuate the posit
engaged in the pr

FIG. 2

FIG. 2 Electron-microscope photo of collagen fibrils.
by courtesy of Professor W. T. Astbury, F.R.S. and *The British Journal of Radiology.*

FIG. 3 Electron-microscope photo of earthworm cuticle collagen fibrils.
by courtesy of the Elsevier Publishing Company, Inc. Amsterdam.

FIG. 4 Electron-microscope photo of toad muscle fibrils (*Bufo marinus*)

FIG. 5 Electron-microscope photo of sarcolemma with overlying fibrils.

Figs. 4 and 5 by courtesy of Dr. Draper and *Australian Journal of Experimental Biology and Medical Science.*

FIG. 3

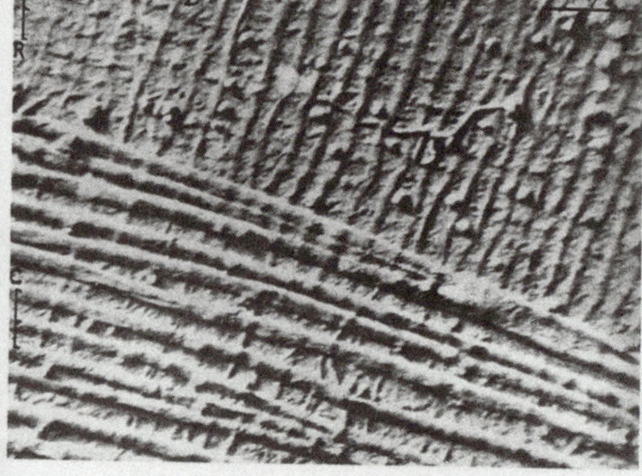

FIG. 4

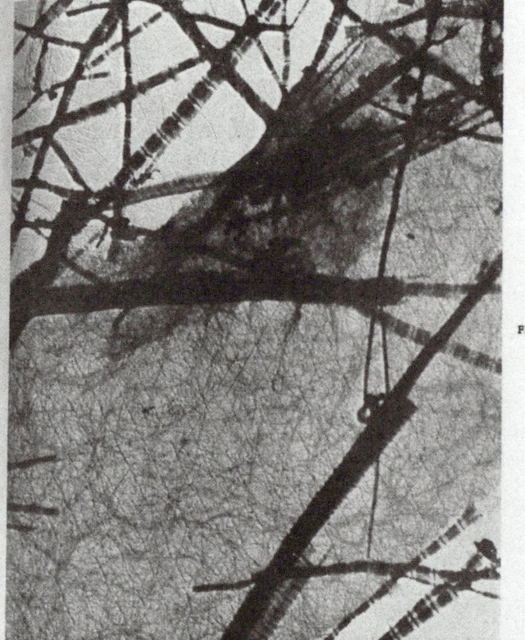

FIG. 5

THE LISTENER JANUARY 24 1952

The Camera and the Artist

By PETER ROSE PULHAM

THE question, whether or not photography is an art, has always seemed to me irritating, meaningless, and beside the point. If photography is used merely as a technical process to record some visible fact, it is an adjunct to science. But if it is used [to] express, since all expression is emotional, selective and personal, it [can]not avoid the use of art.

Art proceeds—it does not progress—by alternate swings of the [pen]dulum. Photography until recently tried to imitate painting. [Le]onardo da Vinci, knowing the principle of the camera-obscura, tried [to] imitate the camera before it was invented. Towards the middle of [the] last century the camera tried to imitate what the painters thought [the] camera could do better than themselves. Towards the end of the [cen]tury the painters began to imitate the camera's defects; Degas, [Mo]net, and Toulouse-Lautrec did that; then the camera started to copy [the] painters' defects, and photographs were made to look like faded [Old] Masters. More recently the photographer has developed a set of [con]ventions of his own, and although these early, mainly German, [atte]mpts are not to my mind very attractive, at least they have severed [the] photograph from painting, have given it autonomy, at any rate for [the] time being.

Nothing is less true than the notion that the camera cannot lie: on [the] contrary, it is incapable of telling the truth, it cannot even reproduce [hu]man vision, and as our idea of human vision is in itself a convention, [a p]hotograph is twice removed from any possible reality; it can only [pre]sent one of the myriad facets of a possible truth. Which facet it [sho]ws depends on the photographer, his attitude both to the camera

Rouen Cathedral: above, as seen by Monet in his painting of 1894; left, in a photograph of about the same date

and to his subject, the mood in which he sees it or the light in which he desires to portray it. A proper comprehension of the possibilities of photography depends, in the first place, on an understanding of the differences between human vision and that of the camera. These are not only mechanical or physical but also intellectual and emotional, for the eye conveys an image to the brain and the lens its image to the film; but whereas the film is passive, and registers finally and without question the instantaneous static image offered to it by the lens, there is always an interplay, a cat's cradle, between the eye and the brain, and between the heart and the head. The eye sees, the brain registers, the mind doubts and questions, the eye quests again, confirms, refutes or modifies its first impression—roves and follows movement and the sequence of events, lingers searching from the heart the character of a face, or is distracted, like a jackdaw by the dazzle of some bright object, or is attracted to a brilliant colour as a bull to a red rag.

The eye sees clearly only the pin-point on which it is momentarily focused; all else, out of the corner of the eye, is vague; but the eye is constantly re-focusing, changing its range from near to far and from far to wide in a hundred darting glances, as quickly as the mind can register the fleeting mobile image: whereas the camera with the fixed stare of its immobile glass eye sees clearly only the objects on the plane

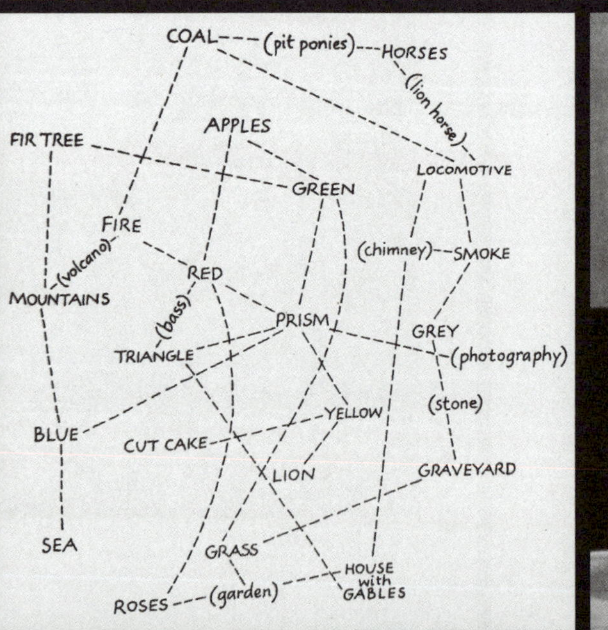

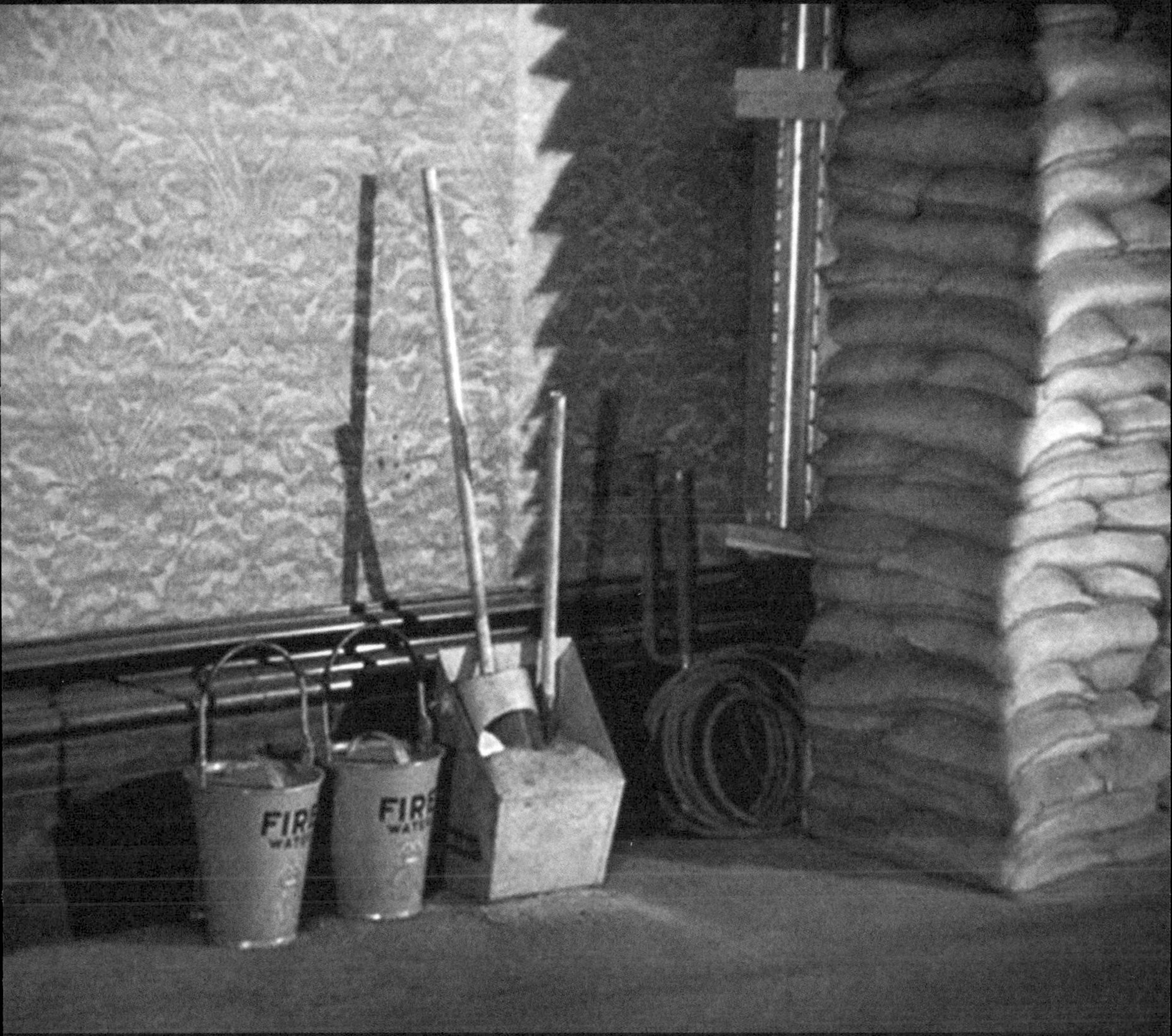

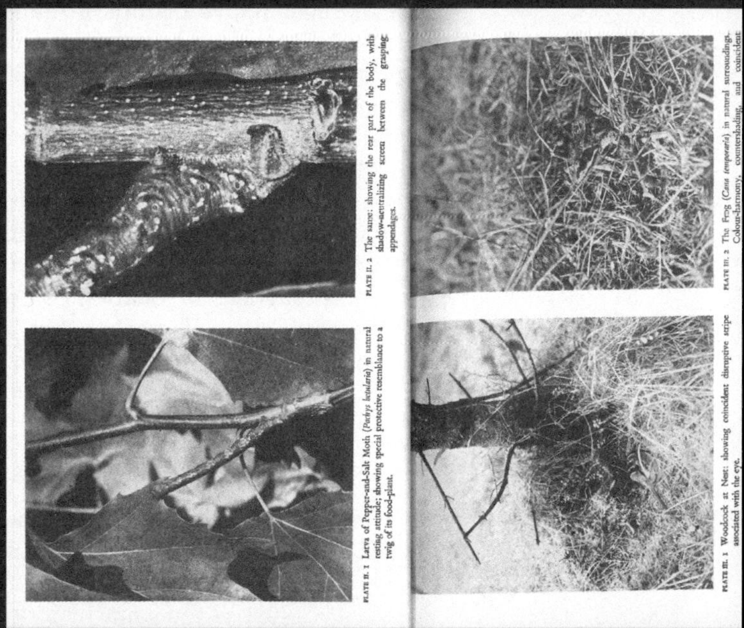

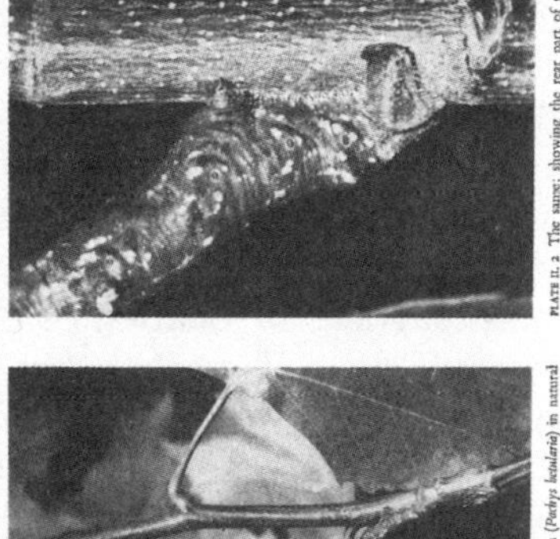

PLATE II. 1 Larva of Pepper-and-Salt Moth (*Pachys betularia*) in natural resting attitude; showing special protective resemblance to a twig of its food-plant.
PLATE II. 2 The same: showing the rear part of the body, with shadow-neutralizing screen between the grasping appendages.

PLATE III. 1 Woodcock at Nest: showing coincident disruptive stripe associated with the eye.
PLATE III. 2 The Frog (*Cana temporaria*) in natural surroundings. Colour-harmony, countershading, and coincident

On January 19, 1952, Pulham presented an influential talk, "The Camera and the Artist," on the BBC's Third Programme, and two months later his provocative ideas were the focus of a panel discussion at the ICA, chaired, somewhat surprisingly, by the architectural historian John Summerson.[58] Pulham had studied architecture at the Architectural Association in the 1920s but turned primarily to painting in 1938 after a brief career as a fashion and portrait photographer. "The Camera and the Artist" focused on the aesthetic affinities and distinctions between painting and photography. Pulham insisted that both mediums facilitate abnormal, and far from objective, vision, and that photography was just as useful for artistic expression as painting. But his contrarian claim was that "a painting can be more realistic than a photograph."[59] He stated: "Nothing is less true than the notion that the camera cannot lie: on the contrary, it is incapable of telling the truth, it cannot even reproduce human vision, and as our idea of human vision is in itself a convention, a photograph is twice removed from any possible reality."[60] In a passage in his notes that he chose not to include in the radio talk or its transcript, he articulated a sensibility closely aligned with the aims of *Parallel of Life and Art*: "Latterly I have been most charmed by really bad Press photographs reproduced through a coarse screen on bad paper; they seem, making an unintentional selection, suppression of detail, much more convincing than the 'see every pore' school."[61]

Jennings was a friend of Nigel Henderson, and in 1951, the year after his accidental death, the ICA staged a show of his Surrealist paintings. But he was better known for making some of the most technically accomplished and formally ambitious documentary films in Britain, such as *Spare Time* (1939) and *Listen to Britain* (1942).[62] As much as Henderson is credited among the four collaborators on *Parallel of Life and Art* for developing their "special use of their word 'image',"[63] Jennings was likely his primary inspiration. Like many close to Jennings, Henderson must have known that he had been at work since 1937 on *Pandaemonium*, a book portraying what he called "the imaginative history of the Industrial Revolution" from 1660 to 1886. The book consisted of a chronologically organized collection of 372 quotations and thirty illustrations, all of which he called "images," along with a thematically organized index with sixteen categories, such as "Poetry and Science," "Miners," "Man-Animal-Machine," "Music and Architecture," and "London." Each image "presents" particular insights into the historical emergence of machines and their effect on society.[64] According to film historian Keith Beattie, "Jennings held that 'the image' (a term he used to refer to unadorned sights capable of bearing referential significance) should not be invented by a filmmaker, but discovered within socio-historical experience."[65] That is also Jennings's approach in *Pandaemonium*, as he explained in the introduction, sounding remarkably like Walter Benjamin in his "Little History of Photography" (1931):

> What I call Images [. . .] contain in little a whole world—they are knots in a great net of tangled time and space—the moments at which the situation of humanity is clear—even if only for the flash of the photographer or lightning. And just as the usual history does not consist of isolated events,

> occurrences—so this "imaginative history" does not consist of isolated images, but each is in a particular place in an unrolling film. [. . .] I do not claim they represent truth—they are too varied, even contradictory, for that. But they represent human experience. They are a record of mental events.[66]

Jennings offered more specific insights into his ideas about photography in a very brief essay in the *London Bulletin* in 1938. His somewhat cryptic remarks were prompted by the National Gallery's decision to begin removing the glass coverings from many of its paintings, which Jennings explained as an acknowledgment of how photography was "breaking down a barrier between the public and the 'sacredness' of images."

> Photography itself—"photogenic drawing"—began simply as the mechanization of realism, and it remains *the* system with which the people can be pictured by the people for the people: simple to operate, results capable of mass reproduction and circulation, effects generally considered truthful ("the camera cannot lie") and so on. But intellectually the importance of the camera lies clearly in the way in which it deals with problems of choice—choice and the avoidance of choice.[67]

Jennings explained the experience of photographing and photographs as analogous to the way Sigmund Freud theorizes déjà vu in *The Psychopathology of Everyday Life* (1901) as an experience that "corresponds to the memory of an unconscious fantasy." For Jennings, "the camera is precisely an instrument for recording the object or image that prompted that memory." Thus photography actualizes Freud's idea of the "impossibility of a voluntarily 'arbitrary' choice or association of objects." By extension, films had the added benefit of linking those involuntary associations, memories, and choices through temporal sequence and montage, as might be inferred from the matrix of "words and images [. . .] with dotted line indications of relationships" that he included as part of the essay.[68]

Gombrich was affiliated with the Warburg Institute in London, and in 1950 had published *The Story of Art*, an accessible and profusely illustrated survey of Western art from prehistory to the twentieth century. His scholarly work advanced an original theory of realism and the conventions of representation that departed from contemporary theories of resemblance or iconography. One of his earliest versions of those ideas, "Meditations on a Hobby Horse, or the Roots of Artistic Form," was published in *Aspects of Form* (1951), a book of essays on "form in nature and art" by distinguished British scientists and intellectuals that was initially intended to serve as the catalogue to Richard Hamilton's *Growth and Form* exhibition at the ICA.[69] The editor Hamilton had chosen, the physicist Lancelot Law Whyte, took the project in a more scholarly direction,[70] yet the range, kinds, and qualities of the images in the book—from scientific diagrams, graphs, and illustrations to diverse types and uses of photography in fields from astronomy to art history—have obvious affinities with the images in *Parallel of Life and Art*. Gombrich's essay, which concludes the book, proposed that every art object operates as an actual, functional image that "substitutes" for something else, in art or in life: "All art is 'image-making' and all image-making is rooted in the creation of substitutes."[71] While Gombrich's central argument in his essay is quite distinct from the imaging interests of the Smithsons, Henderson, and Paolozzi, many of his explanations might be construed as aligned with Jennings's ideas and applicable to the operations and experience of *Parallel of Life and Art*. For example, he writes: "That strange precinct we call 'art' is like a hall of mirrors or a whispering gallery. Each form conjures up a thousand memories or after-images. No sooner is an image presented as art than, by this very act, a new frame of reference is created which it cannot escape."[72] The 122 enlarged images in *Parallel of Life and Art* explicitly demonstrate that idea. Any one image might be replaced by any other in the associative array of figures, textures, patterns, references, and sources, which is as true of the way they were displayed in the gallery space as of the way they were listed in the exhibition catalogue, in eighteen seemingly eccentric categories, the last six of which contained just a single entry each: Anatomy, Architecture, Art, Calligraphy, Date 1901, Landscape, Movement, Nature, Primitive, Scale of Man, Stress, Stress Structure, Football, Science Fiction, Medicine, Geology, Metal, Ceramic.

Ehrenzweig was a colleague of Paolozzi, Henderson, and Peter Smithson at the Central School of Art in the early 1950s. He claimed Gombrich as a mentor and shared his psychological approach to art and theory as well as his skepticism toward generally accepted theories of abstraction and realism. On May 7, 1951, Ehrenzweig gave a lecture at the ICA titled "A Psychoanalytical Evaluation of Abstract Art" that was most likely an introduction to the complex theories in his 1953 book *The Psycho-analysis of Artistic Vision and Hearing* and in his earlier essay "Unconscious Form-Creation in Art" (1948).[73] Ehrenzweig had developed what he called a "new depth-psychological approach to art form," and he credited Gombrich's idea that "our mind [...] works by differentiation rather than generalization" as a basis for his approach.[74] For Ehrenzweig, both aesthetic and ordinary experience require a shuttling between the "unbeautiful gestalt-free vision of the unconscious" and the surface perception of recognizable forms (a basic framework that has been affirmed but radically recast in recent neuroscience): "one refers to strong repressions, the other to strong articulations, both called up by displacements of mental energy between different layers of perception."[75] Like Gombrich, Ehrenzweig's theories are directly applicable to *Parallel of Life and Art*, especially his comments on how spatial perception is generated by the constant interplay between stable surface images and an "unconscious storm of [inarticulate] images"[76] as well as his explanations of how that dialectic can be manipulated with double exposures in photography and by movements of the camera in film.

The theories of Pulham, Jennings, Gombrich, and Ehrenzweig represent varied aspects of the range of thinking about imaging that was circulating around and through the Independent Group meetings. Their ideas and those of others' provided viable alternatives to intellectual trends in postwar British architecture, such as the neo-Palladian enthusiasms that followed Rudolf Wittkower's analyses of symbolic form, the fascination with proportions and mathematics inspired by Le Corbusier's Modulor or Colin Rowe's Neoclassical formal analogies, Richards's insistence on allying modernism with typically British cultural values, Pevsner's and the *Architectural Review*'s promotion of the Picturesque, or Gordon Cullen's techniques of townscape.[77] As Banham made clear in his appeal for *une architecture autre*, or as the Smithsons suggested by characterizing their work as an attempt to pursue "a random aesthetic" or to access "another visual world,"[78] New Brutalism was an exercise in speculative imagination, with its most generative sources and aspirations largely outside the culture of architectural design, history, and criticism. While there are competing assessments of New Brutalism's radicality and influence within architecture, or its peculiar importance as an event in the history of modern architecture and modernism generally, the more necessary and useful questions about the significance of New Brutalism require scrutiny of how architecture was defined and situated in the broader intellectual and popular culture. As Mark Wigley aptly explains the Smithsons' attitude, "Along with their friends, they tried to tune in to the messy energy and gritty material sensuality of the physical and cultural landscape, rejecting every disciplinary and aesthetic limit, opening up the discourse to a wider and wider terrain of objects, images, films and sounds."[79] The ongoing debates, disagreements, and alternative understandings of New Brutalism hinge on how that transdisciplinary field is mapped, and especially on how the architectural significance of New Brutalism is characterized in distinction from, or in alliance with, its significance in art.

Many architectural critics and historians argue that New Brutalism should be understood not as an aesthetic expansion of architecture but as a specific recalibration of architectural values. Irénée Scalbert, who incisively discusses the specific historical relationships between postwar art and New Brutalism, concludes that any substantive exchanges with art were temporary dalliances, in one direction only, with little lasting or useful impact. He recounts how Paolozzi and Henderson introduced the Smithsons and Banham to contemporary Parisian artists and theories, such as Dubuffet's *art brut* and Michel Tapié's *art autre* (both of which were referenced by Banham and were clearly manifest in the sensibility of *Parallel of Life and Art*), but insists that an architecture derived from those aesthetic sources could be no more than "an irresistible conceit and a fascinating paradox." Thus, in agreement with Banham's 1966 conclusions, Scalbert declares that New Brutalism "lasted as long as the collaboration between Paolozzi, Henderson and the Smithsons did. By 1956 [. . .] Brutalism had been spent and the ideology of the modern movement [. . .] became once again determinant in the work of the architects. The demise of Brutalism may have been inevitable. [. . .] Brutalist architecture was an impossible aspiration—like Surrealist architecture [. . .] or Dadaist architecture."[80]

The art historian Alex Kitnick offers a more generous accounting of the transdisciplinary potential of New Brutalism and *Parallel of Life and Art*. Rather than seeing New Brutalism as dependent on or derivative of specific theories or movements in art, Kitnick suggests there was a shared approach among New Brutalists centered on the directness and tangibility of imaging as a productive and meaningful way to engage a changing world:

> The concrete reality of both art and architecture were understood to be fundamentally connected to a world of mediated images, as well as a sundry assortment of cast-off things. [. . .] New Brutalist images lodged in the brain because they had something thing-like about them. [. . .] If New Brutalism in both its artistic and architectural incarnations sought to incorporate the diversity of the world, to compress it and forge it into an image, it also sought to extend outwards, to make plain the systems of circulation and communication that structure life—and it is here that its concerns become more explicitly architectural.[81]

The architectural manifestations of those concerns were hardly confined to buildings or urban designs. The emphasis on imaging engendered an extended range of architectural practices that were crucial to the Smithsons, including the designs of numerous books and exhibitions, but it is especially evident in Alison's lesser-known and varied pursuits, such as her "sensibility primers" and especially her handmade Christmas cards, which were so important to her that she added handwritten notes describing each year's design to a saved set of loose pages cut from the *Arena* monograph.[82] Photographs of many of those Christmas cards and other related "ephemera," such as posters, invitations, and collages, appear on multiple pages of *The Shift* as crucial sources and evidence of the Smithsons' evolving aesthetic. They are described variously as prototypes and tests of the "soft graphics" they developed for project presentations or as "mood carriers" that conveyed complex effects, values, and meanings analogous to those of "the stuff and decoration of the urban scene."[83] Studies of Alison's Christmas cards and the Smithsons' exhibition designs by Ana Ábalos Ramos offer the most extensive and deep analysis of the ways seemingly marginal work was crucial to the development of their sensibility: "Just as the Smithsons made no distinction between writing and building, they distinguished even less between architecture and exhibition, or between reality and dreams when illustrating and materializing their thoughts."[84]

The range and variety of the Smithsons' imaging practices were a way to, in their words, "activate, not merely support, the dressing and interpretation of things and places."[85] Their persistent production of, and insistence on the significance of, work that was "not quite architecture" inspired M. Christine Boyer's historical method for analyzing and understanding their diverse and divergent intentions and ideas. Boyer describes her approach as "a different slant on the materiality of history, on the encounter between persons and objects, landscapes, animals, roads, climate, and buildings. Language, the experience of objects, time and tradition—all become entangled one with another, requiring a flexible, associative, and many-layered form of reading."[86] While Boyer is primarily concerned with all manner of writing, from private notes to essays to books—"received words that must be read as fully as possible"[87]—her approach can be extended and refocused to scrutinize the Smithsons' imaging practices as material that is similarly "not quite architecture" and, perhaps even more than their writing, is crucial to the production and presentation of all of their work and their ongoing development of an aesthetic. It is necessary to understand those practices and materials, and the altered and elevated status of imaging in the broader culture of the second half of the twentieth century as it was examined in philosophy, psychology, and aesthetics or as it was explored in movies, magazines, advertising, and television, to understand what the Smithsons "were all up to" in the 1950s and especially after.

That approach cuts against a more prevalent understanding of the Smithsons' thinking that prioritizes their designs for buildings and cities as the only fully adequate exemplification of their interests. Dirk van den Heuvel, one of the most eloquent advocates of that position, argues that the increasing divergence between the Smithsons and Banham in the late 1950s hinges on differing understandings of the meaning of image and a consequent "falling out [. . .] over Pop and the possibility of a Pop architecture."[88] He maintains that while a fascination with images was a key aspect of New Brutalism, it was never "a central notion" for the Smithsons: "They would rather talk about patterns and clusters, geometries and textures, processes, traces and remembrances. They were looking for structures or systems beyond the singular image or the 'sheer visual'."[89] The questions one might ask, however, are how and why do "structures and systems" go "beyond the singular image or the 'sheer visual'"? Why isn't "talk about patterns and clusters, geometries and textures, processes, traces and remembrances" the best evidence of a fascination with imaging? For Van den Heuvel, "structures" were required for the Smithsons to achieve their "ambition to redesign precisely the system of relationships between the everyday, domestic life, labour and the larger society, including the production and circulation of 'images'."[90] He does not fully embrace imaging practices as substantive or consequential research into, manipulations of, or interventions in "relationships or systems," and he argues that "image" was simply one of many important ideas or terms that the Smithsons favored: "combined notions of form and formlessness, of image and movement, of material and experience, of process, finding processes and the As Found, are key to the aesthetics and aesthetic procedures as proposed by the Smithsons."[91] Van den Heuvel believes that was always the case for the Smithsons, from New Brutalism in the 1950s to their thinking in the 1980s when they proposed "the redefinition of architecture and the urban as the creation of purely sensorial environments, of 'built-places' (and not buildings) that go beyond the sheer visual."[92] Here again, "beyond" is the symptomatic word. Van den Heuvel's emphatic and simple distinction between the environmental robustness of the "built" and the experiential limitations of the "sheer visual" relegates images and imaging practices to a lesser status than conventional design approaches, and justifies his insistence that "the Smithsons defined New Brutalism by laying emphasis on the material qualities of architecture and the aspects of process and making in architectural construction."[93]

That claim leads Van den Heuvel to make some stark distinctions between the Brutalist image and the Pop image, between architecture and art, and between the Smithsons and Banham.[94] While he does not analyze the coherence of Banham's theorization of image (and does not adequately distinguish between the ways the positions of the Smithsons or Banham changed from the 1950s into the 1960s), his claims draw attention to several important yet incomplete formulations in the ways Banham explained the significance of image in "The New Brutalism," which continue to trouble discussion of New Brutalism. The heart of Van den Heuvel's argument is a rejection of what he calls "the Banham Hypothesis": the historical presumption that "Brutalism and Pop must have belonged to the same project, at least in the mid-1950s."[95] But Banham arrived at that position gradually over the next ten years in tandem (and in competition) with others, especially Lawrence Alloway and Richard Hamilton, and eventually rejected it.[96] In 1955 Banham was developing his own version of the Independent Group ideas that only later would come to be understood as the genesis of Pop, and it was not until the early 1960s that Banham would begin to accuse the Smithsons of refusing to take Pop seriously and abandoning the potential he saw in their House of the Future (1956). In any case, Banham's criticism of the Smithsons was not based on a different understanding of image, even if they indeed had differences. His understanding of Pop evolved from other interests—in industrial design, mass-produced products, and technological culture—and a different understanding of their impact on the future of architecture.[97] Most important, Banham never embraced the Pop image in the sense Van den Heuvel defines it.[98] His concerns were directed toward engaging the rapidly evolving realities and values of what he called the Second Machine Age. His ideas about Pop, like most of his writing, developed as an intervention in ongoing debates among architects and in the broader intellectual culture. As Alex Potts explains, Banham and the New Brutalists were negotiating competing impulses between high and low culture, between technical solutions and trendy enthusiasms, between permanence and expendability:

> Banham's writing on architecture and design plays out something very real in 1950s and 1960s culture, as does the interplay in Paolozzi's art between the virtuality of the electronic screen and the hard substance of the metal machine part, the clean styling of the ultra-new and the junk heap of disused and discarded manufactured things. The cultural reality within which Banham and Paolozzi were working was one in which a pop going with the swim was neither more nor less distinctively modern than a fascination with archaic survivals or bloody-minded resistance to consumer demand. Their responsiveness to these heterogeneous and at times conflicting currents testifies to a critical awareness on their part that any valid modern art needed to engage both with [the] consumerist logic of popular visual culture and the anti-consumerist imperatives of a quasi-brutalist high art.[99]

Thus, for both Pop and New Brutalism an image was not simply something to be exchanged or consumed as a product, or to be read and interpreted symbolically or semantically; it was a "visual entity" that could be manipulated and deployed to accentuate and exploit the evasive effects and affects of media representation.

The difficulty of operating within this complex, intertwined condition is apparent in the unresolved, multifaceted way Banham presented his argument for images in "The New Brutalism." He oscillated between a fascination with images as the basis of a generalized "anti-Academic aesthetics" that was "anti-art, or at any rate anti-beauty," and a more specifically architectural proposition that imageability should supersede formality—that a building should be memorable as an image, "should be an immediately apprehensible visual entity, and that the form grasped by the eye should be confirmed by the experience of the building in use."[100] The first, more general, meaning of image is indeed indebted to discussions of aesthetics among the Independent Group (but it is far from either a proto-Pop theory or a celebration of the "single image" or the "sheer visual"), while the second, specifically architectural, meaning is surprisingly close to the visuality of the roving spectator advanced by advocates of the Picturesque and townscape (even as it is intently antagonistic toward both). In "The New Brutalism," Banham was waging a battle on at least two fronts. On the one hand, he was attempting to develop a general theory of New Brutalist aesthetics that could "bridge the gap" between its meaning in architecture and in art; on the other hand, he wanted to distinguish New Brutalism from other understandings of modern architecture that pervaded "the seriously decayed condition in English architectural standards," whether that was the "doldrum of routine-functionalist abdications" in contemporary practice, such as the machine aesthetic, casual form-making, or composition, or whether that was Pevsner's and the *Architectural Review*'s advocacy of the Picturesque as a specifically English source for modernism that might be amenable to the tastes of the journal's readers.[101] Banham's multifaceted argument was thus as much a tactical counterattack on the conventional wisdom of his contemporaries as a strategic attempt to defend or support New Brutalism with sophisticated historical or theoretical explanations—ones that he never fully developed and eventually abandoned.

Banham's clearest points in "The New Brutalism" cleverly and indirectly engaged debates in architectural history, especially the ideas of Pevsner and Wittkower. This is noted by Van den Heuvel, who claims that "the Brutalist image was related to the conceptual or *concetto*" as used by Wittkower to explain how geometric organization was used in Renaissance design as a manipulable and meaningful diagrammatic device: "The Brutalist image is close to a direct manifestation of architectural (or artistic) principles of ordering. This is unlike the Pop image, which celebrates its qualities of surface and exchangeability in the flow of images."[102] Van den Heuvel does not offer specific examples or explanations of either type of image, but his position seems to suggest that Wittkowerian "principles of ordering" are manifested in the kinds of diagrammatic or graphic techniques that appear in the Smithsons' work of the time, ranging
ARRAY 3.7 from the overtly Wittkowerian diagrams for their entry in the Coventry Cathedral competition, to the layout of the CIAM Grille, to the sections, diagrams, and collages for the Golden Lane competition, to the early "Sources" drawing of the installation scheme for *Parallel of Life and Art*. All those examples resonate with Wittkower's ideas and prioritize an approach to spatial organization in which "sheer visual" attention or focus on the "single image" is disrupted or distributed by framing or juxtaposition. In that way, they exemplify Van den Heuvel's argument that the central aim of New Brutalism was "the search for a

3.7

It was necessary in the early '50's to look to the works of painter Pollock and sculptor Paolozzi for a complete image system, for an order with a structure and a certain tension, where every piece was correspondingly new in a new system of relationships.
It is our thesis that for every form of association there is an inherent pattern of building.
The first study was at the relatively simple level of association—the village. It concerned itself with 'infill'—the placing of new dwellings in and around the old village in such a way as to revalidate the existing pattern.
Typical addition to a village irrespective of location
Above: West Burton, Yorkshire.
URBAN
STRUCTURING
STUDIES OF
ALISON & PETER
SMITHSON
Studio Vista: London
Reinhold Publishing Corporation: New York
HOUSE
STREET

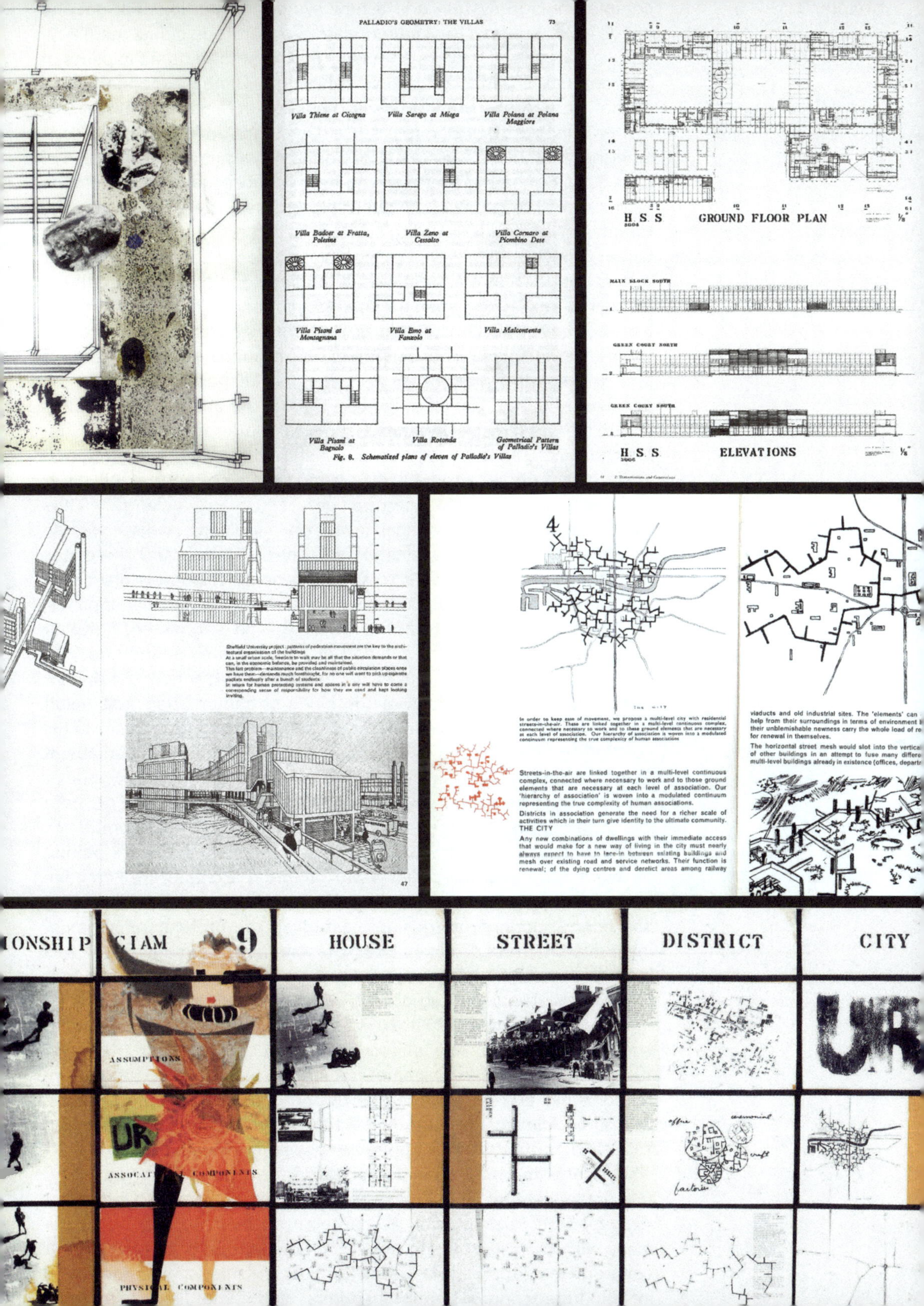

PALLADIO'S GEOMETRY: THE VILLAS
73
Villa Thiene at Cicogna
Villa Sarego at Miega
Villa Poiana at Poiana Maggiore
Villa Badoer at Fratta, Polesine
Villa Zeno at Cessalto
Villa Cornaro at Piombino Dese
Villa Pisani at Montagnana
Villa Emo at Fanzolo
Villa Malcontenta
Villa Pisani at Bagnolo
Villa Rotonda
Geometrical Pattern of Palladio's Villas
Fig. 8. Schematized plans of eleven of Palladio's Villas
H.S.S.
GROUND FLOOR PLAN
MAIN BLOCK SOUTH
GREEN COURT NORTH
GREEN COURT SOUTH
H.S.S.
ELEVATIONS
Sheffield University project: patterns of pedestrian movement are the key to the architectural organisation of the buildings
At a small urban scale, freedom to walk may be all that the situation demands or that can, in the economic balance, be provided and maintained.
This last problem—maintenance and the cleanliness of public circulation places once we have them—demands much forethought, for no one will want to pick up cigarette packets endlessly after a bunch of students.
In return for human protecting systems and spaces in a city will have to come a corresponding sense of responsibility for how they are used and kept looking inviting.
47
4
In order to keep ease of movement, we propose a multi-level city with residential streets-in-the-air. These are linked together in a multi-level continuous complex, connected where necessary to work and to these ground elements that are necessary at each level of association. Our hierarchy of association is woven into a modulated continuum representing the true complexity of human associations
Streets-in-the-air are linked together in a multi-level continuous complex, connected where necessary to work and to those ground elements that are necessary at each level of association. Our 'hierarchy of association' is woven into a modulated continuum representing the true complexity of human associations.
Districts in association generate the need for a richer scale of activities which in their turn give identity to the ultimate community.
THE CITY
Any new combinations of dwellings with their immediate access that would make for a new way of living in the city must nearly always expect to have to lace-in between existing buildings and mesh over existing road and service networks. Their function is renewal; of the dying centres and derelict areas among railway
viaducts and old industrial sites. The 'elements' can
help from their surroundings in terms of environment
their unblemishable newness carry the whole load of re
for renewal in themselves.
The horizontal street mesh would slot into the vertica
of other buildings in an attempt to fuse many differe
multi-level buildings already in existence (offices, depart
ONSHIP
CIAM
9
HOUSE
STREET
DISTRICT
CITY
ASSUMPTIONS
UR
ASSOCIAT AL COMPONENTS
offices
ceremonial
craft
factories
PHYSICAL COMPONENTS

complete image system and a new system of relationship; not the image itself, but how to accommodate the multitude of images."[103]

Van den Heuvel's emphasis on the architectonic aspects of "conceptual" organizing systems draws upon Banham's repeated use of that word in one brief but crucial section of "The New Brutalism." But he misconstrues Banham's intent, which is understandable considering the muddled grammar of Banham's argument in that part of the essay. Banham introduced the term "conceptual" not to build on Wittkower's ideas (which he generally spurned, while the Smithsons found uses for them[104]) but to critique its pejorative use by others for whom "conceptual" implied excessive intellectual sophistication or formal abstraction. Banham was defending sophistication in general as well as endorsing specific intellectual approaches, whether that be "the New Art-History"[105] or contemporary aesthetics and design theory. He was placing himself in a middle ground between Wittkower and those with pragmatic or empiricist dispositions, whom he accused of using "the meaningless phrase 'the conceptual building' [...] to defend the substandard architectural practices of the routine-functionalists, as if 'conceptual buildings' were something new, and something faintly reprehensible in modern architecture. All great architecture has been 'conceptual,' has been image-making."[106] Thus Banham's shrewd theoretical, even philosophical swerve was to redefine "conceptual" as "imageable." That is clear in the sentences that followed, where the scare quotes around the word were discarded and Banham, presumably satisfied he had vanquished his enemies, proceeded with that alternative meaning and suggested, however implicitly and obliquely, that image-making requires a kind of cognition or an aesthetics distinct from geometric abstraction, the pursuit of beauty, the Picturesque, or the kinds of composition that result from pragmatic functionalism. He was also betting, as is clear in his concluding footnote, and clearly influenced in this case by Independent Group discussions, that imageability might be a more popular concept than formality (Wittkower) and a more progressive concept than the Picturesque (Pevsner). While his language was sometimes awkward and his arguments somewhat truncated, Banham's pairing of two broad historical claims—that "all great architecture has been image-making" and "every great building of the Modern Movement has been a conceptual design"—establish the pretext for his most inventive theoretical claim: that the concept of imageability was indeed "something new," especially when used in a "bloody-minded" New Brutalist way to integrate "structure, function and form."[107]

Banham wrote "The New Brutalism" in the months after what would turn out to be the final Independent Group meeting in August 1955. One year earlier, Banham's role in the group had changed from its convener and de facto leader to one of its leading contributors. Lawrence Alloway had assumed Banham's role as convener early in 1955 and soon after was appointed assistant director of the ICA,[108] while Banham had begun to focus on his own writing, including the completion of his dissertation, and his work as an editor at *Architectural Review*, even as he began to work closely but informally with the director, Herbert Read, on various publications.[109] A competitive relationship between Banham and Alloway had developed in the Independent Group meetings, and "The New Brutalism" has to be read as Banham's attempt to distinguish and clarify his position on popular culture and contemporary design from Alloway's.[110] According to the Smithsons, Banham's aim as convener of the Independent Group's 1953–54 seminar series, "Aesthetic Problems of Contemporary Art," had been to "study Techniques," and it was only "in 1955, [when] it was convened by Laurence [*sic*] Alloway and John McHale," that the discussion began to focus on "the relationship of the fine arts and popular art."[111]

Banham also was striving to distinguish his understanding of the modern movement from that of his dissertation adviser Pevsner. In "The New Brutalism" and especially in the language he used in other important essays that year, such as "The Machine Aesthetic"—"symbolic content," "new iconography"—and "Vehicles of Desire"—"symbolic iconographies"—it is evident that Banham remained committed to the methods of architectural history that he had learned from Pevsner and others, even as his evaluative criteria and ideas were radical departures.[112] The circulated description of his March 1955 presentation to the Independent Group of "Borax, or the Thousand Horse-Power Mink" (an early version of a public lecture that he presented again one month later at the ICA titled "Metal in Motion") includes one strikingly Pevsneresque claim about the general acceptance of the "anti-Purist but eye-catching vocabulary"[113] of Detroit automobile design: "Borax is popular art, as well as a *universal style* (in US not in Europe)."[114] But it seems Banham saw refuting the Picturesque as his most urgent challenge, given Pevsner's influence at the *Architectural Review* and in his numerous BBC talks, the most famous of which, the Reith Lectures (seven radio talks and one televised film), were given during the two months before "The New Brutalism" was published.[115] Pevsner's lectures were edited and published as the book *The Englishness of English Art* (1956), which was also the title of the film. His conclusion, in the book, the film, and the lectures, was "a bit of propaganda"[116] championing the Picturesque as a source and model for both national and modern sensibilities as well as design principles for modern architecture and urbanism. Pevsner's advocacy of Picturesque planning had been the more explicit and programmatic topic of an earlier radio talk in January 1954 (a response to Basil Taylor's talks two months prior attacking the *Architectural Review* for promoting a "Picturesque Revival"), which he published, in a significantly reformulated version, as the essay "C20 Picturesque" in the April 1954 issue of the *Architectural Review*. Pevsner defended the Picturesque as both a confirmation of, and a corrective for, modern architecture that emerged in the 1920s "with its free grouping artfully contrived, landscape and building seen as a unity, and care for textures, for surfaces, for finesses of all kind."[117] The Picturesque was also an antidote or alternative to "academic rule of thumb, within whose straight-jacket architecture was confined before the modern movement set it free" by enabling the "free exercise of the imagination stimulated by the disciplines of function and technique."[118] While Banham mentioned neither Pevsner nor the Picturesque in "The New Brutalism," it is not difficult to imagine his introduction of topology as a sly modification of and strategic swerve from Pevsner's appeal to Picturesque landscapes as an implicitly topographic model for contemporary architecture and urban planning, or to read "The New

Brutalism" as an attempt to advance a theory that could claim the higher modernist ground.[119] As Anthony Vidler writes, in support of the idea that Banham was in dialogue with Pevsner, topology can be seen as "a renewed 'picturesque' version of the architectural image and its new technological and material needs [which] would be, for Banham, at least a contingent solution to the impasse of modernist formalism."[120]

Fig. 4

Another compelling affinity between contemporary art and architecture appears in *St Just* (1952–53), a large painting by the modernist British painter of landscapes Peter Lanyon inspired by the Cornwall town with that name which, was the site of a famous 1919 mining disaster. In a letter, Lanyon said of the painting: "I think I have at last painted a picture with no colour like glass." In fact, he had made several glass constructions as studies for the painting, which presents a greenish field cut vertically by a black gash that is both an image of a mineshaft and Christ on the cross. Margaret Garlake describes one of the glass constructions as "a vertiginous edifice, like a house of cards, or fragile sheets of plain glass, held together with Bostik and balanced around an empty centre." The construction has uncanny affinities both with Banham's account of *Figures in a Landscape* and Nigel Henderson's photographs of Hunstanton with its glazing newly installed.

An earlier, more direct attempt by Banham to take on Picturesque theory, and perhaps his most significant statement of an emerging interest in imaging, appeared in the *Architectural Review* two months after Pevsner's "C20 Picturesque." His essay "Object Lesson"[121] was ostensibly a review of *Figures in a Landscape* (1953), a film by Dudley Shaw Ashton that presented Barbara Hepworth's abstract sculptures as seemingly alien objects placed in various settings around Cornwall, such as a garden, a beach, or a hillside. "Object Lesson" was an extension into architecture of the art criticism Banham had been writing for *Art News and Review* since 1950 (his last contribution would be "Art in British Advertising," in November 1955). He argued not only that Hepworth's sculptures offered post-Surrealist lessons about the "particular status of the man-made object in the landscape" but also that those lessons could be a truly modern and presumably post-Picturesque "guide to the siting of buildings" (Fig. 4). But Banham's most provocative and emphatic claim was that "the visual memorability of the screen image" could educate the public most effectively about modernism because it "suggests a way of opening the eyes of those who are blind to the arts of seeing, by offering them simple aesthetic forms under conditions—those of the cinema—where their visual faculties are most alert and receptive."[122] Banham believed that the experience of film magnified the "affective and highly emotive" qualities of any artificial object when placed in an "open-air" setting and demonstrated how those lessons were equally valid for sculpture and architecture,[123] thus anticipating his idea in "The New Brutalism" that image is an aesthetic concept that bridges architecture and art, as well as offering his alternative to Pevsner's theory of the unification of modern art and design. "That one can transfer the experience of sculpture to the large scale experience of architecture in this way, without travestying either art, is a tribute to the essential coherence of the Modern Movement," he wrote.[124] Banham's introduction of the importance of affect and emotion in "Object Lesson" also anticipates the way he would define image in "The New Brutalism" as something "*quod visum perturbat*—that which seen, affects the emotion," as opposed to Thomas Aquinas's "*quod visum placet*—that which seen, pleases" as the experience of beauty.[125]

The distinctive graphic layout of "Object Lesson" visually conveys the imaging lessons Banham was professing: the brief essay's unusually large typeface is interrupted by arrays of stills from the film that are set tight to alternating edges of the page.[126] The grouped images, captions, and empty spaces produce an irregular, interlocking pattern of text and image, of positive and negative blocks. A similar montage strategy appears on the cover of the issue, which also features a series of stills from the film. It would be used yet again later that year in the journal's publication of the Hunstanton School—a now famous series of six images arrayed vertically but oscillating between the right and left sides of the page in an interlocking pattern to convey a cinematic sense of shots taken while moving around the main building, and meant to be distinct from the compositional photographs and drawings that appeared in *Architectural Review* to illustrate the sensibility of the Picturesque or townscape. The montage device would appear yet again on the page opposite the beginning of "The New Brutalism," where seven photographs depict Ronchamp at multiple scales and angles in an attempt to present the building as an ostensibly sculptural object in the landscape that, like Hepworth's sculptures, exemplified Banham's topological theory of space and
ARRAY 3.8
movement.[127] For Banham, the moving image as viewed on a screen or as emulated in graphic design not only simulated spatial experience in architecture; it also stimulated his own heightened, even salacious and decidedly masculine, imagination in "Object Lesson":

> The film is suggestive with its sequences of penetration [. . .] and of progressive involvement with the interior economy of sculptures, for it reminds us that the key view of any building is that of the man who approaches it with the intention of entering it, and that the moment of truth—in any concept of building other than pure facade-making—is the instant when, with one foot still on the pavement and the other on the doormat, he involves himself in its interior economy.[128]

In the final paragraphs of the essay, Banham formulates another evocative image of imaging that would reappear in "The New Brutalism," but only as a faint echo:

> As in quantum physics, where the thing observed and the observer establish, by their presence, a field of relationships

3.8

replace them with the geometrical solids of Paul Nash, neat and clean as machine products, and one has at once a heightened sense of the essential incongruity of Man, the intruder in the landscape, whose pleasure and compulsion is, as Le Corbusier once accidentally defined it, to *faire de la géometrie sous les arbres.* Geometry may be regarded as the key to Nature, but it is a man-made key, and its terrestrial existence reveals the presence of Man as surely as the footprint on the shore of Crusoe's Island. And its relative purity is a sign of his recent presence.

Paul Nash made only passing reference to this subject in a long campaign of object evaluation, in which more time was devoted, with proper Englishry, to the incongruity of the Nature object in a man-made setting, the tree-root in the art gallery, and the worn pebble on the mantelpiece. But these latter are only pathetic exiles, robin redbreasts in aesthetic cages, whereas the man-made object in the landscape is a pioneer outpost, a gesture of defiance in the face of that universal entropy from which human culture has been painfully won. Since his time the subject has remained open but uninvestigated, though it was a sufficiently commonplace war-time experience to see this relationship between ships and the empty wastes of sea, between aircraft and the undifferentiated acres of an aerodrome. But now the aesthetic aspect of the problem has been reopened by a new film of Barbara Hepworth's sculpture in its Cornish landscape setting.* Here one sees forcefully demonstrated the greater persuasiveness of the new-made object, and the difference between any man-made object and any natural one. One sees how much more affective upon human emotion is the perforated sculpture than the perforated rock, and the relative degree to which these affective emotions are stirred by the perforated sculpture, clean, new made, hand made, and the perforated megalith or dolmen, old, tempest-bitten and never so pure in form as the sculpture.

1 2

Whatever their formal similarities, the hand-made perforated sculpture, 1, and the nature-perforated rock, 2, do not play upon our human emotions in the same way—the new-made object, 3, affects us more immediately than man-worked stones, 4 and 5, which, under the action of wind and weather, have become compromised by natural forces.

The introduction of these affective and highly emotive objects into the landscape alters values all round. The object itself becomes far more provocative than it would be in a man-made setting, while the relative values of all the other objects in the landscape are resolved and altered. Correspondences are established, not only between one

* *Figures in a Landscape*, directed by Dudley Shaw Ashton for the British Film Institute.

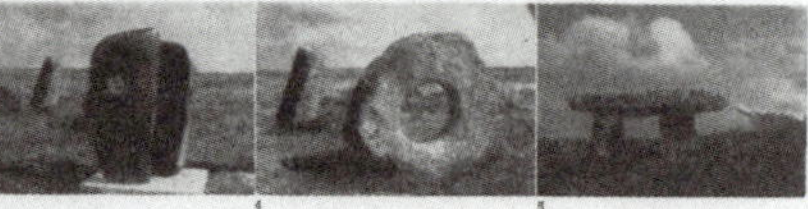
3 4 5

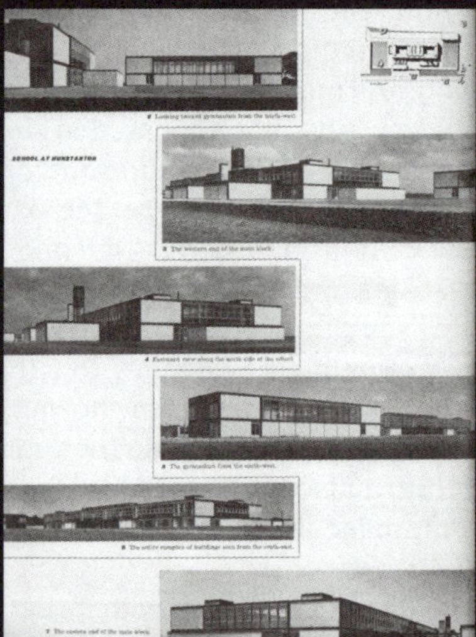

, but between the sculpture and other man-made objects, such as ' china-clay spoil-tips—artefact signals to artefact across the in-ature. Or in a scene where human significance was previously attered timbers of a groyne, the introduction of the uncorroded geometry of the sculptured object dismisses anything which has been compromised by the action of natural forces to a secondary plane of interest. 'Time claims them for the landscape' as the film commentary says.

The lessons which these objects have to teach us have, presumably, been known to every great designer who ever put an object into a landscape with conspicuous success—whether that object was a Pyramid, or the Eiffel Tower, or S. M. della Consolazione at Todi. But the film brings us down to the level of a basic primer, since it offers three different kinds of abstract objects only—new, time-worn, and natural—in various kinds of abstract landscapes. These lessons must be conned and comprehended before one is really fitted to put more complex objects, such as water-towers or office-blocks, into man-compromised landscapes

ape, the man-made object at once ets, whether aesthetic, 6, or indus- human attention had once been artefacts, 8, the new-made object, minishes the status of the old, 10.

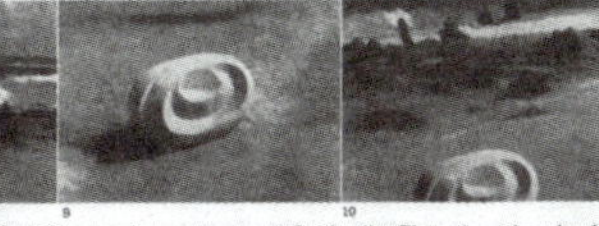

9 10

fordshire or the area east of St. Paul's. There is a time in the any construction when it must be considered as an abstract n relationship to a landscape or town-scape setting, and in rela-ole and obligatory viewpoints from which it may be seen. Here estive with its sequences of penetration (on this month's cover) volvement with the interior economy of sculptures, for it ey view of any building is that of the man who approaches it entering it, and that the moment of truth—in any concept of re façade-making—is the instant when, with one foot still on the er on the doormat, he involves himself in its interior economy. fer the experience of sculpture to the large scale experience of ay, without travestying either art, is a tribute to the essential

In the chapel of Notre Dame du Haut *at Ronchamp, Le Corbusier is generally felt to have achieved one of the most personal and surprising buildings of his career. In the first flurry of excitement at its unexpected forms, consternation has been expressed at the way a master of logical structure has set his great curving roof apparently afloat above the apexes of the massive and perforated walls—the narrow glazed gap between roof and walls can be seen in the exterior views opposite. Maturer consideration will be able to evaluate how far the success of the plastic effect justifies such anti-structural usages and, as a step toward such evaluation, James Stirling will contribute an appreciation of* Notre Dame du Haut *in the new year.*

THE NE

'L'Architecture, c'est, avec des matières brute

Introduce an observer into a field becomes distorted. It is with capitalism, so that Marx spread diffusion of Freud's i any intelligent patient can m influence of contemporary a architecture?

They have created the ide Basil Taylor took up arms ag a rough classification of the main types: One, like *Cubis* historians to a body of work through it, whatever the relat a slogan, a policy consciousl similarity or dissimilarity of t Brutalism—our first native a it should confound these cate

Is Art-History to blame fo other way. One cannot begin the New Art-History has bi teaching methods, into the co between architectural critics.

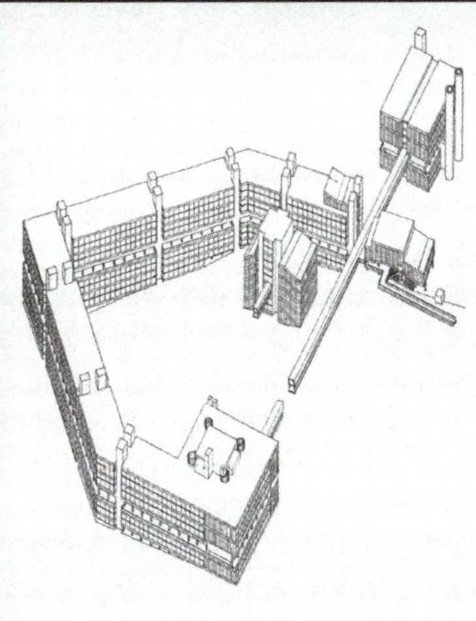

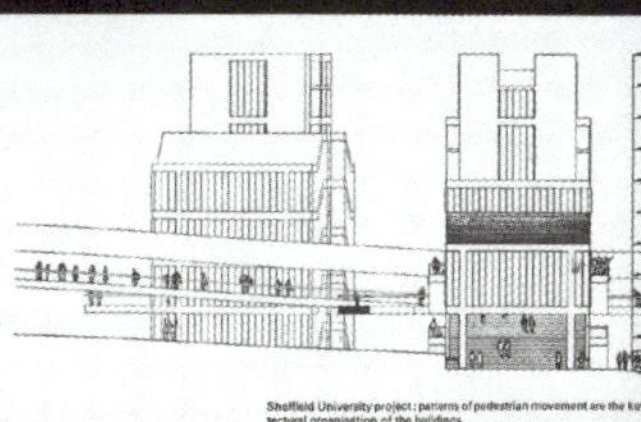

Sheffield University project; patterns of pedestrian movement are the key tectural organisation of the buildings

At a small urban scale, freedom to walk may be all that the situation de can, in the economic balance, be provided and maintained.

This last problem—maintenance and the cleanliness of public circulation we have them—demands much forethought, for no one will want to pic packets endlessly after a bunch of students.

In return for human protecting systems and spaces in a city will hav corresponding sense of responsibility for how they are used and inviting.

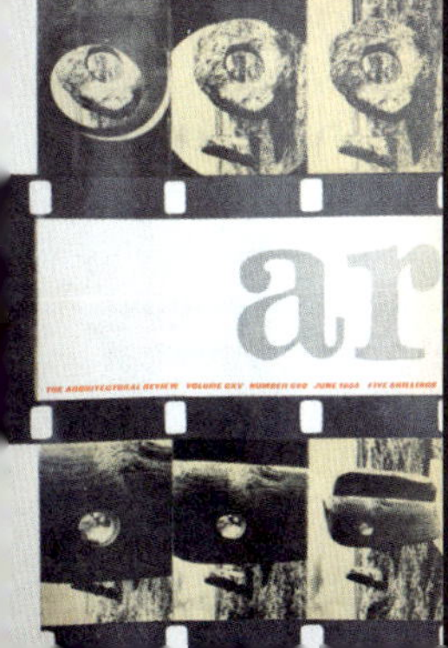

> which their presences distort, so in modern art both the absolute object, unrelated to its setting, and the ideal viewpoint, unrelated to human physiology, have been replaced by the object-in-environment/man-in-environment relationship, a kind of field of aesthetic force. [. . .] But these are lessons for trained aesthetes to learn from landscape objects in general; there is a lesson which a wider public could learn from these objects in particular, as they appear in the film. [. . .] That propitious atmosphere for the exercise of the eye is far more likely, among unsophisticated persons of school age and above, to be generated in front of the cinema or TV screen. Where a verbal discussion of problems of form—this article for instance—would make no impression, the form itself turning before the camera eye within the magic confines of the screen would come to many viewers under conditions when they were most likely to be attending to what they could see, and were most inclined, visually, to accept it—even though they might later, verbally, go through the motions of rejecting it. The visual memorability of the screen image is becoming proverbial, and if that image was an elementary object-form, tied to other images by the kind of simple, though never naïve, comparisons which this film makes, then it could contribute something to the primary education of those who though they have the gift of sight, are blind to the arts of seeing, and to the environment in which they move.[129]

One year later, in "The New Brutalism," whether because his enthusiasm for cinema had waned or because he was more aware of the need to assert "the building" as the medium for his architectural audience, Banham reasserted "human physiology" as the site of experience for the topology and image of architecture. But in "Object Lesson," the gap between sculpture and architecture is bridged by the "visual memorability of the screen image."

Banham never fully transferred the spatial lessons of cinema to his ideas about architecture, and the seeming irreconcilability of architectural experience with photographic and cinematographic media remains a crucial theoretical and practical problem for any understanding of New Brutalism.[130] Claire Zimmerman tackles those issues in her essay "Photographic Images from Chicago to Hunstanton" (2010) and emphasizes a tension between photographic and material practices in architecture. She claims that after World War Two the "new status of the image in building" required "asserting the value of spatial experience over media representation." To do otherwise, she suggests, would have been nothing less than an anticipation of postmodernism's ironies and its treatment of representation as a substitute for building, leading her to conclude that "for the Smithsons, the influence of media representation and dissemination on architecture required the most stringent architectural response, one that opposed the apparent reductions of media society with architecture capable of defying the image, even *through the image*."[131] Banham's ambivalence, or irresolution, on that point certainly invites us to choose sides, or at least attempt clarification. Zimmerman, like Van den Heuvel, Hal Foster, and many others, chooses to reinforce the premise that the efficacy and ethic of postwar modern architecture was challenged and threatened by a culture increasingly saturated by mass media and imaging.[132]

But in 2014 Zimmerman developed a different and more positive understanding of that tension in a collaboration with Victoria Walsh. Their exhibition, *New Brutalist Image, 1949–55* at Tate Britain in London, aimed to "position photography as a primary medium of communication and the photographic image as a remediating tool intended to synthesize the rampant disjunctions of contemporary culture."[133] The multimedia installation attempted to correlate and juxtapose the "visual language" of *Parallel of Life and Art* and the Hunstanton School. Its carefully curated and staged display of physical artifacts and digital projections reactivated "the operations of photographic images in relation to the heterogeneous practices of seeing and viewing which underpinned the cultural sensibility and work of this group of collaborators, and the wider group of practitioners in which they moved as artists, architects, and designers."[134] Zimmerman and Walsh's curatorial approach was motivated in part by a crucial recognition that the conversion of photographic images from the 1950s into digital images allowed a "suspension" of the indexical character of film-based photography, which in turn allowed the exhibition to operate as a heterogenous architectural interplay of projected video, printed text, and physical artifacts (including photographic prints). The result was an intricately choreographed installation that iterated imaging "strategies"—framing, patterning, and staging—analogous to those that Walsh and Zimmermann identified in the photographs of *Parallel of Life and Art* and the Hunstanton School, many of them taken by Henderson. *New Brutalist Image* was an immersive, retrospective simulation of a simultaneous experience of *Parallel of Life and Art* and Hunstanton. In all its dimensions—temporal, visual, formal, textual, material—its display attempted to redeploy the actual beginnings of the Smithsons' aesthetic development.

In her 2006 essay "Brutalism Exposed," Hadas Steiner explores problems related to those that concern Zimmerman. She reconstructs a similarly transdisciplinary but more skeptical understanding of the media and influence of New Brutalism by interrelating the imaging practices of New Brutalism in the 1950s, Archigram's magazines and exhibitions in the 1960s, and Michelangelo Antonioni's 1966 film *Blow-Up*, which opens with a famous sequence filmed in the plaza of the Smithsons' Economist complex (1959–64). Antonioni's film organizes its action and themes around a fashion photographer's attempt to find factual evidence of a murder that he may have accidentally captured on film by serially enlarging his own work. But his efforts are thwarted as the increasingly enlarged images decay into grainy blurs, demonstrating the failure of photography to record reality fully and accurately or to verify experience conclusively. Steiner argues that *Blow-Up* effectively demonstrates both the uses and the limits of the enlargement methods of *Parallel of Life and Art*, which also, but in other ways, operated in the unstable but rich image-world of mass-media photography as well as the presumed objectivity of photojournalism or scientific documentation. For Steiner, this combination of evanescence and elusiveness raises difficult questions about the efficacy of architectural approaches that followed

Parallel of Life and Art, such as the radical magazines *Archigram* (1961–74) and *Megascope* (1964) or exhibitions such as *The Living City* (1963) at the ICA, in which "the jumble of photographic images as signs from across the visual field" began to supplement building as "a medium for ideas" that could effectively "confront radically new structural and social possibilities and explore the contours of intangible entities."[135] Her quotation from Robert Maxwell's review of *The Living City* echoes the dubiousness expressed in many of the reviews of *Parallel of Life and* Art ten years earlier: "In this show, there was no coherent programme, no offer of a policy, no statistics, no rationalisation. Captions were fragmentary, and all the reproductions, whether photographs of real places and things or photographs of photographs of advertising, science, science-fiction or pop-art material, were presented in a deliberately disjointed or random fashion."[136] Steiner's conclusion about the potential of these practices in architecture, like Banham's, is critical: the move from building to imaging invited an aporia in which "the burdens of visual language, those considered intrinsic to the discipline and those still external to it, would continue to vex and have only become more acute."[137]

Ben Highmore looks at the political and social aspects of New Brutalist images from the other direction, treating them not as systems of representation or as media for the communication of messages but as historical materials in need of creative analysis and qualitative interpretation. His political and cultural readings of the entire range of New Brutalist artifacts—buildings, installations, artworks, graphics, writings—draw on the methods of cultural studies, beginning with the work of Raymond Williams and Richard Hoggart. He suggests that it is not coincidental that the "critical project of Cultural Studies emerged at the same moment as the IG and brutalism" because they all involved "an intense attention to cultural forms as a way of exploring the social gravity and orientation of cultural work."[138] He interprets the Smithsons' 1957 statement that New Brutalism was an "attempt to be objective about reality—the cultural objectives of society, its urges, and so on" as an insistence that they, and he, should "look for the characteristics of New Brutalism in the reality of the world."[139] His characterization resonates with Voelcker's assertion in his 1957 letter that "what the Smithsons mean when they say it is necessary to create an architecture of reality or that Brutalism attempts to be objective about reality" is that the architect should be "a kind of resonator that builds in response to a complicated polyincidence of conditions" rather than imposing a "predetermined and pre-planned order."[140] Highmore is interested in the "art of Brutalism" as a "responsive mode rather than a demonstrative one" that provides evidence of the cultural sensibilities engendered by those realities, and he insists its artifacts are only incidentally intended as aesthetic or activist interventions.[141] The aspect of that response that most interests Highmore is how, in the face of the destruction of World War Two and the austerity that followed, New Brutalism was an attempt at "rescuing optimism from the jaws of oblivion, struggling to find a way of inhabiting the wreckage of the past so as to build a future that could somehow come to terms with history."[142] It was an insistently nondogmatic yet assertive way to navigate the transformations, conflicts, and confusion of values occurring in postwar Britain.

Highmore does not question or analyze the specific aesthetic techniques of those responses or their modes of aesthetic production, but he does suggest that New Brutalism was committed to a particular kind of looking aligned with the concepts of "afocalism" and the "multi-evocative image" advanced by David Sylvester in his writings about the paintings, drawings, and teachings of Paul Klee, an artist whose importance to New Brutalism is confirmed by the inclusion of four enlargements of his drawings in *Parallel of Life and Art*. Building on Sylvester, Highmore explains how both afocalism and New Brutalism exercise a "a constant scouring, searching activity" or "restlessness of the eye in looking" that aims to coalesce "a dense field of associations," which he extends to the general attitude toward reality implied in the Smithsons' phrase "as found."[143] That "agitated sense of not quite knowing where to look" was a "promiscuous" way of reworking whatever "was at hand, and crossed the false divide between the material and the representational."[144] Imaging, conceived as afocalism or the multi-evocative image, offered New Brutalists a productive way, in Sylvester's words, "to encounter an attractive chaos" and to generate responses that made sense of what Highmore calls "the condition of the image-field in a mass-media environment."[145]

Highmore's specific interpretations as well as his understanding of aesthetics in ways that "tear that term away from its association with notions of beauty and 'art'" open productive ways to understand New Brutalist aesthetic production as techniques to generate and convey ethical responses to lived cultural, political, and material contexts.[146] It is the presumption of a convergence, or reconfigured relationship, of aesthetics and ethics as imaging practices that makes New Brutalism so intriguing to reconsider and so complicated to understand and unravel. New Brutalism was neither simply responsive nor intently activist, and that attitude never waned in the Smithsons' imaging practices, which were attempts to change their world by acting upon and responding to "the cultural objectives of society." Informed and inspired in large part by their Independent Group experiences and peers, and as an aftereffect of the construction of the Hunstanton School, the Smithsons developed imaging practices that broadened architectural modernism in ways which anticipated the transdisciplinary design aesthetics that continue to emerge and evolve today in work which is generated and deployed with pervasive digital media, from the most arcane experiments with photogrammetry or artificial intelligence in art and architecture to the most popular uses of ubiquitous social media, gaming, and streaming entertainment.

That longer historical trajectory is theorized in the writings of Jacques Rancière. His conceptualization of imaging operations as the basis of post-Enlightenment aesthetics—what he calls "the aesthetic regime of art"—can be used to situate New Brutalist aesthetics as both a specific response to and intervention in a specific historical moment or scene and as an example in architecture of the imaging practices that characterize the aesthetic regime of art. New Brutalism and the Smithsons' approach can be understood as strident, if sometimes naive, struggles to apprehend and productively navigate the reciprocal and isomorphic relationship between aesthetics and politics or dissemblance and "dissensus" theorized by Rancière. For Rancière, both art and politics actively reconfigure what he calls the *partage du sensible*—the partitioning or distributing of the sensible world—by creatively altering our collective sense of what counts and our shared sensibilities toward what matters. Imaging operations are the effective means of that reconfiguration. As he writes in "The Future of the Image," those operations "produce a discrepancy, a dissemblance" that engenders the "transformation of the forms of sensible experience, of ways of perceiving and being affected. They formulate a mode of intelligibility out of these reconfigurations of experience."[147] The dissemblances of imaging produce aesthetic and political effects by enacting a "transitive" capacity to transpose and reconfigure whole and part, or visuality and signification, or a myriad of other categories. In unexpected and productive ways that may frustrate or invigorate, they "create and retract meaning, ensure and undo the link between perceptions, actions and affects."[148]

Rancière maintains that photography and its successors (film, television, video, digital media) introduced a crucial shift into the emergence of the aesthetic regime. But imaging is not confined to or defined by any specific technical medium. It may include any manner of figures, sounds, typography, patterns, colors, or pictures that interrelate through operations of affiliation, juxtaposition, montage, or comparison, "functions whose problematic alignment precisely constitutes the labor of art."[149] The work of art is "pensive" yet "resists thought" because it generates "a set of distances between several image functions present on the same surface."[150] That correlative exchange, or dissemblance, produces a transitive alterity, rather than any kind of normative representation. Dissemblance is distinct from resemblance or mimesis in that all images (whether by iteration or modification) are apprehensible as an effect of their capacity to be different than or opposed to either themselves or other images that might seem very similar or entirely different.

For Rancière, the "aesthetic regime of art" is a deeply historical enterprise that emerges in the Enlightenment, when "Art begins to be named as such, not by closing itself off in some celestial autonomy, but on the contrary by giving itself a new subject, the people, and a new place, history."[151] In *Aisthesis: Scenes from the Aesthetic Regime of Art* (2011), he presents his theorization of aesthetics as a series of distinct historical "scenes," each of which conjoins texts, events, and artifacts in "a moving constellation in which modes of perception and affect, and forms of interpretation defining a paradigm of art, take shape."[152] The present book attempts to make sense of New Brutalism as a scene beginning a decade after the final scene in *Aisthesis*: Rancière's examination of the documentary methods of James Agee and Walker Evans—their words and photographs, respectively—in their book *Let Us Now Praise Famous Men* (1941), which operate in the space between the standards of journalism and the tropes of social realism.

However, it is an earlier scene in *Aisthesis* that is most crucial to understanding how Rancière's theories relate to New Brutalism. The chapter "Decorative Art as Social Art: Temple, House, Factory" interrelates developments in diverse fields of design in the late nineteenth and early twentieth centuries: the decorative objects and spaces of the Art Nouveau, the social aims of the English Arts and Crafts, and Peter Behrens's diverse design work—buildings, products, graphics—for the German corporation AEG. Surprisingly, there are specific affinities between that scene and Pevsner's account of the modern movement, especially as he chronicles it in *The Sources of Modern Architecture and Design* (1968), the last and most thorough of his ongoing revisions of the genealogy he first formulated in 1936 in *Pioneers of the Modern Movement*.[153] While Pevsner's central argument and narrative remained consistent in all editions of *Pioneers* and in *Sources* (that "the three principal lines of progress" leading to the ultimate consolidation of "a universally recognized style" in the architecture of Gropius and the Bauhaus were "the Morris Movement, the development of steel building, and Art Nouveau"[154]), in the latter he significantly expanded the emphasis on modern architecture's sources in the decorative and applied arts that he already had begun in his much-expanded 1960 edition of *Pioneers* and in the revisions to the 1949 edition (including changing "Modern Movement" to "Modern Design" in the title). In *Sources*, Pevsner's discussion of the Arts and Crafts and William Morris was even more attentive to decorative arts than buildings, and he added many images of wallpaper, furniture, and fabrics. But it is the chapter on Art Nouveau that most augments his examples of graphics, printed fabrics, glasswork, ceramics, typography, jewelry, and furniture as the aesthetic and technical precursors of Art Nouveau architecture.[155] It is striking that Art Nouveau, and specifically the glasswork of Émile Gallé, are central for both Pevsner and Rancière, as are their arguments that graphic design was crucial to the development of modernism in the late nineteenth and early twentieth century. But for Rancière, graphic design is both a much broader field than it is for Pevsner and an exceptionally capacious theoretical concept: *graphique* or *graphisme* is a hybrid practice and a precursor for imaging as it emerges in concert with photography in the early twentieth century, operating as a simultaneously abstract and physical "surface of design" with three interrelated traits: "firstly, the equal footing [*plan d'égalité*] on which everything lends itself to art; secondly, the surface of conversion where words, forms, and things exchange roles; and thirdly, the surface of equivalence where the symbolic writing of forms equally lends itself to expressions of pure art and the schematization of instrumental art."[156]

Pevsner's more conventional treatment of graphic art is concerned primarily with formal and stylistic analysis. He always presented his examples as initial, minor sources that enable "the transfer of the style from the small to a larger scale and from design to architecture,"[157] culminating in the work of Art Nouveau architect Victor Horta. Yet his discussions of numerous late nineteenth-century artists touch on the premise of Rancière's aesthetic theory: Otto Eckmann's designs for the German magazine *Pan* (1895); Paul Gauguin's "zincographs" and woodcuts; the calligraphic logos of James Abbott McNeill Whistler and Morris; and Arthur Mackmurdo's designs for theCentury Guild's journal, *The Hobby Horse* (1884–94), and his drawing for the cover of his 1883 book on Christopher Wren, which Pevsner identifies as "the first work of Art Nouveau."[158] Additionally, his increased concern with popular and applied arts has affinities with the attitudes of the Independent Group.[159] In his introduction to *Sources* he makes a claim that emphasizes popular media and culture in a way that is quite unlike the more circumspect tracking of the development of a style in *Pioneers*: "The twentieth century is the century of the masses: mass education, mass entertainment, mass transport [. . .] mass production and consumption, mass communication."[160] Yet Pevsner's emphasis on stylistic analysis leads him to very different judgments and conclusions than Rancière's. *Sources* ends with a dejected statement about the lack of integration in the arts and the vast difference of quality and kind among architecture, design, and the arts in the 1950s and 1960s. He expresses bemusement that a universal style did not achieve dominance in the second half of the twentieth century, and he complains that the "gulf between Jackson Pollock and Mies van der Rohe or even Nervi isbeyond bridging." More so than in *Pioneers*, he excuses his extended discussion of Art Nouveau as necessary to demonstrate that "what is most disastrous in the visual arts of the twentieth century and what is most hopeful was fully in existence by the time the Age of the World Wars dawned."[161]

Rancière's *Aisthesis* attempts not so much to bridge that gulf between disaster and hope as to explore and chart its currents. He argues that the very sources that Pevsner labeled as either disastrous or hopeful are all involved in a complex and continuously evolving historical process of reimagining—and imaging—the redistribution of the available materials and sensible conditions of our worlds. His history is no less synthetic than Pevsner's, but his understanding of aesthetics is much more integrative, inclusive, and disjunctive. His "scenes" share similar tendencies but cannot be unified as a linear narrative or even a common sensibility. Each scene plays out similar kinds of hybrid exchange among media that enable the formation of new kinds of audiences. Like Pevsner, Rancière understands modernity as the emergence of the new conditions and "vibrations of universal life [. . .] the accelerated rhythms of industry, society, and urban life,"[162] but he is dismissive of Pevsner's belief that modernism must coalesce in a "universal style." Instead, Rancière traces the evolution of an aesthetic with roots in graphic design, photography, and other fields that operates on "a common physical surface where signs, forms and acts become equal" and that imultaneously presumes and activates "an equivalence between the forms of art and the forms of objects of everyday living," as well as an "equivalence of the graphic and the visual [*plastique*]."[163] His salient and seemingly divergent examples include Stéphane Mallarmé's typographic poetry, Loïe Fuller's "choreographic spectacles" (which "remodel all the elements of performance: staging, lighting, even the architecture of the place" in what Rancière calls "a formula for the Art Nouveauas such"),[164] and Peter Behrens's development of a "brand image[*image de marque*]" for AEG.[165] He and Pevsner present opposed versions of the relationship between Art Nouveau and Behrens, even as each attempts to work through the interrelationships between social and aesthetic concerns, and each traces Behrens's ideas and work to Ruskin, Morris, Arts and Crafts, and Art Nouveau. But wherePevsner sees Behrens's modernism as a decisive move toward industry, engineering, unadorned surfaces, standardization, and *Sachlichkeit*, and as a radical advance beyond the "blind alley" and the "sultry dreams of Art Nouveau esthetes"[166] with its implicit historicism, individual expression, curvilinearity, decoration, and handicraft, Rancière assembles his distinct scenes as dense historical events that demonstrate a complex, diverse, and often convoluted historical tendency toward the integration of social and aesthetic concerns and a reconfiguration of mediums and disciplines as the surface of design. Far from Pevsner's assertion that "Behrens soon repented these wild oats" in his "revulsion from the Art Nouveau," Rancière characterizes Behrens as a key figure in "the paradoxical genealogy leading from Ruskin to the Werkbund and Bauhaus, and simultaneously the role of debates concerning applied art in the construction of the categories of artistic modernism."[167] However increasingly attentive Pevsner may have been to the decorative and applied arts, he never abandoned the hierarchy that positions architecture as the singular and ultimate exemplar of the historical development of modernism's "universal style."

Rancière imagines architecture after Morris and Behrens transforming into a broader aesthetic engagement with art and design of all kinds: "The model factory designed by Behrens expresses a Ruskinian idea of an essential link between three things: a society, a way of working, and a function of art."[168] But Behrens and the Werkbund "used Ruskin against Ruskin" to convert his valorization of handicraft, the well-being of the individual worker, and the Venetian Gothic as criteria or evidence of a moral society into a focus on the production and design of standardized and commercial objects, from posters to products to buildings, that "define a new texture of communal existence."[169] The crucial tendency of Rancière's aesthetic regime of the arts is its abandonment of the hierarchical representation of ideals, cultural forms, and narratives. Instead, "one builds to shelter and express life, and not to impose a mirror relation between the distinction of a class and the distinction of art."[170] In the aesthetic regime, "there are no noble or base subjects" and "everything is a subject for art."[171] Imaging operations and the surface of design introduce what Rancière calls a "paratactic syntax," which "might also be called montage," which replaces "the parallelism that aligned artistic hierarchies with social hierarchies."[172] Instead, the aesthetic regime generates new "configurations of what can be seen and what can be thought" and new ways "of inhabiting the material [*sensible*] world."[173]

The Smithsons' design approaches exemplify the imaging practices of the aesthetic regime, and many of their later explanations of their motives and their uses of history reveal intriguing affinities with Rancière. Perhaps the most striking is their statement in the introduction to *The Shift* that, as young architects without many opportunities to build, they were instead

> people picking up and quizzically turning things over in our hands, reconsidering [. . .] the things thrown away by our own culture, as yet unrecognized as the carriers of a story of identity, [and which] were transformed in the images made by Nigel Henderson, whose vision through the camera lens made us look differently, and at least twice, at every old door, boot or rusty nail. [. . .] The story of rejection in a society identifies strange, even remote resentments. In written ephemera

> we have tried to identify these blind moves—that are sometimes rages—within a society where they coincide with periods of inventive activity: the heroic period of modern architecture and graphics in Germany; the heroic period of the railways; the British in India; etc. etc. These written explorations of the gestation and realisation of invention in "rough" periods—undertaken to console our own minds—we see as having dual roots: the attractiveness of the ephemera of the period observed, and the powerful imagery of the inventions: that is, we have turned the material into ephemeris.[174]

That reflective and incisive explanation of their notion of the "as found" illuminates the Smithsons' understanding of the aesthetic bond between New Brutalism and the preoccupations of the Independent Group. It is something like a sketch for a scene, like those in *Aisthesis*, each of which functions like "a little optical machine that shows us thought busy weaving together perceptions, affects, names and ideas, constituting the sensible community that makes such weaving possible."[175]

It should not be surprising, therefore, that Rancière, much more than Pevsner or even Banham, provides a theoretical basis for the Independent Group's professed fascination with so-called "non-Aristotelian" approaches. But where the Independent Group was haphazard and inconsistent in its attempts to generate alternatives (by looking for inspiration in sources ranging from pulp science fiction to Alfred Korzybski's "general semantics" to A. J. Ayers's logical positivism), Rancière formulates his aesthetics as first and foremost a subversion of Aristotelian mimesis—what he calls the "representative regime"—and its development as both an aesthetic and a historical paradigm in Western culture. Mimesis imposed a "schema of ideal causality—connection by necessity or verisimilitude" and "a certain form of intelligibility of human actions" that "involved a relationship of subordination between a ruling function—the textual function of intelligibility—and an image-forming function in its service."[176] The aesthetic regime abandons that dominance of text over image and those kinds of common measurement, regulation, and hierarchy that operate as strategies to assign stable values to human actions and artifacts. For Rancière, "*mimesis* was the principle not of resemblance, but of a certain codification and distribution of resemblances."[177]

Rancière's distinction between aisthesis and mimesis (the aesthetic regime and the representative regime) also has rough yet important affinities with Banham's call for *une architecture autre* in 1955 and his revision of those ideas in 1966. Banham's insistence on the dissolution of geometric order and his suspicion of beauty in favor of image and topology, or rejection of structure in favor of environmental performance, resonates with Rancière's theorization of the aesthetic regime as an ongoing "destruction of what lies at the heart of representative logic—namely the organic model of the whole, with its proportions and its symmetries," as well as an "unending break with the hierarchical model of the body, the story, and action."[178] Contrary to Van den Heuvel's account, Banham conceptualized image not as a property of the object but as a result of the individual's

subjective engagement with the architectural situation and the processing of spatial experience. His emphases on "human physiology" in "Object Lesson" and "the presence of human beings as part of the total image" in "The New Brutalism" were shrewd anti-humanist moves that treat the body as the actual and affective site of architectural coherence. When he explained that New Brutalism "requires that the building should be an immediately apprehensible visual entity, and that the form grasped by the eye should be confirmed by the experience of the building in use," or that the aim of New Brutalism is "to create a coherent visual image by non-formal means, emphasizing visible circulation, identifiable units of habitation, and fully validating the presence of human beings as part of the total image," Banham was outlining what could be understood as a unique version of the surface of design as a topological image.[179] The affinity, albeit critical, with Picturesque theory is also apparent. While the architectural conditions that Banham suggested produce the situation of imaging and the experience of the image do not explicitly invoke Picturesque principles of intricacy, variety, or William Hogarth's flowing line (a crucial source for both Pevsner and Rancière),[180] his embrace of topology and image as "more generalized concepts" than beauty and geometry places Banham's aesthetics in the territory of, and in conversation with, the Picturesque. It also resonates with the tendencies of Rancière's aesthetic as epitomized, however differently, in his accounts of Johann Winckelmann's analysis of Greek sculpture,
ARRAY 3.9 Loïe Fuller's "hyper-mediatic"[181] performances, or Agee and Evans's written and photographic descriptions of the living conditions of Alabama sharecroppers. In all three cases, the aesthetic regime was displayed or performed as imaging operations and a play of surfaces.

Fuller's combination of lighting, advertising, flowing fabric, and symbols in her performances epitomized these tendencies toward a surface aesthetic of imaged virtuality and of a "pure display of a play of forms":

> These forms can be called abstract because they tell no stories. But if they get rid of stories, they do so to serve a higher *mimesis*: through artifice they reinvent the very forms in which sensible events are given to us and assembled to constitute a world. [. . .] The body abstracts itself, it dissimulates its own form in the display of veils sketching flight rather than the bird, the swirling rather than the wave, the bloom rather than the flower. What is imitated, in each thing, is the event of its apparition. This is the new fiction: the deployment of appearances as a form of writing.[182]

Fuller's performances were a unique realization of the aspirations that Rancière introduces in the first scene of *Aisthesis*. He claims that Winckelmann's *The History of Ancient Art* (1764) initiates this new paradigm with his "image" of the Belvedere Torso as a virtuously inexpressive, inactive, and incomplete body "whose muscles are not stretched by any action, but melt into one another like waves whose perpetual movement evokes the calm surface of a mirror. [. . .] The tension of many surfaces on one surface, of many kinds of corporality within one body, will define beauty from now on."[183] Most important,

3.9

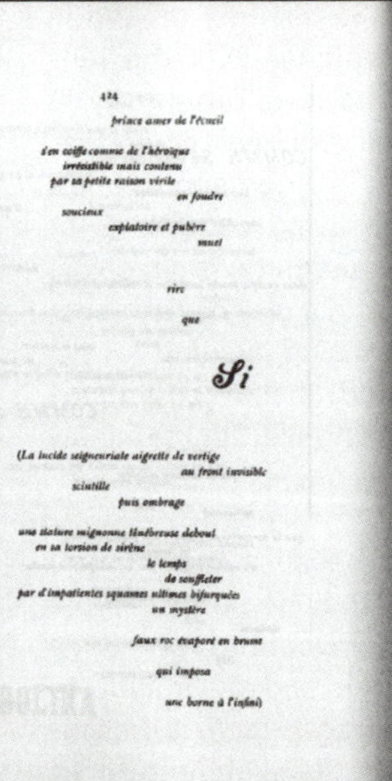
424

prince amer de l'écueil

s'en coiffe comme de l'héroïque
irrésistible mais contenu
par sa petite raison virile
en foudre
soucieux
expiatoire et pubère
muet

rire

que

Si

(La lucide seigneuriale aigrette de vertige
au front invisible
scintille
puis ombrage
une stature mignonne ténébreuse debout
en sa torsion de sirène
le temps
de souffleter
par d'impatientes squames ultimes bifurquées
un mystère

faux roc évaporé en brume

qui imposa

une borne à l'infini)

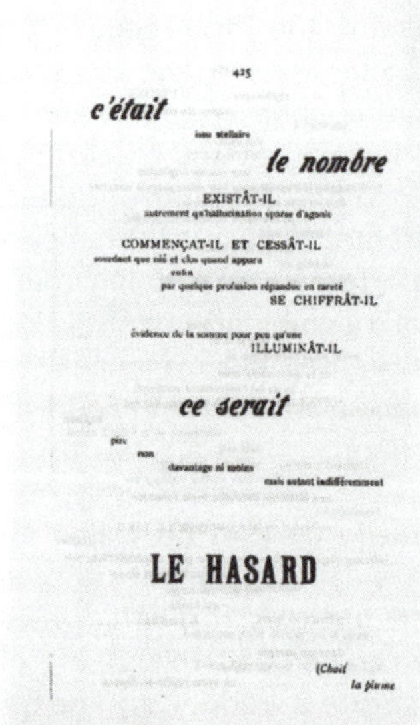
425

c'était

issu stellaire

le nombre

EXISTÂT-IL

COMMENÇAT-IL ET CESSÂT-IL

enfin
par quelque profusion répandue en rareté
SE CHIFFRÂT-IL

ILLUMINÂT-IL

ce serait

pire
non
davantage ni moins
mais autant indifféremment

LE HASARD

(Choit
la plume

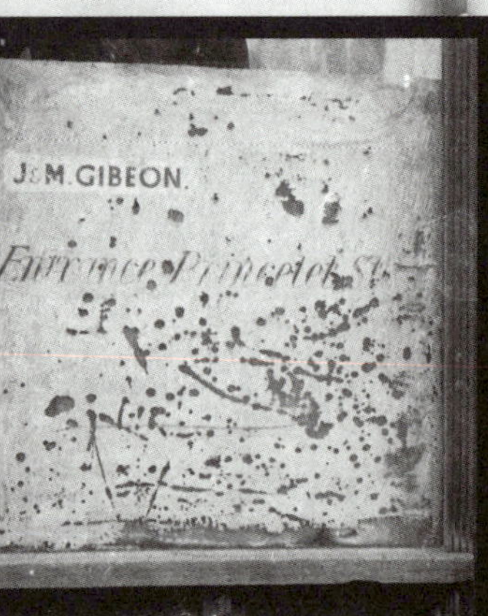

THIS IS THE PICTURE OF THE OLD HOUSE BY THE THAMES TO WHICH THE PEOPLE OF THIS STORY WENT. HEREAFTER FOLLOWS THE BOOK IT SELF WHICH IS CALLED NEWS FROM NOWHERE OR AN EPOCH OF REST & IS WRITTEN BY WILLIAM MORRIS.

NEWS FROM
AN EPOCH O
CHAPTER I. D
BED.
shading off into
various friends, o
of the fully-deve
not listen to eac
could scarcely b
events did not
all together, as i
ordinary polite

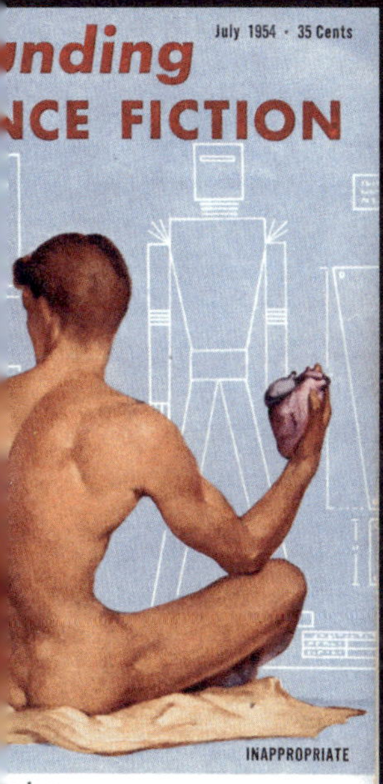

pollock
henderson
burri
cordell

> Winckelmann established an original link between political freedom, the withdrawal of action, and defection from the communitarian body. The aesthetic paradigm was constructed against the representative order, which defined discourse as a body with well-articulated parts, the poem as a plot, and a plot as an order of actions. [. . .] The aesthetic revolution developed as an unending break with the hierarchical model of the body, the story, and action.[184]

Rancière also intends the aesthetic regime as an alternative to the modernist aesthetic of autonomous form famously theorized by Clement Greenberg.[185] While both Greenberg and Rancière characterize their positions as Kantian, Rancière contests Greenberg's idea that modern art, as the pursuit of autonomy and medium-specificity, is a specialized effort to transcend history and ordinary experience. Rancière arrives at "the exact opposite conclusion": "art exists as a separate world since anything whatsoever can belong to it," and, "far from foundering upon these intrusions of the prose of the world, [art] ceaselessly redefined itself—exchanging, for example, the idealities of plot, form and painting for those of movement, light and the gaze, building its own domain by blurring the specificities that define the arts and the boundaries that separate them from the prosaic world."[186] Far from distinguishing the specific traits of each medium, the aesthetic regime operates by "playing on the possibility that each medium could offer to blend its effects with those of others, to assume their role and thereby create new figures, reawakening sensible possibilities which they had exhausted. The new technologies and aids supply these metamorphoses with unprecedented possibilities."[187] Instead of autonomy and transcendence as the unique condition and aim that distinguishes aesthetic objects and experiences from ordinary life, Rancière argues that the kind of separation that enables the pursuit of alternative sensibilities is not negation, not dialectical, not oppositional. Instead, aesthetic production involves a different kind of "withdrawal from action" that is much like the combination of "strategic action and general inaction" in a workers' strike: "Emancipated workers could not repudiate the hierarchical model governing the distribution of activities without taking distance from the capacity to act that subjected them to it, and from the action plans of the engineers of the future."[188] This paradox of emancipation is a central idea of Rancière's "counter-history of artistic modernity," in which "social revolution is the daughter of aesthetic revolution."[189]

Rancière attempts to demonstrate the workings of that uncharacteristically pithy post-Marxist formula for the political potential of art—and involution of aesthetics and ethics, or dissemblance and dissensus—in the final scene of *Aisthesis*, on *Let Us Now Praise Famous Men*. Like the earlier scene on Behrens, Fuller, and Gallé, "The Cruel Radiance of What Is" directly engages architecture. It reworks and elaborates ideas from his earlier writings that interrelate an Evans "photograph of a section of a wooden kitchen wall in Alabama" and Agee's writing about similar houses. Their photography and writing precisely and sensitively describe the "entirely actual, inevitable and unrepeatable" realities of the houses, possessions, and living conditions of Alabama sharecroppers in the 1930s.[190] Agee and Evans insisted on keeping their fundamentally different kinds of imaging distinct, but also understood them as collaborating in tandem: Evans's untitled photographs in the front of the book, each printed on a separate, unnumbered page, grouped in four series, each separated by a single blank page, and Agee's writing, which fills nearly five hundred pages. Rancière's analysis of Agee's description of the graining, machining, and weathering of the wood surfaces of a sharecropper family's house is allied with the details depicted in Evans's photographs. He finds a striking set of dissemblances that not only conjoin the images conveyed by Evans's photographs and Agee's text, but also suggest surprising affinities between the sensibility of the farmers who are the subjects of the book and aspects of functionalist architecture. Thus, the aim of the imaging operations in both Rancière's *Aisthesis* and Agee and Evans's *Let Us Now Praise Famous Men* is to engender an aesthetic and political reconfiguration of the *partage du sensible*. The attentive reader of either book is at once enamored and persuaded by the significant and apparent convergences generated by discerning observations that effectively convey "a new texture of communal existence." Our aesthetic response to, and our political interpretation of, the scene are effectively altered.

> On the one hand, this section of wall in planks, with its small boards nailed askew and its tinplate cutlery and utensils supported by crossbeams [...] form a certain artistic setting. [...] The simplicity of the small nailed board where the cutlery is stored evokes, in its own way, the ideology of modernist architects and designers, in love with simple raw materials and solutions for rational storage, making it possible to expel the horror of bourgeois sideboards. And the arrangement of the askew objects seems to correspond to an aesthetic of the asymmetrical. However, it is impossible for us to know whether all these "aesthetic" elements are accidents of a poor existence or derive from the taste of the occupants. It is likewise impossible for us to know whether the camera has simply recorded them in passing or whether the photographer has consciously framed and highlighted them: whether he has seen this setting as the index of a lifestyle or as a unique, quasi-abstract combination of lines and objects.[191]

The dissemblances that Rancière discerns operate on many registers beyond a close reading of the photograph. They also operate discursively among multiple distinct subjectivities: as a specific artifact of and a particular approach to modern art, as an instance of the circulating and recollected images of modern architecture, as products and documents of differing political positions and subjectivities, and as a sophisticated observer's recording of the sensibility of the occupants' furnishing and use of the room, as well as of the appearance of the materials that form the walls and structure of a sharecropper's house. A further set of dissemblances can be discerned in a section of the book titled "In front of the house: the facade," where Agee describes three intertwined surface characteristics of the unpainted wood:

3.10

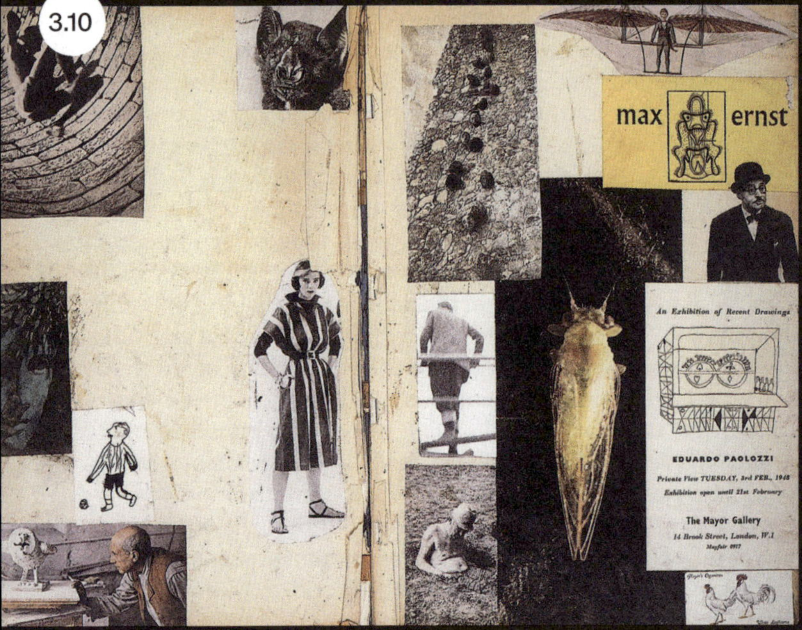

max ernst

An Exhibition of Recent Drawings

EDUARDO PAOLOZZI

Private View TUESDAY, 3rd FEB., 1948

Exhibition open until 21st February

The Mayor Gallery

14 Brook Street, London, W.1

Mayfair 0917

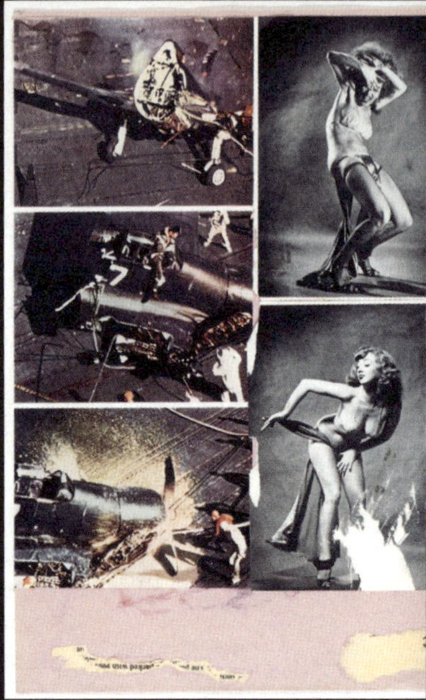

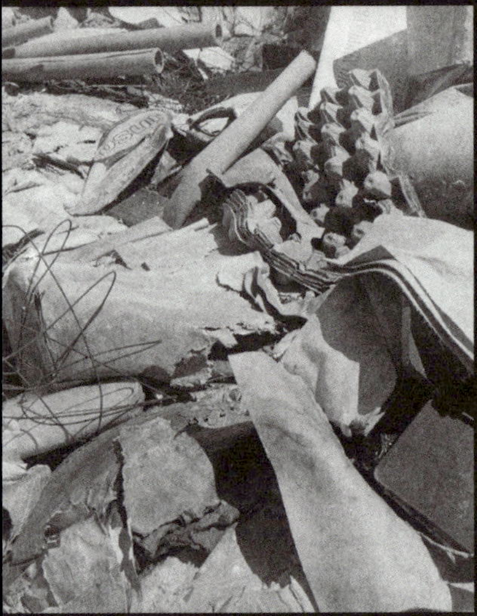

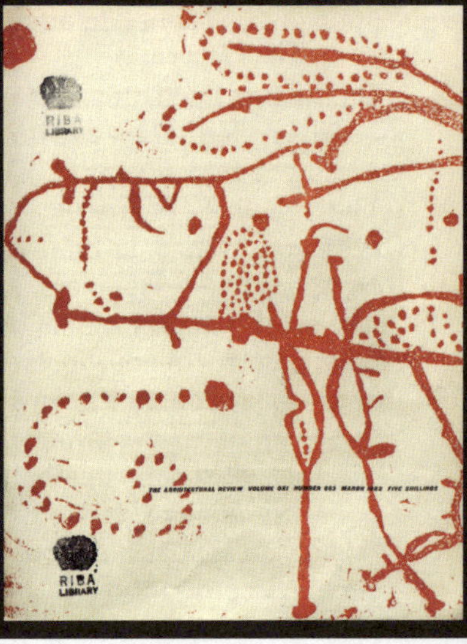

RIBA LIBRARY

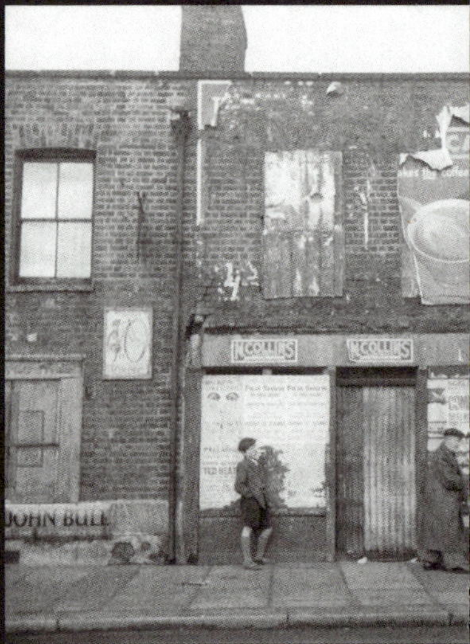

JOHN BULL

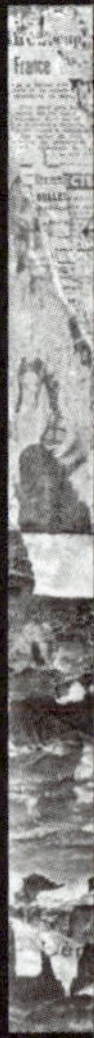

CIGARETTES
1950
FOULSHAMS
OLD MOORES
ALMANACK
1950 EDITION
A.I GUIDE TO
LONDON AND SUBURBS
EVERY STREET AND
ROAD INDEXED.
RONSON
FLINTS
RONSONOL
DRINKS
ORANGE
LEMON
LIME
GINGER BEER
CLARADE

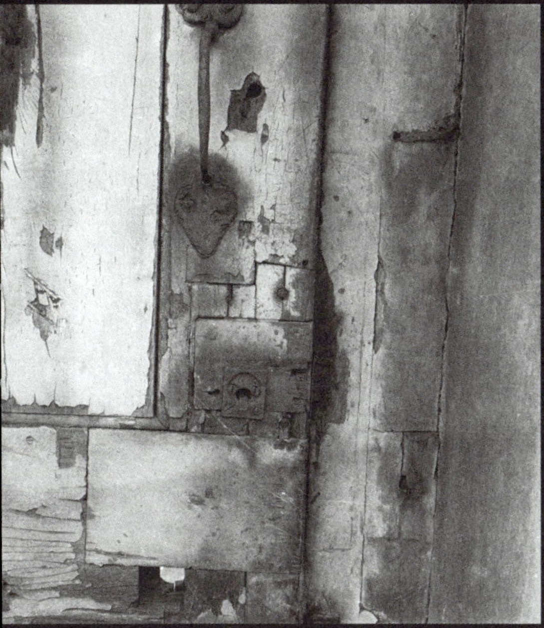

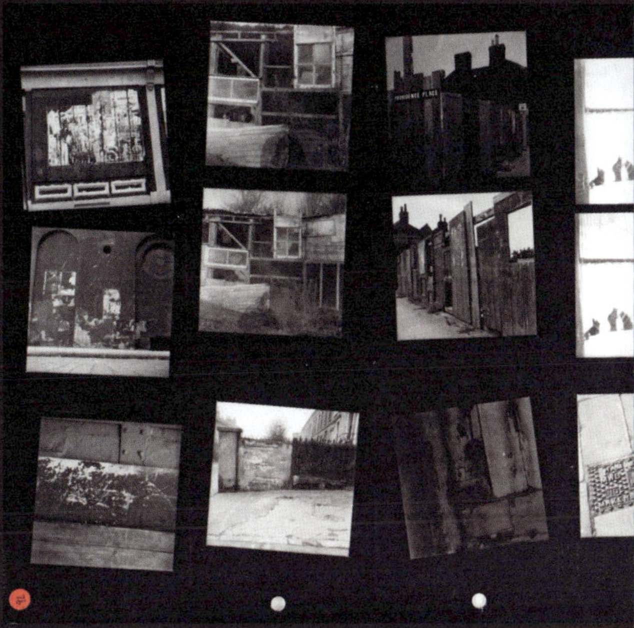

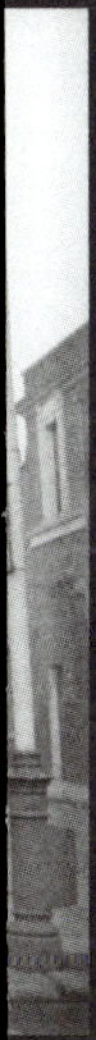

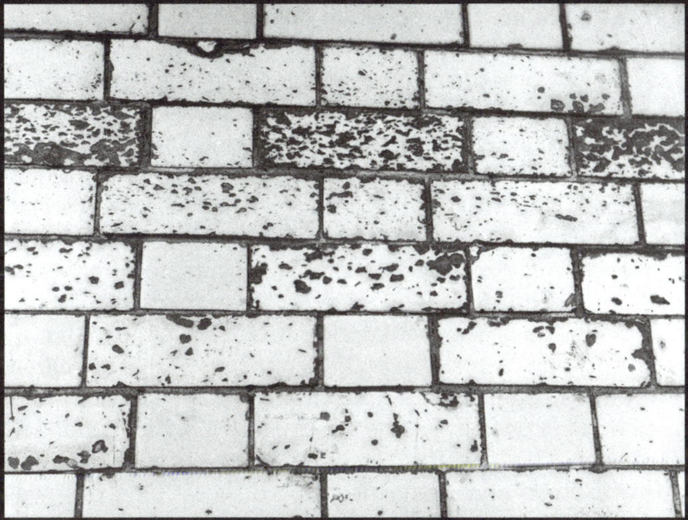

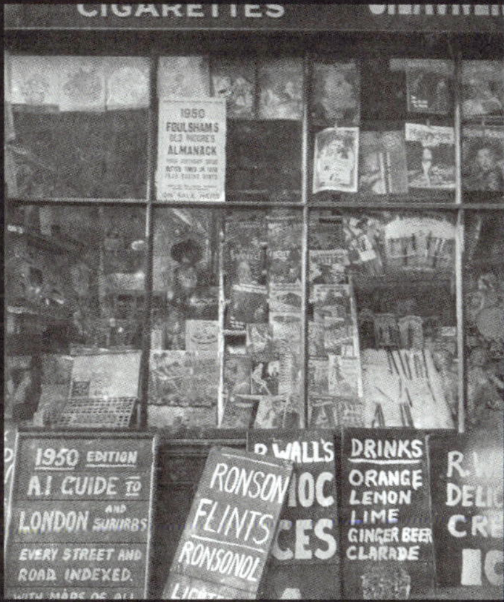

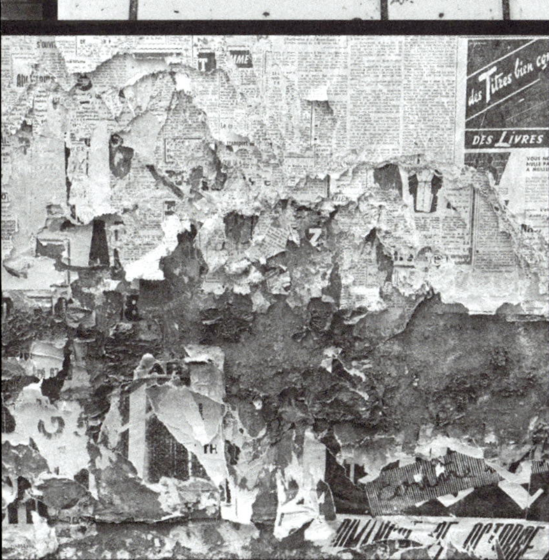

DES LIVRES

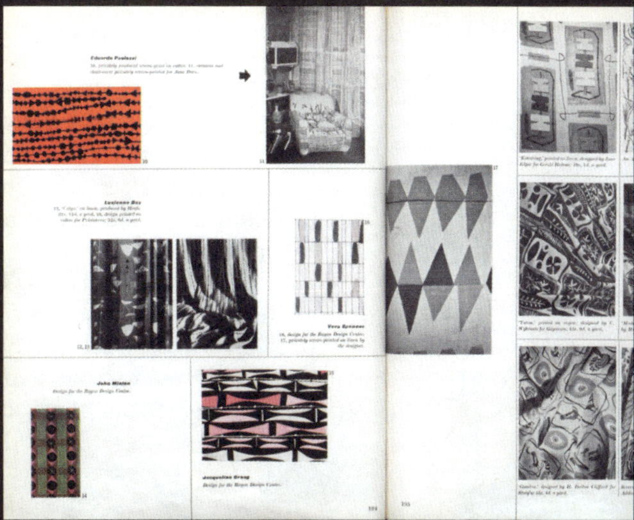

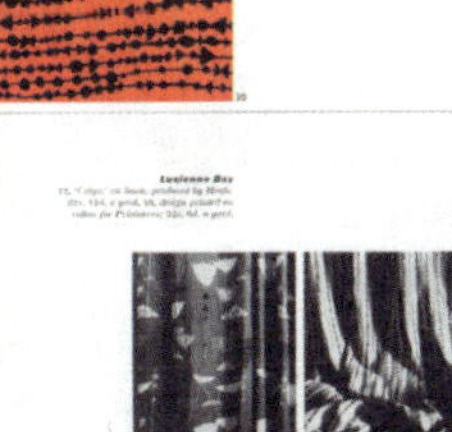

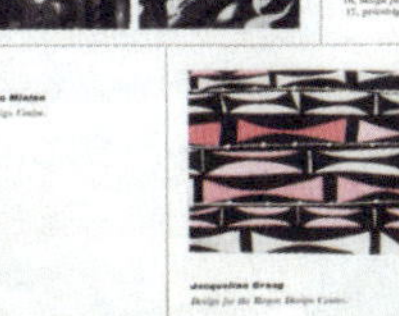

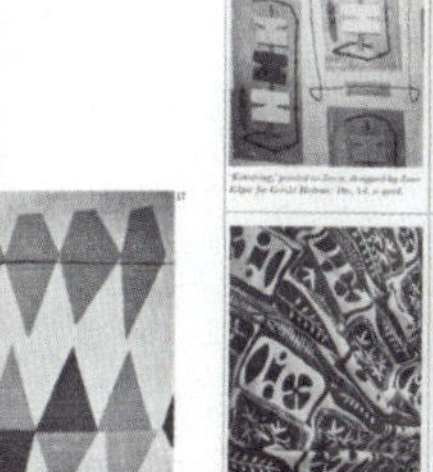

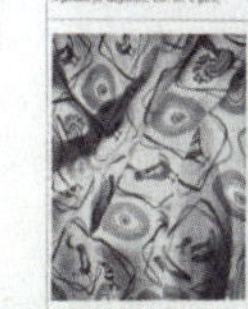

> one is the streaming killed strength of the grain, infinite, talented, and unrepeatable, from inch to inch, the florid genius of nature which is incapable of error: one is the close-set transverse arcs, dozens to the foot, which are shadows of the savage breathings and eatings of the circular saws; little of this lumber has been planed; one is the tone and quality the weather has given it, which is related one way to bone, another to satin, another to unpolished silver.[192]

Evans and Agee, like Winckelmann, Fuller, and Behrens, devised specific variations of the surface of design that offer insights into the aesthetic and ethic of New Brutalism and the imaging operations of the Smithsons. New Brutalism might thus be understood not as a movement or a position in the course of modern architecture, but as a transdisciplinary scene, launched by the Smithsons, with inspiration and instruction from Paolozzi and Henderson, Banham and Alloway, and many others as an evasion of contemporary trends in contemporary British architecture, from the New Empiricism to the Picturesque, and in pursuit of other varieties of modernism that operate aesthetically as a "tension of many surfaces on one surface, of many kinds of corporality within one body."[193] Instead of intentions and causes, actions and effects, or words and principles, the aesthetic regime emerges in concert with photography, which "consecrates the triumph of the gaze over the hand, and the exemplary cinematic body turns out to be one that is constantly bombarded by events, none of which are the result of its intentions."[194] Paolozzi's collages, patterns, and mechanically absurd, comically monstrous, and perversely erotic bodies and Henderson's photography of worked surfaces, from brick walls to wallpapered interiors, and of the shopfronts, signs, people, machines, and detritus of postwar London streets, inspired in part by Evans, provoked a new awareness in the Smithsons of this condition. It is in this way that the foursome's collaborations advanced a "parallel of life and art" and a "transient aesthetic." Hunstanton, New Brutalism, and the Smithsons' later work, from Christmas cards to writings, installations, buildings and urban design, are best understood as instances of what Rancière calls the "transformation of the forms of sensible experience, of ways of perceiving and being affected" and the "paradoxical links between the aesthetic paradigm and political community."[195] Understanding New Brutalism in that way propels its potential beyond architecture, beyond photography and cinema, and beyond the patterns and textures of the enlarged images in *Parallel of Life and Art* in ways that anticipate the electronic imaging of television and video as well as digital media's pulsing, refreshing screens, which operate as the new surface of design of the Mies-image. The Smithsons had virtually no interest in electronic or digital media, yet their imaging practices and their ways of looking responded sensitively and productively, aesthetically and ethically, to "face up to" that "reality" and to "drag a rough poetry out of the confused and powerful forces which are at work" in a world of incessant imaging.[196]

ARRAY 3.10

Notes

1 Reyner Banham, *The New Brutalism: Ethic or Aesthetic?*, New York: Reinhold, 1966, p. 134.
2 Reyner Banham, "The New Brutalism," *Architectural Review*, 118, no. 708 (December 1955), p. 358.
3 Ibid., p. 8.
4 Banham, *The New Brutalism*, p. 134.
5 Banham, "The New Brutalism," p. 358.
6 Peter Smithson, "Team X in Retrospect," quoted in Dirk van Heuvel, "Between Brutalists: The Banham Hypothesis and the Smithson Way of Life," *Journal of Architecture*, 20, no. 2 (2015), p. 303. Van den Heuvel cites "manuscript in GSD archive dated October 1, 1993; revised 1994–2001), p. 2."
7 Banham, "The New Brutalism," p. 357.
8 The Smithsons did include an especially long series of excerpts from Banham's 1955 essay in the *Arena* monograph, which gives a sense of their points of agreement with Banham in early 1966, before his book was published and before they published the books in which they would actively reassess their own beginnings and new trajectories. *Arena: The Architectural Association Journal*, 81, no. 899, special issue: *A Smithson File*, compiled by Jeremy Baker (February 1966), pp. 191–92.
9 Alison and Peter Smithson, "Banham's Bumper Book on Brutalism, Discussed by Alison and Peter Smithson," *Architects' Journal*, 144, no. 26 (December 28, 1966), pp. 1590–91.
10 Banham, *The New Brutalism*, p. 135.
11 Banham, "The New Brutalism," p. 361.
12 Ibid., p. 358.
13 Ibid., pp. 358, 361, 358, 356.
14 Ibid., pp. 357, 358.
15 Banham, *The New Brutalism*, p. 47.
16 Ibid., p. 68.
17 Ibid., pp. 69, 62 ("quest"; "Pop"); Reyner Banham, "Who is This 'Pop'?" *Motif*, 10 (1962–63), p. 13 ("sophistication").
18 Banham, *The New Brutalism*, p. 62.
19 Ibid., p. 89.
20 Banham, "The New Brutalism," pp. 358, 361.
21 Ibid., p. 361.
22 Ibid.
23 Ibid., p. 360.
24 It was Lawrence Alloway who formulated the crucial essays on this condition. See "The Long Front of Culture," *Cambridge Opinion*, 17 (1959), pp. 24–25, and "The Arts and Mass Media," *Architectural Design*, 28, no. 2 (February 1958), pp. 84–85.
25 Alison and Peter Smithson, "But Today We Collect Ads," *Ark*, 18 (November 1956), n.p.
26 Notably, Eduardo Paolozzi was one of the featured actors in *Together* (1956), one of the most acclaimed films by a leader of the Free Cinema movement, Lorenza Mazzetti.
27 Alison and Peter Smithson, *Ordinariness and Light*, Cambridge, MA: MIT Press, 1970, p. 153. The phrase appears in the caption to a photograph of a glamorous couple in evening attire walking between the chrome bumpers of American cars in a parking garage.
28 Alison and Peter Smithson, *Without Rhetoric: An Architectural Aesthetic, 1955–1972*, Cambridge, MA: MIT Press, 1974, p. 92. The statement was likely, at least in part, a retort to the arguments in favor of the "ugly and ordinary" over the "heroic and original" in Robert Venturi and Denise Scott Brown's *Learning from Las Vegas*, which was published one year earlier.
29 As in *The Team 10 Primer* where Alison distinguishes between "carrying text" and "verbal illustrations" in the graphic organization of the book, the Smithsons call some of their writing excerpts in *Changing the Art of Inhabitation* "verbal illustrations." Alison Smithson, ed., *Team 10 Primer*, Cambridge, MA: MIT Press, 1968, p. 2; Alison and Peter Smithson, *Changing the Art of Inhabitation: Mies' Pieces, Eames' Dreams, the Smithsons*, London: Artemis, 1994, pp. 147–48.
30 A. and P. Smithson, *Ordinariness and Light*, p. 10.
31 A. and P. Smithson, "Banham's Bumper Book on Brutalism," pp. 1590–91.
32 Alison and Peter Smithson, "The Aesthetics of Change," *Architects' Yearbook*, 8 (1957), pp. 14–22: pp. 14, 17.
33 Ibid., p. 22.
34 Ibid., pp. 21–22.
35 Ibid., p. 14.
36 A. and P. Smithson, *Ordinariness and Light*, pp. 154–59. The excerpts in *Arena* retain both the IIT reference and Säynätsalo, which suggests that the alteration in their thinking must have occurred later, coincident with the Mies seminar (1967) and its publication (1969).
37 A. and P. Smithson, *Ordinariness and Light*, pp. 158–59. The sensibility of this spread is also explored in *Changing the Art of Inhabitation*, pp. 72–73, 74–75, 76–77, and in *Without Rhetoric*, pp. 82–83.
38 In the Smithsons' *The Charged Void: Urbanism*, New York: Monacelli Press, 2005, a caption to the same drawing attributes it to Alison and dates it to 1978, but it must have been done before *Ordinariness and Light* went to press.
39 The lecture "Phenomenon in Parallel: Eames House, Patio and Pavilion" is published in *Places*, 7 (1991), pp. 19–23 (quote p. 20), using a photograph of the Eames House by Julius Shulman as its opening image that is nearly identical to the one used in *Ordinariness and Light*.
40 A. and P. Smithson, *Ordinariness and Light*, pp. 177–78.
41 Ibid., p. 177.
42 Ibid., p. 179 (my emphasis).
43 Ibid., p. 137 (1958 version, p. 95).
44 Ibid., p. 135.
45 Ibid., p. 141.
46 Ibid., p. 143.
47 As M. Christine Boyer explains, the Smithsons' "ideas retain an ineffable, immaterial, and stubbornly private aspect." Boyer, *Not Quite Architecture: Writing around Alison and Peter Smithson*, Cambridge, MA: MIT Press, 2017, p. xiv.
48 Alison and Peter Smithson, "Thoughts in Progress: The New Brutalism," *Architectural Design*, 27, no. 4 (April 1957), p. 113.

49 Edward J. Armitage, "Letter," *Architectural Design*, 27, no. 6 (June 1957), p. 220. Armitage begins his letter with a famous remark that anticipates Banham's 1966 accusation that the end of New Brutalism is also the end of the Smithsons: "Does the 'New Brutalism' really mean anything other than the architecture of the Smithsons?" The idea is repeated by Robin Boyd in his review of Banham's book, "The Sad End of New Brutalism," *Architectural Review*, 142, no. 845 (July 1967), p. 10. He writes that Banham's catalogue of buildings includes "so much diversity of visual style that one is led finally to the suspicion that the aesthetic of New Brutalism can be found in anything that was built by Alison and Peter Smithson or in anything that in Dr. Banham's opinion looks as if it might have been built by Alison and Peter Smithson in circumstances other than their own."

50 Banham, "The New Brutalism," p. 361. Banham's proposal of an architecture of image and topology, as more general categories than beauty and geometry, is potentially more powerful than Banham himself was able or willing to pursue with persistence in the years that followed.

51 Reyner Banham, "Letter to the Editor," *Architectural Design*, 27, no. 6 (June 1957), p. 220. Banham's ideas in "The New Brutalism" had attained enough recognition and notoriety that, in a May 21, 1957 lecture to the RIBA, John Summerson remarked that "Mr. Banham, in a recent article, has offered us the attractive red herring (I think it's a herring) of topology" as a theoretical alternative to architecture's enduring concern with "regular solids and simple ratios." Summerson, "The Case for a Theory of Modern Architecture," *RIBA Journal* (June 1957), p. 310.

52 John Voelcker, "Letter," *Architectural Design*, 27, no. 6 (June 1957), p. 184.

53 Banham, "The New Brutalism," p. 358.

54 Reyner Banham, "Machine Aesthetes," *New Statesman*, August 1958.

55 Banham, *The New Brutalism*, p. 134.

56 Nigel Henderson and Lawrence Alloway participated in a discussion of *Le Musée imaginaire* at the ICA on May 11, 1954. See David Robbins, ed., *The Independent Group: Postwar Britain and the Aesthetics of Plenty*, Cambridge, MA: MIT Press, 1990, p. 27. On February 23, 1948, Pevsner gave a radio talk on *Le Musée imaginaire*. See Stephen Games, ed., *Pevsner: The Complete Broadcast Talks, Architecture and Art on the Radio and Television, 1945–1977*, Burlington, VT: Ashgate, 2014, pp. 61–66.

57 Ben Highmore has written extensively about Humphrey Jennings and has emphasized his influence on Nigel Henderson. See Highmore, "'Image-breaking, God-making': Paolozzi's Brutalism," *October*, 136 (Spring 2011), pp. 87–104, and his chapter on Jennings and Mass-Observation in *Everyday Life and Cultural Theory*, London: Routledge, 2002.

58 See Anne Massey and Gregor Muir, *ICA London, 1946–1968*, London: Institute of Contemporary Arts, 2014, p. 168. The March 11, 1952 event was titled "Points of View, Photography" and included John Davenport, Douglas Glass, Michael Middleton, Rodrigo Moynihan, and Peter Rose Pulham.

59 Peter Rose Pulham, "The Camera and the Artist," *The Listener*, January 24, 1952, p. 146.

60 Ibid., p. 144.

61 See Martin Harrison, *Transition: The London Art Scene in the Fifties*, exh. cat., Barbican, London: Merrell, p. 54. Harrison offers numerous examples of the increasing interest in art photography in London during the decade after World War Two, as well as the practice of collecting clippings from newspapers and magazines.

62 Jennings was also one of the three founders—with Tom Harrisson and Charles Madge—of Mass-Observation, an adventurous social research project founded in 1937 that enlisted hundreds of untrained volunteers to record everyday life and public conversations in daily diaries or on forms.

63 Banham, *The New Brutalism*, p. 47. Also see Peter Smithson's foreword in Victoria Walsh, *Nigel Henderson: Parallel of Life and Art*, London: Thames and Hudson, 2001, p. 7: "Nigel Henderson's use of 'image' [...] is the key to the period. But why something is 'a good image' cannot be understood outside the persons and the period of its use. Such condensation of meaning into a single word is a characteristic of people campaigning together. Such then were we."

64 Humphrey Jennings, *Pandaemonium, 1660–1886: The Coming of the Machine as Seen by Contemporary Observers* [1985], London: Icon, 2012. Despite being unfinished at the time of his death, and not published until thirty-five years later, his project was well known to his friends. In *Humphrey Jennings, 1907–1950: A Tribute*, London: Humphrey Jennings Memorial Fund, 1951, n.p., Kathleen Raine writes that Jennings hoped to complete it that year. Jennings's introduction to *Pandaemonium* begins: "In this book I present the imaginative history of the Industrial Revolution. Neither the political history, nor the mechanical history, nor the social history, nor the economic history, but the imaginative history. I say 'present', not describe or analyse, because the Imagination is a function of man whose traces are more delicate to handle than the facts and events and ideas of which history is usually constructed. This function I believe is found active in the areas of the arts, of poetry and of religion—but is not necessarily confined to them or present in all their manifestations. I prefer not to try to define its limits at the moment but to leave the reader to agree or not with the evidence which I shall place before him. I present it by means of what I call Images." These ideas resonate in the concluding remarks of Nigel Henderson's introduction to the discussion of *Parallel of Life and Art* at the Architectural Association on December 2, 1953: "It is true that we looked to the material to reveal its own principles of selection—that we ourselves were concerned first of all with the subjective impression, the impact upon our senses rather than upon our

intellects. This may explain our non-dogmatic attitude to the whole thing, and our appreciation of the need of the active participation of the spectators. We should like to bring about a situation in which people felt like undergoing a strong visual experience, without too much reliance on intellectual handrails for their support. And we value the fact that their experience will necessarily differ from our own, being grounded in a different soil. It might be truer of this exhibition than of many to say that you can get out of it what you put into it." See sheets 7 and 8 of the hand-written notes in the Tate Archive, London, 9211.5.1.5.

65 Keith Beattie, *Humphrey Jennings*, Manchester: Manchester University Press, 2010, p. 7.

66 Jennings, *Pandaemonium*, p. xiii. The introduction was assembled by Charles Madge from extensive notes left by Jennings. For an insightful and detailed discussion of how Jennings thought the textual images operated in *Pandaemonium*, see an essay originally written by Madge for a pamphlet published by the ICA on the occasion of his 1951 exhibition: Charles Madge, "A Note on Images," in *Humphrey Jennings: Film-maker, Painter, Poet*, ed. Marie-Louise Jennings, London: Palgrave Press, 2014, pp. 78–82.

67 Humphrey Jennings, "Who Does That Remind You Of?" *London Bulletin* (October 1938). Reprinted in Kevin Jackson, ed., *The Humphrey Jennings Film Reader*, Manchester: Carcanet, 1993, pp. 230–31.

68 Ibid.

69 Ernst Gombrich, "Mediations on a Hobby Horse, or the Roots of Artistic Form," in *Aspects of Form: A Symposium on Form in Nature and Art*, ed. Lancelot Law Whyte, New York: Pellegrini & Cudahy, 1951, pp. 209–28.

70 In an unattributed review of *Growth and Form* (and two other exhibitions, including Barbara Jones's popular arts exhibition *Black Eyes and Lemonade* at the Whitechapel Art Gallery), Banham devotes only one sentence to Hamilton's show and writes at length about Gombrich's essay, calling it an "extraordinarily stimulating [...] 'functional' theory of primitive art." "Exhibitions," *Architectural Review*, 110, no. 658 (October 1951), p. 274.

71 Gombrich, "Mediations on a Hobby Horse," p. 219.

72 Ibid., p. 222.

73 Anton Ehrenzweig, "Unconscious Form-Creation in Art," *British Journal of Medical Psychology*, 21 (1948), pp. 185–214.

74 Ehrenzweig, *The Psycho-analysis of Artistic Vision and Hearing*, Routledge & Kegan Paul, London, 1953, pp. vii, 169.

75 Ibid., pp. xii, x.

76 Ibid., p. 186.

77 The principles underlying townscape were first published as the feature article in the December 1949 issue of *Architectural Review*, pp. 363–74, as "Townscape Casebook," with an introductory essay by Hastings under his pseudonym, I. de Wolfe. As summarized in the issue's table of contents, the article proposes that "the greatest question our society has to face [...] is, of course, the question of our whole physical surroundings as perceived by the eye—in short, landscape," and he proceeds to argue for "the radical canon of English democracy, based on the belief in individualism *per se*," which is embodied in "the Picturesque doctrines of Sir Uvedale Price. [...] It is this *radical* tradition, lying outside both the classical and the romantic movements, which Mr. de Wolfe, and *The Architectural Review* with him, believes must be developed today." The Smithsons found an alternative to townscape in Thomas Sharp, *The Anatomy of the Village* (1946), which is often credited as a source of townscape, but the Smithsons drew other lessons.

78 A. and P. Smithson, *Ordinariness and Light*, p. 11.

79 Mark Wigley, "Alison and Peter Smithson's Quest for the Void," *Bookforum* (Summer 2003), p. 11.

80 Irénee Scalbert, "Parallel of Life and Art," *Daidalos*, 75 (2000), p. 64.

81 Alex Kitnick, "Introduction," *October*, 136 (Spring 2011), p. 5.

82 See folder G081 in the Alison and Peter Smithson Archive at the Loeb Library, Graduate School of Design, Harvard University.

83 Alison and Peter Smithson, *The Shift*, London: Academy Editions, 1982, pp. 52, 58, 61.

84 Ana Ábalos Ramos, "Alison and Peter Smithson: The Transient and the Permanent," PhD thesis, Universitat politèchnica de València, September 2015, p. 59.
Ramos has also written a book, *The Christmas Card Catalogue, 1956–1992*, which is as yet unpublished.

85 A. and P. Smithson, *The Shift*, p. 61.

86 Boyer, *Not Quite Architecture*, p. xii.

87 Ibid., p. xiii.

88 Dirk van den Heuvel, "Between Brutalists: The Banham Hypothesis and the Smithson Way of Life," *Journal of Architecture*, 20, no. 2 (2015), p. 302.

89 Ibid., p. 303.

90 Ibid., p. 305.

91 Dirk van den Heuvel, "Alison and Peter Smithson, "A Brutalist Story Involving the House, the City, and Everyday Life Plus a Couple of Other Things," PhD thesis, Delft Technical Institute, 2013, p. 17.

92 Van den Heuvel, "Between Brutalists," p. 300.

93 Ibid., p. 293.

94 For an insightful and nuanced discussion of the distinctions and relationships between uses of imaging among the Independent Group and the Smithsons, see Ben Highmore, "Brutalist Wallpaper and the Independent Group," *Journal of Visual Culture*, 12 (2013), pp. 205–21.

95 Van den Heuvel, "Between Brutalists," p. 302.

96 Nigel Whiteley claims that "Banham had worked out his theoretical position about pop culture by the end of 1955, but almost a decade passed before he began to write the sort of criticism which did justice to the theory." He synopsizes Banham's position, first offered in his Borax lecture (1955), as a "post-Modern one of product semantics

with forms and colors rich in meaning and association" and with expendability at its center. Whitely, *Historian of the Immediate Future*, Cambridge, MA: MIT Press, 2002, p. 27.

97 In the 1970s Banham would exclude the Smithsons from his film *Fathers of Pop*.

98 Anthony Vidler, for example, summarizes Banham's "theory of the image" as one that goes "beyond the overtly brilliant subterfuges of advertising techniques, pop and op art, collage and montage, supergraphics, and the like." Vidler, *Historians of the Immediate Present: Inventing Architectural Modernism*, Cambridge, MA: MIT Press, 2008, p. 137.

99 Alex Potts, "Realism, Brutalism, Pop," *Art History*, 35 (April 2012), p. 312. In another context with broader aims, Potts offers one of the most eloquent and compelling explanations of the ambivalences and complexities of attitudes toward and uses of images in the late twentieth century: "In both modernist and postmodernist discussions of the image, there was an insistence on distinguishing between the image as something readily apprehended and consumed that lured and deceived the viewer, and as a radically different kind of entity that renounced the easy blandishments of the image in the interests either of engaging the viewer in a process of critical reflection or of offering up something that was unrepresentable in conventional imagistic terms—a kind of non-image that got one beyond the image. In the modernist imaginary, the second alternative played a key role, the utopian idea that a new kind of art might be fashioned that divested itself of the ideological baggage corrupting the image in modern bourgeois or capitalist culture, presenting in its pure but indecipherable immediacy a sense of something that lay beyond or outside the common currency of images circulating in the modern world. But there was also a less utopian, more hard-headed modernism, in which the emphasis was on critical self-awareness—with the task of the artwork being seen as negating the superficial vividness and immediacy of the image and offering up something more complex and authentic, and in the first instance unalluring and unrecognizable, but for all that more compelling in the longer term." Potts, "What Is an Image?," in *What is an Image?*, ed. James Elkins and Maja Naef, University Park: Pennsylvania State University Press, 2011, p. 141.

100 Banham, "The New Brutalism," p. 358.

101 Ibid., pp. 358, 361.

102 Van den Heuvel, "Between Brutalists," p. 308. Van den Heuvel references the insightful analysis of Claire Zimmerman, though his argument does not align with hers, in "From Legible Form to Memorable Image: Architectural Knowledge from Rudolf Wittkower to Reyner Banham," *Candide*, 5 (2012), pp. 93–108.

103 Van den Heuvel, "Between Brutalists," p. 303. Van den Heuvel's statement follows this quote by the Smithsons from 1960: "It was necessary in the early '50s to look to the works of painter Pollock and sculptor Paolozzi for a complete image system, for an order with a structure and a certain tension, where every piece was correspondingly new in a new system of relationship." Alison and Peter Smithson, *Uppercase*, 3: *Urban Structuring* (1960), n.p. Reprinted in a new format as *Urban Structuring: Studies of Alison and Peter Smithson*, New York: Reinhold, 1967, p. 34.

104 In the *Arena* issue quoting from Banham's "The New Brutalism," their only comment was to challenge Banham's attempt to muddle their use of Wittkower's formalist theories. The Smithsons clarify that relationship in a note: "We've always acknowledged our debt and we even quoted Wittkower in our Coventry report." *Arena* special issue, p. 192.

105 Banham, *The New Brutalism*, p. 355.

106 Mark Dorian has noted that in a remark made as a member of the audience at the Conceptual Architecture conference at Art Net, London, in 1975, Banham recollected the importance of the word "conceptual" in the British architectural discourse of the 1950s: "The actual phrase conceptual architecture, some of us may remember, was in in fact in use in England in the middle fifties. It was a word brought into the argument, I think it was brought in from outside England, but it was actually used in England by Jim Richards and Robert Furneaux Jordan to describe any architecture which as they saw it put the expression of an idea over and above or as more important than the service to the expressed needs of the client etc. [...] which is not so different I think than what we've been taking about today, and they certainly saw that as being buildable because for them it makes the Smithsons' Hunstanton School, early Stirling and Gowan housing in particular... I can't reconstruct the rest of it. It only occurred to me while listening to this discussion morning, you should find echoes of it I should think in the Astragal column in about '56, '57 or thereabouts. I don't think what's being said at the moment is at all new, except that in the best Charlie Jencksian sense, the value, the polarities of the words in the caption under the picture have been reversed and what was regarded by both good grown men in 1957 as extremely naughty, naughty and suspect, is now nearly 20 years later regarded as something of potential value, something which might be good for architecture. But the idea of conceptual architecture as buildable is not in any way a new thing, even the actual phrase conceptual architecture was used in that sense though as I say in exactly the opposite sense of value judgment." Dorian, "Art/Architecture/Concept," in *Trading between Architecture and Art*, ed. Wouter Davidts, Susan Holden, and Ashley Payne, Amsterdam: Valiz, 2019, pp. 17–25. While Banham's account may be accurate, there are no columns by Astragal which mention conceptual architecture. For Banham's remarks see "Conceptual Architecture Symposium – Part 5 – Bernard Tschumi, David Stezaker," *Artnet*, London, January 18, 1975, www.youtube.com/watch?v=8jNzbFznLeo&t=423s.

107 Banham, "The New Brutalism," p. 358.

108 Alloway became assistant director in July 1955. Anne Massey, *The Independent Group: Modernism and Mass Culture in Britain, 1945–59*, Manchester: Manchester University Press, 1995, p. 96.

109 On Banham's activities at the ICA and correspondence with Read from 1956 about writing a prospectus and a policy statement for fundraising, see Tate Archives, 955.1.7.1.

110 The only Independent Group event that year that featured both Alloway and Banham was the first, on February 11, 1955, which discussed Hamilton's show of paintings at the ICA and focused on "the use of the photographically defined new reality (with a stress on popular serial imagery) in a fine art context." Otherwise, the events at which they were speakers had somewhat divergent concerns.

111 *Arena* special issue, p. 182.

112 Reyner Banham, "Vehicles of Desire," *Art* (September 1, 1955), p. 3; Banham, "The Machine Aesthetic," *Architectural Review*, 117, no. 700 (April 1955), pp. 224–28

113 Reyner Banham, "Machine Aesthetic," *Architectural Review*, 117, no. 700 (April 1955), p. 228.

114 Massey, *The Independent Group*, p. 143; my emphasis. Banham's "Borax, or the Thousand Horse-Power Mink" was presented to the Independent Group on March 4, and "Metal in Motion" was given as a public lecture on July 7. At that time, as evidenced by Alloway's public lecture on April 7, "The Movies as Mass Medium," Alloway was developing ideas that would appear in his influential essay "The Arts and the Mass Media," *Architectural Design* (February 1958), pp. 84–85. Anecdotally, several Independent Group members have remarked that Banham was noticeably irritated by Paolozzi's epidiascope presentation at the first meeting. Henderson explained that "Banham was very vociferous, rather lecturing, really, about Eduardo Paolozzi's 'show.' I thought it was largely because the visual wasn't introduced and argued (in a linear way) but shovelled, shrivelling in this white hot maw of the epidiascope." Massey, *The Independent Group*, p. 21.

115 The Reith Lectures were broadcast from October 16 through November 27, 1955.

116 Games, ed., *Pevsner: The Complete Broadcast Talks*, p. 312. The phrase appears in the final Reith Lecture, "The Genius of the Place," broadcast on November 27, 1955. This type of caveat does not appear in Pevsner's *The Englishness of English Art*, which contains many strident statements that were not part of his 1955 lectures and culminates with a fuller endorsement of the Picturesque.

117 Nikolaus Pevsner, "The Picturesque and the Twentieth Century," January 31, 1954, in Games, ed., *Pevsner*, pp. 222–23.

118 Nikolaus Pevsner, "C20 Picturesque," *Architectural Review*, 115 (April 1954), p. 229.

119 In "Revenge of the Picturesque," an essay he contributed to a *Festschrift* honoring Pevsner, Banham recounted the ways members of the "anti-Picturesque connexion" embraced topology as an alternative to both the Picturesque and "classical architecture based on elemental geometry." Reyner Banham, "The Revenge of the Picturesque: English Architectural Polemics, 1945–1965," in *Concerning Architecture: Essays on Architectural Writers and Writing Presented to Nikolaus Pevsner*," ed. John Summerson, London: Penguin, 1967, p. 270.

120 Anthony Vidler, *Histories of the Immediate Present: Inventing Architectural Modernism*, Cambridge, MA: MIT Press, 2008, p. 108.

121 Reyner Banham, "Object Lesson," *Architectural Review*, 115, no. 690 (June 1954), pp. 403–6.

122 Reyner Banham, synopsis for "Object Lesson," *Architectural Review*, 115, no. 690 (June 1954), p. 362.

123 Banham, "Object Lesson," p. 404, synopsis p. 362.

124 Ibid., pp. 405–6.

125 Banham, *The New Brutalism*, p. 358. In a footnote, Banham clarifies: "Paraphrasing *Summa Theologica* II (i) xxvii, I. The passage is normally rendered into English as '. . . but that whose very apprehension pleases is called beautiful'."

126 Although she is referring to a somewhat different montage technique, Alison suggested in a 1989 interview how important and influential the Smithsons' use of such cinematic techniques were: "Part of our 1950's influence was a kind of osmosis. One of the things we used very early on, in illustrating *AD* essays, was a mosaic of black and white photographs, i.e., a long, scanning strip of separate, but overlapping, photographs. Now this has become absolutely standard. You go to a students' board in Europe and you get these long scanning strips or mosaics of photographs, either made by one person or by the year, to inform themselves about a site. And of course it even entered into art about ten years ago, with Hockney's mosaics of Polaroid pictures, and when he started this a number of people in England said to us 'Hey, Hockney must have gotten hold of an old *AD* i.e., they recognized where it had come from, so that it is by very secret routes these things influence, take hold and it is for other people to make the connections." Baykan Gunay, "Interview with Alison and Peter Smithson," *METU JFA*, 9, no. 1 (1989), p. 70.

127 The photographs of Ronchamp were a kind of ad or trailer announcing a forthcoming essay by James Stirling.

128 Banham, "Object Lesson," p. 405.

129 Ibid., p. 406.

130 In his 1966 book, and in line with his disavowal of his earlier ideas about images, Banham celebrated the way drive-in theaters, like the "fundamentally 'other' [. . .] approach" of Buckminster Fuller's domes, are "useful environments" that "abandon the dominance of the idea that the prime function of an architect is to employ structure to make space." Rather than seeing the colossal screened images as spatial, Banham describes the drive-in as an environment "where the structure

above ground level encloses no space," and suggests that the projected "cultural symbols are transient light-play." Banham, *The New Brutalism*, pp. 88–89.

131 Claire Zimmerman, "Photographic Images from Chicago to Hunstanton," in *Neo-avant-garde and Postmodern: Postwar Architecture in Britain and Beyond*, ed. Mark Crinson and Claire Zimmerman, New Haven: Yale Center for British Art, 2010, pp. 207–8.

132 See Hal Foster's discussion of "Pop image-ability" and "building as Pop sign" in his account of the historical connection between the emergence of Pop in the Independent Group and its apotheosis in postmodernism and the commercial architecture of the early twenty-first century, in "Image Building," in Foster, *The Art-Architecture Complex*, London and New York: Verso, 2013, pp. 1–16.

133 Victoria Walsh and Claire Zimmerman, "New Brutalist Image, 1949–55: 'atlas to a new world', or, 'trying to look at things today'," *British Art Studies*, 4 (November 2016), http://dx.doi.org/10.17658/issn.2058-5462/issue-04/vwalshczimmerman.

134 Ibid.

135 Hadas Steiner, "Brutalism Exposed: Photography and the Zoom Wave," *Journal of Architectural Education*, 59, no. 3 (February 2006), pp. 21, 20.

136 Ibid., pp. 20–21, quoting from Robert Maxwell, "The Living City Exhibition at the ICA," *Living Arts*, 3 (1964), p. 98.

137 Steiner, "Brutalism Exposed," p. 26.

138 Ben Highmore, *The Art of Brutalism: Rescuing Hope from Catastrophe in 1950s Britain*, New Haven: Yale University Press, 2017, p. 267; Highmore, "'Image-breaking, God-making,'" p. 95.

139 Highmore, "'Image-breaking, God-making,'" p. 95.

140 Voelcker, "Letter," p. 184.

141 Highmore, *The Art of Brutalism*, p. vii.

142 Ibid., p. 27.

143 Highmore, "'Image-breaking, God-making,'" p. 97.

144 Ibid., pp. 97, 96. Highmore suggests that Sylvester's concept is latent in the meaning of the word "image" in Alloway's writing and connects his ideas directly to the influence of Humphrey Jennings.

145 Highmore quotes Sylvester from "Auguries of Experience," *Tiger's Eye*, 6 (December 1948), reprinted as "Late Klee," in Sylvester, *About Modern Art*, New Haven: Yale University Press, 2001, p. 35; Highmore, *The Art of Brutalism*, p. 126.

146 Highmore, *The Art of Brutalism*, p. vii.

147 Jacques Rancière, "The Future of the Image," in *The Future of the Image*, trans. Gregory Elliott, London and New York: Verso, 2007, pp. 6–7; Jacques Rancière, *Aisthesis: Scenes from the Aesthetic Regimes of Art* [2011], trans. Zakir Paul, London and New York: Verso, 2013, p. ix. Although not referring to Rancière, José Luis Brea captures the concept of dissemblance in his characterization of an image as an event that marks "a sheer differing, and even more, a sheer *differing from itself*." Brea, "An Image Is an Image Is an Image (Three Stages)," in *What Is an Image?*, ed. Elkins and Naef, p. 237.

148 Rancière, "The Future of the Image," pp. 3–5.

149 Ibid., p. 1.

150 Ibid., p. 131.

151 Rancière, *Aisthesis*, p. xiii.

152 Ibid., p. xi.

153 Rancière does not reference Pevsner, yet the numerous affinities between Rancière's *Aisthesis* and Pevsner's *Sources* bring focus to Banham's oversights in his understanding of Pevsner. Banham tended to emphasize Pevsner's own oversights in his narratives and "aesthetic preferences" (*The New Brutalism*, 1966, p. 47) and to cast New Brutalism as a reaction against them. Reconstructing what might be called "Rancière's Pevsner" suggests new ways to situate the motives, approaches, and aesthetics of New Brutalism in the history of modern architecture.

154 Nikolaus Pevsner, *Pioneers of the Modern Movement: From William Morris to Walter Gropius*, London: Faber & Faber, 1936, pp. 137 ("three lines"; "Morris"), 38 ("style"); 1949 edition pp. 84, 17.

155 Notably, in *Sources*, Pevsner also eliminates the entire chapter on painting in *Pio-neers*, further reinforcing his emphasis on applied arts and suggesting an intentional move away from fine art sources.

156 Jacques Rancière, "Surface of Design," in *The Future of the Image*, pp. 106–7. First published as "Les Ambivalences du graphisme," in *Design . . . Graphique?*, ed. A. Lantenois, Valence: École Régionale des Beaux-Arts de Valence, 2002.

157 Nikolaus Pevsner, *The Sources of Modern Architecture and Design*, London: Thames & Hudson, 1968, p. 43.

158 For Eckmann: Pevsner, *Pioneers*, 1936, p. 112 (1949, p. 66); for Gauguin: *Pioneers*, 1936, p. 76; for Whistler and Morris: Pevsner, *Sources*, p. 57; and for Mackmurdo: *Sources*, p. 46, and *Pioneers*, 1949, p. 55. The illustration of Mackmurdo's cover drawing appears earlier in the book, on page 30, in a passage that, like the illustration, is not in the 1936 first edition. Pevsner calls the graphic "daringly personal" and of "immense importance." He describes it as "a completely asymmetrical feathery leaf ornament of a kind never seen in Morris or Crane or any of the other representatives of the Arts and Crafts."

159 Pevsner, *Sources*, p. 43. In "Pevsner's Progress," *Times Literary Supplement* (February 17, 1978), pp. 191–92, a review of David Watkin's *Morality and Architecture*, Banham made light of this aspect of Pevsner's story of the stylistic development of the modern movement: "We all have our difficulties in not tittering at his insistence that artists like Gaugin and Douanier [Henri Rousseau] have a place in the progress of modern design 'from William Morris to Walter Gropius'." Yet he defended Pevsner against Watkin's "intention to censure Pevsner for Whiggish historicism in imputing direction and purpose to History, and importing morality into architectural judgment," and defended Pevsner's ability to "generalize convincingly and usefully"

and "to find direction and purpose in history."
160 Pevsner, *Sources*, p. 7.
161 Ibid., p. 201. Pevsner's introduction to the 1960 edition of *Pioneers* is more explicit: "When I wrote this book [...] there was no question that Wright, Garnier, Loos, Behrens, Gropius were the initiators of the style of the century and that Gaudi and Sant'Elia were freaks and their inventions fantastical rantings [...] and once again the validity of the style is queried to whose prehistory this book is dedicated. Historical fairness for that very reson made it imperative to show up the line which runs from Gaudi and the Art Nouveau to the present Neo-Art-Nouveau [...]. But I am as convinced as ever that the style of the Fagus Works and the Cologne model factory is still valid" (pp. 17–18).
162 Rancière, *Aisthesis*, p. 262.
163 Rancière, "Surface of Design," p. 99. I include the original French word here to call attention to one of the idiosyncrasies in Gregory Elliott's English translation.
164 Ibid., p. 97; Rancière, *Aisthesis*, p. 105.
165 Rancière, "Surface of Design," p. 100.
166 For "blind alley": Pevsner, *Pioneers*, 1949, p. 54 (this phrase is not in the 1936 version); for "sultry": ibid., p. 126 (1936, p. 193).
167 Pevsner, *Sources*, p. 71; Pevsner, *Pioneers*, 1949, p. 126 (not in 1936); Rancière, *Aisthesis*, p. 153.
168 Rancière, *Aisthesis*, p. 147.
169 Ibid.; Rancière, "Surface of Design," p. 97.
170 Rancière, *Aisthesis*, p. 135.
171 Rancière, "Surface of Design," p. 106.
172 Jacques Rancière, "Sentence, Image, History," in *The Future of the Image*, p. 48; Rancière, "Surface of Design," p. 106.
173 Rancière, "Surface of Design," p. 91.
174 A. and P. Smithson, *The Shift*, p. 9. The references to "the heroic period of modern architecture and graphics in Germany, the heroic period of the railways; the British in India" are each the subject of Alison's unfinished "sensibility primers."
175 Rancière, *Aisthesis*, p. xi.
176 Rancière, "Sentence, Image, History," pp. 38, 39.
177 Rancière, "Surface of Design," p. 104.
178 Rancière, *Aisthesis*, pp. 7, xiv. The Smithsons write in *The Shift*, p. 9: "The architect feels as a man without arms, and almost without identity, if he cannot build."
179 Banham, "The New Brutalism," pp. 358, 361. There are also intriguing alignments between Banham's 1955 ideas and those developed by John Hejduk in "Out of Time and into Space," in *Mask of Medusa*, ed. K. Shkapich, New York: Rizzoli, 1985, pp. 71–75. (Originally published in French in *L'Architecture d'aujourd'hui* (September–October 1965), pp. 21, 23.)
180 Hogarth is an important source for both Rancière and Pevsner. The latter's *The Englishness of English Art* includes a chapter on Hogarth, whose search for "truth and its everyday paraphernalia" and "mischievous pleasure in debunking" makes him an exemplar of British aesthetics. Pevsner, *The Englishness of English Art*, London: Peregrine Books, 1956, pp. 30–31, 35. Rancière mentions Hogarth and his relationship to English gardens in his discussion of both Winckelmann and Fuller.
181 Rancière, "Surface of Design," p. 98.
182 Rancière, *Aisthesis*, pp. 100–101.
183 Ibid., pp. 8–9.
184 Ibid., p. xiv.
185 See Rancière's "Sentence, Image, History," pp. 39–41, for a brief outline of his characterization and critique of theories of autonomy, from Lessing to Lyotard. For a critique of Greenbergian flatness, see Rancière's "Painting in the Text," in *The Future of the Image*, pp. 69–89.
186 Rancière, *Aisthesis*, pp. x–xi.
187 Jacques Rancière, "The Pensive Image," in *The Emancipated Spectator*, trans. Gregory Elliott, London and New York: Verso, 2009, pp. 131–32.
188 Rancière, *Aisthesis*, pp. xv–xvi.
189 Ibid., pp. xiii–xiv.
190 Rancière, "The Pensive Image," p. 116; Rancière, *Aisthesis*, p. 250.
191 Rancière, "The Pensive Image," pp. 117–18.
192 James Agee and Walker Evans, *Let Us Now Praise Famous Men*, Boston: Houghton Mifflin, 1941, 145, quoted in Rancière, *Aisthesis*, pp. 253–54.
193 Rancière, *Aisthesis*, p. 9.
194 Ibid., p. xv.
195 Ibid., p. xiv.
196 A. and P. Smithson, "Thoughts in Progress," p. 113.

Fig. 4 Margaret Garlake, *Peter Lanyon*, London: Tate Gallery Publishing, 1998, p. 39. *St Just* was first shown in 1953 in *Space in Colour*, a show curated by Patrick Heron at the Hanover Gallery, London. See ibid., p. 68. Also see Margaret Garlake, "The Constructions of Peter Lanyon," in *Peter Lanyon: Air, Land and Sea*, London: South Bank Centre, 1992, pp. 49–61.

Chapter 4

The Smithsons' Mies-image

Alison and Peter Smithson were looking for the latent image of modern architecture. They were looking before they won the competition for the Hunstanton School in 1950, and they kept looking after New Brutalism gained currency and then lost it. Their search was continuous but recursive and thus always both timely and untimely. The specificity of their contrarian stances was their untimely way of making precisely timely statements. They scrutinized their contemporary world while constantly reconsidering history and their own past work within history as the best lens through which to look at history. For the Smithsons, active observation was a way to assemble the potential sources, associations, and ideas that would inform their "random aesthetic" and cultivate a "*general* sensibility"[1] that was "not based on rectangular geometries, but founded on another visual world."[2] Their desire and capacity to discern and to work on that other imaginary was fueled and focused by their experiences of the early 1950s, when their passion for looking, their ways of looking, and their motives for looking became an integral part of their thinking about architecture and the image-world of the built environment. That pursuit can be tracked and examined in the imaging practices that the Smithsons continued to invent and refine in built and unbuilt projects, and which intensified in publications in the latter part of their careers when they attempted to explain and convey their insights as variations and "identifications" of the Mies-image.[3]

BACK ENDPAPER

The Smithsons understood that theirs was a time when looking was changing and things were looking quite different from before. Challenged by and in competition with a diverse range of influences and conditions, from an interest in nineteenth-century travel to the impact of photographic media in the twentieth century, their approach was an assimilation and absorption of evidence through imaging practices and an attempt to generate what might be called a "new look." That phrase, as the social historian Harry Hopkins observed in 1964, gained popular meaning beginning in the late 1940s and into the 1950s—in the years after Christian Dior's New Look arrived in London in 1947, "in flagrant bad taste in the context of [. . .] the puritan discipline of Austerity and Fair Shares."[4] According to Hopkins, "in the newspapers—with that instinct for major social change which popular journalism sometimes shows—'New Look' ('the Government's "New Look" policy') had already begun to replace the long jaded 'New Deal' as a metaphor of all work."[5] Within and against that context, the Smithsons tenaciously pursued the question of what it might mean, in the second half of the twentieth century, for architecture and its practices to be—and to be an effect of—new kinds of persistent looking that challenged professional norms and conventional wisdom. Their way, as always, was contrarian. Just as they had contempt for the Contemporary Style, the "new look" they sought was a counter-project. They looked to history, especially what they called the "heroic period of modern architecture" from "just before to just after the first world war,"[6] but also classical architecture, from the Greeks to the Japanese to Gunnar Asplund. They looked in contemporary magazines, films, art, industrial design, and advertising. They looked at furniture and "*throw away* objects [. . .] that would be worth collecting."[7] They looked in the explanations of anthropology and sociology. They looked, above all, in the work of their professional heroes Charles and

Ray Eames, who "gave us courage to make sense of anything that attracted."[8] Ultimately, they returned to looking at Mies van der Rohe, beginning in the late 1950s and increasingly for the rest of their lives:

> Simply on the basis that successive generations can find something fresh and particular to themselves in any work of art, we should be able to find in Mies' buildings something useful to our immediate course [. . .] although not necessarily what Mies himself intended. We should not look at his buildings for what can be lifted off to paper over the next client's programme or to lose our aesthetic problem: they are to be seen as a vehicle conveying the self-construction, the self-control and the reticence now needed by an architect.[9]

The Smithsons hung on to these realizations as images that were not deployed or developed systematically as a distinct, recognizable design language but as malleable bases for constant revision. They continued their creative and productive looking as a way of reconsidering their encounters with and recollections of the work of Mies. What they achieved was the invention of *un autre* Mies quite unlike what they saw when they first looked at the published photographs and drawings that inspired the design of the Hunstanton School. In light of more knowledge and experience, as well as their changing experiences in a changing culture, generally and in architecture, they looked at their own work to discern their own Mies-image. Their pursuit was gradual but persistent, culminating in the 1980s when Mies's Barcelona Pavilion and the Smithsons' *Patio and Pavilion* were both reconstructed.[10] That coincidence was the last of several key recursive moments over the course of three decades: in late 1953, when the glazing was installed at Hunstanton and the exhibition *Parallel of Life and Art* was installed at the Institute of Contemporary Art; in 1957 and 1958, when Peter first traveled to America and saw many of Mies's buildings; in 1967, when the Garden Building at St. Hilda's College, Oxford (1967–70), was designed and their ideas about Mies coalesced in the Berlin seminar; and in 1982, when *The Shift* was published, their monograph that reconsidered the evolution of and alterations in their thinking and practice, as a process of looking back, looking inward, and looking forward. That shuttling between memories and imagination, recollection and identification, looking and speculating, is vividly exemplified in the arrangement of photographs of *Patio and Pavilion* in their final and definitive monograph, *The Charged Void: Architecture* (2001), where the last two images of the project are their own photographs of the 1990 reconstruction, one of which is itself a reconstruction of one of Nigel Henderson's 1956 photographs (which appears on the prior spread) of the project's installation in the *This Is Tomorrow* exhibition.[11] As Alison explained in a 1990 lecture on the occasion of the *Independent Group* exhibition at the ICA in London (where the reconstructed *Patio and Pavilion* was installed for the second time, after its debut in New York three years earlier), they engaged with the rebuilt project as if they were trying to revive and revise their memories: "We have taken photographs both from the same positions as those we had adopted to take a few colour slides in 1956, and to match the black-and-white

ARRAY 4.1

images by Nigel Henderson."[12] That impulse to revisit the original by making mementos of the rebuilt project is the most overt example of how the Smithsons' imaging practices were procedures for refreshing and generating what could be called photographic memories.

As Peter recollected in 2002, the 1990 reconstruction revealed new but latent potential in *Patio and Pavilion*:

> As a reconstruction it was astonishing, although different to the original, because even industrially produced materials or processes do not stay the same over 34 years. But the truly magical transformation was largely a question of light; whereas in 1956 the natural light was flat, at the ICA we could control the entry of sunlight through the traditional window shutters facing southwards onto the Mall. This light, combined with the increased reflectiveness of the aluminium-faced plywood patio-walls, was astounding.[13]

It is as if Peter is imagining *Patio and Pavilion*—including the building in which it was installed (the lens-like shutters) and the technical capacity of its materials (the film-like surfaces in which aluminum replaces silver)—to operate like a camera and as if the Smithsons processed architecture like photographic memories. Their recursive attitude toward recollection and reproduction, whether of Mies or of their own work, was a complex negotiation with the repetitive potential of mediated experience and their own efforts to convey their sensibility through reproduction. But it took time to realize that:

> Now we seem to be in a situation where an exhibition can—in the manner of music, theatre, film, tapes, photography, books—be replayed (dare one say, conducted?). [. . .] Between 1985 and 1986, while Mies's pavilion was being reconstructed, our attitude was that reconstruction destroys a dream and that it cannot, by way of recompense, recreate for a subsequent generation that excitement, or the impact, experienced by a third-generation architect on first discovering photographs of a lost pavilion from the heroic period of modern architecture. We visited the pavilion through the stages of its reconstruction in Barcelona and had time to consider our attitude in the run-up to Aachen's celebration of the centenary of Mies's birth in 1986.[14]

They eventually realized, no doubt influenced by the outpouring of theory and criticism at the time about the Barcelona reconstruction, that a "facsimile" both affirmed and challenged the "myth" that the original photographs and drawings of the Barcelona Pavilion had built up gradually over decades.[15] The "second life" of *Patio and Pavilion* raised similar questions about what the project once was, how it persisted as "a dream," and what others might now make of it.[16] Alison's 1990 lecture ended with bemusement: "So, we have no idea what a young European architect, walking through *Patio and Pavilion* reconstructed, can find of his—or our—roots in the 1950s; or whether he will recognize a historic connection or have some insight that will provide a tool for his future use."[17]

4.1

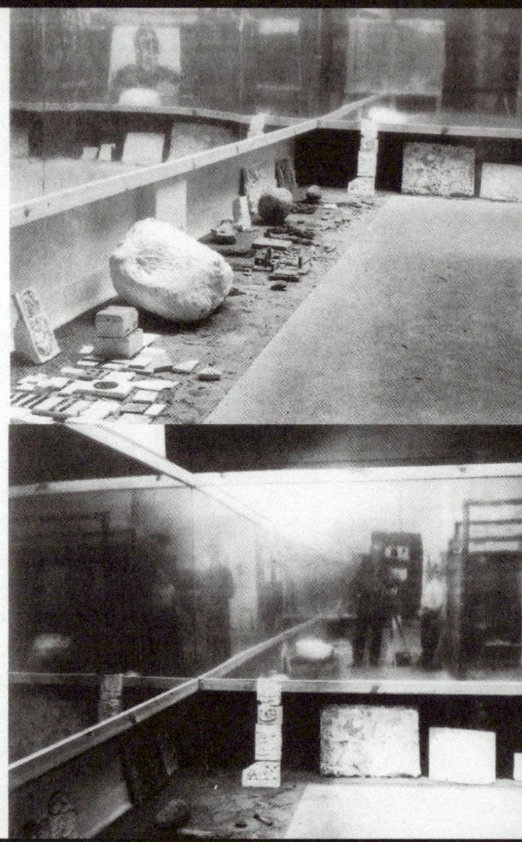

The Architects' Journal for September 15, 1953 [illegible]

l, now nearing completion, will provide secondary school facilities in a large rural area. rve as an evening institute (it has the only decent hall in the district) and a gardening uring primary schools. Designed by Alison and Peter Smithson, for the Norfolk it stands on a 22-acre site on the top "edge" of Hunstanton—an early Victorian seaside that formal teaching areas have south aspect and Sandringham prospect; practical rooms little prospect; "contemplative" rooms face east and west on to the enclosed courts. and the structure—welded steel H-frames—is one of y to be designed according to the "plastic theory." ture were dealt with at the discussion between the ntre in photo) and the engineer and Editors of the elow. The design of the school was the subject of the architects in 1950. It will be described and hen completed.

ARY SCHOOL AT HUNSTANTON

the architects (Alison and Peter Smithson), the engineer (R. S. Jenkins of Ove Arup ditors of the JOURNAL, *referred to below by their respective numbers (see page 305).*

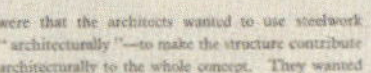

e a brief outline of your n terms both of plan

problem was to provide ty modern secondary additional accommoda- lucation.

ate the normal teaching rectangle with three e being roofed to form pact-noisy elements are e arranged on a raised dominates the site. he upper floor, which is e circulation, adminis- e lower floor, seven feet is by stairs between classrooms, with formal and practical rooms

the assembly hall, into ntrance areas, carrying of the forecourt, green- This allows the circu- g areas and the school , resulting in a compact

o use steel as an archi- void the formalism of piece of steel supports, space it creates. For as jigs and stiffeners to s and transomes to the d copings to the floors fabricated from standard essings.

"terms of reference"

were that the architects wanted to use steelwork "architecturally"—to make the structure contribute architecturally to the whole concept. They wanted

Below, one of the internal "green," courts. N.B., the floor-to-ceiling glazing.

tion as rebuilt, 1990: Reflections resonate the contents II. PS.

Exhibition as rebuilt, 1990: Reflections resonate the contents III. PS.

57

December 1985, AS.

'Mies' Barcelona Pavilion, Myth and Reality', extracts from a lecture, Barcelona, 1986. Unpublished.

The first impression upon entering the Barcelona Pavilion while under reconstruction[58] is that it is all one-third larger than the pavilion-image that the photographs formed in one's mind. That the majority of these photographs are doctored – their backgrounds' whited-out – has possibly contributed to this loss of scale in the image of the myth.

58

In the reconstruction, this apparent increase in scale, the travertine expanse[59, 60] – formally accepted as descendant of the Germanic neo-classical tradition[57] – becomes, because of its colour, some sort of desert; which I connect to the idyll of Saint Jerome's restorative 'place apart'. The Mies Pavilion offers the possibilities: in the open, of Saint Jerome in the desert; under cover, of Saint Jerome in his study. For one can add to those instinctive reasons for accepting the Barcelona Pavilion as myth, an inheritance, by osmosis, of this western idyll.

The old photographs of the Barcelona Pavilion were, naturally enough, black and white, but so were all the photographs of our youth. Our generation was in no doubt as to the nature of the materials – (green) marbles, or (golden) onyx.[61] In fact, directed by the photographs, our myth-image is nearer to what they were than the reconstruction

59

60

61

The Smithsons' path included many visits, trials, detours, revisions, corrections, and reconsiderations. Their unusual compilation of ideas and proposals and judgments, however diverse and unresolved, hangs together because of its complex and opportune aesthetic sensibility, though it often may have been inscrutable to their contemporaries. They were teasing out a sensibility by scrutinizing and looking, an approach Mark Wigley has explained as a kind of delight in the instabilities of their and others' work and the process of design:

> Each presentation, no matter how modest, reworks the work, offering a new singular picture of the design and its "intention", "process", "effect", and so on—words that already imply a unity and clarity in the way architecture is produced and experienced that can never be found in the end. Regardless of the missionary zeal of most architects, the polemical quality of a work is never obvious or stable. It emerges and evolves in the endless selecting and reframing of images and texts that continues long after the work is completed. [...] In fact, the material form turns out to be even more elusive than the drawings. The mysteries delightfully intensify.[18]

Of all their later books, the graphic tactics of *The Shift* exemplify most fully the Smithsons' attempts to negotiate with and profit from recollection. In a brief introduction, they describe their capacious and varying method as "to observe to saturation" and explain that, for them, "to observe was to think ahead and thereby prepare the architectural mind to aim the shaft of invention."[19] They characterize *The Shift* as an attempt to curate "evidence" of a new direction in their work beginning in the late 1960s. Their unusual approach to the monograph and their seemingly idiosyncratic way of organizing its materials were their way of understanding and conveying, for themselves and to their audience, how they got to where they were then, what they believed had changed in "the aesthetic" of their work, and how to look and see what that aesthetic might have been and what it might have become. They identify St. Hilda's as the project that best marks and makes the shift, explaining that in that building "the messages carried by the skin become a first concern. All our previous experiences, and understandings gained in retrospect, of what triggers memory and what sense of time passing and what the wish to take possession and to decorate were thought into its quiet facades."[20] If the interplay of the three adjacent and similar but subtly different towers of their Economist complex was an assertive reaffirmation of their admiration and affection for Mies, St. Hilda's devises yet another, more covert and distinctly personal, Mies-image. Its "treillage'd" skin, inconspicuous siting, straightforward planning, and refined detailing took aspects of the Economist project in directions that explored unique insights into Mies that had been initiated earlier but differently in their design of the Hunstanton School and which would coalesce in the Berlin seminar as their identification of two "separate but reciprocal themes": "an almost autonomous repetitive neutralizing skin; and an open-space-structured [...] recessive, calm, green, urban pattern."[21] From Hunstanton to the Economist complex to St. Hilda's, and facilitated by numerous smaller projects—Christmas cards, small buildings, urban designs—*The Shift*

ARRAY 4.2

presents a complex story of how their Mies-image made its appearance in their work, and how an unbuilt project from the early 1970s, the Lucas Headquarters, may have been, as they remarked years later, "our most ambitious and most fruitful design to date."[22] That project was the culmination of a "clear line of exploration":

> In retrospect, one can detect no special reason why, beginning with the timber lattices of St. Hilda's College, we should be occupied for fifteen years with the exploration of "treillage'd" spaces. In St. Hilda's the timber lattice of the skin was structurally redundant; it was to lead to a conscious deployment of bracings and interlacings that disregard strict structural logic. One can only say perhaps that our generation can see other meanings, other deployments, in the language of modern architecture, including the part of it we had developed ourselves in the 1950s.[23]

The Shift was number 7 in the Academy Editions series of Architectural Monographs but it is less a conventionally curated monograph or retrospective than an autobiographical imaging atlas that reveals how the alterations in the Smithsons' aesthetic are both revisions and returns. Published fifteen years after the Berlin seminar, its presentation insisted on both the lingering importance of New Brutalism (though they entirely avoided the phrase) and extended the sly intensity of their subsequent return to Mies (though almost without ever saying his name). On the rare occasions in *The Shift* when they do mention Mies, it is crucial and revealing. On one spread featuring a large photograph by John Maltby of the housecraft room at Hunstanton along with several drawings and photographs of furniture designs from 1955 and 1958, they remark that their 1955 designs for low tables were never fabricated because "the flat-strip frames" were "too like Mies."[24] The implication, and invitation to look, however subtle it may be, is that the workshop tables in the photograph exemplify another, better version of their Mies-image. Ambivalent juxtapositions, statements, and caveats such as the one on that spread are prompts to look again. When we do, we can see how their design of the laboratory tables in the foreground of Maltby's photo is less "like Mies" than is the rest of the building, and is more "like" the Smithsons' Willys Jeep, which is seen through the glazing in the background of the photograph. Because the vehicle and the furniture appear to be juxtaposed and almost the same size in the photograph, they operate as a version of what Peter, writing about Mies's building layouts in 1966, had called a "gentle, live, equipoise with the people, cars, and trucks of ordinary life."[25] The subtle wit of that and other spreads in *The Shift* shows us that, while the Smithsons' Mies-image did not always look "like Mies," it was by looking at his architecture, more than any other, that they imagined, as a process of "identification," the look of the modernism they were seeking.

ARRAY 4.3

The Shift's one-page introduction begins with the words "looking back" and returns to the beginning of the Smithsons' practice to identify the "first evidence" and "first signs" of their post-1960s approach. That sort of identification is its overt aim, but the Smithsons were looking back from the 1980s with a distinct awareness that their

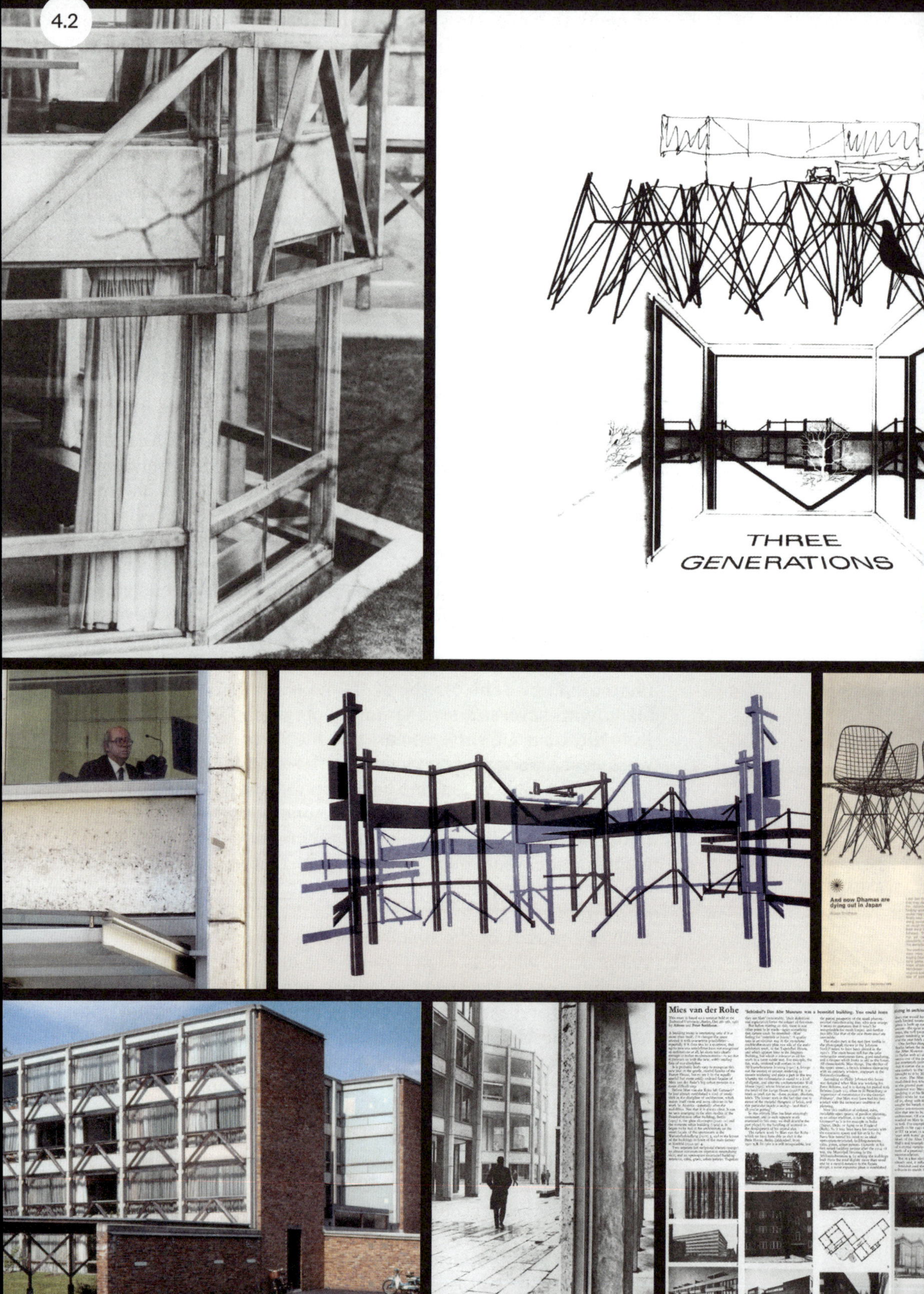
4.2
THREE
GENERATIONS
And now Dhamas are
dying out in Japan
Mies van der Rohe

One knows instinctively that a reduction of urban densities is a human necessity ... This is why we will return so often to Lafayette Park in Detroit, to feel again its decent calm, its openness; to study its methods of putting the car in its place; all achieved without rhetoric ... for us these are the buildings of the hinge-point.

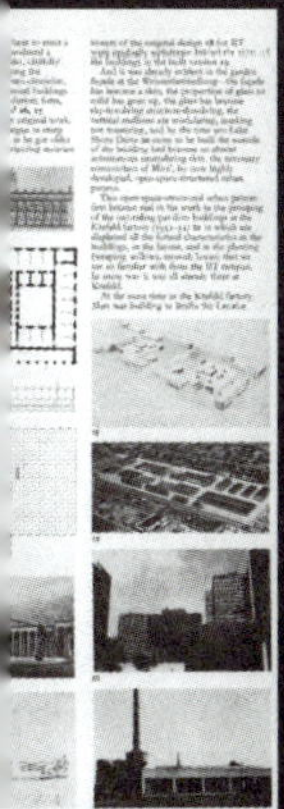

ARCHITECTURAL
Alison +
Smith
A+P Smithson
4.2
Academy Editions

4.3

141. Tokyo Expressway No. 4, near Kandabashi. Built movement

142. Garage; advertisement tear-sheet. Our cities – ar
wish to be?

Series of four photographs of steel details. The extended building period was due to steel rationing; the school took the county's quota for that time. Nigel Henderson.

top left: Green court with ladders.
above left: West green court from top of stairs on the south side.

top right: Gymnasium and reflected gymnasium.
above right: Kitchen yard.

Our repertoire of furniture grew...the Hunstanton serving bench (based on an impression of the hanging mess-bench in the Battleship Potemkin); the cabinet for Jenkins' room; the use of Slingsby Truck parts to make a moveable base to a refurbished marble slab (from a shop front); the sketches made in Limerston Street for tables of marble planks (from fireplace surrounds — the flat-strip frames we thought too like Mies and they were therefore never fabricated); the table base of square rod, painted red oxide (to support the prototype of the Hunstanton door for use as a work table); trestles of rod also painted red oxide (the last two items made by the blacksmith in Dovehouse Street before his smithy was redeveloped as mock-Georgian townhouses); the prototypes of the stick desk lamps attempting to domesticate the fluorescent light; the Pogo chairs of the House of the Future utilising bicycle technology to extend the family of tubular metal chairs of the heroic period

Opposite
Pogo Chair for House of the Future, 1958
(Photos: Sam Lambert)

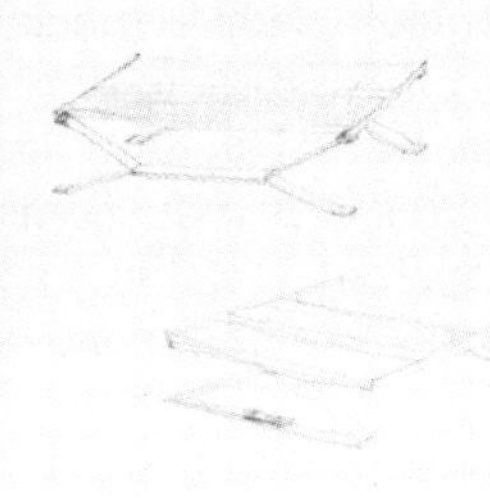

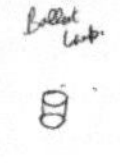

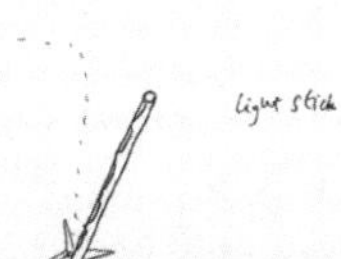

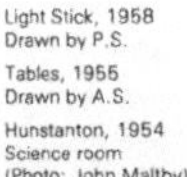

Light Stick, 1958
Drawn by P.S.

Tables, 1955
Drawn by A.S.

Hunstanton, 1954
Science room
(Photo: John Maltby)

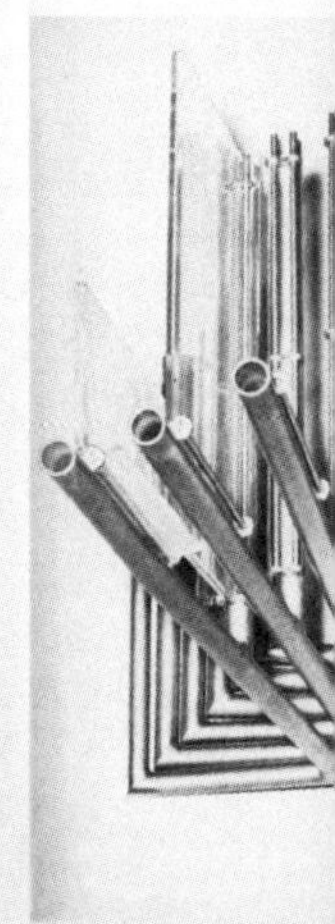

-selves as we now

top: PS with jeep. Nigel Henderson.
above: Checking party, 1953: Clerk of works (Mantelli), PS, and contractor (Crown). Nigel Henderson.

18
Lafayette Park, Detroit: Mies van der Rohe: 1959: photographer C.H. Woodward.

This is why we know instinctively that a reduction of urban densities is a human necessity: we know when we are overcrowded no matter how cleverly stacked one on another.[13] This is why we will return so often to Lafayette Park in Detroit to feel again its decent calm, its openness, to study its methods of putting the car in its place, all achieved without rhetoric. This is why the Chase Manhattan Bank fascinates – its technology and its mechanisms are under control – it has no rhetoric.
This is why we think about the Hochschule fur Gestaltung at Ulm – of its ease, of its ordinariness that has a kind of understated lyricism which is full of potential and does not disturb the peace of the hillside on which it is situated.

13 In ecological terms, crowding means violence: some scientists suggest we shall decline from the stress diseases of overcrowding long before the population increase overruns the food supplies.

19
Chase Manhattan Bank, New York: Skidmore, Owings and Merrill: photographed 1963, P.S.

20
Ulm: Hochschule für Gestaltung: Max Bill: photographed 1956, P.S.

formative ideas and experiences looked different because they were operating in a very different context. "Looking back, it would seem a shift took place in the aesthetic of our architecture in the late 'sixties. The preparation for this shift and the first evidence of it happening—even the first signs of the conviction that there was a need for a shift—can be found in the ephemera of our work," they wrote. The Smithsons recognized that the transformation that had occurred in the 1960s actually had begun a decade earlier when they started to "see things in a new light": "In the early 'fifties, the things thrown away by our own culture, as yet unrecognized as the carriers of a story of identity, were transformed in the images made by Nigel Henderson, whose vision through the camera lens made us look differently, and at least twice, at every old door, boot or rusty nail."[26] That agile and persistent activity of looking was the basis of their interest in and emphasis on ephemera, and was central to their search for an architectural aesthetic and a sensibility "founded on another visual world."

One year after *The Shift*, Alison published a small book intended as a manual demonstrating some of her ways of looking. *AS in DS: An Eye on the Road* was written, but not yet designed, a decade earlier, and its stated focus was the English landscape as seen from a moving car: the family's Citroën DS. Like two other books she had been working on since the late 1960s, which she called

ARRAY 4.4

"sensibility primers" and to which the Smithsons allude in the introduction to *The Shift*—on "the English sensibility of service in India" in the late nineteenth century and the "architecture and graphics" of the modern movement in early twentieth-century Germany,[27] both of which were written from the point of view of a young girl—the actual subject of *AS in DS* is less "the road"—the visual culture and coded history of the English landscape—than "an eye," a graphic elaboration and explanation of Alison's way of observing.[28] As Peter wrote in the book's preface, it is "a diary of car-movement recording the evolving sensibility of a passenger in a car to the post-industrial landscape", or, as Alison wrote in the introduction, "a record of a special recognition by a mind trained to give form: as 'A Diary of a Passenger's View of Movement in a Car'."[29] The book compiles a multitude of observations—sketches, photography, and writing—produced while riding in the Citroën, "a cell of perfected technology" that functioned as a kind of architectural surveillance apparatus—a "room on wheels"—that structured the experience of "car-moved-seeing."[30] *AS in DS* was a creative extension, as Alison explained in an early draft of the introduction, or as Peter stated explicitly in the preface, of the same p articularly British attitude toward viewing and experiencing landscape that had informed the Townscape movement in the 1940s and 1950s, and that Reyner Banham had diagnosed in 1967 as still alive in "the unacknowledged Picturesqueness of the Picturesque's avowed enemies,"[31] including the Smithsons. *AS in DS*, as if responding directly and belatedly to Banham, acknowledged the inescapable latency of that tradition of British seeing and their desire to update it:

> With landscape, we are most encumbered by established English sensibilities, and so deeply involved we have in front of our eyes almost a pre-formed vision, the wherewith-all to relive the whole spirit of the English Picturesque.

> To surmount this fixed-vision, the passenger has behaved towards the scenes passing the windows almost as mechanically as the needle of a seismograph. The result, hopefully, being an unmisted record of the countryside passed through by the car on the road, not unknowingly attuned to the past known aesthetic.[32]

Peter affirmed that position in the book's preface: "In the last quarter of the twentieth century, we have inherited a literature of man and machine in nature but there is as yet no equivalent of the eighteenth-century's understanding which penetrated to all levels of society through the work of writers, artists, landscape designers, and architects."[33] *AS in DS* attempts to assemble that new sensibility and its very different attitude toward the contemporary experience of the built environment through the lens of an oddly French car conceptualized as a moving "camera" or chamber—both a photographic apparatus and a family room.

The Shift is also a sensibility primer but, unlike *AS in DS*, it is not an individual's concentrated study of a particular place, time, and culture but a collaborative and attentive look (though still something of a rough draft, like a carefully assembled scrapbook of images and annotations) at how their work had undergone a major change, from the reverent and rigorous modernism that inspired the initial ethos of New Brutalism as they understood it at the very beginning of their careers, when they designed Hunstanton and the Soho House, to their more recent work in which that modernist ethos was still present but being transformed by new techniques and imagery, as they had already suggested a decade earlier in *Without Rhetoric*:

> The real implications were hidden from us when we started thinking out our position and response to the advertisements contained in the glossy magazines of the 'fifties. Our interest and fascination were a seeming anachronism to our New Brutalist stance unless you read the advertisement images as visual telegrams with a specially loaded message about possibilities of the immediate future.[34]

The Shift is thus a reassessment of how the Smithsons' past ideas and experiences could be, with some precise revision and recombination, still relevant and vital after the emergence of postmodernism and at a time when relatively new forms of media had become commonplace: color television, video, computation, global communications. Those media had been embraced and explored more directly and famously by other London architects, such as Archigram and Cedric Price, or in the performances, installations, and happenings in the contemporary art world and at the Architectural Association's annual Art Net events, organized by Peter Cook from 1974 to 1978. Because all of that was seen at the time, after the demise of New Brutalism, as the legitimate legacy of the Independent Group and Pop, it challenged the Smithsons to venture an honest, open recalibration and reconsideration of the relevance of their current approach, which, in ways that often were seemingly retrograde, celebrated both Mies van der Rohe and "a sort of 'shared'—part national, part European—'memory' of the past."[35]

4.4

ASPECT 2: THE INHERITED SENSIBILITY:
THE WAY WE HAVE BEEN BROUGHT UP TO SEE:

The European sensibility relates to the way we have been taught to see the landscape.
As an 'educated' society we are also able to construct jointly acceptable impressions of previous patterns of use, even previous attitudes, which together form a sort of 'shared' – part national, part European – 'memory' of the past. It is through this largely 'static veil' that we view our inheritance of the landscape.

.... wind from the opposite side-vent blows across the car interior at right-angles to the view driven into .... a half, pumpkin-coloured moon ....
the expanse of road surface has for some reason an American look about it; maybe suggested in sound, perhaps by the colour of the moon ....
road narrows, verge comes close: suddenly the car joins a queue of vehicles in the night: moving fast, their combined displacement-wind washes the herbage of the verge .... the very green weeds of hedgerow foot seen in the close ranked headlights look chilly, damp; how can anyone sleep outside tonight and be a tramp in hedgerows?

LONDON TO FONTHILL: night

.... watchers on bridges over the motorway remind of a Sunday when jeep awaited repair in Montabaur, Germany, and confirm how inviting a late evening this is ....
new houses crowd up to the motorway side ....
then to both sides ....

FONTHILL TO LONDON: M 3: evening

An open society needs an open city. Freedom to move and somewhere to go, both inside and outside the city.
It is this latter aspect which is most worth discussing in detail, for it is in the question of social foci that the difference between the Cluster City idea, and what it is commonly compared with, Los Angeles, can be seen.

19 Social foci and social space[39]

[39] First published in *Architectural Design*, December 1960.

180

178. Advertisements exploiting the desire for relaxation: *a*, t... type; *c*, the open air; *d*, the woods

181

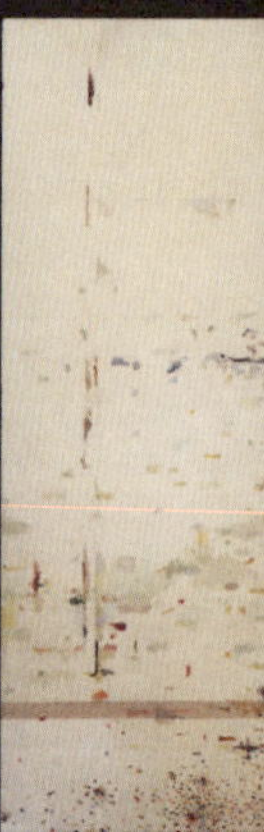

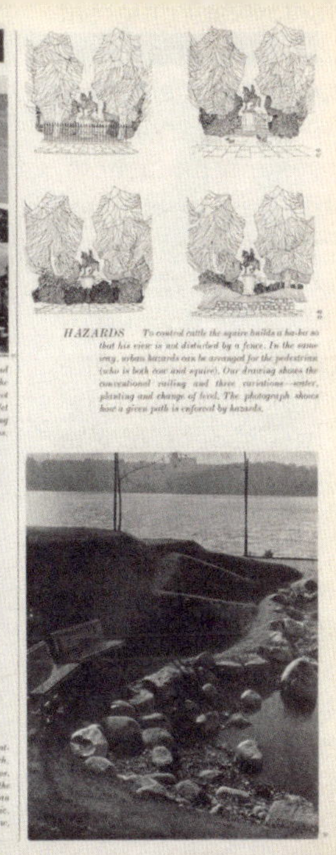

HAZARDS *To control cattle the squire builds a ha-ha so that his view is not disturbed by a fence. In the same way, urban hazards can be arranged for the pedestrian (who is both cow and squire). Our drawing shows the conventional railing and three variations—water, planting and change of level. The photograph shows how a green path is enforced by hazards.*

In small villages in Germany people gather on fine Sundays at vantage points overlooking the autobahn just to see the cars go by. And

134. Flyover near Montabaur. The Cologne-Limburg autobahn through Westewald

this is a very moving experience, for one feels in contact with the life-stream of Europe, and not just of Germany.

So, in this Berlin Plan we have: cars as spectacle ⇓ look down to roads: people as spectacle ⇑ look up to escalators and terraces.

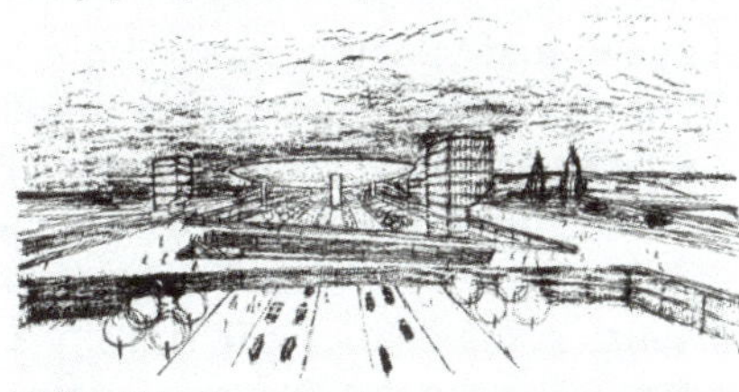

135. Movement systems

To enhance the particular form of movement direct. And the pedestrian platform is free and irr and spaces for the random patterns of pedestrian is directed down to the streets below.

136. Hauptstadt Berlin 1958. In the centre is the upper communication linking the shopping, entertainment and drawing by Peter Sigmond)

Systems of access are also places.

Consider for example the social implications houses around a small parking lot, or turn-aroun ment under continuous social scrutiny.

The opportunity for opting-out of a given soci one of the reasons why people have chosen to bu even if their 'neighbourhood' is in Surrey or New one's associations, and not forced by the size o munity into unchosen relationships from which it is a genuine twentieth-century necessity.

Car movement is flow movement: not the starting, changing direction, turning around, of t

To flow means to move evenly at speeds to sui national roads, to slow on house access roads.

ASPECT 6: CHANGE

As something of a stocktaking ten years after the first writing of THE EYE ON THE ROAD: A DIARY OF A PASSENGER'S VIEW OF CAR MOVEMENT, this selected text covers the improvement of roads in the decade nineteen-seventy to nineteen-eighty.
We know we need to mutate places by building towards an image of towns-in-the-landscape that will satisfy the new sensibilities and allow freedom from pressures of all kinds.

.... pines rest very easily on the mind: a person does not even have to think about the problems of agriculture ....
incredibly mild weather means the yellow of elms is wonderfully perpetuated ....
holly and such shiny evergreens glisten darkly in the rain until obliterated from sight by the rain becoming a downpour ....
gorse in bloom has furry cases against the rain ....
the car slides endlessly forward, past specimen trees of the English landscape, the car movement allows the viewing of each specimen in three-quarters round: if not a mite more ....
odd thickets, perhaps allotment-land intended for poor cottagers to gather faggots in – certainly that sort of [illegible] – seen in rain-and-sack-cloth-weather ....
misty sky touches the ground now and then as the contours rise ....
on the tarmacadam [illegible] as road-hit alters towards the sky-glare .... and the road angle alters wildly, changing continually in passing the car through the countryside under the sky ....
the car moves forever forwards, chasing some tail-lights .... some, but fewer, headlights approach, and pass .... grass bright-wet .... hedgerows alternately line the way .... either make the car's progression an avenue way .... or slip in a glimpse of a ploughed piece of topography ....

BLACKBUSH

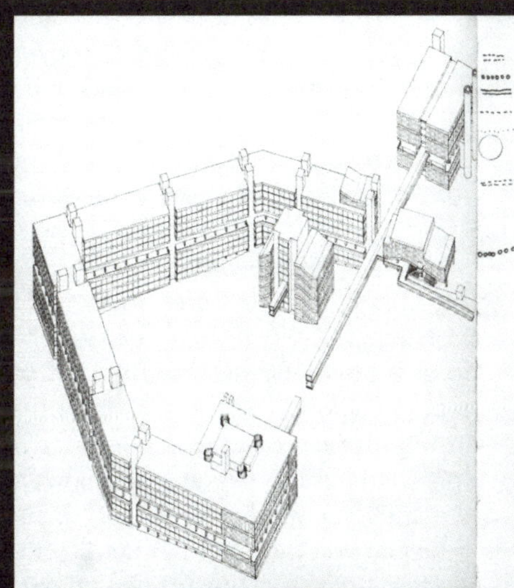

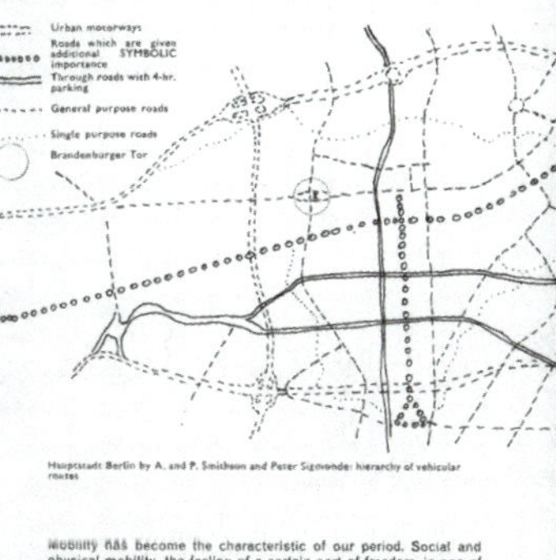

Hauptstadt Berlin by A. and P. Smithson and Peter Sigmonde: hierarchy of vehicular routes

Mobility has become the characteristic of our period. Social and physical mobility, the feeling of a certain sort of freedom, is one of the things that keeps our society together, and the symbol of this freedom is the individually owned motor car. Mobility is the key both socially and organizationally to town planning, for mobility is not only concerned with roads, but with the whole concept of a mobile, fragmented, community. The roads (together with the main power lines and drains) form the essential physical infra-structure of the community. The most important thing about roads is that they are big, and have the same power as any big topographical feature, such as a hill or a river; to create geographical, and in consequence social, divisions. To lay down a road therefore, especially through a built-up area, is a very serious matter for one is fundamentally changing the structure of the community.

The Shift has two sections that each employ very different graphic approaches to imaging. The first section is a sixty-five-page, not quite chronological, predominantly photographic exposition of the evolving look of the Smithsons' work from 1950 to 1978, including buildings, furniture, interiors, exhibition designs, posters, snapshots, drawings, sketches, models, and Christmas cards. It is an attempt to array and annotate images of their work that could demonstrate how their sensibility evolved and ultimately shifted in ways that they still were trying to harness and understand in 1982. By encouraging their "readers" to look carefully at a diverse range of images and to consider them as directly comparable and interrelated in surprising ways (aided by brief texts and captions), the first section of *The Shift* graphically conveys their ways of looking. By evading strict chronology, the Smithsons assembled a shifty story of the particular resonances and specific connections among aspects of their work, identifying themes, devices, and predilections that likely would not otherwise be apparent, even to themselves. For example, Hunstanton appears only intermittently, and usually as the counterpart of other work: in the section's second spread along with Jenkins Room (1952);

ARRAY 4.5

in the ninth spread along with drawings and photographs of furniture (1955 and 1958); in the fourteenth spread along with drawings of the unbuilt Wokingham School (1958), the project which they identified as a crucial precedent for the unbuilt Lucas Headquarters (1974), which is featured on the book's cover; and finally, once as a full spread—a set of four color photographs showing Hunstanton at various stages of construction and from different distances and points of view.

The second, shorter section of the monograph is a precisely chronological selection of thirty-four "Working Drawings" for nine built projects—buildings, exhibitions, and furniture—beginning with Hunstanton. The drawings are presented in three "groups" of two or three projects—dated 1949–54, 1955–58, and 1960–64—plus a fourth part with just one project: "The Shift: The Garden Building at St. Hilda's (1967–1970)." The term "working drawings" is intended to be evocative and precise, but not technical. Six of the drawings are not construction documents but other kinds of hard-lined or freehand architectural projections: perspectives and axonometrics. The implied objectivity of the second section is accentuated by its more descriptive and even briefer texts, as if to say that working drawings are more indexical and factual than the predominantly photographic images of the first section. The writing is direct and declarative, beginning with the first sentence: "The shift became visible in our architecture at St. Hilda's (1967–70): its aesthetic had been built up unknowingly in the ephemera of our work during the whole of the previous decade." The beginning of those ten years, 1957–67, corresponds precisely with the Smithsons' return to Mies, Peter's first trip to America.

The section of working drawings establishes St. Hilda's as the culmination of a process that was initiated by the three projects in the first group, Hunstanton, Jenkins Room, and *Parallel of Life and Art*, which, the Smithsons explain, were "all going on at the same time as the construction period of the Hunstanton School [. . .]. All three are arrangements of straight lines and flat planes overlaid with other sorts of images. [. . .] Our pattern of work has in fact never really changed. It is based on a more Puritan reading (via Mies) of the strip plans and sections and the selected full-size details that our student drawings had to provide."[36] That insistence on deep continuities that "in fact never really changed" sets up their surprising claim that the two seemingly unrelated projects in the second group—the House of the Future (1956) and the Sugden House in Watford (1956–58)—"played the same eyes," even if one "took a straight look at curved panels and gaskets" and the other worked with "true vernacular materials. Marley tiles, stock bricks, Crittall's windows, Batley's up-and-over doors and so on." Equally surprising is their decision not to include their working drawings for *Patio and Pavilion* in that group, as its materials and effects offer a third and perhaps more explicit variation on the "pattern of work" exploring "arrangements of straight lines and flat planes overlaid with other sorts of images."[37] Less surprising, for the same reason, is the Smithsons' description of a small project in the third group, the Occupational Health Unit at Park Royal Hospital, London (1962–63), as a "more complex, more knowing" version of the "frame-and-glass-directly-put-together of Hunstanton. But already the formal organization of the plan is more relaxed and the skin carries many more messages for its users than was carried by the earlier building's well-seamed transparency. This small work is a logical follower [of Hunstanton] but also a forerunner of St. Hilda's."[38]

ARRAY 4.6

The Smithsons intended the collection of working drawings in the second section to tell a story of clear influence, lineage, and development quite unlike the tactical juxtapositions and evocative flashbacks of the first section, which offer a more seductive invitation to look carefully and see precisely the "general sensibility" of the "random aesthetic" they were working on and towards for three decades. The first spread in the first section—the beginning of the telling of the story of the shift—features a brief text, four of Henderson's photographs of *Parallel of Life and Art*, and a reproduction of the show's accordion catalogue unfolded so it can be viewed as one continuous strip. The two-paragraph text in the upper left corner of the spread, with margins justified right and left and aligned top and bottom with the edges of the adjacent photograph, treats the text graphically like an identically sized and similarly striated rectangular image that both looks and reads like what the Smithsons liked to call a "verbal illustration." It begins with a simultaneously clear and uncertain declaration: "The very first (and second?) winter's ephemera, 1949 (1950?), had been Ray-ograms." It continues with an evocative description of those "one-off" photographic prints—the earliest editions of Alison's Christmas cards—which were produced by positioning objects directly on the paper in an enlarger.[39] Each card was a unique photogram that recorded "different compositions of a scatter of Christmas fragments [...] floating down through the photographic print like snow. Scatter as an aesthetic would reappear briefly, 1964, then the theme returns strongly, 1969, and throughout the following years."[40] Thus a series of unique photographic Christmas cards is the first example of work presented—highly allusively, as a verbal illustration—in a monograph covering over thirty years of architectural production. The text's second, much shorter paragraph offers a prosaic description of *Parallel of Life and Art*, as if the Smithsons were content to write differently about it because Henderson's four photographs were more than adequate to convey its significance.

ARRAY 4.7

nages happ… images: the introduction f a plane, th… …o of whose images were ontrapuntal to that of its setting. These spatial anoeuvres interested us (and lay behind our attempt get Norfolk Education Authority to purchase aolozzi fabric curtains for the Assembly Hall at unstanton, 1953). We achieved the upturning and -tuning of existing space to make it indisputably of present in the room for Ronald Jenkins, Charlotte treet, 1952, with its Paolozzi wallpapered ceiling itched up in black poster paint into a single omposition by Eduardo himself (sighing heavily the hile, interspersed by our remarks about ichelangelo's socks). Contrapuntal fragments in ollage decorated the box for the Arup projector, 1952. And from that same period the tuning of pace by the collage of Greek newspapers cut olygonally and stuck on the basement stairwall (after uch repair of plaster) in Limerston Street, winter 953?, a re-play of the temple podium wall, Delphi, if first seen in the dark at the back of that grocer's op but seen by us in summer sun, 1951.

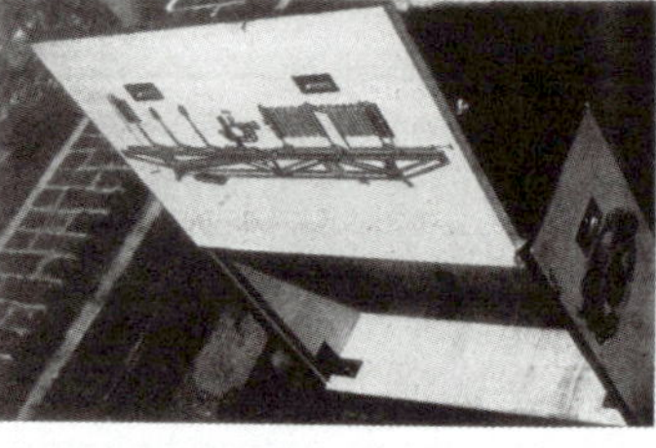

Slide projector box for Ove Arup and Partners, 1952

Ronald Jenkins' room in Charlotte Street, 1952 (Photo: J.R. Pantlin)

Opposite
Hunstanton. Perspective of exterior view of kitchen court with water tower.
Drawn P.S., 1950

Interior view of hall
(Photo: de Burgh Galwey)

Perspective of interior, view through hall.
Drawn P.S., 1950

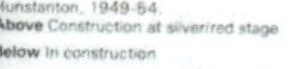

unstanton, 1949-54.
Above Construction at silver/red stage
elow In construction

Above Construction at red/black stage
Below Finished

vices, but just as traditional as those adapted rbusier, were used to delineate Hunstanton's spaces. The school's approach side had the verge to the ha-ha, by which the school was separated from the road (as at 's Seaton Delaval); making clear which was ound and which was the school. The walking were gravel, as befitted a country school, tly formal, echoing the walks of nearby ham. By being raised up, the gravel walk on ng fields' side mastered the field's surface; ed fore-slope took up the difference in the forming a softer edge to the podium on e school stood. At the sides were hard pitches, contained by kitchen-garden-type der the influence of 'The Secret Garden', Hodgson Burnett, Heinemann, 1935, walls in parallel — as at Hunstanton — own to' us only in 1978; Melbourne, e, 1704 to 1711, by Wise (and London?).

n, 1954

The placing of the built elements on the site in th Wokingham Infants' and Primary School design 1958, signalled a further turning away from th immediate pre and post-war school that wa wastefully dumped on its site. The form c Wokingham grasped its territory, holding the line c trees which were remembrances of a previous patter of use, as a hand would a pencil. To reach th doorstep of each class 'street' a child would hav used the angular handspan of paths which throug the different aims of the paths, and increasin distance to objective, would have identified eac class unit and positioned it in the school's hierarch

Wokingham School, 1958

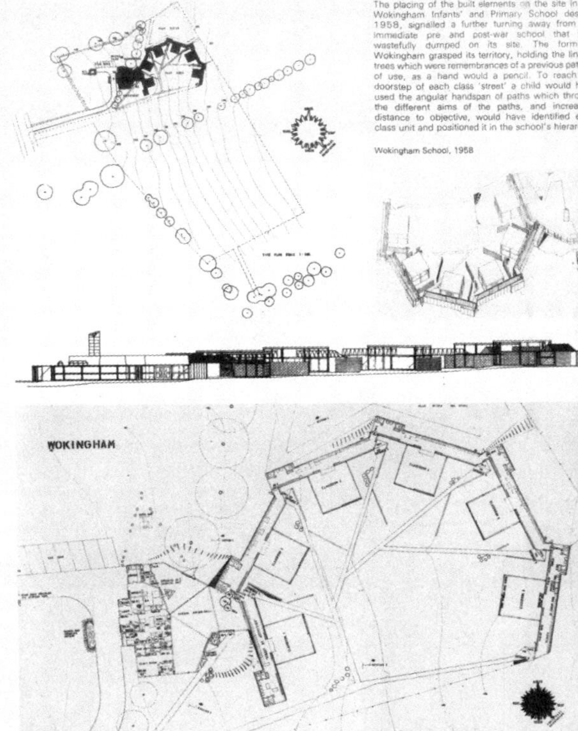

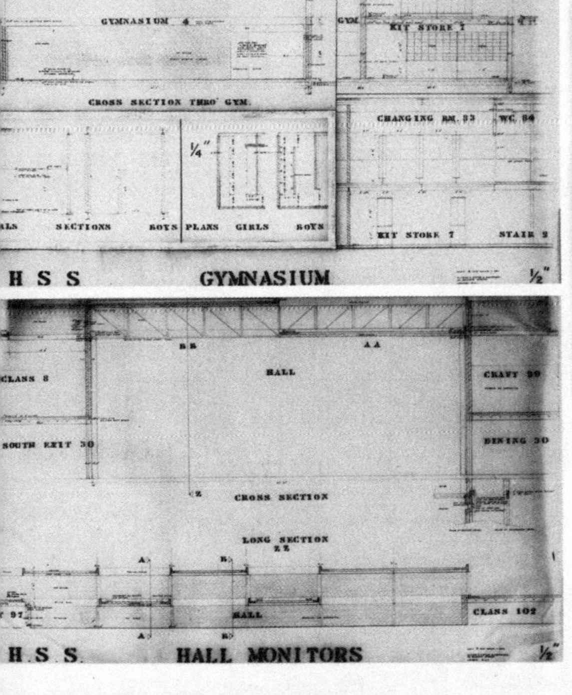

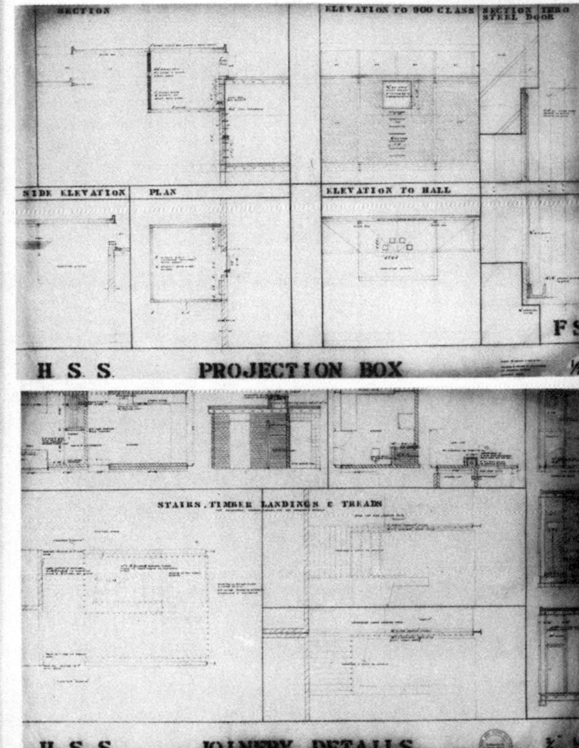

4.6

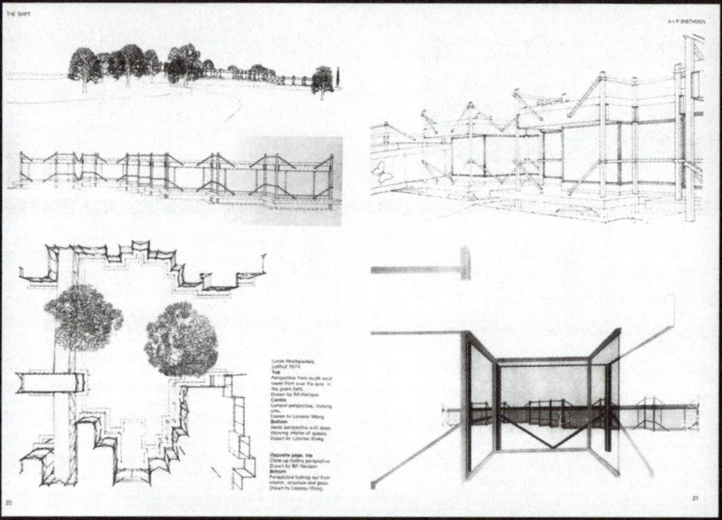

pational Health Clinic, Park Royal

Spring 1962 – 1964
AS
Subsequently demolished

vilion clinic is of the Bayswater/Upper Lawn family. It sits on given land at the foot of an unused Guinness embankment and faces—across a road—the canal. It is a centre for preventative medicine on an industrial

ber-and-glass pavilion is simplicity itself. The treatment rooms are almost secret adjuncts to the prime function mation giving—exhibitions as to the effects of smoking, machine-safety procedures, and so on—which is in a see-through room that can be entered equally well from either side.

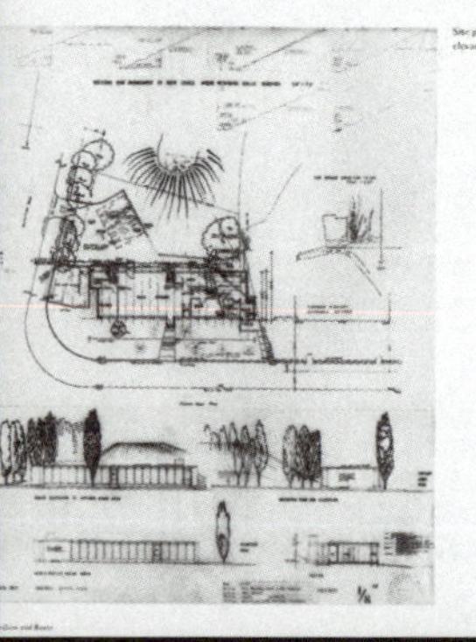

Site plan and plan; elevations. AS.

Elevation towards Guinness railway siding mound. Sam Lambert.

Two views from the road side. The view into the interior was an 'occupational' requirement. PS, 1963.

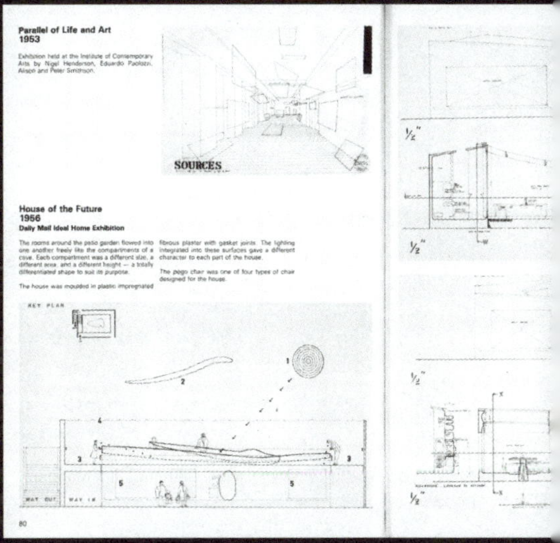

23

Parallel of Life and Art 1953

Exhibition held at the Institute of Contemporary Arts by Nigel Henderson, Eduardo Paolozzi, Alison and Peter Smithson.

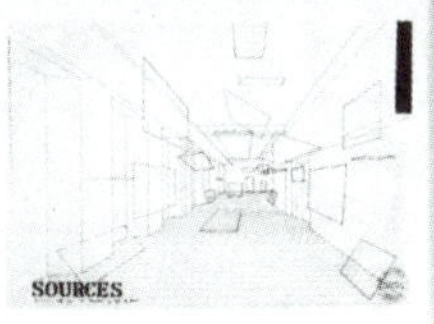

House of the Future 1956

Daily Mail Ideal Home Exhibition

The rooms around the patio garden flowed into one another freely like the compartments of a cave. Each compartment was a different size, a different area, and a different height — a totally differentiated shape to suit its purpose.

The house was moulded in plastic impregnated fibrous plaster with gasket joints. The lighting integrated into these surfaces gave a different character to each part of the house.

The *pogo* chair was one of four types of chair designed for the house.

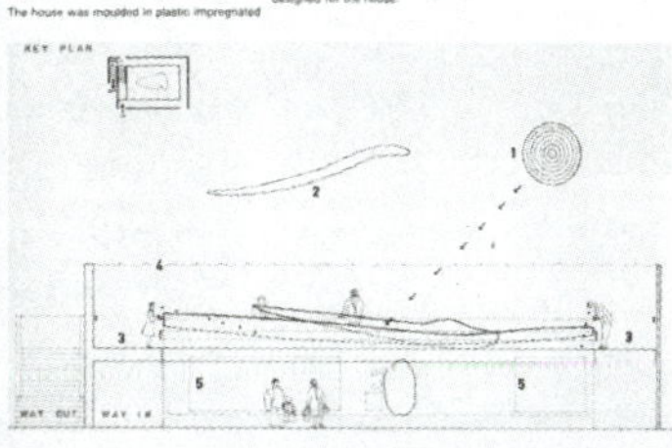

80

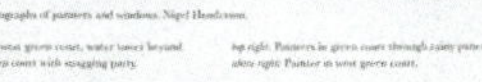

...photographs of painters and windows. Nigel Henderson.

top right: Painters in green court through rainy panes.
above right: Painter in west green court.

Series of four photographs of construction details. The anglicisation of the Mies influence of the Hunstanton is complete. Nigel Henderson.

4.7

he very fir[...]ond?) winter's ephemera, 949 (1950?), [...]een Rayograms: of their one-ff nature, different compositions of a scatter of hristmas fragments...bits of shrub to represent fir ees, glitter and stencilled letters (a set of stencils ought in Italy, August 1949) floating down through e photographic print like snow. Scatter as an esthetic would reappear briefly, 1964, then the eme returns strongly, 1969, and throughout the llowing years. The theme represented by the oating stencilled word 'Xmas' might be said to have eralded the attempt to break free of the trabeated ivisions of space (it was the time of Le Corbusier's ery expensive *Le Poème de l'Angle Droit*). Naturally is ephemera is out of style/phase with the graphic esign of the period in which it happened, for the emes explored are personal; like underground reams which will feed our architecture maybe years ter. In this sense they are genuine ephemera, omething in the air and drifting by, to be caught, oked at and released into other work.

the exhibition Parallel of Life and Art at the Institute f Contemporary Art, September 1953, planes of nages were suspended from the ceiling or angled gainst the walls, as if floating in space (an exhibition ade with Nigel Henderson and Eduardo Paolozzi nd supported by a donation from Ronald Jenkins, unstanton's engineer at Arup).

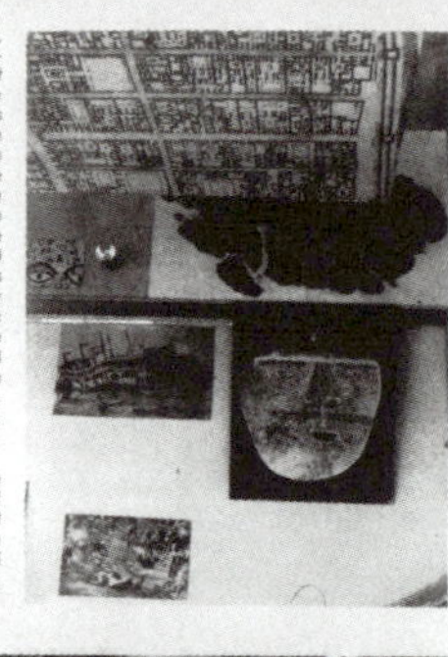

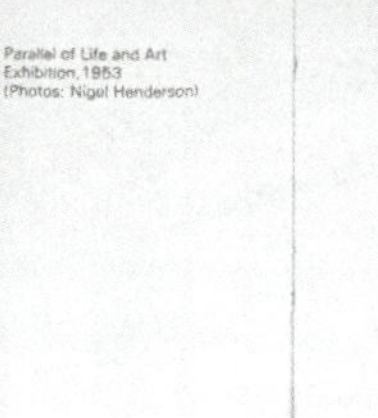

Parallel of Life and Art Exhibition,1953 (Photos: Nigel Henderson)

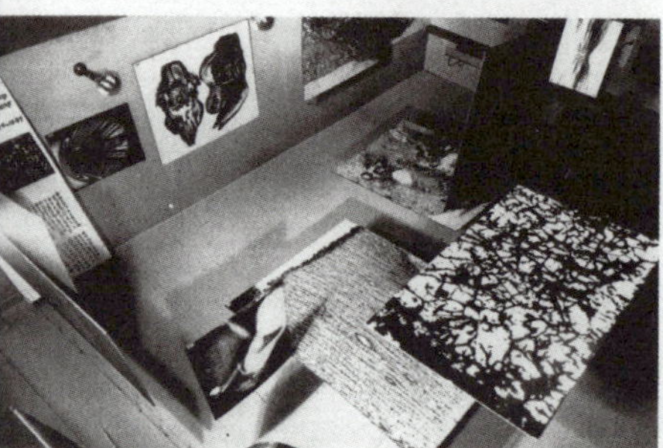

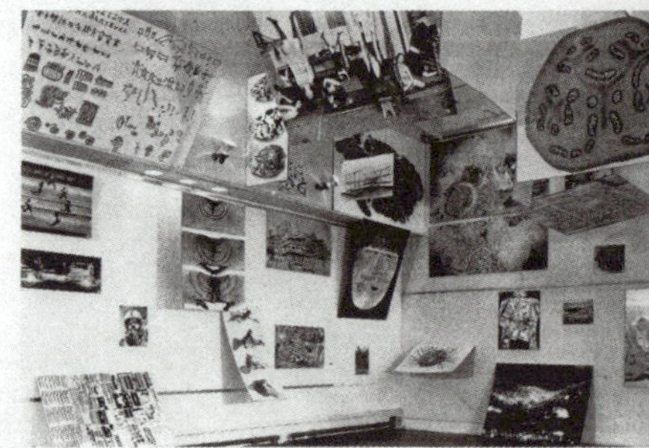

Parallel of Life and Art Catalogue at ICA, 1953

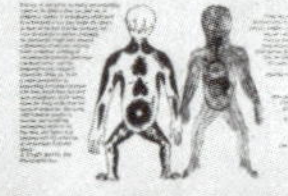
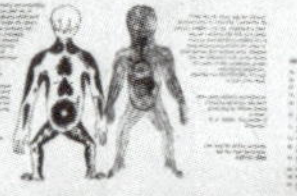

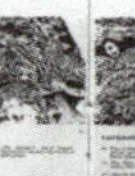

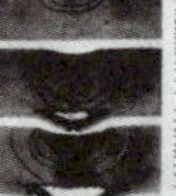

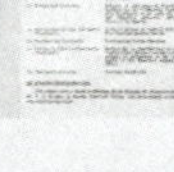

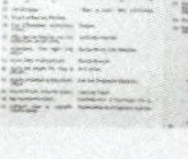

The ephemera of the shift achieved:

1969 Brown larch twigs: lino cut, printed black on light-brown Japanese paper, cut-out perforations, overlaid on chocolate-colour Japanese paper, inserts of cut-out French marbled paper.

1968 Wrapping paper: fircone printed on gold (old woodcut block) and office stamp, printed in gold on brown tissue paper.

1970 Fircones collection: lino-cut, printed in silver on chocolate-brown Japanese paper, cut-out profile.
Wrapping paper: larch twigs (old lino block), printed in gold as layer composition on brown tissue-paper.

1971 Snowman: two lino-cuts, cupressus fringe frame, robin, snowman's face, buttons, printed tan on white, metallic-*eau-de-nil* snowman on white; metallic-red chest to robin, profile cut-out.

1972 Wrapping paper: fircone (old lino block) printed in silver on blue tissue-paper.

1972 Wrapping paper: Christmas tree (old wood block) and robins (old envelope stamp cut from an eraser) printed in indigo on cherry tissue-paper.

1972 Pinecones: zinc block from line drawing, printed black on invitation cards.

1972 Re-used zinc block: printed metallic-*eau-de-nil* on raspberry Japanese paper.

1973 Christmas greenery: large lino-cut, printed in silver on indigo Japanese paper, metallic-red berries.

1973 Wrapping paper: fircones and pine cones (old blocks) metallic-red on blue tissue-paper, in combinations, some as wreaths.

1977 Wrapping paper: fircones (old block) and office stamp, printed in gold on white tissue-paper in the form of wreaths.

1978 Gone swimming... new freedoms discovered in the 'fifties and 'sixties. Art Net Rally, Central School.

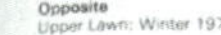

Opposite
Upper Lawn: Winter 1978

Right
Economist Plaza occupied by Paolozzi Sculpture, 1967

Below
Robin Hood Gardens
Interior of hall from deck into flat, Blackwall Tunnel, 1971

Through lift lobby looking into yard of head flat, 1972

Cotton Street: bare trees and trees in blossom, 1976, 1977

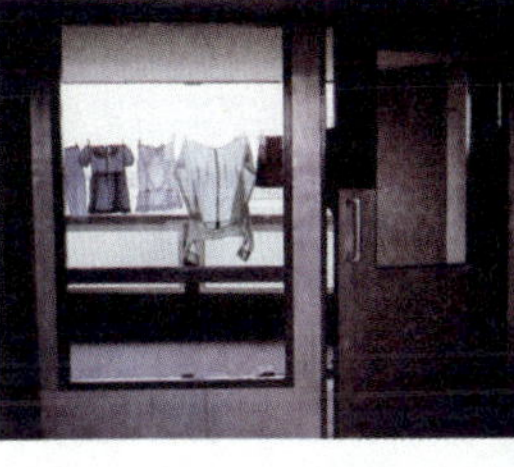

Ephemera of this approach:

1971 Notice of removal, Priory Walk to Gilston Road: zinc block made from line drawing; printed broken black on natural-coloured, light-weight Japanese flock paper. (J?)

1973–77 Re-used zinc block: note/invitation card printed black on gilt-edged card.

1978 Re-used block: twenty-first birthday invitation printed gold on gilt-edge card, gold text.

1974 Ice-theatre: folded box frame in white-flock paper, cut-out icicles of spun-textured foil.

1975 Rustic Christmas vista: lino-cut, printed black on white paper, dye-marbled, faded, blue-jeans colour; silver-blue metallic glitter.

Signs of Occupancy at Christmas: re-work of collage of 1953, a pair of photographs (people received one or the other): hamlet/village, town/city, hand-tinted with blue-silver shadows on snow, metallic gold lights in the windows, red metallic dust on robin and sunset.

Ephemera that spell out our respect for our industrial past utilising the strong sense of connection.

1970–71 Tram flats collages: of people and trams (GLC photographic archives) overlaid by clear acrylic sheet on which red poppies and white daisies are painted; made in Priory Walk, winter before removal.

1976 Mounted enlargement of open-topped tram, depicted as in a field of red poppies: in remembrance of the inventions of our industrial past, whose powerful imagery we have to match with inventions of our own. Art Not Rally, West Central Street.

All these can be thought of as exercises towards the right touch for the event, the response that is so exactly pitched to the scale of the problem that it 'triggers' a reciprocity, a wish in others to take a part – to make the place 'as found' receptive to the new thing.

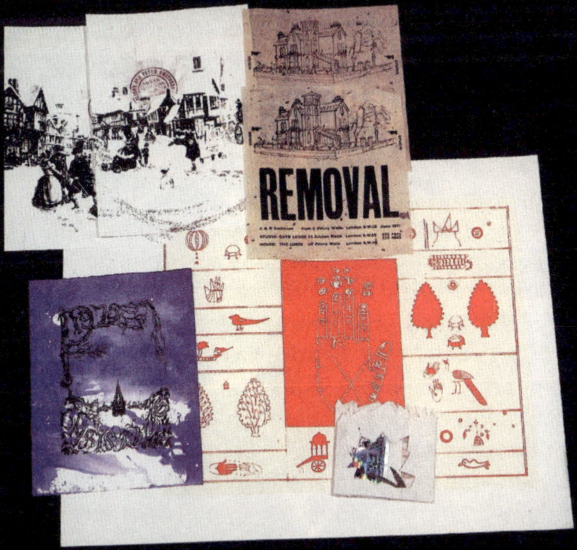

That tactical and versatile manner of imaging was the Smithsons' way of conveying—both in the sense of communicating visually and transporting temporally—the beginnings, development, and alterations of their manner of observing. Looking and imaging were necessarily combined as the productive and expressive means of their "aesthetic" and their "sensibility." Their imaging approach was a way of looking at and looking for architecture anywhere, in anything. Its earliest sources lay in their Independent Group influences, as clearly expressed and synopsized in their 1956 essay "But Today We Collect Ads," but also in their deep, if largely intuitive, inculcation of postwar intellectual culture, exemplified in books such as E. A. Gutkind's *Our World from the Air* (1952) and *The Expanding Environment* (1953), J.R.M. Brumwell's *This Changing World* (1945), or Gordon Rattray Taylor's *Conditions of Happiness* (1949) and *Are Workers Human?* (1950).[41] There also are canny affinities between their ways of looking and the ways visuality was being radically rethought in contemporary British philosophy, particularly the ongoing critiques of the empiricist conception of knowledge as the apprehension of mental images. The Smithsons' manners of formulating design intentions have much in common with one of the most significant of those critical positions. In his influential 1949 book *The Concept of Mind*, Gilbert Ryle explained imagination as the production and performance of what he called "acquired dispositions" or "intelligent capacities."[42] Like many of his British contemporaries—analytic philosophers, ordinary language philosophers, and Ludwig Wittgenstein—Ryle's aim was to subvert what he called the "Official Doctrine" of modern philosophy, which ratified "a polar opposition between mind and matter" and which presumed an analogy or correspondence between inner and outer worlds of experience.[43] Ryle's immediate example of that "dogma of the Ghost in the Machine" was the British empiricist distinction between "sensations and images," in which the latter are "genuine but ghostly likenesses" of the former.[44] For Ryle, that representational model of imagination as an experience of mental images (that are secondary to but also similar to sensory experiences) imposes what he called a "category mistake." He proposed a very different distinction, one that is not categorical but operational, between sensation and *observation*: "Observing is finding out, or trying to find out, something, but having a sensation is neither finding out, nor trying to find out, nor failing to find out, anything."[45] Ryle argued that imagination is not a process of generating and experiencing internalized, representational mental images. Imagination "does not entail the existence of pictures which we contemplate or the existence of a gallery in which such pictures are ephemerally suspended."[46] He sometimes preferred the word "imaging" over either images or imagination for the way it emphasizes "performance" and "actualization" over the "Cartesian Myth" of privatized experiences or the British empiricist emphasis on mental images. Ryle was proposing, as he wrote in one pithy phrasing, that when one is using one's imagination, "imaging occurs, but images are not seen."[47] Or in another, which is equally applicable to the experience of *Parallel of Life and Art* and the production and use of working drawings: "Imaging is not having shadowy pictures before some shadow organ called 'the mind's eye'; but having paper pictures before the eyes in one's face is a familiar stimulus to imaging."[48] In alignment with the Smithsons' claim that "to observe was to think ahead and thereby prepare the architectural mind to aim the shaft of invention," Ryle proposed imagination as achieved intelligence or as dispositions that matter when they are "exercised" as "abilities and propensities."[49]

A sympathy with that sort of looking or observation is evident in the way the Smithsons present Henderson's four photographs of the image arrays in *Parallel of Life and Art* on the first spread of *The Shift*. None of the photographs provides a wide, encompassing view of the room. Each subtly or decidedly crops the original photograph, with the effect of suppressing the containing architecture of the gallery in favor of the play of surfaces of the panel-images in the exhibit and among the four photographs on the spread, each of which offers a different sort of view or "stimulus to imaging": a flattened and foreshortened shot of a portion of a wall and the ceiling that appears horizontally stratified; an oblique shot of the end wall, on which smaller images are packed tightly as if in an eighteenth-century salon of landscapes or portraits; a perspectival shot of a corner where two walls and the ceiling meet; and an oblique close-up of a constellation of images of especially abstract patterns overhead. That last photograph is printed upside down in *The Shift*, and its inversion, whether intended or a printing error, affirms, in effect and in fact, the arrays' enveloping and beguiling qualities as they are replicated in the layout. As mentioned earlier, the spread also includes, along the length of its bottom edge, the miniaturized version of the exhibition catalogue, which includes nine of the exhibition's 122 images and a listing of all of them (though printed too small for the text to be read). It thus no longer serves its original purpose as an annotated inventory or index. In this graphic format it functions as a visual synopsis, or what might be taken as a "POLAA Grille" of the room. The catalogue also has been altered: one page is repeated on each side of the gutter. The spread thus extends the synoptic effect of the catalogue by operating as a fragmentary and sampled reinstallation that restates as directly and succinctly as possible, on just two pages, the visual character and effects of the exhibition. Remembering that the Smithsons thought of each of their books as a kind of architectural project, "like a building in miniature,"[50] the spread is best viewed with the book opened at a 90-degree angle, like the meeting of two walls. This enhances the mirroring effect of the pages' graphic symmetry, which can be imagined as if they were a single double-surfaced photographic image that has been delaminated or can be shuffled and reconstructed in a manner not unlike the way one might play with the accordion catalogue.[51] One might even imagine both the catalogue and *The Shift* as cousins of the Eameses' *House of Cards* (1952), and thus examples of what the Smithsons called the "scaffolding of a graphics of occupation"[52] or the "select and arrange technique" of "the Eames Aesthetic."[53] The complex design of the spread offers a precise yet scrambled sense of how *Parallel of Life and Art* was the beginning or source of a new, shifted imaging aesthetic and an architectural imaginary through which the Smithsons came to see new possibilities in Hunstanton just at the moment it was reaching completion in late 1953.

ARRAY 4.8

The pairing of projects on the next spread continues that logic: two photographs of Jenkins Room on the left page and one

4.8

… other later tradition, that of the Crystal Palace, in which the surface is a regularly seamed glass skin which has no representational function as to structure, or arrangement, or determination of the thing it covers. The decision on the size of the unit of repetition for a seamed glass skin is similar to any other decision on the unit size of sheet material – with stone facings or glass it is traditionally related to the whole of which the units form part, but with plywood or patent-glazing the unit is almost certainly in practice that of the standard economic size (or sizes). When a building is made of standard pieces it would seem that it should be thought about in terms of the standard sizes of those pieces, the whole be derived from the part in some way – an inversion of the classical tradition. When the skin of a building is glass, or tinted glass, what is inside is pretty explicit anyway. That inside can be the carrier of the formal idea in the traditional way, or can become the scaffolding of *a graphics of occupation* in the Eames[24] way, that is, part of a kind of visual conversation between the immovable inside, the seamed glass skin, and a graphic equivalent of the occupiers' activities.

Are there any further traditions or understandings which would help us with repetition?

When we ourselves are *moved* by repetition it is by very grand, very simple affairs; all dominated by big-scaled, repeated forms, and bent or curved on plan so that repetition in a mechanical sense seems melted away.[25]

The amphitheatres at Arles or el Djem . . . the aqueduct outside Tunis . . . any long curved railway viaduct . . . on these

24 Eames Celebration, *Architectural Design*, September 1966.

34
Opposite: Palm House, Kew: Interior from gallery: photographed 1970, S.S.

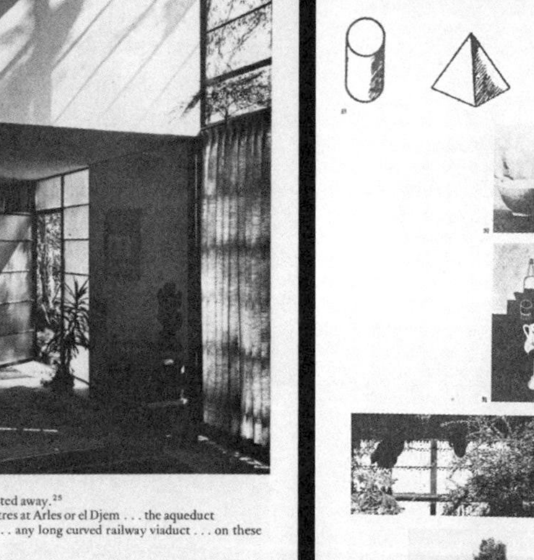

35 Interior of Eames House: visited in 1958, P.S.

25 The use of light in 'Son et Lumière'–shone on only one section and from an 'unnatural' location such as ground level, which can make such unsuccessful flat repetitive buildings as Versailles or Blenheim momentarily seem marvellous–is a related phenomenon.

33

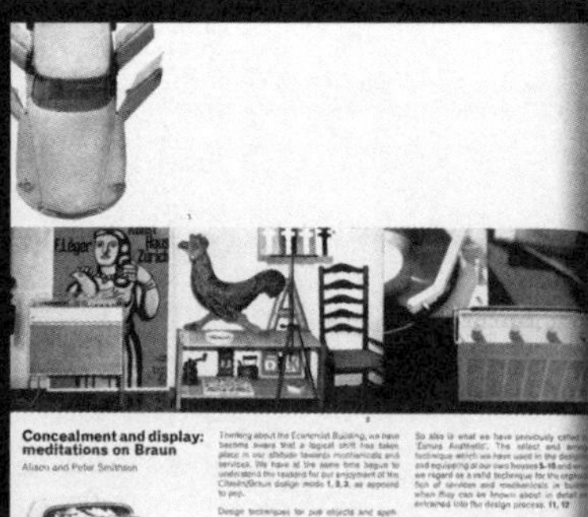

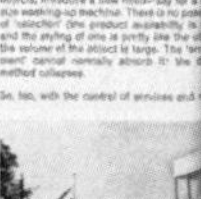

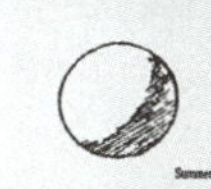

Summer 1966, PS.

'Just a Few Chairs and a House: an Essay on the Eames Aesthetic', Architectural Design, September 1966.

whole design climate was per-
d by the work of Charles and Ray
chairs and a house.
e always been the forward-run-
ange. They have for some mys-
capacity for establishing a new
most overnight. Rietveld estab-
w design mode with a chair. So
th his.
he Eames moved design away
aesthetic and bicycle technol-
d lived since the 1920s, into the
a-eye and the technology of the
t; from the world of the painters
he layout men.
the machine-aesthetic and the
re art forms of ordinary life and
seen with an eye that sees the
nagical.'
sthetic selected with care those
ary life that were based on sim-
– on cones, on spheres, on
s: objects whose commonality
s profiles; that is, pictures could
r arrangement and out of which
ould be erected.''
aesthetic, crystalised in the
Monica Canyon, California,
machine-aesthetic was given
he 'dwelling unit' in the Pavilion
u at the Exposition des Arts Dec-
5), is based on an equally care-
th extra-cultural surprise, rather
rofile, as its criteria. A kind of
of seeing the culturally disparate
happy with each other. This
y, but the basic vehicle – the
in the case of the house, the
our processing in the graphics
s and mouldings in the case of
ordinary to the culture.
separates the Eames' 'selec-
ion' technique from neo-Victo

' This sounds like a description of the role of Hollywood films as myth-maker to America.

'' See Ozenfant's The Foundation of Modern Art.

The Rocket

Peter Smithson

A statement on the present stat
architecture giving a certain ration
to our instinctive judgements on it

The 'Rocket' was recognizably 'made'.
pieces of things which also remained t
selves. We recognize their source, the
untransformed even re-usable, prim
entraining us into the romance of boats
carts, of plate-wagonways and horses.

The modern locomotive is 'designed'. All ap
parts useless for anything else coming tog
to make a complete 'object'. An 'object'
in no way reminds us of the steamers it displ
and if we like it, it is for what it is, not for
emotions it entrains by reminding us of pre
technologies.

It is tempting to use the difference bet
'assembled' and 'designed' as the simpl
criteria to decide what is architecture a
present time. For architecture in this ce
has always stood pretty close both to the
state of technology and to the currently fas
able view of the machine.

In the heroic period of modern architectu
Constructivist/Sachlichkeit faction took
machine products were available from indu
construction—steel beams, industrial gl
ships handrails, stairs and chequerplate
pavement lights, tiles and bricks—a
displayed its machines (lifts, dynamos a
on) very much in the way the Bentley
same period was manifestly made of r
sheets and had its supercharger 'displaye
its front.

The Purist/Bauhaus faction took what had
developed for building proper—standard
windows, flush doors, domestic lighting fi
—was more discreet about its machine
developed a unifying aesthetic which abs
them.

At the present time the admired machines

1
The 'Rocket'

2
English Electric diesel locomotive

3
'Circuit de Dieppe'

4
'Maison de Verre', Paris, 1929. Chareau and Bi

5
Immeuble 'Clarté', Geneva, 1930–32. Le Corbus

Photos: British Railways 2, Work 4, Le Cor
Oeuvre Complet, 1929–34, 5.

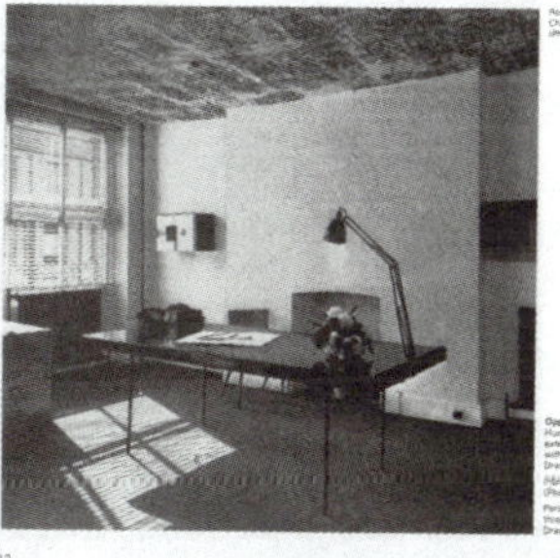

4.8

photograph and two perspective drawings of Hunstanton on the right operate as another example of comparative mirroring. Like the first spread, it offers a block of words in the upper left corner that is paired and aligned with a photograph, in this case an oblique view of the "slide projector box" for Jenkins Room: "Images happening beyond images: the introduction of a plane, the tempo of whose images were contrapuntal to that of its setting. These spatial manoeuvres interested us."[54] The point is as explicit as it is graphic and suggestive. The surfaces, frames, repetitions, patterns, and oblique gridding in the perspectival space of the drawings and photographs resonate among and within them and the spread, which invites us to observe and apprehend similar imaging operations in *Parallel of Life and Art*, Jenkins Room, and Hunstanton.

ARRAY 4.9

The paperback cover of *The Shift* slyly extends that game of photography, recollection, and imagination. It structures an allegory of the shift as the pursuit of the Mies-image across two decades. On the front cover are two images, which are described as: "Coloured essence of the Lucas structures prepared for the Art Net Exhibition, 1975." On the back cover are two color photographs of the Hunstanton School described in the caption as "in construction and finished." The Lucas images, two of many produced in the Smithsons' office by Lorenzo Wong, are highly abstract perspective drawings with applied color, showing the project's rectilinear and diagonal framing systems and the glass surfaces they contain, brace, and screen. The two cover images are cropped portions, much less than half, of larger drawings, as if zoomed in to create an effect of immersion. They have the look of computer renderings at a moment when CAD and video were just emerging as new media of design, culture, and art. In one, red shapes are applied to a line drawing; in the other, there are only the superimposed colored shapes of red, black, and blue. Those drawings and twelve others were featured in the 1975 Art Net exhibition with the title "A Line of Trees . . . A Steel Structure," an attempt to simulate the effect of the building's visual and spatial integration into its landscape, which featured rows of mature trees. The drawings were mounted between large, clear plastic panels, a few of which were suspended as parallel planes in the middle of a gallery, surrounded by the others hung close to the walls.

> The aim of the exhibition was to convey—sketch—an experience of the project for the Lucas Headquarters, Solihull, as if it had an existence. Insubstantial, coloured images sandwiched within transparent screens attempted to penetrate beyond the architectural drawing or model of an unrealised building. The layers of images, many identical apart from their colours, built up into a magical abstracted lattice, suggesting a multicoloured domain: it was possible to walk between the exhibition's screen, to be enclosed by reflective transparency, as if in a real building.[55]

Alison began a presentation of the project, recorded on video as if a performance for television,[56] standing by one of the drawings: a plan of the garden space between two of the project's buildings, with the elevations on either side splayed outward as axonometric projections and with the line of trees running between them depicted as a series of branching networks that filled the space. The crude video recording has oddball, yet charming and appropriate, imaging effects: reflections and burnishing, dayglo-pink discoloration, waveringfocus, and a distorted soundtrack. Her talk begins: "This introductory image is to show that the following images are already in the building as it was projected." Those following images were a series of twenty smaller prints of drawings or photographs of three earlier projects: Peter's thesis project for a new Fitzwilliam Museum (1948–49), the unbuilt Wokingham School (1958), and the Hunstanton School. Continuing with the gallery talk, Alison picked up the prints one by one from a table and held them up to the camera as she explained how each in different ways directly inspired the Lucas project. The first small drawing is an axonometric of Wokingham. Alison says, "This preliminary project is one that is not known about, because we tend to keep projects kind of secret when they are not used because the ideas are a kind of fund of ideas." She simply remarks, "these were steel and glass frames" and characterizes Wokingham as a return to the language of Hunstanton. "But the project that Hunstanton was built on," as she picks up a series of eight small reproductions of Peter's drawings of the Fitzwilliam Museum, "was the first essay that was done by Peter Smithson in the language of Mies van der Rohe." Of crucial importance are the "very large mature trees, which became, as it were, the structuring for the placement of the building in the landscape. And in fact, already, because it was an art gallery," as she shows an interior perspective montage in the manner of Mies,

> you can see that one was playing games with the planar effect that you can find in the language of Mies van der Rohe. But of course, what we did not know at that stage, because Mies buildings tend to be [...] raised up, stood off the ground, is that only in Mies projects you get, as it were, a ground floor related to outside courts. But we didn't know exactly what would begin to happen. It wasn't until we got Hunstanton built that one suddenly realized what was to be found in a steel structure.

She then shows the first photograph of Hunstanton, taken from inside the Craft Room in the northwest corner, looking out past the water tower over the kitchen roof toward the flat landscape in the distance, and begins a discussion of axonometrics while picking up a book to show drawings on several marked pages by "the historical Smythson." She remarks on the "fantastic resistance" of their clients to axonometrics, which she finds "very mysterious" because in the past similar drawings appear to have been quite effective. "We can only imagine that perhaps the English client [now] is very resistant to ideas on architecture. Therefore, this is really why we did this exhibition based on these experiences of Hunstanton," as she begins showing a series of twelve more photos of the school:

> once the building was there we got at least two photographers, Nigel Henderson and [Reginald Hugo de Burgh] Galwey of the [*Architectural*] *Review*, to recognize that this

4.9

ARCHITECTURAL
Monographs 7
Alison + Peter
Smithson
The Shift
Academy Editions · London
A+P Smithson
'A Line of Trees . . . A Steel Structure'
Exhibition at 'Art Net', London and Edinburgh
In this exhibition fourteen transparent panels with coloured latticed images of the Lucas Headquarters project were arranged in space so that many images overlapped to make a simulacrum of the effect aimed at in the real space of a built project.
Set of three perspectives looking out from the interior.
top: Structure only. LW.
second from top: Glass and trees only. LW.
above: Structure, glass, and trees. LW.
Composite 'extract' images of structure, in single and multiple colours. LW, 19

Arrangement in gallery. DW.

'Art Net' exhibition opening. Dennis Crompton.

AS at opening. Dennis Crompton.

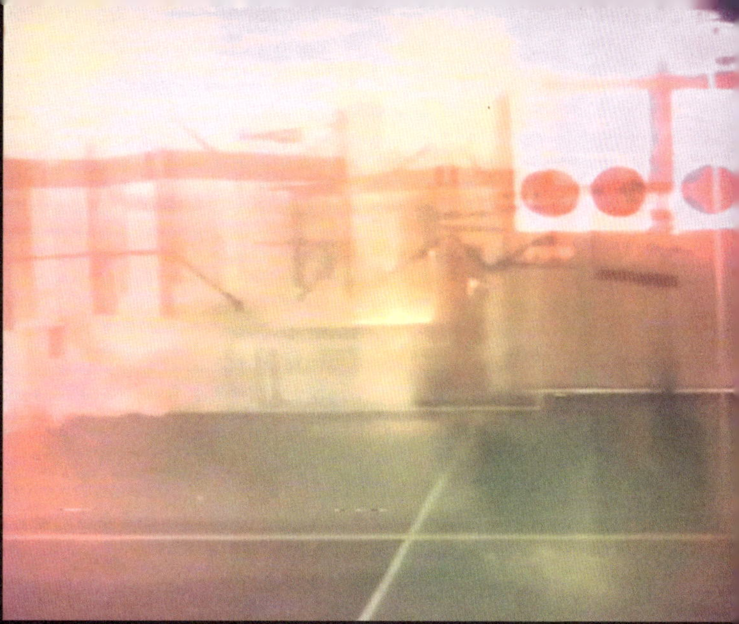

Mies van der Rohe
64

On discovering reflections in H
1953–54, we could better read the
of MIT' and understand what the Bar
ion, the Glass Exhibit, 1934, and so o
been like or intended to be like.

In 1953 we were to see Krefeld."

Mies must have been informed by v
for suddenly (after his Otterlo, the Ou
sion) the plans come apart, walls glid
ice skates – the glass the ice?

Then there is the 'glass-stone'. Is th
ation of the Glasen kette of Taut and S
all architects perhaps since the Goth
about stone, in an artisan-like way it
him; more and more he went as a
mason, dressing with the discretion
undertaker.

> planar effect was happening. That is, because it's on the ground in relation to the green grass you can find things in it that you couldn't actually find in the Mies buildings of the period in America, because, as I said, the Mies buildings are either on stilts or at MIT [*sic*, IIT] had brick walls directly in relation to the ground, so that here at Hunstanton for the first time in England people were able to see this amazing parallel, largely of planes, that you can get all in relationship to green.

As she shows the last two prints, both of which are now famous photographs by Henderson—one of painters on ladders seen through the gridded glazing of a classroom and the second of herself seen through a large sheet of plate glass, her head juxtaposed to a face crudely scratched into a large painted dot on the glass and with the grass fields receding behind her—she says, "You begin to get reflections coming in, too, which of course—here you see the reflections . . ." and, setting the prints down, she walks toward the middle of the gallery: ". . . of other surfaces, which is really why one dared do the business of Perspex, so that really one was building on experience of twenty years of trying to transmit ideas of what happens to steel and glass buildings in the English landscape. And when we say on the back of the card that," reading from the exhibition announcement and moving between the suspended panels, "'the superimposition of transparent colored images creates the illusion of a visit to an actual place,' we are speaking from experience." As she continues to weave among panels she says: "That is, we have developed a sensibility about steel architecture in the English landscape."

She then looks around the room and begins her conclusion, remarking that some people have objected that the exhibition does not actually create the effect of being in a building. But that effect, she says, is only apparent if one already has acquired "this sensibility developed through experience in a steel and glass building with glass planes and all the reflections and the buildup of the transparency, then you can imagine and extend the images into being in a place." The exhibition was an attempt, she continues, to convey that sensibility to the "general public" in a way that avoided both the problems of axonometrics and the "too facile" quality of models and perspectives. But they hoped that in one way the exhibition would be like axonometrics, which can convey the "reality of the ideas without spurious art prettiness," and that "for the architect coming in [. . .] it would open the possibility of a different kind of architecture, an architecture that is anonymous, that speaks of a certain amount of standardization without boredom, that speaks of repetition without it being too obvious (in the sense that an aqueduct is rather obvious repetition)," and that the exhibition could "perhaps start something of [a] dialogue, which is really very difficult when one has to deal with such solid things as buildings." The video ends as Alison walks off screen and the camera pans across the gallery, then stops to zoom in to a view through multiple parallel panels, which ultimately becomes a vaporish pink blur.

"A Line of Trees . . . A Steel Structure" was an effort, like *The Shift* a few years later, to discern and convey *un autre* Mies. The story Alison tells in her gallery talk, looking back at earlier work to explain both the exhibition and the lineage of work that informed the Lucas project, could be seen as an early version of the more complex imaging atlas assembled in *The Shift*. The coupling of the Hunstanton School and the Lucas project on the recto and verso of *The Shift* asserts the significance of Hunstanton and Lucas as two key moments in the Smithsons' pursuit of the Mies-image, as do Hunstanton and St. Hilda's in the working drawings section, where they are the first and last projects, together constituting nearly half of the section's pages. But unlike the chronological presentation of projects in the second half of the book, the covers make priority ambiguous. When the book is closed, Lucas is on the front and Hunstanton is on the back, but when the book is open and laid flat to turn the cover into a spread or diptych, the order is reversed: Hunstanton is on the left, and thus the "first" set of images. The cover stages a game in which Lucas and Hunstanton exchange times and roles as early and late. The front and the back covers display four versions of two different Mies-images that can serve as recent and distant, or New Brutalist and late modern, bookends for the atlas of Mies-images inside. The projects on the cover are neither sequential nor simultaneous but are shifting and shuttling and flickering between past and future, as untimely and uncanny recollections on modern architecture and as a timely and canny curation of the Smithsons' architecture. All begin to look a bit different through the implications of interaction with one another and with the book's contents to convey distinct and elusive Mies-images. The two photographs of Hunstanton on the back cover, one above the other, instigate another temporal pairing: the two phases of Hunstanton before and after the "layering of reflections at the glazed stage" and, by implication, two stages of the time of New Brutalism: one is the IIT Mies-image they initially discovered in Philip Johnson's book and in the *Architects' Journal* and that resonated with the architecture of the "heroic period," and the other is a newer New Brutalism—the Independent Group Mies-image they discovered on the site and in Henderson's photographs as both resonated with experiences of contemporary image culture. A further elaboration of that dialectic appears in the only full spread in the first section of the book devoted to Hunstanton: the two photographs on the back cover appear again, but this time across the gutter from each other and below two others. All four are in color. The caption reads: "Hunstanton, 1949–54. Above: Construction at the silver/red stage. Below: In construction. Above: Construction at the red/black stage. Below: Finished."[57]

The entirety of the first section of *The Shift* plays similar imaging games of shuffling, labeling, juxtaposition, alignment, color, and arraying. In the verbal illustration on the opening spread of the first section, the Smithsons hint at that untimely intent, remarking that the experimental graphics and materials of Alison's handmade Christmas cards were "out of style/phase with the graphic design of the period in which it happened" and thus were "like underground streams which will feed our architecture maybe years later. In this sense they are genuine ephemera, something in the air and drifting by, to be caught, looked at and released into other work."[58] The Smithsons saw the Christmas cards and other examples of "ephemera," whether observed or made, as crucially formative because they initiated the continuous and consequential delayed experimentation that generated their sensibility. The Christmas cards operate in *The Shift*, along with and among their collecting and generating of ephemera, as markers and evidence of specific moments and preoccupations along the way.[59] Their importance was both as parallel explorations of their enduring architectural interests and as generative imaging practices that preserved otherwise transient observations that were as important as the more permanent and better-known built projects or essays. Near the end of the first section of *The Shift* they write: "The Christmas cards as mood carriers took off in 1956."[60] That year's version, "a multi-colored strip or pennion [*sic*], rudely referred to by some recipients as the Christmas toilet roll,"[61] records the earliest intimations of the shift, at the end of the same year they produced *Patio and Pavilion*, House of Tomorrow, and "But Today We Collect Ads."

The Christmas cards appear multiple times near the end of the first section of *The Shift*. On seven pages (52, 56, 58–59, 63, 64, 68), usually with black backgrounds, there are descriptive lists of each year's cards and other ephemera, such as wallpaper, wrapping paper, birthday cards, and collages (categorized by visual theme, not chronology), along with color photographs of selected examples. One of the last of those pages is half of a spread with a particularly untimely and heterogeneous presentation of materials.

ARRAY 4.10

On the left page, on a black background and below a descriptive list of Christmas cards and wrapping paper designs from 1969 to 1978, as an example of "the ephemera of the shift achieved," is a large color image of the 1970 Christmas card (the year St. Hilda's was completed).[62] On the opposite page, with a white background, a thin, vertically cropped, black-and-white photograph of the southwest corner of St. Hilda's runs along the full length of the gutter. It shows the layered building assembly and the visual effects of the skin—the patterns and shadows of the timber framing and the complex reflections in the glass behind it, each juxtaposed with the dark patterns of the bare branches, set against the light gray sky, of the large copper beech adjacent to the building. On the far right of the spread are a caption, a brief descriptive text, and two small diagrams of the Berlin Hauptstadt plan that could also be taken as diagrams of the patterns of tree and twig branches in the linocuts of the Christmas card on the facing page, or of the branches of the copper beech and their reflections on the glazing in the photograph. The text, in the upper right corner of the page, above the diagrams, references work that is not shown in the monograph and can only be imagined:

> Although a series of net/mesh paintings—in ink or red poster paint on white detail paper—date from 1951 to 1957, layering as an aesthetic device had first appeared, it seemed then quite spontaneously in our work for the Berlin Hauptstadt competition design, 1957. In this a pedestrian "platform net" of variable mesh, its threads weaving and diminishing to respond to the irregular movements of persons walking, is superimposed over the largely straight-line rectangular grid of the existing vehicular streets: the effect is of one lattice laid upon another.[63]

Thus the array combines three variations of lattices at vastly different scales (page, building, city) and in very different media (collage, photograph, diagram) as a composite imaging. It conveys the effect and technique of treillage'd space, which the Smithsons would later explain as "something of a return to our first interest in the steel structure."[64] The most assertive effect of the spread is to displace—by making ephemeral and abstruse—the presumed objectivity of two very different kinds of photographs on the two pages, both of which were likely taken at the end of 1970: the color photograph that documents the Christmas card and the black-and-white photograph that frames and focuses attention on the visual and material qualities of St. Hilda's. In those ways the spread offers a model and clues for looking at others in the book, especially those that present arrays combining famous and familiar photographs of buildings with more personal and idiosyncratic images.

The treillage'd aesthetic and its devices are most vividly condensed in the Smithsons' "'Three Generations' image," which they devised in 1981, at the time they were completing work on *The Shift*, as an "ideogram" conveying an architectural lineage from Mies to the Eameses to themselves. Alison and Peter each produced a slightly different version of the stack of three images: a simple sketch by Mies of his House on a Hillside (1934) showing its diagonal bracing; a photograph of the Eameses' wire chairs (1951), cropped to show only the dense lattice of legs with a blackbird standing among them; and one of the drawings of the Lucas Headquarters, showing a view through a large steel frame across a lawn with large trees toward another section of building beyond.[65] Operating like the spread in *The Shift* with the Christmas card, St. Hilda's, and the Hauptstadt diagrams, but with more synoptic theoretical, historical, and biographical intent, the Three Generations ideogram images the Smithsons' "return to our first interest in the steel structure" as a defining
ARRAY 4.11 aspect of modern architecture. They affirm that intent by featuring just that image on the first page of the "Treillage'd Space" chapter in *The Charged Void: Architecture* as a prelude to the presentation on the following pages of the Lucas Headquarters and "A Line of Trees . . . A Steel Structure."[66]

The Smithsons' concept of the "treillage'd space" was an ingenious and willful hybridization of French garden trellises and the modernist frame, drawing attention to "the diagonal brace as an architectural device" that

> enters the language of modern architecture late; by our reckoning, with Mies' sketch for a glass house on a hillside, c. 1934, published in Philip Johnson's book in 1946 (and entering our blood-stream with the purchasing of that book in 1949). [. . .] In our own architecture by the end of the 'sixties the "brace" has been transformed from an expressed structure into a "lattice", and had taken on entirely new meanings: to do with skin-depth, sense of protection; and its use exploits the sense of privacy and the phantasy that the lattice entrains.[67]

Though they do not mention it, the diagonal as an oblique counterpoint to the orthogonal grid actually appears early in the Smithsons'

4.10

The ephemera of the shift achieved:

1969 Brown larch twigs: lino cut, printed black on light-brown Japanese paper, cut-out perforations, overlaid on chocolate-colour Japanese paper, inserts of cut-out French marbled paper.

1968 Wrapping paper: fircone printed on gold (old woodcut block) and office stamp, printed in gold on brown tissue paper.

1970 Fircones collection: lino-cut, printed in silver on chocolate-brown Japanese paper, cut-out profile.
Wrapping paper: larch twigs (old lino block), printed in gold as layer composition on brown tissue-paper.

1971 Snowman: two lino-cuts; cupressus fringe frame, robin, snowman's face, buttons, printed tan on white; metallic-*eau-de-nil* snowman on white; metallic-red chest to robin; profile cut-out.

1972 Wrapping paper: fircone (old lino block) printed in silver on blue tissue-paper.

1972 Wrapping paper: Christmas tree (old wood block) and robins (old envelope stamp cut from an eraser) printed in indigo on cherry tissue-paper.

1972 Pinecones: zinc block from line drawing, printed black on invitation cards.

1972 Re-used zinc block: printed metallic-*eau-de-nil* on raspberry Japanese paper.

1973 Christmas greenery: large lino-cut, printed in silver on indigo Japanese paper, metallic-red berries.

1973 Wrapping paper: fircones and pine cones (old blocks) metallic-red on blue tissue-paper, in combinations, some as wreaths.

1977 Wrapping paper: fircones (old block) and office stamp, printed in gold on white tissue-paper in the form of wreaths.

1978 Gone swimming: new freedoms discovered in the 'fifties and 'sixties. Art Net Rally, Central School.

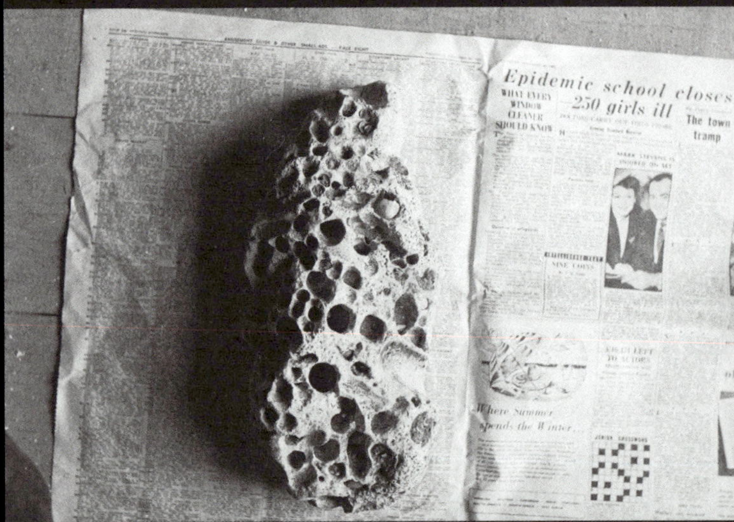

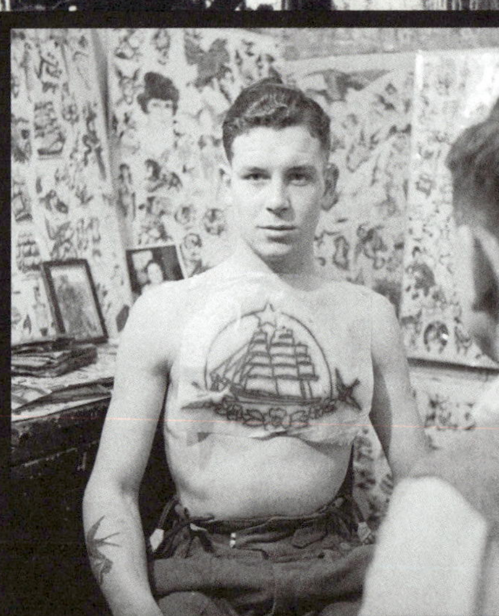

series of net/mesh paintings — ink or red on white detail paper — date from 1951 ayering as an aesthetic device had first t seemed then quite spontaneously in our e Berlin Hauptstadt competition design, his a pedestrian 'platform net' of variable reads weaving and diminishing to respond gular movements of persons walking, is sed over the largely straight-line grid of the existing vehicular streets: the one lattice laid upon another.

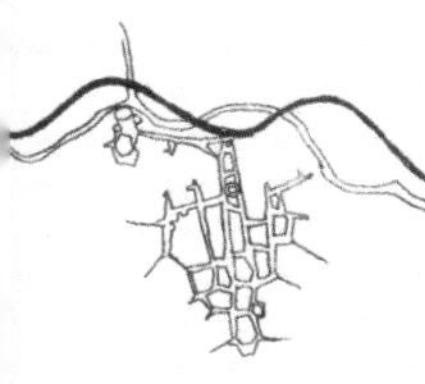

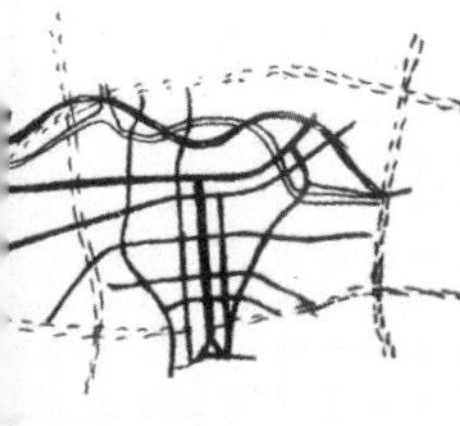

t, Berlin: diagrams of pedestrian and road net

s, Oxford, 1970
est corner with Copper Beech.
Aichael Carapetian)

31 Full page advertisment for toilet paper: Ladies Home Journal, mid 'fifties.

30
Racquet Club, McKim, Mead and White: Lever House, Skidmore Owings and Merrill: Office Building, Emile Roth: photographed 1957, P.S.

reason it has become a universal model: it was not frightening, it made no demands. Lever House did not 'make Mies acceptable' for Mies still had secrets and these frightened; Lever House had none. There was nothing in it which could not be copied by an average team of average architects with a fair amount of money and a fairly developed industry, and a Lever House could give the illusion to a foreign city that it had a genuine technological culture: the glamour without the two centuries of effort.[22]

But no copies of Chase Manhattan Bank will be built; it will never be a model, for it is built with unimaginable wealth and

22 The acceptance of the 'automatic mill' came in the 1790's: see Roger Burlingame, *Machines that built America*, Signet Key Books, 1955.

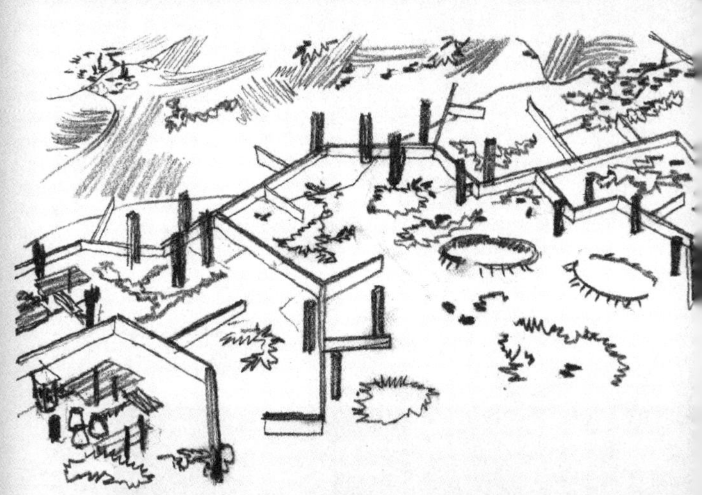

The house, the shell which fits man's back, looks inward to family and outward to society and its organisation should reflect this duality of orientation. The looseness of organisation and ease of communication essential to the largest community should be present in this, the smallest. The house is the first definable city element.

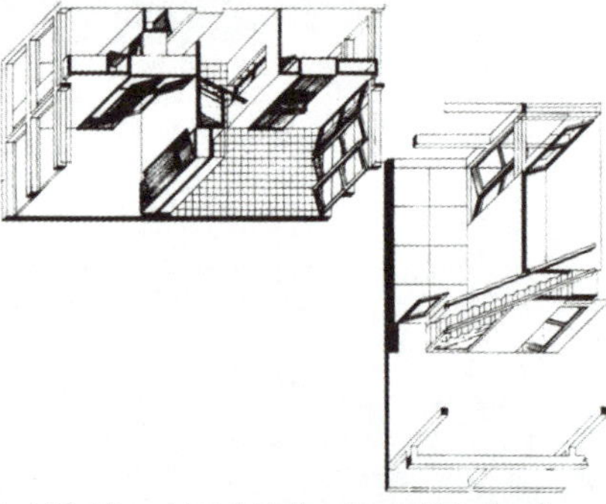

30. The shell that fits man's back. Golden Lane. Axonometric drawing of house cell

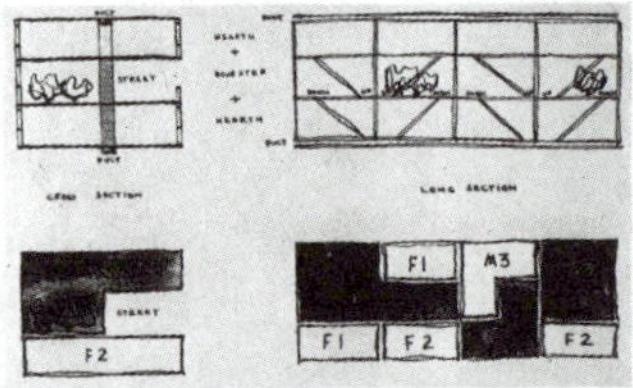

31. Golden Lane. House cell, diagrams

44

Houses can be arranged in such a way that a new thing is created – the 'street'.

The 'street' is our second definable city element.

The 'street' is an extension of the house; in it children learn for the first time of the world outside the family; it is a microcosmic world in which the street games change with the seasons and the hours are reflected in the cycle of street activity.

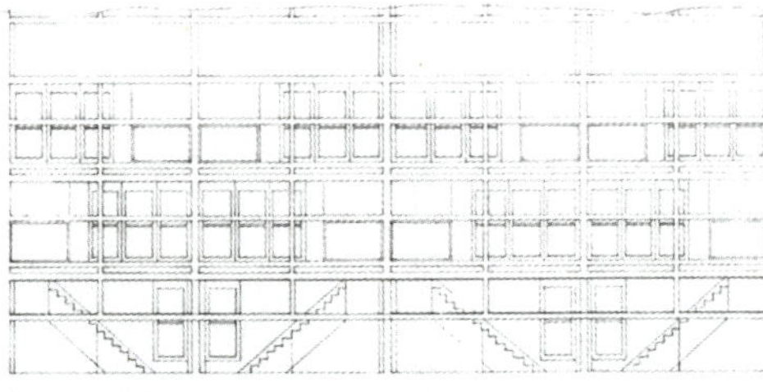

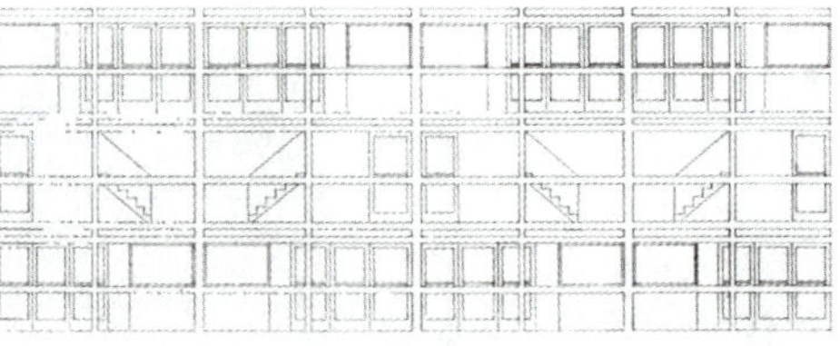

32. Elevations of part of the Golden Lane façade

45

Peter Smithson

The Masque and the Exhibition: Stages toward the Real.

March of this year I gave a 'first erformance' in Gund Hall at Harvard of *hree Generations* .... my last year's aud lecture. I say 'first performance' ecause the real first time is like the elivery of a gift one has made, with ifficulty, oneself. But to do it again hen the idea is cold, requires a critical ame of mind, a re-reading of the text ne by line, a re-screening of the slides lone and in silence: a process which, hen repeated immediately before the cture itself induces a state of mind-lanking panic .... one has become an ctor.

ut after this Gund Hall 'performance', I tarted elaborating one further small arallel between the first three enerations of the Renaissance and ose of Modern Architecture.

o repeat the basic statement of the *hree Generations*:- the architects in the rst three generations of the enaissance established ways of going bout things which we unconsciously llow .... first the architectural idea is ketchily stated as a diagram or a design agment then 'after nine months,' the ooden model. Subsequently the orking-drawings and the shop-drawings nd so on; all as today.

ut in the Renaissance, between the lea sketchily stated and the commission r the permanent real place came the tage-architecture for the Court Masque, e architectural settings and ecorations for the birthday of a avourite prince or the wedding of a ucal daughter; these events were used y the architects of the Renaissance as pportunities for the realisation of the ew style: the new sort of space and the ew forms of decoration made real for ne day only perhaps, but still real. The eal before the real, enjoyably consumed nd creating the taste for more of the ame. Even today in Siena a victorious ontrada prepares its 'stage' to celebrate eir last year's triumph .... a setting vented and decorated for a single vening.

PETER SMITHSON
Architect. London
"THREE GENERATIONS"
Friday March 13. 100pm
Piper Auditorium

Modern architecture follows this old tradition: in the first generation Le Corbusier and Pierre Jeanneret's Pavillion de L'Esprit Nouveau, in 1925, was the first of a series of exhibitions which I believe achieved the real before the real for our period in the same way as did the masque in the Renaissance.

An architect must seize what chances he can; Melnikov's U.S.S.R. pavillion in Paris in the same year made Constructivism real, even if for only a single summer – (and Melnikov had built a market .... all lettering and jagged geometry in wood and canvas .... in Moscow in the previous year, 1924).

In 1927 most of the first generation of Modern Architecture had exhibition houses, temporarily equiped and decorated as if lived in, at the Weissenhofsiedlung exhibition at Stuttgart.

Mies and Lily Reich built and decorated two other 'real-space' exhibits in 1927.

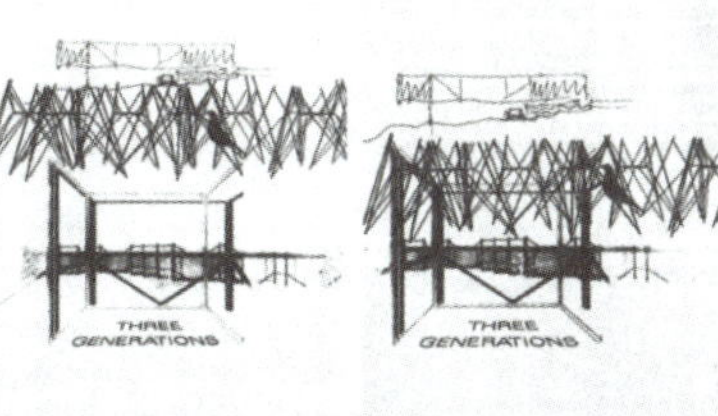

hree Generations, Harvard Lecture Poster.

hree Generations (of Modern Architecture), poster, S. version.

hree Generations (of Modern Architecture) poster, M.S. version.

hese three posters illustrate the theme of my last ar's ILAUD lecture in Urbino called Three Genera-ns. The theme of that lecture was that ere is a curious parallel between the first three nerations of the architects of the Renaissance d those of the Modern Movement. In each case a w architecture suddenly appeared complete and rfect in the 'twenties – in the fourteen twenties for naissance architecture and in the nineteen enties for modern architecture.

A key to the three generations posters.

Renaissance			
From the bottom up:-			
S. Spirito,	1436-82:	Brunelleschi:	First generation.
S. Andrea, Mantua,	1472-1512:	Alberti:	Second generation.
St. Peter's, Rome,	1595:	Bramante:	Third generation (?).
Modern			
From the top downwards:-			
House on a hillside,	1934:	Mies van der Rohe:	First generation.
Legs of wire chairs,	1951:	Charles Eames:	Second generation.
Lucas Headquarters,	1973:	A. & P. Smithson:	Third generation.

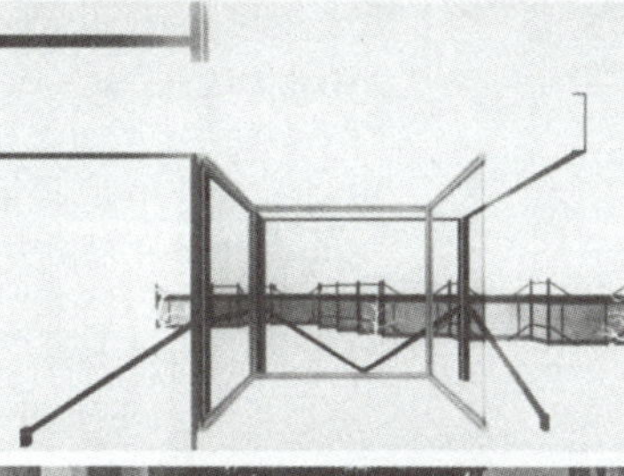

To the Green Fields
"After all, scholarship and precision of operation are only the staff-work of architecture, the aim is to break out to the green-fields, and it is the glimpse of those fresh green fields that the architecture of the 1420's and the 1920's give that allows one to dream that it is possible."
P.S., from a letter to J-M.B. 10/7/79.

buildings – by the Candilis/Woods office were part of the climate of Team X thinking during the late 'fifties and 'sixties – that is in the Le Corbusier's last working years.

And it worked in the same way in the three founding generations of the Renaissance.
Art history has built-up over the last thirty years the documents and the observations necessary to see how Alberti's delicate architecture of the Cappella Rucellai is transported into the etherial architecture of Piero della Francesca's Flagellation.
And some day one will become aware of a suddenly-blindingly-obvious example of influence working the other way round – from the younger to the older; for this is what one has experienced in one's own lifetime amongst architects working within talking and reading and seeing distance of each other.
Giancarlo De Carlo always says that in Francesco di Giorgio's architecture we see a 'deformation of the typology': for example the ideal proportions of the schematic section of San Bernardino are not followed in the real building. Yet, the reality seems to be both 'perfect', and to be descended without interruption, from the ideal geometries of the second generation of the founders – that is from Alberti. But a change has occurred – Francesco di Giorgio's usages of the same forms are less strict, more adapted to terrain and to existing built fabric; yet they retain the resonances those old geometries set in motion.

work, in Hunstanton, in the form of the four open staircases leading to clusters of classrooms on the upper floor, and in the elevations of Golden Lane, where the rhythm of diagonal staircases leading to individual dwellings punctuates the regular rectangular structure of the tower slabs. The diagonal also suggests the kinds of oblique reflections that so often appear in photographs of glass and frame architecture and which the Smithsons accentuate with the truncated corners of the Economist complex and St. Hilda's or the pinwheel planning of the Wokingham School. In all those ways, the Lucas Headquarters is yet another, but the most deliberate and intricate, reconsideration of the modernist grid and the visual qualities of patterns in the Smithsons' work. If St. Hilda's marks a culmination and a shift in that lineage, Lucas is the most explicit and radical reimaging of Hunstanton: it is both a repetition and an initiation of ideas that span and link three generations.

> Layers of latticed structure, the inclusion of a layer of trees, a layering of levels: all speak in turn of connection and separation. The building steps forwards, steps back, performs as it were a stately dance with the trees that lace the site on the lines of old hedgerows [. . .]. The stepping in and out of the building to receive the penetration, or allow the tree line to pass by, offers to the occupants a variety of serrated edge places. In this way the outdoor spaces are possessed differently by each limb of the building.[68]

The Smithsons' ways of looking and observing—their imaging—enabled them to engage their world in ways that, as they claimed in the 1967 Berlin seminar, most architects "have not recognized as architecture at all, let alone seen clearly enough to isolate its characteristics."[69] Their "shift" coincided with the emergence of postmodernism's concern with representation, memory, and history; but the recursive assemblage of images in *The Shift* is an entirely different kind of recollection than historical or mimetic recurrence. It is closer to, but also different from, Banham's emphasis on "memorability as image" in his 1955 essay "The New Brutalism." The recollective and revisionist imaging of projects in *The Shift* plays out the results and potentials of the Smithsons' fascination with Mies's "repetitive almost autonomous neutralizing skin" and operates as a kind of repetition, like the slight variations generated by Pop art's replication of prosaic objects or the kinds of pattern recognition that engender strange familiarity and which first became integrated into their cvarchitecture in Paolozzi's ceiling wallpaper patterns, textures, and figures for Jenkins Room, or the images of famous people inserted into the collages they made for Golden Lane. It is allied with the kind of recognition that the Smithsons called identification, which they learned from Henderson's photography of storefronts, signs, objects, markets, and buildings in postwar London. Other identified sources include Greek stoas, late Italian Gothic, the perspective drawings of the Italian Renaissance, the constant, subtle refinements in the product designs of Citroën, Braun, and Volkswagen, and even Jasper Johns's superimposed flags.[70] Though the Smithsons only reference Johns's work once, there is a strong affinity between the combination of elemental repetition, surface patterning, and sly materiality in both the Smithsons' and Johns's aesthetic sensibilities and their manners of persistent observation of seemingly ordinary things. That kind of identification as repetition is most powerfully epitomized in their Miesian version of American Pop: "Mies has without doubt moved even more towards the use of repetition because the culture he is working in is particularly good at the quality control of serially produced, identical metal objects, and as he has always loved metal he swims freely in this technology."[71] In Mies they saw a model for an architecture "without rhetoric" (as they misleadingly called it) that was attentive to the realities of contemporary culture yet avoided or even sublimated the "object symbolism" of "pop-styling" or of "pop objects and appliances."[72] Central to the Smithsons' shift was an understanding that design could strive for "a unifying aesthetic which absorbed" individual parts and components into "a complete 'object'" which, "if we like it, it is for what it is, not for what emotions it entrains by reminding us of previous technologies."[73] While "in the early days we welcomed such separate and distinct pronouncements" of identity as apparent uniqueness, after the shift they insisted on a distinction between "*assembled* and *designed* as the simplest of criteria to decide what is architecture at the present time."[74] Designed objects, as they came to understand through Mies and the Eameses, aspire to a unity that is other than stylistic and that subsumes "specially designed"[75] parts into something like "an image" as Banham had theorized it in 1955, but one that coheres by virtue of its sensibility, not its topological clarity as a shape or its discrete "apprehensibility and coherence [...] as a visual entity."[76]

If New Brutalism was anything in the 1950s, it was a time when the Smithsons developed a way of looking and when they formed and built complex and intricate imagings that struck them and stuck with them. The Smithsons developed no consistent method or approach to observing or recording their observations. Their imagery production ranged from precisely constructed ink drawings, renderings, and diagrams to witty Christmas cards, children's books, and meticulously curated home decor, to the innovative display and graphic formats they used in exhibitions and books. Their imaging practices were a disparate set of habits, techniques, experiments, and tests that were never settled or codified. Ingenuity and variability were crucial. What they learned, and the sensibility they developed, was played out most productively in their buildings of the 1960s: the Economist complex, the Occupational Health Unit, Robin Hood Gardens, and St. Hilda's, with deep sources in Hunstanton, Golden Lane, Jenkins Room, *Parallel of Life and Art*, and *Patio and Pavilion*. Yet the buildings, as much as they strove to operate and invent within the discipline of architecture, were always testing the potential of architecture to manifest qualities that were first identified as ephemera:

> The shift to thinking about events, and about decorations made for the day, gradually extended the aesthetic of the light touch into the making of designs in which overlay or lattice form part of, or supplement, longer lasting structures and suggest the possibilities of design contributions of their inhabitants: between layers there seems to be room for illusion and for activity.[77]

Reactionary, strident, and dogged, though not at all conservative, impatient, or dogmatic, the Smithsons were peculiarly inventive and innovative in *making* observations, even if they offered little explanation of their political motives, evaluative criteria, or intellectual sources. As much as the Smithsons insisted on refining their aesthetic by looking at sources other than architecture, they were not especially interested in, or attentive to, the theories of visualization, visual art, or technologies of seeing that were rapidly changing in the image culture of the latter half of the twentieth century. Yet numerous comments show how intensively and powerfully those problems and conditions inspired, influenced, and informed the imaging practices they used to tentatively explore the potential of architecture to actively participate in the "dialogic, telematic society of image producers and image collectors" that Vilém Flusser theorized in the 1980s: "When images supplant texts, we experience, perceive, and value the world and ourselves differently [. . .] as surface, context, scene. And our behavior changes: it is no longer dramatic but embedded in fields of relationships."[78]

The Smithsons were focused on the aspects of the reality they saw, and which they engaged through looking and modified through design. Their aim was to work on their reality by imaging it—once they developed the manner of imaging specifically appropriate for each project—and as a way of imagining. That attitude and its sensibility are intently and cogently demonstrated in their books, from *Without Rhetoric* in 1973 to *Changing the Art of Inhabitation* in 1994, which curate diverse materials produced by the Smithsons and others. Beginning with their "Urban Re-identification" document in 1952—which was revised and eventually published in 1970 as the first half of *Ordinariness and Light*—they emphasized the potential of a "random aesthetic." They insisted on decidedly awkward, seemingly casual arrangements, patterns, and juxtapositions. They attempted to convey their intent and values through images and the possibilities of reimagining. Sometimes their images were made of words, such as their description in *Without Rhetoric* of an urban scene in "Kensington or Bath," where the domestic spaces of row homes were visible while walking along the street: "identical doors open to an elegant hall or a laocoan [*sic*] of rusting prams . . . the sounds floating out of upper windows . . . lights on to lined curtains or the old 40-watt bulb over a pensioner's tea . . . the smell of flowers, or old fat, or cats. The richness of the mix within an apparently static format is incredible."[79] The writing continues three pages later:

> The search for a style which can match this ideal has for some time been the floating centre of our design effort—certainly since the mid-Economist years—and explains our mulling over the Eames house and our close watching of the gradually evolving subtly modulated facades of late Mies. What we are looking for is the gentlest of styles, which whilst still giving an adumbration of the measures of internal events and structures (rooms, activities, servicing arrangements, supports), leaves itself open to—even suggests—interpretation, *without itself being changed*.[80]

A footnote in that passage refers the reader not to photographs or drawings of the Eames House, but instead, simply: "See Eames' film, *House*, 1955." Their preoccupation with and affection for *House: After Five Years of Living* (1955), with its sweetness and lightness, bright colors and sunlight, is in some ways puzzling. The Smithsons' images were always more of a sensitively crude and robustly referential "rough poetry." The random aesthetic that united their disparate ideas, approaches, and insights might be identified in banal or anonymous scenes such as "a lengthy climb up a rickety stair" or "up an estate road" or "along an air-conditioned artificially lit corridor" as experiences that are "man's links with society, the vistas down which he looks at his world; they frame his perspective view."[81] But it is precisely the singularity and stability of the perspective view that their random aesthetic attempts to reconsider, not by embracing high modernist modes of visuality, or even the recuperation of the Picturesque, but by reconsidering those modalities and understanding their inherited sensibilities of looking at landscapes or cities or their immersion in the incessant repetitions and mediation of contemporary imaging processes. Their search for a "*general* sensibility," they claimed, "goes against all inherited post-Renaissance ideas [. . .] against the tradition of abstraction."[82] Near the end of *Without Rhetoric*, they write: "We ourselves are still in the hard-slog phase of conscious investigation, conscious self-teaching toward this sensibility," and "the need to re-study" past experiences of work produced, of places visited, and of things observed "arises when we find ourselves working on a problem and the answer we find we recall having seen somewhere before."[83]

That statement follows another in which the Smithsons make a surprising reference: "Very much in the manner of Ruskin we have looked."[84] In a footnote they clarify that that their manner of looking was informed by one of Ruskin's late, lesser-known, and uncharacteristically casual books: "See Ruskin's *Mornings in Florence* for instructions on how to look." It was not unusual for the Smithsons to recommend an obscure source, and in this case it is a revealing, rewarding, and appropriate one. Each chapter In Ruskin's 1875 book is a morning's tour, focused on instructing "English Travellers" how to look at Giotto's frescos. Architecture is a secondary player in the instructions, and Ruskin satirizes some of Florence's most famous monuments but also insists on looking carefully at them to understand their flaws: "Santa Croce is, somehow, the ugliest Gothic church you ever were in. Well, that is really so; and now, will you take the pains to see why?" It is "not beautiful by any means; but deserving, nevertheless, our thoughtfullest examination."[85] Ruskin most brutally dismisses the Duomo. On the "Fourth Morning" he offers a quick but devastating description of the failings of its interior, where:

> you will see nothing whatever in it worth looking at. Nevertheless, look a little longer. But the longer you look, the less you will understand why I tell you to look. It is nothing but a whitewashed ceiling: vaulted indeed—but so is many a tailor's garret window [. . .]. Indeed [. . .] it seems to become so small that you can almost fancy it the ceiling of a good-sized lumber-room in an attic.[86]

He then asks the reader to look at the floor, which "extends round you like a frozen lake," concluding that "the most studious ingenuity could not produce a design for the interior of a building which should more completely hide its extent, and throw away the common advantage of its magnitude, than this Duomo of Florence." By way of relief, he directs the tourist to "quit the cathedral by the western door [. . .] and as quickly as we can walk, return to the Green cloister of Sta. Maria Novella," where he demonstrates that its interior is nearly as large as the Duomo's in plan. But, most important for Ruskin, it achieves grandness through "*dis*proportion [. . .] the *in*equality and immeasurability of the curved lines; and the hiding of the form by the colour."[87] Those architectural qualities are similar to the lessons Ruskin wanted his readers to learn from scrutinizing Giotto's paintings, the first of which is, simply, "You shall see things—as they are. So easy a matter that, you think? [. . .] Easy or not, it is all the sight that is required of you in this world,—to see things, and men, and yourself,—as they are."[88] The virtue of that way of looking, Ruskin continues, is that you become "so heartily interested in them" that, like Giotto, you identify "their decisive *moment*. There is a decisive instant in all matters; and if you look languidly, you are sure to miss it. Nature seems always, somehow, trying to make you miss it."[89]

The passage in *Without Rhetoric* that references Ruskin is an abbreviated version of Peter's 1965 essay "The Slow Growth of Another Sensibility," where he credits Ruskin, in the form of several epigraphs from three sources: *Praeterita* (1885–89), *Modern Painters* (1843), and a letter to the author and critic Charles Eliot Norton (1875), each of which muses on the natural beauty of the Alps. Peter suggests that Ruskin inspired ways of looking that can take us "across the brink of another sensibility" about cities "that I do not have trained into me," because, he claims, it only began to emerge in the years after World War Two. "With luck there will come a literature, an imagery," but it "may take several generations [. . .] to become 'operational'" and will require a "huge personal mental convulsion."

> I now think that it is *reflection*—thought re-thought, lessons re-learned, experiences re-experienced and action taken in the light of reflection—that plays a paramount part in the growth of a sensibility. This might appear to stand oddly against the instant culture we take to be natural to our time. But it is natural in fact only to some part of the entertainment media. All the practical arts from engineering and rocketry to medicine are reflective, concerned with the inner workings of their own discipline.[90]

The Smithsons found a contemporary version of Ruskin's appeal for careful, interested, sophisticated looking at "things as they are," and a compelling variation of the sensibility of contemporary entertainment media, in the Eameses' architecture, furniture, and films, but especially in Ray Eames's "attention to the detail of the collected material, the perseverance in finding exactly what is wanted, although you may not know yourself until you see it."[91] The Eameses tempered the Smithsons' tendency to reject, like Ruskin, the immediacy, intensity, and multiplicity of modern experience, and the Eameses' work encouraged them to find ways to be attentive to complexity, detail, and affect in popular culture and in the twentieth-century city. Thus the Smithsons converted Ruskin's anti-modern descriptions of buildings, nature, and art into their own imagination of architecture, landscapes, and cities. One passage in *Mornings in Florence* may have been a perplexing highlight for the Smithsons. It comes at the end of a digression that critiques modern culture's overestimation of the influence of individual artists and scientists, and its underestimation of the degree to which their achievements build not only on the work of those who preceded them but also on the vitality and richness of the cultures in which they worked, which cannot simply be exported or consumed superficially as "new objects of curiosity to nations who had nothing to look at."[92] Ruskin laments the inability of contemporary publics to appreciate both nature and other cultures, and lambasts the visual poverty and crass hyperbole of advertising and entertainment in modern London.

> Nothing to look at! That indeed—you will find, if you consider it—our sorrowful case. The vast extent of the advertising frescos of London, daily refreshed into brighter and larger frescos by its billstickers, cannot somehow sufficiently entertain the popular eyes. [. . .] Even the excitement of the shop-window, with its too easily attainable splendours, or too easily attainable impostures, cannot maintain itself in the wearying mind of the populace, and I find my charitable friends inviting the children, whom the streets educate only into vicious misery, to entertainments of scientific vision, in microscope or magic lantern; thus giving them something to look at, such as it is;—fleas mostly; and the stomachs of various vermin; and people with their heads cut off and set again;—still *something*, to look at.[93]

The Smithsons' work might be seen as an extended, if sympathetic, retort to Ruskin's anti-modernism, fueled by lessons they had learned about looking at "things as they are" from the Independent Group and from Henderson and Paolozzi. The reality of "advertising frescos" and "shop-windows" described by Ruskin resonates with the kinds of materials and enthusiasms that suffused Paolozzi's epidiascope presentation in 1952 or Henderson's early interest in scientific slides or his many images of London's scruffy urban surfaces. In Hunstanton, *Parallel of Life and Art*, *Patio and Pavilion*, Alison's Christmas cards, and each of their books, the Smithsons were demonstrating that
ARRAY 4.12 there was in fact much "to look at" in the imagery of a city like London if we are inclined and able to look at the advertisements, scientific images, and shop windows not as "too easily attainable" entertainment but with the same discerning fascination and imagination that Ruskin might look at Giotto, or that was evident in ICA exhibitions such as *Growth and Form* (1951), with its models, prints, and projections of scientific images; or *Opposing Forces* (1953), where Jackson Pollock's paintings were first shown in Britain; or *Wonder and Horror of the Human Head* (1953), which assembled art images of busts, faces, and skulls from across history and cultures.

Two similar statements by the Smithsons, published more than a quarter-century apart, affirm the range and the persistence of

4.12

ANATOMY
CATALOGUE OF THE EXHIBITION
Parallel of Life and Art
ACKNOWLEDGEMENTS
ARCHITECTURE

Fifth Day
Eighth Day
Twelfth Day
Sixteenth Day
Nineteenth Day

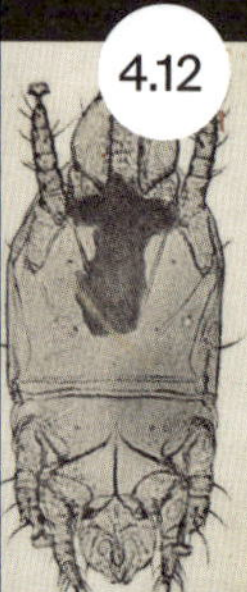

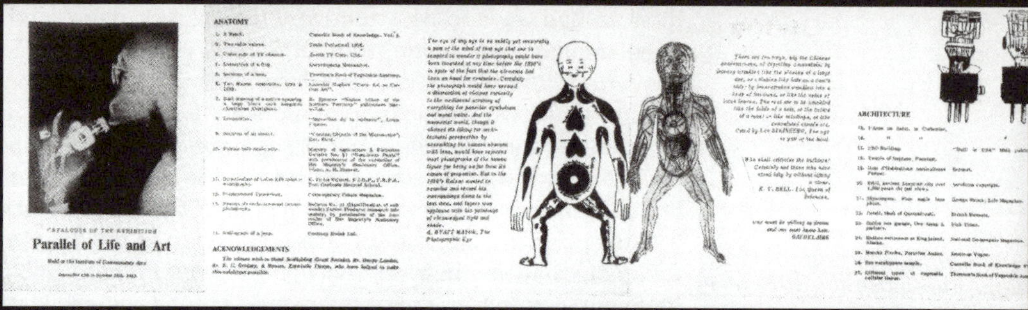

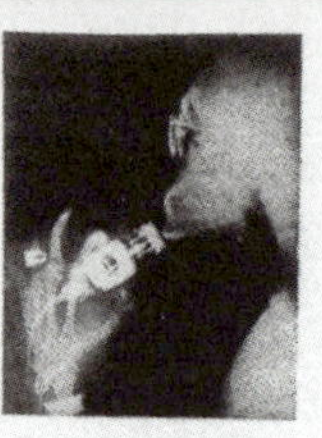

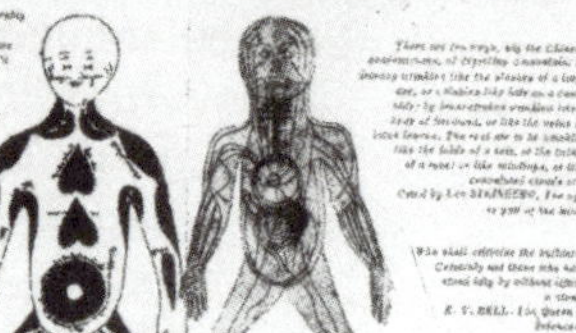

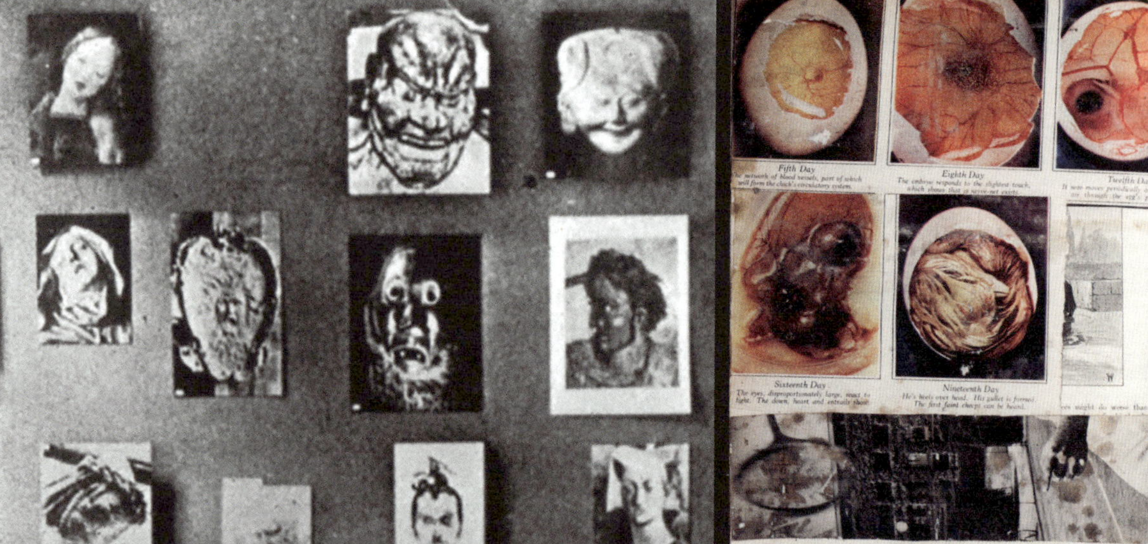

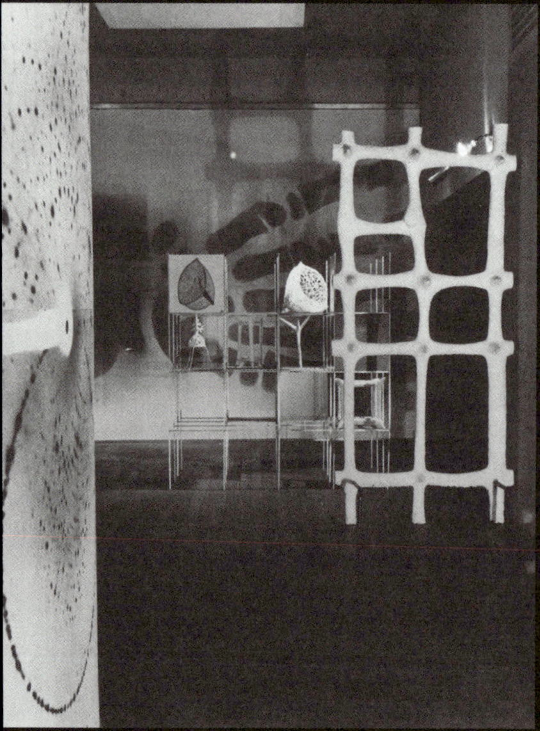

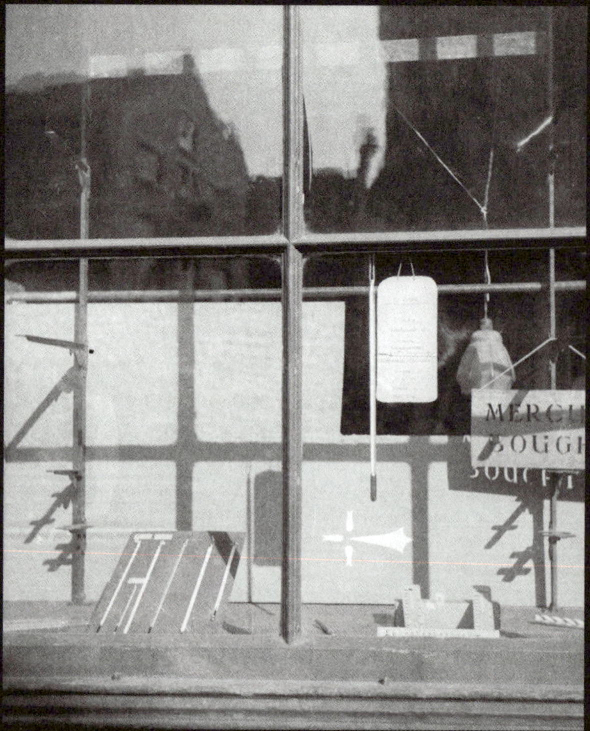

CALLIGRAPHY

CALLIGRAPHY

DATE 1901

LANDSCAPE

MOVEMENT

NATURE

their variations of Ruskinian looking. In their 1956 essay "But Today We Collect Ads," they famously pleaded for architects to look for inspiration in "popular arts advertising" because it is a source of "good 'images' and their technical virtuosity is almost magical. [. . .] Mass-production advertising is establishing our whole pattern of life—principles, morals, aims, aspirations, and standard of living. We must somehow get the measure of this intervention if we are to match its powerful and exciting impulses with our own."[94] In *The Shift* they suggested that one of Alison's *Tram Rats* collages, which was exhibited at Art Net in 1976, had similar motives. They describe it as a "remembrance of the inventions of our industrial past, whose powerful imagery we have to match with inventions of our own."[95] Whether looking at contemporary "mass-production advertising" to inform their own sensibility in the 1950s, or at archival photographs of newspaper sellers, cobblestones, row houses and "an open-topped tram" as materials for a collage in the 1970s, or at cities, buildings, and landscapes in ways that emulated Ruskin or the Eameses, the mode and the product of the Smithsons' search was imaging that was often ambivalent, always nuanced, and rarely explicit. But their intentions and implications become clearer when compared to the contemporaneous, hostile arguments of Reyner Banham. At the same Art Net event where the Smithsons were exhibiting the *Tram Rats* collages as a way of claiming a different and distant resonance with their earlier Independent Group enthusiasms, they were in the audience when Banham presented a "Rally" lecture in which he dismissed the Smithsons as both "traditional" architects and art "sophisticates."[96] Noting that 1976 was the twentieth anniversary of the *This Is Tomorrow* exhibition and that it was still seen by many as the beginning of the Pop art movement in Britain, he promised his audience that his 35 mm slides from 1956 "aren't very often seen in public, which I think will just about blow the eyelids off some of you who have never seen them before." His talk was less a history lesson than a critical assessment of the current scene based on his polemical comparison of the incompatible positions evident in two "performed Smithsons projects" of 1956: *Patio and Pavilion*, their contribution to *This Is Tomorrow*, and House of the Future, from the London Ideal Home Exhibition. He accused the Smithsons of choosing the wrong one—*Patio and Pavilion*—as the model for their subsequent work, arguing that the House of the Future, "irrespective of the architectural quality,"

> may have a stronger claim than anything at *This Is Tomorrow* to have been the first true product of all the Pop art studies that have been going on for so long. It was different than Eduardo Paolozzi's work in tone and style. It was earlier than any of the Pop paintings of Richard Hamilton, and it was different from both in that it was addressed to a pop audience, not to a bunch of gallery sophisticates.

He argued that it was conceived and presented as "a mass-market product addressed to a mass audience" and its design was "treated as styling rather than as art." He praised the ways its "system of paneled construction" emulated "the styling of cars of the period" and "the detailing of automotive technology at that time." The House of the Future "was in the precise sense in which we used to use the word in those days, fabulous. That was a very precise adjective of the period, and this was precisely fabulous."[97]

Banham then began to show slides of *Patio and Pavilion*, and his tone shifted:

> The surviving photographic evidence has precisely the kind of right fine art quality, [which] makes it difficult to read at one level, easy enough to read at a different level, at a purely superficial level, as a kind of celebration of garden shed civilization or garden shed aesthetics [. . .] in which were inexplicably and unexplainedly laid out things, objects, images, shards of real and imaginary civilizations, dredged up from the subconscious of Eduardo Paolozzi, Nigel Henderson, or, I don't know, the Smithsons themselves. A kind of personal archaeology, which you just had to stand and look at and try and make best sense of you could. It did not straight out explain itself like the House of the Future, you needed to know something of what all this was about. And all enclosed in this strange circumvallation of reflecting surfaces in which everything was doubled, in which corners disappeared, in which you yourself appeared as it were redrawn by Eduardo Paolozzi or as photographed underwater or something by Nigel Henderson, was a strange, moving and very, very fine art experience. [. . .] It is clear that ultimately this really would be the route through fine art and traditional art or traditional modern architecture [. . .] the Smithsons were to prefer to pursue.

Banham saw the two projects as representing a stark "choice between two traditions" then operating in contemporary British architecture: "the traditions of the modern movement, and therefore of the traditions of architecture generally," and "the other tradition, the smooth, the rounded corner, high technology," which he saw as architecture's version of "the Beatles and Mary Quant." For Banham, the second tradition as it developed in the 1960s marked "the deprovincialization of British culture,"[98] the "British ascendancy in avant-garde modern architecture," and the moment when British architecture, design, and art "joined the world-wide modern movement as respectable equals [. . .] as part of the cutting edge of that movement." In effect, the House of the Future launched British Pop nearly a decade before it became "world dominant," and the "Smithsons rewrote the scenario for half the British modern movement." With his final two slides, Banham showed how the styling of the House of the Future could be seen as a "pre-echo" of the "Gasket Housing of Archigram of 1964," and thus of the radical ambitions and global influence of that British collective as well as a future of multinational design collaborations such as the "Anglo-Italian team" that won the international competition for the Centre Pompidou in Paris. Banham took the twentieth anniversary of *This Is Tomorrow* as an opportunity to amplify an ongoing debate with the Smithsons about the legacy and future of modern architecture. A few years earlier, in *Without Rhetoric*, the Smithsons had voiced their skepticism toward high-tech architecture, which they accused of a kind of crass modernist nostalgia: "We are right to worry about buildings in which plumbing vents are made to look like ship air-intakes, and towns like oil refineries, where our emotions are engaged by reminders of previous or other technologies."[99] For them, the *Tram Rats* collages were the more productive exploration of the "powerful imagery" of technology; they saw the iconographic expression of technology in the Centre Pompidou as a superficial means of engaging popular culture and saw the *Tram Rats* collages as a more subtle and resonant imagery that was neither nostalgic nor provincial, even if, like *Patio and Pavilion*, the enigmatically allusive collages evaded any explicit suggestions of possible futures and could easily be taken as images of the past rather than intimations of what mattered most now. But unlike Banham, the Smithsons were not interested in images "of the future"; instead, their musings on the currency of past images was their untimely way to say, "this is tomorrow."

As the conclusion to his lecture, Banham offered a surprisingly conventional view of history and of time that, even more than his polemic of two traditions, clarifies his differences with the Smithsons. As he had been hinting all along in the lecture with his references to ten-year time spans, he endorsed a decidedly linear notion of history as a succession of distinct decades. Referring to George Kubler's theories and introducing him as a "chronological structuralist" who is "the one authority on the structure of time in the history of art," Banham set him up with a quote from his 1964 book, *The Shape of Time*: "The decade is only a decimal position in the century. Both the decade and the century are arbitrary integers rather than working durations. There is nothing in the history of art corresponding either to a century or its tenth part."[100] Banham was wholly dismissive: "I don't happen to believe it. I think what I've been talking about this evening suggests there is, in fact, at least in the recent history of British art and architecture, a very clear ten-year structure." Nothing could be further from the Smithsons' understanding of history or their own development and identities as modern architects. Their mining and uses of history and their timely and untimely reimaginings of their own work operated in ways that were much closer to Kubler's theory of replicable "prime" shapes, objects, and images than Banham's endorsement of chronologically bracketed style phases. Their Three Generations idea roughly aligns with Kubler's suggestion that if any regular temporal spacing actually does occur in history, it is either "the length of a generation (25–33 years)" or a period of about fifty or sixty years based on the "productive life-span" of a human adult.[101] For the Smithsons, traditions and influence "are about persistence, about ideas reflected on, carried on, through time. We take persistence to mean not only that ideas persist in the *Three Generations* way, in which the three generations of people at work at the same time learn and absorb from each other, but also that ideas persist from deep time and work within a single long work-life."[102] Or, as Kubler writes in his book's preamble, "An inference from visual images is present in almost all art. Even architecture, which is commonly thought to lack figural intentions, is guided from one utterance to the next by the images of the admired buildings of the past, both far and near in time."[103]

The Smithsons also rejected Banham's characterization of *Patio and Pavilion* as a work of "fine art and traditional art or traditional modern architecture." That is clear in the essays that introduce the idea of Three Generations, such as Peter's "The Masque and the Exhibition: Stages toward the Real" (1981), which places *Patio and Pavilion* in a modernist family (or what Kubler calls a "sequence") of exhibition designs, including those of Le Corbusier, Konstantin Melnikov, Walter Gropius, Mies van der Rohe and Lilly Reich, and the Eameses. All attempt to "realize ideas only as allegory: that is, obliquely, yet in real space."[104] Peter's essay includes a statement by Alison, set in a black box alongside paired images of *Patio and Pavilion* and House of the Future, which invites comparison of and implies affinities between the two projects: (Fig. 5)

Fig. 5

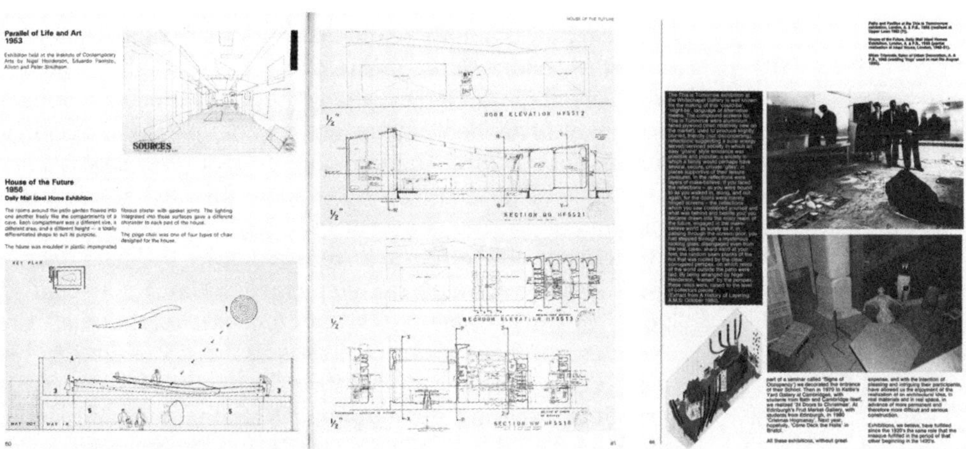

Alison's text in "The Masque and the Exhibition," labeled as an excerpt from "A History of Layering," 1980, appears next to large photos of *Patio and Pavilion* and House of the Future, with a smaller drawing of their Salon of Urban Decoration for the 1968 Milan Triennale. The Smithsons also suggested parallels and affinities between the two 1956 projects in earlier and later publications. In *Ordinariness and Light*, images of the two projects appear on the same page as examples of "embryo appliance houses," which they analogize to mobile homes and caravans. In the first section of *The Shift*, the Smithsons explain their exhibition designs The City by Day, City by Night for the 1953 *Turn Again* exhibition in London; Painting and Sculpture of a Decade of 1964 at the Tate Gallery, London; and Salon of Urban Decoration, Milan Triennale, 1968—as a series: "All these belonged to the family of contrapuntal games stemming from the Parallel of Life and Art." Several spreads later they pair House of the Future and *Patio and Pavilion* as projects concerned with "the re-establishment of a sense of identity. We felt that the sense of belonging could be helped by giving to the dwelling a piece of inviolate territory [...] [that] could be realized as allegory." On the page opposite the images of House of the Future and *Patio and Pavilion* is an alternative version of the famous shot, included in the catalogue of *This Is Tomorrow* along with drawings of *Patio and Pavilion*, of the Smithsons, Henderson, and Paolozzi sitting on modernist chairs in the middle of Limerston Street: this photograph shows just two Tulip Chairs from House of the Future in the street, as an allegorical couple (Alison and Peter) and an allegorical coupling of the two projects.

> The compound screens for *This Is Tomorrow* were aluminum faced plywood (then relatively new on the market); used to produce slightly blurred, friendly (not disconcerting) reflections [...]. In the reflections were layers of make-believe. If you faced the reflections—as you were bound to as you walked in, along, and out again, for the doors were merely hinged screens—the reflections which you saw contained yourself and what was behind and beside you; you became drawn into the misty realm of the future, engaged in the make-believe world as surely as if, in passing through the screen/door, you had stepped through a mysterious looking glass.[105]

The Smithsons saw the project as a staging structure for encounters with elusive and allusive images of the project's contents reflected on its perimeter enclosure, including its occupants and the objects and materials installed in the project by Henderson and Paolozzi.

For both projects, and perhaps for all their work, especially their books, temporal and spatial ambiguities generated by forms and materials were crucial. In the books, those materials are words and images arranged on spreads. The graphics generate recollection and repetition with the aim neither to locate the materials, words, or images at a particular time nor to simply refresh them, but instead to reconsider the interplay and viability of their past and current significance. As the Smithsons explain in the preface to *Ordinariness and Light*, they felt compelled to finally publish their nearly twenty-year-old "Urban Re-identification" manuscript as the first part of the book because they thought the manuscript was "a tumultuous rag-bag of a text, naïve, embarrassingly rhetorical, but stuffed with good things."[106] While it was "intended originally for publication as a popular general statement of an idea" and as an explanation of the design strategies of their unbuilt 1952 Golden Lane project, they saw it as both formative and still generative: "Re-reading this text now is both poignant and painful, for the sense of faith and of energy just waiting to be released can still be felt. In it were laid down the main themes we have been steadily working on ever since without conscious backward looks."[107] Thus *Ordinariness and Light* was intended as a refinishing and reuse of ideas from the 1950s at the same time, between 1966 and 1969, as they were completing the design of the project that came closest to realizing those ideas. Drawings of Robin Hood Gardens and a short chapter explaining its design approach are included as an appendix. The book's subtitle makes explicit the temporal dialectic of their ideas: *Urban Theories, 1952–1960, and Their Application in a Building Project, 1963–1970*. In their acknowledgments, the Smithsons explain: "All the material in the book has been revised [...] to eliminate repetition as much as possible, and to help sequential reading."[108] But that attempt at clarity obscures a more important acknowledgment that is its unspoken subtext: the Smithsons' work was *all* repetition. That is true not only of the contents of *Ordinariness and Light* but also of its design. The book is the Smithsons' first thoroughgoing attempt to develop imaging strategies that convey the latent, interactive potential of diverse visual materials from varied contexts, sources, and times.

As published in *Ordinariness and Light*, each chapter of "Urban Re-identification" operates as an adventurous and witty image series that conveys a sensibility augmenting and even superseding the arguments and ideas in the text. Perhaps the best example is the fourth chapter, "Communications and Dispositions," which begins with a drawing by Antonio Sant'Elia of a design for the Milan Central Station (1913–14). On the facing page is a 1950 photograph of a "helicopter landing with Epiphany gifts in front of the Milan cathedral." The opening spread's pairing of a perspective drawing and a photograph, of trains and helicopters, makes Sant'Elia's Futurism seem less a vision of the future than a now obsolete response to the past: the "immense scale changes" wrought by the "revolution of the railways and canals" in the nineteenth century.[109] By comparison, the almost surreal image of the insect-like Hiller 300 helicopter, hovering just above the heads of a huge crowd gathered in front of a monumental

Gothic-Renaissance facade, conveys "the scale changes consonant with the internal combustion engine, with road and air transport," which is "a problem so difficult that the sooner we start on it the better."[110] The sequence of images on the following pages—a photograph of "the first American jet helicopter," a high-altitude aerial photograph with the caption "beware aircraft crossing," a time-lapse image from *Time* magazine of an aircraft landing, and then more aerial photographs, plans, and bird's-eye view paintings of historical landscapes in Tunisia, Italy, and Britain—is a kind of post-Ruskinian lesson in how to see and inhabit the modern city's complex relationships of spaces, organization, levels, and infrastructures, from gardens, parks, and farms to airfields, ports, and highways. The book conveys the Smithsons' aim as designers and theorists to explore and manipulate existing image-worlds, including recollections of the past as they still exist in landscapes and cities as well as the ways they circulate in popular media. The image series in each chapter effectively "make these groupings apparent as tangible reality" and by extension convey how those groupings might have operated in their Golden Lane project as the "communications and disposition" of the street decks, lifts, balconies, patterns of growth, landscapes, and streetscapes.

The seventh chapter is a more abstract presentation of the patterns, textures, and forms of their "random aesthetic." "The Stuff and Decoration of the Urban Scene" begins with a photograph, again from above, of Jackson Pollock at work on a large canvas covering the floor of his studio—which might be read as yet another image of a landscape or an urban pattern—and then progresses through images of intricately textured sculptures and drawings by Paolozzi, Jean Dubuffet, and Victor Pasmore, the last of which is paired with a 1952 photograph from *Picture Post* (a popular postwar magazine in Britain) showing a worker inside the engine intake of a Comet jet airliner, with only his pants and boots protruding and set against the streamlined and riveted surfaces of the wing. As a clue to the aspirations of their own graphic approach, the Smithsons include the original enthusiastic caption to the image in *Picture Post* (written in the manner of ad copy) and ask, "What religious sect can rival this for intoning while watching its rites?" That series of "stuff and decoration" images, from the famous Pollock painting in his studio to the anonymous man working inside the wing of a Comet, establishes the "general sensibility" for looking at the chapter's remaining pages: a three-image spread with a Corbusier sketch of the Carthusian monastery of Ema, a photograph looking down from a Yorkshire hillside at the ruin of Mount Grace Priory (also a Carthusian monastery), and a plan of Corbusier's design for Saint-Dié published in the *Oeuvre complète*; followed by a four-image spread with two artful photographs of the Unité de Habitation ("Corbusier's 43-year-old dream from Ema realized"), Paestum, and the interior of the Hunstanton School "under construction"; and, on the final page, a single photograph, similar to earlier ones by László Moholy-Nagy of radio towers, looking straight down from the top of a nearly finished television tower in Sutton Coldfield, near Birmingham, with the yet to be installed trusses and beams arrayed on the field below.

The belated publication or republication and revised curation and layout of each series of images in the various chapters of

Ordinariness and Light demonstrate the ways the Smithsons remained intrigued and compelled by the questions, preoccupations, and insights that had guided and inspired them and their aesthetic at the time they initiated and developed New Brutalism. Yet the texts and images in the book almost completely avoid engaging with Mies's work (other than later essays such as "Letter to America" and "Fix: Permanence and Transience"), for the simple reason that almost all the material was originally produced during the mid-1950s, when Le Corbusier served as the architectural exemplar of New Brutalism. On the other hand, the period when they were working on both *Ordinariness and Light* and Robin Hood Gardens coincided with the time they were most assertively returning to Mies, and only in the books that follow, *Without Rhetoric* (which integrates and reworks essays from 1955 to 1970), *The Shift*, and *Changing the Art of Inhabitation*, do the Smithsons track and affirm their return to Mies. That gradual and emphatic return is perhaps the most important aspect of "the great walk back," as they call it in *Without Rhetoric*, which began in 1952 with the "ordinariness and quiet" of their Golden Lane project.

An attempt to chart a chronology of that path appears in "A Smithson File," the February 1966 issue of *Arena: The Architectural Association Journal*, which was "intended to be a definitive description of the Smithsons' work in their first 40 years."[111] Its first spread was an elaborate timeline produced by Jeremy Baker, the editor of the issue, of the Smithsons' ideas, influences, essays, and projects from 1949 to 1965.[112] The main body of the chart lists major projects and writings. Running horizontally across the bottom of the spread are two distinct lines of contemporary influence: "CORB" and "MIES." The Corbusier line breaks off into three thematic tracks in 1951, after which his name disappears and fifteen vertical connections lead from the three parallel tracks to specific projects and writings in the chart above. The Mies line has three segments—"MIES" (in bold typeface) from 1949 to 1950, "AWARENESS OF MIES" from 1950 to 1958, and "awareness of Mies" (in bold typeface) from 1958 to 1965—and only a few vertical connections: to Peter's "Crematorium Thesis" (1949), "Hunstanton Design" (1950), Peter's essay "Footnote on Seagram" (1958), and "Economist" (1963). A line near the top of the chart is labeled "New Brutalism," with a bold segment running from 1950 to 1957 and a lighter segment from 1957 to 1963. Thus, when the two segments of the Mies line are bold, the New Brutalism line is not. That oscillation between Mies and New Brutalism is both revealing and misleading. It clarifies the importance of Mies for the Smithsons' work at various times but suggests that their return to Mies was a departure from New Brutalist preoccupations. Yet those New Brutalist preoccupations were initiated by a fascination with Mies that intensified and evolved through their later, renewed engagement with his work. The fading of the New Brutalism line coincides with Peter's trip to America near the end of 1957, and the Mies line becomes bold just before Peter's second trip in late 1958. The chart also reinforces the understandable, but too simplistic, association of Le Corbusier with the development of New Brutalism after Hunstanton, and the idea that was clearly stated by one of the anonymous participants in a 1957 panel discussion in *Architectural Design*: "The Smithsons realized, after Hunstanton, that this particular manner which derived, with whatever refinements, from Mies van der Rohe, was not capable of extended development. The master himself has really taken it as far as it will go. The Smithsons clearly felt they must move on."[113] In 1961 Banham told another version of the same story:

> There has been much giggling over Alison's alleged farewell to Philip Johnson [in 1951], most distinguished of US followers of Mies, "Goodbye, but keep in touch, there aren't many of us left". If it was said, it was said absolutely straight and level, because it was factually true. The next year, there were two fewer, for they suddenly kicked the Mies-image—an almost unbelievable piece of boldness when they had a virtual corner in the style.[114]

While it is true that the Smithsons abandoned "the style," it is not likely they actually had ever understood Mies's architecture as a style. It was the Mies-image that remained with them.

Banham's more careful and accurate distinction is that the Smithsons "proceeded to offend their own possible supporters by announcing that they had hoped 'to avoid some of Mies's formalisms.'"[115] Banham was reiterating the argument he had made in his letter to the editor in the June 1957 issue of *Architectural Design*: the Smithsons rejected Miesian geometry and his specific idiom, not Hunstanton or the principles of New Brutalism. According to Banham, the only aspect of Hunstanton that they had rejected was "routine-Palladianism" because they "were in search of a wider frame of reference for their design activities."[116] Looking back, as is clear first in their buildings and later in their books, the Smithsons found that wider frame of reference by forgetting Mies's formal and constructional ideas and by returning to the Mies-image. Their return had many looks: it was traced in "the ephemera" of their work, pursued in the concept of "treillage'd space," synopsized in the "Three Generations image," and identified in Mies as the exemplar of the "new, softly smiling face of our discipline," which appears as "a quietness, that up to now our sensibilities have not recognized as architecture at all."

If the design of Golden Lane and the start of the production of the "Urban Re-identification" manuscript—coincident with the launch of the Independent Group in 1952—marked a new beginning in which the Smithsons began to imagine *un autre* Mies, another crucial step was their encounter with one of Mies's lesser-known buildings one year later, on the recommendation of Sam Stevens.[117] In 1953, perhaps on their trip to present the CIAM Grille at the meeting in Aix-en-Provence, France, and then again in September 1955 on their way home from a Team X meeting in La Sarraz, Switzerland,[118] the Smithsons visited the factory complex (1932–33) and Lange House (1928) at Krefeld, Germany. They may have made the visit because that was also when they were beginning to work on *The Heroic Period of Modern Architecture*, and although the Krefeld buildings do not appear in that book,[119] they became fascinated by the subtleties and simplicity of the factory. They eventually came to understand Krefeld not only as a key source for the post-Heroic American work by Mies that had directly inspired Hunstanton and New Brutalism, but also as a direct inspiration for their ideas about New Brutalism which were first explicitly formulated later that year in Alison's text in *Architectural Design* accompanying drawings of their Soho House: "It is our intention in this building to have the structure exposed entirely, without internal finishes wherever practicable. The Contractor should aim at a high standard of basic construction as in a small warehouse."[120] The impact of Krefeld remained latent in the Smithsons' imagination. Their recognition and acknowledgment of the factory's significance for them and for their understanding of the development of Mies's work came later. In early 1966 there was no mention of the visit in the *Arena* special issue. But by the late 1960s, Krefeld would become a key reference. Images and mentions of the factory first appear in the Berlin seminar, held in late 1967 and published two years later, where the Smithsons include Krefeld as the last in a sequence of canonical projects:

> Before Mies van der Rohe left Germany he had already established a kind of mode-shift in the discipline of architecture, which makes itself more and more obvious in his work in America—especially after the mid-fifties. Not that it is always clear. It can be seen emerging in the skin studies of the Friedrichstrasse office building, Berlin (1919), the glass skyscraper (1920–21) and the concrete office building (1922). It began to be real in his architecture on the street façade of the apartments at the Weissenhofsiedlung (1927) and in the layout of the buildings in front of the main factory at Krefeld (1932–33).[121]

Eventually, Krefeld came to exemplify both the insufficiency and the persistence of the Smithsons' early understanding of Mies. This is clear in the first text in their 1994 book *Changing the Art of Inhabitation*. A letter from Peter to Alison, written during his 1958 American trip, contains an ambivalent reference to Krefeld as an important but transitional project: "So it looks as if even Mies can make Miestakes. Certainly at IIT there are many errors. The early buildings [at IIT] in concrete and wood windows (presumably built during the war) and later concrete and steel windows, 1958, are very very Krefeld. [. . .] Krefeld was definitely the starting point."[122] A text that appears later in the book, a 1986 paper by Alison on the Barcelona Pavilion, reiterates the significance of Krefeld: "The Barcelona Pavilion had been—like most Heroic Period buildings—built with the same turn-of-the-century building construction methods which we were taught. So was Krefeld; that we looked at in 1955, returning from La Sarraz."[123] Krefeld appears elsewhere in the book: in an extract from a 1959 lecture by Peter suggesting that "the early buildings on the IIT campus are technically little improvement on their prototype at Krefeld," and in a passage from their 1985 book, *The 1930s*, titled "On Krefeld," tracing the "rough and ready way the rectangle plan form and repetition of bays" were used at IIT and the Krefeld factory. In *Without Rhetoric*, a paragraph on Krefeld is inserted between excerpts from two 1960s essays, the Berlin seminar and Peter's 1966 birthday homage to Mies in *Bauen + Wohnen*,[124] identifying their earliest architectural ideas with the transition from Krefeld to IIT: "Mies was already a third the way through his work in America—what might be said to be his Krefeld period was ending and his truly American period beginning—when we became conscious in architecture."[125] The latency of Krefeld as a memory and an image, which they grasped initially in 1953, the year of Hunstanton's glazed stage and of *Parallel of Life and Art*, and later as a "real" surrogate for the Barcelona Pavilion before it was reconstructed, is a crucial yet subtle, hardly polemical, and easily overlooked example of the Smithsons' persistent reconsideration, documentation, and recollection of the layered complexities and potentialities of the Mies-image.

ARRAY 4.13

Peter's 1958 letter begins as a meditation on the fallacy of considering modernism in terms of simple newness. When he was in Chicago, the towers at 860–880 Lakeshore Drive were being repainted. "The aluminium window frames are being painted grey and the steel black. The result is that the original idea is so re-established it can, just, ride-over the fifty types of air-conditioner and blower which have been put into the lower window panel. This painting business seems to give a solidness and historical existence to things. [...] Smart yet not new. Old things cannot look new."[126] In this case, a fresh coating of paint on a building that was less than ten years "old" renewed its architectural idea by refreshing its image. *Changing the Art of Inhabitation* operates with an analogous imaging operation. An old letter is published in a new book with new annotations and three old photos, taken by Peter in 1958. The kinds of content and its careful organization (the captions for the images, most of which are uncredited, appear only in the back of the book like endnotes) enact a complex oscillation between past and present, old and new, statement and implication, front and back, image and fact, history and contemporaneity, here and there, now and then. That game of fluctuation, which is as crucial to the logic of the Smithsons' imagination as it is to the logic of imaging, continues in the second text in the book: an article on the Seagram Building (1958) that was first published after Peter's second trip to America (when he wrote the letter to Alison), as if to show how an earlier set of observations while in Chicago were modified and reconsidered a few months later when back in London.[127] As the remarks about repainting or the recollections of Krefeld suggest, seeing an actual building can be revelatory, but it is an encounter that is neither more authentic than nor separable from one's previously established imagination of its architecture or the reestablishment of its image. New encounters and new information compel reimagings. The Smithsons' pursuit of the Mies-image is like a documentary film with flashbacks, or a slide lecture given to different audiences with the images slightly remixed and revised each time.

In 1966, in response to questions about the "significance" and "influence" of Mies and his thinking, Peter wrote: "Mies' thought runs very deep and is not easily accessible—not even one suspects to himself—and [...] the re-direction of the main stress of architecture itself, which my instincts tell me lies in his work, will take some years for us to comprehend and grow upon."[128] One year later, in their Berlin seminar, the Smithsons offered their first overt attempt to "comprehend and grow upon" Mies's work. One of the last two slides in that lecture, as it was published two years later in *Architectural Design*, was a photograph of the interior of the Minerals and Metals Research Building that had appeared in the two sources where they first saw Mies: Philip

4.13

Johnson's 1947 book (large and high resolution) and the 1946 article in *Architects' Journal* (small and grainy). The other, and final, image is a photograph by Peter (most likely taken in the early 1960s) of "the unique extrusions of aluminium and neoprene of the Colonnade [Apartments] skin" in Newark, New Jersey. The first image, they write, conveys how the Minerals and Metals Building "that captured our personal interest in Mies when it was first published in England in 1946 [is] a wonderfully clear exposition—because the things it is assembled from are so humble—of how his handling makes us see their richness."[129] That conjuring of "luxury" from humble materials also, and more surprisingly, happens at New Jersey in the low-cost aluminum and neoprene of the Colonnade towers, which abandon the Minerals and Metals Building's "poetry of 'assembled' components—rolled sections and bricks"[130] in favor of the kind of "designed" unity Peter wrote about in "The Rocket" in 1965: "a single clearly designed each-part-specially-developed object" that coheres as an image by virtue of its overall sensibility.[131]

While the photograph of the Minerals and Metals Building is not included in the version of the Berlin seminar published in *Changing the Art of Inhabitation*, the photograph of the Colonnade Apartments (1958–60) is the final image in both the 1969 and 1994 versions of the essay. Fewer than one-third of the 1969 images appear in the 1994 version. Notably, in 1994 a different image of Krefeld, a photograph taken by Peter in 1955 (which also appears in *Without Rhetoric*), is used. It shows a person on a moped leaving one of the smaller buildings on the basement service ramp. Like many others, each of these images reappears multiple times in publications over three decades, but the photograph of the interior of the Minerals and Metals Building is especially potent. It shows a prosaic workspace, with researchers in lab coats, one looking into a microscope in the foreground, another standing in the middle ground in front of a spray booth with its ductwork rising over his head, and a third at the far end of the space, facing the translucent glass wall on the left, seemingly using its light to trace something or to backlight a slide. That same soft, bright light is casting an even glow in a room filled with practical furnishings and equipment. The tables, chairs, shelves, and carts appear to be of the same family of objects as the radiators, lighting fixtures, and conduits. The atmosphere and details of that image reappear incessantly in the Smithsons' work, from the science classrooms of Hunstanton to the street decks of Golden Lane, to *Patio and Pavilion*, their country house, the plaza and offices of the Economist complex, St. Hilda's, the Lucas Headquarters, the Amenity Building at the University of Bath, and their many small projects for Tecta.

The potency of the Smithsons' imaging practices lies in not letting their imagination rest nor ever resting their case. Their evolving efforts to scrutinize, understand, and reconsider Mies were the source of peculiar and persistent preoccupations. Their ways of looking were always ambivalent and mutable, as Alison's reflections on the reconstruction of the Barcelona Pavilion in the 1980s suggest:

> Looking back [...]. In some way we stand with Krefeld, in that we are Europeans with a European morality toward invention. Aware that we are becoming a world of long-arm watchers,

> watching re-enactments; already inheritors of a couple of generations of re-enactment, for beginning in the 1930s, everything was used by Hollywood; advertising followed; television extends this simulation so that even reporting where the explosion rocks the camera is so edited as to be made equal with entertainment: "They took us to" is a phrase one can hear from the elderly to whom television's transportation to an event, a country, is still magic.[132]

Even if their body of work—produced by two quite different individuals working collaboratively and often at cross-purposes—will never be characterized as consistent, the Smithsons' constant effort to reconsider their own work was a sincere and productive effort to wrestle with their earliest and most persistent memories and aspirations, as if New Brutalism might yet be realized and fulfilled in retrospect by curating and collecting—reimaging—their prior thoughts and projects. With a combination of arrogance and vulnerability, insistence and curiosity, their way of looking was also an ongoing effort at autobiography, as if all their work were a comprehensive and synthetic recollection and revision of the lessons of architecture's distant and recent past, of their contemporaries' and collaborators' efforts, and of their own production.

Notes

1 Alison and Peter Smithson, *Without Rhetoric: An Architectural Aesthetic, 1955–1972*, Cambridge, MA: MIT Press, 1974, p. 85.
2 Alison and Peter Smithson, *Ordinariness and Light*, Cambridge, MA: MIT Press, 1970, p. 11.
3 Beginning as early as 1952 in their Urban Re-Identification manuscript, where they write, "we have to try to re-identify man with his environment," and continuing in their later books and essays, the Smithsons characterized their work as a search for "fresh impulses that, given a cultural twist, could re-identify an old society." Alison and Peter Smithson, *Ordinariness and Light*, Cambridge, MA: MIT Press, 1970, p. 38, and Alison and Peter Smithson, *The Shift*, London: Academy Editions, 1982, p. 9.
4 Harry Hopkins, *The New Look: A Social History of the Forties and Fifties in Britain*, London: Readers Union, 1964, p. 95. An opportune example of the phrase's ubiquity is a full-page advertisement for Hermeseal acoustic tiles with the slogan "New Look in Acoustics!" that appears opposite Peter's "Letter to America," *Architectural Design*, 28, no. 3 (March 1958), p. 92.
5 Hopkins, *The New Look*, p. 96. Hopkins is referring to the Eisenhower administration's policy, announced in 1953, to reduce defense expenditures by focusing on international alliances and nuclear deterrence rather than a buildup of conventional weapons. Lesley Jackson extends Hopkins's claims in the catalogue for the 1991 exhibition *The New Look: Design in the Fifties*, arguing that the New Look exemplified a "widespread shift in design aesthetics during the late 1940s and early 1950s" that grew in popularity as "public indignation about wastefulness and indulgence abated. [...] The New Look arrived in two distinct waves. The first wave, organic modernism, took sculpture as its primary source of inspiration and affected the shapes of three-dimensional design and architecture. The second wave [in the early 1950s] transformed patterns, and reflected the influence of recent developments in abstract painting on the decoration of textiles, wallpapers, and ceramics." That influence is clear in the Smithsons' collaborations with Paolozzi on Jenkins Room and with Paolozzi and Henderson on *Parallel of Life and Art*, and especially in Hammer Prints Limited, the product design company focused on patterned textiles and ceramics that Paolozzi and Henderson launched in 1954. Lesley Jackson, *The New Look: Design in the Fifties*, exh. cat., Manchester City Art Galleries and Glasgow Art Gallery and Museum, London: Thames & Hudson, 1991, pp. 8–9.
6 Alison and Peter Smithson, "The Heroic Period of Modern Architecture," *Architectural Design*, 35, no. 12 (December 1965), p. 5.
7 A. and P. Smithson, *The Shift*, p. 9.
8 Alison Smithson, "And Now Dhamas are Dying Out in Japan," *Architectural Design*, 36, no. 9 (September 1966), p. 448.
9 A. and P. Smithson, *Without Rhetoric*, pp. 43–44.
10 The Barcelona Pavilion was reconstructed from 1983 to 1986, and the Smithsons' reconstructed *Patio and Pavilion* was exhibited in 1987 at the Clocktower Gallery in New York and again in 1990 for the Independent Group exhibition at the Institute of Contemporary Arts. That show traveled to Spain and the United States in 1990 and 1991. A version of the lecture by Alison at the ICA in 1990, with annotations by Peter, was published as Alison and Peter Smithson, "'Patio and Pavilion' Reconstructed," *AA Files*, 47 (Summer 2002), pp. 37–44. Also see Peter's lecture "The Two Lives of Patio and Pavilion" at the Architectural Association on October 15, 2001, in which he twice compares the problem of reconstructing *Patio and Pavilion* to the Barcelona Pavilion: "Peter Smithson—The Two Lives of Patio and Pavilion," www.youtube.com/watch?v=f1XqGdOTqsM.
11 Alison and Peter Smithson, *The Charged Void: Architecture*, New York: Monacelli Press, 2001, pp. 198–97.
12 A. and P. Smithson, "'Patio and Pavilion' Reconstructed," p. 39.
13 Ibid., p. 43.
14 Ibid. In Alison's 1984 lecture "Territory of the Pavilion," presented during the reconstruction of the Barcelona Pavilion, she said: "The old photographs of the Barcelona Pavilion were, naturally enough, black and white, but so were the photographs of our youth. Our generation was in no doubt as to the nature of the materials—(green) marbles, or (golden) onyx. In fact, directed by the photographs, our myth-image is nearer to what they were than the reconstruction is [...] my eyes having been conditioned by the photographs." See Alison and Peter Smithson, *Changing the Art of Inhabitation: Mies' Pieces, Eames' Dreams, the Smithsons*, London: Artemis, 1994, pp. 35–37.
15 A. and P. Smithson, "'Patio and Pavilion' Reconstructed," p. 44.
16 Ibid., p. 43.
17 Ibid., p. 44.
18 Mark Wigley, "Alison and Peter Smithson's Quest for the Void," *Bookforum* (Summer 2003), p. 9.
19 A. and P. Smithson, *The Shift*, p. 9.
20 Ibid., p. 73.
21 Alison and Peter Smithson, "Mies van der Rohe," *Architectural Design*, 39, no. 7 (July 1969), p. 363. Inviting their readers to pursue the development of their ideas, a note at the end of the essay reads: "The themes in this essay have been explored previously by Peter Smithson in *Bauen + Wohnen*, May 1966; *Architectural Design*, 8/64, 3/65, 7/65, 8/65, 1[*sic*]/66, 7/66." Much of that material would later be reworked yet again and included in *Without Rhetoric*.
22 A. and P. Smithson, *The Charged Void*, p. 379.
23 Ibid. This idea was elaborated by Peter after Alison's death in "The Lattice Idea," *ILA&UD: Annual Report 1999* (1999), pp. 58–61. Also see Alison Smithson, "Strati e stratificazioni / Layers and layering," *Spazio e Società* (1981), p. 13.

24 A. and P. Smithson, *The Shift*, p. 26.

25 See Peter's contribution to an issue of *Bauen + Wohnen* celebrating Mies's eightieth birthday: vol. 20: *Ludwig Mies van der Rohe 80 Jahre* (May 1966), p. 206.

26 A. and P. Smithson, *The Shift*, p. 9.

27 Max Risselada, "A Critical Chronology," in *Alison and Peter Smithson: A Critical Anthology*, ed. Risselada, Barcelona: Ediciones Polygrafa, 2011, p. 429; A. and P. Smithson, *The Shift*, p. 9.

28 For a detailed discussion of the sensibility primers see M. Christine Boyer, "The 'Sensibility Primers': Revenge of the Picturesque," in Boyer, *Not Quite Architecture: Writing around Alison and Peter Smithson*, Cambridge, MA: MIT Press, 2017, pp. 328–57.

29 Alison Smithson, *AS in DS: An Eye on the Road*, Delft: Delft University Press, 1983, pp. 1, 15.

30 Ibid., pp. 111, 16. Alison's method recalls Richard Hamilton's series of *Trainsition* paintings from the early 1950s. For an insightful account of the Smithsons' automobile interests see M. Christine Boyer, "Vehicles of Desire," in *Not Quite Architecture*, pp. 194–228.

31 Reyner Banham, "Revenge of the Picturesque," in *Concerning Architecture: Essays on Architectural Writers and Writing presented to Nikolaus Pevsner*, ed. John Summerson, London: Penguin, 1967, p. 273.

32 A. Smithson, *AS in DS*, pp. 151–52. Included as "After-Papers" in *AS in DS* are excerpts from William Cobbett, *Rural Rides* (1853), which describes travel in the English countryside in the 1820s. Also see John Betjeman, "The Seeing Eye, or How to Like Everything" [illustrations by John Piper], *Architectural Review*, 86 (July–December 1939), pp. 201–4, as well as John Piper, "London to Bath: A Topographical and Critical Survey of the Bath Road," *Architectural Review*, 85 (May 1939), pp. 229–46.

33 A. Smithson, *AS in DS*, p. 1.

34 A. and P. Smithson, *Without Rhetoric*, p. 1.

35 A. Smithson, *AS in DS*, p. 35.

36 A. and P. Smithson, *The Shift*, p. 73.

37 Ibid.

38 Ibid.

39 In October 1949, Paolozzi purchased an enlarger for Henderson in Paris as a gift, and the two artists spent time together using the enlarger as "a drawing instrument." See Martin Harrison, *Transition: The London Art Scene in the Fifties*, London: Merrell, 2002, pp. 101–2.

40 A. and P. Smithson, *The Shift*, pp. 10–11.

41 Martino Stierli characterizes the Smithsons' visual thinking and writings as "subversive mimicry" of high modernist idioms, and he references the significance of British research on animal mimicry, specifically the writings of the nineteenth-century naturalist Henry Walter Bates. See Stierli, "Taking on Mies: Mimicry and Parody of Modernism in the Architecture of Alison and Peter Smithson and Venturi/Scott Brown," in *Neo-avant-garde and Postmodern: Postwar Architecture in Britain and Beyond*, ed. Mark Crinson and Claire Zimmerman, New Haven: Yale Center for British Art, 2010, pp. 161–62. It should be noted that the zoologist Hugh Cott published an essay on mimicry in *Aspects of Form*, the book published in concert with the 1951 *Growth and Form* exhibition at the ICA, with images that have some visual resemblance to ones often used by the Smithsons.

42 Gilbert Ryle, *The Concept of Mind*, London: Hutchinson, 1949, p. 42. Ryle's book includes an extended discussion of the distinction between "sensation and observation" (pp. 190–231) that precedes the chapter on imagination. For Ryle, intelligence is an achieved disposition for enacting any kind of performance, from simple acts like drawing a diagram or taking a photograph to complex ones like dancing or designing a building.

43 Ibid., p. 15.

44 Ibid., pp. 236, 241.

45 Ibid., p. 195.

46 Ibid., p. 234.

47 Ibid.

48 Ibid., p. 240.

49 A. and P. Smithson, *The Shift*, p. 9; Ryle, *The Concept of Mind*, pp. 44–45.

50 A. and P. Smithson, *The Shift*, p. 62. The Smithsons make the remark in reference to Theo Crosby's design of *Uppercase*, 3: *Urban Structuring* (1960), a small book outlining the Smithsons' urban theories, beginning with Golden Lane, that also included a portfolio of photographs by Henderson. It was republished and redesigned, without Henderson's work, as Alison and Peter Smithson, *Urban Structuring: Studies of Alison and Peter Smithson*, New York: Reinhold, 1967.

51 The idea that the Smithsons might have been interested in the architectural qualities of the opened book is affirmed by Christian Sumi in a postscript to Alison's *AS in DS* that discusses the form of that book (die-cut in the shape of the plan of the Citroën DS): "When the book is opened, the one DS becomes two, bound together at the spine like Siamese twins. If the book is turned 90 degrees, the two cars appear to be racing neck-in-neck." A. Smithson, *AS in DS*, p. 166. Conversely, their suspicion of overt games of reflection and mirroring is captured in the caption to one of Peter's images of glass buildings reflecting one another across a street in New York City in "Letter to America," p. 101 (which also appears in *Ordinariness and Light*): "two curtain wall buildings opposite one another, and bang!"

52 A. and P. Smithson, *Without Rhetoric*, pp. 32–33. A footnote to this phrase reads, "Eames Celebration, *Architectural Design*, September 1966." The Smithsons edited the issue and wrote an introduction and two essays: Peter Smithson, "Just a Few Chairs and a House: An Essay on the Eames-Aesthetic," pp. 443–46, and Alison Smithson, "And Now Dhamas are Dying Out in Japan," pp. 447–48.

53 A. and P. Smithson, *Without Rhetoric*, pp. 44–46. In the original version of the text, "Concealment and Display: Meditations on Braun," *Architectural Design*, 36 (July 1966), pp. 362–63, Peter compares the select and arrange

technique (which he says is a kind of "Pop-styling" that is "in many respects, close to flower-arrangement") to a more integrated kind of "design" in which the repetition of similar objects requires the suppression of symbolism and uniqueness: "It would seem that one of the things that is crucial to large numbers and to repetition is a special sort of anonymity of '*styling*' (a conclusion no-one would have dared even think about in 1952)." Also see Peter Smithson, "The Rocket," *Architectural Design*, 35 (July 1965), pp. 322–23, where he makes a similar argument about "a single clearly designed each-part-specially-developed object" which "reminds us of Mies."

54 A. and P. Smithson, *The Shift*, p. 12.
55 Ibid., p. 22.
56 "Alison Smithson—A Line of Tree [*sic*] ... A Steel Structure," talk at Art Net, London, October 31, 1975, www.youtube.com/watch?v=QHnaEwRWJ-0.
57 A. and P. Smithson, *The Shift*, pp. 38–39.
58 Ibid., p. 10.
59 See Ana Ábalos Ramos, "Alison and Peter Smithson: The Transient and the Permanent," PhD dissertation, Universitat politèchnica de València, September 2015, p. 59.
60 A. and P. Smithson, *The Shift*, p. 58.
61 Ibid.
62 Ibid., p. 64.
63 Ibid., p. 65.
64 A. and P. Smithson, *The Charged Void: Architecture*, p. 377. The Three Generations image appears in *The Charged Void* on the title page of Chapter 8, "The Treillage'd Space," followed by the presentation of the Lucas Headquarters.
65 See ibid., p. 378, and Peter Smithson, "The Masque and the Exhibition: Stages toward the Real," *ILA&UD: Language of Architecture* (1981), p. 62. Peter's essay "The Masque and the Exhibition: Stages toward the Real" includes both Alison's and Peter's versions and mentions *The Shift* as a source to understand the long, oblique arc of their aesthetic development: "We, in the third generation of the *Three Generations*, found (as you can now read in 'The Shift,' a treatise to be published, at last! in 1981) in the 'fifties that we could realize ideas only as allegory, that is obliquely, yet in real space, in exhibitions ... in 'A Parallel of Life and Art' in 1953 at the Institute of Contemporary Arts, in 'Patio and Pavillion' [*sic*] at the *This is Tomorrow* exhibition, and in 'The House of the Future' at the Ideal Homes, the last two both in 1956. We also made a transient real space entirely of pictures and sculptures in the Tate Gallery's '1954–64' exhibition in 1964" (p. 65).
66 Though published in 2001, the Smithsons began working on *The Charged Void* in 1974.
67 Peter Smithson, "Three Generations," *ILA&UD: Annual Report, Urbino 1980* (1980), p. 94. In "The Lattice Idea," p. 58, Peter succinctly characterizes treillage'd space as an "exploration of braces becoming lattices."
68 A. and P. Smithson, *The Charged Void*, p. 380. The Smithsons' first constructed test of the device they proposed for Lucas was the second phase of their Amenity Building at the University of Bath (1984–85), where "the 'bracing' is inside the weather-skin whereas in Lucas Headquarters it was outside." Ibid., p. 443. But the oblique or diagonal appears, whether overt of subdued, in virtually every project after Lucas.
69 A. and P. Smithson, "Mies van der Rohe," p. 363.
70 A small image of Jasper Johns's painting *Three Flags* (1958) (incorrectly captioned "'Flag' by Jasper Johns, 1955") appears in P. Smithson, "The Rocket," p. 323. The article discusses Johns's work as an example of the continued value of "unique hand-crafted objects" in a mass-production society or in prefabricated architecture. The irony of the example—a unique conception and vision of a repeated iconic image as an art object—seems intentional, though it is acknowledged only by the placement of the photograph in an array of perspectival photographs of gridded buildings: prefabricated houses by the London County Council, the interior of the Union Carbide office building in New York by Skidmore, Owings & Merrill, and Mies van der Rohe's Lake Shore Drive Apartments.
71 A. and P. Smithson, "Mies van der Rohe," p. 366.
72 Peter Smithson, "Concealment and Display: Meditations on Braun," *Architectural Design*, 36 (July 1966), p. 362.
73 P. Smithson, "The Rocket," p. 322.
74 A. and P. Smithson, *Without Rhetoric*, pp. 44, 63.
75 Ibid., p. 65.
76 Reyner Banham, "The New Brutalism," *Architectural Review*, 118, no. 708 (December 1955), p. 358. While it seems that it was clearly understood by the Smithsons much later, it is in the sense of assembled components or studied compositions that, at the time of New Brutalism, "*design*, for us, was a dirty word." See A. and P. Smithson, "'Patio and Pavilion' Reconstructed," p. 41.
77 A. and P. Smithson, *The Shift*, p. 67.
78 Vilém Flusser, *Into the Universe of Technical Images*, Minneapolis: University of Minnesota Press, 2011, pp. 4–5.
79 A. and P. Smithson, *Without Rhetoric*, p. 66.
80 Ibid., p. 69. In their introduction to "Eames Celebration", *Architectural Design*, 36, no. 9 (September 1966), p. 432, they write: "There has been much reflection in England on the Eames House. For the Eames House was a cultural gift parcel received here at a particularly useful time. The bright wrapper has made most people —especially Americans—throw the content away as not sustaining. But we have been brooding on it—working on it—feeding from it."
81 A. and P. Smithson, *Ordinariness and Light*, p. 24.
82 A. and P. Smithson, *Without Rhetoric*, p. 85.
83 Ibid., p. 82.
84 Ibid.
85 John Ruskin, *Mornings in Florence* [1881], in *Works of John Ruskin*, 12 vols, New York:

John Wiley & Sons, 1886, vol. 10, p. 14.

86 Ibid., p. 88.

87 Ibid., pp. 91–92.

88 Ibid., pp. 35–36. Ruskin's second and third principles are religious.

89 Ibid., p. 37.

90 Peter Smithson, "The Slow Growth of Another Sensibility: Architecture as Town Building," in *A Continuing Experiment: Learning and Teaching at the Architectural Association*, ed. James Gowan, London: Architectural Press, pp. 56–57, 60.

91 A. Smithson, "And Now Dhamas are Dying Out in Japan," p. 447. "Ourselves and Eduardo Paolozzi know where it came from. It is possible Nigel Henderson alone could have led us to steam engines and the ephemera of life via old boots, bits of sacking, ancient post cards magicked over by photography, but I like to think it is to Ray and Charles Eames we owe the debt of the extravagance of the purchase. The penny whistle, the Woolworths plastic Christmas decoration and toy, on to the German pressed metal toy and the walking robots. [...] The Eames films gave new life to our inherited toys so that they did not have that peculiar front-parlour-collection chill of Black Eyes and Lemonade (Barbara Jones)." Ibid., pp. 447–48.

92 Ruskin, *Mornings in Florence*, p. 44.

93 Ibid., pp. 44–45.

94 Alison and Peter Smithson, "But Today We Collect Ads," *Ark*, 18 (November 1956), n.p.

95 A. and P. Smithson, *The Shift*, p. 56. The collage, which they describe as a "mounted enlargement of [an] open-topped tram, depicted as if in a field of red poppies," was exhibited at Art Net in 1976.

96 "The Rally—Part 1—Reyner Banham," lecture at Art Net, London, www.youtube.com/watch?v=ymYfbuqiVdc. *Architects' Journal* published two reports on Art Net, by Astragal and the editors, both of which focused on Banham's claims about the past and present status of British architecture. Astragal suggested that Banham was "satirising the windy arrogance of the high modern movement" and was arguing that Britain may be "slumping back into the kind of provincialism" of the early twentieth century. An article by the journal's editors characterized the lecture in opposite terms, as a defense of British architecture against the "uninhibited, unabashed, eulogy for British architecture" that was implied by Art Net's lineup of mostly international architects. Neither report acknowledged Banham's ideas about two modernist traditions or his suggestion that the Smithsons could be blamed for taking the wrong path. See Astragal, "Banham's Last Blast," and the editors, "The Rally of Art Net," *Architects' Journal*, 164, no. 28 (July 14, 1976), pp. 89, 92.

97 "The Rally—Part 1—Reyner Banham." Unless noted, subsequent quotations are from this source.

98 In insisting that the Smithsons had made a choice between two sides, Banham was polemicizing their deep ambivalence toward both Pop and Britishness, which is clear in their response in 1990 to a claim by Kenneth Frampton about their debt to Paolozzi: "We always considered ourselves very English and [...] we have always been oriented towards Europe and never deviated, reacting to aspirations beamed out from America that we saw would be irresistible, but also, recognizing these as part of a wider threat to Europe's cultural identity." In a footnote to the statement they add: "A. and P.S. were not under the pop-influence of Eduardo: A.M.S. received American magazines in the form of the *Ladies Home Journal* and the *Companion* respectively through her Grandmother and Great Aunt while evacuated in Edinburgh 1940 onwards, and therefore saw the Green Giant grow, Singer sewing machine become electric, miniaturized; Mama Mia sauce for spaghetti displayed by a fat lady before our troops landed in Italy; and so on, while Eduardo was, from their sea-front stall, still serving wartime ice cream, made by his mother, to us as maroon uniformed school girls coming out of Portobello Baths on Saturday mornings." Alison and Peter Smithson, "Retrospective Statement," in *The Independent Group: Postwar Britain and the Aesthetics of Plenty*, ed. David Robbins, Cambridge, MA: MIT Press, 1990, pp. 194–95. Perhaps the Smithsons protest too much: Alison's scrapbooks of the time have a strong resemblance to Paolozzi's.

99 A. and P. Smithson, *Without Rhetoric*, p. 66.

100 See George Kubler, *The Shape of Time: Remarks on the History of Things*, New Haven: Yale University Press, 1962, p. 100.

101 Ibid., pp. 101–2. Kubler's examples of sixty-year durations include "the development of the pictorial system of the Renaissance in central Italy during about sixty years in the fifteenth century, or the appearance of tall-steel-frame architecture after 1850 in the United States and Europe" (pp. 102–3). Interestingly, Kubler offers this explanation of the patterns of formal sequences in history: "The mathematical analogy for our study is topology, the geometry of relationships without magnitudes or dimensions having only surfaces and directions" (p. 34).

102 Alison and Peter Smithson, "The Nature of Retreat," *Places*, 7, no. 3 (1991), p. 8. The quotation is taken from a one-page introduction to "four texts, edited from lectures given at the University of California, Berkely, College of Environmental Design, in March 1991."

103 Kubler, *Shape of Time*, p. viii.

104 P. Smithson, "The Masque and the Exhibition," p. 65.

105 Ibid., p. 66.

106 A. and P. Smithson, *Ordinariness and Light*, p. 11.

107 Ibid., pp. 10, 9.

108 Ibid., p. 13.

109 Ibid., p. 62.

110 Ibid., p. 63.

111 *Arena: The Architectural Association Journal*, 81, no. 899, special issue: *A Smithson File*, compiled by Jeremy Baker (February 1966), p. 177.

112 Ibid., pp. 178–79.

113 Alison and Peter Smithson, "Thoughts in Progress," *Architectural Design*, 27, no. 4 (April 1957), p. 111.

114 Reyner Banham, "Apropos the Smithsons," *New Statesman* (September 8, 1961), p. 317. The farewell Banham is referring to most likely occurred at the time of Philip Johnson's "Modern Architecture" lecture at the ICA on July 12, 1951.

115 Ibid.

116 Reyner Banham, "Letter to the Editor," *Architectural Design*, 27, no. 6 (June 1957), p. 220.

117 See note on page 64 in *Changing the Art of Inhabitation*. In the *Arena* monograph, the Smithsons list Stevens among the IG members (p. 182). The only other source I know of that includes Stevens among the group's members is Harrison, *Transition*, p. 124: "Outside the original nine or ten members of the Independent Group, the fringe membership was comprised almost entirely of architects: Alison and Peter Smithson, Colin St John Wilson, James Stirling, Sam Stevens, Cedric Price and Theo Crosby." Stevens participated with Banham, Lawrence Alloway, and William Howell in a discussion of Corbusier's Modulor at the ICA on March 18, 1954. See "Chronology" in Anne Massey and Gregor Muir, *Institute of Contemporary Arts, 1946–1968*, London: ICA, 2014. Kenneth Frampton, in an interview with Stan Allen and Hal Foster, says, "In London there was this fertile figure named Thomas (Sam) Stevens, who had taught at the Liverpool School of Architecture, a leading training ground in the postwar period (it produced Colin Rowe, among others). At the AA he was a talking head par excellence with a BA in art history from the Courtauld and a photographic memory. Stevens was the kind of person who stimulates young students better than most academics." "A Conversation with Kenneth Frampton," *October* (Fall 2003), pp. 41–42. Rem Koolhaas, in an interview with Bob Somol, says: "Stevens was a friend of Rowe's from Liverpool where they had studied together; I think that a large part of what Rowe thought, and of the brilliance of the 'Transparency' essays, were things that had been elaborated together with Sam Stevens. Stevens [...] could hold forth on almost anything in the most unbelievably brilliant way [...]. He had a stunning erudition that went from everything modern to everything baroque and back." See "Being OMU's Ghostwriter: Rem Koolhaas in Conversation with Robert Somol," in *Reckoning with Colin Rowe: Ten Architects Take a Position*, ed. Emmanuel Petit, New York: Routledge, 2015, pp. 87–88.

118 See A. and P. Smithson, *Changing the Art of Inhabitation*, p. 42. The *Arena* chronology lists two "La Sarraz" entries for September 1955.

119 The last projects in *The Heroic Period* are from 1937, and the last Mies project is the Tugendhat House (1930). But it is more likely that the Krefeld buildings were not included because there were no well-known images.

120 Alison and Peter Smithson, "House in Soho, London," *Architectural Design*, 23, no. 12 (December 1953), p. 342. The Lange House may have been closest to the ethos of the Soho House. In the Berlin seminar they wrote: "The brick of the Lange House is as brick as brick can be—dour, puritan, absolute, brick." A. and P. Smithson, "Mies van der Rohe," p. 363.

121 A. and P. Smithson, "Mies van der Rohe," p. 363.

122 A. and P. Smithson, *Changing the Art of Inhabitation*, p. 9.

123 Ibid., p. 42.

124 P. Smithson, contribution to *Bauen + Wohnen*, 20: *Ludwig Mies van der Rohe 80 Jahre*, p. 206. Contributors were asked: "1. What is your view of the general significance of Mies van der Rohe? 2. What influence has the architectural thinking of Mies van der Rohe had on your own work?"

125 A. and P. Smithson, *Without Rhetoric*, p. 20.

126 A. and P. Smithson, *Changing the Art of Inhabitation*, p. 8.

127 Peter Smithson, "Footnote on the Seagram Building," *Architectural Review*, 124 (December 1958), p. 382.

128 P. Smithson, contribution to *Bauen + Wohnen*, 20: *Ludwig Mies van der Rohe 80 Jahre*, p. 206.

129 A. and P. Smithson, "Mies van der Rohe,", p. 366.

130 Ibid., p. 366.

131 P. Smithson, "The Rocket," p. 323.

132 A. and P. Smithson, *Changing the Art of Inhabitation*, pp. 43–44. Text written "December 1985 and April/May 1986" and labeled: "'Mies' Barcelona Pavilion: Myth and Reality', paper given at Aachen, 6, 7 June 1986. Unpublished."

Fig. 5 Peter Smithson, "The Masque and the Exhibition: Stages toward the Real," *ILA&UD: Language of Architecture* (1981); Alison and Peter Smithson, *The Shift*, London: Academy Editions, 1982

Chapter 5

Banham's Mieses

Reyner Banham was both the most right and the most wrong theorist of New Brutalism, from his overt enthusiasm in "The New Brutalism" (1955) to his peculiar sublimation of New Brutalist issues in *A Concrete Atlantis* (1986). Banham was right in 1955 that "image [. . .] is one of the most intractable and the most useful terms in contemporary aesthetics" and that the "concept of *Image* is common to all aspects of The New Brutalism in England." He would be proven right—more than he could have imagined then, or anticipated—that "the manner in which it works out in architectural practice has some surprising twists to it."[1] Banham's initial support for New Brutalism, his gradual cooling, and his eventual dismissal position him as the Smithsons' collaborator and their antagonist. In both roles, and with many (occasionally heated) disagreements between them along the way, most notably about the meaning of Pop, the role of technology, and the potential of modernism, Banham's changing polemics, arguments, and claims clarify the Smithsons' evolving ideas, attitudes, and practice. His 1955 theory, inspired by the discussions and projects of the Independent Group (1952–55), that a New Brutalist "building should be an immediately graspable visual entity, and that the form grasped by the eye should be confirmed by experience of the building in use,"[2] is the best place to start to assemble a historical understanding of New Brutalism's legacy, both at its beginning and as it developed in the Smithsons' persistent reformulations in the following decades. It is even the best place to begin to understand the importance of Mies van der Rohe for the Smithsons, despite the fact that Banham consistently dissociated Mies from any potential he imagined for the future of modern architecture as "*une architecture autre*."[3]

But Banham's theorization of New Brutalism was hardly consistent. In 1955 he proposed "Memorability as an Image" as its first principle and topology as its organizational "discipline."[4] In 1956, in his review of the group show *This Is Tomorrow*, he proposed the provocative concept of "concrete images" as a new direction for modern architecture.[5] Less than one year later, in a letter to *Architectural Design* in which he defended the work of the Smithsons and most of his earlier ideas about New Brutalism, he avoided using the word "image."[6] By 1966, at the end of his book *The New Brutalism: Ethic or Aesthetic?*, he explicitly rejected his 1955 "attempt to father some of my own pet notions on the movement."[7] But he did attempt to recuperate his 1955 call for *une architecture autre*, this time on very different terms. Inspired by examples ranging from the "fundamentally other" work of Buckminster Fuller to the "drive-in cinema, where the structure above ground level encloses no space, and the cultural symbols are transient light-play,"[8] Banham's revised version of *une architecture autre* somewhat puzzlingly avoided his earlier concepts of memorability as image and topology. Instead, he made a radical swerve. He argued for the wholesale rejection of the "structure/space synthesis [. . .] that has been current since the Renaissance [. . .] because it has nothing to do with the architect's function in relation to society," and advocated what he called a "genuinely functional approach" for achieving "ever-higher environmental performance"[9] with "no cultural preconceptions and the full battery of modern mechanical services."[10] Banham's chapter titled "A Note on 'une architecture autre'" ends with an unequivocal dismissal: "In the last resort they

[Brutalists] are dedicated to the traditions of architecture as the world has come to know them: their aim is not 'une architecture autre' but, as ever, 'vers une architecture'."[11] New Brutalism had proceeded on the wrong path and failed to achieve its radical potential.

It could also be said that Banham failed to achieve the potential of his own ideas. His theorization of image remained undeveloped beyond the compelling idea of "concrete images" in 1956 or the rudimentary, if incisive, formulation the previous year in "The New Brutalism" in which he conflated "image" and "concept": "All great architecture has been 'conceptual,' has been image-making."[12] Banham's 1966 book attempted to account for the surprising twists that had actually occurred in the prior decade, which were not the topological ones he imagined in 1955. But there is an alternative to Banham's story that could recuperate and advance his "pet notions" by demonstrating that the most developed and compelling, if somewhat surreptitious, variations of *une architecture autre* were wrapped up in the twists and turns of the afterlife of New Brutalism: in the varieties of the Smithsons' Mies-image and the imaging practices they developed to pursue *un autre* Mies. Banham's writings aimed to foreclose even the possibility of that alternative, as did the two-page image array in his 1955 essay of New Brutalist sources in and beyond architecture. The array had no images of work by Mies. Even the Miesian Hunstanton School appeared only at the bottom of the array as a small photograph (smaller than any of the composite images of four other Smithsons projects). The inclusion and content of the array thus affirmed both his theorization of images and his attempt in the essay's only two mentions of Mies to dissociate his work from New Brutalism.[13] Both cast his architecture in strictly formal terms and overlook the materialist, technical, and imagistic aspects with which Banham defined New Brutalism. The first reference is a curt estimation of Mies's significance for the Smithsons as merely opportunistic: Mies's Chicago work, he claimed, was nothing more than "one of the few recent examples of conceptual, form-giving design to which a young architect could turn at the time of its [Hunstanton's] conception."[14] The second occurs near the end of the essay after Banham had made his case for New Brutalism as an architecture that aims "to create a coherent visual image by non-formal means [...] and fully validating the presence of human beings as part of the total image."[15] He expanded on the earlier reference to Mies and insisted that "Miesian or Wittkowerian geometry was only an *ad hoc* device for the realization of 'Images'" and, most important, suggested that "formality was discarded" after the Smithsons, working with the artists Eduardo Paolozzi and Nigel Henderson, developed an alternative approach in *Parallel of Life and Art* (1953), their all-over installation of enlarged photographic and photographed images from diverse sources (artworks, X-rays, newspapers, magazines, and science) at the Institute for Contemporary Arts. That use of images, he wrote, converted the "camera-eyed western" imaginary—"the common visual currency of our time"—into "a deliberate flouting of the traditional concept of beauty" and "enabled Brutalists to define their relationship to the visual world in terms of something other than geometry."[16] For Banham, that aesthetic realization was the first crucial twist in the development of New Brutalism. But it was one that seemed to be lost on many observers.

As Banham would remind the readers of his 1957 letter to *Architectural Design*, his 1955 essay ended with a "second version of the deducible principles (not dogmas) of Brutalism [that] in no way excludes Hunstanton School, but simply recognizes the fact—made clear by A. and P. S. on p. 113 of April *A.D.*—that the Brutalists were in search of a wider frame of reference for their design activities. They rejected routine-Palladianism, not Hunstanton."[17] Apparently, many readers had only got as far in the essay as the first version of New Brutalist principles: "formal legibility of plan," "clear exhibition of structure," and "valuation of materials for their inherent qualities 'as found.'"[18] Banham's letter was a reminder that he bracketed Hunstanton within the first, "formal" stage of New Brutalism, and his sly twist was to argue in the conclusion to the essay (with the crucial ideas in a footnote) that geometry is only a "special case" of the "more generalized concept" of topology.[19] That theoretical "gearshift from formality to memorability, from geometry to topology" (Banham does not mention the shift from beauty to image),[20] was best exemplified in the Smithsons' entry in the Sheffield University competition (1953), which created multiple views by moving users along a system of ramps and by wrapping the new building around and among those already existing on the site. As he explains in the final caption in the array, Sheffield was the "furthest development of New Brutalist architecture toward the completely a-formal, anti-geometric, yet systematic compositional methods exemplified in painting by Pollock and Burri."[21] Most important, Banham's 1955 theorization of a newer New Brutalism based in topology and image was a way to write Mies out of the story, but to keep Hunstanton in. "The definition of a New Brutalist building derived from Hunstanton [...] must be modified so as to exclude formality as a basic quality if it is to cover future developments and should more properly read: 1, Memorability as an Image; 2, Clear Exhibition of Structure; and 3, Valuation of Materials 'as found.'"[22] Banham was constructing an argument to allow certain qualities of Hunstanton to remain valued as prototypically New Brutalist, but to suppress any association with Mies.

But it would be more plausible, accurate, and intriguing to infer that the Smithsons had not rejected Mies. Instead, their interest in his architecture had shifted away from its formal aspects yet remained committed to others, which they discovered in Hunstanton only as it was being built—in the "layering of reflections in the glazed stage"—and which they developed persistently afterwards. That less exclusive understanding of the Smithsons' development after designing Hunstanton was not apparent initially to Banham, the Smithsons, or other observers. At the end of a brief essay introducing a thirteen-page presentation of the finished building in the September 1954 issue of *Architectural Review*, Philip Johnson wrote: "I like to think of them as youngsters who utilize what they can of their elders' philosophies [...] and who then proceed, having, one hopes, digested their early lessons, to go on from there."[23] Like Banham, Johnson was searching for a way to reconcile the Smithsons' success in designing "a plan that is not only radical but good Mies van der Rohe" with their turn "against such formalistic and 'composed' designs toward an Adolf Loos type of Anti-Design which they call New Brutalism."[24] An uncredited editor's note, most likely written by Banham, was appended to Johnson's remark with an asterisk: "The architects themselves would certainly disagree with Mr. Johnson's separation of Hunstanton from the New Brutalist canon, even though that term had not been coined when the school was designed."[25] That note, and the "design principles" included on the following two pages, also likely written by Banham, anticipate some of the arguments he would devise one year later in "The New Brutalism" to simultaneously solve the problem of Hunstanton's New Brutalist *bona fides* and to exclude Mies. The design principles attempted to situate Hunstanton within the historical tendencies of British architecture (such as the "radicalism" of Hardwick Hall in Derbyshire (1590–97) and All Saints Margaret Street in London (1850–59), or the qualities of surface achieved with brick by "Queen Anne builders" and with stone by "Regency engineers"), but in a way that "owes nothing to precedent, and everything to the inner mechanisms of the Modern Movement."[26] Paradoxically, Hunstanton exemplifies "a peculiar ruthlessness—overriding gentlemen's agreements and routine solutions—which pervades the whole design from original conception to finished details," but also is a "traditional building, free from the sentimentalism of Frank Lloyd Wright or the formalism of Mies van der Rohe. This might seem a hard saying since Mies is the obvious comparison."[27] The explanation of design principles was an adaptation of the Smithsons' own characterization of Hunstanton. In one of the first articles to feature photographs of the still unfinished building, a 1953 interview with the Smithsons and Ronald Jenkins, the building's structural engineer, in the *Architects' Journal*, the Smithsons explained that they wanted "to use steel as an architectural material, but to avoid the formalism of Mies van der Rohe."[28] They claimed, "we are using steel in the same way mediaeval builders used wood" (in pegged post and beam construction) and insisted at the end of the interview, "ours is a 'traditional' method of building."[29] That interview was published in September, as was an article in *Architectural Design*,[30] the same month *Parallel of Life and Art* went on view at the ICA. Both articles include photographs, some taken as early as June, showing the glazing and bricks being installed in the steel structure.[31] Both focus on practical issues of cost and building systems, as did the very first publication on the building, in the April 1953 issue of *The National Builder*, which focused solely on the innovative uses of welding in the fabrication and plastic theory in the design of the steel structure.[32] In that context, it is not surprising that the conclusion of the explanation of the building's "design principles" in *Architectural Review* the following year was an endorsement of Hunstanton for "performing structurally, functionally and decoratively as [. . .] an integrated architecture." Here, "literally every structural and functional element is visible, and, since there is nothing else to see, they are the totality of the architectural elements. This imposes an existential responsibility upon the architect for every brick laid, every joint welded, every panel offered up" and requires:

> a new aesthetic of materials, which must be valued for the surfaces they have on delivery to the site [. . .] a valuation like that of the Dadaists, who accepted their materials "as found", a valuation built into the Modern Movement by Moholy-Nagy at the Bauhaus. [. . .] In this sense, this is probably the first truly modern building in England, fully accepting

> the moral load which the Modern Movement lays upon the architect's shoulders.[33]

What *is* surprising, however, is how similar that assessment is to the one Banham would offer a decade later in a very different context. At the end of his 1966 book, after declaring New Brutalism "a disappointment in the end" and dismissing his "pet notions," Banham offered a limited endorsement of its original virtues: "The relationships of the parts and materials of a building are a working morality—this, for me, is the continuing validity of the New Brutalism."[34] It is striking that Banham's final "historical" assessment of New Brutalism regressed to a formulation devised before he offered his theorization of images, as if the final word on New Brutalism should embrace only its first phase and could ignore virtually all of the "surprising twists" that had occurred afterwards. Thus Mies remained Banham's problem, and Banham's problem was taken on by the Smithsons in their pursuit of the Mies-image.

In all his writings, Banham would cast Mies as a great architect but "a Master of the past."[35] Mies operated for Banham as an emblem of the old modern, not the new *autre*, or even the New Brutal, and the more the Smithsons reengaged Mies—beginning in the late 1950s and intensifying in the 1960s—the more Banham distanced himself from their work. That divergence turned on two different attitudes toward Mies as well as toward architectural history (both distant and recent) and toward "Pop" as the legacy of the Independent Group. But even in the early years of New Brutalism, the tensions and contradictions between refusing Mies and explaining Hunstanton as the predecessor of the definitive New Brutalist projects that followed raised complex issues of influence and history. Those were precisely the problems Banham posed at the beginning of "The New Brutalism." The synopsis of the essay in the table of contents begins with the assertion that "the New Brutalism needs to be seen in a double historical context—that of post-war architectural thought, and that of post-war historical writings on architecture,"[36] and the essay itself begins with the accusation that the contemporary situation in Britain had been "distorted" by "the influence of contemporary historians on the history of contemporary architecture."[37] "The New Art History" had "created the idea of a Modern Movement" and had introduced a new self-awareness—both nuanced insights and tired myths—into the British scene. Thus any discussion of "our first native art-movement since the new Art-History arrived here" had to be "seen against the background of the recent history of history, and, in particular, the growing sense of the inner history of the Modern Movement itself."[38] Banham, who was then pursuing his doctorate under Nikolaus Pevsner at the Courtauld Institute, was projecting his own ambivalence—about scholarship, Englishness, and modernism—onto the situation. The Courtauld, along with the Warburg Institute, had been established in London in 1932 and 1933, respectively, and the faculties of both were dominated by European scholars who had fled the Nazi regime before the war. Banham's arguments and evaluations were fueled by sophistication and suspicion about that intellectual legacy and its contemporary potential, and were launched in opposition to what he saw as its degraded but pervasive reception among British professionals: the "substandard practices of routine-functionalists" who presumed that modernism meant that "if structure and function are served the result must be architecture."[39] Banham's aim was to both challenge the narratives of authorities like Pevsner (as he did in his dissertation) and call out the reductive reception of historical scholarship, believing that both the narratives and their reception encumbered any new movement's capacity to be as radical as earlier modernists.

Banham's two mentions of Mies in his 1955 essay aim to do much more than dismiss his influence; they reduce his architecture to a version of formalism, they categorically exclude Mies from the theories he launched in the latter part of his essay, and they implicate him in the problems of history-writing and its influence that he was attempting to work himself out of. Yet Banham got the salient significance of New Brutalism right in 1955 in *Architectural Review*, even if he never did quite get the story straight. But how could he? In 1955 there really was no story yet to tell. There were only pronouncements, affiliations, a lot of attitude, and a few Smithsons' projects that seemed more divergent than similar. But Banham was not one for telling it straight anyway, especially if that got in the way of getting it right. His tendency was to mix it up in the moment, to take a position with polemical purpose, and to attempt to impact a field still in formation. "The New Brutalism" was his attempt to claim the narrative and define the principles and potential of the movement. His provocative question about "the influence of contemporary architectural historians on the history of contemporary architecture" set up a fervent attempt to assert some of his own. But a decade later, he made clear that he felt his 1955 essay had failed to influence the contemporary field. Still hoping to get it right, but this time far from getting the story straight, he revised his earlier ideas about New Brutalism and what he saw as the best prospects for modern architecture.

In both 1955 and 1966 Banham's motives worked at cross-purposes to the Smithsons', although they all were in their own ways revisionists. The Smithsons were trying to get it right too, by coalescing an unstable field and inserting their own ideas into the present, including their ideas about the past. The Smithsons were historians also, but not scholars.[40] In 1955 they had begun work on their book *The Heroic Period of Modern Architecture* (1965), an atlas of iconic images from a time of "absolute conviction" (1910–37). They always insisted on integrating and synthesizing prior ideas, including their own, into the present as a way to move into the future. Banham, on the other hand, was eager to discard prior ideas and projects as last year's models, and to focus on history as a resource for identifying a desired "immediate future," as he famously explained in a 1961 lecture to the RIBA.[41] As it worked out, Banham's 1955 desires for the future of New Brutalism did not materialize. He may not have had the influence he hoped for, or perhaps he had an influence that he did not hope for, but in neither case does it mean he was not right the first time. Today it seems clear that, on this topic at least, Banham was better at contemporary history (in 1955) than recent history (in 1966). "The New Brutalism" was one of those rare prognostications that was as audacious as it was prescient. Banham's insights into postwar, mid-century design culture were not only astute and discerning at the time, but also identified trends and offered explanations that remained, and remain today, vital as contemporary possibilities. Even if writing contemporary histories like Banham's is hardly plausible in today's world of the ever-present, a brief time-out to get his ideas straight might show that New Brutalism is still (or is once again) a source for the kind of twisted image that he suspected might hold promise for modern architecture. Today, it may be possible to make sense of how what he thought then might matter now in new ways.

Banham's theorization of *une architecture autre* as topological "image-making"[42] is increasingly pertinent in today's world of dense, instantaneous, superficial actualities, which are as prevalent, and as necessary to grapple with, in architecture's production, reception, and dissemination as in any other field. Whether encountered online, in exhibitions, or in cities, examples that explore the architectural potential of that reality are wildly diverse in quality and kind. The surfaces and images of those architectures are the products of, and are calibrated to thrive in, the altered modes of media and exchange that became pervasive after World War Two and have become immersive today. Banham's claim in 1955 that a New Brutalist "building should be an immediately apprehensible visual entity, and that the form grasped by the eye should be confirmed by experience of the building in use," attempted to reconcile an emerging image culture in which anything that circulates as "a coherent and apprehensible visual entity" counts as an actual artifact,[43] with the fact that those image-entities continue to make their appearances only by virtue of a brute hardware of materials, structures, and organizations. Attention to the effects of technological systems was an enduring theme for Banham, but even though his fascination with images quickly waned and the implications and potential of imaging are now quite unlike what they were in 1955, his ideas remain vital and apt. The image environment of product design, magazines, movies, and advertising that intrigued Banham, the Smithsons, and others in the Independent Group must have seemed just as perplexing and astounding to architects then as our computational, networked, and globalized systems of social networks and big data do to us now. The economic, social, and geopolitical shifts that occurred after World War Two were very different, but hardly more extreme than those that are underway in the early twenty-first century. Banham's attempt to navigate and make sense of that complex time was unapologetically speculative. His aspiration was not to resist the rapidly evolving technologies, economies, and cultures of imaging, but to write the contemporary history of what might be called theory and design in the first imaging age.

Banham's enthusiasm for New Brutalism gradually faded as he reconsidered his reasons and revised his estimate of "the immediate future." His commitment to image and topology would wane, and his writing would rarely be as unapologetically intellectualized as it was in "The New Brutalism." (In 1961 he would declare that "an up-to-date book on architectural theory [...] is un-writable" because architectural theory "has now become what some linguistic philosophers would call a vacuous category."[44]) His continued writing, and rewriting, of contemporary history led him to other topics, concepts, and conclusions, and the differences between his 1955 article and 1966 book must be understood in the context of evolving contemporaneities and new attempts at historical revision. Both were the unstated subtexts of his second, more assiduous and critical attempt to get New Brutalism right in his 1966 book, which recounts the story of how it was initially developed and promoted in the early 1950s by the Smithsons and a few others in Britain, and which assembles an international lineage of its offspring and dispersion over the next decade. Banham diligently reassembles the facts, texts, and projects of the beginnings of New Brutalism in a way that was not possible ten years earlier, but he made a brilliant muddle of how it had worked out in practice in England and beyond, as well as of the radical theoretical speculations on New Brutalism that he had got so brilliantly right in the midst of the real muddle of its beginnings.

Banham's 1966 account takes his thoughts on *une architecture autre* in new directions and treats image and topology as if they were generic, benign architectural concepts rather than the fuzzy, subversive, and challenging ideas they had been in 1955. He excused himself in 1966 for getting his contemporary history wrong in 1955, and explicitly dismissed his earlier article as "not representative of the state of the [New] Brutalist movement at that important time in its evolution."[45] Preoccupied as he was with contemporary history, as the best way to anticipate the immediate future, and confident he had it right the second time, Banham was no longer interested in, or had forgotten, why his pet notions once had seemed so compelling and auspicious. In 1966 he was telling the end of a story that he believed had not fulfilled the promise of his earlier ideas, and he was willing to let them pass. He also was distancing himself from the Smithsons, who had developed other ideas of their own, and he was willing to let them pass too.

But for architects as historically savvy and intellectually contrarian in their approach and interests as the Smithsons, it is crucial to revisit the possible sources for their sensibility and attitudes—as well as Banham's—in order to make sense of New Brutalism and the still latent potential of its aspirations. Banham nearly got it right the first time, in real time, and those theories had, and still have, more currency than he acknowledged in 1966 or wanted others to remember. In fact, the theoretical framework he advanced in 1955 remained part of the discourse for several years, as evidenced in many journal articles and, perhaps most notably, in John Summerson's 1957 lecture to the RIBA, "A Case for a Theory of Modern Architecture," in which he makes light of "Mr. Banham [who] in a recent article has offered us the attractive red herring (I think it's a herring) of topology."[46] At the very least, his 1966 humility and circumspection about his 1955 ideas were only half-hearted: earlier in the book he confidently revived and revised some of those pet notions to make clear what he still thought New Brutalism could have been and what he still hoped modern architecture might become. Most important, Banham had already been putting distance between himself and the Smithsons in 1955: that was the actual reason why his pet notions were "not representative [...] at that important time." Then, as in 1966, he knew he was getting ahead of the Smithsons theoretically, and perhaps even historically. Banham wrote his history of New Brutalism in 1966 not because he had got it wrong in 1955 but because the Smithsons and others had not followed his lead.

Banham's two versions of New Brutalism's contemporary history in his 1955 article both got it right: the first, tamer version was indeed representative of the movement at that time, while the second version offers astute speculations that were representative of its *potential* at that time. The first situates New Brutalism in the context of recent debates among British architects about their relationship to the legacy of "the classic Modern Movement"[47] and builds on the Smithsons' public statements and two of their earliest projects, Hunstanton and the Soho House. Despite the difference between the steel, glass, and brick Miesian idiom of Hunstanton and the concrete and masonry "warehouse aesthetic" of the Soho House, Banham's earnestly modernist criteria that define those two projects—"formal legibility of plan," "clear exhibition of structure," and "valuation of materials for their inherent qualities 'as found'"—establish the more or less familiar characteristics—a caricature, really—of New Brutalism that were taken up by others and persisted, reductively, as "Brutalism."[48] Banham argued that the Hunstanton–Soho "first phase" of New Brutalism was too reactionary (a tough-minded intensification of "the basic moral imperatives of the Modern Movement") and too amenable to "crypto-academicism" (a new orthodoxy of formal logics and neo-Palladianism).[49] It was those weaknesses that led Banham to replace, later in the article, the first principle with a more radical and progressive one: "Memorability as an Image." By 1955, Banham's negative assessment of formality was shared by the Smithsons, whose interests and involvements (urbanism with CIAM and mass culture with the Independent Group) were evolving and broadening. But the latter part of "The New Brutalism" launches polemical and theoretical trajectories that are all Banham. He introduced and correlated the concepts of image and topology (as alternatives, in effect, to the current vogue of the Picturesque and proportional systems) as generative ideas for a newer New Brutalism that could engage a range of extra-architectural influences, collaborators, and audiences.

Banham was riding the wave of his leading role in the Independent Group as its third and most energetic "convener" from 1952 to 1954. The so-called "pet notions" in his 1955 article clearly draw on the varied interests in mass media, popular culture, new technologies, and product design that were shared by the intellectually adventurous young artists, critics, and architects in the Independent Group and were aligned with their interest in "anti-Academic aesthetics" and developments in the arts such as Jackson Pollock's painting, *art autre*, and musique concrète (all of which he also mentioned in his 1966 book). In attempting to explain the potential of this approach, Banham took a path the Smithsons had not yet taken—as they were focused then on urban issues and housing—and articulated, though not entirely consistently, definitively, or explicitly, a theory of the newer New Brutalism that is somewhat different from the definition he offered at the end of his essay. That theory can be pieced together from three evocative phrases that appear in various places in the essay: "memorability as an image," "obsessive emphasis on basic structure," and "abstemious under-designing of the details, and [. . .] ineloquence."[50]

Banham's clear intent in his 1966 account was to distance himself from the directions the Smithsons and others had taken. But to do so, he selectively revised, refuted, revived, and redefined his earlier ideas and assessments. He downwardly revised his estimation of the significance and influence of the Golden Lane and Sheffield projects, refuted the boldest aspects of his own theorization of a newer New Brutalism, and revived and redefined his idea of *une architecture autre*, making it even more radical and explicit. In 1966 Banham was no longer writing the contemporary history of New Brutalism because he no longer viewed it as timely. He thought only its history was left to write. New Brutalism was as much a past movement as Mies was a past master. Despite his distinct role in the emergence of New Brutalism, Mies's influence on the course of modern architecture in postwar Britain was hardly pervasive. The Chicago Mies would reverberate uncertainly in British modernism but regain acceptance in the late 1950s when he was awarded the RIBA Gold Medal (1959). That shift is evidenced in changes to the 1962 edition of J. M. Richards's popular Penguin paperback *Modern Architecture* (first edition 1940), which not only featured the Minerals and Metals Building on its cover for the first time, but replaced the plates, plans, and descriptions of Barcelona and Tugendhat that had appeared in earlier editions with Mies's Chicago projects. The revised text discussed the newer buildings as exemplars of his work and reiterated the caricature of Mies as simultaneously "rational and matter-of-fact" and a poet of building technology.[51] Richards described the buildings at IIT and the Lakeshore Drive towers as "masterpieces of precise engineering, devoid of ornament, or of qualities (such as those arising from the effects of the weather or from the varying textures of materials) that cannot be precisely controlled. They rely for their aesthetic effect on subtlety of proportion and mechanical precision of finish."[52] They are "precise, logical studies in pure geometry" that "transform the cold mechanical rhythms which arise from these methods into a quite magical feeling for the interplay of enclosed and semi-enclosed space," thereby "evoking the same sort of aesthetic satisfaction as a neatly balanced mathematical equation."[53]

Banham was intent on dismantling that conventional modernist wisdom. In the concluding chapter of *Theory and Design in the First Machine Age* (1960) he discussed the Barcelona Pavilion as the beginning of a "purely symbolic" aesthetic aligned with the International Style and a departure from the strident claims and polemical strictures that Mies voiced in the early 1920s.[54] For Banham, the Barcelona Pavilion exemplified the unfortunate swerve from functionalism and "technological culture" that was the fate of the architecture of the first machine age.[55] But his most provocative criticism of the time addressed Mies's Chicago work. In a 1962 article—the final entry in his six-part "On Trial" series in *Architectural Review*, which prosecuted his case against the current state of "the relationship between architecture and technology"[56]—Banham argued that Mies's genius indeed could be found in the details, but a "close student of Miesian detailing will soon be forced to the conclusion that a perfected system is not the goal. This may sound blasphemous, but it will stand examination."[57] Banham discerned a "peculiar authority" in Mies's Chicago work that derives not from a desire for control but rather from persistent technical ingenuity and a willingness to "define his goal in the light of what he has learned to do better since the last time he designed a comparable product."[58] It is as if Banham was suggesting that in Chicago, Mies recuperated some aspects of his Dada-affiliated ethos from the 1920s, as expressed in his famous statement: "We reject all aesthetic speculation, all doctrine, all formalism."[59] But in Chicago, Mies's anti-aesthetic was less Dada than ad hoc. It was manifest as pragmatic R&D prototyping, in the manner of a hot-rod tinkerer whose work is "built up from catalogued parts and adapters."[60] Banham's 1962 Mies was not a heroic genius, a stylist, or a mere formalist: he was the ingenious master not only of curtain walls but also of prosaic technologies like the suspended ceiling,[61] and was, in fact, a practical imperfectionist, a claim Banham made stridently and vividly: "The closer one stands to Mies's actual buildings, the less likely does a perfected system appear—the blobby slurps of black mastic down the side of the glazing bars to the front of the Campus Chapel at IIT make it clear that there are occasions when almost nothing is nothing like enough."[62]

In the same year, Banham's *Guide to Modern Architecture* offered a similar, if more tempered and adulatory, characterization of Mies. The book ends with a presentation of IIT's Crown Hall and the conclusion that the "sheer space" produced by the abstractness of the structure forces us to "fix on the details" that join steel to glass. Those joints "work" but are not "the final and perfect joint" and never will be. They are the "best-possible solutions for today," and "it is in details such as those at Crown Hall, perfected today but perfectible tomorrow, that one sees what kind of God is modern architecture's."[63] It would seem Banham intended "On Trial" as a double entendre: both an interrogation of the accused and an advocacy of design research as trial and error.

When the *Guide to Modern Architecture* was revised and republished in 1975 with an altered title that implicitly consigns its content to the past—*Age of the Masters*—Banham did not significantly alter his examples, arguments, or assessment of Mies. But he did amend them in ways that correlate with his revised historical narrative of modern architecture. He reintroduced the fraught affiliation of Mies and New Brutalism, and was more explicit than ever in his characterization of Mies as the master of "the True Style" that could "embrace both the classical and the romantic, the plain and the devious, the fancy and the naked. All these, in the service of function, are within the range of modern architectural possibilities. All you need is nerve, and those old Masters had it!"[64] To acclaim Mies as a "Master" meant that he was not, and never could have been, a vital source for the next generation. If in 1955 Banham diminished Mies, his reconsideration of Mies in the 1960s and 1970s was realigned with his ambivalent judgment that New Brutalism was truly ambitious, though not as forward-looking as it may have seemed, which was proven by its failure to develop its most radical potential. Only after New Brutalism was no longer an ongoing movement, and then again after Mies's death, did direct connections between Mies and New Brutalism return to Banham's accounts and explanations, but with a new twist. In 1975 his aim was not to dissociate Mies and New Brutalism, but to imply guilt by association. Banham came to explicitly acknowledge the significance of Mies's influence on the Smithsons, both in their choice to emulate Mies in 1950 and in their increasing engagement with his work beginning in the late 1950s. While there are no projects by the Smithsons in the 1962 book, the 1975 revision includes two. Each is paired with one of the Mies buildings that had appeared in the first version. The Economist complex (1959–64) is added to Banham's comparison of the Seagram Building (1958) and Gordon Bunshaft's Lever House (1950–52) in New York, while an image of Hunstanton is included with those of Crown Hall.[65]

Banham's 1975 revisions were entries in an ongoing discourse that saw Banham, the Smithsons, and Banham's student Charles Jencks engaged in a vibrant contestation of modernism's identity and legacy, its promise or its failure, in part through their divergent evaluations of Mies and explanation of his connections to New Brutalism. Banham amplified his criticism, first offered following the completion of the Smithsons' Economist complex in an article in the *New Statesman*, that their embrace of the formal, classicizing, and commercial aspects of Mies was the definitive end of New Brutalism. Following an accusation that Mies's Seagram Building had inspired and excused many American commercial buildings of much lower quality, Banham turned his sights on the Smithsons:

> If one seeks a true development of this concept of commercial public space it is most notably found in a work by two of Mies's more remote admirers. The crop-cornered towers that cluster around a raised pedestrian yard off St. James Street in London's clubland to form the premises of that grand old weekly paper *The Economist*, are the work of Alison and Peter Smithson. Their early reputation depended on a building that frankly imitated Mies—the school at Hunstanton —but their pursuit of their ever-admired master became less and less obvious, and at The Economist the tell-tale traces tend to lurk half-hidden, like the metal sections behind the stone facing of the columns. [...] To move forward from Mies, the Smithsons were prepared to take a long step backward, to return to the sources of the Classical tradition that was always the backbone of Mies's designing. They know and love the sacred sites of ancient Greece; they have views on how and why they were planned as they were. Any visitor who stands at the foot of the steps that rise from St. James Street to the piazza and compares the grouping of the buildings with what he can remember of the view up to the Acropolis of Athens through the Propylaea may decide that what he sees could be the subtlest and craftiest piece of learning from Antiquity this century has produced.[66]

Banham was aware that the Economist complex revealed Peter Smithson's long-standing interest, as a self-professed "buff" and "consumer," in the arrangement of ancient Greek buildings.[67] Yet it was after the completion of the Economist complex that the Smithsons began to write most explicitly and originally about the contemporary significance of Mies: first in Peter's 1966 contribution to an issue of *Bauen + Wohnen* celebrating Mies's eightieth birthday, in which he wrote that Mies represented "the re-direction of the main stream of architecture itself,"[68] and then in the 1967 seminar in Berlin, which would be published in July 1969 as a homage to Mies one month before he died, and revised once again for inclusion in *Without Rhetoric*

(1974).[69] The Mies that the Smithsons admired and emulated was "surprisingly tuned-in to our culture": an ingenious exemplar of "repetition as a quality in itself" and "ordered sameness" who understood how to assert fundamental architectural coherence and integrity in a mass-production society.[70] The Smithsons had adopted an attitude similar to Banham's in the "On Trial" critique, and began to understand Mies as continuously "working though available technologies" with the result that "a building of Mies can be placed with ease, certainly dated within three years by the dozens of signs to do with changing building technique."[71] They also seemed to have adopted certain of Banham's ideas from the fifth "On Trial" essay, titled "Towards a Pop Architecture," where he wrote: "It is up to architects to make what they can of conditions in which it is temporarily possible for them to mould the creation of a keen Pop taste [...] and to operate the amoral techniques of technology according to the morality of architecture."[72] For the Smithsons, Mies achieved this possibility in his use of standardized elements. They saw this in two aspects of his work, beginning as early as 1919 in the Friedrichstrasse office buildings—"an almost autonomous, repetitive, neutralizing skin" and "an open-space-structured building-recessive, calm, green, urban pattern"—and seemed to suggest, with comparisons to Karl Schinkel's Altes Museum in Berlin and the Stoa of Attalus in Athens, that Mies had found a way to replace the elements of the classical orders with "serially produced, identical metal objects."[73] They saw those components of Mies's architecture as just one aspect of the "prevalent technology" that he engaged and manipulated skillfully. When the Smithsons insisted, with an intent to shock, that "Mies is surprisingly tuned-in to our culture," they were not just talking about construction systems and industrial materials. They were also talking about art and design more generally: things like "a Braun toast-maker," and "Volkswagens," and modern paintings, and "show-business." They were slyly aligning Mies with Pop in a way that refuted both Banham and Jencks on that score. Their statement that "with Mies, repetition is life-including; his feel for it can make the multiplied thing magical in its very multiplication" puts a canny Pop twist, in the manner of Andy Warhol's Brillo Boxes or Jasper Johns's flags and targets, on his sensibility. Whether the medium was inexpensive "extrusions of aluminum and neoprene [...] at New Jersey," where "a high level of formal sophistication is achieved on the same budget as 'conventional speculative builders' projects," or the honorific "big-box" of "his Museum of the Twentieth Century in Berlin," the Smithsons' Mies operated iteratively and effectively through multiple technologies and pervasive media to offer "the new, softly smiling face of our discipline," as though the repetition of mass-produced building elements could be an architectural version of the flickering frames of a soft-focus face in a Hollywood close-up.[74]

Jencks was less sly than either Banham or the Smithsons, and agreed with neither. He saw Mies's work as the epitome of impoverished and repressive modern dogmas. Jencks's 1971 book *Modern Movements in Architecture* (which was based on his thesis, supervised by Banham at the Bartlett School of Architecture in London) developed the basic semiotic premise that all good architecture must generate multivalent readings, and he launched the key claims of his argument in its second chapter, "The Problem of Mies," which framed

Mies as a negative example of "univalent literalism" and "reductivism" who "demands an absolute commitment to the Platonic world-view in order to appreciate his buildings."[75] As Banham also would do a few years later, Jencks brought New Brutalism back into the mix, arguing that "critics and architects are prepared to inhabit this world as if it were complete: none more so than Peter and Alison Smithson."[76] Later in the book he returned to this accusation, and his exemplar is none other than the Hunstanton School: "Brutalism was never more than a dramatization of honest literalism," he wrote, and in his caption to a photograph of Hunstanton that recollects similar photographs of the Minerals and Metals Building at IIT, he added: "The formal ordering is academic, both Palladian and Miesian, but the underlying attitude is ascetic and literalist: bricks are bricks, steel is steel and never a metaphor they shall become. Except Brutalist."[77] Like Banham in 1966, Jencks was returning to New Brutalism's first phase. He was echoing Banham's 1955 characterization that "Hunstanton *appears* to be made of glass, brick, steel and concrete and is in fact made of glass, brick, steel and concrete. [. . .] One can see what Hunstanton is made of, and how it works, and there is not another thing to see except the play of spaces."[78]

But Banham not only endorsed the literalism of building materials and technologies in both 1955 and 1966: he aligned it with Pop and his augmented idea of *une architecture autre*, which added structure to his list of proscribed "traditional" space-making devices: "*une architecture autre* [. . .] ought to abandon the idea that the prime function of the architect is to employ structure to make spaces."[79] His cursorily referenced example of "a drive-in cinema, where the structure above ground level encloses no space, and the cultural symbols are transient light play,"[80] suggests a range of possible Pop trajectories in which image and topology return in different guises, from the Eameses' installation of their multiscreen film *Glimpses of the USA* in a Fuller dome at the 1959 American National Exhibition in Moscow, to Cedric Price's Fun Palace (1961–74), to Robert Venturi's "Bill-Ding-Board" (1967), to John Hejduk's Wall House (1968).

In 1966 Banham seems to have realized it had been a mistake in 1955 to list "clear exhibition of structure" as one of his three New Brutalist principles, declaring that "since the Renaissance" structure was conceptually inextricable from geometry in architecture.[81] The problematic nature of this "traditional" association of geometry and structure may have first occurred to Banham less than a year after writing "The New Brutalism." His review of *This Is Tomorrow*, where he introduced the concept of concrete images, begins by identifying a disappointingly traditional collusion between structure and geometry in most of the twelve collaborative installations by groups of architects and artists: "Some concept of structure—geometry clothed in substance—proved to be the basic, or unifying postulate of most groups' offerings."[82] As a result, those installations did not fulfill the ambitions of the show "to smash all boundaries between the arts" and to "embrace all the available channels of human perception."[83] Most installations were disappointingly limited to a "technique of category-smashing" that had only two channels, amounting in most cases to the construction of what he called "structure-sculptures." That critique implicated *Patio and Pavilion*, the project produced by the Smithsons, Henderson, and Paolozzi. Banham took issue with the Smithsons' simple rectilinear shed and enclosure because they "showed the New Brutalists at their most submissive to traditional values" and were "a confirmation of accepted values and symbols."[84] In that respect, *Patio and Pavilion* was entirely unlike the project in the exhibition that Banham admired most, by Richard Hamilton, John McHale, and John Voelker, which comprised "optical illusions, ultra-violet light, CinemaScope, recorded sound, squashy floors, collage, science-fiction, van Gogh, topology, expanded metal, a juke box [. . .] and a general desire to break down all barriers, prise open all watertight conventions, and get ideas and sensory responses on the move."[85] The assemblage of patterned surfaces, printed and projected images, mass-produced objects, and sounds required the visitor to take "individual responsibility for his own atomized sensory awareness of images of only local and contemporary significance."[86]

Yet in the end, Banham identified a crucial similarity between the two projects that superseded their divergent attitudes toward structure. The Hamilton-McHale-Voelker project, "curiously, seemed to have more in common with the New Brutalists than any other, and the clue to this kinship would appear to lie in the fact that neither relied on abstract concepts, but on concrete images—images that can carry the mass of tradition and association, or the energy of novelty and technology, but resist classification by the geometrical disciplines."[87] That last phrase, "resist classification by the geometrical disciplines," is the crux. In 1956 Banham understood *Patio and Pavilion* as an environment of concrete images *despite* its conventionality and its overt use of basic geometry and structure. Its evasion of "geometrical discipline" was partial and sublimated, while the unconventional design of Hamilton-McHale-Voelker fully engaged mass media and resisted the very possibility of being classified as geometric. In 1956 Banham had a more expansive idea of New Brutalism that included a broader range of structural attitudes than he would accept ten years later. When he discussed *This Is Tomorrow* in his book, he did not mention, or recollect, his earlier claim of a "kinship" between the two projects based on their production of "concrete images." Instead, he characterized them as irreconcilably opposed. In 1966 he saw only the Hamilton-McHale-Voelker project as contemporary and praised it as "the first Pop-Art manifestation to be seen in any art gallery anywhere in the world."[88] Ten years later, in his 1976 "Rally" lecture celebrating the twentieth anniversary of *This Is Tomorrow*, Banham would amend that historical claim, adding the Smithsons' House of the Future to that lineage. It had been displayed in the London Ideal Home Exhibition a few months before *Patio and Pavilion*, and, he claimed, "its importance, irrespective of the architectural quality, is that it may have a stronger claim than anything at *This Is Tomorrow* to have been the first true product of all the pop art studies that have been going on for so long."[89] Yet Banham offered that high praise precisely to set up an attack on the Smithsons for turning away from Pop styling in *Patio and Pavilion* and after: "Fine art and traditional art or traditional modern architecture was the route the Smithsons were to prefer to pursue." That acknowledgment of the historical significance of House of the Future went beyond the positive assessment in his 1966 book—"a serious attempt at 'Pop

Architecture' comparable to the 'Pop Art' which has subsequently appeared in Britain and America"—and Banham's revisionist hyperbole was calculated to make the sting of his negative assessment of *Patio and Pavilion* that much more painful. Looking back, in both 1976 and 1966, Banham saw *Patio and Pavilion* as "an appeal to fundamentals in architecture [and] an appeal to tradition and the past." It was the first indication that the Smithsons had "abandoned their extreme anti-traditionalist position of 1953" (in *Parallel of Life and Art* and in the Sheffield competition) and "were withdrawing imperceptibly from their close approach to an Other Architecture."[90] In 1966 Banham had concluded that the simple structure and geometry of *Patio and Pavilion* were no more than a return to the first phase of New Brutalism and were the antithesis of the radical qualities that he had found contemporary and compelling in 1956. Most important, he now saw *Patio and Pavilion* as inseparable from the obsolete logic of architectural structure and incompatible with his updated Pop version of *une architecture autre*.

Thus Banham failed to see, or looked past, how *Patio and Pavilion* could be understood to exemplify the devices and effects of his drive-in cinema. The imaging that Banham had commended in 1956 was not simply an effect of the pavilion and other artifacts in the space. A crucial aspect of the project was how the environment was reflected and multiplied by the aluminum-faced plywood surface of the patio enclosure. This was the most active feature of the design, producing a complex extension of the surfaces of the pavilion and the contents of the patio as experienced by the circulating visitors. The geometry and structure of the pavilion were indeed extremely basic, but in that way they actually were more like the structure and space of the drive-in than were the multimedia, fun-house tactics of the Hamilton-McHale-Voelker project. They also were remarkably similar to Banham's characterization of the "sheer space" of Crown Hall, in which "order is made manifest only by the structure."[91] But unlike Mies, in *Patio and Pavilion* one is not left with "nothing else to see" except "the details."[92] The reflective enclosing surface of the enclosure (which Banham did not mention in 1956 and which in 1966 he saw simply as a use of "non-traditional materials"[93]) activated the space and its contents (which were installed by Henderson and Paolozzi as the project's final elements without the involvement of the Smithsons) in a way that was distinctly aligned with the drive-in environment's screening of cultural images. It also produced virtually the same effects as the staging of the image environment of *Parallel of Life and Art*, although in 1966 Banham described only the qualities of the enlarged photographs, not their installation in a traditional room.[94]

The Smithsons certainly saw it that way in retrospect. When *Patio and Pavilion* was reconstructed in the late 1980s, they emphasized precisely those aspects of the project in their lectures and in their decision to take photographs that restaged the views they and Henderson had shot in 1956.[95] Most interesting is that, looking back, especially after the reconstructions of *Patio and Pavilion* (1987) and the Barcelona Pavilion (1983–86), they saw distinct affiliations between the spatial and imaging effects of *Patio and Pavilion* and those of Mies's buildings. The Smithsons' attitudes had come full circle, from taking Mies's Chicago idiom as the inspiration in 1950 for the first New Brutalist project to their reaffirmation of his influence in their lectures and essays from the late 1960s into the 1990s. What the Smithsons saw in the reconstructed Barcelona Pavilion was conceptually similar to Banham's 1966 proscription against structure as a space-making device. There is a powerful connection between the ordinary elements and environment of *Patio and Pavilion* and Mies's polished onyx surfaces, as well as, and even more intriguingly, his famous chrome-plated cruciform columns, all of which seem to offer a literalization of Banham's call for a new dissociation between structure and space.

Banham did not have to see *Patio and Pavilion* reductively in terms of his hyperbolic rejection of structure: he could simply have reiterated his judgment that after the Hunstanton–Soho phase of New Brutalism, architects needed to reject the criterion of an integrated "relationship between structure, form and function [as] the basic commonplace of all good building."[96] He could have refined and amplified his earlier appeal for architects to seek more radical attitudes toward the relationships between structure and images. In fact, he could have found numerous possibilities to support a more capacious position in none other than Richard Hamilton's early work, such as his drawing *Structure* (1950), his series of *Trainsition* paintings (1954), and his *Growth and Form* exhibition (1951). Hamilton continued to pursue those ideas productively even into the 1970s and 1980s, for example in the peculiar spatial effects produced by his diverse models, drawings, installations, paintings, and prints based on a postcard image of the oddly banal lobby of the Hotel Europa in Berlin. Banham had it right in 1956 when he saw *Patio and Pavilion* and the Hamilton-McHale-Voelker installations not as opposed, but as occupying different positions on a New Brutalist spectrum: together, those projects demonstrate a range of possible convergences between basic structure and *une architecture autre*, as well as with the qualities of Mies that the Smithsons identified in their 1967 Berlin seminar: "an almost autonomous repetitive neutralizing skin" and "an open-space-structured building—recessive, calm, green, urban pattern" that "charge[s] the space around it with connective possibilities" that "up to now our sensibilities have not recognized as architecture at all, let alone seen clearly enough to isolate its characteristics."[97]

Patio and Pavilion, like the Hunstanton School, the competition entry for Sheffield University, and *Parallel of Life and Art*, is an insistently rational yet idiosyncratic and contingent architecture that produces intensely elusive and uncanny images. Its New Brutalist insistence on being both contemporary and rudimentary tempts us to consider the ways in which the aspiration of *Patio and Pavilion* to convey an image of dwelling in a culture emerging from a world war expands the robust versatility of basic modernist sources and principles, the openness and directness of basic structure and raw details, an awareness of history and its place in contemporary history, and, most important, the contemporary possibilities of imaging in architecture that Banham identified in 1955.

While Banham's attempt to track that lineage in his book is ultimately dismissive, one of his examples opens especially poignant affiliations. He mentions the building designs of the engineer and "great British anti-aesthete Sir Owen Williams" as the only "conceivable precedent" for the Smithsons' Sheffield project. Banham's attempt to affiliate New Brutalism with an engineer's advanced and innovative use of concrete is more wily and insightful—and implicitly aligned with his Pop understanding of Mies's details—than his extremely limited observation about the Sheffield project suggests: "The relationship of structure to glazing may have been remotely suggested by [...] the 'Dry' manufacturing block [1935–38] (but not the well-known 'Wet' factory alongside [1930–32]) of the Boots chemical plant [in Beeston, Nottinghamshire]."[98] Yet there are both trivial and powerful affiliations between Williams's work and New Brutalism that go beyond Banham's. Perhaps the closest relative to New Brutalism among Williams's projects is the Pioneer Health Centre in Peckham, south London (1935). Unlike either of the Boots factories (which the Smithsons denied knowledge of until Banham mentioned them[99]), the Pioneer Health Centre (which the Smithsons certainly knew) shares a scale and perhaps a structural and even a social and political ethic with the Hunstanton School. The rigorous application of concrete structure as the primary organizational device for its plan is conceptually analogous to the Smithsons' use of steel frames (and their application of "plastic theory" in collaboration with Ronald Jenkins) at Hunstanton. More significant, however, is how Williams's seemingly "formal" plan, like Hunstanton, activates an entirely unconventional disposition of program—such as medical and dental exam rooms, social lounges and cafeteria, exercise areas including a swimming pool, and a library, lecture room, and study areas—and subdivision of space in the service of a progressive social program that offered holistic preventive medicine in the form of annual memberships to the center for working-class families.[100]

Banham's presumption in his book that a turn toward 1960s Pop was in effect a turn away from New Brutalism was an unfortunate erasure of his earlier insights and led him to propose the diametrical contrast between the two *This Is Tomorrow* projects that he once had seen as "kin." Yet Pop, or at least a different understanding of the legacy of the Independent Group, was the wedge between Banham and the Smithsons. Even as early as 1961 Banham suggested that "if one interprets recent pronouncements correctly, they [the Smithsons] have pulled out of the pro-Pop camp."[101] But in his desire to be current, he both falsely settled and further confused the issue by overly simplifying the relationship between New Brutalism and the Independent Group, insisting that Pop was first and foremost a matter of technological styling and sophisticated consumer taste. A decade earlier, in his review of *This Is Tomorrow*, Banham was closer to the truth and his understanding of Pop architecture was closer to the Smithsons' than he allowed. In the half-century since Banham's book was published, numerous examples—in architecture, art, and art history—help us see Banham's oversight. But in the 1960s, artists outside Britain were exploring a parallel, or some might say aberrant, version of the Pop image that is close to New Brutalism. While it may be more visible and pertinent today than it was then, the varied work of Gerhard Richter emerged out of his own twisted relationship to Pop. It first coalesced in the 1963 exhibition he co-organized in Düsseldorf, *Living with Pop: A Demonstration for Capitalist Realism*, which polemically explored politically ambivalent attitudes toward the ongoing emergence and historical evolution of the replicable image in mass media that resonate with those of the Independent Group a decade earlier. More recently, Richter's work seems even closer to the Smithsons' sensibility. Examples range from his blurred photo paintings to his scrape paintings to his more recent *Strip* paintings, even to his glass sculptures. Richter's imagings are not representational but more like echoes or repetitions of immanent organization at multiple scales. Troels Wörsel has explained Richter's early work, which involved the painting of altered but entirely recognizable images of photographs, as "pictures of pictures, pictures of pictures associated with text, pictures of press photos, amateur photos, aerial photos—all of this material that advertises its 'imageness.'"[102] Richter's simultaneous evasion and iteration of representation brings painting closer to architecture's—and the Smithsons' —allusive manner of dealing with visual analogy and affiliation. Intriguingly, Richter once explained his own attitude toward painting in quasi-architectural terms: "The act of making should occur without inner involvement, like crushing stones or painting a building."[103]

Looking back from the 1980s, with eyes and attitudes shaped by several decades of changes in image culture and imaging practices, the Smithsons similarly described what they, Paolozzi, and Henderson were after in their approach to *Parallel of Life and Art*, where "planes of images were suspended from the ceiling or angled against the walls, as if floating in space," and that approach was expanded in other contemporaneous designs for interiors:

> Images happening beyond images: the introduction of a plane, the tempo of whose images were contrapuntal to that of its setting. These spatial manoeuvres interested us (and lay behind our attempt to get Norfolk Education Authority to purchase Paolozzi fabric curtains for the assembly hall at Hunstanton, 1953). We achieved the upturning and re-tuning of existing space to make it indisputably of its present in the room for Ronald Jenkins, Charlotte Street, 1952, with its Paolozzi wallpapered ceiling stitched up in black poster paint into a single composition by Eduardo himself (sighing heavily the while, interspersed by our remarks about Michelangelo's socks). Contrapuntal fragments of collage decorated the box for the Arup projector, c. 1952. And from that same period the tuning of space by the collage of Greek newspapers cut polygonally and stuck in the basement stairwell (after much repair of plaster) in Limestone Street, winter 1953?, a re-play of the temple podium wall, Delphi, as if first seen in the dark at the back of that grocer's shop but seen by us in summer sun, 1951.[104]

That statement, the entire text on the second spread in *The Shift*, which featured photographs of Jenkins Room and Hunstanton, invokes another which appears in *The Charged Void: Architecture* as a caption to a photograph by Peter of the interior of their house on Limerston Street showing the "decoration of the WC on the landing with wallpaper by Eduardo Paolozzi, in style later used by Nigel Henderson at Bethnal Green and Thorpe-le-Soken. A classic Brutalist image."[105] All of these imagings are both iterative (the arrays, patterns, and grids that distribute and connect their discrete components) and cohesive (the diagrams, uses, and assembly processes of the structure and spaces). This somewhat elusive and abstruse understanding of New Brutalist imaging can be augmented by Roland Barthes's concept of "the neutral," which he describes as a strategy of "outplaying the paradigm" or that "baffles the paradigm."[106] By paradigm, Barthes means a fundamental semiotic "structural" opposition, which normally operates by actualizing one term over the other to produce meaning. The neutral evades prioritizing either term. One of his myriad examples of outplaying a paradigm is the Taoist explanation of human minds as mirrors, but not in the sense of a mechanical and passive device that replicates, imitates, and responds in kind. Instead, this sort of cognitive reflection imparts an "action without appropriation" by "replying without retaining."[107] This kind of neutral mirroring is more like mimicry than *mimesis*. It intensifies image as reflection without recollection in the service of evasion or concealment. This kind of empty repetition produces an *imago* that refuses the concepts of character or identity and their implication of uniqueness, autonomy, or individuality. The concept resonates with the Smithsons' characterization of Mies's "almost autonomous repetitive neutralizing skin" or Peter's statement that Mies's architecture conveys "a kind of loving neutrality. This is for me the great lesson of his later years."[108] Similarly, Richter's images are all unique, but also all seemingly similar, or even after the same image, and thus after each other. Richter's images baffle and twist meaning. They are released from the oppositional logic of the negative, the paradigms of reproduction or copying. Richter's images echo, or repeat without retaining, their source images and their specific claims on reality.[109] He insists on this by using a variety of devices of reflection or doubling as a schema. Some are internal to the format of the painting; some occur as part of its production or process; some operate in relationship to a source image. Some operate quite literally as architecture: in his exhibition layouts, which he devises using scale models, or the design of his own house in Cologne (1994–96) with its overt and partial symmetries.[110] It is a strategy that simultaneously clarifies and blurs, distributes and materializes, specifies and multiplies the image. Perhaps Barthes, as usual, says it best: "One doesn't protest against an image, that is useless. What can be done is to drift by displacing the paradigm."[111]

For the Smithsons and Richter, the brutal, the neutral, or the neutral brutal, are wryly contrarian and anti-dogmatic, taking an interest in key issues and preoccupations of the moment but with a twist, with a difference and with deference. "Everything about the neutral is about sidestepping assertion," Barthes writes, but not by neutering, or being nondescript: rather, the neutral is capable of "intense, strong, unprecedented states."[112] That sounds and looks like the Smithsons' New Brutalist pursuit of the Mies-image.

Notes

1 Reyner Banham, "The New Brutalism," *Architectural Review*, 118, no. 708 (December 1955), p. 358.
2 Ibid.
3 Ibid., p. 361.
4 Ibid. Banham writes, "topology becomes the dominant and geometry the subordinate discipline."
5 Reyner Banham, "This Is Tomorrow," *Architectural Review*, 120, no. 716 (September 1956), p. 188.
6 Reyner Banham, "Letter to the Editor," *Architectural Design*, 27, no. 6 (June 1957), p. 185.
7 Reyner Banham, *The New Brutalism: Ethic or Aesthetic?*, New York: Reinhold, 1966, p. 134.
8 Ibid., pp. 69, 68.
9 Intimations of Banham's concern with structure that relate to both image and Fuller appear in his 1955 essay in his discussion of Louis Kahn's Yale Art Gallery (1947–53) as the "only other building" comparable to Hunstanton at that time. "Here is a building which is uncompromisingly frank about its materials, which is inconceivable apart from its boldly exhibited structural method which—being a concrete space-frame—is as revolutionary and unconventional as the use of the Plastic Theory in stressing Hunstanton's steel H-frames." But Banham's high praise for the building is limited to Kahn and Anne Tyng's use of tetrahedral trusses in the structural design, which was inspired by Fuller as well as Konrad Wachsmann's structures. The rest of the building "does not quite answer to the standard set by Hunstanton," with its "abstemious under-designing of the details, and [...] the ineloquence, but absolute consistency, of such components as the stairs and hand-rails. By comparison, Kahn's detailing is arty, and [...] jarringly out of key with the rough-shuttered concrete of the main structure. [...] Every Smithson design has been, obviously or subtly, a coherent and apprehensible visual entity, but this Louis Kahn's design narrowly fails to be." Banham, "The New Brutalism," p. 357. Thus Banham's discussion of problems of form and structure lead directly to his interest in image. His theorization of image in the essay follows immediately after the critique of Kahn.
10 Banham, *The New Brutalism*, pp. 68–69.
11 Ibid., p. 69.
12 Banham, "The New Brutalism," p. 358.
13 The degree to which Banham participated in the design of the array (printed on two sides of one sheet) is not known, but its careful composition and simple captions were an appropriate, effective way to convey both the potential of Banham's ideas and the affiliation between New Brutalism and the Independent Group. The array emulated a manner of aesthetic exploration and visual explanation that was increasingly common in "picture books," such as André Malraux's *The Voices of Silence* (1953), Marshall McLuhan's *The Mechanical Bride* (1951), E. A. Gutkind's *Our World from the Air* (1952), Rex Wailes's *Windmills in England* (1948), and Fritz Saxl and Rudolf Wittkower's *British Art and the Mediterranean* (1948), or in private research ranging from Aby Warburg's *Mnemosyne Atlas* (1924–29) to the scrap-books produced by Eduardo Paolozzi and Alison Smithson.
14 Banham, "The New Brutalism," p. 358.
15 Ibid., p. 361.
16 Reyner Banham, "Photography: Parallel of Life and Art," *Architectural Review*, 114, no. 682 (October 1953), pp. 260, 261; Banham, "The New Brutalism," p. 361.
17 Banham, "Letter to the Editor," p. 185. Banham was referring to the Smithsons' response published at the end of the "Thoughts in Progress" discussion, which has become perhaps the most quoted, and misunderstood, of their statements on New Brutalism.
18 Banham, "The New Brutalism," p. 357.
19 Ibid., p. 361.
20 Banham, "Letter to the Editor," p. 185.
21 Banham, "The New Brutalism," p. 360. In 1966 Banham wrote: "the term was coined by analogy with Tapié's concept of 'un art autre', and was intended to stand for something equally radical. That is, an architecture whose vehemence transcended the norms of architectural expression as violently as the paintings of Dubuffet transcended the norms of pictorial art; an architecture whose concepts of order were as far removed from those of 'architectural composition' as those of Pollock were removed from the routines of painterly composition (i.e. balance, congruence or contrast of forms within a dominant rectangular format—we argued much whether Pollock paid any regard to the edges of the canvas when dribbling his action paintings); an architecture as uninhibited in its response to the nature of materials 'as found', as were the composers of 'musique concrète' in their response to natural sounds 'as recorded'." Banham, *The New Brutalism*, p. 68.
22 Banham, "The New Brutalism," p. 361.
23 Philip Johnson, "Comment by Philip Johnson as an American Follower of Mies van der Rohe," *Architectural Review*, 116, no. 693 (September 1954), p. 152.
24 Ibid., pp. 148, 152.
25 [Reyner Banham], editorial note in Philip Johnson, "School at Hunstanton Norfolk," *Architectural Review*, 116, no. 693 (September 1954), p. 152. Banham includes Johnson's remark and the editor's note in his 1966 book but does not acknowledge authorship: Banham, *The New Brutalism*, p. 20.
26 [Reyner Banham], "Design Principles," in Philip Johnson, "School at Hunstanton Norfolk," *Architectural Review*, 116, no. 693 (September 1954), p. 152.
27 Ibid., p. 153.
28 "Secondary School at Hunstanton," interview with Alison and Peter Smithson and Ronald Jenkins, *Architects' Journal* (September 10, 1953), p. 323.
29 Ibid., pp. 325, 328.
30 Dargan Bullivant, "Hunstanton Secondary Modern School," *Architectural Design*, 23, no. 9 (September 1953), pp. 238–47.

31 The caption to a photograph of the south elevation with the glazing installed on the first page of the article in *Architectural Design* dates the photograph to "June 1953." Ibid.
32 "Welded Steel Fabrication Used at Hunstanton Secondary Modern School," *The National Builder* (April 1953), pp. 280–81. In both his 1955 essay and 1966 book, Banham incorrectly cites the 1954 publication in *Architectural Review* as the first publication of Hunstanton and suggests that much confusion about the meaning of New Brutalism was a result of the building being first published more than one year after the name "New Brutalism" first appeared in print and the Sheffield and Golden Lane projects were designed. He is correct insofar as the images in the September 1953 publications showed an unfinished (but nearly complete) building.
33 [Banham], "Design Principles," in Johnson, "School at Hunstanton Norfolk," p. 153.
34 Banham, *The New Brutalism*, pp. 134, 135.
35 Banham, "The New Brutalism," p. 361.
36 A different version of the concern with historicization appeared in Walter Segal's letter in *Architectural Design* (February 1954, p. 7). Responding to the publication of the Soho House two months earlier, Segal—a 1936 Swiss-German émigré—asserted his authority based on direct experiences and knowledge of German modernism. He identified a strain of strident belief in the Smithsons that was quite unlike the usual (and to his mind, admirable) English tendency to be "consumers rather than producers of 'isms.'" Segal's tone is sarcastic, suggesting that New Brutalism has "stern parentage" in Hannes Meyer, who "supplanted" Walter Gropius "in Dessau and paved the way for the 'Mies Influence,' after having driven out the Moholy Influence largely by the use of clean white paint and purges." Segal suggests that Meyer and others have "demonstrated [...] that the path of the true Western brutalist eventually led to Mies van der Rohe. The English brutalism, that little phoenix, is still obsessed by concrete, brick and wood. Will the glass stage follow?" It is not clear if Segal knew only of the Soho House and was unaware of Hunstanton, or if he was just feigning naivete.
37 Banham, "The New Brutalism," pp. 353, 355.
38 Ibid., pp. 355, 356.
39 Ibid., p. 358.
40 Peter published three articles in 1954 and 1955 on the past and present of European architecture: "Modern Architecture in Holland," *Architectural Design*, 24, no. 8 (August 1954), p. 225; "The Lesson of Le Havre: Perret," *Architectural Design*, 24, no. 9 (September 1954); and "Sculpture Pavilion, Arnhem, Holland, by Rietveld," *Architectural Design*, 25, no. 12 (December 1955).
41 Reyner Banham, "The History of the Immediate Future," *RIBA Journal*, 68 (May 1961), pp. 252–57.
42 Banham, "The New Brutalism," p. 358.
43 Ibid., p. 357.
44 Banham, "The History of the Immediate Future," p. 252.
45 Banham, *The New Brutalism*, p. 134.
46 John Summerson, "A Case for a Theory of Modern Architecture," *RIBA Journal*, 64 (May 1957), p. 310.
47 Banham, "The New Brutalism," p. 357.
48 Ibid.
49 Ibid., p. 361.
50 The phrases appear in Banham, "The New Brutalism," pp. 357, 361.
51 J. M. Richards, *An Introduction to Modern Architecture*, London: Penguin, 1962, p. 85.
52 Ibid., p. 110.
53 Ibid., pp. 87, 111, 158.
54 Reyner Banham, *Theory and Design in the First Machine Age*, Cambridge, MA: MIT Press, 1980, p. 321.
55 When the Barcelona Pavilion was reconstructed in the 1980s, the Smithsons began to see how it, along with the factory in Krefeld, was a hinge from Mies's earliest work to his American idiom.
56 Reyner Banham, "On Trial: What Architecture of Technology?," *Architectural Review*, 131, no. 780 (February 1962), p. 97. In his introduction to the series, Banham singles out Peter Smithson's statement, "We are really at the very beginning of the architecture of technology," in the first paragraph as "the kind of nonsense that could only be written by one architect for other architects [...] after some two hundred years of architecture variously influenced by the rise of industrial technology," but then adds a few paragraphs later: "Yet architectural nonsense has a habit of containing veins of perverse truth, and it may be that something is happening, something which architects, if nobody else, believe to be of consequence, in the no-man's land between technology and architecture."
57 Reyner Banham, "On Trial: Mies van der Rohe: Almost Nothing Is Too Much," *Architectural Review*, 132, no. 786 (August 1962), p. 126.
58 Ibid., pp. 128, 126.
59 Quoted in Banham, *Theory and Design in the First Machine Age*, p. 271. The original quotation appears in the first issue of *G* (July 1923), while the translation matches that in Philip Johnson's book.
60 Banham, "On Trial: Mies van der Rohe," p. 126. Banham's explanation that "the development from one *ad hoc* compromise solution to another without an ultimate goal, is something that has come in only with the rise of mass-production technology and research" was building on ideas in the previous essay in the series, "On Trial: The Spec-Builders: Towards a Pop Architecture," *Architectural Review*, 132, no. 787 (July 1962), pp. 43–46. The Pop essay begins: "The presence of an article on Pop-Art in a series devoted to architectural realizations of the potentials of technology, may appear to need some justification, but this is not so. Justification is needed only in the eyes of those who have tried to build up technology as a moral discipline, following a mistaken reading of the intentions of Mies van der Rohe, or an accurate reading of the mistaken conclusion of *Vers une Architecture*.

Technology is morally, socially and politically neutral, though its exploitation may require adjustments of social and political structures, and its consequences may call moral attitudes in question. And the Pop-Arts, being almost all of them inconceivable without a high level of mechanization and mass-production, are integral with technology, which does not discriminate between recording of John Glenn heard through the ionosphere, and recording of Cliff Richard heard through an echo-chamber." The essay concludes: "It is up to architects to make what they can of conditions in which it is temporarily possible for them to mould the creation of a keen Pop taste in architecture without coming under the discipline of those commercial rituals that normally operate the amoral techniques of technology according to the morality of architecture."

61 Banham offers the example of the suspended ceiling as the "Pop" alternative to architects' fascination with the curtain wall in the first article of the "On Trial" series. Suspended ceilings have "long since achieved a degree of industrialization and interchangeabilty of parts that is not remotely rivaled by exterior panelling systems. With a flexibility the more remarkable for going unremarked, they accommodate a greater variety of services than any other membrane [...] and in the process they dispense a level of power (expressed in wattage per square foot) that puts them in a class of mechanical services that are commonly supposed to be a Utopian or Dymaxion dream." Banham, "On Trial: What Architecture of Technology?", p. 99.

62 Banham, "On Trial: Mies van der Rohe," p. 126.

63 Reyner Banham, *Guide to Modern Architecture*, London: Architectural Press, 1962, p. 154.

64 Reyner Banham, *Age of the Masters: A Personal View of Modern Architecture*, New York: Harper & Row (Icon Editions), 1975, p. 168.

65 A third Mies building, the Berlin Neue Nationalgalerie, was added in the 1975 book, unpaired with a project by the Smithsons, as the conclusion of the book and replacing Crown Hall as the exemplar of mastery.

66 Banham, *Age of the Masters*, p. 115.

67 Peter Smithson, "Theories Concerning the Layout of Classical Greek Buildings," *Architectural Association Journal*, 74, no. 829 (February 1959), p. 194.

68 Peter Smithson, contribution to *Bauen + Wohnen*, 20: *Ludwig Mies van der Rohe 80 Jahre* (May 1966), p. 206.

69 "The Heroic Period of Modern Architecture" first appeared in the December 1965 issue of *Architectural Design*. The 1967 seminar was held in December at the Technische Universität Berlin and published as "Mies van der Rohe," also in *Architectural Design* (July 1969), as well as in a somewhat different form in *Without Rhetoric.*

70 Alison and Peter Smithson, "Mies van der Rohe," *Architectural Design*, 39, no. 7 (July 1969), pp. 365, 366.

71 Ibid., p. 366.

72 Banham, "On Trial: The Spec-Builders," p. 46.

73 A. and P. Smithson, "Mies van der Rohe," pp. 363, 366.

74 Ibid., pp. 365–66.

75 Charles Jencks, *Modern Movements in Architecture*, New York: Anchor Press, 1971, pp. 22, 95.

76 Ibid., p. 98.

77 Ibid., p. 251. Jencks sets up the Smithsons, as exemplified by the Miesian "univalence" of Hunstanton and the Economist complex, as the opposite of the Pop architecture that he celebrates, thus reinforcing the irreconcilability of the Smithsons' New Brutalism and their involvement in the Independent Group. Banham and Jencks advanced different arguments but agreed on this crucial point.

78 Banham, "The New Brutalism," p. 357.

79 Banham, *The New Brutalism*, p. 68.

80 Ibid.

81 Ibid.

82 Banham, "This Is Tomorrow," p. 187.

83 Ibid., p. 186.

84 Ibid., pp. 187–88.

85 Reyner Banham, "Not Quite Architecture: Not Quite Painting or Sculpture Either," *Architects' Journal*, 124 (August 16, 1956), p. 219.

86 Banham, "This Is Tomorrow," p. 188.

87 Ibid.

88 Banham, *The New Brutalism*, p. 64.

89 "The Rally—Part 1—Reyner Banham," lecture at Art Net, London, www.youtube.com/watch?v=ymYfbuqiVdc.

90 Ibid., pp. 65–66.

91 Banham, *Guide to Modern Architecture*, pp. 153–54.

92 [Banham], 'Design Principles," in "School at Hunstanton Norfolk," p. 153; Banham, *Guide to Modern Architecture*, p. 154.

93 Banham, *The New Brutalism*, p. 64.

94 Ibid., pp. 41, 61.

95 See Alison and Peter Smithson, "'Patio and Pavilion' Reconstructed," *AA Files*, 47 (Summer 2002), pp. 37–44.

96 Banham, "The New Brutalism," p. 358.

97 A. and P. Smithson, "Mies van der Rohe," p. 363.

98 Banham, *The New Brutalism*, p. 43.

99 Alison and Peter Smithson, "Banham's Bumper Book on Brutalism, Discussed by Alison and Peter Smithson," *Architects' Journal*, 144 (December 28, 1966), p. 1591.

100 See Innes Pearse and Lucy Crocker, *The Peckham Experiment: A Study in the Living Structure of Society*, London: George Allen & Unwin, 1944, and "The Pioneer Health Centre," *Architectural Review* 77, no. 462 (May 1935), pp. 203–16.

101 Reyner Banham, "Apropos the Smithsons," *New Statesman* (September 8, 1961), vp. 317.

102 Troels Wörsel, "Image, Window, Mirror," in *Gerhard Richter: Image after Image*, ed. Michael Holm et al., exh. cat., Humlebaek: Louisiana Museum of Art, 2005, p. 79.

103 The remark, made in 1971, is quoted in Coosje van Bruggen, "Gerhard Richter: Painting as a Moral Act," *Artforum*, 9 (May 1985), p. 86.

104 A. and P. Smithson, *The Shift*, p. 10.

105 Alison and Peter Smithson, *The Charged*

Void: Architecture, New York: Monacelli Press, 2001, p. 81. Ben Highmore's essay "Brutalist Wallpaper and the Independent Group," *Journal of Visual Culture*, 12, no. 2 (2013), pp. 205–21, begins with this photograph and offers a fascinating and precise "phenomenological" analysis of a visual sensibility shared by New Brutalism and the Independent Group.

106 Roland Barthes, *The Neutral: Lecture Course at the Collège de France (1977–1978)* [2002], trans. Rosalind Krauss and Denis Hollier, New York: Columbia University Press, 2005, p. 6.

107 Ibid., p. 182.

108 P. Smithson, contribution to *Bauen + Wohnen*, 20: *Ludwig Mies van der Rohe 80 Jahre*, p. 206.

109 Alex Bacon offers a compelling version of the visual neutrality of Richter's work. "Like the child that crawls into a discarded cardboard box to take imaginative respite in its neutrality from the intense pressures to conform to one cultural demand or another, the best abstract work makes no impositions on, or demands of, the viewer, but instead allows him or her to reflect back on the nature of these demands, and on his or her place within them. [...] In this way certain abstract work like Richter's is not merely compensatory, because it does not in fact offer to replenish something proposed to be lacking—phenomenological plenitude, for example—but rather suggests to hold, as best it can, all of these terms momentarily in abeyance—that is its radical neutrality." Alex Bacon, "Reflections on Gerhard Richter: *Painting 2012*," *Brooklyn Rail* (November 2012), www.brooklynrail.org/2012/11/art/reflections-on-gerhard-richter-painting-2012.

110 See Gerhard Richter, *Atlas*, New York: DAP, 2011, plates 481–82 (design drawings and model) and 620–28 (photographs).

111 Barthes, *The Neutral*, p. 73.

112 Ibid., pp. 44, 7.

Chapter 6

Imaging Theory

Images are intractable, elusive, indefatigable, and indefinable. They are vague, ephemeral, and shape-shifting. They operate with both stupidity and intelligence. They threaten stability and circulate surreptitiously. They are a source of consternation and controversy. Images are charged. They invite and activate forms of discourse that test the limits of presumed authority and expert knowledge.

In comparison to their equally ubiquitous and useful companions such as language, data, formulas, graphs, or things, images are perplexing as a subject of inquiry and undervalued as an object of exchange, even as they pervade our world not only as representations but, especially now in our increasingly mediated and virtual realities, as actual, informational, reproducible entities.

At the very least, images are now a special case of the regular stuff that constitutes our worlds. But even more important than images' new status as regular stuff are the myriad imaging practices and imaging technologies that produce, distribute, manipulate, record, and activate this stuff. Images may be perplexing, but imaging is both enervating and invigorating. Images are our common currency and imaging technologies are our standard operating systems. Images are instances of imaging.

Focusing on entities or operations as profuse, abstruse, incessant, and evasive as images or imaging presents many difficulties for any field of study. For architecture, the challenges of images and imaging as a subject of research or the media of architectural production are as daunting as they are obvious. Attempting to understand and pursue their appearances and potential puts a great deal of pressure on our usual ways of describing, defining, explaining, and identifying our architectural subjects and objects of study. Yet imaging is increasingly a productive way to understand the kinds of thinking architects do as well as the kinds of thinking that permeate our broader culture. Architects, like everyone else, have shifted from understanding and using visual material as discrete figurations or practical depictions to inhabiting and altering our worlds as matters and acts of effective and affective imaging. The astounding imaging capacities of digital technologies and the imaging practices they have generated are extreme alterations in human culture and experience that engage and immerse us, as casual and expert users, in imaging products and environments.

We live in an increasingly imaging-saturated, imaging-effected, and imaging-influenced world, which is altering our habits of communication and interpretation. Yet imaging is still implicitly or explicitly disparaged as deceitful, shallow, and vague. That skeptical attitude has ancient roots. It is not easy to shake. Its dogged persistence in today's world of incessant image transmission, exchange, and production is perplexing and incongruous, to say the least. It is also counterproductive. The pervasion of images and the ubiquity of imaging requires the adjustment of our fundamental assumptions about the intricacies of communication, the formation of identities, the operations of languages, the efficacy of politics, the production of knowledge, the negotiation of values, and the media of art. Can imaging ever triumph over iconoclastic sophistication or suspicion and achieve what Jacques Rancière has called its "destiny": the political, aesthetic, and communicative potential, or capacity, to circulate on a triple register "between the social production of resemblances, artistic operations of dissemblance, and the discursiveness of symptoms"?[1] Is it possible that our future will be, as Vilém Flusser has proposed, a "dialogic, telematic society of image producers and image collectors" where the "calculated and computed mosaics" that he calls "technical images" will "play the mediating role that texts once played" as "surfaces where information is produced and through which people can enter into dialog"?[2] How can we meet Barbara Stafford's challenge "to understand images and the intricate processes of imaging [as] a deeply connected body of non-verbal knowledge with specific cognitive and formal properties, rules and techniques, that need to be learned"?[3] How plausible is Mark Hansen's claim that neuroscience can inform "a comprehensive theory of the image [. . .] capable of addressing the *continuum* connecting mental and material images" and which characterizes "the image as a temporal process rather than a spatial/visual figure"?[4] Or, is it the fate of images and imaging to provoke uncertainty and evade understanding, to always be taken as ambiguous, paradoxical, and irrelevant in comparison to words and language, numbers and calculation, or things and materials?

Perhaps the frustrating slipperiness of imaging explains why the most ardent imaging advocates in fields as diverse as philosophy, art history, biology, and neuroscience have been and remain some of our most controversial, uncategorizable, and creative thinkers: Francis Galton, Henri Bergson, Walter Benjamin, Aby Warburg, Frances Yates, Ludwig Wittgenstein, Frederick Kiesler, Adolf Portmann, Gilles Deleuze, Georges Didi-Huberman, Antonio Damasio, as well as Stafford, Flusser, Hansen, and Rancière. Of course, it is much easier to malign the abstruseness of imaging than to develop precise arguments that explain its operations or endorse its virtues. Most imaging advocates pose confounding questions and raise perplexing issues that are fraught with misunderstandings and folded into layers of historical debate. The constant, rapid advances of technology, science, and globalization compound the problems and intensify the pace at which we must revise our thinking about imaging, our uses of imaging and images, and our capacity to manage and exchange images both as information and as currency. It is not easy to know where or when to begin a positive, productive discussion of imaging today. Imaging and its effects seem to emerge everywhere and pervade everything. Imaging is a complex subject of inquiry that is as quickly evolving as it is historically deep, technically challenging, and discursively sophisticated. The final decades of the twentieth century and the first decades of the twenty-first have witnessed a virtual explosion of image theories in art history and other fields, such as Stafford on the coevolution of the human brain and visual cultures, Hans Belting's efforts to redefine his discipline as an "anthropology of images," James Elkins's expansive effort to apply art historical methods to the study of scientific images, Whitney Davis's theorization of "neurovisuality," research programs such *Bildwissenschaft* in Germany,[5] neurologist Antonio Damasio on images as the media of consciousness, the science historians Lorraine Daston and Peter Galison on images of objectivity, or Michael Lynch's research on the production and use of images in scientific practice.

For architects and everyone else, imaging and images are peculiarly influential aspects of contemporary life. Today, the power of images and imaging is greater than, and different from, ever before. In both the distant and recent past, images were understood and valued primarily as instrumental means toward architecture as a material or intellectual practice. They were projective representations that used conventional languages or encoded information to convey ideas or legible meanings: iconography and iconology, typography and typology, forms and figures, projections and renderings. But today, images and imaging have a new status as actuality and as nonhuman actors. They are neither media- nor medium-specific and operate through association, affect, and processing, not through reading, delineation, and interpretation. As a result, fundamental disciplinary assumptions about how architecture makes its appearance—in its production and its reception—face radical challenges. Age-old questions about architecture's efficacy and operations—as physical and social environments, as forms and spaces, as embodied energy, as property—are more confounding than ever.

Imaging theory is first of all an ongoing search to understand the evolving meanings and uses of the words "image" and "imaging" in general and in specific fields from philosophy to medicine. Images are distinct from pictures, icons, or representations, and imaging departs from the modernist theories of vision, visuality, or optics that have long been used to analyze and understand, and even to operate as paradigms of, cognition and abstraction. Imaging involves modalities and instances of appearances and exchange that require serial processing and pattern recognition rather than the delineation of objects, the apprehension of abstract form, and the comprehension of legible content. Treating images and imaging as the subjects and material of investigation virtually necessitates operating without precise definitions of those terms. The motto for such a project might be, "I don't 'know' one when I don't 'see' one."

For over five hundred years, orthographic projections, perspectives, and other delineations have been understood as architectural images par excellence, but since the advent of photography, mass media, and computing architects increasingly employ surfaces, patterns, diagrams, fields, atmospheres, and graphs as imaging formats. This radical evolution of architectural imaging is a necessary response to the effects and potential of digital technology and media. Yet its emergence can be traced as a long lineage of the many innovations in the history of architectural representation, from the spectral projections of the camera obscura and the visual pleasures of other optical devices, to Sebastiano Serlio's iconic woodcut of the five orders, to Giovanni Battista Piranesi's puzzling and sublime etchings, to the legible forms of *architecture parlante*, to Antoine-Chrysostome Quatremère de Quincy's type, to John Ruskin's theory of resemblance, to Mies van der Rohe's uncanny photomontages and Le Corbusier's canny use of commercial photographs, to Frederick Kiesler's fantastic plans for a vision machine,[6] to the Smithsons' populist claims in "But Today We Collects Ads," to Aldo Rossi's oneiric sketchbooks, to Robert Venturi and Denise Scott Brown's "Bill-Ding-Board," to the diagrams, renderings, animations, and models that now circulate globally as architecture's most pervasive design modes and memes. Architecture has become a *matter* of imaging, as has virtually every aspect of contemporary life.

Serious and sophisticated speculation on architectural imaging provokes a string of difficult and consequential questions. What are these ubiquitous entities and enigmatic things we call images? How are they related to, but not simply aligned with, photography, representation, visuality, pictures, icons, screening, mimesis, concepts, figures, cartoons, or shapes? How are they produced, and how do they operate in architecture? What are the relationships between imaging and imagination? How have computing and networked media altered our answers to these questions? What is needed to deal productively with images today? How might a direct and deep commitment to imaging change the discipline and practice of architecture? What would architectural practice become if its acknowledged means and ends were imaging? How are imaging technologies and practices altering our customs of discourse, inhabitation, exchange, and production? How does architecture provoke and enable peculiar aspects of imaging? How have imaging techniques emerged in architecture's history, and how has image culture altered the operational protocols and perceptual habits of the discipline or its relations with other disciplines?

Fully embracing the potential of imaging would require architects to suspend the operative logic of imitation or reference in a visual or linguistic sense, and in turn to suspend disabling and now intellectually unsustainable dichotomies: real and virtual, form and concept, medium and material, presence and absence, and, most radically, architecture's distinction from other design fields. But we need not assume that the proliferation and ubiquity of imaging in today's culture effaces and denigrates rational discourse or architecture's basic value. As contemporary artists, neuroscientists, and theorists suggest, we have many compelling ways to focus and clarify our understanding of the contemporary status of imaging.

Despite the diversity of their projects, most imaging theorists are looking back to a few key figures, such as Henri Bergson and Walter Benjamin, as the first generation to begin to embrace image thinking as a peculiarly modern adaptation of cognition, communication, and speculation that supersedes Platonic (idealist) or Humean (empiricist) concepts of "mental images." In very different ways, Bergson and Benjamin each attempted to explain modernity in terms of a new potential to engage and manipulate the reality of images. Benjamin's famous concept of the dialectical image proposed that historical change can be understood, engaged, experienced, and achieved through mechanically fabricated images—from photographs to glass and iron constructions—that collapse anticipation and recollection. These images offer a flash of recognition of the present as it was prefigured in the past.[7] Benjamin identified the most intense and complex example of these technically specific and temporally stable instances of "dialectics at a standstill"—like snapshots in time—in the urban architecture of the Parisian arcades.[8] His insistence on the dialectical and technically determined sites of these images is distinct from the immaterial and durational images vividly theorized by Bergson, whose 1896 book *Matter and Memory* offered an evasion of philosophical models focused on language, representation, or logic. For Bergson, thinking is first and foremost the conscious and unconscious processing of perceived and recollected images as a means toward action. He claimed that "matter is an aggregate of 'images'"[9] and proposed a notoriously abstract and radical recasting of the mind as a "cinematicographical" flow of images that we "reel off" and "wind up."[10] Bergson's images condense stuff and mind into a single entity (of which the body is a unique instance) that is neither a representation of reality nor a projected mental state.

Two of the most expansive and original image theorists in recent decades, Gilles Deleuze and Jacques Rancière, explicitly look back to the time of Bergson for the beginnings of the concepts or conditions that might be useful to explain and engage the potential of today's image world. Though Deleuze's early book on Bergson (*Bergsonism*, 1966) focused on his concepts of temporality and multiplicity, he soon after proposed his concept of "the image of thought," and about two decades later produced two books on the cinema image which take Bergson as the explicit point of departure.[11] More recently, Rancière has offered an alternative trajectory for image theory in essays such as "The Future of the Image," "The Pensive Image," and "The Surface of Design."[12] He locates the emergence of new varieties of imaging practices contemporaneous with Bergson's major works: the typographic poetry of Stéphane Mallarmé and the diverse design work of Peter Behrens. Aiming to disturb the now orthodox distinction between modernist autonomy and the politics of the avant-garde, Rancière argues that "the practice and idea of design, as they develop at the beginning of the twentieth century, redefine the place of artistic activities in the set of practices that configure the shared material world."[13] Whether "drawing lines, arranging words or distributing surfaces, one also designs divisions of communal space." Thus the kinds of imaging that most people conceive reductively as branding, lifestyle, or virtual identities are for Rancière potential arenas for dissensual politics. For him, "images are not primarily manifestations of the properties of a certain technical medium but operations: relations between a whole and parts, between a visibility and a power of signification and affect associated with it; between expectations and what happened to meet them [...]. The images of art are operations that produce a discrepancy, a dissemblance."[14] His philosophical writings on film, literature, photography, and design as they are practiced in what he calls the "aesthetic regime" of modernity conceptualize a mode of transdisciplinary aesthetic production that deploys imaging operations as devices to enact and exploit "an ambivalence in which the same procedures create and retract meaning, ensure and undo the link between perceptions and affects."[15] Imaging thus subverts and refuses recognition, representation, and conceptualization. Instead, it involves "the interplay of operations that produces what we call art: or precisely an alteration of resemblance [...] operations that produce a discrepancy, a dissemblance."[16] Imaging as dissemblance (and as a means of political "dissensus") is always an incessant montage of relations, repetitions, and conversions.

Sunil Manghani reminds us that "invariably an image offers plurality,"[17] and media theorist Mark Hansen extends that insistence on inexorable multiplicity to include the neurological and technological temporalities of imaging. He argues that in our digital era it is not possible to stabilize the "temporal process" of imaging by treating an image as "a spatial/visual figure."[18] Digital images are "irreducibly temporal entities or processes," and "with the invention of video [...] the material image becomes dynamic in itself."[19] Imaging has become a kind of reflexive process of mediation between machines and brains, and Hansen challenges us to find ways "to correlate the neuroscientific revolution in imaging with the computational revolution in media" in ways that "position the human—human imagination—as a hinge between mental processing and technical networks."[20] His phenomenological framing of imaging proposes that our bodies have "a newly specified function within the regime of the digital image, namely, the function of filtering information in order to create images."[21] For Hansen, digital imaging is defined as something that "can no longer be restricted to the level of surface appearances, but must be extended to encompass the entire process by which information is made perceivable though embodied experience."[22] He theorizes new media as events that convert "information into corporeally apprehensible images,"[23] an apt and capacious definition that might also be extended to the processes, platforms, and products of digital design and architecture. How can architects build on this intersection of imaging in computation and neuroscience to better explain and exploit the kinds of design imagination involved in the actual modification and virtual manipulation of reality?

Brains and machines are evolving in tandem, but too rapidly and too thoroughly for the effects of either to be understood, fully, in real time. Yet each pressures our understanding of the other in ways that fuel advanced research in both computation and neuroscience. New knowledge about the partitioned and networked anatomy of the brain has developed in tandem with burgeoning advances in imaging technology, including not only specific tools such as fMRI but also new media of production, distribution, storage, and reception as well as the subfield of artificial intelligence known as artificial imagination, which ranges from machine vision to novel image generation using neural networks. Artificial imagination strives to engage and produce images in ways that mimic the complexities, powers, and applications of human vision and visual cognition. It is thus as much research into computational potential as an investigation into the ways our brains process visual information and assemble images. Like Hansen's approach to media theory and Stafford's approach to art history, efforts to achieve artificial imagination generate insights into the evolved imaging capacities of our brains and suggest that understanding creativity requires understanding how imagination depends on the neural and artificial processes and capacities of imaging. Each of those projects invites us to understand, precisely and comprehensively, how creativity literally *involves* imaging across multiple media and fields of knowledge, not only with our brains and bodies but also with pervasive technologies.

That insight, which challenges us to rethink our traditional understanding of mental and material images as functional representations of either consciousness or reality, has been ongoing at least since the late nineteenth century in science and in art. Key questions that emerged at that time remain compelling and unanswered today. How is thinking imaging? How is imaging thinking? How is imaging not what modern philosophy and theory have conceptualized as "seeing"? How can a better understanding of imaging offer insights into thinking? How are technologies of observation launching new research approaches and imaging practices in science, art, and daily life? The increasing ubiquity and reliance on technologies of observation that objectivize and exteriorize imaging—from photography to X-rays to microscopy to cinema to video to scanning—have disrupted the traditional notion of images as mental objects that can be experienced and manipulated "in our heads."[24] Among the first to begin to comprehensively theorize this "universe of technical images" was the philosopher Vilém Flusser. Writing near the end of the twentieth century, his speculative and progressive phenomenology offered an accessible, ambitious, and programmatic set of ideas and claims about a "new imagination" that "produces images of calculations instead of facts." Those technical images are synthesized from data, programs, and coding, and will supplant writing's "historical" and "linear" basis.[25] Unlike the past, when writing aimed to decipher representational images in reasoned acts of iconoclasm, Flusser argued that today's images are "computations of concepts" and "mosaics assembled from particles."[26] He insisted that the proliferation of images after photography and mass media is not a retrogressive return to past forms of imagination but a new condition in which technical images are "disembodied surfaces" and "transmissions" that operate in and as networks for "programming the behavior of functionaries in a post-industrial society."[27] He proposed in 1985, at the moment of the advent of the personal computer, that we are either moving "toward a centrally programmed, totalitarian society of image receivers and image administrators" or "toward a dialogic, telematic society of image producers and image collectors."[28]

Damasio's most recent writings seem to offer a neurological explanation and degree of plausibility to the second of Flusser's prognostications. He explains consciousness as an effect of the brain's conversion of neural networks into maps, and of those maps into images of thought: "when brains make maps, they are also creating images, the main currency of our minds. Ultimately consciousness allows us to experience maps as images, to manipulate those images, and to apply reasoning to them."[29] For Damasio, the sense of a body image is an effect of the conscious and unconscious mapping of the neural networks in—and even beyond—the brain as it interacts with others, the physical world, and information. The body is functionally an extension and housing of a neurological network that converges in the brain but is not limited to it. The crucial example is the eyes, or more specifically the retinas, which are "an elaborate outpost of the brain" with a gridded neural structure much like that of the cerebral cortex.[30] The retinas produce neural map-images that feed directly into the brain, where they are processed into subsequent maps. Brain plasticity thus is related in specific and deep ways to the plasticity of images, as actual entities and as mental material. Damasio also comes very close to offering a neurological basis for Bergson's radical thesis in *Matter and Memory* that images are the stuff of consciousness, suspended between mind and matter, and that memory is the place or medium that is the most "real" proof of thinking. I remember, therefore I am. I image, therefore I think.

The beginnings of New Brutalism, in the context of the discussions among the Independent Group, align with that post-Cartesian manner of thinking, although they were inspired by different intellectual sources.[31] As Nigel Henderson explained in his speech at the opening of *Parallel of Life and Art* in September 1953, the collaborators on the exhibition—himself, Alison and Peter Smithson, Eduardo Paolozzi, and the usually unmentioned engineer Ronald Jenkins—were interested in whether "others too responded in the same way to the visual impact of a particular image."[32] Referencing André Malraux's book *Le Musée imaginaire* (1947, translated into English in 1949 as *Museum without Walls*), Henderson described the installation of suspended and wall-mounted images as a "virtual ceiling" that allowed them to "avoid the uniform plain flat wall-display with its 2-dimensional juxtapositions, and instead to use space as one ally in the attempt to touch off as many and as varied associations as the responsiveness [of] our audience allowed."[33] Henderson also referenced the biologist D'Arcy Wentworth Thompson's attempt in his book *On Growth and Form* (1917, expanded edition 1942) to explain "recurrent themes in nature, the tensions and forces which, operating at different levels of intensity, on material of varying composition, produce visually startling, but physically inevitable resemblances."[34] Henderson's reference to Thompson was also an implicit reference to *Growth and Form*, the 1951 exhibition that he and Paolozzi had initially conceived with the artist Richard Hamilton (and which also was inspired by Thompson's book). While *Parallel of Life and Art* consisted entirely of photographic enlargements of intentionally uncategorizable found images, *Growth and Form* was intended to be a literally dynamic display of mostly biomorphic images ranging from physical models to film projections. The installation was "a prototype multimedia or environmental art event that included film-loop projections and the stroboscopic lighting of water droplets. Assembled largely from non-fine-art materials [...] the exhibits included radiographs, electron micrographs and film stills."[35] Both *Parallel of Life and Art* and *Growth and Form* aimed to demonstrate the experience and effects of mediated images and drew on a range of influences from philosophy, art theory, and science. As explained in the proposals, notebooks, and correspondence that Hamilton and Henderson compiled in the process of developing the exhibition, *Growth and Form* was less a presentation of Thompson's theories of organic morphology than a demonstration of the potential of emerging imaging technologies to investigate and display the formal principles of natural systems, from atomic particles to astronomical phenomena. When Le Corbusier, who was in Britain for the eighth CIAM meeting at Hoddesdon, spoke at the opening of *Growth and Form*, he pointedly remarked, in French, that he was relieved not to see yet another exhibition of abstract art and was "delighted to find an exhibition of fantastically 'Concrete Art'" that made use of the "magnificent tools of science, instruments of measurement, and the apparatus of photography and the cinema."[36]

Growth and Form was organized with the assistance of an advisory committee chaired by J.R.M. Brumwell, an advertising innovator, art collector, and the founder—with architect Misha Black and designer Milner Gray in 1943—of the Design Research Unit. The ICA leadership's imposition of the advisory committee, packed with established intellectual and cultural figures, was an attempt to both legitimate and oversee Hamilton's adventurous ideas. Brumwell was best known as the editor of the popular and influential book *This Changing World* (1945), which aimed "to cast light upon the pattern of the modern world"[37] and contained essays by well-known figures in the arts (Herbert Read, art theorist and director of the ICA, wrote both the prologue and epilogue) and the natural and social sciences, several of whom also were on the advisory committee for *Growth and Form* as well as contributors to *Aspects of Form*, the book that was published to accompany the exhibition. Hamilton invited Lancelot Law Whyte, the scientist and philosopher, to edit that book, which includes nine essays by scientists (in the fields of physics, astronomy, biology, biochemistry, embryology, animal mimicry, and neuroscience) and only two by art scholars: Rudolf Arnheim (who might as easily be characterized as a representative of psychology) and Ernst Gombrich. In an otherwise sarcastic review of *Growth and Form* in the *Sunday Times*, art critic John Russell noted how the tendency to integrate science and art had shifted the initiative to the scientists: "It is now the biologists and the geneticists who encourage the view that aesthetics is no longer an isolated science of beauty and that science can no longer neglect the intimations of aesthetics."[38] That attitude is clear in a typed proposal for *Growth and Form*:

> The visual interest of this field, where biology, chemistry, physics and mathematics overlap, was considered an excellent subject for presentation in purely visual terms. The laws of growth and form pertaining to the processes of nature are [. . .] the result of very precise physical laws; the complexities of art, on the other hand, are the products of involved psychological processes. [. . .] Nevertheless, the painter and sculptor have much to gain from the enlargement of their world of experience by an appreciation of the forms in nature beyond their immediate visual environment. It is the enlarged environment opened by scientific studies that we would reveal for its visual qualities.[39]

An aversion to established aesthetic theory and an interest in empirical experimentation is also clear in Henderson's concluding remark in his *Parallel of Life and Art* speech:

> It is true that we looked to the material to reveal its own principles of selection—that we ourselves were concerned first of all with the subjective impression, the impact upon our senses rather than upon our intellects. This may explain our non-dogmatic attitude to the whole thing, and our appreciation of the need of the active participation of the spectators. We should like to bring about a situation in which people felt like undergoing a strong visual experience, without too much reliance on intellectual handrails for their support. And we value the fact that their experience will necessarily differ from our own, being grounded in a different soil. It might be truer of this exhibition than of many to say that you can get out of it what you put into it.[40]

Like the other members of the Independent Group, Henderson's explanation of imaging, which would be recast two years later in the provocations and speculations of Banham's "The New Brutalism," were an acknowledgment and product of art and architecture's immersion in the evolving intellectual culture of post-war Britain. Image was an especially contested and fashionable term and issue that had attracted attention in many fields, including academic philosophy. Although there were no direct affiliations of the Independent Group with the philosophers most engaged in those debates, the positions and the perplexities that fueled the philosophers' interests help to illuminate the ways the image was significant for both the Independent Group and New Brutalism, and how their thinking was an explicit reaction against the Surrealist-inspired attitude toward images promoted by Herbert Read and Roland Penrose at the ICA and evident in shows such as *The Wonder and Horror of the Human Head* (1953). The differences between the ICA leadership and the Independent Group ultimately were aired publicly in two identically titled lectures on "The Human Image" given almost exactly one year apart by Read (January 29, 1953) and Lawrence Alloway (January 28, 1954). The two generations were promoting competing claims on the long and rich legacy of the study and theorization of images in British intellectual history, going back to the beginnings of British empiricism in the early nineteenth century and William Hogarth's *Analysis of Beauty* (1753) in the previous century.

One of the most groundbreaking if idiosyncratic scientific researchers on images was the late nineteenth-century polymath Francis Galton. Even though Galton's interests and presumptions always treated imagination as a purely mental capacity "to think in visual images," and his intention was to conduct experiments that could "elicit the degree and manner in which different persons possess the power of seeing images in the mind's eye," his projects suggested other imaging possibilities to many in the twentieth century.[41] A comparison of two studies by Galton on "visualized numerals" and "composite portraits" demonstrates the potential implications of a shift away from the concept of mental images. Writing in *Nature* in 1880, Galton hypothesized that "persons who are

ARRAY 6.1

imaginative almost invariably think of numerals in visual imagery."[42] Based entirely on the introspective testimony of participants who described the ways they visualized number sequences "in definite and constant arrangements or schemes,"[43] he catalogued and published numerous diagrams of what he called "visualized numerals" or "number forms," showing how varied kinds of symbols, not only numerals, could be integrated into graphic images as a not quite logical way to comprehend and utilize mathematical relationships. Imagination, in this case, serves as a kind of mental crutch, or "convenience for mnemonic purposes,"[44] and a purely private and idiosyncratic way to understand logical relationships that are normally, and more precisely, understood through abstractions like mathematics or language. For Galton, number forms demonstrated the mental phenomenon of imaging, but were ultimately a less than sophisticated kind of cognition that is unevenly and seemingly randomly distributed among individuals and can only be studied based on reports of subjective experience.[45]

Galton's interest in composite portraits utilized an entirely different approach to understanding visual imagination and yielded a very different understanding of the potential of imaging. Those studies attempted to use photography to simulate—and even produce—non-reductive generalizations by combining multiple, partially exposed photographs of different faces, or different photographs or photographs of representations of the same face, in a single printed image. Galton explained that technique as a simulation of a possible mental faculty: "A composite portrait represents the picture that would rise before the mind's eye of a man who had the gift of pictorial imagination in an exalted degree [. . .] the merit of the photographic composite is its mechanical precision being subject to no errors beyond those incidental to all photographic productions."[46] But unlike his research on number forms, composite portraiture was an entirely technical method of imaging. In addition, and more important, it activated a kind of imagination or imaging that enables simultaneous perception of both specific and general visual features or aspects. Galton even speculated that these technical imagings have the capacity to mediate dichotomies such as good and evil, or beauty and ugliness. For example, and recalling that Galton was the inventor of the term "eugenics," he suggested that a composite portrait of several presumably evil and ugly criminals would be "better looking" than a portrait of any of the individuals because their defects fade out and their common humanity emerges. Less scandalous examples are composites of multiple portraits of a single individual—such as a series of photographs or the various imprints of a historical figure on different coins—which he argued would offer "a really good likeness" because they are not restricted to a "single expression." Galton concluded that any composite would be a truer "resemblance" than a single photograph, because it contains not one aspect or instance but instead generates "varied suggestiveness."[47] Thus, while Galton imagined composite portraits as an approximation of mental images, they also exemplify the aesthetic operations of dissemblance that Rancière theorizes. They can be simultaneously vague and rich, accurate and suggestive, mimetic and metamorphic, type and model, ideal and individual.[48]

Though far from his intentions, Galton's investigations also prefigure recent neuroscientific insights about our brains' constant processing of massive numbers of perceived images as the basis of facial recognition or higher order conceptual thought. Most important, Galton's creative application of photography to synthesize and visualize qualitative data sets and generate non-reductive statistical averages (which literally portray "standard deviations") is distinct from the approaches of his more famous contemporaries, such as Étienne-Jules Marey's use of his "chronophotographic gun" or Eadweard Muybridge's related efforts to record animal motion, which were preoccupied with the use of photography to visualize time and motion accurately and objectively as a series of discrete and stable images.[49] Galton not only challenged established assumptions about mental images, but also introduced an application and understanding of photographic or technical images that was quite different from the usual presumption of the camera's mechanical objectivity. The fact that Galton thought of composite portraiture as a mechanical simulation

6.1

It was necessary in the early '50's to look to the works of painter Pollock and sculptor Paolozzi for a complete image system, for an order with a structure and a certain tension, where every piece was correspondingly new in a new system of relationships.

It is our thesis that for every form of association there is an inherent pattern of building.

The first study was at the relatively simple level of association—the village. It concerned itself with 'infill'—the placing of new dwellings in and around the old village in such a way as to revalidate the existing pattern.

ypical addition to a village
respective of location

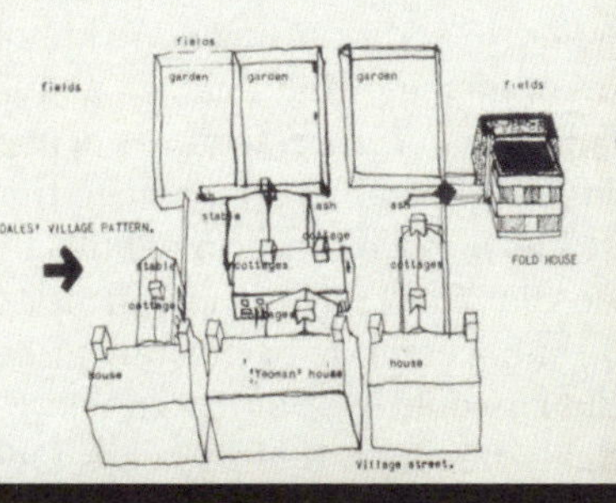

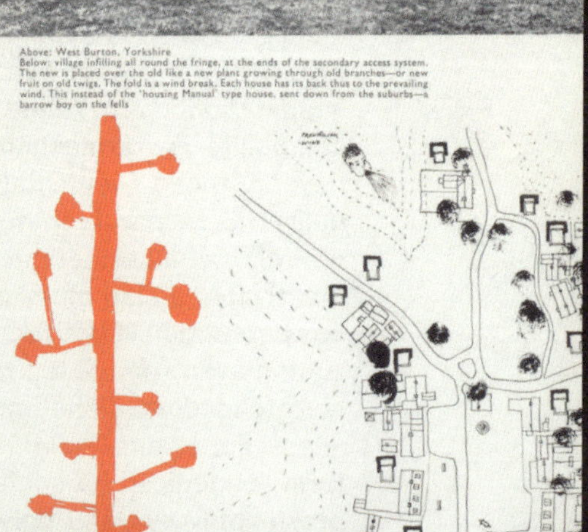

Above: West Burton, Yorkshire
Below: village infilling all round the fringe, at the ends of the secondary access system. The new is placed over the old like a new plant growing through old branches—or new fruit on old twigs. The fold is a wind break. Each house has its back thus to the prevailing wind. This instead of the 'housing Manual' type house, sent down from the suburbs—a barrow boy on the fells

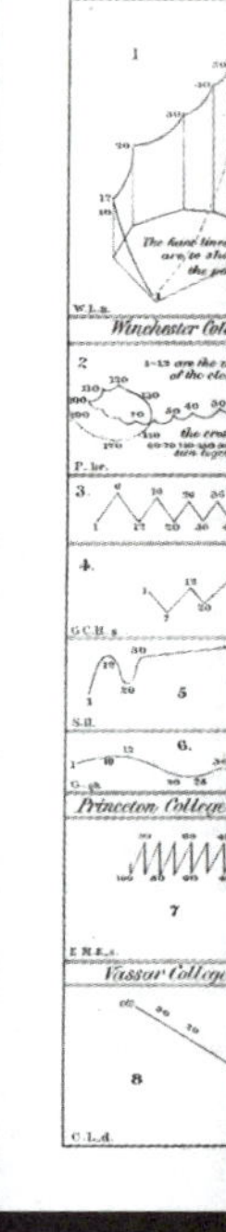

PLATE XXXI

Composites of the Members of a Family.

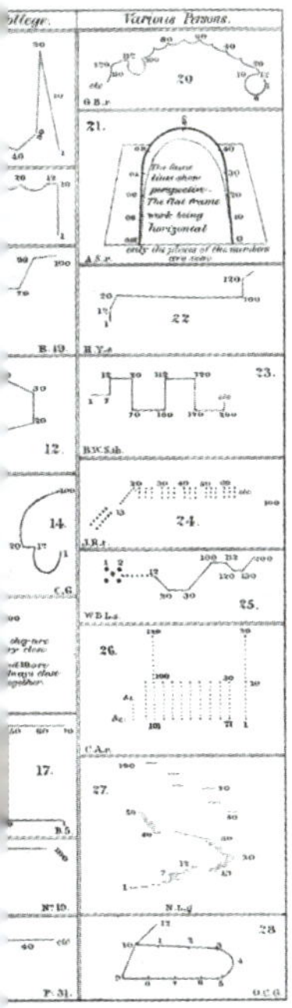

ollege. Various Persons.

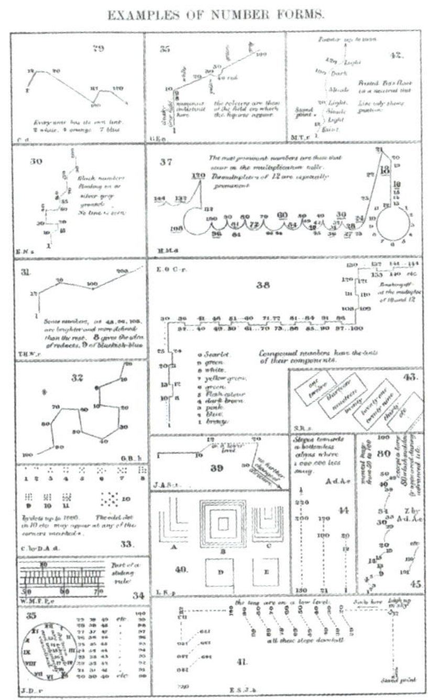

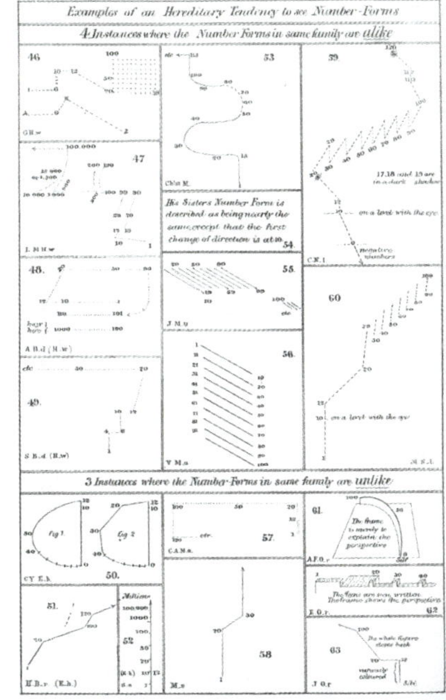

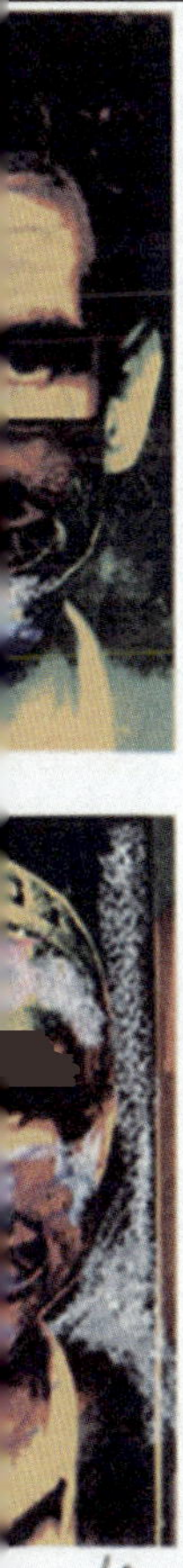

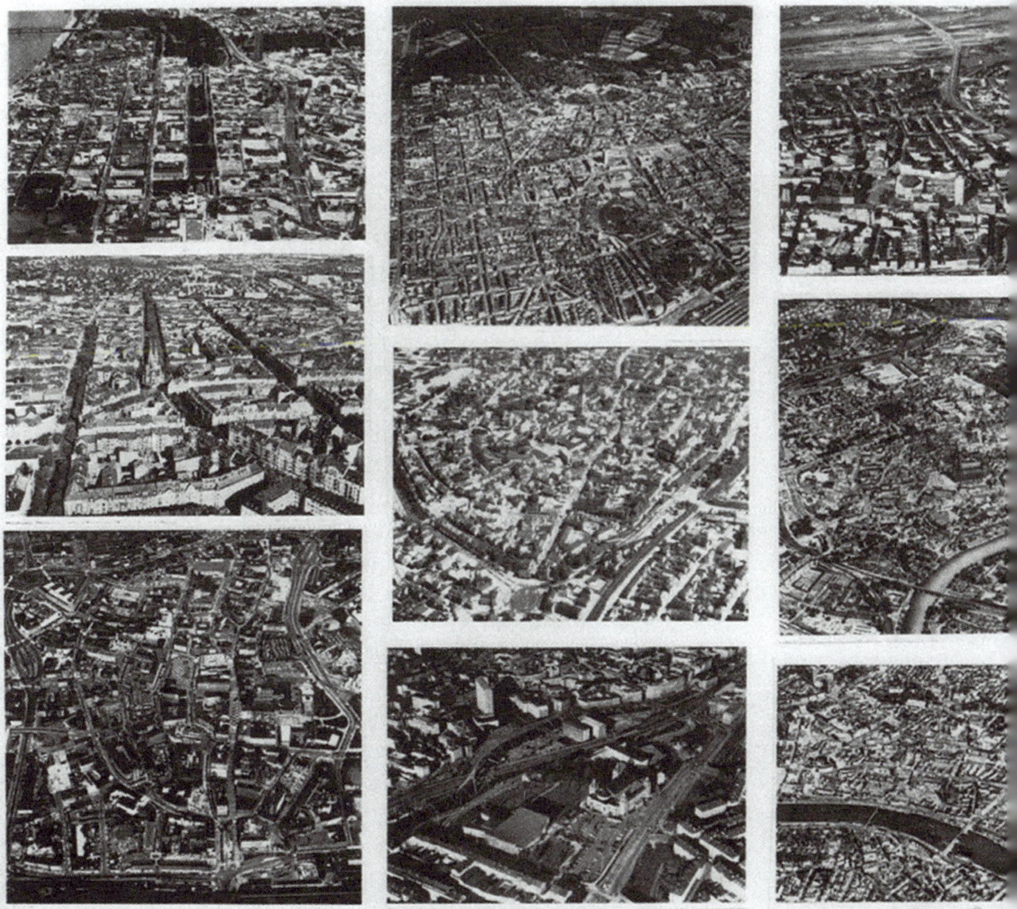

of a possible mental function does not abrogate his method's anticipation of the ways that montage or other photographic techniques would later be championed as imaging practices that suggest new modes of consciousness, or even function as devices to construct or modify realities.

Ironically, photography initially had proved to be a major impediment or distraction (in the ordinary and the Benjaminian sense) to the emergence of speculative imaging practices.[50] Throughout the nineteenth century, photography all too easily was assumed to affirm, or was captivated by, the model of mechanical imaging as an objective representation or reflection of things in the world. The use of photography seemed to promise automatic, indexical realism. But every imaging theorist struggles against this simplicity, and instead attempts to comprehend either the incapacities of technical imaging to rival human imagination or, more intriguingly, its capacities to evoke ever more artificial imaginative possibilities that challenge the evolved and learned capacities of our brains.

Postwar British philosophy revived Galton's preoccupation with mental images. An intriguing example was the Oxford philosopher H. H. Price's 1952 lecture titled "Image Thinking" at the Aristotelian Society in London.[51] Price did not advance a prescient theory, nor even craft a particularly intriguing argument. In fact, his lecture might best be described as a lucid, candid apologia for the ways mental images operate as a central concept in the tradition of British empiricism. Yet the lecture was important and timely enough to be the subject of a symposium at the Aristotelian Society the next year, a fact that might be attributed as much to native philosophers' support for Price's position in a moment when Britain was modernizing and internationalizing as to the general significance of the topic in the broader culture.[52] Price's conservatism was matched by progressive attitudes, not only in philosophy but also in art theory, such as those of Read, who, two years prior to Price's lecture, professed a dogmatic and symptomatic theory of images: "That which we call reality is a chain of images invented by man [...]. Reality is man-made, and the maker is the image maker, the poet. Reality accords with the images the artist makes and derives its validity from such values as integrity, self-consistency, viability, pragmatic satisfaction, aesthetic satisfaction, etc."[53] To support his claim, Read offered an even more strident statement, quoted from a personal letter from the sculptor Naum Gabo: "We know only what we do, what we make, what we construct; and all that we make, all that we construct, are realities; I call them *images*, not in Plato's sense (namely, that they are only reflections of reality), but I hold that these images are the reality itself and that there is no reality beyond this reality except when we in our creative process change the images."[54]

Price likely would have found Read's and Gabo's statements philosophically naive; his own essay is a useful and revealing philosophical reflection on the deeper issues and cultural stakes latent in the discourse on images. Price argued that the intellectual controversies about mental images were largely academic, were nothing new, and that they could be dispelled by attentive explanation of ordinary experience. Curiously, this is an attitude Price shared with the unnamed antagonist of his lecture, though he offered enough clues for his audience to understand that he was motivated by a distaste for the work, and especially the influence, of Ludwig Wittgenstein (as he would explicitly acknowledge several years later).[55] Both Wittgenstein and Price built their arguments on analyses and descriptions of experience, but Price respectfully revised the introspective tradition, while Wittgenstein proposed a radical attack on the notion of private mental states. While Price proudly turned to his British predecessors to construct his arguments, Wittgenstein viewed philosophy and its history as so thoroughly bungled that wholesale revolution was needed. The vast differences between the writings of these two very different philosophers, each claiming to attend to, and to explain, the role of images in ordinary thinking and experience, offer fascinating insights into the diversity of postwar attitudes about the importance, elusiveness, and insistence of images in modern life.

Price launched his philosophical argument as a populist appeal to common sense or conventional wisdom, and endorsed images as actual elements of thinking and of experience. For Price, the apparent ease and naturalness of image thinking was worthy of philosophical inquiry, and his "Imagist" theory was a protest against the theories and influence of the "modernist" philosophers' efforts to limit philosophical speculation to the analysis of language as the primary evidence of thinking.[56] He embraced the imprecision, indistinctness, indeterminacy, and elusiveness of images as objects of thought, and his essay affirmed the many ways that imaging is simultaneously an inescapably obvious feature of human experience and a deeply confusing and evasive topic. Price built his "imagist theory of thinking" on the common understanding that nearly every one of us "*uses* images in our thinking [. . .] rather as we use maps or sketch-plans to find our way about":

> An engineer engaged in inventing a new machine, a garage-mechanic considering how to take an old one to pieces, a surgeon planning a difficult operation, a housewife wondering how that new picture would look over the mantelpiece in the spare bedroom, or even a student of elementary geometry who is told by his teacher to bisect an angle—all these people whose thoughts are concerned with the spatial relations of things, with their shapes and colours, use visual images to solve their problems.[57]

Price accepted the idea that logic and language are higher-order thinking, but argued they are built on the basis of image thinking: "Mental images are the primary symbols, and all other symbols are secondary and derivative."[58]

Most important, Price wanted to defend the popular understanding of consciousness and thinking as private and internal against those among his contemporaries who attempted to refute it—Gilbert Ryle being the most prominent and respected among them.[59] Price embraced pervasive understandings of mental images—just as, in his later writings, he would tackle topics such as religious belief, parapsychology, and concepts of the afterlife—in order to align philosophy with, and bring it closer to, the beliefs of what he called "ordinary unintellectual mankind."[60] At stake for Price were the ancient questions of whether human experience and thought directly engage individuals in their world in obvious ways; he wanted to explain simply and directly how it is possible to have private experiences, such as memories and imagination, that resemble experiences of reality. He was opposed to both the behaviorist trend, which aimed to dissolve all presumptions of cognition or intention into analyses of actions, or what Ryle called "dispositions," and the linguistic trend, which either converted all cognition into symbol-based logic or focused on language as the empirical evidence of thinking.[61] Imagism, for Price, provided a relatively simple way to preserve the concept of individual consciousness while also avoiding complicated abstractions and technical language. He did not conceal his frustration with his "anti-Imagist" academic peers, who "lose no opportunity of telling us how unimportant mental images are" and who "repeat *ad nauseum* that a mental image is not like a picture; and then they proceed to tell us that the entity-word 'image' ought not to be used at all."[62]

Price was right that Wittgenstein not only saw philosophy as a means to challenge conventional wisdom but also was perhaps the most ruthless critic of philosophical and psychological theories of consciousness that presumed interior mental states. Yet Wittgenstein was as fascinated as Price by images and vision, though for very different reasons. While he was entirely dismissive of popular or traditional understandings of mind, thinking, or imagination, he carefully and seriously scrutinized how our ordinary and specialized uses of language necessarily affirm those pervasive assumptions and make it extremely difficult to achieve alternate understandings. For Wittgenstein, conventional wisdom, whether academic or popular, and however misguided, was empirical evidence that both revealed and obscured the puzzling quality of all thinking. His attempts to play out the implications of those puzzles, and to attend to the problems posed by images and imaging, or by vision and perception, were his way of showing that those inscrutable conditions are the basis for the varieties of sophisticated thinking that enable everyday uses of language. While he conceived of language as fundamentally logical and as the best evidence of the structure of reality, he also conceived of that logic as complex and ultimately elusive of rational explication.

Wittgenstein's move away from characterizing mental images as representations is a key part of his evasion of any categorical distinction between language and image. For Wittgenstein, there is no clear difference between writing or speaking and drawing or seeing. Linguistic thinking is a kind of envisioning. It is not a matter of sheer logic, nor a matter of mental images or picturing. The most succinct version of Wittgenstein's attitude and approach appears in his famous aphorisms, which were offered as advice to philosophers: "Don't think, but look!"; "*look* and *see.*"[63] Curiously, his famous discussion of pain in the *Philosophical Investigations*—which is usually understood as a meditation on the skeptical problem of whether, or how, one can know that another person is in pain because we are unable to feel it ourselves—also revolves around a question of imaging, or imagination. At one point, he suggests that our ability to understand others' pain involves a capacity to envision an "image of pain."[64] What could that kind of image or imagination be? It is not a concept or a statement. Most importantly, he says, it is not a picture. Any specific image—or imaging, or experience, or awareness—

of pain "is not replaceable in this language-game by anything we should call a picture.—The image of pain certainly enters into the language game in a sense; only not as a picture."[65] This may be Wittgenstein's most important and provocative claim about imagination. For Wittgenstein, a mental image is neither a mental picture nor a private experience. It is a form of communication and behavior—"a grammatical movement"[66]—that is accessible only as a description, and the best description is actual behavior, from gestures to the uses of language to the productions or performances of art. Yet it is ultimately impossible to objectify: "The mental picture is the picture which is described when someone describes what he imagines."[67] Wittgenstein was not simply dismissing the concept of the mental image. As we see in his discussion of pain, there is something he calls an image: it is just not a picture, or even like a picture, though our language often seems to suggest that is what it seems to be when we explain it or describe it. This mistake applies not only to pain but also to visualization.

The fact that imagination seems like a picture is an important mistake. This becomes clear in his discussion of what he calls a "visual room."[68] In an attempt to show that experiences like imagination, pain, or memory should not be understood as interior or private, and more importantly should not be described with the same "grammatical moves" as physical objects that individuals can "have," Wittgenstein offers the example of a "visual room" that two people in an actual room can imagine, share and discuss. Simply put, the visual room is not a representation but an imaging. It is not something you can have, but it is something you can get. It is almost nothing. You might even say it is aesthetic. What you "get" when you imagine, share, and describe the visual room is

> like a discovery, but what its discoverer really found was a new way of speaking, a new comparison; it might even be called a new sensation. You have a new conception and interpret it as seeing an object. You interpret a grammatical movement made by yourself as a quasi-physical phenomenon which you are observing. [. . .] But [. . .] what you have primarily discovered is a new way of looking at things. As if you had invented a new way of painting; or, again, a new metre, or a new kind of song.[69]

For Wittgenstein, the problem of imaging the visual room is not unlike that of imaging pain. One can occupy a room with another person and share that experience in language or actions, but of course, no one can see what another sees, just as one can understand that another person is in pain without actually feeling it, even if it sometimes seems as if we can. Wittgenstein explains that we image rooms as we image pain; in both cases, imaging is a "grammatical movement" of description and discourse. To image is to play a spatial, temporal language game. This is not a mere game of grammar; the strange and wonderful thing about imaging is that it is like "a discovery": the visual room did not exist before we discussed it, described it, or designed it. Like pain, the visual room does not quite exist *after* we discuss, describe, or design it, either. Think, for example, of the various ways medical practitioners ask patients to rate or describe pain.

Think also of the ingenious ways architects and filmmakers convey the space of a room.

For Wittgenstein, those kinds of imaging are startling, remarkable, or amazing articulations or modes of expression, while for Price they are a kind of discernible and useful entity. Wittgenstein's overtly aesthetic formulation has much to teach architects who design digital models or produce simulations, renderings, and animations. He warns against treating the visual room as either a "quasi-physical phenomenon" or as a kind of representational language like a drawing. The visual room is a virtual room, and Wittgenstein doubles down on the puzzle of mental interiority and privacy by saying that the visual room "has no master outside it, and none inside it either."[70] It is not only imaginary; it is a spatially involuted and virtually inhabited image. Another aspect of Wittgenstein's example may be even more remarkable and pertinent to both architecture and the New Brutalist fascination with imaging. The reciprocity between the visual room and the actual room could be seen as a compelling figure of what it means to "get" architecture. It is likely Wittgenstein's discussion of the visual room was drawing—or building—on his experience, from 1926 to 1929, of designing a house in Vienna for his sister, and it is intriguing to imagine New Brutalist projects such as *Parallel of Life and Art*, Jenkins Room, *Patio and Pavilion*, and *House of the Future*, or even the Smithsons' books such as *The Shift*, *AS in DS*, and *Changing the Art of Inhabitation*, as visual rooms in Wittgenstein's sense. His linking of aesthetics and pain is a curious recasting of the Kantian separation of aesthetic experience and pleasure that resonates with the New Brutalist fascination with, in the minds of its critics (according to Banham), "a cult of ugliness," "denying the spiritual in Man," or the "deliberate flouting of the traditional concepts of photographic beauty."[71]

ARRAY 6.2

Unlike Wittgenstein, who aimed to radically subvert the very distinction between imaging and language, Price's aim was to develop a comprehensive and workable account of image thinking as the basis of language. Ultimately, Price claimed, modern philosophies such as Wittgenstein's were part of a broader attack on what he called "the inner life" of the individual.[72] He saw himself as a defender not only of the tradition of British empiricism but also of the manner in which ordinary people think, which aligns him with J. M. Richards's defense of suburbia in *The Castles on the Ground* (1946) or with the policy of *Architectural Review* and the writings of Pevsner to recuperate the Picturesque (1944–c. 1958). Price wrote in protest against what he saw as the drastic social, political, and technological changes taking place in Britain in the wake of World War Two: "Perhaps there is some connection between this attack on the inner life and the attack on *private life* which was made by the politicians, social reformers, and economic planners" who have "gone a long way towards a kind of 'dehumanisation' of man; and this seems to me one of the darkest features of the very dark age in which we live."[73]

Price's hyperbole is not unusual in the arguments of image advocates, although his conservatism is. The conflict between Price's and Wittgenstein's philosophies was intertwined in complex and seemingly paradoxical ways with the rise of image culture. Wittgenstein, despite his interest in photography and his love of popular movies, was working against the conventions of popular culture. Price, despite his traditionalism, was reminding philosophers that their insistence on a purely linguistic or logical model of thinking was remarkably esoteric. Yet the two men shared a deep concern with the popular and the ordinary, and both made references to Galton's imaging research. Price mentioned Galton in the second paragraph of "Image Thinking" and drew on his composite portraits as a model of what he called "generic images" and on his number forms as examples of what he called "diagrammatic images." Wittgenstein referenced composite portraiture in his later philosophy to exemplify his notion of family resemblance. He even had a Galton-like composite photograph made of himself and his three sisters that he reportedly carried with him in a photo album. The differences between Wittgenstein's interests in imaging (as an analogy for language) and Price's interests in images (as mental entities more basic than language) are huge. Yet both take on images as evidence of a deep, endemic problem of modernity.

At one point in "Image Thinking," Price observed that "words can be manipulated far more quickly and more easily than images can," which was certainly true at the time Price was speaking, but not for much longer and not for an artist like Eduardo Paolozzi, who, in that same year, presented his epidiascope lecture at the first Independent Group meeting with comments that amounted to not much more than "heavy breathing and painful sighs."[74] Paolozzi's series of projected collages and magazine clippings was a crude attempt at mediated image thinking, and a small step toward today's ubiquitous digital image manipulation and transmission, when images "can be manipulated far more quickly and more easily" than words, especially by those whom Price patronized as "ordinary unintellectual mankind." In that condition, image thinking begins to merge not only with the anti-psychologizing aims of Wittgenstein but also with the writings of Stafford, Flusser, Rancière, Hansen, and Damasio, all of whom offer innovative theories that can illuminate the ways our brains are now being called upon, in both new and old ways, to operate with imaging in a changed world and how, as architects, artists, or designers, we can change the ways an imaged world operates.

Although Banham did not maintain his interest in images for long after his initial enthusiasm in 1955, he did, in his last, posthumously published essay, implicitly raise many of the same problems that Wittgenstein and Price discussed. In "A Black Box," Banham accused architects of maintaining a "secret value system" based in their drawing techniques. That "exercise of an arcane and privileged aesthetic code" allowed the profession to function as a cult of *disegno*: the six-hundred-year architectural tradition that conflates design and drawing.[75] His intent was noble, at least in part. With the advent of computer-aided design (CAD), the tradition of *disegno* and the "mystique of drawing" were in danger. The new technology made it possible to "design buildings without making drawings at all [...]. Not by mechanizing the act of drawing itself, but by rendering it unnecessary."[76] But another of Banham's insights offers more intriguing implications. He suggested that the computer has a crucial flaw. The problem, at least in the late 1980s when he wrote the essay, was that while computers could make, copy, manipulate, and remember

6.2

drawings, they could not "remember them in imagery that the eye can read."[77] That incapacity revealed what Wittgenstein would call an "aspect" of *disegno* that is much more salient and significant than its representational uses by, or cult value for, the profession. *Disegno* is as much an imaging device as the black box of CAD, which, intriguingly, could be characterized as a version of Wittgenstein's visual room. Certainly, computation has fundamentally altered the mystique of drawing, but it has also renewed and intensified the importance of Banham's warning to the profession, and the attention that warning draws to imaging in architecture. The reasons have less to do with the accuracy or insight of Banham's positions or claims than his own changing allegiances and prognostications. Considering Banham's insistent advocacy of an architecture of technology, it seems he jettisoned New Brutalism and images too soon. Nothing today is more technological than imaging.

The architectural historian Mario Carpo offers historical and theoretical explanations of the implications of imaging technologies for the design and production of architecture quite unlike Banham's. In his book *The Second Digital Turn: Design beyond Intelligence* (2017), he argues that the systems of parallel projection that have long dominated architectural representation, from the Renaissance systemization of perspective through the uses of photography beginning in the nineteenth century, are now in the process of being superseded by digital scanning (photogrammetry) and point cloud modeling: "Today, at long last, the demise of projected images may be happening for good—this time around, however, not by proclamation but by sheer technological obsolescence [. . .]: parallel projections, long favored by the technical and design professions, have already been mostly replaced by computer-based 3-D modeling."[78] A crucial point for Carpo is that the most advanced type of spatial modeling, 3-D scanning, is unlike perspective or photography, or, before that, writing and printing, because inexpensive data storage has alleviated the practical need for data compression. For each of the prior technologies, compression is achieved by transposing three-dimensional information to a two-dimensional surface, but scanning is not encumbered by the specificity of media: "Today, for most practical applications, the marginal cost of advanced computation is close to zero [. . .] [and] there is now less urgency to laboriously cull, select, and compress data to make information leaner and easier to deal with. [. . .] We no longer need [. . .] to compress oral or visual data due to technical limitations or cost. Today, we can digitally record and process sound and images as images, as need be."[79] Scanning takes advantage of these advances and efficiencies to record information as millions of spatially registered points that cohere as an entirely different kind of imaging: point cloud models that are not pictures or projections but data sets that are "navigable and scalable at will," in real time, and that can be "visualized using perspective images or axonometric or parallel projections" using virtual reality or augmented reality tools.[80] Carpo characterizes this development historically—both the long process of millennia, from the invention of writing to the invention of perspective, photography, and digital media, and the decades-long process in computation, from word processing to image processing to scanning—as an evolution from "verbal to visual to spatial operations."[81] The advent of scanning thus radically alters the relationship between material and image: it is no longer a process of translation but has become an *actually coincidental* interface or interaction. Most important, scanning has the potential to radically alter architectural imagination by construing data as infinitely malleable spatially. Point cloud models enable a kind of artificial imagination that can seamlessly move from actual to virtual to material, or from scanning to modeling to fabrication.[82]

Yet Carpo is reticent to discuss those models as imagings. He implies that scanning promises to make obsolete the "arcane and privileged code" and "the mystique of drawing" that Banham despised, and suggests that it also makes images, at least the kinds of images generated by parallel projection, obsolete too. Thus, like Banham's abandonment of his early interest in images, Carpo does not go so far as to claim that scanning and the point cloud models it produces are an unprecedented kind of imaging process. Instead, he claims that this "conflation of new technologies for capturing and reproducing reality directly in three dimensions, without the mediation of images [. . .] ha[s] replaced text and images as our tools of choice for the notation and replication, representation and quantification of the physical world around us: born verbal, then gone visual, knowledge can now be recorded and transmitted in a new spatial format."[83]

But what Carpo calls a new spatial format is better understood as a new kind of image, or imaging, or imagination.[84] It epitomizes the variations and advances of technologies that have made imaging inarguably ubiquitous in general public use and in architecture. It furthers the irony that while imaging practices have become ridiculously easy, the puzzles of imaging have become no less perplexing, and not only in architecture. The inscrutable glass wall or visual room we incessantly face today is a computer screen or modeling program, and our black boxes, only four decades after desktop computers began to be no longer considered esoteric hardware, are increasingly capable of "thinking" in images. As has always been true, advancing technologies, and the cultures they spawn, pose challenges for architecture. Imaging and artificial imagination are as crucially compelling and conceptually complex for architects today as advertising was for the Smithsons in the 1950s. As they wrote then, "We must somehow get the measure of this intervention if we are to match its powerful and exciting impulses with our own."[85]

Imaging perpetuates a kind of dissipation and persists as the long, slow burn of afterimages. Imaging is a kind of persistent, insatiable looking, much different from modernist acts or concepts of visualizing or gazing. With imaging, there is almost nothing to "see," which means there is almost nothing to write about, which is precisely what makes it so difficult. This gives a somewhat different understanding of Mies's imagings of almost nothing, from Berlin to Barcelona to New York to Chicago. As imagings, they have been endlessly reiterated in stories, reports, remakes, covers, pictures, theories, criticism, and pilgrimages. Mies's buildings, photomontages, and drawings are best taken as serial revisionings of memorable and exemplary architectures that repeat as an overload of afterimages. That makes it seem that the Mies-image is ubiquitous. But actually, and literally, it is rare, like Marcel Duchamp's readymades or Andy Warhol's Brillo Boxes. With Mies there is almost nothing worth copying, but much worth repeating. That is how Mies exemplifies the contrarian claim of the Smithsons that his "coldly ordered facades" offer us the "new, softly smiling face of our discipline."[86] What we might get from what the Smithsons were saying, or almost seeing, fifty years ago is that Mies may be the best and most amazing exemplar of architecture as imaging. The Mies-image may be nothing other, or less, or more, than an extended essay on Wittgenstein's (that other Ludwig) curious puzzle of the "visual room." Mies's relentless and focused pursuit of that puzzle is the brilliant dissemblance of his buildings. Their effect is the Mies-image. That version of *une architecture autre* may be as close as we can get to what Mies does, and how the Mies-image performs: almost nothing, like a building, and almost something, like an image. Another way to understand this might be to suggest that we should follow Wittgenstein's advice to "look and see" how Mies's buildings operate as transactions between imaging and architecture. Mies never stopped making photomontages. In that way, looking back from today, New Brutalism reappears in a new guise as a case study in the emergence of a deeper imaging culture.

Notes

1 Jacques Rancière, "The Future of the Image," in *The Future of the Image* [2003], trans. Gregory Elliott, London and New York: Verso, 2007, p. 22.

2 Vilém Flusser, *Into the Universe of Technical Images* [1985], trans. Nancy Ann Roth, Minneapolis: University of Minnesota Press, 2011, pp. 4, 170, 85.

3 Barbara Maria Stafford, *Good Looking: Essays on the Virtues of Images*, Cambridge, MA: MIT Press, 1996, p. 127.

4 Mark Hansen, "From Fixed to Fluid: Material-Mental Images between Neural Synchronization and Computational Mediation," in *Releasing the Image: from Literature to New Media*, ed. Jacques Khalip and Robert Mitchell, Stanford: Stanford University Press, 2011, p. 104; italics original.

5 For a brief introduction to the complex meanings of the term *Bildwissenschaft* and an account of its emergence as a research approach to the history of art, see Horst Bredekamp, "A Neglected History? Art History as *Bildwissenschaft*," *Critical Inquiry*, 29, no. 3 (Spring 2003), pp. 418–28.

6 Frederick Kiesler's ambitious and preposterous project between 1937 and 1945 at Columbia University to devise a vision machine based on his complex understanding of "photo-graphy" as "design by light" offers a strange case study in the emergence of image culture and was one of the first efforts to explore architecture as a technologically driven imaging practice. By the mid-1930s Kiesler had begun to swerve and stumble toward the edges of a kind of image architecture as a "tectonic" problem of constructing imaging environments that could supersede cinematic or theatrical projections. Inspired by both Surrealism and his friend Marcel Duchamp, Kiesler seems to have understood, and was actively building on, a moment in history when ambitious and adventurous architects, artists, and others, driven by necessity and desire, began to see and act in ways that inserted imaging into architectural practices, such as Mies van der Rohe's photomontages, Robert Mallet Stevens's film sets, or László Moholy-Nagy's uses of scientific or avant-garde photography in *Von Material zu Architektur* (1929). The actual operations of the vision machine combined, among other things, the logic of perspective diagrams and the structure of cathode ray tubes to convey and simulate the human imagination as a complex interplay between optics and imaging. Its central effect, or focal point, was the overlay of two opposing light sources onto a transparent screen: actual reflections from a physical object on one side, and projected images that were intended to simulate those produced in the brain on the other. Conceptually, this overlay constructed imaging as instances of double exposure—between perception and imagination, light rays and memories, or sense-impressions and aftereffects—and subtly, but overtly, asserts montage as the very basis of visual experience. The vision machine attempted to convey a calibrated relationship between object, perceiving eye, projection device, and produced image. It was both a camera-projection-environment imaging machine and a conceptual model, or a schema of imagination with architectural space as its medium. Kiesler's fantastic and failed example of those possibilities was one of the few early attempts to think seriously and originally about the technical means and spatial effects of a kind of "photographic" transdisciplinary aesthetic production. For more on the vision machine see Frederick Kiesler, "The Vision-Machine" and "Brief Description of the Vision Machine," typescripts, n.d., in Vision Machine Box, VM_ Descriptions and Memorandum, Frederick and Lillian Kiesler Private Foundation Archive, Vienna; Stephen Phillips, "Toward a Research Practice: Frederick Kiesler's Design-Correlation Laboratory," *Grey Room* 38 (Winter 2010), pp. 109–13; Frederick Kiesler, "Design Correlation: Certain Data Pertaining to the Genesis of Design by Light (Photo-graphy), Part 1," *Architectural Record* (July 1937), pp. 89–92; and Frederick Kiesler, "Design Correlation: Certain Data Pertaining to the Genesis of Design by Light (Photography), Part 2," *Architectural Record* (August 1937), pp. 79–84; Mark Linder, "Wild Kingdom: Frederick Kiesler's Display of the Avant-Garde," in *Autonomy and Ideology: Positioning an Architectural Avant-Garde in America*, ed. Robert E. Somol, New York: Monticelli Press, 1997.

7 Walter Benjamin writes in section V of "Theses on the Philosophy of History": "The true picture of the past flits by. The past can be seized only as an image which flashes up at the instant when it can be recognized, and is never seen again. [...] For every image of the past that is not recognized by the present as one of its own threatens to disappear irretrievably." Walter Benjamin, *Illuminations: Essays and Reflections*, ed. Hannah Arendt, trans. Harry Zohn, New York: Schocken Books, 1968, p. 255.

8 Benjamin explains: "It's not that what is past casts its light on what is present, or what is present its light on the past; rather, image is that wherein what has been comes together in a flash with the now to form a constellation. In other words, image is dialectics at a standstill. For while the relation of the present to the past is a purely temporal, continuous one, the relation of what-has-been to the now is dialectical: is not progression but image, suddenly emergent.—Only dialectical images are genuine images (that is, not archaic)." Walter Benjamin, *The Arcades Project*, trans. Howard Eiland and Kevin McLaughlin, Cambridge, MA: Harvard University Press, 1999, p. 462 (N2a, 3).

9 Henri Bergson, *Matter and Memory*, trans. Nancy Margaret Paul and W. Scott Palmer, London: George Allen & Unwin, 1911, p. xiv. "Matter is an aggregate of 'images.' And by 'image' we mean a certain existence which is more than that which the idealist calls a *representation*, but less than that which a realist calls a *thing*."

10 The term "cinematographical" appears in Bergson's *Creative Evolution* (1907), and the descriptive image of thinking as something we "reel off" and "wind up" is introduced in *Matter and Memory* (p. xiv).
11 Deleuze introduces the concept of the image of thought in the third chapter of *Difference and Repetition*, originally published in French in 1968. See Gilles Deleuze, *Difference and Repetition*, trans. Paul Patton, New York: Columbia University Press, 1994. Also see Gilles Deleuze, *Cinema 1: The Movement Image* [1983], trans. Hugh Tomlinson and Barbara Habberjam, Minneapolis: University of Minnesota, 1986, and Gilles Deleuze, *Cinema 2: The Time Image* [1985], trans. Hugh Tomlinson and Robert Galeta, Minneapolis: University of Minnesota, 1989. One of the very few attempts to conceptualize architecture as image builds directly on Deleuze. Bernard Cache's *Earth Moves*, Cambridge, MA: MIT Press, 1995, defines architecture as the manipulation of territorializing images (or in Deleuzian terms, a "cinema of things"), including frame, vector, and inflection, which "can become crystal-clear while never entering the realm of the identical" (pp. 16, 29).
12 "The Future of the Image" and "The Surface of Design" were both written in 2002 and are published in Rancière, *The Future of the Image*. "The Pensive Image" was published in *The Emancipated Spectator*, trans. Gregory Elliott, London and New York: Verso, 2009, pp. 107–32.
13 Rancière, "The Surface of Design," p. 91.
14 Ibid., pp. 3, 7.
15 Rancière, "The Future of the Image," pp. 3–5.
16 Ibid., pp. 6–7.
17 Sunil Manghani, "Images: An Imaginary Problem," in *What is an Image?*, ed. James Elkins and Maja Naef, University Park: Penn State University Press, 2011, p. 226.
18 Hansen, "From Fixed to Fluid," p. 104.
19 Ibid., pp. 89, 90.
20 Ibid., pp. 105, 106.
21 Mark Hansen, *New Philosophy for New Media*, Cambridge, MA: MIT Press, 2004, p. 12.
22 Ibid., p. 10.
23 Ibid., p. 11.
24 Critiques of the concept of mental images have been persistent over the past century, other than a revival of interest in philosophy and cognitive psychology in the 1960s and 1970s.
25 Vilém Flusser, "A New Imagination" [1990], in Flusser, *Writings*, ed. Andreas Strohl, trans. Erik Eisel, Minneapolis: University of Minnesota Press, 2002, pp. 110–16.
26 Flusser, *Into the Universe of Technical Images*, pp. 10, 6.
27 Vilém Flusser, "Images in the New Media" [1989], in *Writings*, pp. 73–74.
28 Flusser, *Into the Universe of Technical Images*, p. 4.
29 Antonio Damasio, *Self Comes to Mind: Constructing the Conscious Brain*, New York: Vintage Books, 2010, p. 67.
30 Ibid., p. 71.
31 Anne Massey notes the use of the term "non-Aristotelian" within the Independent Group to indicate their aversion to "teleological" or "essentializing" modes of thought and their interest in alternatives such as logical positivism (A. J. Ayer gave a talk at the second meeting of the IG), existentialism, Dada (the April 29, 1955 session discussed the question, Were the Dadaists non-Aristotelians?), or experimental science. She argues that enthusiasm for D'Arcy Thompson was motivated by his Darwinian "rejection of teleological, universal explanations of the environment." Anne Massey, *The Independent Group: Modernism and Mass Culture in Britian, 1945–59*, Manchester: Manchester University Press, 1995, p. 44.
32 Nigel Henderson speech, sheet 2, Tate Archive, London, 9211.5.1.5. Jenkins was listed as one of the collaborators on *Parallel of Life and Art* on one of the first proposals to the ICA, the press release, and the invitation. See "Memorandum, March 27th, 1953," 9211.5.1.1; "Press Release August 311953," 9211.5.1.2; and invitation, 9211.5.1.3, Tate Archive. Henderson mentions Paolozzi's "work in the field of textiles, wallpaper, etc." as the way the Smithsons had become acquainted with him, leading to his ceiling wallpaper in Jenkins's office in 1952, designed by the Smithsons. Massey, in *The Independent Group*, p. 57, notes that Paolozzi then introduced the Smithsons to Henderson that same year.
33 Henderson speech, sheet 2. On May 11, 1954, the ICA hosted a discussion of Malraux's book *Voices of Silence* (1951), which coincided with an exhibition of Henderson's work, *Photo-Images*, in the members' room.
34 Henderson speech, sheet 6.
35 Martin Harrison, *Transition: The London Art Scene in the Fifties*, London: Merrell, 2002, p. 96.
36 Translation of Le Corbusier's remarks in the Tate Archive, London, 955.1.12.26.
37 J.R.M. Brumwell, ed., *Our Modern World*, London: George Routledge & Sons, 1945.
38 John Russell, *Sunday Times*, July 15, 1951. He continues: "These lofty speculations come curiously and sometimes comically to earth in the darkened halls of Dover Street [and] we leave convinced that we have seen infinity in the Medusa of a jellyfish and eternity in the pelvis of a goat."
39 Richard Hamilton, outline for *Growth and Form* exhibition, December 20, 1949, Tate Archive, London, 9211.6.1.4.
40 Henderson speech, sheets 7–8.
41 Francis Galton, "Visualised Numerals," *Journal of the Anthropological Institute*, 10 (1881), p. 85; Francis Galton, "Visualised Numerals," *Nature*, 21 (January 15, 1880), p. 252.
42 Galton, "Visualised Numerals" (1881), p. 86.
43 Galton, "Visualised Numerals" (1880), p. 253.
44 Galton, "Visualised Numerals" (1881), p. 95.
45 Galton was aware of the problems inherent in "introspective" psychological research: "Although philosophers may have written to show the impossibility of our discovering what goes on in the minds of others, I maintain the opposite opinion. I do not see why the report of a person upon his own

mind would not be as intelligible and trustworthy as that of a traveller upon a new country, whose landscapes and inhabitants are of a different type to any which we ourselves have seen." Galton, "Visualised Numerals" (1880), p. 256.

46 Francis Galton, "Composite Portraits," *Nature*, 18 (May 23, 1878), p. 97.

47 Ibid., pp. 99–100.

48 A related kind of ambivalence appears in the literalisms of Minimalist art, in which the concept is inseparable from the object and the actual is inseparable from the conceptual. "One concise definition of literalism is representation without idealization." See Mark Linder, *Nothing Less than Literal: Architecture after Minimalism*, Cambridge, MA: MIT Press, 2004.

49 Another intriguing expression of these ideas is articulated by J. G. Ballard in *The Atrocity Exhibition* (1970): "Using a series of photographs of the most commonplace objects [...] he treated them as if they already were chronograms and *extracted* the element of time. [...] The results were extraordinary. A very different world was revealed." Ballard, *The Atrocity Exhibition*, London: Fourth Estate, [1970] 2014, p. 6. Galton's experiments also align with the ideas of Gerald Edelman (the theories of "neural Darwinism," "neuronal group selection," and "reentry") or Ray Kurzweil (the "pattern recognition theory of mind"). See Gerald Edelman, "Neural Darwinism: Selection and Reentrant Signaling in Higher Brain Function," *Neuron*, 10 (February 1993), pp. 115–25; Gerald Edelman and Joseph Gally, "Reentry: A Key Mechanism for Integration of Brain Function," *Frontiers in Integrative Neuroscience* (August 27, 2013), doi: 10.3389/fnint.2013.00063; Ray Kurzweil, *How to Create a Mind: The Secret of Human Thought Revealed*, New York: Penguin, 2013.

50 Benjamin famously described distraction as a characteristically modern mode of aesthetic reception that is epitomized by film as well as experienced in the metropolis, but also by architecture even before the advent of modernity. "Architecture has always offered the prototype of an artwork that is received in a state of distraction and through the collective. [...] Under certain circumstances, this form of reception acquires canonical value. For the tasks which face the human apparatus of perception at historical turning points cannot be performed solely by optical means—that is, by way of contemplation. They are mastered gradually—taking their cue from tactile reception—through habit. [...] Reception in distraction—the sort of reception which is increasingly noticeable in all areas of art and is a symptom of profound changes in apperception—finds in film its true training ground. Film, by virtue of its shock effects, is predisposed to this form of reception. In this respect, too, it proves to be the most important subject matter, at present, for the theory of perception which the Greeks called aesthetics." Walter Benjamin, "The Work of Art in the Age of Mechanical Reproducibility, Second Version" [1936], trans. Edmund Jephcott and Harry Zohn, in *The Work of Art in the Age of Mechanical Reproducibility, and Other Writings on Media*, ed. Michael Jennings, Brigid Doherty, and Thomas Levin, Cambridge, MA: Harvard University Press, 2008, pp. 40–41.

51 H. H. Price, "Image Thinking," *Proceedings of the Aristotelian Society*, n.s., 52 (1951–52), pp. 135–66. "Image Thinking" would be published as a chapter titled "The Imagist Theory of Thinking" in his 1953 book *Thinking and Experience*, London: Hutchinson's University Library, 1953.

52 "Symposium: Abstract Ideas and Images," *Proceedings of the Aristotelian Society*, suppl. vol., 27 (1953), pp. 121–58. Untitled papers were presented by E. J. Furlong, C. A. Mace, and D. J. O'Connor.

53 Herbert Read, "Realism and Abstraction in Modern Art," *Eidos*, 1 (May–June 1950), p. 33. An effort to update a more conservative position was promoted by the magazine *Image*, which was launched in 1949 as a successor to *Alphabet and Image*. Focused on drawing and woodcuts as well as "photography and lithography, colour stencil patterns and copper engraving," the magazine aimed "to deal in an interesting and authoritative (yet not too dustily academic) manner with various aspects of the visual arts of our time and of our own rich past" and to address audiences "concerned with the visual arts as normal interests of our daily lives and not as recondite studies for antique pundits armed with microscopes and microfilm." See *Image*, 1 (Summer 1949).

54 Read, "Realism and Abstraction in Modern Art," p. 31.

55 Price lays bare not only his intellectual motives but also his cultural attitudes and political stance, in response to a late review (September 1957) of this book in *The Review of Metaphysics*: "I really am just an old-fashioned British empiricist" and "the 'climate of opinion' in which I was writing [c. 1952], and against which I was reacting" was one that aimed to transform "the empiricist epistemology into a *linguistic* epistemology, a transformation initiated by the Logical Positivists of the 1930s, and completed by Wittgenstein and his disciples" in Cambridge before, during, and after World War Two. H. H. Price, "Comment On: 'Price's Theory of the Concept'," *Review of Metaphysics*, 12, no. 3 (March 1959), pp. 481–85.

56 A counter-example is a recent protest by philosophers of the linguistic tradition against the terminologies of neuroscience: Maxwell Bennet and Peter Hacker, *Philosophical Foundations of Neuroscience*, Oxford: Blackwell Publishing, 2003.

57 Price, "Image Thinking," p. 137.

58 Ibid., p. 140. Price qualifies this broad statement in the later chapters of *Thinking and Experience*.

59 See Gilbert Ryle, *The Concept of Mind*, London: Hutchinson, 1949.

60 Price, "Image Thinking," p. 139.

61 Although Price was certainly unaware of the Swiss zoologist Adolf Portmann's

contemporary writings on animal appearances, it is intriguing to place Portmann's phenomenological theory of animal appearances between Price and Wittgenstein. Portmann argued for an image-based theory of animal behavior and evolution as opposed to a Darwinian functionalism. For Portmann, animal life is fundamentally a matter of external appearances, and he proposed that internal functions sustain external forms, that physiology serves morphology. In other words, life is manifested in acts of "self-display" for others. Images are functional. An organism's vital signs are not numerical indexes—heart rate, temperature, or respiration—but visual images: gestures, colors, shapes, and patterns. Survival is a matter of self-presentation, not self-preservation. According to Portmann: "The surface's display is a part of the self-presentation of a living being [.. .]. We should not depreciate what appears on this surface by thinking of it as a ' front,' an incidental extra which is plastered over a far more genuine and authentic ' inside' Adolf Portmann, "The Living Thing as Pre-arranged Relationship," in *Essays in Philosophical Zoology by Adolf Portmann: The Living Form and the Seeing Eye*, trans. R. Carter, Lewiston, NY: Edward Mellen Press, 1990, p. 25.

62 Price, "Image Thinking," pp. 136, 145.

63 Ludwig Wittgenstein, *Philosophical Investigations*, trans. G.E.M. Anscombe, New York: Macmillan, 1953, §66.

64 Ibid., §300.

65 Ibid. Wittgenstein's German phrase is "die Vorstellung des Schmerzes" and is translated in the new version of *Philosophical Investigations* as "pain in the imagination" or "imagined pain." Ludwig Wittgenstein, *Philosophical Investigations*, trans. G.E.M. Anscombe, P.M.S. Hacker, and Joachim Schulte, London: Blackwell, 2009.

66 Wittgenstein, *Philosophical Investigations*, §401.

67 Ibid., §367.

68 Ibid., §398–400. Wittgenstein's German phrase is "visuelle Zimmer."

69 Ibid., §400–401.

70 Ibid., §398.

71 Banham, "The New Brutalism," *Architectural Review*, 118, no. 708 (December 1955), p. 356.

72 Price, "Comment On: 'Price's Theory of the Concept,'" p. 481.

73 Ibid., p. 482.

74 Nigel Henderson, "Notes Written in Response to Peter Karpinski," in *The Independent Group: Postwar Britain and the Aesthetics of Plenty*, ed. David Robbins, Cambridge, MA: MIT Press, 1990, p. 21.

75 Reyner Banham, "A Black Box: The Secret Profession of Architecture," *New Statesman and Society* (October 1990), pp. 23–24.

76 Ibid., p. 25.

77 Ibid.

78 Mario Carpo, *The Second Digital Turn: Design beyond Intelligence*, Cambridge, MA: MIT Press, 2017, p. 99.

79 Ibid., p. 101.

80 Ibid., p. 124.

81 Ibid., p. 99.

82 See Mark Linder, "Literal Digital," in *Architecture In Formation: On the Nature of Information in Digital Architecture*, ed. Pablo Lorenzo-Eiroa and Aaron Sprecher, London: Routledge, 2013, pp. 69–71.

83 Carpo, *The Second Digital Turn*, p. 129.

84 A wonderful example of point cloud modeling as imaging is the project "Melting Landscapes" led by Christophe Girot at the landscape modeling and visualization lab of the ETH Zurich, which uses lasers, lidar, drones, and microphones to generate point cloud models of shrinking glaciers and their sounds in the Alps. While Girot often describes these point cloud models as incredibly accurate modes of visualization, they are also time-based media that enable qualitative visualization of both the appearance and disappearance of a vast landscape. See Christophe Girot, "Landscape Topology: Digital Landscape Design and Analysis Based on Pointcloud Modelling Technology," https://girot.arch.ethz.ch/research/digital-landscape-design-and-analysis. "Melting Landscapes" can be understood as an advance upon an equally amazing precedent: Viollet-le-Duc's project to understand both the geology and processes of glacial erosion of Mont Blanc. See Eugène Emmanuel Viollet-le-Duc, *Le Massif du Mont Blanc: Étude sur sa constitution géodésique et géologique sur ses transformationss et sur l'état ancien et moderne de ses glaciers*, Paris: Librairie Polytechnique, 1876.

85 Alison and Peter Smithson, "But Today We Collect Ads," *Ark*, 18 (November 1956), n.p.

86 Alison and Peter Smithson, "Mies van der Rohe," *Architectural Design*, 39, no. 7 (July 1969), pp. 363–66.

Acknowledgments

This book is the result of a too-long process fraught with misdirection, meandering, and interregnums. Along the way other projects spun out of it and many more were drawn into it, especially those of others whose ideas, questions, and talents nourished, provoked, and inspired me. Yet however twisted and delayed that path was, its origin is perfectly clear. My intrigue with New Brutalism and Mies emerged out of a lecture I was invited to give in 2006 at the Illinois Institute of Technology as part of the celebration of the reopening of the renovated Crown Hall. While doing the research for that talk, I became fascinated by the disagreements between Reyner Banham and Charles Jencks in the 1960s about the interrelated significance and legacy of New Brutalism, Mies, and the Smithsons. In divergent ways, and for reasons that ran deep in their competing polemics about modern architecture, both men judged all three harshly. It was only a few years later, when I started reading and teaching imaging theory, that the specificities and logics of their differences began to fall away and I began to appreciate, and find value in, the Smithsons' peculiar, persistent, and productive affection for Mies. Along the way, I developed my own for New Brutalism.

I am thankful to many people who helped push this book along by providing speaking opportunities and encouragement along the way, beginning with Donna Robertson's invitation to the IIT. Others followed that were equally important: the project was advanced and improved by invitations to present and discuss the work in progress by Jon Yoder at Kent State, Bob Somol and Walter Benn Michaels at UIC, Eugene Han at Yale, Aaron Sprecher at McGill, Jonathan Louie at Texas A&M, Elizabeth Miller at UCSD, and Andrew Colopy at Rice. Although a trip to speak in Australia was a casualty of the Covid pandemic, my work was buoyed by invitations from John Macarthur in Brisbane, Don Bates and Julie Willis in Melbourne, and Francesca Hughes in Sydney. My greatest thanks go to Mark Robbins and Nancy Cantor at Syracuse for the honor of serving as Chancellor's Fellow in the Humanities for three years, which allowed me to dive into my interest in imaging, and to be educated by the scholars I was able to invite to speak in the "Images? Precisely!" series, including, Barbara Maria Stafford, James Elkins, Brigid Doherty, Mark Hansen, Tom Gunning, Sunil Manghani, and Aud Sissel Hoel.

The project would never have been completed without the work of many research assistants—Greg Hauck, Ashley Nowicki, Erick Sanchez, Nusrat Mim, Priyal Chheda, Alexandra Grisanti, Andrea Hinajosa—or the invitations to publish early versions of the material in this book from Mehrdad Hadigi, Tsz Yan Ng, Aaron Sprecher, Wouter Davidts, Penelope Dean, Alexander Eisenschmidt, and Mathew Bohne. I also was consistently inspired by the adventurous projects and curiosity of my students in the School of Architecture and my humanities seminars. At the top of that list are Robin Janik, Anna Acklin, Daina Swagerty, Stefan Zoller, Ian Herrmann, A.J. Hauck, Brian Scheib, Muwen Li, and Kristabel Chung.

Many colleagues, often without even knowing it, made crucial contributions and suggestions. Chief among them are Britt Eversole, Jonathan Louie, Nicole McIntosh, Kyle Miller, Emily Pellicano, McLain Clutter, Jesus Vasallo, David Ruy, Catherine Ingraham, Michael Hays, Claire Zimmermann, David Turturo, Daniele Profeta, Andrew Holder, and

Joe Day. None of this would have been possible without the Syracuse University School of Architecture's consistent financial support and the selfless efforts of Barbara Opar and her staff at the Architecture Reading Room. I am in debt to Simon and Soraya Smithson who located and made available materials from the Smithson Family Collection. Julie Cirelli and Sophie Kullmann were wonderful collaborators at Park Books, Aimee Selby was a generous and tireless editor, and I am thrilled with the book design by Mattias Jakobsson of Konst & Teknik. Thanks also to Jonathan Sergison and Ian Cartlidge for arranging a visit to Upper Lawn and to the guys at HIONFI for keeping the volume down when I was working at the firehouse.

More than anyone or anything, I needed the love, understanding, and encouragement of my family. My late parents will never hold this book in their hands but the wish that they could kept me going. Azriel and Lili kept me grounded, committed, and hopeful. Finally, above all, Julia's unending patience, enthusiasm, and optimism were amazing, especially when I was running out of all three.

Select Bibliography

Key books and articles only. Information on other sources can be found in the end-notes.

"The Baroque—Photographed Well and Photographed Badly," *Architectural Review*, 94 (July 1943), p. 25

"Drawings for the Library and Administration Building, Illinois Institute, Designed by Mies van der Rohe," *Architects' Journal*, 103 (January 3, 1946), pp. 11–15

"Ludwig Mies van der Rohe: An Address of Appreciation by H. T. Cadbury-Brown to the Guest of Honor, Professor Mies van der Rohe. Illustrated by Slides of his Work," *Architectural Association Journal*, 75, no. 834 (1959), pp. 26–46

"Metals and Minerals Research Building, Illinois Institute of Technology, Designed by Mies Van Der Rohe," *Architects' Journal*, 103 (January 3, 1946), pp. 7–10

"[Photographs of SS *Mexico* and Aztec Ornament]," *Architectural Review*, 95 (January 1944), p. 33

"School at Hunstanton Norfolk," *Architectural Review*, 116 (September 1954), pp. 149–62

"Secondary School at Hunstanton," *Architects' Journal*, 118 (September 10, 1953), pp. 323–28

"The Telekinema Building," *The Builder* (July 6, 1951), pp. 11–13

Ábalos Ramos, Ana, "Alison and Peter Smithson: The Transient and the Permanent," dissertation, Universitat Politècnica de València, 2015

Aldrich, Virgil C., "Images as Things and Things as Imaged," *Mind*, 64 (April 1955), pp. 261–63

Allen, Brian, ed., *Towards a Modern Art World*, New Haven: Yale University Press, 1995

Alloway, Lawrence, "Eduardo Paolozzi," *Architectural Design*, 26, no. 4 (April 1956), p. 133

Alloway, Lawrence, "The Arts and Mass Media," *Architectural Design*, 28, no. 2 (February 1958), pp. 84–85

Alloway, Lawrence, "The Long Front of Culture," *Cambridge Opinion*, 17 (1959), pp. 25–26

Astragal, "Banham's Last Blast?," *Architects' Journal*, 164 (July 14, 1976), p. 89

Astragal, "The Rally at Art Net: Banham Boosts the Brits," *Architects' Journal*, 164 (July 14, 1976), p. 92

Baker, Jeremy, ed., *Arena: The Architectural Association Journal*, 81, no. 899, special issue: *A Smithson File*, pp. 177–218

Banham, Reyner, "Exhibitions [*Growth and Form*]," *Architectural Review*, 110 (October 1951), pp. 273–74

Banham, Reyner, "Howard Robertson," *Architectural Review*, 114 (September 1953), pp. 161–68

Banham, Reyner, "Photography: *Parallel of Life and Art*," *Architectural Review*, 114 (October 1953), pp. 259–61

Banham, Reyner, "Klee's 'Pedagogical Sketchbook'," *Encounter* (April 1954), pp. 53–58

Banham, Reyner, "Object Lesson," *Architectural Review*, 115 (June 1954), pp. 403–6

Banham, Reyner, "The Machine Aesthetic," *Architectural* Review, 117 (April 1955), pp. 224–28

Banham, Reyner, "Vehicles of Desire," *Art* (September 1, 1955), p. 3

Banham, Reyner, "The New Brutalism," *Architectural Review*, 118 (December 1955), pp. 355–61

Banham, Reyner, "Not Quite Architecture: Not Quite Painting or Sculpture Either," *Architects' Journal*, 124 (August 16, 1956), pp. 61, 218–19

Banham, Reyner, "This Is Tomorrow," *Architectural Review*, 120 (September 1956), pp. 186–88

Banham, Reyner, "Machine Aesthetes," *New Statesman* (August 16, 1958), pp. 192–93

Banham, Reyner, *Theory and Design in the First Machine Age*, London: Architectural Press, 1960

Banham, Reyner, "The History of the Immediate Future," *Journal of the Royal Institute of British Architects*, 68 (May 1961), pp. 252–57

Banham, Reyner, "Apropos the Smithsons," *New Statesman* (September 8, 1961), pp. 317–18

Banham, Reyner, *Guide to Modern Architecture*, London: Architectural Press, 1962

Banham, Reyner, "On Trial 6: Mies van der Rohe, Almost Nothing Is Too Much," *Architectural Review*, 132 (August 1962), pp. 125–28

Banham, Reyner, "Who Is This Pop?" *Motif*, 10 (1962–63), pp. 3–13

Banham, Reyner, "Crowther's Acropolis," *New Statesman* (January 15, 1965), pp. 83–84

Banham, Reyner, *The New Brutalism: Ethic or Aesthetic?*, London: Architectural Press, 1966

Banham, Reyner, "Revenge of the Picturesque: English Architectural Polemics, 1945–1965," in *Concerning Architecture: Essays on Architectural Writers and Writing Presented to Nikolaus Pevsner*, ed. J. Summerson, London: Penguin Press, 1968, pp. 265–73

Banham, Reyner, *Age of the Masters: A Personal View of Modern Architecture*, New York: Harper & Row (Icon Editions), 1975

Banham, Reyner, "Pevsner's Progress," *Times Literary Supplement* (February 17, 1978), pp. 191–92

Banham, Reyner, *A Concrete Atlantis: US Industrial Building and European Architecture, 1900–1925*, Cambridge, MA: MIT Press, 1986

Banham, Reyner, "A Black Box: The Secret Profession of Architecture," *New Statesman and Society* (October 12, 1990), pp. 22–25

Barthes, Roland, *The Neutral: Lecture Course at the Collège de France (1977–1978)* [2002], trans. Rosalind Krauss and Denis Hollier, New York: Columbia University Press, 2005

Benjamin, Walter, "Little History of Photography [1931]," in *The Work of Art in the Age of Its Mechanical Reproducibility, and Other Writings on Media*, ed. Michael W. Jennings, Brigid Doherty, and Thomas Y. Levin, trans. Edmund Jephcott, Rodney Livingstone, and Howard Eiland, Cambridge, MA: Harvard University Press, 2008, pp. 274–98

Berger, John, "For the Future," *New Statesman and Nation* (January 19, 1952), pp. 64, 66

Select Bibliography

Berger, John, "The Unknown Political Prisoner," *New Statesman and Nation* (March 21, 1953), pp. 337–38

Bergson, Henri, *Matter and Memory* [1896], trans. Nancy M. Paul and W. Scott Palmer, London: George Allen & Unwin, 1911

Borutti, Silvana, "Aesthetic Family Resemblances between Wittgenstein and Paolozzi," in *Paolozzi and Wittgenstein: The Artist and the Philosopher*, ed. Diego Mantoan and Luigi Perissinotto, London: Palgrave, 2019, pp. 15–29

Boyd, Robin, "The Sad End of New Brutalism," *Architectural Review*, 142 (July 1967), pp. 9–11

Boyer, M. Christine, *Not Quite Architecture: Writing around Alison and Peter Smithson*, Cambridge, MA: MIT Press, 2017

Brumwell, J.R.M. *This Changing World*, London: Readers Union; George Routledge & Sons, 1945

Bullivant, Dargan, "Hunstanton Secondary Modern School," *Architectural Design*, 23 (September 1953), pp. 238–48

Bullock, Nicholas, *Building the Post-war World: Modern Architecture and Reconstruction in Britain*, London: Routledge, 2002

Burbridge, David, "Galton's 100: An Exploration of Francis Galton's Imagery Studies," *British Journal for the History of Science*, 27 (1994), pp. 443–63

Casson, Hugh, "The Aesthetics of Camouflage," *Architectural Review*, 96 (September 1944), pp. 63–68

Collins, Peter, "The New Brutalism of the 1920s," in *Concrete: The Vision of a New Architecture*, 2nd edn, Montreal: McGill-Queen's University Press, 1975, pp. 315–40

Colomina, Beatriz, "Eames' Images," *Daidalos*, 66 (December 1997), pp. 40–53

Colomina, Beatriz, "Couplings," *OASE*, 51 (1999), pp. 20–33

Colomina, Beatriz, "Friends of the Future: A Conversation with Peter Smithson," *October*, 94 (Fall 2000), pp. 3–30

Conekin, Becky, *'The Autobiography of a Nation': The 1951 Festival of Britain*, Manchester: Manchester University Press, 2003

Cooke, Lynne, "The Independent Group: British and American Pop art, a 'Palimpcestuous' Legacy," in *Modern Art and Popular Culture: Readings in High and Low*, ed. Adam Gopnik and Kirk Varnedoe, exh. cat., New York: Museum of Modern Art and Harry N. Abrams, 1990, pp. 192–216

Corbett, David, *The Modernity of English Art, 1914–1930*, Manchester: Manchester University Press, 1997

Crinson, Mark, and Claire Zimmerman, ed., *Neo-Avant-Garde and Postmodern: Postwar Architecture in Britain and Beyond*, New Haven: Yale Center for British Art, 2010

Crosby, Theo, "The New Brutalism," *Architectural Design*, 25 (January 1955), p. 1

Crosby, Theo, "This Is Tomorrow," *Architectural Design*, 26 (September 1956), pp. 302–4

Crosby, Theo, ed., *This Is Tomorrow*, exh. cat., London: Whitechapel Art Gallery, 1956

Crosby, Theo, *Uppercase*, 3, London: Whitefriars Press, 1960

Curley, John J., *A Conspiracy of Images: Andy Warhol, Gerhard Richter, and the Art of the Cold War*, New Haven: Yale University Press, 2013

Damasio, Antonio, *Self Comes to Mind: Constructing the Conscious Brain*, New York: Vintage Books, 2010

Darling, Elizabeth, *Re-Forming Britain Narrative of Modernity before Reconstruction*, New York: Routledge, 2007

Daston, Lorraine, and Peter Galison, "The Image of Objectivity," *Representations*, 40 (Autumn 1992), pp. 81–128

de Maré, Eric, "Et Tu, Brute?," *Architectural Review*, 119 (August 1956), p. 72

Didi-Huberman, Georges, *Atlas: How to Carry the World on One's Back?*, exh. cat., Madrid: Museo Nacional Centro de Arte Reina Sofía, 2010

Dodds, George, *Building Desire: On the Barcelona Pavilion*, London: Routledge, 2005

Dover, Harriet, *Home Front Furniture: British Utility Design, 1941–1951*, Aldershot: Scolar Press, 1991

Ehrenzweig, Anton, "Unconscious Form Creation in Art," *British Journal of Medical Psychology*, 21 (1948), pp. 185–214

Ehrenzweig, Anton, "Unconscious Mental Imagery in Art and Science," *Nature*, 21 (June 16, 1962), pp. 1008–12

Ehrenzweig, Anton, *The Hidden Order of Art: A Study in the Psychology of Artistic Imagination*, Berkeley: University of California Press, 1967

Eisenman, Peter, "From Golden Lane to Robin Hood Gardens; or, If You Follow the Yellow Brick Road, It May Not Lead to Golders Green," *Oppositions*, 1 (1973), pp. 27–56

Farnham, Jonathan E., "Pure Pop for New People: Reyner Banham, Science Fiction and History," *Lotus International*, 104 (2000), pp. 112–31

Flusser, Vilém, *Into the Universe of Technical Images* [1985], trans. Nancy Ann Roth, Minneapolis: University of Minnesota Press, 2011

Flusser, Vilém, *Writings*, ed. Andreas Strohl, trans. Erik Eisel, University of Minnesota Press, 2002

Foster, Hal, "Savage Minds (A Note on Brutalist Bricolage)," *October*, 136 (Spring 2011), pp. 182–91

Fry, Maxwell, "Twenty-Five Years of Modern Architecture in England," *Architectural Design*, 25 (November 1955), pp. 338–41

Furlong, E. J., C.A. Mace, and D. J. O'Connor, "Symposium: Abstract Ideas and Images," *Proceedings of the Aristotelian Society, Supplementary Volumes*, 27 (1953), pp. 121–58

Galton, Francis, "Composite Portraits," *Nature* (May 23, 1878), pp. 97–100

Galton, Francis, "Visualised Numerals," *Nature* (January 15, 1880), pp. 252–56

Galton, Francis, "Visualised Numerals," *Journal of the Anthropological Institute* (March 9, 1880), pp. 85–102

Galton, Francis, "Thought without Words," *Nature* (May 12, 1887), pp. 28–29

Games, Stephen, ed., *Pevsner: The Complete Broadcast Talks, Architecture and Art on Radio and Television, 1945–1977*, Burlington, VT: Ashgate, 2014

Garlake, Margaret, "The Constructions of Peter Lanyon," in *Peter Lanyon: Air, Land and Sea,* exh. cat., London: South Bank Centre, 1992, pp. 49–61

Goldhagen, Sarah, "Freedom's Domiciles: Three Projects by Alison and Peter Smithson," in *Anxious Modernisms: Experimentation in Postwar Architectural Culture*, ed. Sarah Williams Goldhagen and Réjean Legault, Cambridge, MA: MIT Press, 2000, pp. 74–95

Grigson, Geoffrey, "The Aesthetic of Lichens," *Architectural Review*, 101 (March 1947), pp. 79–82

Günay, Baykan, "Interview with Alison and Peter Smithson," *Middle East Technical University Journal of the Faculty of Architecture*, 9 (1989), pp. 67–104

Hamilton, Richard, "Persuading Image," *Design*, 134 (February 1960), pp. 28–32

Hansen, Mark, "From Fixed to Fluid: Material-Mental Images between Neural Synchronization and Computational Mediation," in *Releasing the Image: From Literature to New Media*, ed. Jacques Khalip and Robert Mitchell, Stanford: Stanford University Press, 2011, pp. 83–11

Harrison, Charles, *English Art and Modernism, 1900–1939*, Bloomington, IN: Indiana University Press, 1981

Harrison, Martin, *Transition: The London Art Scene in the Fifties*, London: Merrell, 2002

Hastings, Hubert de Cronin [I. de Wolfe], "Townscape," *Architectural Review*, 106 (December 1949), pp. 354–74

Hatherley, Owen, *Militant Modernism*, Winchester: Zero Books, 2008

Henderson, Nigel, Manuscript [Speech at the opening of *Parallel of Art and Life*], Tate Archives, 9211.5.1.5, 8pp.

Heron, Patrick, "Space in Painting and Architecture," in *Architects' Year Book 5*, ed. Trevor Dannatt, London: Elek Books, 1953, pp. 19–26

Hewison, Robert, *In Anger: British Culture in the Cold War, 1945–60*, Oxford: Oxford University Press, 1981

Hewison, Robert, *Culture and Consensus: England, Art and Politics since 1940*, London: Methuen, 1995

Higgott, Andrew, "Memorability as Image: The New Brutalism and Photography," in *Mediating Modernism: Architectural Cultures in Britain*, London: Routledge, 2007, pp. 283–94

Higgott, Andrew, "Visual Sensibility and the Search for Form: The *Architectural Review* in Postwar Britain," in *Modernism and the Professional Architecture Journal: Reporting, Editing, and Reconstructing in Postwar Europe*, ed. Torsten Schmiedeknecht and Andrew Peckham, Routledge, 2019, pp. 93–111

Highmore, Ben, "Mass-Observation: A Science of Everyday Life," in *Everyday Life and Cultural Theory*, London: Routledge, 2002, pp. 75–112

Highmore, Ben, "Rough Poetry: *Patio and Pavilion* Revisited," *Oxford Art Journal*, 29 (2006), pp. 269–90

Highmore, Ben, "Hopscotch Modernism: On Everyday Life and the Blurring of Art and Social Science," *Modernist Cultures*, 2 (May 2006), pp. 70–79

Highmore, Ben, "'Image-Breaking, God-Making': Paolozzi's Brutalism," *October*, 136 (Spring 2011), pp. 87–104

Highmore, Ben, "Brutalist Wallpaper and the Independent Group," *Journal of Visual Culture*, 12 (2013), pp. 205–21

Highmore, Ben, *The Art of Brutalism: Rescuing Hope from Catastrophe in 1950s Britain*, New Haven: Yale University Press, 2017

Hitchcock, Henry-Russell, "The Place of Painting and Sculpture in Relation to Modern Architecture," in *Architects' Year Book 2*, ed. Jane B. Drew, London: Paul Elek, 1947, pp. 12–23

Holt, Robert, "Imagery: The Return of the Ostracized," *American Psychologist*, 19 (April 1964), pp. 254–64

Hopkins, Harry, *The New Look: A Social History of the Forties and Fifties*, London: Secker & Warburg, 1964

Jackson, Anthony, *The Politics of Architecture*, Toronto: University of Toronto Press, 1970

Jackson, Lesley, *The New Look: Design in the Fifties*, London: Thames & Hudson, 1991

Janik, Robin, "Wittgenstein, Banham, and the Literal Image," unpublished manuscript, 2009

Janik, Robin, "Images of Pure Space and Chalk Dust," unpublished manuscript, 2011

Jencks, Charles, *Modern Movements in Architecture*, New York: Anchor Books, 1973

Jennings, Humphrey, *Pandaemonium, 1660–1886: The Coming of the Machine as Seen by Contemporary Observers*, ed. Mary-Lou Jennings and Charles Madge, New York: The Free Press, 1985

Johnson, Philip, *Mies van der Rohe*, New York: Museum of Modern Art, 1947

Johnson, Philip, "Comment by Philip Johnson as an American Follower of Mies van der Rohe," *Architectural Review*, 116 (September 1954), pp. 148, 152

Jones, Barbara, *The Unsophisticated Arts*, London: Architectural Press, 1951

Kaniari, Assimina, "Brutalist Image as Humanist Form: Reyner Banham, Erwin Panofsky and the Turn to Spatio-Temporal Structures in 1950s Histories of (Modern) Art," *Punctum*, 2 (2016), pp. 60–68

Kepes, Gyorgy, *Language of Vision*, Chicago: Paul Theobald, 1944

Kitnick, Alex, "The Brutalism of Life and Art," *October*, 136 (Spring 2011), pp. 63–86

Linder, Mark, "Wild Kingdom: Fredrick Kiesler's Display of the Avant-Garde," in *Autonomy and Ideology: Positioning an Avant-Garde in America*, ed. Robert Somol, New York: Monacelli Press, 1997, pp. 122–53, 337–43

Linder, Mark, "Transdisciplinarity," *Hunch*, 9 (2005), pp. 12–15

Linder, Mark, "Images and Other Stuff," *Journal of Architectural Education*, 66 (October 2012), pp. 3–8

Linder, Mark, "Literal Digital," in *Architecture In Formation: On the Nature of Information in Digital Architecture*, ed. Pablo Lorenzo-Eiroa and Aaron Sprecher, New York: Routledge, 2013, pp. 69–71

Macarthur, John, "Townscape, Anti-Scrape and Surrealism: Paul Nash and John Piper in *Architectural Review*," *Journal of Architecture*, 14 (2009), pp. 387–406

Select Bibliography

Macarthur, John, "'The Revenge of the Picturesque,' *Redux*," *Journal of Architecture*, 17 (2012), pp. 643–53

Macarthur, John, and Aitchison, Matthew, "Oxford versus the Bath Road: Empiricism and Romanticism in *The Architectural Review*'s Picturesque Revival," *Journal of Architecture*, 17 (2012), pp. 51–68

Madge, Charles, "A Note on Images," in *Humphrey Jennings: Film-maker, Painter, Poet*, ed. Mary-Lou Jennings, London: British Film Institute, 1982, pp. 78–82

Manghani, Sunil, *Image Studies: Theory and Practice*, London: Routledge, 2013

Massey, Anne, *The Independent Group: Modernism and Mass Culture in Britain, 1945–59*, Manchester: Manchester University Press, 1995

Massey, Anne, "The Mother of Pop? Dorothy Morland and the Independent Group," *Journal of Visual Culture*, 12 (2013), pp. 262–78

Massey, Anne, and Gregor Muir, ed., *Institute of Contemporary Arts, 1946–1968*, London: Institute of Contemporary Arts, 2014

Massey Anne, and Penny Sparke, "The Myth of the Independent Group," *Block*, 10 (1985), pp. 48–56

May, John, *Signal. Image. Architecture*, New York: Columbia Books on Architecture and the City, 2019

McLuhan, Herbert Marshall, *The Mechanical Bride: Folklore of Industrial Man*, New York: Vanguard Press, 1951

Mertins, Detlef, ed., *Presence of Mies*, New York: Princeton Architectural Press, 1994

Middleton, Robin, "The New Brutalism; or, A Clean, Well-Lighted Place," *Architectural Design*, 37 (January 1967), pp. 7–8

Moffat, Isabelle, "'A Horror of Abstract Thought': Postwar Britain and Hamilton's 1951 *Growth and Form* Exhibition," *October*, 94 (Autumn 2000), pp. 89–112

Moholy-Nagy, László, *The New Vision and Abstract of an Artist* [1928], New York: George Wittenborn, 1947

Moholy-Nagy, László, *Vision in Motion*, Chicago: Paul Theobald, 1947

Orwell, George, *The Lion and the Unicorn: Socialism and the English Genius*, London: Martin Secker and Warburg, 1941

Paolozzi, Eduardo, *The Metallization of a Dream*, London: Lion and Unicorn Press, 1963

Parnell, Steve, "*AR*'s and *AD*'s Post-war Editorial Policies: The Making of Modern Architecture in Britain," *Journal of Architecture*, 17 (2012), pp. 763–75

Pearson, Brook, "Ontology in Collage: Paolozzi's Wittgenstein and Film," *Rivista di esthetica*, 46 (January 2011), pp. 103–21

Penrose, Roland, *The Wonder and Horror of the Human Head*, London: Lund Humphries, 1953

Pevsner, Nikolaus, *Pioneers of the Modern Movement: From William Morris to Walter Gropius*, London: Faber & Faber, 1936

Pevsner, Nikolaus, "1860–1930," *Architectural Record* (March 1937), pp. 1–6

Pevsner, Nikolaus, *Pioneers of Modern Design: From William Morris to Walter Gropius*, New York: Museum of Modern Art, 1949

Pevsner, Nikolaus, "C20 Picturesque: An Answer to Basil Taylor's Broadcast," *Architectural Review*, 115 (April 1954), pp. 237–39

Pevsner, Nikolaus, *The Englishness of English Art*, London: Peregrine Books, 1956

Pevsner, Nikolaus, *The Sources of Modern Architecture and Design*, London: Thames & Hudson, 1968

Potts, Alex, "Realism, Brutalism, Pop," *Art History*, 35 (April 2012), pp. 288–313

Potts, Alex, "Paolozzi's Pop New Brutalist World," *Tate Papers*, 21 (April 3, 2014), www.tate.org.uk/research/tate-papers/21

Potts, Alex, "The Image Valued 'As Found' and the Reconfiguring of Mimesis in Post-war Art," *Art History*, 37 (September 2014), pp. 784–805

Price, H. H., "Symposium on Thinking and Language," *Proceedings of the Aristotelian Society*, 51 (1950–51), pp. 329–38

Price, H. H., *Thinking and Experience*, Cambridge, MA: Harvard University Press, 1953

Price, H. H., "Comment On: 'Price's Theory of the Concept,'" *Review of Metaphysics*, 12 (March 1959), p. 481

Pulham, Peter Rose, "The Camera and the Artist," *The Listener* (January 24, 1952), pp. 144–46

Rancière, Jacques, *The Politics of Aesthetics*, trans. Gabriel Rockhill, London and New York: Continuum, 2000

Rancière, Jacques, *The Future of the Image*, trans. Gregory Elliott, London and New York: Verso, 2007

Rancière, Jacques, *Aisthesis: Scenes from the Aesthetic Regime of Art* [2011], trans. Zakir Paul, London and New York: Verso, 2013

Rancière, Jacques, "Art of the Possible" [2007], in *Dissenting Words: Interviews with Jacques Rancière, 1976–2015*, ed. and trans. Emiliano Battista, New York: Bloomsbury, 2017

Read, Herbert, "Realism and Abstraction in Modern Art," *Eidos*, 1 (May–June 1950)

Read, Herbert, "Farewell to Formalism," *Art News*, 51 (June–August 1952), p. 36

Richards, J. M., *The Castles on the Ground*, London: Architectural Press, 1946

Richards, J. M., "The Pioneer Health Centre: The Idea Behind the Idea," *Architectural Review*, 77 (May 1935), pp. 207–16

Risselada, Max, ed., *Alison and Peter Smithson: A Critical Anthology*, Barcelona: Edicones Poliigrada, 2011

Robbins, David, ed., *The Independent Group: Postwar Britain and the Aesthetics of Plenty*, Cambridge, MA: MIT Press, 1991

Rosso, Michela, "Between History, Criticism, and Wit: Texts and Images of English Modern Architecture (1933–36)," *Journal of Art Historiography*, 14 (June 2016), pp. 1–22

Ryle, Gilbert, *The Concept of Mind*, London: Hutchinson, 1949

Schonfield, Katherine, "Glossing with Graininess: Cross Occupations in Postwar British Film and Architecture," *Journal of Architecture*, 3 (Winter 1998), pp. 355–75

Sisson, Edward O., "Things, Images, Ideas," *Journal of Philosophy*, 45 (July 15, 1948), pp. 405–11

Sissons, Michael, and French, Philip, ed., *Age of Austerity, 1945–51*, Harmondsworth: Penguin, 1964

Smithson, Alison, "And Now Dhamas Are Dying Out in Japan," *Architectural Design*, 36 (September 1966), pp. 447–48
Smithson, Alison, *AS in DS: An Eye on the Road*, Delft: Delft University Press, 1983
Smithson, Alison, and Peter Smithson, "House in Soho, London," *Architectural Design*, 23 (December 1953), p. 342
Smithson, Alison, and Peter Smithson, "The New Brutalism," *Architectural Review*, 115 (April 1954), pp. 274–75
Smithson, Alison, and Peter Smithson, "But Today We Collect Ads," *Ark*, 18 (November 1956), n.p.
Smithson, Alison, and Peter Smithson, "The Aesthetics of Change," in *Architects' Year Book 8*, ed. Trevor Dannatt, London: Elek Books, 1957, pp. 14–22
Smithson, Alison, and Peter Smithson, "The New Brutalism: Alison and Peter Smithson Answer the Criticisms on the Opposite Page [to 'Thoughts in Progress: The New Brutalism']," *Architectural Design*, 27 (April 1957), p. 113
Smithson, Alison, Peter Smithson, Jane B. Drew, and Maxwell Fry, "Conversation on Brutalism," *Zodiac*, 4 (1959), pp. 73–81
Smithson, Alison, and Peter Smithson, "The Heroic Period of Modern Architecture, 1917–1937," *Architectural Design*, 35 (December 1965), pp. 587–641
Smithson, Alison, and Peter Smithson, "Banham's Bumper Book on Brutalism, Discussed by Alison and Peter Smithson," *Architects' Journal*, 144 (December 28, 1966), pp. 1590–91
Smithson, Alison, and Peter Smithson, "Mies van der Rohe," *Architectural Design*, 39 (July 1969), pp. 363–66
Smithson, Alison, and Peter Smithson, *Ordinariness and Light: Urban Theories, 1952–1960, and Their Application in a Building Project, 1963–1970*, Cambridge, MA: MIT Press, 1970
Smithson, Alison, and Peter Smithson, *Without Rhetoric: An Architectural Aesthetic, 1955–1972*, Cambridge, MA: MIT Press, 1974
Smithson, Alison, and Peter Smithson, *The Shift*, Architectural Monographs 7, London: Academy Editions, 1982
Smithson, Alison, and Peter Smithson, "The Nature of Retreat," *Places*, 7 (1991), pp. 8–23
Smithson, Alison, and Peter Smithson, *Changing the Art of Inhabitation: Mies' Pieces, Eames' Dreams, The Smithsons*, London: Artemis, 1994
Smithson, Alison, and Peter Smithson, *The Charged Void: Architecture*, New York: Monacelli Press, 2001
Smithson, Alison, and Peter Smithson, "'Patio and Pavilion' Reconstructed," *AA Files*, 47 (Summer 2002), pp. 37–44
Smithson, Peter, "Letter to America," *Architectural Design*, 28 (March 1958), pp. 93–102
Smithson, Peter, "The Rocket," *Architectural Design*, 35 (July 1965), pp. 322–23
Smithson, Peter, "[On Mies van der Rohe]," *Bauen + Wohnen*, 20: *Ludwig Mies van der Rohe 80 Jahre* (May 1966), p. 206
Smithson, Peter, "Concealment and Display: Meditations on Braun," *Architectural Design* (July 1966), pp. 362–63
Smithson, Peter, "Just a Few Chairs and a House: An Essay on the Eames-Aesthetic," *Architectural Design*, 36 (September 1966), pp. 443–46
Smithson, Peter, "The Slow Growth of Another Sensibility: Architecture as Townbuilding," in *A Continuing Experiment: Learning and Teaching at the Architectural Association*, ed. James Gowan, London: Architectural Press, 1975, pp. 55–63
Smithson, Peter, "Three Generations," *ILA&UD: Annual Report, Urbino 1980* (1980), pp. 88–95
Smithson, Peter, "The Masque and the Exhibition: Stages Toward the Real," *ILA&UD: Language of Architecture* (1981), pp. 62–67
Smithson, Peter, "Reflections on Hunstanton," *ARQ*, 2 (Summer 1997), pp. 32–43
Smithson, Peter, "The Lattice Idea," *ILA&UD: Annual Report 1999* (2000), pp. 58–61
Smithson, Peter, "Foreword," in *Nigel Henderson: Parallel of Life and Art*, ed. Victoria Walsh, London: Thames & Hudson, 2001
Sontag, Susan, "The Image-World," in *On Photography*, New York: Farrar, Straus & Giroux, 1977, pp. 153–80
Spencer, Catherine, "The Independent Group's 'Anthropology of Ourselves,'" *Art History*, 35 (April 2012), pp. 314–35
Sperling, Joshua, *A Writer of Our Time: The Life and Work of John Berger*, London and New York: Verso, 2018
Stafford, Barbara Maria, "Crystal and Smoke: Putting Image Back in Mind," in *A Field Guide to a New Meta-Field: Bridging the Humanities-Neuroscience Divide*, ed. B. M. Stafford Chicago: University of Chicago Press, 2011, pp. 1–63
Stalder, Laurent, "'New Brutalism,' 'Topology' and 'Image': Some Remarks on the Architectural Debates in England around 1950," *Journal of Architecture*, 13 (2008), pp. 263–81
Steiner, Hadas, "Brutalism Exposed: Photography and the Zoom Wave," *Journal of Architectural Education*, 59 (2006), pp. 15–27
Steiner, Hadas, "Life at the Threshold," *October*, 136 (Spring 2011), pp. 133–55
Steyn, Juliet, "Realism versus Realism in British Art of the 1950s," *Third Text*, 22 (March 2008), pp. 145–56
Stonard, John-Paul, "The 'Bunk' Collages of Eduardo Paolozzi," *The Burlington Magazine*, 150, no. 1261 (April 2008), pp. 238–49
Stonard, John-Paul, "Eduardo Paolozzi's *Psychological Atlas*," *October*, 136 (Spring 2011), pp. 51–62
Summerson, John, "Bread & Butter and Architecture," *Horizon*, 6 (October 1940), pp. 233–43
Summerson, John, "The Case for a Theory of Modern Architecture," *RIBA Journal* (June 1957), pp. 307–13
Sylvester, A.D.B., "Architecture in Modern Painting," *Architectural Review*, 109 (February 1951), pp. 80–89
Sylvester, David, "Curriculum Vitae," in *About Modern Art: Critical Essays, 1948–1997*, New York: Henry Holt, 1997, pp. 13–17

Thomas, Mark Hartland, "Mies van der Rohe," *Architectural Design*, 23 (December 1953), pp. 331–39

Trevelyan, Julian, "The Technique of Camouflage," *Architectural Review*, 96 (September 1944), pp. 68–70

Van den Heuvel, Dirk, "Between Brutalists: The Banham Hypothesis and the Smithson Way of Life," *Journal of Architecture*, 20 (2015), pp. 293–308

Van den Heuvel, Dirk, and Max Risselada, ed., *Alison and Peter Smithson: From the House of the Future to a House of Today*, Rotterdam: 010 Publishers, 2004

Vassallo, Jesús, *Epics in the Everyday: Photography, Architecture, and the Problem of Realism*, Zurich: Park Books, 2019

Venturi, Robert, "Photographs from the American Academy in Rome, 1954–56," *AA Files*, 56 (2007), pp. 56–63

Vidler, Anthony, *Histories of the Immediate Present: Inventing Architectural Modernism*, Cambridge, MA: MIT Press, 2008

Vidler, Anthony, "Another Brick in the Wall," *October*, 136 (Spring 2011), pp. 105–32

Vidler, Anthony, "Troubles in Theory V: The Brutalist Moment(s)," *Architectural Review*, 235 (February 2014), pp. 96–101

Voelker, John, "Letter to the Editor," *Architectural Design*, 27 (June 1957), pp. 184

Walsh, Victoria, *Nigel Henderson: Parallel of Life and Art*, London: Thames & Hudson, 2002

Walsh, Victoria, "Reordering and Redistributing the Visual: The Expanded 'Field' of Pattern-Making in *Parallel of Life and Art* and Hammer Prints," *Journal of Visual Culture*, 12 (2013), pp. 222–44

Walsh, Victoria, and Claire Zimmerman, "New Brutalist Image, 1949–55: 'Atlas to a New World' or, 'Trying to Look at Things Today,'" *British Art Studies*, 4 (Autumn 2016), https://doi.org/10.17658/issn.2058-5462/issue-04/vwalsh-czimmerman

Wells, M. J., "The Practice of History: the Smithsons, Colin St. John Wilson, and the Writing of Architectural History," *Journal of Art Historiography*, 14 (June 2016), pp. 1–9

Whiteley, Nigel, "Banham and 'Otherness,'" *Architectural History*, 33 (1990), pp. 188–221

Whyte, Lancelot Law, ed., *Aspects of Form: A Symposium on Form in Nature and Art*, London: Lund Humphries, 1951

Wigley, Mark, "Editor's Notes: Alison and Peter Smithson's Quest for the Void," *Bookforum* (Summer 2003), pp. 8–12

Williamson, Beth, "Paolozzi, Anton Ehrenzweig and Art Education in Post-war London," in *Eduardo Paolozzi*, ed. Daniel F. Herrmann, exh. cat., London: Whitechapel Gallery, 2017, pp. 43–48

Wittgenstein, Ludwig, *Philosophical Investigations*, trans. G.E.M. Anscombe, 3rd edn, New York: Macmillan, 1953

Zimmerman, Claire, "Mies in Photos," *MoMA*, 4.5 (June 2001), pp. 2–5

Zimmerman, Claire, "From Legible Form to Memorable Image: Architectural Knowledge from Rudolf Wittkower to Reyner Banham," *Candide: Journal for Architectural Knowledge*, 5 (February 2012), pp. 93–108

Zimmerman, Claire, "Photography into Building in Post-war Architecture: The Smithsons and James Stirling," *Art History*, 35 (April 2012), pp. 270–87

Zimmerman, Claire, *Photographic Architecture in the Twentieth Century*, Minneapolis: University of Minnesota Press, 2014

Image Credits

© 2025 Artists Rights Society (ARS), New York: 162, 165
© 2025 Artists Rights Society (ARS), New York /VG Bild-Kunst, Bonn: 94, 125, 294
© Nigel Henderson Estate: 195, 299
© Nigel Henderson Estate/Tate. Photo: Tate: 10, 18, 20, 24, 27, 33, 34, 53, 54, 55, 56, 57, 59, 61, 63, 64, 66, 67, 72, 82, 85, 89, 90, 92, 95, 96, 98, 99, 100, 103, 106, 107, 110, 114, 116, 118, 139, 173, 190, 197, 198, 199, 201, 202, 203, 204, 207, 259, 264, 267, 268, 277, 278, 285, 287, 289, 290
© Nigel Henderson Estate/Tate © Westinghouse Electric Corporation & © reserved. Photo: Tate: 5, 108, 112
© Nigel Henderson Estate/The Eduardo Paolozzi Foundation. Photo: Tate: 111
© R. Hamilton. All Rights Reserved, DACS and ARS 2025: 230
© R. Hamilton. All Rights Reserved, DACS and ARS 2025. Photo: Tate: 240
© Smithson Family Collection: 4, 16, 17, 21, 28, 35, 36, 41, 44, 45, 46, 52, 68, 69, 73, 74, 75, 79, 81, 83, 88, 102, 113, 117, 119, 135, 140, 142, 143, 144, 145, 146, 147, 148, 149, 151, 153, 154, 168, 170, 171, 172, 178, 209, 210, 212, 213, 215, 218, 219, 220, 225, 226, 228, 229, 231, 233, 235, 236, 237, 238, 243, 244, 245, 246, 249, 251, 252, 253, 254, 255, 257, 258, 260, 261, 262, 265, 269, 271, 273, 274, 276, 279, 280, 301
© Tate. Photo: Tate: 180
© The Estate of Eduardo Paolozzi, 2018. All Rights Reserved DACS © Nigel Henderson Estate/Tate. Photo: Tate: 108
© The Estate of Nigel Henderson/Tate & © reserved. Photo: Tate: 70, 105, 115, 234
© The Paolozzi Foundation, Licensed by DACS/ ARS 2025: 58, 62, 65, 150, 196, 206, 296
© The Paolozzi Foundation, Licensed by DACS/ ARS 2025. Photo: Tate: 101
© Walker Evans Archive, The Metropolitan Museum of Art: 185, 205
© Walker Evans Archive, The Metropolitan Museum of Art Photo: RISD Museum: 192
Architectural Press Archive/RIBA Collections: 43, 49, 71
Canadian Centre for Architecture: 300
Chicago History Museum, HB-07327-A, Hedrich-Blessing Collection: 51
Chicago History Museum, HB-07327-G, Hedrich-Blessing Collection: 15
Chicago History Museum, HB-07890-C1, Hedrich-Blessing Collection: 124
City Archives Krefeld: 130, 134, 227, 292
Courtesy of the Architectural Association: 13, 76, 77, 87, 242, 270, 272, 273, 275, 304, 305
Courtesy Shelley Power Literary Agency Ltd.: 7, 8, 14
John Maltby/RIBA Collections: 22, 26, 97
Photograph Peter Smithson © Smithson Family Collection: 6, 9, 12, 31, 284, 308
Scottish National Gallery of Modern Art: 288

Imprint

Concept: Mark Linder
Copy editing: Aimee Selby
Proofreading: Linda Schofield
Design: Konst & Teknik
Image processing: Dexter Pre-Media, London
Printing and binding: Printer Trento, Italy

Park Books AG
Niederdorfstrasse 54
8001 Zurich
Switzerland
www.park-books.com
+41 44 262 16 62
info@park-books.com

Product Safety:
Responsible person according to
EU regulation 2023/988 (GPSR):
GVA Gemeinsame Verlagsauslieferung
Göttingen GmbH & Co. KG
P.O. Box 2021
37010 Göttingen, Germany
+49 551 384 200 0
info@gva-verlage.de

Park Books is being supported by the Federal Office of Culture with a general subsidy for the years 2021–2025.

ISBN 978-3-03860-401-3

Index of Arrays

30 87 255 88 10
15 94 11 307 104 176
81 25 273 77 234 55

Front Endpaper

82 145 85 242 301
306 28 299 264 215
2 146 271 16 4 84

Back Endpaper

1 2 3 4 5
6 7 8 9
10 11 12 13

0.1

14 15 16
17 18 19 20 21
22 23 24 25

0.2

26 27 28 29
30 31 32 33 34
35 36 37 38

0.3

40 42 43
44 45 46 47
48 30 50 51 52

1.1

53 54 55 41
56 57 58 59 60
61 62 63 64 65

1.2

5 66 67 68
69 70 71 72
73 74

1.3

75 76 77
78 79 80

1.4

81 82 83 84
85 86 87 88 89
90 91 92 93

1.5

10 94 95
96 97 98 99 100
101 102 103

1.6

72 105 106 107
108 6 109
110 111 73

1.7

112 27 113
114 115 116 11 117
12 118 55 119 66

1.8

120 121
122 123

2.1

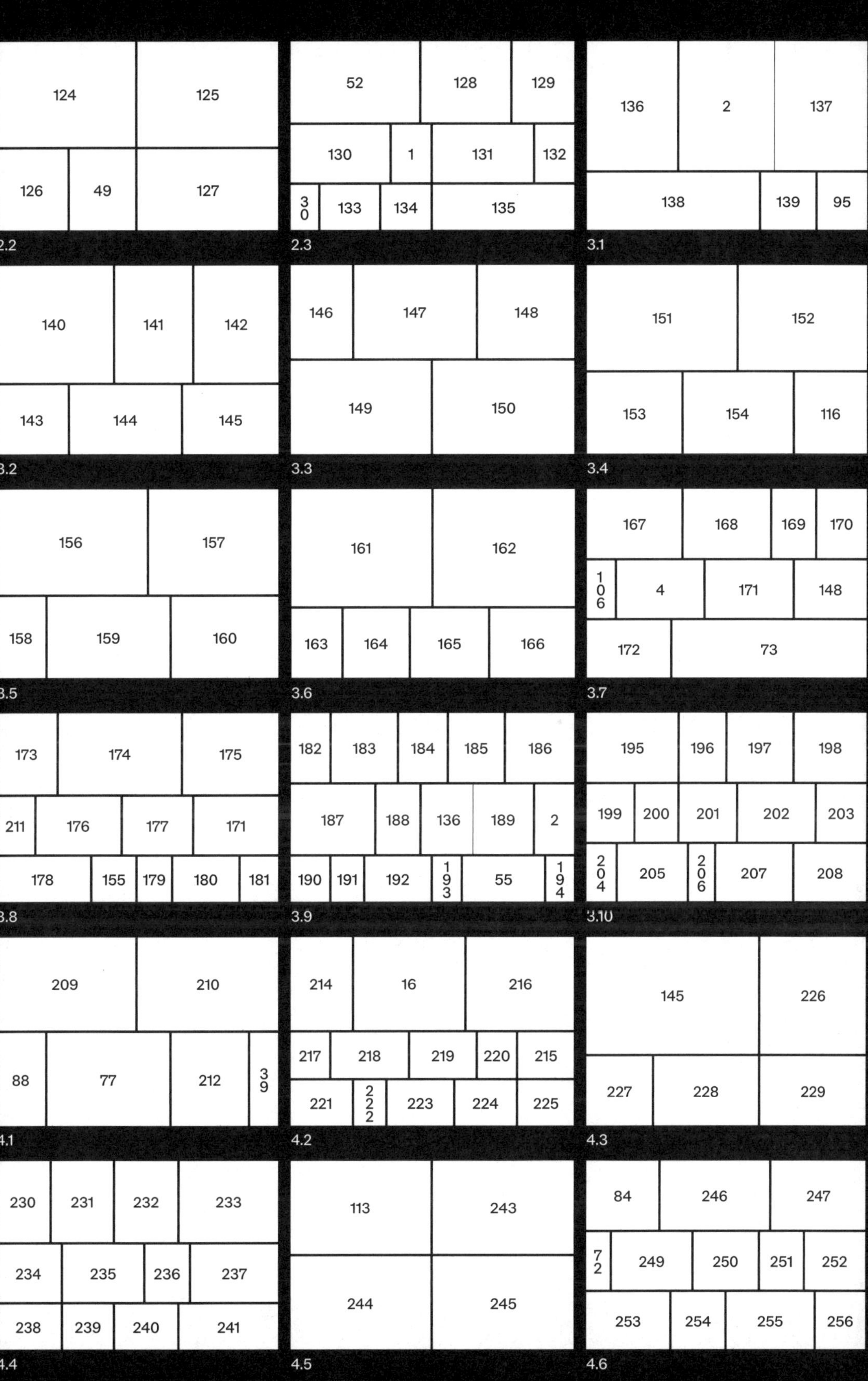

124 125
126 49 127
2.2
52 128 129
130 1 131 132
30 133 134 135
2.3
136 2 137
138 139 95
3.1
140 141 142
143 144 145
3.2
146 147 148
149 150
3.3
151 152
153 154 116
3.4
156 157
158 159 160
3.5
161 162
163 164 165 166
3.6
167 168 169 170
106 4 171 148
172 73
3.7
173 174 175
211 176 177 171
178 155 179 180 181
3.8
182 183 184 185 186
187 188 136 189 2
190 191 192 193 55 194
3.9
195 196 197 198
199 200 201 202 203
204 205 206 207 208
3.10
209 210
88 77 212 39
4.1
214 16 216
217 218 219 220 215
221 222 223 224 225
4.2
145 226
227 228 229
4.3
230 231 232 233
234 235 236 237
238 239 240 241
4.4
113 243
244 245
4.5
84 246 247
72 249 250 251 252
253 254 255 256
4.6

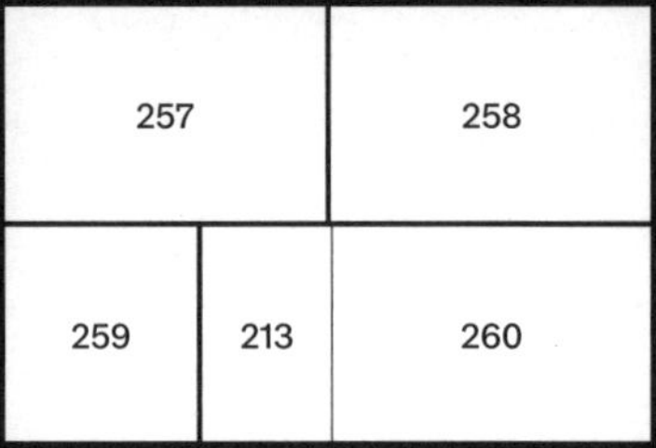

257 258
259 213 260

4.7

261 262 263
264 257 29 113
265 266 267 268

4.8

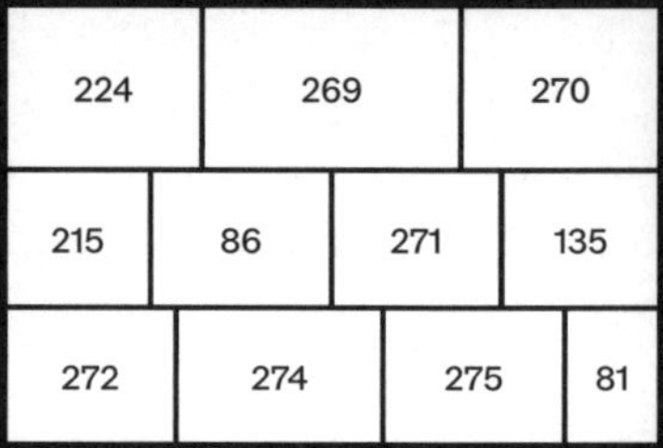

224 269 270
215 86 271 135
272 274 275 81

4.9

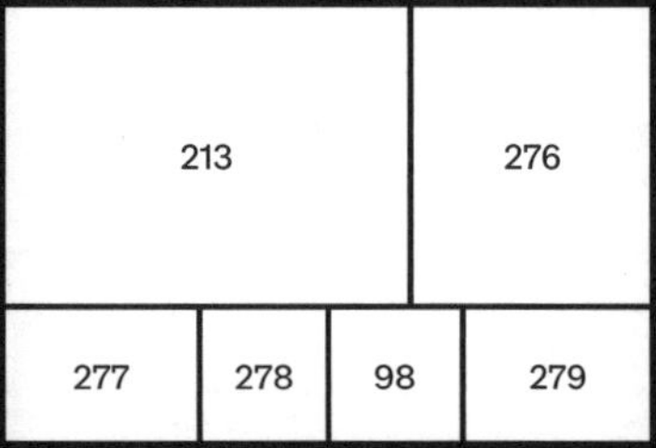

213 276
277 278 98 279

4.10

280 281 282
216 283 284

4.11

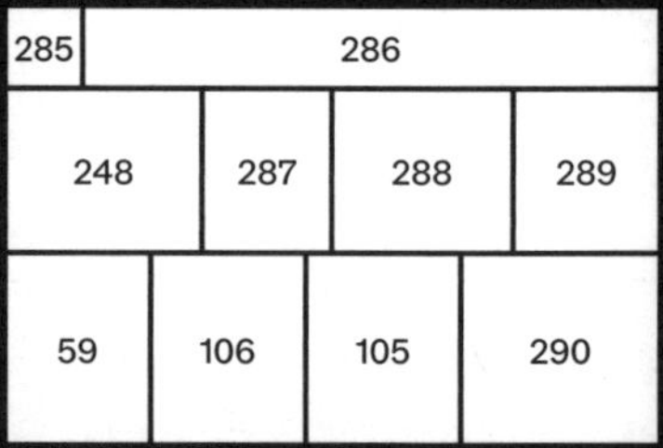

285 286
248 287 288 289
59 106 105 290

4.12

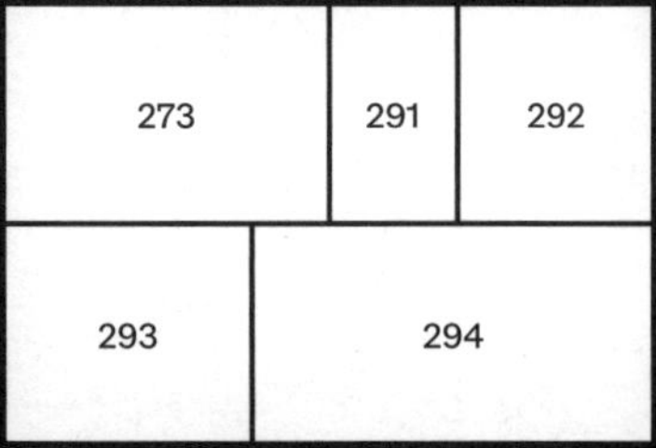

273 291 292
293 294

4.13

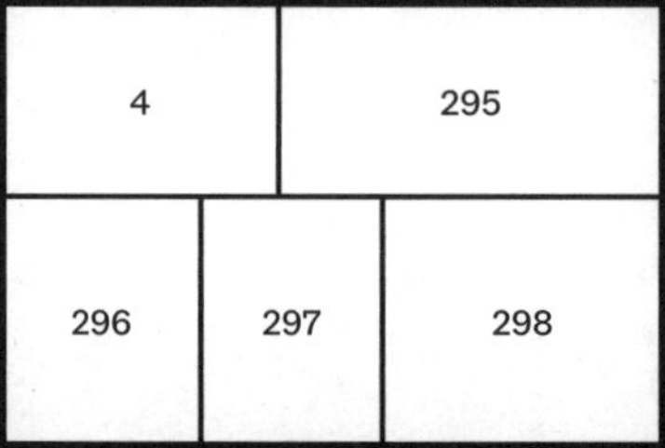

4 295
296 297 298

6.1

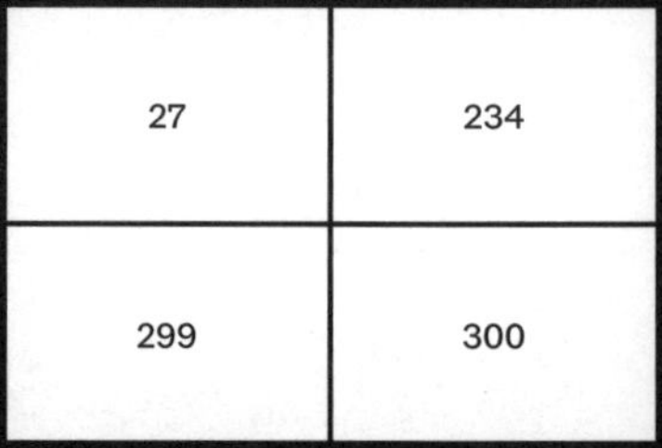

27 234
299 300

6.2

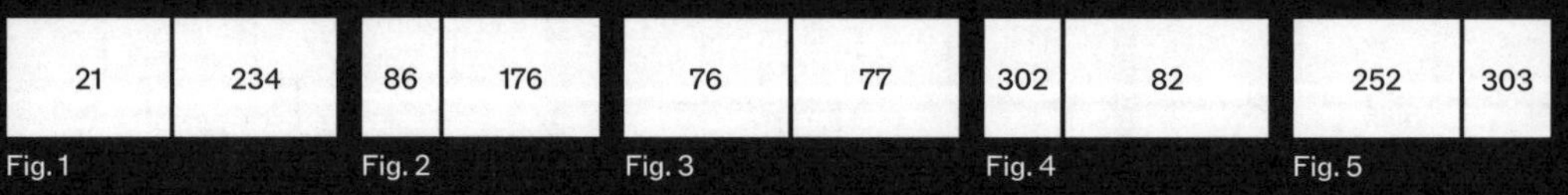

Fig. 1 Fig. 2 Fig. 3 Fig. 4 Fig. 5

Captions

1 *AJ*, January 1946, p. 7
2 *AR*, December 1955, p. 359
3 *AR*, September 1956, p. 187
4 *UP*
5 *PLA*, Nigel Henderson photograph, 1953
6 Photomontage, Golden Lane Competition, Peter Smithson, 1952
7 Reyner Banham, *A Concrete Atlantis*, MIT Press, 1986, p. 5
8 Reyner Banham, *A Concrete Atlantis*, MIT Press, 1986, pp. 250–51
9 Verseidag Silk Factory, Krefeld. Mies van der Rohe, Peter Smithson photograph, 1955
10 *PP*, Nigel Henderson photograph, 1956
11 *PLA*, Nigel Henderson photograph, 1953
12 Alison Smithson in Jenkins Room, London. Peter Smithson photograph, 1952
13 Reyner Banham lecture at Artnet, London 1976. Video still
14 Abandoned oil tanks and concrete structure, Monterey, California. Reyner Banham photograph, c. 1982
15 Interior, Minerals and Metals Building, Mies van der Rohe, Illinois Institute of Technology, Chicago. Kenneth Hedrich photograph
16 Three Generations image, Alison and Peter Smithson and Lorenzo Wong, 1980
17 Hunstanton School under construction. Nigel Henderson photograph, 1953
18 Construction site, London. Nigel Henderson photograph, c. 1949–56
19 Hunstanton School, servery and washup, in *AR*, September 1954, p. 161
20 Hunstanton School under construction. Nigel Henderson photograph, 1953
21 Hunstanton School under construction. Nigel Henderson photograph, 1953
22 Hunstanton School. John Maltby photograph, 1954
23 Science Room, Hunstanton School. John Maltby photograph, 1954
24 Hunstanton School under construction. Nigel Henderson photograph, c. 1952
25 Science Room, Hunstanton School. John Maltby photograph, 1954
26 Washroom sinks, Hunstanton School. John Maltby photograph, 1954
27 Jenkins Room, London. Nigel Henderson photograph, 1952
28 Limerston Street watercloset. Peter Smithson photograph, 1956
29 *AJ*, January 1946, p. 10
30 *TS*, pp. 10–11. Photographed "as if a corner."
31 Tissue-paper "confetti" for Christmas cards, Alison and Peter Smithson, c. 1957
32 *ILAUD Yearbook*, 1980, p. 95
33 Interior, Henderson House at 46 Chisenhale Road. Nigel Henderson photograph, c. 1952
34 Interior, Hunstanton School. Nigel Henderson photograph, c. 1953
35 *WR*, pp. 44–45
36 Alison Smithson, Tram Rats collage, 1975
37 Poster for *PLA*, 1953
38 *ILAUD Yearbook*, 1978, pp. 78–79
39 Garden Building, St. Hilda's College, Oxford. Michael Carapetian photograph, 1970
40 *AJ*, January 1946, pp. 8–9
41 Locker Room, Hunstanton School. Nigel Henderson photograph
42 Philip Johnson, *Mies van der Rohe*, Museum of Modern Art, 1947, pp. 148–49
43 Interior, Hunstanton School. John Maltby photograph, 1954
44 Interior during construction, Hunstanton School. Nigel Henderson photograph, c. 1953
45 Perspective, Hunstanton School, Peter Smithson, 1950
46 Section, Fitzwilliam Museum Project, Peter Smithson, 1949
47 Hunstanton School. Mark Linder photograph, 2013
48 Gymnasium interior, Hunstanton School. Mark Linder photograph, 2013
49 Flats, Albert Drive Estate, Wimbledon, London, 1956. John Pantlin photograph
50 *AJ*, January 1946, p. 11
51 Interior, Minerals and Metals Building, Mies van der Rohe, Illinois Institute of Technology, Chicago. Kenneth Hedrich photograph
52 Perspective collage, Fitzwilliam Museum Project, Peter Smithson, 1949
53 Hunstanton School under construction. Nigel Henderson photograph, 1953
54 Wall painter. Nigel Henderson photograph, c. 1949–56
55 Jenkins Room, London. Nigel Henderson photograph, 1952
56 Eduardo Paolozzi with object. Nigel Henderson photograph, c. 1949–56
57 Nigel Henderson with printed papers. Nigel Henderson photograph, c. 1952
58 Eduardo Paolozzi, *North Dakota's Lone Skyscraper; Will Alien Powers Invade the Earth?*, 1950
59 *Growth and Form* exhibition, Institute of Contemporary Arts, London. Nigel Henderson photograph, 1951
60 *AJ*, June 5, 1952, p. 690
61 Hunstanton School under construction. Nigel Henderson photograph, 1953
62 Eduardo Paolozzi, *Refreshing and Delicious* (plate 12 from *Bunk!*), 1972, lithograph of 1952 collage
63 Football players at Stoke-on-Trent potteries. Nigel Henderson photograph, c. 1950
64 Contact sheet. Nigel Henderson photograph, c. 1952
65 Eduardo Paolozzi, collage, 1952
66 Jenkins Room, London. Nigel Henderson photograph, 1952
67 Interior, Hunstanton School. Nigel Henderson photograph, c. 1953
68 Photomontage of yard-garden, Golden Lane Competition, Alison Smithson, 1952
69 Street deck perspective, Golden Lane Housing, Peter Smithson, 1952
70 *PLA*, Nigel Henderson photograph, 1953
71 Hunstanton School under construction. D. Firth photograph, 1954
72 Hunstanton School under construction. Nigel Henderson photograph, 1953
73 *Urban Re-identification Grid* (CIAM Grille), Alison and Peter Smithson, 1953
74 Elevation, Sheffield University Competition, Alison and Peter Smithson, 1953
75 *CA*, pp. 8–9
76 *Architectural Association Journal*, 1959, p. 44 (with Peter Smithson photographs)
77 *Architectural Association Journal*, 1959, p. 45 (with Peter Smithson photographs)
78 *AD*, February 1958, pp. 92–93

79 *OL*, p. 138
80 *AD*, February 1958, pp. 94–95
81 *CA*, p. 64
82 Hunstanton School under construction. Nigel Henderson photograph, 1953
83 *Patio and Pavilion* reconstructed, Alison and Peter Smithson. Peter Smithson photograph, 1990
84 Garden Building, St. Hilda's College, Oxford. Michael Carapetian photograph, 1970
85 Interior, Hunstanton School. Nigel Henderson photograph, c. 1953
86 *AJ*, September 1953, p. 323
87 *A Line of Trees . . . A Steel Structure* exhibition, video still from gallery talk, 1975
88 Hunstanton School. Nigel Henderson photograph, 1953
89 Nigel Henderson photograph, c. 1949–54
90 Nigel Henderson photograph, c. 1949–54
91 Hunstanton School. John Maltby photograph, 1954
92 *PP*, Nigel Henderson photograph, 1956
93 Hunstanton School. Mark Linder photograph, 2013
94 Perspective, German Pavilion, International Exposition, Barcelona, Spain, Ludwig Mies van der Rohe, c. 1928–29
95 Hunstanton School under construction. Nigel Henderson photograph, 1953
96 Nigel Henderson photograph, c. 1949–54
97 *PP*, John Maltby photograph, 1956
98 Hunstanton School under construction. Nigel Henderson photograph, c. 1952
99 Nigel Henderson photograph, c. 1949–54
100 *PP*, Nigel Henderson photograph, 1956
101 Eduardo Paolozzi, *Collage Mural*, 1952
102 Perspective collage, Fitzwilliam Museum Project, Peter Smithson, 1949
103 Hunstanton School under construction. Nigel Henderson photograph, c. 1953
104 Soho House, Alison and Peter Smithson, in *AD*, December 1953, p. 342
105 *PLA*, Nigel Henderson photograph, 1953
106 Nigel Henderson photograph, c. 1949–54
107 Nigel Henderson photograph, c. 1949–56
108 Nigel Henderson and Eduardo Paolozzi, *Untitled (Study for Parallel of Life and Art)*, 1952
109 Nigel Henderson photograph, c. 1951
110 Panel 108, *PLA*, "Plaster Blocks, Eduardo Paolozzi, 1952," Nigel Henderson photograph
111 Study for *PLA*, Nigel Henderson and Eduardo Paolozzi, 1952
112 *PLA*, Nigel Henderson photograph, 1953
113 *TS*, pp. 12–13
114 Nigel Henderson, Page from scrapbook, c. 1952
115 *PLA*, Nigel Henderson photograph, 1953
116 Nigel Henderson photograph, c. 1949–56
117 Section/Elevation, Golden Lane Competition, Peter Smithson drawing, 1952
118 Interior, Henderson House at 46 Chisenhale Road. Nigel Henderson photograph, c. 1952
119 Perspective, Proposed layout for *PLA*, Peter Smithson, 1952
120 *AR*, July 1943, pp. 24–25
121 *AR*, September 1944, pp. 62–63
122 *AR*, January 1944, pp. 32–33
123 *AR*, March 1947, pp. 80–81
124 Interior, Minerals and Metals Building, Mies van der Rohe, Illinois Institute of Technology, Chicago
125 Interior perspective, Convention Hall Project, Chicago, Ludwig Mies van der Rohe, 1954
126 22–26 Ovington Square, Walter Segal, London. Mark Linder photograph, 2012
127 Interior perspective, Coventry Cathedral Competition, Colin St. John Wilson and Peter Carter, 1951
128 Gymnasium, Hunstanton School. Mark Linder photograph, 2010
129 Verseidag Silk Factory, Krefeld, Mies van der Rohe. Mark Linder photograph, 2023
130 Verseidag Silk Factory, Krefeld, Mies van der Rohe, 1935
131 Verseidag Silk Factory, Krefeld, Mies van der Rohe. Mark Linder photograph, 2023
132 Hunstanton School under construction. Photograph in *AD* September 1953, p. 244
133 Verseidag Silk Factory, Krefeld, Mies van der Rohe. Mark Linder photograph, 2023
134 Verseidag Silk Factory, Krefeld, Mies van der Rohe, 1935
135 Photocollage, Fitzwilliam Museum Project, Peter Smithson, 1949
136 Cover, *Astounding Science Fiction*, July 1954
137 *AR*, December 1955, pp. 359–60
138 Footnote, *AR*, December 1955, p. 361
139 Interior, Henderson House at 46 Chisenhale Road. Nigel Henderson photograph, c. 1952
140 *HP*, pp. 56–57
141 *AD*, October 1958, p. 388
142 *OL*, p. 181
143 HP, pp. 6–7
144 *WR*, pp. 2–3
145 *OL*, pp. 152–53
146 *OL*, p. 10
147 *OL*, pp. 148–49
148 *UP*
149 *OL*, pp. 86–87
150 Eduardo Paolozzi, *Marine Composition*, 1950
151 *OL*, pp. 158–59
152 Eames House, photograph in *Architects Yearbook*, June 1957, p. 22
153 *Architects Yearbook*, June 1957, pp. 18–19
154 *OL*, pp. 84–85
155 Hunstanton School. Mark Linder photograph, 2013
156 Lazlo Moholy-Nagy, *Vision in Motion*, Paul Theobald, 1947, pp. 46–47
157 Sigfried Giedion, *Mechanization Takes Command*, Oxford University Press, 1948, pp. 576–77
158 André Malraux, *Les Voix du Silence*, Editions Gallimard, 1951, p. 13
159 Paul Klee, *Pedagogical Sketchbook*, translation by Sibyl Moholy-Nagy, Praeger, 1953, pp. 20–21
160 Marshall McLuhan, *The Mechanical Bride*, Vanguard Press, 1951, pp. 12–13
161 Lancelot Law Whyte (ed.), *Aspects of Form*, Lund Humphries, 1951, pp. 88–89
162 Humphrey Jennings, *Listen to Britain*, 1942, film still

243 *TS*, pp. 36–37
244 *TS*, pp. 38–39
245 *TS*, pp. 76–77
246 Occupational Health Unit at Park Royal Hospital, London. Peter Smithson photograph
247 Hunstanton School. John Maltby photograph. 1954
248 Panel detail, *Wonder and Horror of the Human Head* exhibition, Institute of Contemporary Arts, London, 1953
249 *TS*, pp. 20–21
250 Economist Building. Henk Snoek photograph, 1964
251 *TS*, pp. 28–29
252 *TS*, pp. 80–81
253 *CV*, pp. 314–15
254 Sugden House, 1956
255 *CV*, pp. 52–53
256 Economist Building. Mark Linder photograph, 2013
257 *TS*, pp. 10–11
258 *TS*, pp. 34–35
259 Nigel Henderson photograph, c. 1949–56
260 *TS*, pp. 56–57
261 *WR*, pp. 32–33
262 *CA*, pp. 72–73
263 *AD*, July 1965, p. 322
264 Nigel Henderson photograph, c. 1949–56
265 *UP*, spread showing last two of six progressive enlargements of a Nigel Henderson photograph
266 *AD*, July 1966, pp. 362–63
267 Hammer Prints Limited, Ceramics. Nigel Henderson photograph, c. 1954–61
268 Nigel Henderson photograph, c. 1949–56
269 *CV*, pp. 386–87
270 *A Line of Trees . . . A Steel Structure* exhibition, video still from gallery talk, 1975
271 Nigel Henderson photograph, c. 1953
272 *A Line of Trees . . . A Steel Structure* exhibition, video still from gallery talk, 1975
273 Verseidag Silk Factory, Krefeld, Mies van der Rohe, 1935. Peter Smithson photograph, 1955
274 Image of structure for "A Line of Trees... A Steel Structure," Lorenzo Wong, 1975
275 *A Line of Trees . . . A Steel Structure* exhibition, video still from gallery talk, 1975
276 *WR*, pp. 26–27
277 Nigel Henderson photograph, c. 1949–56
278 Nigel Henderson photograph, c. 1949–56
279 Alison Smithson, *Cluster City (Random Aesthetic) Diagram*, 1953
280 *OL*, pp. 44–45
281 *ILAUD Yearbook*, 1981, p. 62
282 *ILAUD Yearbook*, 1980, p. 93
283 TECTA Cantilever Chair Museum, Lauenförde, Peter Smithson, 2001–8
284 Amenity Building, University of Bath, Alison and Peter Smithson. Peter Smithson photograph, 1985
285 Panel 10, *PLA*, "Female Bulb Scale Mite," Nigel Henderson photograph, 1953
286 Catalog, *PLA*, 1953
287 Nigel Henderson, Page from scrapbook, c. 1952
288 *Wonder and Horror of the Human Head* exhibition, installation photo, Institute of Contemporary Arts, London, 1953
289 Nigel Henderson photograph, c. 1949–56
290 Nigel Henderson photograph, c. 1949–56
291 Door detail, Lange House, Krefeld, Mies van der Rohe. Mark Linder photograph, 2023
292 Verseidag Silk Factory, Krefeld, Mies van der Rohe, 1935
293 Detail, Hunstanton School. Mark Linder photograph, 2013
294 Perspective, Ludwig Mies van der Rohe. Concrete Office Building Project, Berlin, Germany, 1923
295 "Number Forms," plate XXIV from Karl Pearson, *The Life, Letter and Labours of Francis Galton*, Volume 2, Cambridge University Press, 1924
296 "Composite Photographs of a Family," plate XXXI from Karl Pearson, *The Life, Letter and Labours of Francis Galton*, Volume 2, Cambridge University Press, 1924
297 Eduardo Paolozzi, *Studies on Wittgenstein*, 1994
298 Gerhard Richter, *Atlas*, Sheet 112, "Cities," 1968
299 *PP*, Nigel Henderson photograph, 1956
300 Alison and Peter Smithson, *House of the Future, Daily Mail Ideal Homes Exhibition*, London, 1956
301 *OL*, p. 88
302 Peter Lanyon, construction for St. Just, c. 1950
303 *ILAUD Yearbook*, 1981, p. 66
304 *A Line of Trees . . . A Steel Structure* exhibition, video still from gallery talk, 1975
305 *A Line of Trees . . . A Steel Structure* exhibition, video still from gallery talk, 1975

Abbreviations

AJ *Architects' Journal*
AR *Architectural Review*
AD *Architectural Design*
CA *Changing the Art of Inhabitation: Mies' Pieces, Eames' Dreams, The Smithsons*, Artemis, 1994
CV *The Charged Void: Architecture*, Alison and Peter Smithson, The Monacelli Press, 2001
HP *The Heroic Period of Modern Architecture*, Alison and Peter Smithson, Rizzoli, 1981
OL *Ordinariness and Light: Urban Theories, 1952–1960, and Their Application in a Building Project ,1963–1970*, Alison and Peter Smithson, MIT Press, 1970
PLA *Parallel of Life and Art*, Institute of Contemporary Arts, Alison and Peter Smithson, Nigel Henderson, Eduardo Paolozzi, 1953
PP *Patio and Pavilion*, *This is Tomorrow Exhibition*, Whitechapel Gallery, Alison and Peter Smithson, Nigel Henderson, Eduardo Paolozzi, 1956
TS *The Shift*, Alison and Peter Smithson, Academy Editions, 1982
UP *Uppercase 3*, edited by Theo Crosby, Whitefriars Press, 1960 (unpaginated spreads)
WR *Without Rhetoric: An Architectural Aesthetic, 1955–1972*, Alison and Peter Smithson, Latimer New Dimensions, 1973

141. Tokyo Expressway No. 4, near Kandabashi. Built movement

152

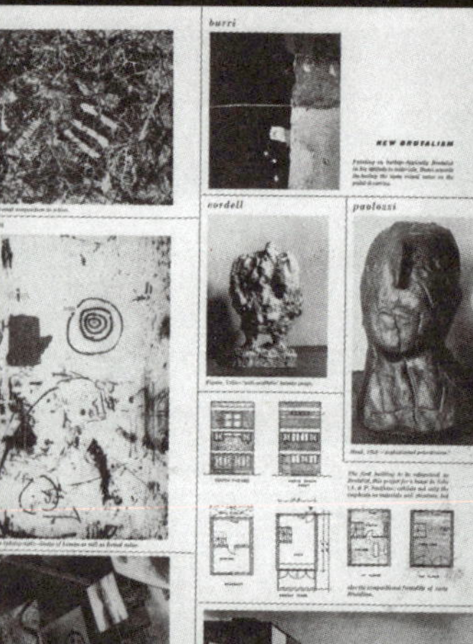

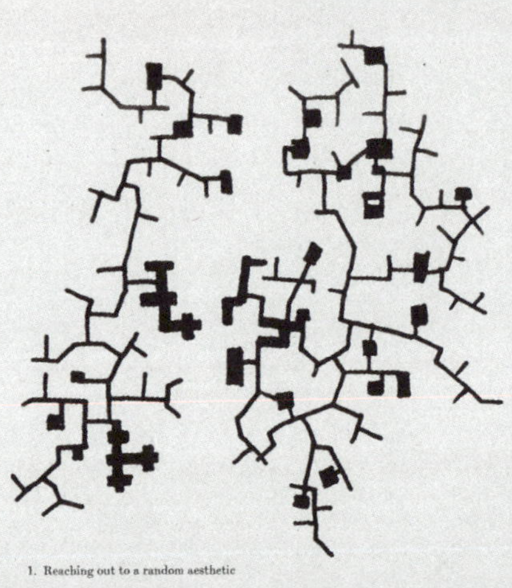

1. Reaching out to a random aesthetic